JOSEPHUS

LCL 203

JOSEPHUS

THE JEWISH WAR
BOOKS I–II

WITH AN ENGLISH TRANSLATION BY

H. ST. J. THACKERAY

HARVARD UNIVERSITY PRESS
CAMBRIDGE, MASSACHUSETTS
LONDON, ENGLAND

First published 1927
Reprinted 1956, 1961, 1967, 1976, 1989, 1997
Jewish War bound in three volumes beginning 1997

LOEB CLASSICAL LIBRARY® is a registered trademark
of the President and Fellows of Harvard College

ISBN 0-674-99568-6

Printed in Great Britain by St Edmundsbury Press Ltd,
Bury St Edmunds, Suffolk, on acid-free paper.
Bound by Hunter & Foulis Ltd, Edinburgh, Scotland.

CONTENTS

INTRODUCTION

THE *History of the Jewish War* is the earliest and the most famous of the works of Josephus. The first-fruits of the leisure which he found in Rome after the war, it was written with all the advantages possessed by an ex-combatant and eyewitness, now a pensioner quartered in the former palace of Vespasian, with the "commentaries" of his imperial patrons, the commanders in the recent campaign, placed at his disposal.[a]

The *title* by which the author refers to his work is Title. "Concerning the Jewish War" (Περὶ τοῦ Ἰουδαϊκοῦ πολέμου *Vita* 412, *A.* xx. 258, *cf.* xviii. 11). Laqueur, *Der jüd. Historiker Flavius Josephus*, Giessen, 1920, p. 255 and p. 98, considers that this heading plainly betrays the purely *Roman* point of view of the Jewish turncoat. The expanded form, Ἰουδαϊκοῦ πολέμου πρὸς Ῥωμαίους, found at the head of the first two books in Niese's principal MS P, may, it has been suggested, be an attempt of the author to neutralize the offensive character of the former superscription. But the majority of the MSS employ another title, "Concerning (the) capture" (Περὶ ἁλώσεως), often with the addition of Ἰουδαϊκῆς ἱστορίας. The title Περὶ ἁλώσεως is found also in Origen and Jerome, the latter of whom attributes it to the author himself: "quae Josephus Judaicae scriptor historiae septem explicat uoluminibus, quibus imposuit titulum Captiui-

[a] *Ap.* i. 50, *Vita* 358, 423.

INTRODUCTION

tatis Judaicae id est Περὶ ἁλώσεως " (*Comm. in Isaiam*, cap. 64, *sub fin.*). Niese (vol. i. p. vi) regarded this as a title of Christian origin, introduced at a time when our author's principal works, the *War* and the *Antiquities*, were collected into a single *corpus*, bearing the general title Ἰουδαϊκὴ ἱστορία, and sub-titles Περὶ ἁλώσεως and Ἀρχαιολογία. Yet the short title is one which the author might well have employed himself; ἅλωσις, often without the article, is constantly used of the final tragedy, *e.g.* ii. 454 (προοίμιον ἁλώσεως), iv. 318, and v. 3 (ἁλώσεως ἄρξαι, ἀλ. κατῆρξεν τῇ πόλει).

Dr. Robert Eisler, to whom the present writer is indebted for many suggestions in this Introduction, and whose forthcoming volume on the important Old Russian version of the *War* will throw much light on the genesis of the work, draws a distinction between an older and simpler draft, the *Halosis*, and a later and more elaborate edition, the *Polemos*.

He thinks that " Jewish history " or " histories " (ἱστορίαι *Vita* 345 ; Euseb. *Histor. Eccl.* i. 8) was the general title of Josephus's " collected works " as they were finally published by Epaphroditus. He emphasizes the fact that all mss of the Russian version are entitled " On the Capture of Jerusalem " and that a hitherto unidentified quotation from Josephus, ἐν τῷ πέμπτῳ λόγῳ τῆς ἁλώσεως, in the *Chron. Pasch.* i. 263 Dind., can be traced to certain of those mss. He hopes to prove in his forthcoming work that the Russian version, as well as the so-called " Egesippus " (Heg.)—a Christianized Latin translation by a converted Jew, Isaac *alias* Gaudentius or Hilarius, a contemporary of Pope Damasus—is based on a lost earlier, somewhat different edition of our work— first published in A.D. 72 for the celebration of the triumph of Titus—which bore the title Φλανίου Ἰωσήπου περὶ ἁλώσεως τῆς Ἱερουσαλήμ. This was gradually added to, revised, curtailed, and expanded in subsequent years. He considers Ἰουδαϊκὸς πόλεμος to be the title of the

INTRODUCTION

thoroughly revised edition, published during the reign of Domitian, as it survives in the MSS PA and L, while VR and MC represent earlier, less carefully revised editions of the original Ἅλωσις, such as were used also by the Slavonic translator.

We learn from the proem that the Greek text was not the first draft of the work. It had been preceded by a narrative written in Aramaic and addressed to "the barbarians in the interior," who are more precisely defined lower down as the natives of Parthia, Babylonia, and Arabia, the Jewish dispersion in Mesopotamia, and the inhabitants of Adiabene, a principality of which the reigning house, as was proudly remembered, were converts to Judaism (*B.* i. 3, 6). Of this Aramaic work the Greek is described as a "version" (Ἑλλάδι γλώσσῃ μεταβαλών), made for the benefit of the subjects of the Roman Empire, *i.e.* the Graeco-Roman world at large.

The Aramaic is lost, but two probable inferences may be drawn with regard to (i) its relation to the Greek text, and (ii) its purpose. First, the Greek was not a literal translation. This may be inferred from the language of the historian elsewhere. He describes his *Antiquities* as a translation from the Hebrew Scriptures (ἐκ τῶν Ἑβραϊκῶν μεθηρμηνευμένην γραμμάτων, *A.* i. 5), and again as a rendering of the Hebrew books into Greek (μεταφράζειν εἰς τὴν Ἑλλάδα γλῶτταν) without material addition or omission on his own part (*A.* x. 218) ; but we know in fact that that work is a free paraphrase of the Biblical story, made with the assistance of the LXX translation, and including considerable additions derived from other sources. The *Jewish War* in its Greek form was, we are told, produced with the aid of Greek assistants and shows no trace whatever of Semitic phraseology; we may infer that the older work has been practically rewritten.

With regard to its purpose, written as it was almost immediately after the war under the patronage of Vespasian, there is good ground for believing that it was officially " inspired " (see Laqueur, *Der jüd. Historiker Fl. Josephus*, 126 f.). It was a manifesto intended as a warning to the East of the futility of further opposition and to allay the after-war thirst for revenge, which ultimately led to the fierce out-breaks under Trajan and Hadrian. The danger of a Parthian rising was a constant menace, and it is significant that the Parthians stand in the forefront of the list of contemplated readers (i. 6). Such a motive is in fact admitted in the remark with which Josephus closes his description of the Roman army : " If I have dwelt at some length on this topic, my intention was not so much to extol the Romans as *to console those whom they have vanquished and to deter others who may be tempted to revolt* " (iii. 108 ; *cf.* Agrippa's speech ii. 345 ff., with the reference to the Jewish hopes of aid from Mesopotamia).

The Old Russian version.

The original Aramaic edition was at an early date lost to the Western world. A theory advanced by H. Kottek in 1886 that part of it has survived in the 6th century Syriac version of Book vi was shown by Nöldeke to be untenable. More recently, however, A. Berendts (*ap.* Harnack, *Texte und Untersuchungen*, xiv. 1, 1906) has maintained that it survives in the Old Russian version. That version contains some remarkable deviations from, and additions to, the Greek text of the *War*, including in particular passages relating to John the Baptist, Christ, and the early Christians.

The full text of the Slavonic version has not yet been made available to scholars ; but the first four books of the *War* have appeared in a German translation by the late

INTRODUCTION

A. Berendts, edited by K. Grass (Dorpat, 1924–27). This work reached the hands of the present translator too late for use to be made of it in the volume now issued. He hopes, however, to print in an Appendix to vol. iii a translation of the more important additions in the Slavonic text, together with a list of the passages which it omits.

The theory of Berendts can, according to Dr. Eisler, be accepted only with reservations. The Slavonic text is interpolated, but even after certain Christian interpolations have been detected and set aside, it cannot be derived *directly* from the lost Aramaic; numerous indications prove that it is a translation from a *Greek* text, allied to that contained in the mss VRC. But below this Greek text Dr. Eisler finds, in certain transliterated words, traces of an underlying *Semitic* original. According to him,[a] the Greek was translated into Slavonic in Lithuania between A.D. 1250 and 1260 by a Judaizing heretic priest of the Russian Church, who by chance obtained a copy, or copies, of Josephus's first rough Greek version of the original Aramaic (the *Halosis*), before it was rewritten in the form in which it has come down to us.

The first draft of the Greek work was produced in parts and formed the subject of a long correspondence between the author and King Agrippa, two of whose 62 complimentary letters, one offering further oral information, are reproduced (*Vita* 364 ff.); we may suspect that Agrippa was also consulted on the earlier Aramaic edition. On its completion copies were presented by the author to his imperial patrons and others, Titus giving it his imprimatur: "indeed so anxious was the Emperor Titus that my volumes should be the sole authority from which the world

Production of Greek edition.

[a] "Les Origines de la traduction slave de Josèphe, l'hérésie judaisante en Russie et la secte des Joséphinistes en Asie Mineur, en Italie et en Provence." Communication au Congrès des Historiens Français le 22 Avril 1927 (*Revue des Études slaves*, Paris, 1927).

should learn the facts, that he affixed his own signature to them and gave orders for their publication " (*ib.* 363, *Ap.* i. 50 ff.).

The date of publication is commonly regarded as falling within the latter half of the reign of Vespasian, between A.D. 75 and 79, before the death of that Emperor, who received a copy, but after the dedication of the Temple of *Pax* (*B.* vii. 158 ff.) in the year 75 (Dio Cassius, lxvi. 15). It had, we know, been preceded by other narratives of the war (*B.* i. 1 ff., *A.* i. 4).

These limits cannot, however, be pressed and may be applicable only to a single edition. Josephus, as we have come to learn, like other ancient authors, must have constantly retouched and added to his works as fresh copies were called for. We know that in A.D. 93-4, towards the end of his life, he was contemplating a new edition of the *War*, which was to include the after events of his nation's history brought up to date (*A.* xx. 267). Similarly our extant text was not improbably preceded by a shorter draft. From the fact that the " table of contents " in the Greek proem (*B.* i. 29) concludes with the triumph, Dr. Eisler infers that the first Greek edition ended with that event and appeared as early as A.D. 71. He acutely suggests that Josephus strove to complete his work by the day of the triumph and to present a copy to the two emperors on that memorable occasion. The sequel, including the penultimate chapter about the destruction of the other Jewish temple, that of Onias in Egypt, in A.D. 73 (*B.* vii. 420-436), was, in Dr. Eisler's opinion, added after that event, the opportunity being taken at the same time to prefix to the whole work a corresponding chapter about its foundation (*B.* i. 33) and contemporary Hasmonaean history.

Contents. A brief preface includes a somewhat inadequate and unsystematic summary of the whole work (i. 19-29) ; the topics mentioned are probably selected primarily to catch the imperial eye and also to

xii

attract the general reader. Then follows an in-ordinately long introduction, occupying the whole of the first and nearly half the second Book, containing a sketch of Jewish history from the previous capture of the Temple by Antiochus Epiphanes down to the outbreak of the war with Rome, nearly 250 years later. When in later life the author undertook a complete history of his nation, this portion of the narrative was expanded in the *Antiquities*, where it fills seven and a half books (*A*. xiii-xx). A comparison of these two narratives forms an instructive study ; the parallel passages in the *Antiquities* are indicated at the head of the pages of the present translation.

Book i extends from the time of Antiochus Epiphanes (*c.* 170 B.C.) to the death of Herod ; ii continues the history down to the outbreak of war in A.D. 66, the rout of Cestius, and the preparations of Josephus for a campaign in Galilee. Book iii narrates Vespasian's Galilaean campaign of A.D. 67, including the siege of Jotapata and the capture of Josephus ; iv the conclusion of the Galilaean campaign, the isolation of Jerusalem, and the inter-ruption of operations by the acclamation of Vespasian as Emperor (68-69) ; v and vi describe the siege and capture of Jerusalem by Titus in A.D. 70 ; vii the return of the conquerors to Rome, the triumphal procession, the extermination of the last strongholds of the rebels and some later events.

Considered as a literary work the *Jewish War* as a whole possesses great merits. The style is an excellent specimen of the Atticistic Greek fashionable in the first century, introduced by the school which sought to stem the development of the language that set in with the Alexandrian age and to revive the

Greek style.

xiii

INTRODUCTION

Attic of the age of Pericles. A choice vocabulary, well-knit sentences and paragraphs, niceties in the use of particles and in the order of words, a uniformly classical style but without slavish imitation of classical models, these and other excellences tax and often defy the powers of a translator.

> *Vocabulary.*—The following words, among others, are characteristic of the *War*, and do not occur elsewhere in Josephus: ἀδιάλειπτος (-ως), ἀνέδην, ἄτονος (-ως), βασιλειᾶν, δημότης, διεκπαίειν, διέχειν (*distare*, in preference to ἀπέχειν), εἰκαῖος (-ως), ἐξαπίνης (in preference to ἐξαίφνης), ἑωθινός, θανατᾶν, καταλήγειν, καταντιβολεῖν, κατορρωδεῖν and ὀρρωδεῖν, κοπιᾶν, λαθραῖος (-ως), λεωφόρος, μεσημβρινός ("southern"), μεταγενέστερος and προγενέστερος, μόνον οὐκ ("almost"), ὀλόφυρσις (from Thuc.), παλινδρομεῖν, πανοῦργος (and derivatives), παράστημα ("intrepidity"), πολίχνη and πολίχνιον, πρὸς δέ (adverb: where καὶ προσέτι), προσαμύνειν, προσάρκτιος, προσιτός, πτοεῖσθαι, συμμίσγειν, συστάδην, διὰ τάχους and κατὰ τάχος, τονοῦν, ὑποδείδειν (epic), χθαμαλός, χωρισμός ("departure"), χῶρος.

Writing for educated readers, Josephus boasts of having immersed himself in Greek literature (*A.* xx. 263), and taken extraordinary pains to cultivate style. "Among other qualifications," he writes, "the historian . . . needs charm of style, in so far as this is attainable by the choice and nice adjustment (ἁρμονία) of words and whatever else may serve to embellish the narrative for his readers" (*A.* xiv. 2); in the " nice adjustment " he refers to the careful avoidance of hiatus or harsh clashing of vowels, which is a marked feature, particularly in the *War*. But such mastery could only have been gradually acquired, and that an author, who had hitherto written solely in Aramaic, should open his literary career with a work showing such a thorough command of Greek

xiv

INTRODUCTION

niceties would be astonishing, were it not explained by an *obiter dictum* in a later work.

In the *Contra Apionem*, written perhaps a quarter Literary
of a century after the *War*, the historian makes a assistants.
welcome, if tardy, acknowledgement of the help which he had received in the composition of the earlier work. He employed, he tells us, some assistants for the sake of the Greek (χρησάμενός τισι πρὸς τὴν Ἑλληνίδα φωνὴν συνεργοῖς, *Ap.* i. 50). The immense debt which he owes to these admirable collaborators is apparent on almost every page of the work. Book vii stands apart ; the style here shows many of the characteristics of the *Antiquities*, and the author seems to have been more dependent on his own resources. The author's own style may also perhaps be detected in some autobiographical passages and occasional insertions.

> The admission made in the *Contra Apionem* serves to explain the inequalities in the work of Josephus as a whole, and puts us on the track of other " assistants." The cruder style of the *Life* appears to represent the *ipsissima verba* of the author. The *Antiquities* also seem to have been largely written with little assistance, until towards the close, when, having reached the narrative already partially covered in the *War*, the author for nearly five books (xv-xix) entrusts the work to other hands : xv-xvi appear to betray the style of one of the able assistants in the *War*; xvii-xix. 275 exhibit the marked mannerisms of a hack, a slavish imitator of Thucydides. In the *Contra Apionem* the choice diction, recondite classical lore, and excellent arrangement of subject matter again suggest that assistance has been obtained.

Josephus, by the time that he wrote the *Antiquities*, Classical
claims to have been thoroughly conversant with the models.
best Greek literature, including, according to the reading of some MSS, Greek poetry : τῶν Ἑλληνικῶν

INTRODUCTION

δὲ γραμμάτων ἐσπούδασα μετασχεῖν τὴν γραμματικὴν
ἐμπειρίαν ἀναλαβών A. xx. 263, where after γραμμάτων
Cod. A and the epitome add the words καὶ ποιητικῶν
μαθημάτων (+πολλὰ A). The last words may have
dropped out of the other MSS through homoioteleuton, or possibly, as Dr. Eisler suggests, through
the deliberate malice of his assistant slaves, who knew
the truth about these boasted achievements of their
master. In his earlier work we may well believe that
he is indebted for an occasional classical phrase or
allusion to his learned secretaries. Thucydides was
naturally a model to which most historians turned.[a]
In the *Antiquities* Josephus quarries freely from this
mine, and his assistant in Books xvii-xix deserves
the ridicule already cast by Cicero on such plagiarists
(" ecce autem aliqui se Thucydidios esse profitentur,
novum quoddam imperitorum et inauditum genus,"
Orator 30). In the *War*, on the contrary, the use of
this source is far more restrained, being confined to an
occasional reminiscence or phrase. Similar use is made
of Herodotus, Xenophon, Demosthenes, and Polybius.

More interesting is the familiarity shown with
Greek poetry, Homer and the tragedians. The
poignant narrative of the domestic troubles of Herod
the Great is told in the manner of a Greek drama :[b]
we hear of Nemesis at the outset (i. 431), of the pollution of the house (μύσος 638, *cf.* 445), the tempest
lowering over it (488), the villain and stage-manager

---

[a] Dr. Eisler draws my attention to Lucian's strictures on
such borrowing in his *Quomodo historia sit conscribenda.*
The quotation from Cicero I owe to Drüner, *Untersuchungen
über Josephus*, 1896.

[b] Eusebius describes this portion of the narrative as τραγικὴ
δραματουργία (*H.E.* i. 8). I am again indebted for the reference to Dr. Eisler.

INTRODUCTION

of the plot (τὸν λυμεῶνα τῆς οἰκίας καὶ δραματουργὸν ὅλου τοῦ μύσους 530), the anxious waiting for " the end of the drama " (543), the avenging deity (καθ' ᾅδου φέρειν τὸν ἀλάστορα 596), the ghosts (δαίμονες) of the murdered sons roaming the palace and dragging secrets to light (599) or sealing the lips of others (607). But there are other more precise allusions. Sophocles was evidently a favourite; the allusions to this tragedian, being mainly confined to the *War* and to portions of the *Antiquities*, especially Books xv-xvi, written in the style of the *War*, are probably attributable rather to the assistant than to the historian. From him also doubtless come some apparent allusions to Virgil.

THUCYDIDES.—The proem of Josephus (i. 4 γενομένου γὰρ . . . μεγίστου τοῦδε τοῦ κινήματος . . . ἀκμάζον) echoes that of Thucydides (i. 1 κίνησις γὰρ αὕτη μεγίστη . . . ἐγένετο with preceding ἀκμάζοντες); Herod's speech to his troops disheartened by defeat followed by earthquake (i. 373 ff.) recalls that of Pericles to the Athenians exasperated by invasion and the plague (ii. 60 ff.); the reception at Jerusalem of the news of the fall of Jotapata (iii. 432) is reminiscent of the reception at Athens of the news of the Sicilian disaster (viii. 1). In phraseology the following parallels are noteworthy: βύζην *B.* iii. 296, vi. 326, Thuc. iv. 8; ἀναρριπτεῖν κίνδυνον *B.* iv. 217, Thuc. vi. 13; περιαλγεῖν τῷ πάθει *B.* iv. 590, Thuc. iv. 85, 95; δουλεία ἀκίνδυνος *B.* vii. 324, cf. Thuc. vi. 80; τὸ (μὴ) βουλόμενον τῆς γνώμης *B.* vii. 338, Thuc. i. 90; στεριφώτερ(ον) ποιεῖν *B.* vii. 314, Thuc. vii. 36.

HERODOTUS supplies the following: τέμενος ἀποδεικνύναι *B.* i. 403; προκαθίζειν (ἐπὶ θρόνου) ii. 27, cf. Hdt. i. 14 (ἐς θρόνον); τὴν ἐπὶ θανάτῳ (sc. ὁδόν) ii. 231, vi. 155; πάντες ἡβηδόν iii. 133, cf. iv. 554; τροχοειδὴς λίμνη iii. 511; ἄκεσις "cure" iv. 11, vii. 189; πρὸς ἀλκὴν τρέπεσθαι vi. 14, vii. 232; ἀναμάρτητος πρός τινα γίνεσθαι vii. 329; λήματος πλήρης vii. 340, cf. λήματος πλέος Hdt. v. 111.

XENOPHON, *Cyropaedia*, probably furnishes θήγειν ψυχὰς

INTRODUCTION

iv. 174; ἀντιμέτωπος v. 56 and ἀντιπρόσωπος v. 62, 136;
τάραχος (for ταραχή) iv. 495; διαδωρεῖσθαι vi. 418; ῥιψο-
κίνδυνος vii. 77.

DEMOSTHENES provides phrases for speeches such as
ἐπιτετειχισμένη τυραννίς iv. 172, τιμωρίας διακρούεσθαι iv.
257; perhaps also ἀναισθητεῖν iv. 165, ἐκ τῶν ἐνόντων
vi. 183, βρόχον ἐπισπᾶν vii. 250, σκευώρημα vii. 449.

From HOMER come ἀναιμωτί ii. 495, iv. 40 etc.;
εἴχοντο καὶ μετὰ κωκυτῶν iii. 202, cf. κωκυτῷ τ᾽ εἴχοντο
Il. xxii. 409; ἐκφορεῖν = "carry out corpse for burial,"
iv. 330; ἄκολος "morsel" v. 432; ἀμάρα "conduit" and
ὄνθος "dung" v. 571; πεπαρμέν(α) ἥλοις vi. 85; φυλακτήρ
(for φύλαξ) vii. 291.

SOPHOCLES.—From the *Electra* come ἀφειδεῖν ψυχῆς B.
iii. 212, *El.* 980, and θράσος ὁπλίζειν B. iii. 153, *El.* 995 f.,
and we may confidently infer that we have a paraphrase
of a line in the near context of that play (ὅρα πόνου
τοι χωρὶς οὐδὲν εὐτυχεῖ *El.* 945) in B. iii. 495, v. 501;
reminiscences of this play and of the *Ajax* occur also in
A. xv-xvi. We find also θάρσος προξενεῖν B. v. 66 from
Trach. 726; ἐνσκήπτειν θεός B. v. 408, probably from
O.T. 27; προσψαύειν B. vii. 348, cf. *O.C.* 330 etc., and
immediately after ζῇ καὶ τέθηλεν from *Trach.* 235; οὐδὲν
ὑγιὲς φρονεῖν, B. v. 326, cf. *Phil.* 1006.

VIRGIL.—Like a rather younger historian of the same
period—Tacitus—the συνεργός (for Josephus can here
hardly be responsible) seems to have interwoven some
Virgilian reminiscences into the narrative. The sack of
Jotapata (as in Tacitus the siege of the Capitol under
Vitellius, Mackail, *Latin Literature* 219) recalls the sack
of Troy. Compare B. iii. 319 περὶ γὰρ τὴν ἐσχάτην φυλακήν,
καθ᾽ ἣν ἀνεσίν τε τῶν δεινῶν ἐδόκουν ἔχειν καὶ καθάπτεται
μάλιστα κεκοπωμένων [= mortalibus aegris] ἑωθινὸς ὕπνος
. . . 323 ff. ᾔεσαν ἡσυχῇ πρὸς τὸ τεῖχος. καὶ πρῶτος ἐπιβαίνει
Τίτος . . .᾽ ἀποσφάξαντες δὲ τοὺς φύλακας εἰσίασιν εἰς τὴν
πόλιν with *Aen.* ii. 263 ff. ". . . primusque Machaon
. . . Invadunt urbem somno vinoque sepultam;
| caeduntur uigiles. . . . Tempus erat quo prima quies
mortalibus aegris | incipit et dono divum gratissima
serpit." The personified Φήμη B. iii. 433 f. (with the
allusion to facts embroidered by fiction, προσεσχεδιάζετό γε
μὴν τοῖς πεπραγμένοις καὶ τὰ μὴ γενόμενα) recalls the picture

of Fama in *Aen.* iv. 173 ff. ("et pariter facta atque infecta canebat" 190); *cf. B.* i. 371.

The portrait of John of Gischala in *B.* ii. 585 ff. curiously resembles that of Catiline in Sallust, *Cat.* 5.

The *War* contains no allusions to authorities such as are interspersed throughout the *Antiquities*. The historian in this earlier work is silent as to his sources, merely leading us to infer from his proem that his information is largely first-hand and based on his own recollections as an eyewitness (i. 3), that he had new materials and constructed the framework of the narrative himself (φιλόπονος . . . ὁ μετὰ τοῦ καινὰ λέγειν καὶ τὸ σῶμα τῆς ἱστορίας κατασκευάζων ἴδιον), and that he collected the facts with laborious care (i. 15 f.).

These scanty hints can be supplemented by a few notices in the works produced in later life, the *Contra Apionem* and the *Life*. Here again he emphasizes the personal part which he took in the contest, as commander in Galilee in the opening campaign, after his capture in constant touch with the Roman generals, and during the siege of Jerusalem associated with Titus behind the Roman lines. He tells us that throughout the siege he made careful notes of the proceedings in the Roman camp and was kept aware of events within the city by deserters, whose information he was alone in a position to understand (*Ap.* i. 47-49). We know, moreover, from the *War*, that he was employed on more than one occasion as intermediary to urge his besieged compatriots to surrender. We learn further that King Agrippa, who was kept supplied with a copy of the *War* as it appeared in parts, was in correspondence with the author throughout its production and offered to

Sources.

furnish him with information about facts not generally known (*Vita* 364 ff.).

The *Commentaries* of Vespasian and Titus.

But, besides his own notes and recollections and such further information as he may have obtained from Agrippa, the author appears to have had access to another document of the first importance, the "memoirs" or "commentaries" (ὑπομνήματα) of Vespasian and Titus. No reference to this source is made in the *War* itself; this silence is in accordance with the historian's consistent practice of naming no authorities in this work, but may, perhaps without injustice, be partly attributed to vanity. He would have us know that the framework of the narrative is his own (σῶμα ἴδιον), and a mention of this source, whatever weight it might add to his authority, might detract from his personal fame. At any rate, like his acknowledgement of indebtedness to his Greek assistants, his allusions to the *Commentaries* only appear in his later works, in reply to the adverse criticism which his *Jewish War* evoked from Justus and other rival historians. His previous silence on other matters (τὰ μέχρι νῦν σεσιωπημένα) evidently formed one of the complaints of his critics (*Vita* 338 f.).

The *Commentaries* are thrice mentioned. Replying to the criticisms of Justus of Tiberias, Josephus reminds him of hostilities for which he and his fellow-citizens were responsible at the opening of the war before Vespasian's arrival, and which were afterwards brought to that general's notice. He adds: " This is no unsupported assertion of my own. The facts are recorded in the *Commentaries* of the emperor Vespasian, which further relate how insistently the inhabitants of Decapolis pressed Vespasian, when at Ptolemais, to punish you as the culprit " (*Vita* 342).

INTRODUCTION

Ptolemais was the first place to which Vespasian led his army from Antioch, his original base (*B*. iii. 29); we here learn that the *Commentaries* went back to the opening of the campaign. Again, attacking the same opponent, Josephus writes : " Perhaps, however, you will say that you have accurately narrated the events which took place at Jerusalem. How, pray, can that be, seeing that neither were you on the scene of action, nor had you perused the *Commentaries* of Caesar, as is abundantly proved by your account which conflicts with those *Commentaries* ? " (*Vita* 358). Again, of certain malignant critics who have dared to compare his *Jewish War* to a schoolboy's prize composition (ὥσπερ ἐν σχολῇ μειρακίων γύμνασμα προκεῖσθαι νομίζοντες), the author writes : " Surely, then, one cannot but regard as audacious the attempt of these critics to challenge my veracity. Even if, as they assert, they have read the *Commentaries* of the imperial commanders, they at any rate had no first-hand acquaintance with our position in the opposite camp" (*Ap*.i.53-56). These two last passages, in which Josephus is contrasting his own qualifications with those of others, clearly imply that the *Commentaries* were before him when he wrote the *War*.

Indeed, as has been suggested by a recent writer (W. Weber, *Josephus und Vespasian*, 1921), there is reason to think that our author has made extensive use of these documents. The *Commentarii principales*, it may be supposed, were the notes, presumably in Latin, made on the field of action by the Roman commanders and their staff, which might sometimes be put out in a more literary shape as the official record of the campaign, like the *Commentarii de Bello Gallico* of Julius Caesar. From this or from some other official source must come the information with regard to the disposition of the Roman legions in A.D. 66, which is strikingly confirmed by other evidence and is here worked up into the great speech of King Agrippa (*B.* ii. 345 ff.). Another passage which looks like a direct extract from the *Commentaries* of Titus is the concise itinerary of the march of that general from Egypt to Caesarea, with its bare enumeration of the various stages, though it must be remembered that Josephus accompanied him (*B.* iv. 658-end). Whether Weber is right in referring to this source the geographical sketches of Palestine interspersed throughout the narrative may perhaps be questioned, but the description of the Dead Sea with the mention of Vespasian's visit of inspection (*B.* iv. 477) lends support to his view (*cf.* the rather similar account in Tacitus, *Hist.* v. 6).

> Weber goes so far as to maintain that the backbone of the whole history is a " Flavian work," of which the theme was the rise to power of the Flavian dynasty. In his opinion, this work opened with a sketch of the disposition of the legions in A.D. 66 (utilized in Agrippa's speech), included much of the material of *B.* iii-vi, and ended with the passage which stands in Josephus at vii. 157 ; it was used by Pliny the Elder and Tacitus. In his review of Weber, Laqueur denies the existence of any such literary work, on the ground that Josephus severely criticizes all previous publications on the war (*B.* i. *ad init.*).

Nicolas of Damascus. For the pre-war period (Books i-ii) we can confidently name one writer, frequently mentioned in the *Antiquities,* as having furnished material also for the *War*—Nicolas of Damascus (*c.* 64 B.C. to the end of the century), the intimate friend of Herod the Great and of Augustus, and author of a universal history in 144 books and other works, including probably a

xxii

separate life of Herod. From Nicolas undoubtedly is derived the detailed history of Herod's house, which fills two-thirds of Book i, and of the accession of Archelaus (opening of Book ii), in which he himself played an important part. Here again Josephus had the advantage of a first-rate, if somewhat biased, contemporary authority. After Archelaus the narrative unfortunately becomes meagre, expanding into rather greater fullness when the reign of Agrippa I is reached. With regard to him the historian would obtain information from his son, Agrippa II, and for the events leading up to the war he might draw on his own recollections. For the slight sketch of the Hasmonaean house the history of Nicolas is perhaps again the authority ; the historian shows no acquaintance in the *War* with the first book of Maccabees, of which he afterwards made large use in the *Antiquities*.

As historian of the Jewish War Josephus thus Credibility. comes before us with apparently high credentials ; at any rate few war historians in ancient or modern times can have enjoyed so rare a combination of opportunities for presenting a veracious narrative of events. How does his work appear when tested by the highest of standards, the *History of the Peloponnesian War* ? It is natural to compare the Jew and the Athenian because, widely different as were the characters of the two, there were points of similarity in their careers. Like Thucydides, Josephus combined the functions of general and historian ; like him he failed as a commander and was consequently brought into close contact with the enemy and enabled to view the war from the standpoint of both belligerents (Thuc. iv. 104 ff., v. 26 " associating with both sides, with the Peloponnesians quite as much as with

INTRODUCTION

the Athenians, because of my exile," *cf.* Jos. *B.* i. 3);
while the Jewish historian, unlike the Greek, had the
further advantage of the use of the official record of
the campaign compiled by, or under the supervision
of, the enemy's generals.

With access to these first-hand sources, with the
weighty authority both of his imperial patrons and
of King Agrippa behind him, and with the possibly
more questionable benefit of good literary assistants,
the historian's narrative *as a whole* cannot but be
accepted as trustworthy. Unfortunately reservations must be made. Josephus lacks the sober im-
partiality of Thucydides and, with all his boasted zeal
for truth, shows on occasions, when his statements
are subject to control, a lax sense of the meaning
of that word. The *Commentaries* themselves were
written from the Roman standpoint, and the pro-
Roman bias of this client of the conquerors, who
from the first had recognized the hopelessness of
resistance to imperial Rome, is frequently evident.
His repeated references to the clemency of the
Roman generals, his hero Titus in particular, and his
representation of them as the saviours of an oppressed
people, are specially open to suspicion.

In one crucial instance, a statement of Josephus—
that Titus desired to spare the temple—is directly
contradicted by a later historian. The fourth-
century Christian writer, Sulpicius Severus, who has
been thought to be here dependent on the lost work
of Tacitus, states, like Josephus, that a council of war
was held on the subject, at which different opinions
were expressed, but here the rôles are reversed and
it is Titus who sanctions the destruction of the
building. The passages are as follows:

INTRODUCTION

Josephus, *B.* vi.

238 βουλὴν περὶ τοῦ ναοῦ
239 προυτίθει. τοῖς μὲν οὖν
ἐδόκει χρῆσθαι τῷ τοῦ
πολέμου νόμῳ· μὴ γὰρ ἄν
ποτε Ἰουδαίους παύσασθαι
νεωτερίζοντας τοῦ ναοῦ
μένοντος, ἐφ' ὃν οἱ παν-
240 ταχόθεν συλλέγονται. τινὲς
δὲ παρῄνουν, εἰ μὲν κατα-
λίποιεν αὐτὸν Ἰουδαῖοι καὶ
μηδεὶς ἐπ' αὐτοῦ τὰ ὅπλα
θείη, σώζειν, εἰ δὲ πολεμοῖεν
ἐπιβάντες, καταφλέγειν ...
241 ὁ δὲ Τίτος οὐδ' ἂν ἐπιβάντες
ἐπ' αὐτοῦ πολεμῶσιν Ἰου-
δαῖοι φήσας ἀντὶ τῶν ἀνδρῶν
ἀμυνεῖσθαι τὰ ἄψυχα οὐδὲ
καταφλέξειν ποτὲ τηλικοῦ-
τον ἔργον· Ῥωμαίων γὰρ
ἔσεσθαι τὴν βλάβην, ὥσπερ
καὶ κόσμον τῆς ἡγεμονίας
αὐτοῦ μένοντος ...

Sulpicius, *Chron.* ii. 30.

Fertur Titus adhibito consilio
prius deliberasse, an templum
tanti operis euerteret. Etenim
nonnullis uidebatur, aedem
sacratam ultra omnia mortalia
illustrem non oportere deleri,
quae seruata modestiae
Romanae testimonium, diruta
perennem crudelitatis notam
praeberet. At contra alii *et
Titus ipse euertendum in primis
templum censebant*, quo plenius
Iudaeorum et Christianorum
religio tolleretur: quippe has
religiones, licet contrarias sibi,
isdem tamen ab auctoribus
profectas; Christianos ex
Iudaeis extitisse: radice sub-
lata stirpem facile perituram.

The evidence of Sulpicius is somewhat vitiated by
the final allusion to Christianity which can hardly be
correct ; [a] but the known partiality of Josephus leaves
him under the suspicion of having misrepresented
the attitude of Titus, in order to clear him of the
imputation of cruelty. Weber (*Josephus und Vespasian* 72 f.) with others upholds Sulpicius against
Josephus ; Schürer (*Gesch. des jüd. Volkes*, ed. 3,
i. 631 f.) inclines to the middle view of Valeton
that Josephus, without actual mendacity, has by
the suppression of important facts created a false
impression.

[a] Dr. Eisler suggests that " Christiani " may be a general
designation for Jewish " Messianist " rebels ; but here I
hesitate to follow him.

INTRODUCTION

For the earlier pre-war history Josephus has himself provided us with a certain check upon his statements and enabled us to form some estimate of his treatment of his sources by the double narrative which he has left us. The precise relation between the two narratives cannot here be considered. The fuller account in the *Antiquities* was based partly on the same sources which he had used in the *War*, partly on new information since obtained. The subject matter has sometimes been re-arranged, notably in the latter part of Herod's reign, where the *War* separates the external history from the domestic tragedies, while the *Antiquities* keep the chronological order. There are, as is natural, inconsistencies between the two accounts ; but, generally speaking, it may be said that the author faithfully follows his written authorities.

It is otherwise with the passages in which the *War* overlaps with the *Life*. Here there are unaccountable discrepancies, and the autobiographical notices of the historian must be pronounced the least trustworthy portion of his writings. The numerous inconsistencies, of a minor or a graver character, between the two accounts of his command in Galilee, to which attention is called in the footnotes to *B.* ii. 569-646, betray either gross carelessness or actual fraud.[a] Laqueur, who holds the *Life*, or certain portions of it, to be the earlier and more faithful record, suspects the author of deliberate misrepresentation of some details in the *War* in order

---

[a] The latter alternative, Dr. Eisler informs me, is rendered a certainty through his critical comparison of the third, and again quite distinct, account in the Slavonic *Halosis*.

to ingratiate himself with another patron, King
Agrippa.

Nothing, unfortunately, has survived of the earliest, Other
probably Roman, histories of the war criticized by narratives
Josephus in his proem, nor yet of the Jewish history of the war.
of Justus of Tiberias produced soon after A.D. 100,
in which his own work was criticized. We possess,
however, from the pen of Tacitus early in the second
century a brief sketch of the campaign up to the
preparations for the siege of Jerusalem (*Hist.* v. 1-13);
the sequel is lost. We have also the lives of Vespasian and Titus written at about the same time by
Suetonius, and an epitome of this portion (Book lxvi)
of the great Roman history of Dion Cassius (early
third century) made in the eleventh century by
Xiphilinus. The account of Tacitus presents some
interesting parallels not only with the *War*, but also,
on the origin of the Jewish nation, with the *Contra
Apionem* of our author. Though the *Histories* were
written at Rome almost within the lifetime of
Josephus, the Roman's antipathy to the Jews makes
it improbable that he ever consulted his works. But
both writers may be dependent on a common source,
such as the Flavian *Commentaries*.

The Greek text here printed is based on that of Greek text
Niese, but is the outcome of a careful and independent and MSS.
investigation of the MS evidence collected in his great
edition. The MSS and other ancient authorities
for the text, in so far as they have been used by
Niese, are quoted in the present work with his
abbreviations as follows : [a]

[a] For particulars with regard to the versions I am indebted
to Dr. Eisler.

INTRODUCTION

P Codex Parisinus Graecus 1425, cent. x. or xi.

A Codex Ambrosianus (Mediolanensis) D. 50 sup., cent. x. or xi.

M Codex Marcianus (Venetus) Gr. 383, cent. xi. or xii.

L Codex Laurentianus, plut. lxix. 19, cent. xi. or xii.

V Codex Vaticanus Gr. 148, about cent. xi.

R Codex Palatinus (Vaticanus) Gr. 284, cent. xi. or xii.

C Codex Urbinas (Vaticanus) Gr. 84, cent. xi.

Exc. Excerpts made in the tenth century by order of Constantine VII Porphyrogenitus.

Lat. A Latin version known to Cassiodorus in the fifth century and commonly ascribed to Rufinus in the preceding century.

Heg. Hegesippus, a corruption of Josepus or Josippus : another Latin version, wrongly ascribed to S. Ambrose, written about 370 A.D. by a converted Jew, Isaac, as a Christian called Hilarius or Gaudentius, the so-called Ambrosiaster, a contemporary of Pope Damasus (see Jos. Wittig in Max Sdralek's *Kirchengesch. Abhandlungen* iv ; ed. Keber-Caesar, Marburg, 1864). A new edition by Vinc. Ussani for the Vienna Corpus is forthcoming.

Syr. A Syriac translation of Book vi in Translatio Syra Pescitto Vet. Test. ex cod. Ambrosiano sec. fere vi phololith. edita cura et adnotationibus Antonii Maria Ceriani, Milan, 1876–1883.

To these may be added :

Yos. = Josephus Gorionides or Yosippon, a Hebrew
paraphrase, derived from Heg., ed. Breit-
haupt, Gotha, 1727.

Slav. A critical edition of the Old Russian Version
by Vladimir Istrin is nearing completion.
The first four books are published in a German
version by Konrad Grass (see above, p. xi).

Among other MSS occasionally quoted by Niese
are :

N Codex Laurentianus, plut. lxix. 17, about
cent. xii.

T Codex Philippicus, formerly belonging to the
library of the late Sir Thomas Phillips,
Cheltenham, about cent. xii.

The MSS fall into two main groups, PA(ML) and
VR(C) ; M, L, and, to a less extent, C are inconstant
members, siding now with one group, now with the
other. The first group is decidedly superior to the
second. The two types of text go much further back
than the date of Niese's oldest MSS, since traces of
the " inferior " type appear already in Porphyry
(3rd century) ; the diversity of readings must therefore have begun very early. Indeed some variants
appear to preserve corrections gradually incorpor-
ated by the author himself in later editions of
his work.[a] Mixture of the two types also began
early, a few instances of " conflation " occurring

---

[a] A striking instance occurs in *B.* vi. 369, where, beside
the neater τόπος . . . πᾶς λιμοῦ νεκρὸν εἶχεν ἢ στάσεως, a more
prolix and apparently older phrase καὶ πεπλήρωτο νεκρῶν ἢ διὰ
στάσιν ἢ διὰ λιμὸν ἀπολωλότων has been left undeleted. See
Laqueur, *Der jüd. Historiker Fl. Josephus,* p. 239, whose
theory is confirmed, I am told, by Dr. Eisler's analysis of
the Old Russian.

already in the fourth-century Latin version. P and A, on which Niese mainly relies, appear to have been copied from an exemplar in which the terminations of words were abbreviated, and are to that extent untrustworthy. The true text seems to have been not seldom preserved in one of the MSS of mixed type, L in particular. The mixture in that MS is peculiar: throughout Book i and down to about ii. 242 it sides with VRC, from that point onwards more often with the other group or with the Latin version. In the later books L becomes an authority of the first rank and seems often to have preserved alone, or in combination with the Latin version, the original text.

The translator must finally express his grateful acknowledgement for the assistance which he has received from the labours of many previous workers, of various nationalities, in the same field: notably Dr. Robert Eisler, of whose forthcoming work on the Slavonic version an English version is expected from Messrs. Methuen, Benedict Niese (on whose edition the Greek text is based), the Rev. Robert Traill, D.D., who fell a victim to his devoted exertions for his parishioners during the Irish famine of 1846–47 (for his excellent translation), the Rev. William Whiston (for his pioneering version, produced nearly two centuries ago, as revised by the Rev. A. R. Shilleto, 1889–90), and last, but not least, Dr. Théodore Reinach and his collaborators (for his French translation and invaluable notes, *Œuvres complètes de Flavius Josèphe*, tome v, *Guerre des Juifs*, livres i-iii, Paris, 1912). Dr. Reinach has graciously permitted me to make use of this work with its admirable commentary, and

INTRODUCTION

my constant indebtedness to this brilliant scholar will be evident to the reader from the references in the footnotes throughout this volume. The works of R. Laqueur and W. Weber must also be mentioned.

ABBREVIATIONS

A. = *Antiquitates Judaicae.*
Ap. = *Contra Apionem.*
B. = *Bellum Judaicum.*
V. = *Vita.*
conj. = conjectural emendation.
ed. pr. = *editio princeps* (Basel, 1544).
Eus. (*H.E. ; P.E.*) = Eusebius (*Historia Ecclesiastica ; Praeparatio Evangelica*).
ins. = inserted by.   *om.* = omit.

Conjectural insertions in the Greek text are indicated by angular brackets, < > ; doubtful MS readings and apparent glosses by square brackets, [ ].

The smaller sections introduced by Niese are shown in the left margin of the Greek text. References throughout are to these sections. The chapter-division of earlier editions is indicated on both pages (Greek and English).

Editorial Note (1979): Readers should note that the theory of Robert Eisler, that the Slavonic version of the *Jewish War* preserves in some places a genuine tradition overlaid in our Greek manuscripts by Christian interpolation, has failed to win any authoritative support. Nevertheless the Appendix to this edition has been retained for its intrinsic interest. See also the notes and appendix on the *Testimonium Flavianum* in the Loeb edition of *Jewish Antiquities*. Comprehensive bibliographies are given in those volumes, to which may be added R. J. H. Shutt, *Studies in Josephus* (1961).

THE JEWISH WAR

ΙΣΤΟΡΙΑ ΙΟΥΔΑΪΚΟΥ ΠΟΛΕΜΟΥ ΠΡΟΣ ΡΩΜΑΙΟΥΣ

ΒΙΒΛΙΟΝ Α

(1) Ἐπειδὴ τὸν Ἰουδαίων πρὸς Ῥωμαίους πόλεμον συστάντα μέγιστον οὐ μόνον τῶν καθ᾽ ἡμᾶς, σχεδὸν δὲ καὶ ὧν ἀκοῇ παρειλήφαμεν ἢ πόλεων πρὸς πόλεις ἢ ἐθνῶν ἔθνεσι συρραγέντων, οἱ μὲν οὐ παρατυχόντες τοῖς πράγμασιν, ἀλλ᾽ ἀκοῇ συλλέγοντες εἰκαῖα καὶ ἀσύμφωνα διηγήματα σοφι- 2 στικῶς ἀναγράφουσιν, οἱ παραγενόμενοι δὲ ἢ κολακείᾳ τῇ πρὸς Ῥωμαίους ἢ μίσει τῷ πρὸς Ἰουδαίους καταψεύδονται τῶν πραγμάτων, περι- έχει δὲ αὐτοῖς ὅπου μὲν κατηγορίαν ὅπου δὲ ἐγκώ- μιον τὰ συγγράμματα, τὸ δ᾽ ἀκριβὲς τῆς ἱστορίας 3 οὐδαμοῦ, προυθέμην ἐγὼ τοῖς κατὰ τὴν Ῥωμαίων ἡγεμονίαν, Ἑλλάδι γλώσσῃ μεταβαλὼν ἃ τοῖς ἄνω βαρβάροις τῇ πατρίῳ συντάξας ἀνέπεμψα πρότερον, ἀφηγήσασθαι, Ἰώσηπος Ματθίου παῖς, [γένει Ἑβραῖος,]¹ ἐξ Ἱεροσολύμων ἱερεύς, αὐτός

¹ om. P Eus.

2

HISTORY OF THE JEWISH WAR
AGAINST THE ROMANS

BOOK I

(1) THE war of the Jews against the Romans—the greatest not only of the wars of our own time, but, so far as accounts have reached us, well nigh of all that ever broke out between cities or nations—has not lacked its historians. Of these, however, some, having taken no part in the action, have collected from hearsay casual and contradictory stories which they have then edited in a rhetorical style ; while others, who witnessed the events, have, either from flattery of the Romans or from hatred of the Jews, misrepresented the facts, their writings exhibiting alternatively invective and encomium, but nowhere historical accuracy. In these circumstances, I— Josephus, son of Matthias, a Hebrew by race, a native of Jerusalem and a priest, who at the opening of the war myself fought against the Romans and in the sequel was perforce an onlooker—propose to provide the subjects of the Roman Empire with a narrative of the facts, by translating into Greek the account which I previously composed in my ver-

τε Ῥωμαίους πολεμήσας τὰ πρῶτα καὶ τοῖς ὕστερον παρατυχὼν ἐξ ἀνάγκης·

4 (2) γενομένου γάρ, ὡς ἔφην, μεγίστου τοῦδε
τοῦ κινήματος, ἐν Ῥωμαίοις μὲν ἐνόσει τὰ οἰκεῖα,
Ἰουδαίων δὲ τὸ νεωτερίζον τότε τεταραγμένοις
ἐπανέστη τοῖς καιροῖς ἀκμάζον κατά τε χεῖρα καὶ
χρήμασιν, ὡς δι᾽ ὑπερβολὴν θορύβων τοῖς μὲν ἐν
ἐλπίδι κτήσεως τοῖς δ᾽ ἐν ἀφαιρέσεως δέει γίνε-
5 σθαι τὰ πρὸς τὴν ἀνατολήν, ἐπειδὴ Ἰουδαῖοι μὲν
ἅπαν τὸ ὑπὲρ Εὐφράτην ὁμόφυλον συνεπαρθήσεσ-
θαι σφίσιν ἤλπισαν, Ῥωμαίους δ᾽ οἵ τε γείτονες
Γαλάται παρεκίνουν καὶ τὸ Κελτικὸν οὐκ ἠρέμει, μεστὰ δ᾽ ἦν πάντα θορύβων μετὰ Νέρωνα, καὶ
πολλοὺς μὲν βασιλειᾶν ὁ καιρὸς ἀνέπειθεν, τὰ
στρατιωτικὰ δὲ ἦρα μεταβολῆς ἐλπίδι λημμάτων·
6 ἄτοπον ἡγησάμενος[1] περιιδεῖν πλαζομένην ἐπὶ
τηλικούτοις πράγμασι τὴν ἀλήθειαν, καὶ Πάρθους
μὲν καὶ Βαβυλωνίους Ἀράβων τε τοὺς πορρωτάτω
καὶ τὸ ὑπὲρ Εὐφράτην ὁμόφυλον ἡμῖν Ἀδιαβηνούς
τε γνῶναι διὰ τῆς ἐμῆς ἐπιμελείας ἀκριβῶς, ὅθεν
τε ἤρξατο καὶ δι᾽ ὅσων ἐχώρησεν παθῶν ὁ πόλεμος
καὶ ὅπως κατέστρεψεν, ἀγνοεῖν δὲ Ἕλληνας ταῦτα
καὶ Ῥωμαίων τοὺς μὴ ἐπιστρατευσαμένους, ἐντυγχάνοντας ἢ κολακείαις ἢ πλάσμασι.

---

[1] Some mss. have ἄτοπον οὖν ἡγησάμην. But chaps. (1) and
(2) apparently form a single sentence, §§ 4 and 5 being a
parenthesis.

---

[a] Aramaic.

[b] The " up-country barbarians " intended are more precisely specified in § 6.

[c] As Reinach points out, this is exaggerated. At the outbreak of war the Roman Empire was free from disorder.

[d] *i.e.* the Germans. The references are respectively to

nacular tongue *a* and sent to the barbarians in the interior.*b*

(2) I spoke of this upheaval as one of the greatest magnitude. The Romans had their own internal disorders. The Jewish revolutionary party, whose numbers and fortunes were at their zenith, seized the occasion of the turbulence of these times for insurrection.*c* As a result of these vast disturbances the whole of the Eastern Empire was in the balance ; the insurgents were fired with hopes of its acquisition, their opponents feared its loss. For the Jews hoped that all their fellow-countrymen beyond the Euphrates would join with them in revolt ; while the Romans, on their side, were occupied with their neighbours the Gauls, and the Celts *d* were in motion. Nero's death, moreover, brought universal confusion ; many were induced by this opportunity to aspire to the sovereignty, and a change which might make their fortune was after the heart of the soldiery.

I thought it monstrous, therefore, to allow the truth in affairs of such moment to go astray, and that, while Parthians and Babylonians and the most remote tribes of Arabia with our countrymen beyond the Euphrates and the inhabitants of Adiabene *e* were, through my assiduity, accurately acquainted with the origin of the war, the various phases of calamity through which it passed and its conclusion, the Greeks and such Romans as were not engaged in the contest should remain in ignorance of these matters, with flattering or fictitious narratives as their only guide.

Critical condition of affairs in East and West.

June A.D. 68.

the revolt of Gaul under Vindex (A.D. 68) and to that of the Batavi under Civilis (69).

e In the upper Tigris region.

7 (3) Καίτοι γε ἱστορίας αὐτὰς ἐπιγράφειν τολ-
μῶσιν, ἐν αἷς πρὸς τῷ μηδὲν ὑγιὲς δηλοῦν καὶ τοῦ
σκοποῦ δοκοῦσιν ἔμοιγε διαμαρτάνειν. βούλονται
μὲν γὰρ μεγάλους τοὺς Ῥωμαίους ἀποδεικνύειν,
καταβάλλουσιν δὲ ἀεὶ τὰ Ἰουδαίων καὶ ταπεινοῦ-
8 σιν· οὐχ ὁρῶ δέ, πῶς ἂν εἶναι μεγάλοι δοκοῖεν οἱ
μικροὺς νενικηκότες· καὶ οὔτε τὸ μῆκος αἰδοῦνται
τοῦ πολέμου οὔτε τὸ πλῆθος τῆς Ῥωμαίων καμού-
σης στρατιᾶς οὔτε τὸ μέγεθος τῶν στρατηγῶν, οἳ
πολλὰ περὶ τοῖς Ἱεροσολύμοις ἱδρώσαντες, οἶμαι,
ταπεινουμένου τοῦ κατορθώματος αὐτοῖς ἀδο-
ξοῦσιν.

9 (4) Οὐ μὴν ἐγὼ τοῖς ἐπαίρουσι τὰ Ῥωμαίων
ἀντιφιλονεικῶν αὔξειν τὰ τῶν ὁμοφύλων διέγνων,
ἀλλὰ τὰ μὲν ἔργα μετ' ἀκριβείας ἀμφοτέρων διέξειμι, τοὺς δ' ἐπὶ τοῖς πράγμασι λόγους ἀνα-
τίθημι τῇ[1] διαθέσει, καὶ τοῖς ἐμαυτοῦ πάθεσι διδοὺς
10 ἐπολοφύρεσθαι ταῖς τῆς πατρίδος συμφοραῖς. ὅτι
γὰρ αὐτὴν στάσις οἰκεία καθεῖλεν, καὶ τὰς Ῥωμαίων χεῖρας ἀκούσας καὶ τὸ πῦρ ἐπὶ τὸν [ἅγιον][2]
ναὸν εἵλκυσαν οἱ Ἰουδαίων τύραννοι, μάρτυς αὐτὸς
ὁ πορθήσας Καῖσαρ Τίτος, ἐν παντὶ τῷ πολέμῳ
τὸν μὲν δῆμον ἐλεήσας ὑπὸ τῶν στασιαστῶν φρου-
ρούμενον, πολλάκις δὲ ἑκὼν τὴν ἅλωσιν τῆς
πόλεως ὑπερτιθέμενος καὶ διδοὺς τῇ πολιορκίᾳ
11 χρόνον εἰς μετάνοιαν τῶν αἰτίων. εἰ δέ τις ὅσα
πρὸς τοὺς τυράννους ἢ τὸ ληστρικὸν αὐτῶν κατη-
γορικῶς λέγοιμεν ἢ τοῖς δυστυχήμασι τῆς πατρίδος
ἐπιστένοντες συκοφαντοίη, διδότω παρὰ τὸν τῆς

---

[1] Holwerda inserts ⟨ἰδίᾳ⟩. [2] om. PM*.

(3) Though the writers in question presume to give their works the title of histories, yet throughout them, apart from the utter lack of sound information, they seem, in my opinion, to miss their own mark. They desire to represent the Romans as a great nation, and yet they continually depreciate and disparage the actions of the Jews. But I fail to see how the conquerors of a puny people deserve to be accounted great. Again, these writers have respect neither for the long duration of the war, nor for the vast numbers of the Roman army that it engaged, nor for the prestige of the generals, who, after such herculean labours under the walls of Jerusalem, are, I suppose, of no repute in these writers' eyes, if their achievement is to be underestimated. *Erroneous disparagement of Jews by previous historians.*

(4) I have no intention of rivalling those who extol the Roman power by exaggerating the deeds of my compatriots. I shall faithfully recount the actions of both combatants ; but in my reflections on the events I cannot conceal my private sentiments, nor refuse to give my personal sympathies scope to bewail my country's misfortunes. For, that it owed its ruin to civil strife, and that it was the Jewish tyrants who drew down upon the holy temple the unwilling hands of the Romans and the conflagration, is attested by Titus Caesar himself, who sacked the city ; throughout the war he commiserated the populace who were at the mercy of the revolutionaries, and often of his own accord deferred the capture of the city and by protracting the siege gave the culprits time for repentance. Should, however, any critic censure me for my strictures upon the tyrants or their bands of marauders or for my lamentations over my country's misfortunes, I ask *The author's personal feelings.*

ἱστορίας νόμον συγγνώμην τῷ πάθει· πόλιν [μὲν]¹
γὰρ δὴ τῶν ὑπὸ Ῥωμαίοις πασῶν τὴν ἡμετέραν
ἐπὶ πλεῖστόν τε εὐδαιμονίας συνέβη προελθεῖν καὶ
12 πρὸς ἔσχατον συμφορῶν αὖθις καταπεσεῖν. τὰ
γοῦν πάντων ἀπ᾽ αἰῶνος ἀτυχήματα πρὸς τὰ
Ἰουδαίων ἡττῆσθαι δοκῶ κατὰ σύγκρισιν, καὶ
τούτων αἴτιος οὐδεὶς ἀλλόφυλος, ὥστε ἀμήχανον
ἦν ὀδυρμῶν ἐπικρατεῖν. εἰ δέ τις οἴκτου σκλη-
ρότερος εἴη δικαστής, τὰ μὲν πράγματα τῇ ἱστορίᾳ
προσκρινέτω, τὰς δ᾽ ὀλοφύρσεις τῷ γράφοντι.

13 (5) Καίτοι γε ἐπιτιμήσαιμ᾽ ἂν αὐτὸς δικαίως
τοῖς Ἑλλήνων λογίοις, οἳ τηλικούτων κατ᾽ αὐτοὺς
πραγμάτων γεγενημένων, ἃ κατὰ σύγκρισιν ἐλα-
χίστους ἀποδείκνυσι τοὺς πάλαι πολέμους, τούτων
μὲν κάθηνται κριταὶ τοῖς φιλοτιμουμένοις ἐπηρεά-
ζοντες, ὧν εἰ καὶ τῷ λόγῳ πλεονεκτοῦσι, λεί-
πονται τῇ προαιρέσει· αὐτοὶ δὲ τὰ Ἀσσυρίων καὶ
Μήδων συγγράφουσιν ὥσπερ ἧττον καλῶς ὑπὸ
14 τῶν ἀρχαίων συγγραφέων ἀπηγγελμένα. καίτοι
τοσούτῳ τῆς ἐκείνων ἡττῶνται δυνάμεως ἐν τῷ
γράφειν, ὅσῳ καὶ τῆς γνώμης· τὰ γὰρ καθ᾽ αὑτοὺς
ἐσπούδαζον ἕκαστοι γράφειν, ὅπου καὶ τὸ παρα-
τυχεῖν τοῖς πράγμασιν ἐποίει τὴν ἀπαγγελίαν
ἐναργῆ καὶ τὸ ψεύδεσθαι παρ᾽ εἰδόσιν αἰσχρὸν ἦν.
15 τό γε μὴν μνήμῃ τὰ [μὴ]² προϊστορηθέντα διδόναι
καὶ τὰ τῶν ἰδίων χρόνων τοῖς μεθ᾽ ἑαυτὸν συν-
ιστάνειν ἐπαίνου καὶ μαρτυρίας ἄξιον· φιλόπονος δὲ
οὐχ ὁ μεταποιῶν οἰκονομίαν καὶ τάξιν ἀλλοτρίαν,

---

¹ PAM: om. the rest: Destinon conj. μίαν (after Lat.
solam). ² A^corr Lat.: om. the rest.

ᵃ Literally " which is contrary to the law of history ";
cf. B. v. 20.

his indulgence for a compassion which falls outside an historian's province.[a] For of all the cities under Roman rule it was the lot of ours to attain to the highest felicity and to fall to the lowest depths of calamity. Indeed, in my opinion, the misfortunes of all nations since the world began fall short of those of the Jews ; and, since the blame lay with no foreign nation, it was impossible to restrain one's grief. Should, however, any critic be too austere for pity, let him credit the history with the facts, the historian with the lamentations.

(5) Yet I, on my side, might justly censure those erudite Greeks who, living in times of such stirring actions as by comparison reduce to insignificance the wars of antiquity, yet sit in judgement on these current events and revile those who make them their special study—authors whose principles they lack, even if they have the advantage of them in literary skill. For their own themes they take the Assyrian and Median empires, as if the narratives of the ancient historians were not fine enough. Yet, the truth is, these modern writers are their inferiors no less in literary power than in judgement. The ancient historians set themselves severally to write the history of their own times, a task in which their connexion with the events added lucidity to their record ; while mendacity brought an author into disgrace with readers who knew the facts. In fact, the work of committing to writing events which have not previously been recorded and of commending to posterity the history of one's own time is one which merits praise and acknowledgement. The industrious writer is not one who merely remodels the scheme and arrangement of another's work, but one

The historian of contemporary events is superior to the compiler of ancient history.

9

ἀλλ᾽ ὁ μετὰ τοῦ καινὰ λέγειν καὶ τὸ σῶμα τῆς
16 ἱστορίας κατασκευάζων ἴδιον. κἀγὼ μὲν ἀνα-
λώμασι καὶ πόνοις μεγίστοις ἀλλόφυλος ὢν Ἕλ-
λησί τε καὶ Ῥωμαίοις τὴν μνήμην τῶν κατορθωμάτων ἀνατίθημι· τοῖς δὲ γνησίοις πρὸς μὲν τὰ
λήμματα καὶ τὰς δίκας κέχηνεν εὐθέως τὸ στόμα
καὶ ἡ γλῶσσα λέλυται, πρὸς δὲ τὴν ἱστορίαν, ἔνθα
χρὴ τἀληθῆ λέγειν καὶ μετὰ πολλοῦ πόνου τὰ
πράγματα συλλέγειν, πεφίμωνται παρέντες τοῖς
ἀσθενεστέροις καὶ μηδὲ γινώσκουσι τὰς πράξεις
τῶν ἡγεμόνων γράφειν. τιμάσθω δὴ παρ᾽ ἡμῖν τὸ
τῆς ἱστορίας ἀληθές, ἐπεὶ παρ᾽ Ἕλλησιν ἠμέληται.
17 (6) Ἀρχαιολογεῖν μὲν δὴ τὰ Ἰουδαίων, τίνες τε
ὄντες καὶ ὅπως ἀπανέστησαν Αἰγυπτίων, χώραν
τε ὅσην ἐπῆλθον ἀλώμενοι καὶ πόσα ἑξῆς κατ-
έλαβον καὶ ὅπως μετανέστησαν, νῦν τε ἄκαιρον
ᾠήθην εἶναι καὶ ἄλλως περιττόν, ἐπειδήπερ καὶ
Ἰουδαίων πολλοὶ πρὸ ἐμοῦ τὰ τῶν προγόνων
συνετάξαντο μετ᾽ ἀκριβείας καί τινες Ἑλλήνων
ἐκεῖνα τῇ πατρίῳ φωνῇ μεταβαλόντες οὐ πολὺ
18 τῆς ἀληθείας διήμαρτον. ὅπου δ᾽ οἵ τε τούτων
συγγραφεῖς ἐπαύσαντο καὶ οἱ ἡμέτεροι προφῆται,
τὴν ἀρχὴν ἐκεῖθεν ποιήσομαι τῆς συντάξεως.
τούτων δὲ τὰ μὲν τοῦ κατ᾽ ἐμαυτὸν πολέμου δι-
εξοδικώτερον καὶ μεθ᾽ ὅσης ἂν ἐξεργασίας δύνω-
μαι δίειμι, τὰ δὲ προγενέστερα τῆς ἐμῆς ἡλικίας
ἐπιδραμῶ συντόμως·
19 (7) ὡς Ἀντίοχος ὁ κληθεὶς Ἐπιφανὴς ἑλὼν

---

[a] Perhaps " successively."
[b] An allusion to the works of Demetrius, Philo the elder,
Eupolemus, etc. ; cf. Ap. i. 218, where Josephus speaks
in the same terms. Subsequently he thought that these

who uses fresh materials and makes the framework of the history his own. For myself, at a vast expenditure of money and pains, I, a foreigner, present to Greeks and Romans this memorial of great achievements. As for the native Greeks, where personal profit or a lawsuit is concerned, their mouths are at once agape and their tongues loosed; but in the matter of history, where veracity and laborious collection of the facts are essential, they are mute, leaving to inferior and ill-informed writers the task of describing the exploits of their rulers. Let us at least hold historical truth in honour, since by the Greeks it is disregarded.

(6) To narrate the ancient history of the Jews, the origin of the nation and the circumstances of their migration from Egypt, the countries which they traversed in their wanderings, the extent of the territory which they subsequently [a] occupied, and the incidents which led to their deportation, would, I considered, be not only here out of place, but superfluous; seeing that many Jews before me have accurately recorded the history of our ancestors, and that these records have been translated by certain Greeks into their native tongue without serious error.[b] I shall therefore begin my work at the point where the historians of these events and our prophets conclude. Of the subsequent history, I shall describe the incidents of the war through which I lived with all the detail and elaboration at my command; for the events preceding my lifetime I shall be content with a brief summary.

(7) I shall relate how Antiochus, surnamed

Limits of present work: early Jewish history neglected.

earlier works still left room for a new " archaeology " (*A.* i. proem).

11

κατὰ κράτος Ἱεροσόλυμα καὶ κατασχὼν ἔτεσι
τρισὶ καὶ μησὶν ἓξ ὑπὸ τῶν Ἀσαμωναίου παίδων
ἐκβάλλεται τῆς χώρας· ἔπειθ᾽ ὡς οἱ τούτων ἔγ-
γονοι περὶ τῆς βασιλείας διαστασιάσαντες εἵλκυσαν εἰς τὰ πράγματα Ῥωμαίους καὶ Πομ-
πήιον· καὶ ὡς Ἡρώδης ὁ Ἀντιπάτρου κατέλυσε
20 τὴν δυναστείαν αὐτῶν ἐπαγαγὼν Σόσσιον, ὅπως
τε ὁ λαὸς μετὰ τὴν Ἡρώδου τελευτὴν κατεστα-
σίασεν Αὐγούστου μὲν Ῥωμαίων ἡγεμονεύοντος,
Κυιντιλίου δὲ Οὐάρου κατὰ τὴν χώραν ὄντος, καὶ
ὡς ἔτει δωδεκάτῳ τῆς Νέρωνος ἀρχῆς ὁ πόλεμος
ἀνερράγη, τά τε συμβάντα κατὰ Κέστιον καὶ ὅσα
κατὰ[1] τὰς πρώτας ὁρμὰς ἐπῆλθον οἱ Ἰουδαῖοι τοῖς
ὅπλοις·

21   (8) ὅπως τε τὰς περιοίκους ἐτειχίσαντο, καὶ
ὡς Νέρων ἐπὶ τοῖς Κεστίου πταίσμασι δείσας περὶ
τῶν ὅλων Οὐεσπασιανὸν ἐφίστησι τῷ πολέμῳ,
καὶ ὡς οὗτος μετὰ τοῦ πρεσβυτέρου τῶν παίδων
εἰς τὴν Ἰουδαίων χώραν ἐνέβαλεν, ὅση τε χρώμενος Ῥωμαίων στρατιᾷ καὶ †ὅσοις συμμάχοις
εἰσέπαισεν†[2] εἰς ὅλην τὴν Γαλιλαίαν, καὶ ὡς τῶν
πόλεων αὐτῆς ἃς μὲν ὁλοσχερῶς καὶ κατὰ κράτος
22 ἃς δὲ δι᾽ ὁμολογίας ἔλαβεν· ἔνθα δὴ καὶ τὰ περὶ
τῆς Ῥωμαίων ἐν πολέμοις εὐταξίας καὶ τὴν ἄσκη-
σιν τῶν ταγμάτων, τῆς τε Γαλιλαίας ἑκατέρας
τὰ διαστήματα καὶ τὴν φύσιν καὶ τοὺς τῆς Ἰουδαίας ὅρους, ἔτι τε τῆς χώρας τὴν ἰδιότητα,
λίμνας τε καὶ πηγὰς τὰς ἐν αὐτῇ, καὶ τὰ περὶ
ἑκάστην πόλιν τῶν ἁλισκομένων πάθη μετὰ ἀκρι-

----

[1] παρὰ LVNC.

[2] ὅσοις συμμάχοις εἰσέπαισεν conj. (after Niese and Naber):
ὅσοι σύμμαχοι ἐκόπησαν MSS.

Epiphanes, took Jerusalem by storm and, after hold- Summary of whole work: Book i.
ing it for three years and six months, was expelled
from the country by the Hasmonaeans [a]; next how
their descendants, in their quarrel for the throne,
dragged the Romans and Pompey upon the scene;
how Herod, son of Antipater, with the aid of Sossius,
overthrew the Hasmonaean dynasty; of the revolt Book ii.
of the people, after Herod's death, when Augustus
was Roman Emperor and Quintilius Varus provincial
governor; of the outbreak of war in the twelfth
year of Nero's principate, the fate which befell
Cestius and the success which attended the Jewish
arms in overrunning the country in the opening
engagements.

(8) Then I shall proceed to tell how they fortified
the neighbouring towns; how Nero, apprehensive for Book iii.
the Empire in consequence of the reverses of Cestius,
entrusted the conduct of the war to Vespasian; of
his invasion of Jewish territory, accompanied by his
elder son; of the strength of the forces, Roman and
auxiliary, with which he penetrated into Galilee, and
of the towns of that province which he captured
either by main force or by negotiation. In this
connexion I shall describe the admirable discipline iii. 70 ff.
of the Romans on active service and the training
of the legions; the extent and nature of the two iii. 35 ff.
Galilees,[b] the limits of Judaea, the special features
of the country, its lakes and springs. I shall give a cf. iii. 506 ff.
precise description of the sufferings of the prisoners
taken in the several towns, from my own observation

---

[a] Gr. " the sons of Asamonaeus."
[b] Upper and Lower.

βείας, ὡς εἶδον ἢ ἔπαθον, δίειμι. οὐδὲ γὰρ τῶν
ἐμαυτοῦ τι συμφορῶν ἀποκρύψομαι, μέλλων γε
πρὸς εἰδότας ἐρεῖν.

23 (9) Ἔπειθ' ὡς ἤδη καμνόντων Ἰουδαίοις τῶν
πραγμάτων θνήσκει μὲν Νέρων, Οὐεσπασιανὸς δὲ
ἐπὶ Ἱεροσολύμων ὡρμημένος ὑπὸ τῆς ἡγεμονίας
ἀνθέλκεται· τά τε γενόμενα περὶ ταύτης αὐτῷ
24 σημεῖα καὶ τὰς ἐπὶ Ῥώμης μεταβολάς, καὶ ὡς
αὐτὸς ὑπὸ τῶν στρατιωτῶν ἄκων αὐτοκράτωρ
ἀποδείκνυται, καὶ ἀποχωρήσαντος ἐπὶ διοικήσει
τῶν ὅλων εἰς τὴν Αἴγυπτον ἐστασιάσθη τὰ τῶν
Ἰουδαίων, ὅπως τε ἐπανέστησαν αὐτοῖς οἱ τύραννοι, καὶ τὰς τούτων πρὸς ἀλλήλους διαφοράς·

25 (10) καὶ ὡς ἄρας ἀπὸ τῆς Αἰγύπτου Τίτος
δεύτερον εἰς τὴν χώραν ἐνέβαλεν, ὅπως τε τὰς
δυνάμεις καὶ ὅπου συνήγαγε καὶ ὁπόσας, καὶ
ὅπως ἐκ τῆς στάσεως ἡ πόλις διέκειτο παρόντος
αὐτοῦ, προσβολάς τε ὅσας ἐποιήσατο καὶ ὁπόσα
χώματα, περιβόλους τε τῶν τριῶν τειχῶν καὶ τὰ
μέτρα τούτων, τήν τε τῆς πόλεως ὀχυρότητα καὶ
26 τοῦ ἱεροῦ καὶ τοῦ ναοῦ τὴν διάθεσιν, ἔτι δὲ καὶ
τούτων καὶ τοῦ βωμοῦ τὰ μέτρα πάντα μετ'
ἀκριβείας, ἔθη τε ἑορτῶν ἔνια καὶ τὰς ἑπτὰ
ἁγνείας καὶ τὰς τῶν ἱερέων λειτουργίας, ἔτι
δὲ τὰς ἐσθῆτας τῶν ἱερέων καὶ τοῦ ἀρχιερέως,
καὶ οἷον ἦν τοῦ ναοῦ τὸ ἅγιον, οὐδὲν οὔτε

ᵃ Lit. " the seven purifications," referring doubtless, as

or personal share in them. For I shall conceal nothing even of my own misfortunes, as I shall be addressing persons who are well aware of them.

(9) I shall next relate how, at the moment when the Jewish fortunes were on the decline, Nero's death occurred, and how Vespasian's advance upon Jerusalem was diverted by the call to imperial dignity; the portents of his elevation which he received, and the revolutions which took place in Rome; his proclamation by his soldiers as Emperor against his will; the civil war which, on his departure for Egypt to restore order to the realm, broke out among the Jews, the rise of the tyrants to power and their mutual feuds. Book iv 491. iv. 601. iv. 656. Book v; cf. iv. 121.

(10) My narrative will proceed to tell of the second invasion of our country by Titus, starting from Egypt; how and where he mustered his forces, and their strength; the condition to which civil war had reduced the city on his arrival; his various assaults and the series of earthworks which he constructed; further, the triple line of our walls and their dimensions; the defences of the city and the plan of the temple and sanctuary, the measurements of these buildings and of the altar being all precisely stated; certain festival customs, the seven degrees of purity,[a] the ministerial functions of the priests, their vestments and those of the high priest, with a description of the Holy of Holies.[b] Nothing shall be concealed, iv. 658. v. 47. v. 1. v. 136. v. 184. v. 231.

Reinach suggests, to the zones or rings into which the Holy City was divided, and accessible to persons of various degrees of ceremonial purity. A list of these, omitting the innermost ring (the Holy of Holies), is given in the Mishna, *Kelim*, i. 8 (quoted in Schürer, *GJV*³, ii. 273); Josephus gives an incomplete enumeration in *B.* v. 227, *cf. Ap.* ii. 102 ff.

[b] " The holy [place] of the sanctuary."

ἀποκρυπτόμενος οὔτε προστιθεὶς τοῖς πεφωρα-
μένοις.

27 (11) Ἔπειτα διέξειμι τήν τε τῶν τυράννων πρὸς
τοὺς ὁμοφύλους ὠμότητα καὶ τὴν Ῥωμαίων
φειδὼ πρὸς τοὺς ἀλλοφύλους, καὶ ὁσάκις Τίτος
σῶσαι τὴν πόλιν καὶ τὸν ναὸν ἐπιθυμῶν ἐπὶ δεξιὰς
τοὺς στασιάζοντας προυκαλέσατο. διακρινῶ δὲ
τὰ πάθη τοῦ δήμου καὶ τὰς συμφοράς, ὅσα τε
ὑπὸ τοῦ πολέμου καὶ ὅσα ὑπὸ τῆς στάσεως καὶ
28 ὅσα ὑπὸ τοῦ λιμοῦ κακωθέντες ἑάλωσαν. παραλείψω δὲ οὐδὲ τὰς τῶν αὐτομόλων ἀτυχίας οὐδὲ
τὰς τῶν αἰχμαλώτων κολάσεις, ὅπως τε ὁ ναὸς
ἄκοντος ἐνεπρήσθη Καίσαρος καὶ ὅσα τῶν ἱερῶν
κειμηλίων ἐκ τοῦ πυρὸς ἡρπάγη, τήν τε τῆς ὅλης
πόλεως ἅλωσιν καὶ τὰ πρὸ ταύτης σημεῖα καὶ
τέρατα, καὶ τὴν αἰχμαλωσίαν τῶν τυράννων, τῶν
τε ἀνδραποδισθέντων τὸ πλῆθος καὶ εἰς ἣν ἕκα-
29 στοι τύχην διενεμήθησαν· καὶ ὡς Ῥωμαῖοι μὲν
ἐπεξῆλθον τὰ λείψανα τοῦ πολέμου καὶ τὰ ἐρύματα τῶν χωρίων καθεῖλον, Τίτος δὲ πᾶσαν ἐπελθὼν τὴν χώραν κατεστήσατο, τήν τε ὑποστροφὴν αὐτοῦ τὴν εἰς Ἰταλίαν καὶ τὸν θρίαμβον.
30 (12) Ταῦτα πάντα περιλαβὼν ἐν ἑπτὰ βιβλίοις
καὶ μηδεμίαν τοῖς ἐπισταμένοις τὰ πράγματα καὶ
παρατυχοῦσι τῷ πολέμῳ καταλιπὼν ἢ μέμψεως
ἀφορμὴν ἢ κατηγορίας, τοῖς γε τὴν ἀλήθειαν
ἀγαπῶσιν, ἀλλὰ μὴ πρὸς ἡδονὴν[1] ἀνέγραψα. ποιήσομαι δὲ ταύτην τῆς ἐξηγήσεως ἀρχήν, ἣν καὶ
τῶν κεφαλαίων ἐποιησάμην.

31 (i. 1) Στάσεως τοῖς δυνατοῖς Ἰουδαίων ἐμπε-

[1] +ἀφορῶσιν M.

16

nothing added to facts which have been brought to light.[a]

(11) I shall then describe the tyrants' brutal treatment of their fellow-countrymen and the clemency of the Romans towards an alien race, and how often Titus, in his anxiety to save the city and the temple, invited the rival parties to come to terms with him. I shall distinguish between the sufferings and calamities of the people, culminating in their defeat, as attributable respectively to the war, the sedition, and the famine. Nor shall I omit to record either Book vi. the misfortunes of the deserters or the punishments inflicted on the prisoners ; the burning of the Temple, contrary to Caesar's wishes, and the number of the sacred treasures rescued from the flames ; the taking of the whole city and the signs and portents that vi. 288. preceded it ; the capture of the tyrants, the number of the prisoners and the destiny allotted to each ; vi. 414. nor yet how the Romans crushed the last remnants Book vii. of the war and demolished the local fortresses ; how Titus paraded the whole country and restored order ; and lastly his return to Italy and triumph.

(12) All these topics I have comprised in seven books. While I have left no pretext for censure or accusation to persons who are cognisant of the facts and took part in the war, my work is written for lovers of the truth and not to gratify my readers. I will now open my narrative with the events named at the beginning of the foregoing summary.

(i. 1) At the time[b] when Antiochus, surnamed

---

[a] Cf. Ap. ii. 80, 107, for the " discoveries " of Antiochus Epiphanes in the Holy of Holies and the " unspeakable mysteries " supposed to take place there.   [b] c. 171 B.C.

17

σούσης καθ᾽ ὃν καιρὸν Ἀντίοχος ὁ κληθεὶς Ἐπιφανὴς διεφέρετο περὶ ὅλης Συρίας πρὸς Πτολεμαῖον τὸν ἕκτον (ἡ φιλοτιμία δ᾽ ἦν αὐτοῖς περὶ
δυναστείας, ἑκάστου τῶν ἐν ἀξιώματι μὴ φέρον-
τος τοῖς ὁμοίοις ὑποτετάχθαι), Ὀνίας μὲν εἷς τῶν
ἀρχιερέων ἐπικρατήσας ἐξέβαλε τῆς πόλεως τοὺς
32 Τωβία υἱούς. οἱ δὲ καταφυγόντες πρὸς Ἀντίοχον
ἱκέτευσαν αὐτοῖς ἡγεμόσι χρώμενον εἰς τὴν Ἰουδαίαν ἐμβαλεῖν. πείθεται δ᾽ ὁ βασιλεὺς ὡρμημένος πάλαι, καὶ μετὰ πλείστης δυνάμεως αὐτὸς
ὁρμήσας τήν τε πόλιν αἱρεῖ κατὰ κράτος καὶ πολὺ
πλῆθος τῶν Πτολεμαίῳ προσεχόντων ἀναιρεῖ,
ταῖς τε ἁρπαγαῖς ἀνέδην ἐπαφιεὶς τοὺς στρατιώτας αὐτός καὶ τὸν ναὸν ἐσύλησε καὶ τὸν ἐνδελε-
χισμὸν τῶν καθ᾽ ἡμέραν ἐναγισμῶν ἔπαυσεν ἐπ᾽
33 ἔτη τρία καὶ μῆνας ἕξ. ὁ δ᾽ ἀρχιερεὺς Ὀνίας
πρὸς Πτολεμαῖον διαφυγὼν καὶ παρ᾽ αὐτοῦ λαβὼν τόπον ἐν τῷ Ἡλιοπολίτῃ νομῷ πολίχνην τε
τοῖς Ἱεροσολύμοις ἀπεικασμένην καὶ ναὸν ἔκτισεν
ὅμοιον· περὶ ὧν αὖθις κατὰ χώραν δηλώσομεν.
34 (2) Ἀντιόχῳ γε μὴν οὔτε τὸ παρ᾽ ἐλπίδα κρατῆσαι τῆς πόλεως οὔθ᾽ αἱ ἁρπαγαὶ καὶ ὁ τοσοῦτος
φόνος ἤρκεσεν, ὑπὸ δὲ ἀκρασίας παθῶν καὶ κατὰ
μνήμην ὧν παρὰ[1] τὴν πολιορκίαν ἔπαθεν ἠνάγκαζεν Ἰουδαίους, καταλύσαντας τὰ πάτρια, βρέφη
τε αὐτῶν φυλάττειν ἀπερίτμητα καὶ σῦς ἐπιθύειν
35 τῷ βωμῷ· πρὸς ἃ πάντες μὲν ἠπείθουν, ἐσφάττοντο δὲ οἱ δοκιμώτατοι. καὶ Βακχίδης ὁ πεμ-

---

[1] παρὰ Naber, Niese: περὶ mss.

---

[a] "The regular course," literally "continuity," *i.e.* the
Tāmīd or continuous (standing) burnt offering. "Sacrifices";
18

Epiphanes, was disputing with Ptolemy VI. the Antiochus
suzerainty of Syria, dissension arose among the (IV)
Epiphanes
Jewish nobles. There were rival claims to supreme takes
Jerusalem
power, as no individual of rank could tolerate sub- and inter-
jection to his peers. Onias, one of the chief priests, rupts the
temple
gaining the upper hand, expelled the sons of Tobias worship.
from the city. The latter took refuge with Antiochus
and besought him to use their services as guides
for an invasion of Judaea. The king, having long c. 170 B.C.
cherished this design, consented, and setting out at
the head of a huge army took the city by assault,
slew a large number of Ptolemy's followers, gave his
soldiers unrestricted licence to pillage, and himself
plundered the temple and interrupted, for a period
of three years and six months, the regular course of
the daily sacrifices.[a] The high priest Onias made
his escape to Ptolemy and, obtaining from him a site
in the nome of Heliopolis, built a small town on the
model of Jerusalem and a temple resembling ours.
We shall revert to these matters in due course.[b]

(2) Not content with his unlooked for success in Religious
capturing the city and with the plunder and whole- persecution.
sale carnage, Antiochus, carried away by his ungovernable passions and with the rankling memory of
what he had suffered in the siege, put pressure upon
the Jews to violate the code of their country by leaving their infants uncircumcised and sacrificing swine
upon the altar. These orders were disobeyed by all,
and the most eminent defaulters were massacred.
Bacchides,[c] who was sent by Antiochus to command

the Greek word is that elsewhere used for the Lat. *parentatio*
or offering to the *manes* of the dead.   [b] *B.* vii. 421 ff.
  [c] The mention of Bacchides is, as Reinach notes, an
anachronism ; he did not appear on the scene till some
years later, *A.* xii. 393, 1 Macc. vii. 8.

φθεὶς ὑπ' Ἀντιόχου φρούραρχος, τῇ φυσικῇ προσλαβὼν ὠμότητι τὰ ἀσεβῆ παραγγέλματα παρανομίας οὐδεμίαν κατέλιπεν ὑπερβολήν, καὶ κατ'
ἄνδρα τοὺς ἀξιολόγους αἰκιζόμενος καὶ κοινῇ καθ'
ἡμέραν ἐνδεικνύμενος ὄψιν ἁλώσεως τῇ πόλει,
μέχρι ταῖς ὑπερβολαῖς τῶν ἀδικημάτων τοὺς πά-
σχοντας εἰς ἀμύνης τόλμαν ἠρέθισε.

36 (3) Ματθίας γοῦν υἱὸς Ἀσαμωναίου τῶν ἱερέων
εἷς ἀπὸ κώμης Μωδεεὶν ὄνομα, συνασπίσας μετὰ
χειρὸς οἰκείας, πέντε γὰρ υἱεῖς ἦσαν αὐτῷ, κοπίσιν
ἀναιρεῖ τὸν Βακχίδην. καὶ παραχρῆμα μὲν δείσας
τὸ πλῆθος τῶν φρουρῶν εἰς τὰ ὄρη καταφεύγει,
37 προσγενομένων δὲ ἀπὸ τοῦ δήμου πολλῶν ἀναθαρ-
σήσας κάτεισι καὶ συμβαλὼν μάχῃ νικᾷ τε τοὺς
Ἀντιόχου στρατηγοὺς καὶ τῆς Ἰουδαίας ἐξελαύνει.
παρελθὼν δὲ ἀπὸ τῆς εὐπραγίας εἰς δυναστείαν
καὶ διὰ τὴν ἀπαλλαγὴν τῶν ἀλλοφύλων ἄρξας τῶν
σφετέρων ἑκόντων, τελευτᾷ Ἰούδᾳ τῷ πρεσβυ-
τάτῳ τῶν παίδων καταλιπὼν τὴν ἀρχήν.

38 (4) Ὁ δέ, οὐ γὰρ ἠρεμήσειν Ἀντίοχον ὑπελάμβανε, τάς τ' ἐπιχωρίους συγκροτεῖ δυνάμεις
καὶ πρὸς Ῥωμαίους πρῶτος ἐποιήσατο φιλίαν,
καὶ τὸν Ἐπιφανῆ πάλιν εἰς τὴν χώραν ἐμβάλ-
39 λοντα[1] μετὰ καρτερᾶς πληγῆς ἀνέστειλεν. ἀπὸ δὲ
θερμοῦ τοῦ κατορθώματος ὥρμησεν ἐπὶ τὴν ἐν τῇ
πόλει φρουράν, οὔπω γὰρ ἐκκέκοπτο, καὶ ἐκβαλὼν ἀπὸ τῆς ἄνω πόλεως συνωθεῖ τοὺς στρατιώτας εἰς τὴν κάτω· τοῦτο δὲ τοῦ ἄστεος τὸ μέρος

---

[1] A Lat. (vid.) : εἰσβαλόντα the rest.

[a] Mattathias (1 Macc.).
[b] Apelles according to A. xii. 270 ; the officer is unnamed
in 1 Macc. ii. 25.

the garrison, with these impious injunctions to back
his innate brutality, was guilty of every excess of
iniquity, torturing distinguished individuals one after
another, and daily parading before the eyes of all
the appearance of a captured city, until by the
extravagance of his crimes he provoked his victims
to venture on reprisals.

(3) These began with Matthias,[a] son of Asa- Rising of
monaeus, a priest of a village called Modein, who Matt(at)-
forming an armed band of himself and his family of hias.
five sons, slew Bacchides [b] with choppers. Fear of
the large garrison drove him to seek refuge at the
moment in the hills ; but, on being joined by many
of the common people, he summoned courage to
descend, fought and defeated the generals of
Antiochus, and drove them out of Judaea. This
success brought him supreme power ; his expulsion
of the foreigners led his countrymen willingly to
submit to his rulership, which, on his death, he be- c. 167 B.C.
queathed to Judas, the eldest [c] of his sons.

(4) Judas, assuming that Antiochus would not re- Exploits
main inactive, besides recruiting a native force, and death
of JUDAS
made an alliance—he was the first to do so—with MACCA-
the Romans ; [d] and when Epiphanes [e] again invaded BAEUS.
the country struck hard and forced him to retire.
Flushed with this success, he attacked the garrison,
not yet ousted from the capital, expelled the troops
from the upper city and confined them to the lower
portion of the town, known as Acra. Being now 165 B.C.

[c] According to 1 Macc. ii. 4, Judas was the third of the
five sons.
[d] Another anachronism : the treaty with Rome, if the
narrative of 1 Maccabees (viii.) is to be trusted, fell under
Demetrius (162–150 B.C.).
[e] Or rather his generals Lysias and Gorgias (1 Macc.).

Ἄκρα κέκληται· κυριεύσας δὲ τοῦ ἱεροῦ τόν τε
χῶρον ἐκάθηρε πάντα καὶ περιετείχισε, καὶ τὰ
πρὸς τὰς λειτουργίας σκεύη καινὰ κατασκευάσας
εἰς τὸν ναὸν εἰσήνεγκεν ὡς τῶν προτέρων μεμιαμ-
μένων, βωμόν τε ᾠκοδόμησεν ἕτερον καὶ τῶν
40 ἐναγισμῶν ἤρξατο. λαμβανούσης δὲ ἄρτι τὸ ἱερὸν
κατάστημα τῆς πόλεως τελευτᾷ μὲν Ἀντίοχος,
κληρονόμος δὲ τῆς βασιλείας αὐτοῦ καὶ τῆς πρὸς
Ἰουδαίους ἀπεχθείας ὁ υἱὸς Ἀντίοχος γίνεται.

41   (5) Συναγαγὼν γοῦν πεζῶν μὲν¹ μυριάδας πέντε,
ἱππεῖς δ' εἰς² πεντακισχιλίους, ἐλέφαντας δὲ ὀγδοήκοντα ἐμβάλλει διὰ τῆς Ἰουδαίας εἰς τὴν ὀρεινήν.
Βηθσουρὸν μὲν οὖν πολίχνην αἱρεῖ, κατὰ δὲ τόπον
ὃς καλεῖται Βεθζαχαρία, στενῆς οὔσης τῆς παρόδου,
42 Ἰούδας ὑπαντᾷ μετὰ τῆς δυνάμεως. πρὶν δὲ συν-
άψαι τὰς φάλαγγας Ἐλεάζαρος ὁ ἀδελφὸς αὐτοῦ
προϊδὼν τὸν ὑψηλότατον τῶν ἐλεφάντων πύργῳ
τε μεγάλῳ καὶ περιχρύσοις προτειχίσμασι κεκοσμημένον, ὑπολαβὼν ἐπ' αὐτοῦ τὸν Ἀντίοχον εἶναι
τῶν τε ἰδίων ἐκτρέχει πολὺ καὶ διακόψας τὸ
στῖφος τῶν πολεμίων ἐπὶ τὸν ἐλέφαντα διήνυσεν.
43 ἐφικέσθαι μὲν οὖν τοῦ δοκοῦντος εἶναι βασιλέως
οὐχ οἷός τε ἦν διὰ τὸ ὕψος, ὁ δὲ τὸ θηρίον ὑπὸ
τὴν γαστέρα πλήξας ἐπικατέσεισεν ἑαυτῷ καὶ συν-
τριβεὶς ἐτελεύτησεν, μηδὲν πλέον δράσας τοῦ μεγάλοις ἐπιβαλέσθαι, θέμενος εὐκλείας ἐν δευτέρῳ τὸ
44 ζῆν. ὅ γε μὴν κυβερνῶν τὸν ἐλέφαντα ἰδιώτης ἦν·
κἂν εἰ συνέβη δὲ εἶναι τὸν Ἀντίοχον, οὐδὲν πλέον

____
¹ Text emended by Destinon.   ² om. εἰς AM.

master of the temple, he cleansed the whole area and
walled it round, replaced the old and polluted vessels
for the services by others which he caused to be made
and brought into the sanctuary, built another altar
and reinstalled the expiatory sacrifices.[a] The city
was just recovering its hallowed character when Antiochus died, leaving his son Antiochus heir, alike to 164 B.C.
his kingdom, and to his detestation of the Jews.

(5) The latter, accordingly, having collected 50,000
infantry, some 5000 horse and 80 elephants, pushed
through Judaea into the hill country.[b] After capturing the small town of Bethsuron,[c] he was met at
a spot called Bethzacharia, where there is a narrow
defile, by Judas at the head of his forces. Before
the opposing armies came into action, Eleazar,
brother of Judas, observing the tallest of the elephants, surmounted by a huge howdah [d] and an
array of gilded battlements, and concluding that it
bore Antiochus, rushed out far beyond his own
lines and, cutting through the enemy's ranks, made
his way to the elephant. Being unable to reach the
supposed monarch because of his height from the
ground, he struck the beast below the belly, brought
its whole weight down upon himself, and was crushed
to death ; having achieved nothing more than to
attempt great things, holding life cheaper than renown. The elephant-rider was, in fact, a commoner ;
yet, even had he happened to be Antiochus, his

[a] See note on § 32.
[b] There is an independent account of this battle of the
elephants in 1 Macc. vi. 28 ff., of which Josephus made use
in his later work (A. xii.).
[c] According to 1 Macc. vi. 50 (A. xii. 376) Bethsuron
was not taken until after the battle.
[d] Greek " tower."

ἤνυσεν ἂν ὁ τολμήσας τοῦ δοκεῖν ἐπ' ἐλπίδι μόνῃ
λαμπροῦ κατορθώματος ἑλέσθαι τὸν θάνατον.
45 γίνεται δὲ καὶ κληδὼν τἀδελφῷ τῆς ὅλης παρα-
τάξεως· καρτερῶς μὲν γὰρ οἱ Ἰουδαῖοι καὶ μέχρι
πολλοῦ διηγωνίσαντο, πλήθει δὲ ὑπερέχοντες οἱ
βασιλικοὶ καὶ δεξιᾷ χρησάμενοι τύχῃ κρατοῦσι,
καὶ πολλῶν ἀναιρεθέντων τοὺς λοιποὺς ἔχων
Ἰούδας εἰς τὴν Γοφνιτικὴν τοπαρχίαν φεύγει.
46 Ἀντίοχος δὲ παρελθὼν εἰς Ἱεροσόλυμα καὶ καθίσας ὀλίγας ἡμέρας ἐν αὐτῇ κατὰ σπάνιν τῶν
ἐπιτηδείων ἀπανίσταται, καταλιπὼν μὲν φρουρὰν
ὅσην ἀποχρήσειν ὑπελάμβανε, τὴν δὲ λοιπὴν δύναμιν ἀπαγαγὼν χειμεριοῦσαν εἰς τὴν Συρίαν.
47 (6) Πρὸς δὲ τὴν ὑποχώρησιν τοῦ βασιλέως
Ἰούδας οὐκ ἠρέμει, προσγενομένων δ' ἐκ τοῦ
ἔθνους πολλῶν καὶ τοὺς διασωθέντας ἐκ τῆς μάχης
ἐπισυγκροτήσας κατὰ κώμην Ἀκέδασαν[1] συμβάλ-
λει τοῖς Ἀντιόχου στρατηγοῖς, καὶ φανεὶς ἄριστος
κατὰ τὴν μάχην πολλούς τε τῶν πολεμίων ἀποκτείνας ἀναιρεῖται. καὶ μεθ' ἡμέρας ὀλίγας ὁ
ἀδελφὸς αὐτοῦ Ἰωάννης ἐπιβουλευθεὶς ὑπὸ τῶν
τὰ Ἀντιόχου φρονούντων τελευτᾷ.

48 (ii. 1) Διαδεξάμενος δὲ τοῦτον ὁ ἀδελφὸς Ἰωνάθης τά τε ἄλλα πρὸς τοὺς ἐπιχωρίους διὰ φυλακῆς ἦγεν ἑαυτόν, καὶ τῇ πρὸς Ῥωμαίους φιλίᾳ
τὴν ἀρχὴν ἐκρατύνατο, πρός τε τὸν Ἀντιόχου

—————
[1] *Adasa* Lat., perhaps rightly ; *cf. A.* xii. 408.

[a] One of the eleven sub-districts of Judaea (*B.* iii. 55) ;
according to *A.* xii. 375 Judas withdrew to Jerusalem and
prepared for a siege.

[b] Strictly Nicanor, the general of Demetrius, 1 Macc.
vii. 39 ff.

daring assailant would have gained but the reputation of courting death in the bare expectation of a brilliant exploit. To Eleazar's brother the incident proved an omen of the issue of the engagement. For, long and stubborn as was the resistance of the Jews, the king's forces, with superior numbers and favoured by fortune, were victorious ; and, after the loss of many of his men, Judas fled with the remainder to the province of Gophna.[a] Antiochus proceeded to Jerusalem, where, owing to a shortage of supplies, he stayed but a few days ; he then left what he considered a sufficient garrison and withdrew the rest of his army to winter quarters in Syria.

(6) After the king's retreat, Judas did not remain inactive. Rallying the survivors of the combat and joined by numerous new recruits from his nation, he gave battle to the generals of Antiochus[b] at the village of Acedasa ; where, after winning the honours of the day and slaying a large number of the enemy, he was slain himself.[c] A few days later his brother 161 B.C. John also perished, a victim of a conspiracy of the partisans of Antiochus.[d]

(ii. 1) Jonathan, his brother, who succeeded him, JONATHAN amongst other safeguards against his countrymen, Jewish strengthened his authority by an alliance with leader Rome[e] and made a truce with the young Antiochus.[f] 161-143 B.C.

[c] Judas was slain, not at the battle of A(ce)dasa, but in a later engagement at Elasa (1 Macc. ix. 5) or Berzetho (A. xii. 422). [d] Cf. 1 Macc. ix. 35 f.; A. xiii. 10 f.
[e] 1 Macc. xii. 1-4; A. xiii. 164 f.
[f] Greek " the son of Antiochus," i.e. presumably of Antiochus IV Epiphanes. But the reference must be to the treaty of Jonathan with Antiochus VI Dionysus, 1 Macc. xi. 57, A. xiii. 145. Josephus has confused Antiochus V and Antiochus VI.

παῖδα διαλλαγὰς ἐποιήσατο. οὐ μήν τι τούτων
49 ἤρκεσεν αὐτῷ πρὸς ἀσφάλειαν· Τρύφων γὰρ ὁ
τύραννος, ἐπίτροπος μὲν ὢν τοῦ Ἀντιόχου παιδός,
ἐπιβουλεύων δ' αὐτῷ καὶ πρόσθεν, ἀποσκευάζε-
σθαι τοὺς φίλους αὐτοῦ πειρώμενος, ἥκοντα τὸν
Ἰωνάθην σὺν ὀλίγοις εἰς Πτολεμαΐδα πρὸς Ἀντίοχον δόλῳ συλλαμβάνει καὶ δήσας ἐπὶ Ἰουδαίαν
στρατεύει· εἶτ' ἀπελαθεὶς ὑπὸ τοῦ Σίμωνος, ὃς ἦν
ἀδελφὸς τοῦ Ἰωνάθου, καὶ πρὸς τὴν ἧτταν ὠργι-
σμένος κτείνει τὸν Ἰωνάθην.

50 (2) Σίμων δὲ γενναίως ἀφηγούμενος τῶν πραγμάτων αἱρεῖ μὲν Γάζαρά[1] τε καὶ Ἰόπην καὶ Ἰάμνειαν τῶν προσοίκων, κατέσκαψε δὲ καὶ τὴν
ἄκραν τῶν φρουρῶν κρατήσας. αὖθις δὲ γίνεται
καὶ Ἀντιόχῳ σύμμαχος κατὰ Τρύφωνος, ὃν ἐν
Δώροις πρὸ τῆς ἐπὶ Μήδους στρατείας ἐπολιόρ-
51 κει. ἀλλ' οὐκ ἐξεδυσώπησεν τὴν τοῦ βασιλέως
πλεονεξίαν Τρύφωνα συνεξελών· μετ' οὐ πολὺ
γὰρ Ἀντίοχος Κενδεβαῖον τὸν αὐτοῦ στρατηγὸν
μετὰ δυνάμεως δῃώσοντα τὴν Ἰουδαίαν ἔπεμψεν
52 καὶ καταδουλωσόμενον Σίμωνα. ὁ δὲ καίτοι γη-
ραιὸς ὢν νεανικώτερον ἀφηγήσατο τοῦ πολέμου·
τοὺς μέν τοι γε υἱεῖς αὐτοῦ[2] μετὰ τῶν ἐρρωμενε-
στάτων προεκπέμπει, αὐτὸς δὲ μοῖραν τῆς δυνά-
53 μεως ἀναλαβὼν ἐπῄει κατ' ἄλλο μέρος. πολλοὺς
δὲ πολλαχοῦ κἂν τοῖς ὄρεσι προλοχίσας πάσαις
κρατεῖ ταῖς ἐπιβολαῖς, καὶ νικήσας λαμπρῶς
ἀρχιερεὺς ἀποδείκνυται καὶ τῆς Μακεδόνων ἐπι-

---

[1] Bernard (cf. A. xiii. 215): Γάζαν or Ζαρά mss.
[2] M Lat.: ἐπ' αὐτὸν the rest.

[a] Cf. 1 Macc. xii. 39 ff.; A. xiii. 187 ff.

None, however, of these precautions proved a sufficient protection. For the tyrant Trypho, guardian of the young Antiochus, who was already conspiring against his ward and attempting to make away with his friends, treacherously arrested and imprisoned Jonathan, when on a mission with a small retinue to Antiochus at Ptolemais, and started on a campaign against Judaea. Repulsed by Simon, Jonathan's brother, and indignant at his defeat he then put his captive to death.[a]

(2) Simon's administration of affairs was excellent. He captured the towns of Gazara, Joppa, and Jamnia, in the vicinity of the capital, and, after overpowering the garrison at Jerusalem, razed the citadel [b] to the ground. Subsequently, he made alliance with Antiochus [c] against Trypho, whom the king, before his expedition against the Medes, was besieging at Dora. Yet Simon's contribution to the fall of Trypho failed to shame the king out of his cupidity ; for not long after Antiochus sent his general Cendebaeus at the head of an army to ravage Judaea and make a vassal of Simon. The latter, though advanced in years, took command of the war with juvenile energy ; and, sending his sons ahead with the most able-bodied of his troops, proceeded himself, with a division of his army, to the attack on another front. Having, further, posted numerous ambuscades in different parts of the hills, he was successful in all the engagements, and after a brilliant victory was appointed high-priest and liberated the Jews from

SIMON's leadership 142–135 B.C.

---

[b] Greek " Acra " ; A. xiii. 215 shows that Jerusalem is referred to.

[c] Antiochus VII Sidetes, A. xiii. 223. From this point the two narratives in B. and A. are closely parallel.

κρατείας μετὰ ἑκατὸν καὶ ἑβδομήκοντα ἔτη τοὺς
Ἰουδαίους ἀπαλλάττει.

54 (3) Θνήσκει δὲ καὶ αὐτὸς ἐπιβουλευθεὶς ἐν
συμποσίῳ ὑπὸ Πτολεμαίου τοῦ γαμβροῦ, ὃς
αὐτοῦ τήν τε γυναῖκα καὶ τοὺς δύο παῖδας ἐγκαθ-
είρξας ἐπὶ τὸν τρίτον Ἰωάννην, ὃς καὶ Ὑρκανὸς
55 ἐκαλεῖτο, τοὺς ἀναιρήσοντας ἔπεμψεν. προγνοὺς
δὲ τὴν ἔφοδον ὁ νεανίσκος παραγενέσθαι εἰς τὴν
πόλιν ἠπείγετο, πλεῖστον τῷ λαῷ πεποιθὼς κατά
τε μνήμην τῶν πατρῴων κατορθωμάτων καὶ
μῖσος τῆς Πτολεμαίου παρανομίας. ὥρμησε δὲ
καὶ Πτολεμαῖος εἰσελθεῖν καθ' ἑτέραν πύλην,
ἐξεκρούσθη γε μὴν ὑπὸ τοῦ δήμου ταχέως δεδεγ-
56 μένων ἤδη τὸν Ὑρκανόν. καὶ ὁ μὲν παραχρῆμα
ἀνεχώρησεν εἴς τι τῶν ὑπὲρ Ἱεριχοῦντος ἐρυμάτων, ὃ Δαγὼν καλεῖται· κομισάμενος δὲ τὴν
πατρῴαν ἀρχιερωσύνην Ὑρκανὸς καὶ θύσας τῷ
θεῷ μετὰ τάχους ἐπὶ Πτολεμαῖον ὥρμησεν βοηθήσων τῇ μητρὶ καὶ τοῖς ἀδελφοῖς.

57 (4) Καὶ προσβαλὼν τῷ φρουρίῳ τὰ μὲν ἄλλα
κρείττων ἦν, ἡττᾶτο δὲ δικαίου πάθους. ὁ γὰρ
Πτολεμαῖος ὁπότε καταπονοῖτο, τήν τε μητέρα
καὶ τοὺς ἀδελφοὺς αὐτοῦ προάγων ἐπὶ τοῦ τείχους
εἰς εὐσύνοπτον ᾐκίζετο καὶ κατακρημνιεῖν, εἰ μὴ
58 θᾶττον ἀπανασταίη, διηπείλει. πρὸς ἃ τὸν μὲν
Ὑρκανὸν ὀργῆς πλείων οἶκτος εἰσῄει καὶ δέος, ἡ
δὲ μήτηρ οὐδὲν οὔτε πρὸς τὰς αἰκίας οὔτε πρὸς
τὸν ἀπειλούμενον αὐτῇ θάνατον ἐνδιδοῦσα χεῖρας
ὤρεγε καὶ κατηντιβόλει τὸν παῖδα μήτι πρὸς τὴν

---

the Macedonian supremacy which had lasted for 170 years.[a]

(3) He too, however, fell a victim to treachery, being murdered at a banquet by his son-in-law Ptolemy. The latter, after incarcerating Simon's wife and two of his sons, sent a body of men to kill the third, John, also called Hyrcanus. This youth, forewarned of their approach, hastened to reach the city, fully confident of the people's support, both from their recollection of his father's achievements and their hatred of Ptolemy's enormities. Ptolemy also rushed to gain entrance by another gate, but was repelled by the populace, who had with alacrity already admitted Hyrcanus. Ptolemy forthwith withdrew to one of the fortresses above Jericho, called Dagon ; while Hyrcanus, having gained the high priestly office held by his father before him, offered sacrifice to God and then started in haste after Ptolemy to bring aid to his mother and brethren.

(4) Attacking the fort, he proved superior in other ways, but was overcome by his righteous feelings. For Ptolemy, as often as he was hard pressed, brought forward his mother and brothers upon the ramparts and tortured them within full view of Hyrcanus, threatening to hurl them over the battlements, if he did not instantly retire. At this spectacle indignation in the breast of Hyrcanus gave way to pity and terror. His mother, unshaken by her torments or the menace of death, with outstretched hands implored her son not to be moved

JOHN HYRCANUS (135–105 B.C.) opposes his brother-in-law Ptolemy.

dates from c. 142 B.C., i.e. from the *beginning* of his leadership, where it is placed in the parallel account in *A.* xiii. 213. *Cf.* 1 Macc. xiii. 41 f., " In the hundred and seventieth year was the yoke of the heathen taken away from Israel," and Jerusalem started a new era of its own.

αὐτῆς ὕβριν ἐπικλασθέντα φείσασθαι τοῦ δυσ-
σεβοῦς, ὡς αὐτῇ γε κρείττονα τὸν ἐκ Πτολεμαίου
θάνατον ἀθανασίας εἶναι δόντος δίκας ἐφ᾽ οἷς εἰς
59 τὸν οἶκον αὐτῶν παρηνόμησεν. ὁ δὲ Ἰωάννης
ὁπότε μὲν ἐνθυμηθείη τὸ παράστημα τῆς μητρὸς
καὶ κατακούσειε τῆς ἱκεσίας, ὥρμητο προσβάλ-
λειν, ἐπειδὰν δὲ[1] κατίδοι τυπτομένην τε καὶ σπα-
ραττομένην, ἐθηλύνετο καὶ τοῦ πάθους ὅλος ἦν.
60 τριβομένης δὲ διὰ ταῦτα τῆς πολιορκίας ἐπέστη
τὸ ἀργὸν ἔτος, ὃ κατὰ ἑπταετίαν ἀργεῖται παρὰ
Ἰουδαίοις ὁμοίως ταῖς ἑβδομάσιν ἡμέραις. κἂν
τούτῳ Πτολεμαῖος ἀνεθεὶς τῆς πολιορκίας ἀναιρεῖ
τοὺς ἀδελφοὺς Ἰωάννου σὺν τῇ μητρὶ καὶ φεύγει
πρὸς Ζήνωνα τὸν ἐπικληθέντα Κοτυλᾶν· Φιλ-
αδελφείας δ᾽ ἦν τύραννος.
61 (5) Ἀντίοχος δὲ κατ᾽ ὀργὴν ὧν ὑπὸ Σίμωνος
ἔπαθεν στρατεύσας εἰς τὴν Ἰουδαίαν ἐπολιόρκει
τὸν Ὑρκανὸν προσκαθεζόμενος τοῖς Ἱεροσολύμοις. ὁ δὲ τὸν Δαυίδου τάφον ἀνοίξας, ὃς δὴ
πλουσιώτατος βασιλέων ἐγένετο, καὶ ὑφελόμενος
ὑπὲρ τρισχίλια τάλαντα χρημάτων τόν τε Ἀντίοχον ἀνίστησι τῆς πολιορκίας πείσας τριακοσίοις
τάλαντοις, καὶ δὴ καὶ ξενοτροφεῖν πρῶτος Ἰουδαίων ἐκ τῆς περιουσίας ἤρξατο.
62 (6) Αὖθίς γε μὴν ὡς Ἀντίοχος ἐπὶ Μήδους
στρατεύσας καιρὸν ἀμύνης αὐτῷ παρεῖχεν, εὐθέως
ὥρμησεν ἐπὶ τὰς ἐν Συρίᾳ πόλεις, κενάς, ὅπερ ἦν,

---

[1] ἐπειδὰν δὲ mss.: ἐπεὶ δ᾽ αὖ Niese.

---

[a] The sabbatical year: Lev. xxv. 4.
[b] So A. vii. 393 ; in the parallel account in A. xiii. 249,

by her outrageous treatment to spare the monster ; to her, death at Ptolemy's hands would be better than immortality, if he paid the penalty for the wrongs which he had done to their house. John, as often as he took his mother's unflinching courage to heart and gave ear to her entreaties, was impelled to the assault ; but, when he beheld her beaten and mangled, he was unmanned and quite overcome by emotion. The siege consequently dragged on until the year of repose came round, which is kept septennially by the Jews as a period of inaction, like the seventh day of the week.[a] Ptolemy, now relieved of the siege, put John's brethren and their mother to death and fled to Zeno, surnamed Cotulas, the despot of Philadelphia.

(5) Antiochus, smarting under the blows which His war Simon had dealt him, led an army into Judaea and, with Antiochus sitting down before Jerusalem, besieged Hyrcanus ; (VII) Sidetes. who, opening the tomb of David, wealthiest of kings, extracted therefrom upwards of three thousand talents, with three hundred of which he bribed Antiochus to raise the blockade.[b] The surplus he used to pay a mercenary force, being the first Jew to start this practice.

(6) Subsequently, however, the campaign of Anti- His ochus against the Medes gave him an opportunity victories. for revenge.[c] He at once flew upon the cities of Syria, expecting to find them, as he did, drained of efficient

Hyrcanus did not open the tomb until after the departure of Antiochus.

[c] The account in *A*. xiii. 250 ff., is more trustworthy. There Hyrcanus joins Antiochus in his expedition against the Parthians (here called " Medes ") in 130 B.C. ; his attack on the Syrian cities only began after the death of Antiochus in 129 B.C.

63 ὑπολαμβάνων τῶν μαχιμωτέρων εὑρήσειν. Μεδά-
βην μὲν οὖν καὶ Σαμαγὰν ἅμα ταῖς πλησίον, ἔτι
δὲ Σίκιμα καὶ Ἀργαριζὶν αὐτὸς¹ αἱρεῖ, πρὸς αἷς τὸ
Χουθαίων γένος, οἳ περιῴκουν τὸ εἰκασθὲν τῷ ἐν
Ἱεροσολύμοις ἱερόν.² αἱρεῖ δὲ καὶ τῆς Ἰδουμαίας ἄλλας τε οὐκ ὀλίγας καὶ Ἀδωρεὸν καὶ
Μάρισαν.

64 (7) Προελθὼν δὲ καὶ μέχρι Σαμαρείας, ἔνθα
νῦν ἐστιν Σεβαστὴ πόλις ὑφ' Ἡρώδου κτισθεῖσα
τοῦ βασιλέως, καὶ πάντοθεν αὐτὴν ἀποτειχίσας
τοὺς υἱεῖς ἐπέστησε τῇ πολιορκίᾳ Ἀριστόβουλον
καὶ Ἀντίγονον· ὧν οὐδὲν ἀνιέντων λιμοῦ μὲν εἰς
τοσοῦτον προῆλθον οἱ κατὰ τὴν πόλιν, ὡς ἅψα-
65 σθαι καὶ τῶν ἀηθεστάτων. ἐπικαλοῦνται δὲ βοηθὸν Ἀντίοχον τὸν ἐπικληθέντα Ἀσπένδιον·³ κἀκεῖνος ἑτοίμως ὑπακούσας ὑπὸ τῶν περὶ Ἀριστόβουλον ἡττᾶται. καὶ ὁ μὲν μέχρι Σκυθοπόλεως
διωχθεὶς ὑπὸ τῶν ἀδελφῶν ἐκφεύγει, οἱ δ' ἐπὶ
τοὺς Σαμαρεῖς ὑποστρέψαντες τό τε πλῆθος
πάλιν εἰς τὸ τεῖχος συγκλείουσιν καὶ τὴν πόλιν
ἑλόντες αὐτήν τε κατασκάπτουσιν καὶ τοὺς ἐν-
66 οικοῦντας ἐξηνδραποδίσαντο. προχωρούντων δὲ
τῶν κατορθωμάτων τὴν ὁρμὴν οὐ κατέψυξαν, ἀλλὰ
προελθόντες ἅμα τῇ δυνάμει μέχρι τῆς Σκυθοπόλεως ταύτην τε κατέδραμον καὶ τὴν ἐντὸς Καρ-
μήλου τοῦ ὄρους χώραν ἅπασαν κατενείμαντο.

67 (8) Πρὸς δὲ τὰς εὐπραγίας αὐτοῦ τε Ἰωάννου
καὶ τῶν παίδων φθόνος ἐγείρει στάσιν τῶν ἐπιχωρίων, καὶ πολλοὶ κατ' αὐτῶν συνελθόντες
οὐκ ἠρέμουν, μέχρι καὶ πρὸς φανερὸν πόλεμον ἐκ-

---

¹ A. (in parallel passage) has εὐθὺς: ? read οὕτως.
² Niese: ἱερῷ mss.   ³ Ἀσπόνδιον mss.

troops. He thus captured Medabe and Samaga with
the neighbouring towns, also Sichem and Argarizin,
besides defeating the Cuthaeans,[a] the race inhabiting
the country surrounding the temple modelled on
that at Jerusalem. He further took numerous cities
in Idumaea, including Adoreon and Marisa.

(7) Advancing to Samaria, on the site of which
now stands the city of Sebaste, founded by King
Herod, he blockaded it by a surrounding wall and
entrusted the siege to his sons Aristobulus and
Antigonus, who pressed it so vigorously that the
inhabitants were reduced by the extremities of
famine to make use of the most unheard of food.
They summoned to their aid Antiochus, surnamed
Aspendius,[b] who, readily complying, was defeated by
the forces of Aristobulus. Pursued by the brothers
as far as Scythopolis he got away ; they on their
return to Samaria again confined its people within
the walls, captured the town, razed it to the ground,
and reduced the inhabitants to slavery. Not allowing
the flowing tide of success to cool their ardour, they
proceeded with their army to Scythopolis, overran
that district, and laid waste the whole country south
of [c] Mount Carmel.

(8) The prosperous fortunes of John and his sons, His
however, provoked a sedition among his envious prosperous
countrymen, large numbers of whom held meetings gift of
to oppose them and continued to agitate, until the prophecy.
smouldering flames burst out in open war and the

[a] The foreigners imported into Samaria at the time of the
exile, *A.* ix. 288, 2 Kings xvii. 24.

[b] Antiochus of Aspendus (in Pamphylia) = Antiochus VIII
or Grypus ; *A.* xiii. 276 names, instead of him, his half-
brother and rival, Antiochus IX Cyzicenus.

[c] Literally " within," *i.e.* " this side of."

68 ῥιπισθέντες ἡττῶνται. τὸ λοιπὸν δ' ἐπιβιοὺς ἐν
εὐδαιμονίᾳ Ἰωάννης καὶ τὰ κατὰ τὴν ἀρχὴν κάλλιστα διοικήσας ἑνὶ[1] καὶ τριάκοντα ὅλοις ἔτεσιν
ἐπὶ πέντε υἱοῖς τελευτᾷ, μακαριστὸς ὄντως καὶ
κατὰ μηδὲν ἐάσας ἐφ' ἑαυτῷ μεμφθῆναι τὴν τύχην.
τρία γοῦν τὰ κρατιστεύοντα μόνος εἶχεν, τήν τε
ἀρχὴν τοῦ ἔθνους καὶ τὴν ἀρχιερωσύνην καὶ προ-
69 φητείαν. ὡμίλει γὰρ αὐτῷ τὸ δαιμόνιον ὡς μηδὲν
τῶν μελλόντων ἀγνοεῖν, ὅς γε καὶ περὶ δύο τῶν
πρεσβυτέρων υἱῶν ὅτι μὴ διαμενοῦσι κύριοι τῶν
πραγμάτων προεῖδέν τε καὶ προεφήτευσεν· ὧν
τὴν καταστροφὴν ἄξιον ἀφηγήσασθαι, παρ' ὅσον
τῆς πατρῴας εὐδαιμονίας ἀπέκλιναν.

70 (iii. 1) Μετὰ γὰρ τὴν τοῦ πατρὸς τελευτὴν ὁ
πρεσβύτατος αὐτῶν Ἀριστόβουλος, τὴν ἀρχὴν εἰς
βασιλείαν μεταθείς, περιτίθεται μὲν διάδημα πρῶτος μετὰ τετρακοσιοστὸν καὶ ἑβδομηκοστὸν πρῶτον ἔτος, πρὸς δὲ μῆνας τρεῖς, ἐξ οὗ κατῄει[2] ὁ
λαὸς εἰς τὴν χώραν ἀπαλλαγεὶς τῆς ἐν Βαβυλῶνι
71 δουλείας· τῶν δὲ ἀδελφῶν τὸν μὲν μεθ' ἑαυτὸν
Ἀντίγονον, ἐδόκει γὰρ ἀγαπᾶν, ἦγεν ἰσοτίμως,
τοὺς δ' ἄλλους εἷργνυσι δήσας. δεσμεῖ δὲ καὶ τὴν
μητέρα διενεχθεῖσαν περὶ τῆς ἐξουσίας, ταύτην
γὰρ κυρίαν τῶν ὅλων ὁ Ἰωάννης ἀπολελοίπει, καὶ
μέχρι τοσαύτης ὠμότητος προῆλθεν, ὥστε καὶ
λιμῷ διαφθεῖραι δεδεμένην.

72 (2) Περιέρχεται δὲ αὐτὸν[3] ἡ ποινὴ[4] εἰς τὸν

---

[1] ἑνὶ (with Hegesippus) Niese, cf. A. xiii. 299, xx. 240: ἐν
τρισὶν MSS. Lat., ENI having perhaps been read as EN Ι'.
[2] AM: κατῆλθεν the rest.
[3] AMC: αὐτῶ(ν) the rest.　　　　[4] AM: τίσις the rest.

---

[a] 481 years according to A. xiii. 301. Both numbers are

rebels were defeated. For the rest of his days John lived in prosperity, and, after excellently directing the government for thirty-one whole years, died leaving five sons ; truly a blessed individual and one who left no ground for complaint against fortune as regards himself. He was the only man to unite in his person three of the highest privileges : the supreme command of the nation, the high priesthood, and the gift of prophecy. For so closely was he in touch with the Deity, that he was never ignorant of the future ; thus he foresaw and predicted that his two elder sons would not remain at the head of affairs. The story of their downfall is worth relating, and will show how great was the decline from their father's good fortune.

(iii. 1) On the death of Hyrcanus, Aristobulus, the eldest of his sons, transformed the government into a monarchy, and was the first to assume the diadem, four hundred and seventy-one years [a] and three months after the return of the people to their country, when released from servitude in Babylon. Of his brothers, he conferred upon Antigonus, the next in seniority, for whom he had an apparent affection, honours equal to his own ; the rest he imprisoned in chains. His mother also, who had disputed his claim to authority, John having left her mistress of the realm, he confined in bonds, and carried his cruelty so far as to starve her to death in prison.

(2) Retribution, however, overtook him [b] in the

ARISTO-
BULUS I
105–104 B.C.

too large ; the decree of Cyrus for the return of the Jews is dated 537 B.C., 432 years before Aristobulus I. The chronology of Josephus appears to be based on the " seventy weeks " (=490 years) of Dan. ix. 24.

[b] See §§ 81 ff.

ἀδελφὸν Ἀντίγονον, ὃν ἠγάπα τε καὶ τῆς βασιλείας κοινωνὸν εἶχεν· κτείνει γὰρ καὶ τοῦτον ἐκ
διαβολῶν, ἃς οἱ πονηροὶ τῶν κατὰ τὸ βασίλειον
ἐνεσκευάσαντο. τὰ μὲν δὴ πρῶτα διηπίστει τοῖς
λεγομένοις ὁ Ἀριστόβουλος, ἅτε δὴ καὶ τὸν ἀδελφὸν ἀγαπῶν καὶ διδοὺς φθόνῳ τὰ πολλὰ τῶν
73 λογοποιουμένων. ὡς δ᾽ ὁ Ἀντίγονος λαμπρὸς
ἀπὸ στρατείας ἦλθεν εἰς τὴν ἑορτήν, ἐν ᾗ σκηνο-
ποιεῖσθαι πάτριον τῷ θεῷ, συνέβη μὲν κατ᾽
ἐκείνας τὰς ἡμέρας νόσῳ χρήσασθαι τὸν Ἀριστόβουλον, τὸν δὲ Ἀντίγονον ἐπὶ τέλει τῆς ἑορτῆς
ἀναβάντα μετὰ τῶν περὶ αὐτὸν ὁπλιτῶν, ὡς ἐνῆν
μάλιστα κεκοσμημένον, προσκυνῆσαι τὸ πλέον
74 ὑπὲρ τἀδελφοῦ. κἀν τούτῳ προσιόντες οἱ πονηροὶ τῷ βασιλεῖ τήν τε πομπὴν τῶν ὁπλιτῶν ἐδήλουν καὶ τὸ παράστημα τοῦ Ἀντιγόνου μεῖζον ἢ
κατ᾽ ἰδιώτην, ὅτι τε παρείη[1] μετὰ μεγίστου συντάγματος ἀναιρήσων αὐτόν· οὐ γὰρ ἀνέχεσθαι
τιμὴν μόνον ἐκ βασιλείας ἔχων, παρὸν αὐτὴν
κατασχεῖν.
75   (3) Τούτοις κατὰ μικρὸν ἄκων ἐπίστευσεν ὁ
Ἀριστόβουλος, καὶ προνοῶν τοῦ μήθ᾽ ὑποπτεύων
φανερὸς γενέσθαι καὶ προησφαλίσθαι πρὸς τὸ
ἄδηλον καθίστησι[2] μὲν τοὺς σωματοφύλακας ἔν
τινι τῶν ὑπογαίων ἀλαμπεῖ, κατέκειτο δ᾽ ἐν τῇ
Βάρει πρότερον αὖθις δ᾽ Ἀντωνίᾳ μετονομα-
σθείσῃ, προστάξας ἀνόπλου μὲν ἀπέχεσθαι, κτείνειν δὲ τὸν Ἀντίγονον, εἰ μετὰ τῶν ὅπλων προσίοι,
καὶ πρὸς αὐτὸν ἔπεμψεν τοὺς προεροῦντας ἄν-
76 οπλον ἐλθεῖν. πρὸς τοῦτο πάνυ πανούργως ἡ
βασίλισσα συντάσσεται μετὰ τῶν ἐπιβούλων·

---

[1] C: παρήει the rest.   [2] διίστησι LVN.

person of his brother Antigonus, whom he loved and
had made partner of his kingdom ; for he slew him murders his
also, owing to calumnies concocted by knavish brother
courtiers. Aristobulus at first distrusted their state- Antigonus.
ments, out of affection for his brother and because
he attributed most of these fabricated reports to
envy. But one day when Antigonus had come in
pomp from a campaign to attend the festival at
which, according to national custom, tabernacles are
erected in God's honour,[a] Aristobulus happened to
be ill ; and, at the close of the ceremony, Antigonus,
surrounded by his bodyguard and arrayed with the
utmost splendour, went up (to the Temple) and
offered special worship on his brother's behalf.
Thereupon these villains went off to the king and
told him of the military escort and of Antigonus's air
of assurance, grander than became a subject, and
that he was coming with an immense body of troops
to put him to death, disdaining the mere honours of
royalty when he might occupy the throne itself.

(3) Gradually and reluctantly Aristobulus came to
believe these insinuations. Taking precautions at
once to conceal his suspicions and to secure himself
against risks, he posted his bodyguards in an unlit
subterranean passage—he was lying at the time in
the castle formerly called Baris, afterwards Antonia
—with orders to let Antigonus pass, if unarmed, but
to kill him if he approached in arms. To Antigonus
himself he sent instructions to come unarmed. To
meet the occasion the queen concerted with the
conspirators a very crafty plot. They induced the

---

[a] The autumn feast of *Sukkoth* or Tabernacles.

τοὺς γὰρ πεμφθέντας πείθουσιν τὰ μὲν παρὰ τοῦ
βασιλέως σιωπῆσαι, λέγειν δὲ πρὸς τὸν Ἀντίγονον ὡς ὁ ἀδελφὸς ἀκούσας ὅπλα τε αὐτῷ παρ-
εσκευακέναι κάλλιστα καὶ πολεμικὸν κόσμον ἐν τῇ
Γαλιλαίᾳ, διὰ μὲν τὴν ἀσθένειαν αὐτὸς ἐπιδεῖν
ἕκαστα κωλυθείη, νῦν δ' ἐπεὶ καὶ χωρίζεσθαι
μέλλοις, θεάσαιτ' ἂν ἥδιστά σε ἐν τοῖς ὅπλοις.

77 (4) Ταῦτ' ἀκούσας ὁ Ἀντίγονος, ἐνῆγεν δ' ἡ
τοῦ ἀδελφοῦ διάθεσις μηδὲν ὑποπτεύειν πονηρόν,
ἐχώρει μετὰ τῶν ὅπλων, ὡς πρὸς ἐπίδειξιν.
γενόμενος δὲ κατὰ τὴν σκοτεινὴν πάροδον, Στράτωνος ἐκαλεῖτο πύργος, ὑπὸ τῶν σωματοφυλάκων ἀναιρεῖται, βέβαιον ἀποδείξας ὅτι πᾶσαν εὔνοιαν καὶ φύσιν κόπτει διαβολὴ καὶ οὐδὲν οὕτως
τῶν ἀγαθῶν παθῶν ἰσχυρόν, ὃ τῷ φθόνῳ μέχρι
παντὸς ἀντέχει.

78 (5) Θαυμάσαι δ' ἄν τις ἐν τούτῳ καὶ Ἰούδαν,
Ἐσσαῖος ἦν γένος οὐκ ἔστιν ὅτε πταίσας ἢ ψευ-
σθεὶς ἐν τοῖς προαπαγγέλμασιν, ὃς ἐπειδὴ καὶ τότε
τὸν Ἀντίγονον ἐθεάσατο παριόντα διὰ τοῦ ἱεροῦ,
πρὸς τοὺς γνωρίμους ἀνέκραγεν, ἦσαν δ' οὐκ
ὀλίγοι παρεδρεύοντες αὐτῷ τῶν μανθανόντων,

79 "παπαί, νῦν ἐμοὶ καλόν," ἔφη, "τὸ θανεῖν, ὅτε
μου[1] προτέθηκεν ἡ ἀλήθεια καί τι τῶν ὑπ' ἐμοῦ
προρρηθέντων διέψευσται· ζῇ γὰρ Ἀντίγονος
οὑτοσὶ σήμερον ὀφείλων ἀνῃρῆσθαι. χωρίον δὲ
αὐτῷ πρὸς σφαγὴν Στράτωνος πύργος εἵμαρτο·
καὶ τοῦτο μὲν ἀπὸ ἑξακοσίων ἐντεῦθεν σταδίων
ἐστίν, ὧραι δὲ τῆς ἡμέρας ἤδη τέσσαρες. ὁ δὴ
80 χρόνος ἐκκρούει τὸ μάντευμα." ταῦτ' εἰπὼν σκυθρωπὸς ἐπὶ συννοίας ὁ γέρων διεκαρτέρει, καὶ

_____
[1] Niese: μοι MSS.

messengers to keep the king's orders to themselves, and instead to tell Antigonus that his brother had heard that he had procured for himself some very fine armour and military decorations in Galilee ; that illness prevented him from paying a visit of inspection ; " but, now that you are on the point of departure, I shall be very glad to see you in your armour."

(4) On hearing this, as there was nothing in his brother's disposition to arouse his suspicions, Antigonus went off in his armour as for a parade. On reaching the dark passage, called Strato's Tower, he was slain by the bodyguard ; affording a sure proof that calumny severs all ties of affection and of nature, and that of our better feelings none is strong enough to hold out interminably against envy.

(5) Another feature of this case which may well excite astonishment was the conduct of Judas. He was of Essene extraction, and his predictions had never once proved erroneous or false.[a] On this occasion, seeing Antigonus passing through the court of the temple, he exclaimed to his acquaintances— a considerable number of his disciples were seated beside him—" Ah me ! now were I better dead, since truth has died before me and one of my prophecies has been falsified. For yonder is Antigonus alive, who ought to have been slain to-day. The place predestined for his murder was Strato's Tower, and that is 600 furlongs from here ; and it is already the fourth hour of the day. So time frustrates the prophecy." Having said this, the old man remained plunged in gloomy meditation. A

Prediction of the murder by Judas the Essene.

---

[a] For the Essenes as prophets see *B.* ii. 159 with note.

μετ' ὀλίγον ἀνῃρημένος Ἀντίγονος ἠγγέλλετο
κατὰ τὸ ὑπόγαιον χωρίον, ὃ δὴ καὶ αὐτὸ Στράτωνος ἐκαλεῖτο πύργος, ὁμωνυμοῦν τῇ παραλίῳ
Καισαρείᾳ. τοῦτο γοῦν τὸν μάντιν διετάραξεν.

81 (6) Ἀριστοβούλῳ γε μὴν εὐθὺς ἡ περὶ τοῦ
μύσους μεταμέλεια νόσον ἐνσκήπτει καὶ πρὸς
ἔννοιαν τοῦ φόνου τὴν ψυχὴν ἔχων ἀεὶ τεταραγ-
μένην συνετήκετο, μέχρι τῶν σπλάγχνων ὑπ'
ἀκράτου τῆς λύπης σπαραττομένων ἄθρουν αἷμα
82 ἀναβάλλει. τοῦτό τις τῶν ἐν τῇ θεραπείᾳ παίδων
ἐκφέρων δαιμονίῳ προνοίᾳ σφάλλεται καθ' ὃν
τόπον Ἀντίγονος ἔσφακτο, καὶ φαινομένοις ἔτι
τοῖς ἀπὸ τοῦ φόνου σπίλοις τὸ αἷμα τοῦ κτείναντος
ἐπεξέχεεν. ἤρθη δ' εὐθὺς οἰμωγὴ τῶν θεασα-
μένων, ὥσπερ ἐπίτηδες τοῦ παιδὸς ἐκεῖ ἐπικατα-
83 σπείσαντος τὸ αἷμα. τῆς δὲ βοῆς ἀκούσας ὁ
βασιλεὺς τὴν αἰτίαν ἐπυνθάνετο, καὶ μηδενὸς
τολμῶντος εἰπεῖν μᾶλλον ἐνέκειτο μαθεῖν ἐθέλων·
τέλος δ' ἀπειλοῦντι καὶ βιαζομένῳ τἀληθὲς εἶπον.
ὁ δὲ τοὺς ὀφθαλμοὺς ἐμπίπλησι δακρύων καὶ
84 στενάξας ὅσον ἦν αὐτῷ δύναμις εἶπεν· "οὐκ
ἄρα θεοῦ μέγαν ὀφθαλμὸν ἐπ' ἔργοις ἀθεμίτοις
λήσειν ἔμελλον, ἀλλά με ταχεῖα μέτεισι δίκη
φόνου συγγενοῦς. μέχρι τοῦ[1] μοι, σῶμα ἀναιδέ-
στατον, τὴν ἀδελφῷ καὶ μητρὶ κατάκριτον ψυχὴν
καθέξεις; μέχρι τοῦ[1] δ' αὐτοῖς[2] ἐπισπείσω κατὰ
μέρος τοὐμὸν αἷμα; λαβέτωσαν ἀθρόον τοῦτο,
καὶ μηκέτι ταῖς ἐκ τῶν ἐμῶν σπλάγχνων χοαῖς

[1] Niese: ποῦ mss.
[2] Destinon (with Lat.): αὐτὸς mss.

little later came the news that Antigonus had been
slain in the underground quarter, also called, like
the maritime Caesarea, Strato's Tower.[a] It was this
identity of names which had disconcerted the seer.

(6) Remorse for his foul deed had the instant effect The end of
of aggravating the malady of Aristobulus. His mind Aristobulus.
ever distracted with thoughts of the murder, he fell
into a decline ; until, sheer grief rending his entrails,
he threw up a quantity of blood. While removing
this, one of the pages in attendance slipped, so
divine providence willed, on the very spot where
Antigonus had been assassinated, and spilt on the
yet visible stains of the murder the blood of the
murderer. An instantaneous cry broke from the
spectators, believing that the lad had intentionally
poured the bloody libation on that spot. The king,
hearing the cry, inquired what was its cause, and,
when no one ventured to tell him, became more
insistent in his desire to be informed. At length,
under pressure of threats, they told him the truth.
With tears filling his eyes and a groan such as his
remaining strength permitted, he said : " My law-
less deeds, then, were not destined to escape God's
mighty eye ; swift retribution pursues me for my
kinsman's blood. How long, most shameless body,
wilt thou detain the soul that is sentenced to a
brother's and a mother's vengeance ? How long
shall I make them these drop-by-drop libations of
my blood ? Let them take it all at once, and let
heaven cease to mock them with these dribbling

[a] For Strato's Tower on the coast, afterwards rebuilt by
Herod the Great and renamed Caesarea, see *B.* i. 408 ff.
The quarter in Jerusalem so called is not mentioned else-
where except in the parallel passage in *A.* xiii.

ἐπειρωνευέσθω τὸ δαιμόνιον.'' ταῦτ' εἰπὼν εὐθέως τελευτᾷ βασιλεύσας οὐ πλεῖον ἐνιαυτοῦ.

85 (iv. 1) Λύσασα δ' ἡ γυνὴ τοὺς ἀδελφοὺς αὐτοῦ
βασιλέα καθίστησιν Ἀλέξανδρον, τὸν καὶ καθ'
ἡλικίαν καὶ μετριότητι προύχειν δοκοῦντα. ὁ δὲ
παρελθὼν εἰς τὴν ἐξουσίαν τὸν ἕτερον μὲν τῶν
ἀδελφῶν βασιλειῶντα κτείνει, τὸν δὲ καταλιμ-
πανόμενον ἀγαπῶντα τὸ ζῆν δίχα πραγμάτων
εἶχεν <ἐν τιμῇ>.[1]

86 (2) Γίνεται δ' αὐτῷ καὶ πρὸς τὸν Λάθουρον
ἐπικληθέντα Πτολεμαῖον συμβολὴ πόλιν Ἀσωχὶν
ᾑρηκότα, καὶ πολλοὺς μὲν ἀνεῖλεν τῶν πολεμίων,
ἡ δὲ νίκη πρὸς Πτολεμαῖον ἔρρεψεν. ἐπεὶ δ'
οὗτος ὑπὸ τῆς μητρὸς Κλεοπάτρας διωχθεὶς εἰς
Αἴγυπτον ἀνεχώρησεν, Ἀλέξανδρος Γαδάρων τε
πολιορκίᾳ κρατεῖ καὶ Ἀμαθοῦντος, ὃ δὴ μέγιστον
μὲν ἦν ἔρυμα τῶν ὑπὲρ Ἰορδάνην, τὰ τιμιώτατα
δὲ τῶν Θεοδώρου τοῦ Ζήνωνος κτημάτων ἦν ἐν
87 αὐτῷ. ἐπελθὼν δ' ἐξαίφνης ὁ Θεόδωρος τά τε
σφέτερα καὶ τὴν τοῦ βασιλέως ἀποσκευὴν αἱρεῖ,
τῶν δ' Ἰουδαίων εἰς μυρίους κτείνει. γίνεται δ'
ἐπάνω τῆς πληγῆς Ἀλέξανδρος καὶ τραπόμενος
εἰς τὴν παράλιον αἱρεῖ Γάζαν τε καὶ Ῥάφιαν καὶ
Ἀνθηδόνα τὴν αὖθις ὑφ' Ἡρώδου τοῦ βασιλέως
Ἀγριππιάδα ἐπικληθεῖσαν.

88 (3) Ἐξανδραποδισαμένῳ δὲ ταύτας ἐπανίσταται
τὸ Ἰουδαϊκὸν ἐν ἑορτῇ· μάλιστα γὰρ ἐν ταῖς

---

[1] ἐν τιμῇ om. mss. : inserted by Hudson from *A.* xiii. 323.

---

[a] Salina (*v.l.* Salome) or Alexandra, *A.* xiii. 320. Though
Josephus never expressly says so, it appears certain that,
besides the throne, she gave Alexander Jannaeus her hand
in marriage. For her subsequent reign see § 107.

offerings from my entrails." With these words on his lips he expired, after a reign of no more than a year.

(iv. 1) The widow of Aristobulus [a] released his imprisoned brothers and placed on the throne Alexander, who had the double advantage over the others of seniority and apparent moderation of character. However, on coming into power, he put to death one brother, who had aspirations to the throne ; the survivor, who was content with [b] a quiet life, he held in honour.

ALEXANDER JANNAEUS 104–78 B.C.

(2) He also had an encounter with Ptolemy, surnamed Lathyrus, who had taken the town of Asochis ; although he killed many of the enemy, victory inclined to his opponent. But when Ptolemy, pursued by his mother Cleopatra, retired to Egypt,[c] Alexander besieged and took Gadara and Amathus, the latter being the most important of the fortresses beyond Jordan and containing the most precious possessions of Theodorus, son of Zeno. Theodorus, however, suddenly appearing, captured both his own treasures and the king's baggage and put some ten thousand Jews to the sword. Alexander, nevertheless, recovering from this blow, turned towards the coast and captured Gaza, Raphia, and Anthedon, a town which subsequently received from King Herod the name of Agrippias.[d]

His early wars.

(3) After his reduction of these places to servitude, the Jewish populace rose in revolt against him at

The Jews revolt against him.

[b] Or " loved."
[c] More correctly to Cyprus, where he reigned after his expulsion by Cleopatra from the throne of Egypt ; *A.* xiii. 328, 358.
[d] See *B.* i. 416 (where the name is given as Agrippeion).

εὐωχίαις αὐτῶν στάσις ἅπτεται. καὶ ἐδόκει μὴ
ἂν κρείττων γενέσθαι τῆς ἐπιβουλῆς, εἰ μὴ τὸ
ξενικὸν αὐτῷ παρεβοήθει· Πισίδαι καὶ Κίλικες
ἦσαν· Σύρους γὰρ οὐκ ἐδέχετο μισθοφόρους διὰ
τὴν ἔμφυτον αὐτῶν πρὸς τὸ ἔθνος ἀπέχθειαν.
89 κτείνας δὲ τῶν ἐπαναστάντων ὑπὲρ ἑξακισχιλίους
Ἀραβίας ἥπτετο, καὶ ταύτης ἑλὼν Γαλααδίτας
καὶ Μωαβίτας, φόρον τε αὐτοῖς ἐπιτάξας, ἀνέστρεψεν ἐπὶ Ἀμαθοῦντα. Θεοδώρου δὲ πρὸς τὰς
εὐπραγίας αὐτοῦ[1] καταπλαγέντος ἔρημον λαβὼν τὸ
φρούριον κατέσκαψεν.
90   (4) Ἔπειτα συμβαλὼν Ὀβέδᾳ τῷ Ἀράβων
βασιλεῖ προλοχίσαντι κατὰ τὴν Γαυλάνην ἐνέδρας
αὐτῷ γενομένης πᾶσαν ἀποβάλλει τὴν στρατιάν,
συνωσθεῖσαν κατὰ βαθείας φάραγγος καὶ πλήθει
καμήλων συντριβεῖσαν. διαφυγὼν δ’ αὐτὸς εἰς
Ἱεροσόλυμα τῷ μεγέθει τῆς συμφορᾶς πάλαι
91 μισοῦν τὸ ἔθνος ἠρέθισεν εἰς ἐπανάστασιν. γίνεται
δὲ καὶ τότε κρείττων καὶ μάχαις ἐπαλλήλοις οὐκ
ἔλαττον πεντακισμυρίων Ἰουδαίων ἀνεῖλεν ἐν ἓξ
ἔτεσιν. οὐ μὴν εὐφραίνετό γε ταῖς νίκαις τὴν
ἑαυτοῦ βασιλείαν ἀναλίσκων· ὅθεν παυσάμενος
τῶν ὅπλων λόγοις ἐπεχείρει διαλύεσθαι πρὸς τοὺς
92 ὑποτεταγμένους. οἱ δὲ μᾶλλον ἐμίσουν τὴν μετάνοιαν αὐτοῦ καὶ τοῦ τρόπου τὸ ἀνώμαλον, πυνθανομένῳ τε [τὸ αἴτιον][2] τί ἂν ποιήσας καταστείλειεν
αὐτούς, ἀποθανών, ἔλεγον· νεκρῷ γὰρ ἂν διαλ-
λαγῆναι μόλις τῷ τοσαῦτα δράσαντι. ἅμα δὲ καὶ
τὸν Ἄκαιρον ἐπικληθέντα Δημήτριον ἐπεκαλοῦντο.

---

[1] αὐτοῦ Lat., Hegesippus: αὐτὸν mss.
[2] omit Destinon: has probably arisen out of τε τί ἂν.

one of the festivals ; for it is on these festive occasions that sedition is most apt to break out. It was thought that he would never have quelled this conspiracy, had not his mercenaries come to his aid. These were natives of Pisidia and Cilicia ; Syrians he did not admit to the force on account of their innate hatred of his nation. After slaying upwards of six thousand of the insurgents, he attacked Arabia ; there he subdued the people of Galaad and Moab and imposed tribute upon them, and then returned once more to Amathus. Theodorus being overawed by his victories, he found the fortress abandoned and razed it to the ground.

(4) He next attacked Obedas, king of Arabia. The latter having laid an ambuscade near Gaulane, Alexander fell into the trap and lost his entire army, which was cooped into a deep ravine and crushed under a multitude of camels. He himself escaped to Jerusalem, but the magnitude of his disaster provoked the nation, which had long hated him, to insurrection. Yet once again he proved a match for them, **His long war with his subjects** and in a succession of engagements in six years killed no fewer than fifty thousand Jews. His victories, however, by which he wasted his realm, brought him little satisfaction ; desisting, therefore, from hostilities, he endeavoured to conciliate his subjects by persuasion. But his change of policy and inconsistency of character only aggravated their hatred ; and when he inquired what he could do to pacify them, they replied " Die ; even death would hardly reconcile us to one guilty of your enormities." They **and with Demetrius the Unready.** simultaneously appealed for aid to Demetrius, sur-

45

ῥᾳδίως δὲ ὑπακούσαντος κατ' ἐλπίδα μειζόνων
καὶ μετὰ στρατιᾶς ἥκοντος συνέμισγον οἱ Ἰουδαῖοι
τοῖς συμμάχοις περὶ Σίκιμα.

93 (5) Δέχεται δ' ἑκατέρους Ἀλέξανδρος ἱππεῦσι
μὲν χιλίοις, μισθοφόροις δὲ πεζοῖς ὀκτακισχιλίοις·
παρῆν δὲ αὐτῷ καὶ τὸ εὐνοοῦν Ἰουδαϊκὸν εἰς
μυρίους. τῶν δ' ἐναντίων ἱππεῖς μὲν ἦσαν τρισχίλιοι, πεζῶν δὲ μύριοι τετρακισχίλιοι. καὶ πρὶν
εἰς χεῖρας ἐλθεῖν διακηρύσσοντες οἱ βασιλεῖς ἐπειρῶντο τῶν παρ' ἀλλήλοις ἀποστάσεων, Δημήτριος
μὲν τοὺς Ἀλεξάνδρου μισθοφόρους, Ἀλέξανδρος
δὲ τοὺς ἅμα Δημητρίῳ Ἰουδαίους μεταπείσειν
94 ἐλπίσας. ὡς δ' οὔτε οἱ Ἰουδαῖοι θυμῶν,[1] οὔτε οἱ
Ἕλληνες ἐπαύσαντο πίστεως, διεκρίνοντο ἤδη τοῖς
95 ὅπλοις συμπεσόντες. κρατεῖ δὲ τῇ μάχῃ Δημήτριος, καίτοι πολλὰ τῶν Ἀλεξάνδρου μισθοφόρων
καὶ ψυχῆς ἔργα καὶ χειρὸς ἐπιδειξαμένων. χωρεῖ
δὲ τὸ τέλος τῆς παρατάξεως παρὰ δόξαν ἀμφοτέ-
ροις· οὔτε γὰρ Δημητρίῳ παρέμειναν νικῶντι οἱ
καλέσαντες, καὶ κατ' οἶκτον τῆς μεταβολῆς Ἀλεξάνδρῳ προσεχώρησαν εἰς τὰ ὄρη καταφυγόντι
Ἰουδαίων ἑξακισχίλιοι. ταύτην τὴν ῥοπὴν οὐκ
ἤνεγκεν Δημήτριος, ἀλλ' ὑπολαβὼν ἤδη μὲν ἀξιό-
μαχον εἶναι πάλιν Ἀλέξανδρον, μεταρρεῖν δὲ καὶ
πᾶν τὸ ἔθνος εἰς αὐτόν, ἀνεχώρησεν.

96 (6) Οὐ μὴν τό γε λοιπὸν πλῆθος ὑποχωρη-
σάντων τῶν συμμάχων κατέθεντο τὰς διαφοράς,
συνεχὴς δὲ πρὸς Ἀλέξανδρον ἦν αὐτοῖς ὁ πόλεμος,

---

[1] C: ὅρκων PAM Lat., whence Destinon restores ὀργῶν.

[a] Demetrius III, king of Syria; his nickname is elsewhere given as Eukairos, "the timely," here Akairos, "the
untimely."

named the Unready.[a] Hopes of aggrandizement brought from him a prompt response. Demetrius arrived with an army, and the Jews joined their allies in the neighbourhood of Sichem.

(5) Their combined forces, amounting to three thousand horse and fourteen thousand foot, were met by Alexander with one thousand horse and eight thousand foot, mercenaries; besides these he had some ten thousand Jews who were still loyal to him.[b] Before action the two kings endeavoured by proclamations to cause desertion from the opposite ranks; Demetrius hoped to win over Alexander's mercenaries, Alexander the Jewish allies of Demetrius. But, when neither would the Jews abate their resentment nor the Greeks their fidelity, they ended by referring the issue to the clash of arms. The battle was won by Demetrius, notwithstanding many feats of gallantry and strength displayed by Alexander's mercenaries. The upshot, however, proved contrary to the expectations of both combatants. For Demetrius, the victor, found himself abandoned by those who summoned him; while Alexander, who took refuge in the hills, was joined by six thousand Jews, moved by compassion for his reverse of fortune. This turn of affairs was more than Demetrius could stand; and in the belief that Alexander was now once more his match and that the whole nation was streaming back to him, he withdrew.

(6) The remainder of the people, however, did not, on the withdrawal of their allies, drop their quarrel, but waged continuous war with Alexander,

---

[b] The numbers in *A.* xiii. 377 are different: there Demetrius has 3000 horse and 40,000 foot, Alexander 6200 mercenaries and about 20,000 Jews.

μέχρι πλείστους ἀποκτείνας τοὺς λοιποὺς ἀπήλασεν
εἰς Βεμέσελιν πόλιν, καὶ ταύτην καταστρεψάμενος
97 αἰχμαλώτους ἀνήγαγεν εἰς Ἱεροσόλυμα. προύκοψεν δ᾽ αὐτῷ δι᾽ ὑπερβολὴν ὀργῆς εἰς ἀσέβειαν
τὸ τῆς ὠμότητος· τῶν γὰρ ληφθέντων ὀκτακοσίους ἀνασταυρώσας ἐν μέσῃ τῇ πόλει γυναῖκάς τε
καὶ τέκνα αὐτῶν ἀπέσφαξεν ⟨ἐν⟩[1] ταῖς ὄψεσι, καὶ
ταῦτα πίνων καὶ συγκατακείμενος ταῖς παλλακίσιν
98 ἀφεώρα. τοσαύτη δὲ κατάπληξις ἔσχεν τὸν δῆμον,
ὥστε τῶν ἀντιστασιαστῶν κατὰ τὴν ἐπιοῦσαν
νύκτα φυγεῖν ὀκτακισχιλίους ἔξω Ἰουδαίας ὅλης,
οἷς ὅρος τῆς φυγῆς ὁ Ἀλεξάνδρου θάνατος κατέστη.
τοιούτοις ἔργοις ὀψὲ καὶ μόλις ἡσυχίαν τῇ βασιλείᾳ
πορίσας ἀνεπαύσατο τῶν ὅπλων.

99   (7) Γίνεται δὲ αὐτῷ πάλιν ἀρχὴ θορύβων Ἀντίοχος ὁ καὶ Διόνυσος[2] ἐπικληθείς, Δημητρίου
μὲν ἀδελφὸς ὤν, τελευταῖος δὲ τῶν ἀπὸ Σελεύκου.
τοῦτον γὰρ δείσας στρατεύεσθαι ἐπὶ τοὺς Ἄραβας
ὡρμημένον, τὸ μὲν μεταξὺ τῆς ὑπὲρ Ἀντιπατρίδος
παρωρείου καὶ τῶν Ἰόπης αἰγιαλῶν διαταφρεύει
φάραγγι βαθείᾳ, πρὸ δὲ τῆς τάφρου τεῖχος ἤγειρεν
ὑψηλὸν καὶ ξυλίνους πύργους ἐνετεκτήνατο τὰς
100 εὐμαρεῖς ἐμβολὰς ἀποφράττων. οὐ μὴν εἶρξαί γε
τὸν Ἀντίοχον ἴσχυσεν· ἐμπρήσας γὰρ τοὺς πύργους
καὶ τὴν τάφρον χώσας διήλαυνε μετὰ τῆς δυνάμεως. θέμενος δ᾽ ἐν δευτέρῳ τὴν πρὸς τὸν κωλύ-
101 σαντα ἄμυναν εὐθὺς ἐπὶ τοὺς Ἄραβας ᾔει. τῶν
δ᾽ ὁ βασιλεὺς ἀναχωρῶν εἰς τὰ χρησιμώτερα τῆς

---

[1] ins. Herwerden.
[2] Διονύσιος mss.: for text cf. A. xiii. 387.

[a] In A. xiii. 380 Bethome (unidentified).

until, after killing a very large number of them, he
drove the rest into Bemeselis [a]; having subdued
this town, he brought them up to Jerusalem as
prisoners. So furious was he that his savagery went His
to the length of impiety. He had eight hundred of massacre of
his captives crucified in the midst of the city, and the Jews.
their wives and children butchered before their eyes,
while he looked on, drinking, with his concubines
reclining beside him. Such was the consternation
of the people that, on the following night, eight
thousand of the hostile faction fled beyond the pale
of Judaea; their exile was terminated only by
Alexander's death. Having, by such deeds, at last
with difficulty secured tranquillity for the realm, he
rested from warfare.

(7) A fresh cause of disturbance, however, arose His last
in the person of Antiochus, surnamed Dionysus, wars.
brother of Demetrius and the last of the Seleucid
line.[b] This prince having set out on a campaign
against the Arabs, Alexander, in alarm, dug a deep
dyke to intercept him, extending from the mountain-
side above Antipatris to the coast at Joppa, and in
front of the trench erected a high wall with wooden
towers inserted, in order to bar the routes where
attack was easy. However, he failed to check
Antiochus, who burnt the towers, levelled the trench
and marched across with his army. Deferring his
vengeance on the author of this obstruction he at
once pushed on against the Arabs. The Arabian
king began by retiring to territory more favourable

[b] Antiochus XII Dionysus, c. 86–85 B.C. The last of the
Seleucid line, before Syria became a Roman province in
64 B.C., was actually Antiochus XIII Asiaticus (Bevan,
House of Seleucus, ii. 266 f.).

χώρας πρὸς τὴν μάχην, ἔπειτα τὴν ἵππον ἐξαίφνης
ἐπιστρέψας, μυρία δ' ἦν τὸν ἀριθμόν, ἀτάκτοις
ἐπιπίπτει τοῖς περὶ τὸν Ἀντίοχον. καρτερᾶς δὲ
μάχης γενομένης, ἕως μὲν περιῆν Ἀντίοχος ἀντ-
εἶχεν ἡ δύναμις αὐτοῦ, καίπερ ἀνέδην ὑπὸ τῶν
102 Ἀράβων φονευόμενοι· πεσόντος δέ, καὶ γὰρ προ-
εκινδύνευεν ἀεὶ τοῖς ἡττωμένοις παραβοηθῶν,
ἐγκλίνουσι[1] πάντες, καὶ τὸ μὲν πλεῖστον αὐτῶν
ἐπί τε τῆς παρατάξεως κἂν τῇ φυγῇ διαφθείρεται,
τοὺς δὲ λοιποὺς καταφυγόντας εἰς Κανὰ[2] κώμην
σπάνει τῶν ἐπιτηδείων ἀναλωθῆναι συνέβη πλὴν
ὀλίγων ἅπαντας.

103   (8) Ἐκ τούτου Δαμασκηνοὶ διὰ τὸ πρὸς Πτολεμαῖον τὸν Μενναίου μῖσος Ἀρέταν ἐπάγονται καὶ
καθιστῶσιν κοίλης Συρίας βασιλέα. στρατεύεται
δ' οὗτος ἐπὶ τὴν Ἰουδαίαν καὶ μάχῃ νικήσας
104 Ἀλέξανδρον κατὰ συνθήκας ἀνεχώρησεν. Ἀλέξανδρος δὲ Πέλλαν ἑλὼν ἐπὶ Γέρασαν ᾔει πάλιν
τῶν Θεοδώρου κτημάτων γλιχόμενος, καὶ τρισὶ
τοὺς φρουροὺς περιβόλοις ἀποτειχίσας δίχα[3] μάχης
105 τὸ χωρίον παραλαμβάνει. καταστρέφεται δὲ καὶ
Γαυλάνην καὶ Σελεύκειαν καὶ τὴν Ἀντιόχου
φάραγγα καλουμένην, πρὸς οἷς Γάμαλαν φρούριον
καρτερὸν ἑλών, τὸν ἄρχοντα Δημήτριον ἐν αὐτῷ
παραλύσας[4] ἐκ πολλῶν ἐγκλημάτων, ἐπάνεισιν εἰς
Ἰουδαίαν, τρία πληρώσας ἔτη τῆς στρατείας.
ἀσμένως δ' ὑπὸ τοῦ ἔθνους ἐδέχθη διὰ τὴν εὐ-

---

[1] Bekker: ἐκκλίνουσι(ν) mss.
[2] From A. xiii. 391: Ἀνὰν or Ἄννα mss.
[3] Destinon: διὰ mss.; cf. A. xiii. 393 ‖ ἀμαχί, and for the
phrase διὰ μάχης B. iv. 372.
[4] A^{corr}: the other mss. have περιλύσας or περιδύσας (cf.
A. περιέδυσεν).

50

for battle, and then suddenly wheeling round his cavalry, ten thousand strong, fell upon the troops of Antiochus while in disorder. A hard fought battle ensued. So long as Antiochus lived, his forces held out, though mercilessly cut up by the Arabs. When he fell, after constantly exposing himself in the front while rallying his worsted troops, the rout became general. The bulk of his army perished either on the field or in the flight; the rest took refuge in the village of Cana, where all save a few succumbed to starvation.

(8) On the death of Antiochus, the inhabitants of Damascus, from hatred of Ptolemy, son of Mennaeus, brought in Aretas and made him king of Coele-Syria.[a] The latter made an expedition into Judaea, defeated Alexander in battle, and after concluding a treaty withdrew. Alexander, for his part, captured Pella and proceeded against Gerasa, hankering once more after the treasures of Theodorus.[b] Having blockaded the garrison by a triple line of walls, he carried the place without a battle. He also conquered Gaulane and Seleuceia and took the so-called "Ravine of Antiochus." He further captured the strong fortress of Gamala and dismissed its commander, Demetrius, in consequence of numerous accusations. He then returned to Judaea after a campaign of three whole years. His successful career brought him a cordial welcome from the nation; yet

---

[a] Ptolemy was king of Chalcis and the surrounding district in Coele-Syria (c. 85–40 B.C.); Aretas was king of the Nabataean Arabs.
[b] Cf. § 86.

πραγίαν, καὶ λαμβάνει τὴν ἀνάπαυσιν τοῦ πολεμεῖν
106 ἀρχὴν νόσου. τεταρταίαις δὲ περιόδοις πυρετῶν
ἐνοχλούμενος ᾠήθη διακρούσεσθαι[1] τὴν νόσον
πάλιν ἁψάμενος πραγμάτων. διὸ δὴ στρατείαις
ἀκαίροις ἑαυτὸν ἐπιδιδοὺς καὶ βιαζόμενος παρὰ
δύναμιν τὸ σῶμα πρὸς τὰς ἐνεργείας ἀπήλλαξεν.
τελευτᾷ γοῦν ἐν μέσοις τοῖς θορύβοις στρεφόμενος
βασιλεύσας ἑπτὰ πρὸς τοῖς εἴκοσιν ἔτη.
107 (v. 1) Καταλείπει δὲ τὴν βασιλείαν Ἀλεξάνδρᾳ
τῇ γυναικὶ πεπεισμένος ταύτῃ μάλιστ' ἂν ὑπακοῦσαι τοὺς Ἰουδαίους, ἐπειδὴ τῆς ὠμότητος αὐτοῦ
μακρὰν ἀποδέουσα καὶ ταῖς παρανομίαις ἀνθ-
108 ισταμένη τὸν δῆμον εἰς εὔνοιαν προσηγάγετο.[2] καὶ
οὐ διήμαρτεν τῆς ἐλπίδος· ἐκράτησεν γὰρ τῆς
ἀρχῆς τὸ γύναιον διὰ δόξαν εὐσεβείας. ἠκρίβου
γὰρ δὴ μάλιστα τοῦ ἔθνους[3] τὰ πάτρια καὶ τοὺς
πλημμελοῦντας εἰς τοὺς ἱεροὺς νόμους ἐξ ἀρχῆς
109 προεβάλλετο. δύο δ' αὐτῇ παίδων ὄντων ἐξ Ἀλεξάνδρου, τὸν μὲν πρεσβύτερον Ὑρκανὸν διά τε
τὴν ἡλικίαν ἀποδείκνυσιν ἀρχιερέα καὶ ἄλλως ὄντα
νωθέστερον ἢ ὥστε ἐνοχλεῖν περὶ τῶν ὅλων, τὸν
δὲ νεώτερον Ἀριστόβουλον διὰ θερμότητα κατεῖχεν
ἰδιώτην.
110 (2) Παραφύονται δὲ αὐτῆς εἰς τὴν ἐξουσίαν
Φαρισαῖοι, σύνταγμά τι Ἰουδαίων δοκοῦν εὐσεβέστερον εἶναι τῶν ἄλλων καὶ τοὺς νόμους ἀκρι-
111 βέστερον ἀφηγεῖσθαι. τούτοις περισσὸν δή τι
προσεῖχεν · ἡ Ἀλεξάνδρα σεσοβημένη[4] περὶ τὸ
θεῖον. οἱ δὲ τὴν ἁπλότητα τῆς ἀνθρώπου κατὰ

---

[1] Bekker: διακρούσασθαι MSS.
[2] προηγάγετο AM: προσ- is supported by B. i. 153.
[3] νόμου PAM*.   [4] M margin: σεβομένη the rest.

rest from war proved but the beginning of disease. Afflicted by a quartan ague, he hoped to shake off the malady by a return to active life. He, accordingly, plunged into ill-timed campaigns and, forcing himself to tasks beyond his strength, hastened his end. He died, at any rate, amid stress and turmoil, after a reign of twenty-seven years. His death 78 B.C.

(v. 1) Alexander bequeathed the kingdom to his wife Alexandra, being convinced that the Jews would bow to her authority as they would to no other, because by her utter lack of his brutality and by her opposition to his crimes she had won the affections of the populace. Nor was he mistaken in these expectations ; for this frail woman firmly held the reins of government, thanks to her reputation for piety. She was, indeed, the very strictest observer of the national traditions and would deprive of office [a] any offenders against the sacred laws. Of the two sons whom she had by Alexander, she appointed the elder, Hyrcanus, high priest, out of consideration alike for his age and his disposition, which was too lethargic to be troubled about public affairs ; the younger, Aristobulus, as a hot-head, she confined to a private life. Queen ALEXANDRA 78-69 B.C.

(2) Beside Alexandra, and growing as she grew, arose [b] the Pharisees, a body of Jews with the reputation of excelling the rest of their nation in the observances of religion, and as exact exponents of the laws. To them, being herself intensely religious, she listened with too great deference ; while they, gradually taking advantage of an ingenuous woman, Growing power of the Pharisees.

---

[a] Or perhaps " banish from the realm."
[b] Literally, " grew up beside into her power " (like suckers round a tree).

μικρὸν ὑπιόντες ἤδη καὶ διοικηταὶ τῶν ὅλων
ἐγίνοντο, διώκειν τε καὶ κατάγειν οὓς ἐθέλοιεν,
λύειν τε καὶ δεσμεῖν. καθόλου δ' αἱ μὲν ἀπολαύ-
σεις τῶν βασιλείων ἐκείνων ἦσαν, τὰ δ' ἀναλώ-
112 ματα καὶ αἱ δυσχέρειαι τῆς Ἀλεξάνδρας. δεινὴ
δ' ἦν τὰ μείζω διοικεῖν, δύναμίν τε ἀεὶ συγ-
κροτοῦσα διπλασίονα κατέστησεν καὶ ξενικὴν συνήγαγεν οὐκ ὀλίγην, ὡς μὴ μόνον κρατύνεσθαι τὸ
οἰκεῖον ἔθνος, φοβερὰν δὲ καὶ τοῖς ἔξωθεν εἶναι
δυνάσταις. ἐκράτει δὲ τῶν μὲν ἄλλων αὐτή,
Φαρισαῖοι δ' αὐτῆς.

113   (3) Διογένην γοῦν τινα τῶν ἐπισήμων, φίλον
Ἀλεξάνδρῳ γεγενημένον, κτείνουσιν αὐτοί,[1] σύμ-
βουλον ἐγκαλοῦντες γεγονέναι περὶ τῶν ἀνασταυρωθέντων ὑπὸ τοῦ βασιλέως ὀκτακοσίων. ἐνῆγον δὲ
τὴν Ἀλεξάνδραν εἰς τὸ καὶ τοὺς ἄλλους διαχειρίσασθαι τῶν παροξυνάντων ἐπ' ἐκείνους τὸν Ἀλέξ-
ανδρον· ἐνδιδούσης δ' ὑπὸ δεισιδαιμονίας ἀνῄρουν
114 οὓς ἐθέλοιεν αὐτοί. προσφεύγουσι δὲ Ἀριστοβούλῳ τῶν κινδυνευόντων οἱ προύχειν δοκοῦντες,
κἀκεῖνος πείθει τὴν μητέρα φείσασθαι μὲν διὰ τὸ
ἀξίωμα τῶν ἀνδρῶν, ἐκπέμψαι δ' αὐτούς, εἰ μὴ
καθαροὺς ὑπείληφεν, ἐκ τῆς πόλεως. οἱ μὲν οὖν
δοθείσης ἀδείας ἐσκεδάσθησαν ἀνὰ τὴν χώραν.
115 Ἀλεξάνδρα δὲ ἐκπέμψασα ἐπὶ Δαμασκὸν στρατιάν,
πρόφασις δ' ἦν Πτολεμαῖος ἀεὶ θλίβων τὴν πόλιν,
ταύτην μὲν ὑπεδέξατο μηθὲν ἀξιόλογον ἐργασα-
116 μένην· Τιγράνην δὲ τὸν Ἀρμενίων βασιλέα προσ-
καθεζόμενον Πτολεμαΐδι καὶ πολιορκοῦντα Κλεο-

----

[1] οὗτοι Destinon.

became at length the real administrators of the state, at liberty to banish and to recall, to loose and to bind, whom they would. In short, the enjoyments of royal authority were theirs ; its expenses and burthens fell to Alexandra. She proved, however, to be a wonderful administrator in larger affairs, and, by continual recruiting doubled her army, besides collecting a considerable body of foreign troops ; so that she not only strengthened her own nation, but became a formidable foe to foreign potentates. But if she ruled the nation, the Pharisees ruled her.

(3) Thus they put to death Diogenes, a distinguished man who had been a friend of Alexander, accusing him of having advised the king to crucify his eight hundred victims.[a] They further urged Alexandra to make away with the others who had instigated Alexander to punish those men ; and as she from superstitious motives always gave way, they proceeded to kill whomsoever they would. The most eminent of the citizens thus imperilled sought refuge with Aristobulus, who persuaded his mother to spare their lives in consideration of their rank, but, if she was not satisfied of their innocence, to expel them from the city. Their security being thus guaranteed, they dispersed about the country.

Alexandra sent an army to Damascus, on the pretext of the constant pressure put upon that city by Ptolemy ; the troops, however, returned to her without having achieved anything remarkable. On the other hand, by means of treaties and presents, she won over Tigranes, king of Armenia, who was

Alexandra's foreign policy.

c. 70–69 B.C.

---

[a] § 97.

πάτραν συνθήκαις καὶ δώροις ὑπηγάγετο. φθάνει
δ' ἐκεῖνος ἀναστὰς διὰ τὰς οἴκοι ταραχὰς ἐμ-
βεβληκότος εἰς τὴν Ἀρμενίαν Λευκόλλου.

117 (4) Κἂν τούτῳ νοσούσης Ἀλεξάνδρας ὁ νεώτερος τῶν παίδων Ἀριστόβουλος τὸν καιρὸν
ἁρπάσας μετὰ τῶν οἰκείων,[1] εἶχεν δὲ πολλοὺς καὶ
πάντας εὔνους διὰ τὴν θερμότητα, κρατεῖ μὲν τῶν
ἐρυμάτων ἁπάντων, τοῖς δ' ἐκ τούτων χρήμασιν
μισθοφόρους ἀθροίσας ἑαυτὸν ἀποδείκνυσι βασιλέα.

118 πρὸς ταῦτα ὀδυρόμενον τὸν Ὑρκανὸν ἡ μήτηρ
οἰκτείρασα τήν τε γυναῖκα καὶ τοὺς παῖδας Ἀριστοβούλου καθείργνυσιν εἰς τὴν Ἀντωνίαν· φρούριον
δ' ἦν τῷ βορείῳ κλίματι τοῦ ἱεροῦ προσκείμενον,
πάλαι μέν, ὡς ἔφην, Βᾶρις ὀνομαζόμενον, αὖθις
δὲ ταύτης τυχὸν τῆς προσηγορίας ἐπικρατήσαντος
Ἀντωνίου, καθάπερ ἀπό τε τοῦ Σεβαστοῦ καὶ
Ἀγρίππα Σεβαστὴ καὶ Ἀγριππιὰς πόλεις ἐπ-
119 ωνομάσθησαν. πρὶν δὲ ἐπεξελθεῖν Ἀλεξάνδρα τὸν
Ἀριστόβουλον τῆς τἀδελφοῦ καταλύσεως τελευτᾷ
διοικήσασα τὴν ἀρχὴν ἔτεσιν ἐννέα.

120 (vi. 1) Καὶ κληρονόμος μὲν ἦν τῶν ὅλων Ὑρκανός, ᾧ καὶ ζῶσα τὴν βασιλείαν ἐνεχείρισεν,
δυνάμει δὲ καὶ φρονήματι προεῖχεν ὁ Ἀριστόβουλος. γενομένης δὲ αὐτοῖς περὶ τῶν ὅλων συμβολῆς περὶ Ἱεριχοῦντα καταλιπόντες οἱ πολλοὶ τὸν
Ὑρκανὸν μεταβαίνουσιν πρὸς τὸν Ἀριστόβουλον.

121 ὁ δὲ μετὰ τῶν συμμεινάντων φθάνει συμφυγὼν
ἐπὶ τὴν Ἀντωνίαν καὶ κυριεύσας τῶν πρὸς σωτη-

---

[1] οἰκείων Herwerden : οἰκετῶν mss. and Niese.

[a] Cleopatra or Selene (Α. xiii. 420), daughter of Ptolemy
Physcon, and married to several of the Seleucid kings. We

seated before Ptolemais, besieging Cleopatra.[a] He, however, had to beat a hasty retreat, recalled by domestic troubles in Armenia, which Lucullus had invaded.

(4) Alexandra now falling ill, her younger son Aristobulus seized his opportunity and with the aid of his followers—a numerous body, every one of whom was devoted to him because of his fiery nature—took possession of all the fortresses and, with the money which he found there, recruited a mercenary force and proclaimed himself king. The complaints of Hyrcanus at these proceedings moved the compassion of his mother, who shut up the wife and children of Aristobulus in Antonia. This was a fortress adjoining the north side of the temple, which, as I said,[b] was formerly called Baris, but afterwards took this new name under Antony's supremacy ; just as Augustus and Agrippa gave their names to the cities of Sebaste [c] and Agrippias.[d] But before Alexandra could take action against Aristobulus for his deposition of his brother, she expired, after a reign of nine years.

(vi. 1) Hyrcanus, to whom even in her lifetime his mother had entrusted the kingdom, was sole heir to the throne, but in capacity and courage was surpassed by Aristobulus. A battle for the crown took place near Jericho, when most of the troops of Hyrcanus deserted him and went over to Aristobulus. Hyrcanus, with those who remained with him, hastily took refuge in Antonia and secured hostages for his

Revolt of her son Aristobulus.

Her death.

HYRCANUS II abdicates in favour of ARISTO- BULUS II 69–63 B.C.

learn from Strabo, xvi. 749, that Tigranes on his retreat from Syria carried off Cleopatra as a prisoner and subsequently put her to death.

[b] § 75.   [c] Samaria.

[d] Formerly Anthedon, § 87.

ρίαν ὁμήρων· ταῦτα δ' ἦν ἡ 'Αριστοβούλου γυνὴ
μετὰ τῶν τέκνων. ἀμέλει πρὶν ἀνηκέστου πάθους
διελύθησαν, ὥστε βασιλεύειν μὲν 'Αριστόβουλον,
'Υρκανὸν δὲ ἐκστάντα τῆς ἄλλης ἀπολαύειν τιμῆς
122 ὥσπερ ἀδελφὸν βασιλέως. ἐπὶ τούτοις διαλλαγέν-
τες ἐν τῷ ἱερῷ καὶ τοῦ λαοῦ περιεστῶτος φιλοφρόνως ἀλλήλους ἀσπασάμενοι διήμειψαν τὰς οἰκίας·
'Αριστόβουλος μὲν γὰρ εἰς τὰ βασίλεια, 'Υρκανὸς
δ' ἀνεχώρησεν εἰς τὴν 'Αριστοβούλου οἰκίαν.
123 (2) Δέος δὲ τοῖς τε ἄλλοις τῶν 'Αριστοβούλου
διαφόρων ἐμπίπτει παρ' ἐλπίδα κρατήσαντος καὶ
μάλιστα 'Αντιπάτρῳ πάλαι διαμισουμένῳ. γένος
δ' ἦν 'Ιδουμαῖος, προγόνων τε ἕνεκα καὶ πλούτου
124 καὶ τῆς ἄλλης ἰσχύος πρωτεύων τοῦ ἔθνους. οὗτος
ἅμα καὶ τὸν 'Υρκανὸν 'Αρέτᾳ προσφυγόντα τῷ
βασιλεῖ τῆς 'Αραβίας ἀνακτήσασθαι τὴν βασιλείαν
ἔπειθεν, καὶ τὸν 'Αρέταν δέξασθαί τε τὸν 'Υρκανὸν
καὶ καταγαγεῖν ἐπὶ τὴν ἀρχήν, πολλὰ μὲν τὸν
'Αριστόβουλον εἰς τὸ ἦθος διαβάλλων, πολλὰ δ'
ἐπαινῶν τὸν 'Υρκανὸν [παρῄνει δέξασθαι],[1] καὶ
ὡς πρέπον εἴη τὸν οὕτω λαμπρᾶς προεστῶτα
βασιλείας ὑπερέχειν χεῖρα τῷ ἀδικουμένῳ[2]· ἀδι-
κεῖσθαι δὲ τὸν 'Υρκανὸν στερηθέντα τῆς κατὰ τὸ
125 πρεσβεῖον αὐτῷ προσηκούσης ἀρχῆς. προκατα-
σκευάσας δὲ ἀμφοτέρους, νύκτωρ ἀναλαβὼν τὸν
'Υρκανὸν ἀπὸ τῆς πόλεως ἀποδιδράσκει καὶ συν-
τόνῳ φυγῇ χρώμενος εἰς τὴν καλουμένην Πέτραν
διασώζεται· βασίλειον αὕτη τῆς 'Αραβίας ἐστίν.
126 ἔνθα τῷ 'Αρέτᾳ τὸν 'Υρκανὸν ἐγχειρίσας καὶ
πολλὰ μὲν καθομιλήσας, πολλοῖς δὲ δώροις ὑπ-
ελθών, δοῦναι δύναμιν αὐτῷ πείθει τὴν κατάξουσαν

---

[1] om. Bekker.   [2] τῶν ἀδικουμένων Destinon.

safety in the persons of the wife and children of Aristobulus. However, before any irreparable harm was done, the brothers came to terms, to the effect that Aristobulus should be king and Hyrcanus, while abdicating the throne, should enjoy all his other honours as the king's brother. The reconciliation on these terms took place in the temple. In the presence of the surrounding crowd they cordially embraced each other, and then exchanged residences, Aristobulus repairing to the palace, Hyrcanus to the house of Aristobulus.

(2) The unexpected triumph of Aristobulus alarmed his adversaries, and, in particular, Antipater, an old and bitterly hated foe. An Idumaean by race, his ancestry, wealth, and other advantages put him in the front rank of his nation. It was he who now persuaded Hyrcanus to seek refuge with Aretas, king of Arabia, with a view to recovering his kingdom, and at the same time urged Aretas to receive him and to reinstate him on the throne. Heaping aspersions on the character of Aristobulus and encomiums on Hyrcanus, he represented how becoming it would be in the sovereign of so brilliant a realm to extend a protecting hand to the oppressed ; and such, he said, was Hyrcanus, robbed of the throne which by right of primogeniture belonged to him.

Having thus prepared both parties for action, Antipater one night fled with Hyrcanus from the city, and, pushing on at full speed, safely reached the capital of the Arabian kingdom, called Petra. There he committed Hyrcanus into the hands of Aretas, and, by dint of conciliatory speeches and cajoling presents, induced the king to furnish an

Antipater with the aid of Aretas, seeks to reinstate Hyrcanus.

59

αὐτόν· ἦν δ' αὕτη πεζῶν τε καὶ ἱππέων πέντε
μυριάδες. πρὸς ἢν οὐκ ἀντέσχεν Ἀριστόβουλος,
ἀλλ' ἐν τῇ πρώτῃ συμβολῇ λειφθεὶς εἰς Ἱερο-
127 σόλυμα συνελαύνεται. κἂν ἔφθη κατὰ κράτος λη-
φθείς, εἰ μὴ Σκαῦρος ὁ Ῥωμαίων στρατηγὸς ἐπ-
αναστὰς αὐτῶν τοῖς καιροῖς ἔλυσε τὴν πολιορκίαν·
ὃς ἐπέμφθη μὲν εἰς Συρίαν ἀπὸ Ἀρμενίας ὑπὸ
Πομπηίου Μάγνου πολεμοῦντος πρὸς Τιγράνην,
παραγενόμενος δὲ εἰς Δαμασκὸν ἑαλωκυῖαν προσ-
φάτως ὑπὸ Μετέλλου καὶ Λολλίου καὶ τούτους
μεταστήσας, ἐπειδὴ τὰ κατὰ τὴν Ἰουδαίαν ἐπύθετο,
καθάπερ ἐφ' ἕρμαιον ἠπείχθη.

128   (3) Παρελθόντος γοῦν εἰς τὴν χώραν πρέσβεις
εὐθέως ἧκον παρὰ τῶν ἀδελφῶν, ἑκατέρου δεο-
μένου βοηθεῖν αὐτῷ. γίνεται δ' ἐπίπροσθεν τοῦ
δικαίου τὰ παρὰ Ἀριστοβούλου τριακόσια τάλαντα·
τοσοῦτον γὰρ λαβὼν Σκαῦρος ἐπικηρυκεύεται πρός
τε Ὑρκανὸν καὶ τοὺς Ἄραβας, ἀπειλῶν Ῥωμαίους
καὶ Πομπήιον, εἰ μὴ λύσειαν τὴν πολιορκίαν.
129 ἀνεχώρει δ' ἐκ τῆς Ἰουδαίας εἰς Φιλαδέλφειαν
Ἀρέτας καταπλαγείς, καὶ πάλιν εἰς Δαμασκὸν
130 Σκαῦρος. Ἀριστοβούλῳ δ' οὐκ ἀπέχρησεν τὸ μὴ
ἁλῶναι, πᾶσαν δὲ τὴν δύναμιν ἐπισυλλέξας εἵπετο
τοῖς πολεμίοις καὶ περὶ τὸν καλούμενον Παπυρῶνα
συμβαλὼν αὐτοῖς ὑπὲρ ἑξακισχιλίους κτείνει, μεθ'
ὧν καὶ τὸν ἀδελφὸν τὸν Ἀντιπάτρου Φαλλίωνα.

131   (4) Ὑρκανὸς δὲ καὶ Ἀντίπατρος τῶν Ἀράβων
ἀφαιρεθέντες μετέφερον ἐπὶ τοὺς ἐναντίους τὴν
ἐλπίδα, κἀπειδὴ Πομπήιος ἐπιὼν τὴν Συρίαν εἰς

---

[a] *A.* xiv. 19, " 50,000 cavalry besides infantry."

army, fifty thousand strong, both cavalry and infantry,[a] to reinstate his ward. This force Aristobulus was unable to resist. Defeated in the first encounter he was driven into Jerusalem, and would there have been speedily captured through the storming of the city, had not Scaurus the Roman general, intervening at this critical moment, raised the siege. The latter had been sent into Syria from Armenia by Pompey the Great, then at war with Tigranes. On reaching Damascus, which had recently been captured by Metellus and Lollius, he superseded those officers,[b] and then, hearing of the position of affairs in Judaea, hastened thither to snatch what seemed a god-sent opportunity.

Intervention of Scaurus in the brothers' quarrel. 65 B.C.

(3) Sure enough, no sooner had he entered Jewish territory, than he received deputations from the brothers, each imploring his assistance. Three hundred talents offered by Aristobulus outweighed considerations of justice ; Scaurus, having obtained that sum, dispatched a herald to Hyrcanus and the Arabs, threatening them with a visitation from the Romans and Pompey if they did not raise the siege. Aretas, terror-struck, retired from Judaea to Philadelphia, and Scaurus returned to Damascus. Aristobulus, however, not content with having escaped capture, mustered all his forces, pursued the enemy, fought them in the neighbourhood of a place called Papyron, and killed upwards of six thousand. Among the slain was Phallion, Antipater's brother.

(4) Deprived of their Arab allies, Hyrcanus and Antipater turned their hopes to the opposite party, and when Pompey entered Syria and reached

Both brothers appeal to Pompey 63 B.C.

---

[b] The meaning of the phrase καὶ τούτους μεταστήσας (omitted in *A*.) is uncertain.

Δαμασκὸν ἧκεν, ἐπ' αὐτὸν καταφεύγουσιν, καὶ
δίχα δωρεῶν, αἷς καὶ πρὸς τὸν Ἀρέταν δικαιο-
λογίαις χρώμενοι, κατηντιβόλουν μισῆσαι μὲν τὴν
Ἀριστοβούλου βίαν, κατάγειν δ' ἐπὶ τὴν βασιλείαν τὸν καὶ τρόπῳ καὶ καθ' ἡλικίαν προσήκοντα.
132 οὐ μὴν οὐδ' Ἀριστόβουλος ὑστέρει πεποιθὼς τῇ
Σκαύρου δωροδοκίᾳ, παρῆν τε καὶ αὐτὸς ὡς οἷόν
τε βασιλικώτατα κεκοσμηκὼς ἑαυτόν. ἀδοξήσας
δὲ πρὸς τὰς θεραπείας καὶ μὴ φέρων δουλεύειν
ταῖς χρείαις ταπεινότερον τοῦ σχήματος ἀπὸ Δίου
πόλεως[1] χωρίζεται.
133   (5) Πρὸς ταῦτ' ἀγανακτήσας Πομπήιος, πολλὰ
καὶ τῶν περὶ Ὑρκανὸν ἱκετευόντων, ὥρμησεν ἐπ'
Ἀριστόβουλον, ἀναλαβὼν τήν τε Ῥωμαϊκὴν δύνα-
134 μιν καὶ πολλοὺς ἐκ τῆς Συρίας συμμάχους. ἐπεὶ
δὲ παρελαύνων Πέλλαν καὶ Σκυθόπολιν ἧκεν εἰς
Κορέας, ὅθεν ἡ Ἰουδαίων ἄρχεται χώρα κατὰ τὴν
μεσόγειον ἀνιόντων, ἀκούσας συμπεφευγέναι τὸν
Ἀριστόβουλον εἰς Ἀλεξάνδρειον, τοῦτο δ' ἐστὶν
φρούριον τῶν πάνυ φιλοτίμως ἐξησκημένων ὑπὲρ
ὄρους ὑψηλοῦ κείμενον, πέμψας καταβαίνειν αὐτὸν
135 ἐκέλευσεν. τῷ δ' ἦν μὲν ὁρμὴ καλουμένῳ δεσπο-
τικώτερον διακινδυνεύειν μᾶλλον ἢ ὑπακοῦσαι,
καθεώρα δὲ τὸ πλῆθος ὀρρωδοῦν, καὶ παρῄνουν
οἱ φίλοι σκέπτεσθαι τὴν Ῥωμαίων ἰσχὺν οὖσαν
ἀνυπόστατον. οἷς πεισθεὶς κάτεισιν πρὸς Πομπήιον καὶ πολλὰ περὶ τοῦ δικαίως ἄρχειν ἀπο-
136 λογηθεὶς ὑπέστρεψεν εἰς τὸ ἔρυμα. πάλιν τε
τἀδελφοῦ προκαλουμένου καταβὰς καὶ διαλεχθεὶς

---

[1] Δίου πόλεως Spanheim : Διὸς ἡλίου πόλεως (probably arising
from a glossed text Διὸς ἢ Δίου π.) or Διοσπόλεως mss.

Damascus, took refuge with him. Coming without presents and resorting to the same pleas which they had used with Aretas, they implored him to show his detestation of the violence of Aristobulus, and to restore to the throne the man whose character and seniority entitled him to it. Nor was Aristobulus behindhand ; relying on the fact that Scaurus was open to bribery, he too appeared, arrayed in the most regal style imaginable. But feeling it beneath his dignity to play the courtier, and scorning to further his ends by a servility that humiliated his magnificence, he, on reaching the city of Dium, took himself off. [a]

(5) Indignant at this behaviour, and yielding to the urgent entreaties of Hyrcanus and his friends, Pompey started in pursuit of Aristobulus, with the Roman forces and a large contingent of Syrian auxiliaries. Passing Pella and Scythopolis, he reached Coreae, at which point a traveller ascending through the interior enters the territory of Judaea. There he heard that Aristobulus had taken refuge in Alexandreion, one of the most lavishly equipped of fortresses, situated on a high mountain, and sent orders to him to come down. At this imperious summons Aristobulus felt disposed to brave the risk rather than obey ; but he saw that the people were terrified, and his friends urged him to reflect on the irresistible power of the Romans. He gave way, came down to Pompey, and after making a long defence in support of his claims to the throne, returned to his stronghold. He descended again on his brother's invitation, discussed the rights of his

Aristobulus recalcitrant prepares for war with Pompey.

---

[a] *A.* has " he went off (from Damascus) to Dium and thence to Judaea."

περὶ τῶν δικαίων ἄπεισιν μὴ κωλύοντος τοῦ
Πομπηίου. μέσος δ' ἦν ἐλπίδος καὶ δέους, καὶ
κατῄει μὲν ὡς δυσωπήσων Πομπήιον πάντ' ἐπιτρέπειν αὐτῷ, πάλιν δ' ἀνέβαινεν εἰς τὴν ἄκραν,
137 ὡς μὴ προκαταλύειν δόξειεν αὐτόν. ἐπεὶ μέντοι
Πομπήιος ἐξίστασθαί τε τῶν φρουρίων ἐκέλευεν
αὐτῷ καί, παράγγελμα τῶν φρουράρχων ἐχόντων
μόναις πειθαρχεῖν ταῖς αὐτογράφοις ἐπιστολαῖς,
ἠνάγκαζεν αὐτὸν ἑκάστοις γράφειν ἐκχωρεῖν, ποιεῖ
μὲν τὰ προσταχθέντα, ἀγανακτήσας δὲ ἀνεχώρησεν
εἰς Ἱεροσόλυμα καὶ παρεσκευάζετο πολεμεῖν πρὸς
Πομπήιον.

138 (6) Ὁ δ', οὐ γὰρ ἐδίδου χρόνον ταῖς παρα-
σκευαῖς, εὐθέως εἵπετο, καὶ προσεπέρρωσεν τὴν
ὁρμὴν ὁ Μιθριδάτου θάνατος ἀγγελθεὶς αὐτῷ περὶ
Ἱεριχοῦντα, ἔνθα τῆς Ἰουδαίας τὸ πιότατον φοινικά
τε πάμπολυν καὶ βάλσαμον τρέφει. τοῦτο λίθοις
ὀξέσιν ἐπιτέμνοντες τὰ πρέμνα συνάγουσιν[1] κατὰ
139 τὰς τομὰς ἐκδακρῦον. καὶ στρατοπεδευσάμενος
ἐν τῷ χωρίῳ μίαν ἑσπέραν ἔωθεν ἠπείγετο πρὸς
τὰ Ἱεροσόλυμα. καταπλαγεὶς δὲ τὴν ἔφοδον Ἀριστόβουλος ἱκέτης ἀπαντᾷ, χρημάτων τε ὑποσχέσει
καὶ τῷ μετὰ τῆς πόλεως ἐπιτρέπειν καὶ ἑαυτὸν
140 χαλεπαίνοντα καταστέλλει τὸν Πομπήιον. οὐ μήν
τι τῶν ὡμολογημένων ἐγένετο· τὸν γὰρ ἐπὶ τὴν
κομιδὴν τῶν χρημάτων ἐκπεμφθέντα Γαβίνιον οἱ τὰ
Ἀριστοβούλου φρονοῦντες οὐδὲ τῇ πόλει δέχονται.

141 (vii. 1) Πρὸς ταῦτα ἀγανακτήσας Πομπήιος
Ἀριστόβουλον μὲν ἐφρούρει, πρὸς δὲ τὴν πόλιν
ἐλθὼν περιεσκόπει ὅπως δεῖ προσβαλεῖν, τήν τε
ὀχυρότητα τῶν τειχῶν δυσμεταχείριστον ὁρῶν καὶ

[1] συλλέγουσι VNC.

case, and withdrew, unimpeded by Pompey. Torn
between hope and fear, he would come down determined by importunity to force Pompey to deliver
everything to him, and as often ascend to his
citadel, lest it should be thought that he was pre-
maturely throwing up his case. In the end, Pompey
commanded him to evacuate the fortresses and knowing that the governors had orders only to obey
instructions given in Aristobulus's own hand, insisted
on his writing to each of them a notice to quit.
Aristobulus did what was required of him, but in-
dignantly withdrew to Jerusalem and prepared for
war with Pompey.

(6) Pompey, allowing him no time for these pre- Pompey
parations, followed forthwith. A further impetus to advances on
his pace was given by the death of Mithridates, news Jerusalem.
of which reached him near Jericho. (The soil here
is the most fertile in Judaea and produces abundance
of palms and balsam-trees ; the stems of the latter
are cut with sharp stones and the balsam is collected
at the incisions, where it exudes drop by drop.) At
this spot Pompey encamped for an evening only and
at daybreak pressed on to Jerusalem. Terrified at
his approach, Aristobulus went as a suppliant to
meet him, and by the promise of money and of the
surrender of himself and the city pacified Pompey's
wrath. However, none of his undertakings was fulfilled ; for when Gabinius was dispatched to take
over the promised sum, the partisans of Aristobulus
refused even to admit him to the city.

(vii. 1) Indignant at this treatment, Pompey kept Pompey
Aristobulus under arrest and, advancing to the city, besieges
carefully considered the best method of attack. He Jerusalem
noted the solidity of the walls and the formidable 63 B.C.

τὴν πρὸ τούτων φάραγγα φοβερὰν τό τε ἱερὸν
ἐντὸς τῆς φάραγγος ὀχυρώτατα τετειχισμένον,
ὥστε τοῦ ἄστεος ἁλισκομένου δευτέραν εἶναι
καταφυγὴν τοῦτο τοῖς πολεμίοις.

142   (2) Διαποροῦντος δ' ἐπὶ πολὺν χρόνον στάσις
τοῖς ἔνδον ἐμπίπτει, τῶν μὲν Ἀριστοβούλου
πολεμεῖν ἀξιούντων καὶ ῥύεσθαι τὸν βασιλέα, τῶν
δὲ τὰ Ὑρκανοῦ φρονούντων ἀνοίγειν Πομπηίῳ τὰς
πύλας· πολλοὺς δὲ τούτους ἐποίει τὸ δέος, ἀφ-
143 ορῶντας εἰς τὴν τῶν Ῥωμαίων εὐταξίαν. ἡττώ-
μενον δὲ τὸ Ἀριστοβούλου μέρος εἰς τὸ ἱερὸν
ἀνεχώρησεν καὶ τὴν συνάπτουσαν ἀπ' αὐτοῦ τῇ
πόλει γέφυραν ἀποκόψαντες ἀντισχεῖν εἰς ἔσχατον
παρεσκευάζοντο. τῶν δὲ ἑτέρων δεχομένων Ῥωμαίους τῇ πόλει καὶ τὰ βασίλεια παραδιδόντων,
ἐπὶ μὲν ταῦτα Πομπήιος ἕνα τῶν ὑφ' ἑαυτῷ
στρατηγῶν Πείσωνα εἰσπέμπει μετὰ στρατιᾶς·
144 ὃς διαλαβὼν φρουραῖς τὴν πόλιν, ἐπειδὴ τῶν εἰς
τὸ ἱερὸν καταφυγόντων οὐδένα λόγοις ἔπειθεν
συμβῆναι, τὰ πέριξ εἰς προσβολὰς εὐτρέπιζεν
ἔχων τοὺς περὶ τὸν Ὑρκανὸν εἴς τε τὰς ἐπινοίας
καὶ τὰς ὑπηρεσίας προθύμους.

145   (3) Αὐτὸς δὲ κατὰ τὸ προσάρκτιον κλίμα τὴν
τε τάφρον ἔχου καὶ τὴν φάραγγα πᾶσαν, ὕλην
συμφορούσης τῆς δυνάμεως. χαλεπὸν δ' ἦν τὸ
ἀναπληροῦν διὰ βάθος ἄπειρον καὶ τῶν Ἰουδαίων
146 πάντα τρόπον εἰργόντων ἄνωθεν. κἂν ἀτέλεστος
ἔμεινεν τοῖς Ῥωμαίοις ὁ πόνος, εἰ μὴ τὰς ἑβδομάδας ἐπιτηρῶν ὁ Πομπήιος, ἐν αἷς παντὸς ἔργου
διὰ τὴν θρησκείαν χεῖρας ἀπίσχουσιν Ἰουδαῖοι, τὸ
χῶμα ὕψου τῆς κατὰ χεῖρα συμβολῆς εἴργων τοὺς

task of their assault, the frightful ravine in front of them, and within the ravine the temple also so strongly fortified as to afford, after the capture of the town, a second line of defence to the enemy.

(2) However, during his long period of indecision, sedition broke out within the walls ; the partisans of Aristobulus insisting on a battle and the rescue of the king, while those of Hyrcanus were for opening the gates to Pompey. The numbers of the latter were increased by the fear which the spectacle of the perfect order of the Romans inspired. The party of Aristobulus, finding themselves beaten, re-tired into the temple, cut the bridge which con-nected it with the city, and prepared to hold out to the last. The others admitted the Romans to the city and delivered up the palace. Pompey sent a body of troops to occupy it under the command of Piso, one of his lieutenant-generals. That officer distributed sentries about the town and, failing to induce any of the refugees in the temple to listen to terms, prepared the surrounding ground for an assault. In this work the friends of Hyrcanus keenly assisted him with their advice and services.

(3) Pompey himself was on the north side, en-gaged in banking up the fosse and the whole of the ravine with materials collected by the troops. The tremendous depth to be filled, and the impediments of every sort to which the work was exposed by the Jews above, rendered this a difficult task. Indeed, the labours of the Romans would have been endless, had not Pompey taken advantage of the seventh day of the week, on which the Jews, from religious scruples, refrain from all manual work, and then proceeded to raise the earthworks, while forbidding

67

στρατιώτας· ὑπὲρ μόνου γὰρ τοῦ σώματος ἀμύ-
147 νονται[1] τοῖς σαββάτοις. ἤδη δ' ἀναπεπληρωμένης
τῆς φάραγγος πύργους ὑψηλοὺς ἐπιστήσας τῷ
χώματι καὶ προσαγαγὼν τὰς ἐκ Τύρου κομισθείσας
μηχανὰς ἐπειρᾶτο τοῦ τείχους· ἀνέστελλον δὲ αἱ
πετροβόλοι τοὺς καθύπερθεν κωλύοντας. ἀντεῖχον
δ' ἐπὶ πλεῖον οἱ κατὰ τοῦτο τὸ μέρος πύργοι
μεγέθει τε καὶ κάλλει διαφέροντες.

148 (4) Ἔνθα δὴ πολλὰ τῶν Ῥωμαίων κακοπα-
θούντων ὁ Πομπήιος τά τε ἄλλα τῆς καρτερίας
τοὺς Ἰουδαίους ἀπεθαύμαζεν, καὶ μάλιστα τοῦ
μηδὲν παραλῦσαι τῆς θρησκείας ἐν μέσοις τοῖς
βέλεσιν ἀνειλημένους· ὥσπερ γὰρ εἰρήνης βαθείας
κατεχούσης τὴν πόλιν αἵ τε θυσίαι καθ' ἡμέραν
καὶ οἱ ἐναγισμοὶ καὶ πᾶσα θεραπεία κατὰ τἀκριβὲς
ἐξετελεῖτο τῷ θεῷ. καὶ οὐδὲ κατ' αὐτὴν τὴν
ἅλωσιν περὶ τῷ βωμῷ φονευόμενοι τῶν καθ'
ἡμέραν νομίμων εἰς τὴν θρησκείαν ἀπέστησαν.
149 τρίτῳ γὰρ μηνὶ τῆς πολιορκίας μόλις ἕνα τῶν
πύργων καταρρίψαντες εἰσέπιπτον εἰς τὸ ἱερόν.
ὁ δὲ πρῶτος ὑπερβῆναι τολμήσας τὸ τεῖχος Σύλλα
παῖς ἦν Φαῦστος Κορνήλιος καὶ μετ' αὐτὸν ἑκατοντάρχαι δύο Φούριος[2] καὶ Φάβιος. εἵπετο δὲ
ἑκάστῳ τὸ ἴδιον στῖφος, καὶ περισχόντες πανταχῆ
τὸ ἱερὸν ἔκτεινον οὓς μὲν τῷ ναῷ προσφεύγοντας,
οὓς δὲ ἀμυνομένους πρὸς ὀλίγον.

[1] + καὶ VRNC Lat. (etiam).
[2] Lat., Heg.: Φρούριος MSS.

---

[a] Military engines for flinging stones and other missiles.
[b] A. xiv. 66 gives the precise year (Olympiad 179 and
the Roman consuls of 63 B.C.) and adds "on the day of the
fast," i.e. probably the Day of Atonement (10th Tishri,
September-October). Dio Cassius, xxxvii. 16, says "on the

his troops to engage in hostilities; for on the sabbaths the Jews fight only in self-defence. The ravine once filled up, he erected lofty towers on the earthworks, brought up the battering engines which had been conveyed from Tyre, and tried their effect upon the walls; the *ballistae*,[a] meanwhile, beating off resistance from above. However, the towers, which in this sector were extraordinarily massive and beautiful, long resisted the blows.

(4) While the Romans were undergoing these severe hardships, Pompey was filled with admiration for the invariable fortitude of the Jews, and in particular for the way in which they carried on their religious services uncurtailed, though enveloped in a hail of missiles. Just as if the city had been wrapt in profound peace, the daily sacrifices, the expiations and all the ceremonies of worship were scrupulously performed to the honour of God. At the very hour when the temple was taken, when they were being massacred about the altar, they never desisted from the religious rites for the day. It was the third month of the siege[b] when, having with difficulty succeeded in overthrowing one of the towers, the Romans burst into the temple. The first to venture across the wall was Faustus Cornelius, son of Sulla; after him came two centurions, Furius and Fabius. Followed by their respective companies, they formed a ring round the court of the temple and slew their victims, some flying to the sanctuary, others offering a brief resistance.

Capture of the Temple.

sabbath " (ἐν τῇ τοῦ Κρόνου ἡμέρᾳ); and it has been held by some that " the fast " named in Josephus's non-Jewish source meant the sabbath, according to a mistaken and widespread idea in the Graeco-Roman world that the Jews fasted on the sabbath (Schürer).

150 (5) Ἔνθα πολλοὶ τῶν ἱερέων ξιφήρεις τοὺς
πολεμίους ἐπιόντας βλέποντες ἀθορύβως ἐπὶ τῆς
θρησκείας ἔμειναν, σπένδοντες δὲ ἀπεσφάττοντο
καὶ θυμιῶντες [καὶ] τῆς πρὸς τὸ θεῖον θεραπείας
ἐν δευτέρῳ τὴν σωτηρίαν τιθέμενοι. πλεῖστοι δ᾽
ὑπὸ τῶν ὁμοφύλων ἀντιστασιαστῶν ἀνηροῦντο καὶ
κατὰ τῶν κρημνῶν ἔρριπτον ἑαυτοὺς ἄπειροι· καὶ
τὰ περὶ τὸ τεῖχος δ᾽ ἔνιοι μανιῶντες ἐν ταῖς
151 ἀμηχανίαις ὑπέπρησαν καὶ συγκατεφλέγοντο. Ἰουδαίων μὲν οὖν ἀνηρέθησαν μύριοι καὶ δισχίλιοι,
Ῥωμαίων δὲ ὀλίγοι μὲν πάνυ νεκροί, τραυματίαι
δ᾽ ἐγένοντο πλείους.

152 (6) Οὐδὲν δ᾽ οὕτως ἐν ταῖς τότε συμφοραῖς
καθήψατο τοῦ ἔθνους ὡς τὸ τέως ἀόρατον ἅγιον
ἐκκαλυφθὲν ὑπὸ τῶν ἀλλοφύλων. παρελθὼν γοῦν
σὺν τοῖς περὶ αὐτὸν ὁ Πομπήιος εἰς τὸν ναόν,
ἔνθα μόνῳ θεμιτὸν ἦν παριέναι τῷ ἀρχιερεῖ, τὰ
ἔνδον ἐθεάσατο, λυχνίαν τε καὶ λύχνους καὶ τρά-
πεζαν καὶ σπονδεῖα καὶ θυμιατήρια, ὁλόχρυσα
πάντα, πλῆθός τε ἀρωμάτων σεσωρευμένον καὶ
153 ἱερῶν χρημάτων εἰς τάλαντα δισχίλια. οὔτε δὲ
τούτων οὔτε ἄλλου τινὸς τῶν ἱερῶν κειμηλίων
ἥψατο, ἀλλὰ καὶ μετὰ μίαν τῆς ἁλώσεως ἡμέραν
καθᾶραι τὸ ἱερὸν τοῖς νεωκόροις προσέταξεν καὶ
τὰς ἐξ ἔθους ἐπιτελεῖν θυσίας. αὖθις δ᾽ ἀποδείξας
Ὑρκανὸν ἀρχιερέα, τά τε ἄλλα προθυμότατον
ἑαυτὸν ἐν τῇ πολιορκίᾳ παρασχόντα, καὶ διότι τὸ
κατὰ τὴν χώραν πλῆθος ἀπέστησεν Ἀριστοβούλῳ
συμπολεμεῖν[1] ὡρμημένον, ἐκ τούτων, ὅπερ ἦν
προσῆκον ἀγαθῷ στρατηγῷ, τὸν λαὸν εὐνοίᾳ πλέον
154 ἢ δέει προσηγάγετο. ἐν δὲ τοῖς αἰχμαλώτοις

_____
[1] συμπονεῖν C.

(5) Then it was that many of the priests, seeing the enemy advancing sword in hand, calmly continued their sacred ministrations, and were butchered in the act of pouring libations and burning incense; putting the worship of the Deity above their own preservation. Most of the slain perished by the hands of their countrymen of the opposite faction; countless numbers flung themselves over the precipices; some, driven mad by their hopeless plight, set fire to the buildings around the wall and were consumed in the flames. Of the Jews twelve thousand perished; the losses of the Romans in dead were trifling, in wounded considerable.

(6) Of all the calamities of that time none so deeply affected the nation as the exposure to alien eyes of the Holy Place, hitherto screened from view. Pompey indeed, along with his staff, penetrated to the sanctuary, entry to which was permitted to none but the high priest, and beheld what it contained: the candelabrum and lamps, the table, the vessels for libation and censers, all of solid gold, an accumulation of spices and the store of sacred money amounting to two thousand talents. However, he touched neither these nor any other of the sacred treasures and, the very day after the capture of the temple, gave orders to the custodians to cleanse it and to resume the customary sacrifices. He reinstated Hyrcanus as high priest, in return for his enthusiastic support shown during the siege, particularly in detaching from Aristobulus large numbers of the rural population who were anxious to join his standard. By these methods, in which goodwill played a larger part than terrorism, he, like the able general he was, conciliated the people. Among the prisoners was

Hyrcanus reinstated as high priest.

71

ἐλήφθη καὶ ὁ Ἀριστοβούλου πενθερός, ὃ δ᾽ αὐτὸς
ἦν καὶ θεῖος αὐτῷ. καὶ τοὺς αἰτιωτάτους μὲν τοῦ
πολέμου πελέκει κολάζει, Φαῦστον δὲ καὶ τοὺς
μετ᾽ αὐτοῦ γενναίως ἀγωνισαμένους λαμπροῖς
ἀριστείοις δωρησάμενος τῇ τε χώρᾳ καὶ τοῖς
Ἱεροσολύμοις ἐπιτάσσει φόρον.

155 (7) Ἀφελόμενος δὲ τοῦ ἔθνους καὶ τὰς ἐν κοίλῃ
Συρίᾳ πόλεις, ἃς εἷλον, ὑπέταξεν τῷ κατ᾽ ἐκεῖνο
Ῥωμαίων στρατηγῷ κατατεταγμένῳ καὶ μόνοις
αὐτοὺς τοῖς ἰδίοις ὅροις περιέκλεισεν. ἀνακτίζει
δὲ καὶ Γάδαραν ὑπὸ Ἰουδαίων κατεστραμμένην,
Γαδαρίτῃ τινὶ τῶν ἰδίων ἀπελευθέρων Δημητρίῳ
156 χαριζόμενος. ἠλευθέρωσεν δ᾽ ἀπ᾽ αὐτῶν καὶ τὰς
ἐν τῇ μεσογείῳ πόλεις, ὅσας μὴ φθάσαντες κατ-
έσκαψαν, Ἵππον Σκυθόπολίν τε καὶ Πέλλαν καὶ
Σαμάρειαν καὶ Ἰάμνειαν καὶ Μάρισαν Ἄζωτόν τε
καὶ Ἀρέθουσαν, ὁμοίως δὲ καὶ τὰς παραλίους
Γάζαν Ἰόππην Δῶρα καὶ τὴν πάλαι μὲν Στράτωνος
πύργον καλουμένην, ὕστερον δὲ μετακτισθεῖσάν
τε ὑφ᾽ Ἡρώδου βασιλέως λαμπροτάτοις κατα-
157 σκευάσμασιν καὶ μετονομασθεῖσαν Καισάρειαν. ἃς
πάσας τοῖς γνησίοις ἀποδοὺς πολίταις κατέταξεν
εἰς τὴν Συριακὴν ἐπαρχίαν. παραδοὺς δὲ ταύτην
τε καὶ τὴν Ἰουδαίαν καὶ τὰ μέχρις Αἰγύπτου καὶ
Εὐφράτου Σκαύρῳ διέπειν καὶ δύο τῶν ταγμάτων,
αὐτὸς διὰ Κιλικίας εἰς Ῥώμην ἠπείγετο τὸν
Ἀριστόβουλον ἄγων μετὰ τῆς γενεᾶς αἰχμάλωτον.
158 δύο δ᾽ ἦσαν αὐτῷ θυγατέρες καὶ δύο υἱεῖς, ὧν ὁ
ἕτερος μὲν Ἀλέξανδρος ἐκ τῆς ὁδοῦ διαδιδράσκει,

---

[a] Named Absalom (Δ. xiv. 71).

the father-in-law of Aristobulus, who was also his
uncle.[a] Those upon whom lay the main responsibility
for the war were executed. Faustus and his brave Judaea
companions in arms were presented with splendid made
tributary
rewards. The country and Jerusalem were laid to Rome.
under tribute.

(7) Pompey, moreover, deprived the Jews of the Redistribu-
cities which they had conquered in Coele-Syria, tion of
territory.
placing these under the authority of a Roman
governor appointed for the purpose,[b] and thus confined the nation within its own boundaries. To
gratify Demetrius, one of his freedmen, a Gadarene,
he rebuilt Gadara, which had been destroyed by the
Jews. He also liberated from their rule all the
towns in the interior which they had not already
razed to the ground, namely Hippos, Scythopolis,
Pella,[c] Samaria, Jamnia, Marisa, Azotus, and Are-
thusa; likewise the maritime towns of Gaza, Joppa,
Dora, and the city formerly called Strato's Tower,
which afterwards, when reconstructed by King
Herod with magnificent buildings, took the name of
Caesarea. All these towns he restored to their
legitimate inhabitants and annexed to the province
of Syria. That province, together with Judaea and
the whole region extending as far as Egypt and the
Euphrates, he entrusted, along with two legions, to
the administration of Scaurus; and then set out in
haste across Cilicia for Rome, taking with him his
prisoners, Aristobulus and his family. That prince Aristobulus
had two daughters and two sons. Of the latter, taken
captive to
one, Alexander, made his escape on the journey; Rome.

[b] κατ' ἐκεῖνο, "ad hoc," or perhaps "of the Roman
governor placed over that region."
[c] A. adds Dium.

σὺν δὲ ταῖς ἀδελφαῖς ὁ νεώτερος Ἀντίγονος εἰς
Ῥώμην ἐκομίζετο.

159　(viii. 1) Κἀν τούτῳ Σκαῦρος εἰς τὴν Ἀραβίαν
ἐμβαλὼν τῆς μὲν Πέτρας εἴργετο ταῖς δυσχωρίαις,
ἐπόρθει δὲ τὰ πέριξ πολλὰ κἀν τούτῳ κακοπαθῶν·
ἐλίμωττεν γὰρ ἡ στρατιά. καὶ πρὸς τοῦτο Ὑρκανὸς ἐπεβοήθει διὰ Ἀντιπάτρου τἀπιτήδεια πέμπων,
ὃν καὶ καθίησι Σκαῦρος ὄντα συνήθη πρὸς Ἀρέταν,
ὅπως ἐπὶ χρήμασιν διαλύσαιτο τὸν πόλεμον.
πείθεται δ' ὁ Ἄραψ τριακόσια δοῦναι τάλαντα,
κἀπὶ τούτοις Σκαῦρος ἐξῆγεν τῆς Ἀραβίας τὴν
δύναμιν.

160　(2) Ὁ δ' ἀποδρὰς τῶν Ἀριστοβούλου παίδων
Πομπήιον Ἀλέξανδρος χρόνῳ συναγαγὼν χεῖρα
συχνὴν βαρὺς ἦν Ὑρκανῷ καὶ τὴν Ἰουδαίαν
κατέτρεχεν, ἐδόκει τε ἂν καταλῦσαι ταχέως αὐτόν,
ὅς γε ἤδη καὶ τὸ καταρριφθὲν ὑπὸ Πομπηίου
τεῖχος ἐν Ἱεροσολύμοις ἀνακτίζειν ἐθάρρει προσ-
ελθών, εἰ μὴ Γαβίνιος εἰς Συρίαν πεμφθεὶς
Σκαύρῳ διάδοχος τά τε ἄλλα γενναῖον ἀπέδειξεν
ἑαυτὸν ἐν πολλοῖς καὶ ἐπ' Ἀλέξανδρον ὥρμησεν.

161　ὁ δὲ δείσας πρὸς τὴν ἔφοδον δύναμίν τε πλείω
συνέλεγεν, ὡς γενέσθαι μυρίους μὲν ὁπλίτας
χιλίους δὲ καὶ πεντακοσίους ἱππεῖς, καὶ τὰ ἐπιτήδεια τῶν χωρίων ἐτείχιζεν, Ἀλεξάνδρειόν τε
καὶ Ὑρκανίαν[1] καὶ Μαχαιροῦντα πρὸς τοῖς Ἀρα-
βίοις ὄρεσιν.

162　(3) Γαβίνιος δὲ μετὰ μέρους τῆς στρατιᾶς
Μᾶρκον Ἀντώνιον προπέμψας αὐτὸς εἵπετο τὴν

---

[1] Niese (so it is called elsewhere): Ὑρκάν(ε)ιον mss.

[a] According to Appian, Syr. 51, there were two inter-
mediate governors of Syria between Scaurus and Gabinius,

Antigonus, the younger, was conducted with his sisters to Rome.

(viii. 1) Meanwhile Scaurus had invaded Arabia. Being held up at Pella by the difficulties of the ground, he proceeded to lay waste the surrounding country, but here again suffered severely, his army being reduced to starvation. To relieve his wants Hyrcanus sent Antipater with supplies. Antipater being on intimate terms with Aretas, Scaurus dispatched him to the king to induce him to purchase release from hostilities. The Arab monarch consenting to pay three hundred talents, Scaurus on these conditions withdrew his troops from the country.

Antipater assists Scaurus against Aretas.

(2) Alexander, son of Aristobulus, the one who escaped from Pompey, in course of time mustered a considerable force and caused Hyrcanus serious annoyance by his raids upon Judaea. Having already advanced to Jerusalem and had the audacity to begin rebuilding the wall which Pompey had destroyed, he would in all probability have soon deposed his rival, but for the arrival of Gabinius, who had been sent to Syria as successor to Scaurus.[a] Gabinius, whose valour had been proved on many other occasions, now marched against Alexander. The latter, alarmed at his approach, raised the strength of his army to ten thousand foot and fifteen hundred horse, and fortified the strategic positions of Alexandreion, Hyrcania, and Machaerus, adjacent to the Arabian mountains.

Revolt of Alexander, son of Aristobulus.

Government of Gabinius 57–55 B.C.

(3) Gabinius sent Mark Antony ahead with a division of his army, following himself with the main

He defeats Alexander

viz. Marcius Philippus (61–60 B.C., Schürer) and Lentulus Marcellinus (59–58 B.C.).

75

ὅλην ἔχων δύναμιν. οἱ δὲ περὶ τὸν Ἀντίπατρον
ἐπίλεκτοι καὶ τὸ ἄλλο τάγμα τῶν Ἰουδαίων, ὧν
Μάλιχος ἦρχεν καὶ Πειθόλαος, συμμίξαντες τοῖς
περὶ Μᾶρκον Ἀντώνιον ἡγεμόσιν ὑπήντων Ἀλεξάνδρῳ. καὶ μετ᾽ οὐ πολὺ παρῆν ἅμα τῇ φάλαγγι
163 Γαβίνιος. ἐνουμένην δὲ τὴν τῶν πολεμίων δύναμιν
οὐχ ὑπομείνας Ἀλέξανδρος ἀνεχώρει καὶ πλησίον
ἤδη Ἱεροσολύμων γενόμενος ἀναγκάζεται συμβαλεῖν, καὶ κατὰ τὴν μάχην ἑξακισχιλίους ἀπο-
βαλών, ὧν τρισχίλιοι μὲν ἔπεσον τρισχίλιοι δὲ
ἐζωγρήθησαν, φεύγει σὺν τοῖς καταλειφθεῖσιν εἰς
Ἀλεξάνδρειον.

164   (4) Γαβίνιος δὲ πρὸς τὸ Ἀλεξάνδρειον ἐλθὼν
ἐπειδὴ πολλοὺς εὗρεν ἐστρατοπεδευμένους, ἐπειρᾶτο συγγνώμης ὑποσχέσει περὶ τῶν ἡμαρτημένων πρὸ μάχης αὐτοὺς προσαγαγέσθαι· μηδὲν
δὲ μέτριον φρονούντων ἀποκτείνας πολλοὺς τοὺς
165 λοιποὺς ἀπέκλεισεν εἰς τὸ ἔρυμα. κατὰ ταύτην
ἀριστεύει τὴν μάχην ὁ ἡγεμὼν Μᾶρκος Ἀντώνιος,
πανταχοῦ μὲν γενναῖος ἀεὶ φανείς, οὐδαμοῦ δ᾽
οὕτως. Γαβίνιος δὲ τοὺς ἐξαιρήσοντας τὸ φρούριον
καταλιπὼν αὐτὸς ἐπῄει τὰς μὲν ἀπορθήτους πόλεις
καθιστάμενος, τὰς δὲ κατεστραμμένας ἀνακτίζων.
166 συνεπολίσθησαν γοῦν τούτου κελεύσαντος Σκυθό-
πολίς τε καὶ Σαμάρεια καὶ Ἀνθηδὼν καὶ Ἀπολ-
λωνία καὶ Ἰάμνεια καὶ Ῥάφεια Μάρισά τε καὶ
Ἀδώρεος καὶ Γάμαλα[1] καὶ Ἄζωτος καὶ ἄλλαι
πολλαί, τῶν οἰκητόρων ἀσμένως ἐφ᾽ ἑκάστην
συνθεόντων.
167   (5) Μετὰ δὲ τὴν τούτων ἐπιμέλειαν ἐπανελθὼν
πρὸς τὸ Ἀλεξάνδρειον ἐπέρρωσεν τὴν πολιορκίαν,

[1] VC : Γάβαλα the rest : Gadara Lat. : Gaza *A*. ||

body. Antipater's picked troops and the rest of the
Jewish contingent under the command of Malichus
and Peitholaus joined forces with Antony's generals
and proceeded against Alexander. Gabinius appeared before long with the heavy infantry. Alexander, unable to withstand the combined forces of
the enemy, retired, but when approaching Jerusalem
was forced into an engagement. In this battle he
lost six thousand of his men, three thousand killed,
and as many prisoners. With the remnant of his
army he fled to Alexandreion.

(4) Gabinius, following him thither, found many of
his men camping outside the walls. Before attacking
them, he endeavoured, by promise of pardon for past
offences, to bring them over to his side ; but, on
their proudly refusing all terms, he killed a large
number of them and confined the remainder in the
fortress. The honours of this combat went to the
commanding officer, Mark Antony ; his valour, displayed on every battlefield, was never so conspicuous
as here. Leaving the reduction of the fort to his
troops, Gabinius made a parade of the country,
restoring order in the cities which had escaped *and restores*
devastation, and rebuilding those which he found in *order in the country.*
ruins. It was, for instance, by his orders that
Scythopolis, Samaria, Anthedon, Apollonia, Jamnia,
Raphia, Marisa, Adoreus, Gamala, Azotus, and many
other towns were repeopled, colonists gladly flocking
to each of them.

(5) After supervising these arrangements, Gabinius
returned to Alexandreion and pressed the siege so

ὥστε Ἀλέξανδρος ἀπογνοὺς περὶ τῶν ὅλων ἐπικηρυκεύεται πρὸς αὐτόν, συγγνωσθῆναί τε τῶν ἡμαρτημένων δεόμενος καὶ τὰ συμμένοντα[1] φρούρια παραδιδοὺς Ὑρκανίαν καὶ Μαχαιροῦντα· αὖθις δὲ
168 καὶ τὸ Ἀλεξάνδρειον ἐνεχείρισεν. ἃ πάντα Γαβίνιος ἐναγούσης τῆς Ἀλεξάνδρου μητρὸς κατέστρεψεν, ὡς μὴ πάλιν ὁρμητήριον γένοιτο δευτέρου πολέμου· παρῆν δὲ μειλισσομένη τὸν Γαβίνιον κατὰ δέος τῶν ἐπὶ τῆς Ῥώμης αἰχμαλώτων, τοῦ τε
169 ἀνδρὸς καὶ τῶν ἄλλων τέκνων. μετὰ δὲ ταῦτα εἰς Ἱεροσόλυμα Γαβίνιος Ὑρκανὸν καταγαγὼν καὶ τὴν τοῦ ἱεροῦ παραδοὺς κηδεμονίαν αὐτῷ καθίστατο τὴν ἄλλην πολιτείαν ἐπὶ προστασίᾳ τῶν ἀρίστων.
170 διεῖλεν δὲ πᾶν τὸ ἔθνος εἰς πέντε συνόδους,[a] τὸ μὲν Ἱεροσολύμοις προστάξας, τὸ δὲ Γαδάροις, οἱ δ' ἵνα συντελῶσιν εἰς Ἀμαθοῦντα, τὸ δὲ τέταρτον εἰς Ἱεριχοῦντα κεκλήρωτο, καὶ τῷ πέμπτῳ Σέπφωρις ἀπεδείχθη πόλις τῆς Γαλιλαίας. ἀσμένως δὲ τῆς ἐξ ἑνὸς ἐπικρατείας ἐλευθερωθέντες τὸ λοιπὸν ἀριστοκρατίᾳ διῳκοῦντο.
171 (6) Μετ' οὐ πολύ γε μὴν αὐτοῖς ἀρχὴ γίνεται θορύβων Ἀριστόβουλος ἀποδρὰς ἐκ Ῥώμης, ὃς αὖθις πολλοὺς Ἰουδαίων ἐπισυνίστη, τοὺς μὲν ἐπιθυμοῦντας μεταβολῆς, τοὺς δ' ἀγαπῶντας αὐτὸν πάλαι. καὶ τὸ μὲν πρῶτον καταλαβόμενος τὸ Ἀλεξάνδρειον ἀνατειχίζειν ἐπειρᾶτο· ὡς δὲ Γαβίνιος ὑπὸ Σισέννᾳ καὶ Ἀντωνίῳ καὶ Σερουιανῷ

[1] συλληφθέντα PAM.

[a] συνόδους; Reinach would read συνέδρια, " councils," as in the parallel passage A. xiv. 91.

[b] So the mss. in B. and A.; but we should rather read Gazara, i.e. the O.T. Gezer, about half-way between Jerusalem and Joppa. The Hellenistic town Gadara in N.

vigorously that Alexander, despairing of success, sent
him a herald with a petition for pardon for his
offences and an offer to surrender the fortresses of
Hyrcania and Machaerus, still in his possession ;
subsequently he gave up Alexandreion as well. All
these places Gabinius demolished, to prevent their
serving as a base of operations for another war. He
was instigated to take this step by Alexander's
mother, who had come to propitiate him, in her
concern for her husband and remaining children,
then prisoners in Rome. After this Gabinius re- Aristocratic
instated Hyrcanus in Jerusalem and committed to constitution
of Judaea.
him the custody of the Temple. The civil administration he reconstituted under the form of an aristocracy. He divided the whole nation into five
unions ; *a* one of these he attached to Jerusalem,
another to Gadara,*b* the third had Amathus as its
centre of government, the fourth was allotted to
Jericho, the fifth to Sepphoris, a city of Galilee.
The Jews welcomed their release from the rule of an
individual and were from that time forward governed
by an aristocracy.

(6) They were soon, however, involved in fresh Fresh revolt
troubles through the escape of Aristobulus from and re-
capture of
Rome. Once more he succeeded in mustering a Aristobulus
large body of Jews, some eager for revolution, others
long since his devoted admirers. He began by
seizing Alexandreion and attempting to restore the
fortifications ; but on hearing that Gabinius had
dispatched an army against him, under the command

Peraea had been severed from Jewish territory by Pompey.
The names are elsewhere confused (Schürer). Judaea proper
is thus represented by three towns, Galilee by one, and
Peraea by one (Amathus), a little E. of Jordan, to the N. of
the river Jabbok.

στρατιὰν ἔπεμψεν ἐπ' αὐτόν, γνοὺς ἀνεχώρει ἐπὶ
172 Μαχαιροῦντος. καὶ τὸν μὲν ἄχρηστον ὄχλον
ἀπεφορτίσατο, μόνους δ' ἐπήγετο τοὺς ὡπλισμένους, ὄντας εἰς ὀκτακισχιλίους, ἐν οἷς καὶ
Πειθόλαος ἦν ὁ ἐξ Ἱεροσολύμων ὑποστράτηγος
αὐτομολήσας μετὰ χιλίων. Ῥωμαῖοι δ' ἐπηκο-
λούθουν, καὶ γενομένης συμβολῆς μέχρι πολλοῦ
μὲν οἱ περὶ τὸν Ἀριστόβουλον διεκαρτέρουν γενναίως ἀγωνιζόμενοι, τέλος δὲ βιασθέντες ὑπὸ τῶν
Ῥωμαίων πίπτουσι μὲν πεντακισχίλιοι, περὶ δὲ
δισχιλίους ἀνέφυγον εἴς τινα λόφον, οἱ δὲ λοιποὶ
χίλιοι σὺν Ἀριστοβούλῳ διακόψαντες τὴν φάλαγγα
τῶν Ῥωμαίων εἰς Μαχαιροῦντα συνελαύνονται.
173 ἔνθα δὴ τὴν πρώτην ἑσπέραν ὁ βασιλεὺς τοῖς
ἐρειπίοις ἐναυλισάμενος ἐν ἐλπίσι μὲν ἦν ἄλλην
συναθροίσειν δύναμιν, ἀνοχὴν τοῦ πολέμου διδόντος,
καὶ τὸ φρούριον κακῶς ὠχύρου· προσπεσόντων δὲ
Ῥωμαίων ἐπὶ δύο ἡμέρας ἀντισχὼν ὑπὲρ δύναμιν
ἁλίσκεται καὶ μετ' Ἀντιγόνου τοῦ παιδός, ὃς ἀπὸ
Ῥώμης αὐτῷ συναπέδρα, δεσμώτης ἐπὶ Γαβίνιον
ἀνήχθη καὶ ἀπὸ Γαβινίου πάλιν εἰς Ῥώμην.
174 τοῦτον μὲν οὖν ἡ σύγκλητος εἷρξεν, τὰ τέκνα δ'
αὐτοῦ διῆκεν[1] εἰς Ἰουδαίαν, Γαβινίου δι' ἐπιστολῶν
δηλώσαντος τῇ Ἀριστοβούλου γυναικὶ τοῦτο ἀντὶ
τῆς παραδόσεως τῶν ἐρυμάτων ὡμολογηκέναι.
175   (7) Γαβινίῳ δ' ἐπὶ Πάρθους ὡρμημένῳ στρα-
τεύειν γίνεται Πτολεμαῖος ἐμπόδιον, ὃν[2] ὑπο-
στρέψας ἀπ' Εὐφράτου κατῆγεν εἰς Αἴγυπτον,

---

[1] διῆκεν Destinon (after Lat.; cf. ἀνῆκεν A. ‖) : διῆγεν
MSS.   [2] Hudson : ὃς MSS.

---

[a] Servilius, A. xiv. 92, and many MSS. of B.   [b] Cf. § 168.
[c] Ptolemy Auletes, driven from the throne of Egypt by

of Sisenna, Antony, and Servianus,[a] he retreated towards Machaerus. Disencumbering himself of his rabble of inefficient followers, he retained only those who were armed, numbering eight thousand ; among these was Peitholaus, the second in command at Jerusalem, who had deserted to him with a thousand men. The Romans pursued and an engagement took place. Aristobulus and his men for long held their ground, fighting valiantly, but were ultimately overpowered by the Romans. Five thousand fell ; about two thousand took refuge on a hill ; Aristobulus and the remaining thousand cut their way through the Roman lines and flung themselves into Machaerus. There, as he camped among the ruins on that first evening, the king entertained hopes of raising another army, given but a respite from war, and proceeded to erect some weak fortifications ; but, when the Romans attacked the place, after holding out beyond his strength for two days, he was taken, and, with his son Antigonus, who had shared his flight from Rome, was conducted in chains to Gabinius, and by Gabinius was sent back once more to Rome. The 56 B.C. Senate imprisoned the father, but allowed his children to return to Judaea, Gabinius having written to inform them that he had promised this favour to the wife of Aristobulus in return for the surrender of the fortresses.[b]

(7) An expedition against the Parthians, on which Gabinius had already started, was cut short by Ptolemy,[c] to effect whose restoration to Egypt the former returned from the banks of the Euphrates.

Further revolt and defeat of Alexander 55 B.C.

his subjects, induced Gabinius by a large bribe to undertake his restoration (55 B.C.). He had since his expulsion in 58 been working for this at Rome and had obtained the influential support of Cicero.

ἐπιτηδείοις εἰς ἅπαντα χρώμενος κατὰ τὴν στρατείαν Ὑρκανῷ καὶ Ἀντιπάτρῳ· καὶ γὰρ χρήματα
καὶ ὅπλα καὶ σῖτον καὶ ἐπικούρους Ἀντίπατρος
προσῆγεν, καὶ τοὺς ταύτῃ Ἰουδαίους φρουροῦντας
τὰς κατὰ τὸ Πηλούσιον ἐμβολὰς παρεῖναι Γαβίνιον
176 ἔπεισεν. τῆς δ' ἄλλης Συρίας πρὸς τὸν Γαβινίου
χωρισμὸν κινηθείσης καὶ Ἰουδαίους πάλιν ἀπέστησεν Ἀλέξανδρος ὁ Ἀριστοβούλου, μεγίστην δὲ
συγκροτήσας δύναμιν ὥρμητο πάντας τοὺς κατὰ
177 τὴν χώραν Ῥωμαίους ἀνελεῖν. πρὸς ὃ Γαβίνιος
δείσας, ἤδη δὲ παρῆν ἀπ' Αἰγύπτου τοῖς τῇδε
θορύβοις ἠπειγμένος, ἐπὶ τινὰς μὲν τῶν ἀφεστώτων
Ἀντίπατρον προπέμψας μετέπεισεν, συνέμενον δὲ
Ἀλεξάνδρῳ τρεῖς μυριάδες, κἀκεῖνος ὥρμητο
πολεμεῖν. οὕτως ἔξεισιν πρὸς μάχην. ὑπήντων
δ' οἱ Ἰουδαῖοι, καὶ συμβαλόντων περὶ τὸ Ἰταβύριον
ὄρος μύριοι μὲν ἀναιροῦνται, τὸ δὲ λοιπὸν πλῆθος
178 ἐσκεδάσθη φυγῇ. καὶ Γαβίνιος ἐλθὼν εἰς Ἱεροσόλυμα πρὸς τὸ Ἀντιπάτρου βούλημα κατεστήσατο
τὴν πολιτείαν. ἔνθεν ὁρμήσας Ναβαταίων τε
μάχῃ κρατεῖ καὶ Μιθριδάτην καὶ Ὀρσάνην φυ-
γόντας ἐκ Πάρθων κρύφα μὲν ἀπέπεμψεν, παρὰ
δὲ τοῖς στρατιώταις ἔλεγεν ἀποδρᾶναι.
179   (8) Κἂν τούτῳ Κράσσος αὐτῷ διάδοχος ἐλθὼν
παραλαμβάνει Συρίαν. οὗτος εἰς τὴν ἐπὶ Πάρθους στρατείαν τόν τε ἄλλον τοῦ ἐν Ἱεροσολύμοις
ναοῦ χρυσὸν πάντα περιεῖλεν καὶ τὰ δισχίλια
τάλαντα ἦρεν, ὧν ἀπέσχετο Πομπήιος. διαβὰς

<hr />

ᵃ Or " river-mouths." For the charge of the river Nile
entrusted to the Jews cf. Ap. ii. 64.

ᵇ As Reinach remarks, this detail, which has no relevance to
Jewish history, shows that Josephus is abridging a general
history. The language, both here (κρύφα ἀπέπεμψεν) and

For this campaign Hyrcanus and Antipater put their services entirely at his disposal. In addition to providing money, arms, corn, and auxiliaries, Antipater further induced the local Jewish guardians of the frontiers [a] at Pelusium to let Gabinius through. His departure, however, was the occasion for a general commotion in Syria ; and Alexander, son of Aristobulus, heading a new Jewish revolt, collected a vast army and proceeded to massacre all Romans in the country. Gabinius was alarmed. He was already on the spot, news of the local disturbances having hastened his return from Egypt. Sending Antipater in advance to address some of the rebels he brought them over to reason. Alexander, however, had still thirty thousand left and was burning for action. Gabinius, accordingly, took the field, the Jews met him, and a battle was fought near Mount Tabor, in which they lost ten thousand men ; the remainder fled and dispersed. Gabinius then proceeded to Jerusalem, where he reorganized the government in accordance with Antipater's wishes. From there he marched against the Nabataeans, whom he fought and defeated. Two fugitives from Parthia, Mithridates and Orsanes, he privily dismissed, giving out to his soldiers that they had made their escape.[b]

(8) The government of Syria now passed into the hands of Crassus, who came to succeed Gabinius. To provide for his expedition against the Parthians, Crassus stripped the temple at Jerusalem of all its gold, his plunder including the two thousand talents left untouched by Pompey.[c] He then crossed the

Crassus plunders the temple 54-53 B.C.

in the parallel *A*. xiv. 103 (τῷ δὲ λόγῳ ἀπέδρασαν αὐτόν), is based on Thuc. i. 128.   [c] §§ 152 f.

δὲ τὸν Εὐφράτην αὐτός τε ἀπώλετο καὶ ὁ στρατὸς αὐτοῦ, περὶ ὧν οὐ νῦν καιρὸς λέγειν.

180 (9) Πάρθους δὲ μετὰ τὸν Κράσσον ἐπιδιαβαίνειν εἰς Συρίαν ὡρμημένους ἀνέκοπτεν Κάσσιος εἰς τὴν ἐπαρχίαν διαφυγών. περιποιησάμενος δ' αὐτὴν ἐπὶ Ἰουδαίας ἠπείγετο, καὶ Ταριχαίας μὲν ἑλὼν εἰς τρεῖς μυριάδας Ἰουδαίων ἀνδραποδίζεται, κτείνει δὲ καὶ Πειθόλαον τοὺς Ἀριστοβούλου στασιαστὰς ἐπισυνιστάντα· τοῦ φόνου

181 δὲ ἦν σύμβουλος Ἀντίπατρος. τούτῳ γήμαντι[1] γυναῖκα τῶν ἐπισήμων ἐξ Ἀραβίας, Κύπρον[1] τοὔνομα, τέσσαρες μὲν υἱεῖς γίνονται, Φασάηλος καὶ ὁ βασιλεὺς αὖθις Ἡρώδης, πρὸς οἷς Ἰώσηπος καὶ Φερώρας καὶ Σαλώμη θυγάτηρ. ἐξῳκειωμένος δὲ τοὺς πανταχοῦ δυνατοὺς φιλίαις τε καὶ ξενίαις μάλιστα προσηγάγετο τὸν Ἀράβων βασιλέα διὰ τὴν ἐπιγαμβρίαν, κἀπειδὴ τὸν πρὸς τὸν Ἀριστόβουλον ἀνείλετο πόλεμον, ἐκείνῳ παρα-

182 καταθήκην ἔπεμψεν τὰ τέκνα. Κάσσιος δὲ κατὰ συνθήκας ἡσυχάζειν Ἀλέξανδρον ἀναγκάσας ἐπὶ τὸν Εὐφράτην ὑπέστρεψεν, Πάρθους διαβαίνειν ἀνείρξας, περὶ ὧν ἐν ἑτέροις ἐροῦμεν.

183 (ix. 1) Καῖσαρ δὲ Πομπηίου καὶ τῆς συγκλήτου φυγόντων ὑπὲρ τὸν Ἰόνιον Ῥώμης καὶ τῶν ὅλων κρατήσας ἀνίησι μὲν τῶν δεσμῶν τὸν Ἀριστόβουλον, παραδοὺς δ' αὐτῷ δύο τάγματα κατὰ τάχος ἔπεμψεν εἰς Συρίαν, ταύτην τε ῥᾳδίως ἐλπίσας καὶ τὰ περὶ τὴν Ἰουδαίαν δι' αὐτοῦ προσ-

---

[1] Hudson : Κύπριν mss.

---

[a] i.e. the Euphrates (§ 182).
[b] This promise is not fulfilled; the corresponding phrase

Euphrates and perished with his whole army; but of those events this is not the occasion to speak.

(9) After the death of Crassus the Parthians rushed to cross the river [a] into Syria, but were repulsed by Cassius, who had made his escape to that province. Having secured Syria, he hastened towards Judaea, capturing Tarichaeae, where he reduced thirty thousand Jews to slavery and put to death Peitholaus, who was endeavouring to rally the partisans of Aristobulus. His execution was recommended by Antipater. Antipater had married a lady named Cypros, of an illustrious Arabian family, by whom he had four sons—Phasael, Herod afterwards king, Joseph, and Pheroras—and a daughter, Salome. He had, by kind offices and hospitality, attached to himself persons of influence in every quarter; above all, through this matrimonial alliance, he had won the friendship of the king of Arabia, and it was to him that he entrusted his children when embarking on war with Aristobulus. Cassius, having bound over Alexander by treaty to keep the peace, returned to the Euphrates to prevent the Parthians from crossing it. Of these events we shall speak elsewhere.[b]

(ix. 1) When Pompey fled with the Senate across the Ionian Sea, Caesar, now master of Rome and the empire, set Aristobulus at liberty; and, putting two legions at his service, dispatched him in haste to Syria, hoping by his means to have no difficulty in bringing over both that province and Judaea with

Cassius
53-51 B.C.

Rise of
ANTIPATER.

Julius
CAESAR
49 B.C.

in *A.* xiv. 122 is ὡς καὶ ὑπ' ἄλλων δεδήλωται. It is uncertain whether Josephus in this and kindred phrases, mainly relating to Parthia and the Seleucids, has thoughtlessly taken over a formula from his source, or whether he actually wrote, or contemplated writing, a work which has not come down to us.

184 ἄξεσθαι. φθάνει δ' ὁ φθόνος καὶ τὴν Ἀριστοβούλου προθυμίαν καὶ τὰς Καίσαρος ἐλπίδας·
φαρμάκῳ γοῦν ἀναιρεθεὶς ὑπὸ τῶν τὰ Πομπηίου
φρονούντων μέχρι πολλοῦ μὲν οὐδὲ ταφῆς ἐν τῇ
πατρῴᾳ χώρᾳ μετεῖχεν, ἔκειτο δὲ μέλιτι συν-
τηρούμενος ὁ νεκρὸς [αὐτοῦ] ἕως ὑπ' Ἀντωνίου
Ἰουδαίοις ἐπέμφθη τοῖς βασιλικοῖς μνημείοις
ἐνταφησόμενος.

185 (2) Ἀναιρεῖται δὲ καὶ ὁ υἱὸς αὐτοῦ Ἀλέξανδρος πελέκει ὑπὸ Σκιπίωνος ἐν Ἀντιοχείᾳ, Πομπηίου τοῦτ' ἐπιστείλαντος καὶ γενομένης κατηγορίας
πρὸ τοῦ βήματος ὧν Ῥωμαίους ἔβλαψεν. τοὺς
δ' ἀδελφοὺς αὐτοῦ Πτολεμαῖος ὁ Μενναίου παραλαβών, ὃς ἐκράτει τῆς ὑπὸ τῷ Λιβάνῳ Χαλκίδος,
Φιλιππίωνα τὸν υἱὸν ἐπ' αὐτοὺς εἰς Ἀσκάλωνα
186 πέμπει. κἀκεῖνος ἀποσπάσας τῆς Ἀριστοβούλου
γυναικὸς Ἀντίγονον καὶ τὰς ἀδελφὰς αὐτοῦ πρὸς
τὸν πατέρα ἀνήγαγεν. ἁλοὺς δ' ἔρωτι γαμεῖ τὴν
ἑτέραν[1] καὶ μετὰ ταῦθ' ὑπὸ τοῦ πατρὸς δι' αὐτὴν
κτείνεται· γαμεῖ γὰρ Πτολεμαῖος τὴν Ἀλεξάνδραν ἀνελὼν τὸν υἱὸν καὶ διὰ τὸν γάμον κηδεμονικώτερος αὐτὸς ἦν πρὸς τοὺς ἀδελφούς.

187 (3) Ἀντίπατρος δὲ μετὰ τὴν Πομπηίου τελευτὴν μεταβὰς ἐθεράπευεν Καίσαρα, κἀπειδὴ Μιθριδάτης ὁ Περγαμηνὸς μεθ' ἧς ἦγεν ἐπ' Αἴγυπ-
του δυνάμεως εἰργόμενος τῶν κατὰ τὸ Πηλούσιον ἐμβολῶν ἐν Ἀσκάλωνι κατείχετο, τούς τε
Ἄραβας ξένος ὢν ἔπεισεν ἐπικουρῆσαι καὶ αὐτὸς

---

[1] PA Heg. : νεωτέραν the rest (perhaps rightly).

[a] Q. Caecilius Metellus Scipio, father-in-law of Pompey
and governor of Syria ; defeated by Julius Caesar at the
battle of Thapsus 46 B.C.

the surrounding country to his side. But the zeal of Aristobulus and the hopes of Caesar were thwarted by malice. Poisoned by Pompey's friends, it was long before Aristobulus obtained even burial in his native land ; the corpse lay preserved in honey until it was sent to the Jews by Antony for interment in the royal sepulchres. Death of Aristobulus

(2) His son Alexander also perished ; under Pompey's orders, he was beheaded at Antioch by Scipio,[a] after a trial in which he was accused of the injuries which he had caused to the Romans. Alexander's brother and sisters were taken under the roof of Ptolemy,[b] son of Mennaeus, prince of Chalcis in the Lebanon valley, who sent his son Philippion to Ascalon to fetch them. The latter succeeded in tearing Antigonus and his sisters from the arms of Aristobulus's widow and escorted them to his father. Becoming enamoured of one [c] of the princesses, the young man married her, but was subsequently slain by his father on account of this same Alexandra, whom Ptolemy, after murdering his son, married himself. His marriage made him a more attentive guardian to her brother and sister. and of Alexander.

(3) Antipater, on the death of Pompey, went over to his opponent and paid court to Caesar. When Mithridates of Pergamus, with the army which he was leading to Egypt, was forbidden to pass the Pelusiac frontier [d] and was held up at Ascalon, it was Antipater who induced his friends the Arabs to lend their assistance, and himself brought up an army of three Services rendered by Antipater to Caesar in Egypt 48–47 B.C.

---

[b] See § 103.   [c] Another reading " the younger."
[d] Or "arm of the Nile." The authorities at Pelusium must have sent early notice refusing him a passage ; Ascalon was six days' march from that mouth of the Nile (B. iv. 661 ff.).

ἧκεν ἄγων Ἰουδαίων εἰς τρισχιλίους ὁπλίτας.
188 παρώρμησεν δὲ καὶ τοὺς ἐν Συρίᾳ δυνατοὺς ἐπὶ
τὴν βοήθειαν τόν τ' ἔποικον τοῦ Λιβάνου Πτολεμαῖον καὶ Ἰάμβλιχον, δι' οὓς αἱ ταύτῃ πόλεις
189 ἑτοίμως συνεφήψαντο τοῦ πολέμου. καὶ θαρρῶν
ἤδη Μιθριδάτης τῇ προσγενομένῃ δι' Ἀντίπατρον ἰσχύϊ πρὸς τὸ Πηλούσιον ἐξελαύνει, κω-
λυόμενός τε διελθεῖν ἐπολιόρκει τὴν πόλιν. γίνεται
δὲ κἀν τῇ προσβολῇ διασημότατος Ἀντίπατρος·
τὸ γὰρ καθ' αὑτὸν μέρος τοῦ τείχους διαρρήξας
πρῶτος εἰσεπήδησεν εἰς τὴν πόλιν μετὰ τῶν σὺν
αὐτῷ.
190   (4) Καὶ τὸ Πηλούσιον μὲν ἑάλω, πρόσω δ'
αὐτὸν ἰόντα εἶργον αὖθις οἱ τὴν Ὀνίου προσαγορευομένην χώραν κατέχοντες· ἦσαν δὲ Ἰουδαῖοι
Αἰγύπτιοι. τούτους Ἀντίπατρος οὐ μόνον μὴ
κωλύειν ἔπεισεν, ἀλλὰ καὶ τἀπιτήδεια τῇ δυνάμει
παρασχεῖν· ὅθεν οὐδὲ οἱ κατὰ Μέμφιν ἔτι εἰς
χεῖρας ἦλθον, ἑκούσιοι δὲ προσέθεντο Μιθριδάτῃ.
191 κἀκεῖνος ἤδη τὸ Δέλτα περιελθὼν συνέβαλλεν
τοῖς λοιποῖς Αἰγυπτίοις εἰς μάχην κατὰ χῶρον
ὃς Ἰουδαίων στρατόπεδον καλεῖται. κινδυνεύοντα
δ' αὐτὸν ἐν τῇ παρατάξει σὺν ὅλῳ τῷ δεξιῷ
κέρατι ῥύεται περιελθὼν Ἀντίπατρος παρὰ τὸν
192 αἰγιαλὸν τοῦ ποταμοῦ· τῶν γὰρ καθ' ἑαυτὸν
ἐκράτει τὸ λαιὸν ἔχων κέρας· ἔπειτα προσπεσὼν
τοῖς διώκουσι Μιθριδάτην ἀπέκτεινεν πολλοὺς καὶ
μέχρι τοσούτου τοὺς καταλειπομένους ἐδίωξεν,
ὡς καὶ τὸ στρατόπεδον αὐτῶν ἑλεῖν. ὀγδοήκοντα

---

a Son of Sohemus (A. xiv. 129), not the son of Mennaeus
mentioned above (§ 185), though living in the same region.
Nothing more is known of him and Jamblichus.

thousand Jewish infantry. It was he who roused in
support of Mithridates persons so powerful in Syria
as Ptolemy,[a] in his Lebanon home, and Jamblichus,
through whose influence the cities in those parts
readily took their share in the war. Emboldened
by the reinforcements which Antipater had brought
him, Mithridates now marched on Pelusium, and,
being refused a passage, laid siege to the town. In
the assault it was Antipater again who won the
greatest distinction ; for he made a breach in
the portion of the wall which faced him and was
the first to plunge into the place at the head of his
troops.

(4) Thus Pelusium was taken ; but the conqueror's
advance was again barred by the Egyptian Jews who
occupied the district which took its name from Onias.[b]
Antipater, however, prevailed on them not only to
refrain from opposition, but even to furnish supplies
for the troops ; with the result that no further resistance was encountered even at Memphis, whose
inhabitants voluntarily joined Mithridates. The
latter, having now rounded the Delta, gave battle to
the rest of the Egyptians at a spot called " Jews'
camp." In this engagement he, with the whole of
his right wing, was in serious danger, when Antipater,
victorious on the left where he was in command,
wheeled round and came along the river bank to his
rescue. Falling upon the Egyptians who were pursuing Mithridates he killed a large number of them
and pushed his pursuit of the remainder so far that
he captured their camp. He lost only eighty[c] of

[b] For the Jewish temple built in Egypt by Onias, a re-
fugee from Jerusalem, see *B*. vii. 421 ff.

[c] *A*. " fifty."

δὲ μόνους τῶν ἰδίων ἀπέβαλεν, καὶ Μιθριδάτης ἐν
τῇ τροπῇ περὶ ὀκτακοσίους. σωθεὶς δ' αὐτὸς παρ'
ἐλπίδα μάρτυς ἀβάσκανος γίνεται πρὸς Καίσαρα
τῶν Ἀντιπάτρου κατορθωμάτων.

193 (5) Ὁ δὲ τότε μὲν τὸν ἄνδρα τοῖς ἐπαίνοις καὶ
ταῖς ἐλπίσιν εἰς τοὺς ὑπὲρ ἑαυτοῦ κινδύνους ἐπέρρωσεν, ἐν οἷς πᾶσιν παραβολώτατος ἀγωνιστὴς
γενόμενος καὶ πολλὰ τρωθεὶς ἐφ' ὅλου σχεδὸν τοῦ
194 σώματος εἶχεν τὰ σημεῖα τῆς ἀρετῆς. αὖθις δὲ
καταστησάμενος τὰ κατὰ τὴν Αἴγυπτον ὡς ἐπ-
ανῆκεν εἰς Συρίαν, πολιτείᾳ τε αὐτὸν τῇ Ῥωμαίων
ἐδωρήσατο καὶ ἀτελείᾳ, τῆς τε ἄλλης τιμῆς καὶ
φιλοφρονήσεως ἕνεκεν ζηλωτὸν ἐποίησεν, καὶ τὴν
ἀρχιερωσύνην δὲ δι' αὐτὸν ἐπεκύρωσεν Ὑρκανῷ.

195 (x. 1) Κατ' αὐτὸ δὲ καὶ Ἀντίγονος ὁ Ἀριστοβούλου πρὸς τὸν Καίσαρα παρὼν γίνεται παρα-
δόξως Ἀντιπάτρῳ μείζονος προκοπῆς αἴτιος· δέον
γὰρ[1] ἀποδύρεσθαι περὶ τοῦ πατρὸς πεφαρμάχθαι
δοκοῦντος ἐκ τῶν πρὸς Πομπήιον διαφορῶν
καὶ περὶ τἀδελφοῦ τὴν Σκιπίωνος ὠμότητα
μέμφεσθαι καὶ μηδὲν εἰς τὸν ἔλεον παραμῖξαι
φθονερὸν πάθος, ὁ δ' ἐπὶ τούτοις Ὑρκανοῦ καὶ
196 Ἀντιπάτρου κατηγόρει παρελθών, ὡς παρανο-
μώτατα μὲν αὐτὸν μετὰ τῶν ἀδελφῶν πάσης
ἀπελαύνοιεν τῆς πατρίου γῆς, πολλὰ δ' εἰς τὸ
ἔθνος αὐτοὶ διὰ κόρον ἐξυβρίζοιεν, καὶ ὅτι[2] τὴν
εἰς Αἴγυπτον συμμαχίαν οὐκ ἐπ' εὐνοίᾳ αὐτῷ
πέμψειαν, ἀλλὰ κατὰ δέος τῶν πάλαι διαφορῶν

_____

[1] γοῦν LVRC.   [2] διότι LVR.

his men; Mithridates in the rout had lost about eight hundred. Thus saved beyond all expectation, Mithridates bore to Caesar's ears ungrudging witness of Antipater's prowess.

(5) The praise bestowed by Caesar at the time on the hero of the day and the hopes which it excited spurred Antipater to further ventures in his service. Showing himself on all occasions the most daring of fighters, and constantly wounded, he bore the marks of his valour on almost every part of his person. Later, when Caesar had settled affairs in Egypt and returned to Syria, he conferred on Antipater the privilege of Roman citizenship with exemption from taxes, and by other honours and marks of friendship made him an enviable man. It was to please him that Caesar confirmed the appointment of Hyrcanus to the office of high-priest.

Honours conferred on Antipater.

(x. 1) About this time Antigonus, son of Aristobulus, waited upon Caesar and, contrary to his intentions, became the means of Antipater's further promotion. Antigonus ought to have confined himself to lamentation over his father's fate, believed to have been poisoned on account of his differences with Pompey, and to complaints of Scipio's cruelty to his brother,[a] without mixing up with his plea for compassion any sentiments of jealousy. But, not content with that, he came forward and accused Hyrcanus and Antipater. They had, he said, in utter defiance of justice, banished him and his brothers and sisters from their native land altogether; they had, in their insolence, repeatedly done outrage to the nation; they had sent supports into Egypt, not from any goodwill to Caesar, but from fear of the consequences

Antigonus accuses Antipater before Caesar.

---

[a] §§ 184 f.

καὶ τὴν πρὸς τὸν Πομπήιον φιλίαν ἀποσκευαζό-
μενοι.

197 (2) Πρὸς ταῦθ' ὁ Ἀντίπατρος ἀπορρίψας τὴν
ἐσθῆτα τὸ πλῆθος ἐπεδείκνυεν τῶν τραυμάτων,
καὶ περὶ μὲν τῆς εἰς Καίσαρα εὐνοίας οὐκ ἔφη
λόγου δεῖν αὐτῷ· κεκραγέναι γὰρ τὸ σῶμα σιω-
198 πῶντος· Ἀντιγόνου δὲ θαυμάζειν τὴν τόλμαν, εἰ
πολεμίου Ῥωμαίων υἱὸς ὢν καὶ Ῥωμαίων δρα-
πέτου καὶ τὸ νεωτεροποιὸς εἶναι καὶ στασιώδης
αὐτὸς πατρῷον ἔχων, παρὰ τῷ Ῥωμαίων ἡγεμόνι
κατηγορεῖν ἐπικεχείρηκεν ἑτέρων καὶ πειρᾶται
τυχεῖν ἀγαθοῦ τινος, δέον ἀγαπᾶν ὅτι ζῇ· καὶ γὰρ
νῦν ἐφίεσθαι πραγμάτων οὐ τοσοῦτον δι' ἀπορίαν,
ἀλλ' ἵνα Ἰουδαίους διαστασιάσῃ παρελθὼν καὶ χρή-
σηται κατὰ τῶν δόντων ταῖς ἀφορμαῖς.

199 (3) Τούτων Καῖσαρ ἀκούσας Ὑρκανὸν μὲν
ἀξιώτερον τῆς ἀρχιερωσύνης ἀπεφήνατο, Ἀντιπάτρῳ δὲ δυναστείας αἵρεσιν ἔδωκεν. ὁ δ' ἐπὶ
τῷ τιμήσαντι τὸ μέτρον τῆς τιμῆς θέμενος πάσης
ἐπίτροπος Ἰουδαίας ἀποδείκνυται, καὶ προσεπι-
τυγχάνει τὰ τείχη τῆς πατρίδος ἀνακτίσαι κατ-
200 εστραμμένα. τὰς μὲν δὴ τιμὰς ταύτας Καῖσαρ
ἐπέστελλεν ἐν τῷ Καπετωλίῳ χαραχθῆναι, τῆς τε
αὐτοῦ δικαιοσύνης σημεῖον καὶ τῆς τἀνδρὸς ἐσο-
μένας[1] ἀρετῆς.

201 (4) Ἀντίπατρος δὲ Καίσαρα προπέμψας ἐκ τῆς
Συρίας εἰς Ἰουδαίαν ὑπέστρεψεν. καὶ πρῶτον
μὲν τὸ τεῖχος ἀνεδείματο τῆς πατρίδος ὑπὸ Πομπηίου κατεστραμμένον καὶ τοὺς ἀνὰ τὴν χώραν
θορύβους ἐπιὼν κατέστελλεν, ἀπειλητὴς ἅμα καὶ

---

[1] Niese : ἐσομένης or ἐσόμενον MSS.

[a] Or " procurator."

of old quarrels and to obliterate the memory of their friendship for Pompey.

(2) At these words Antipater stripped off his clothes and exposed his numerous scars. His loyalty to Caesar needed, he said, no words from him ; his body cried it aloud, were he to hold his peace. But the audacity of Antigonus astounded him. The son of an enemy of the Romans, son of a fugitive from Rome, one who inherited from his father a passion for revolution and sedition, presuming to accuse others in the presence of the Roman general and looking for favours when he ought to be thankful to be alive ! Indeed (said Antipater), his present ambition for power was not due to indigence ; he wanted it in order to sow sedition among the Jews and to employ his resources against those who had provided them.

(3) After hearing both speakers, Caesar pronounced Hyrcanus to be the more deserving claimant to the high-priesthood, and left Antipater free choice of office. The latter, replying that it rested with him who conferred the honour to fix the measure of the honour, was then appointed viceroy [a] of all Judaea. He was further authorized to rebuild the ruined walls of the metropolis.[b] Orders were sent by Caesar to Rome for these honours to be graven in the Capitol, as a memorial of his own justice and of Antipater's valour. *Caesar upholds Antipater and makes him viceroy of Judaea.*

(4) After escorting Caesar across Syria, Antipater returned to Judaea. There his first act was to rebuild the wall of the capital which had been overthrown by Pompey. He then proceeded to traverse the country, quelling the local disturbances, and every- *Antipater takes the government of Judaea into his own hands.*

[b] In *A.* xiv. 144 this permission is given to Hyrcanus.

σύμβουλος ὢν ἑκάστοις, ὅτι τὰ μὲν Ὑρκανοῦ
φρονοῦντες ἐν ὄλβῳ καὶ καθ᾽ ἡσυχίαν βιώσονται,
τῶν τε ἰδίων κτημάτων καὶ κοινῆς εἰρήνης ἀπο-
202 λαύοντες· εἰ δὲ πείθοιντο ταῖς ψυχραῖς ἐλπίσιν
τῶν νεωτερίζειν ἐπὶ κέρδεσιν οἰκείοις ἐθελόντων,
ὡς αὐτόν τε πειράσουσιν ἀντὶ κηδεμόνος δεσπότην
καὶ Ὑρκανὸν ἀντὶ βασιλέως τύραννον, Ῥωμαίους
γε μὴν καὶ Καίσαρα πολεμίους ἀνθ᾽ ἡγεμόνων καὶ
φίλων· οὐ γὰρ ἀνέξεσθαι μετακινούμενον ἐκ τῆς
203 ἀρχῆς ὃν αὐτοὶ κατέστησαν. ἅμα δὲ ταῦτα λέγων
καὶ δι᾽ αὑτοῦ καθίστατο τὴν χώραν, ὁρῶν τὸν
Ὑρκανὸν νωθῆ τε καὶ βασιλείας ἀτονώτερον.
Φασάηλον μὲν δή, τῶν παίδων τὸν πρεσβύτατον,
Ἱεροσολύμων καὶ τῶν πέριξ στρατηγὸν καθίστησιν, τὸν δὲ μετ᾽ αὐτὸν Ἡρώδην ἐπὶ τοῖς ἴσοις
ἔστειλεν εἰς Γαλιλαίαν κομιδῇ νέον.
204 (5) Ὁ δὲ ὢν φύσει δραστήριος ὕλην εὐθέως
εὑρίσκει τῷ φρονήματι. καταλαβὼν οὖν Ἐζεκίαν
τὸν ἀρχιλῃστὴν τὰ προσεχῆ τῇ Συρίᾳ κατα-
τρέχοντα μετὰ μεγίστου στίφους, αὐτόν τε συλ-
205 λαβὼν ἀποκτείνει καὶ πολλοὺς τῶν λῃστῶν. ὃ δὴ
μάλιστα τοῖς Σύροις ἠγάπητο[1] κεχαρισμένον· ὑμ-
νεῖτο γοῦν ἀνά τε τὰς κώμας καὶ ἐν ταῖς πόλεσιν
Ἡρώδης ὡς εἰρήνην αὐτοῖς καὶ τὰς κτήσεις
ἀνασεσωκώς. γίνεται δ᾽ ἐκ τούτου καὶ Σέξτῳ
Καίσαρι γνώριμος ὄντι συγγενεῖ τοῦ μεγάλου
206 Καίσαρος καὶ διοικοῦντι τὴν Συρίαν. πρὸς δὲ τὸν
ἀδελφὸν εὐδοκιμοῦντα καὶ Φασάηλος ἐφιλοτιμεῖτο
τὴν ἀγαθὴν ἔριν, τοὺς ἐν τοῖς Ἱεροσολύμοις εὐ-

---

[1] ἠγάπητο conj. (cf. A. ‖ ἠγάπησαν): ἡγεῖτο PAM: κατώρθωκε
the rest.

where combining menaces with advice. Their support of Hyrcanus, he told them, would ensure them a prosperous and tranquil existence, in the enjoyment of their own possessions and of the peace of the realm. If, on the contrary, they put faith in the vain expectations raised by persons who for personal profit desired revolution, they would find in himself a master instead of a protector, in Hyrcanus a tyrant instead of a king, in the Romans and Caesar enemies instead of rulers and friends ; for they would never suffer their own nominee to be ousted from his office. But, while he spoke in this strain, he took the organization of the country into his own hands, finding Hyrcanus indolent and without the energy necessary to a king.[a] He further appointed his eldest son, Phasael, governor of Jerusalem and the environs ; the second, Herod,[b] he sent with equal authority to Galilee, though a mere lad.

(5) Herod, energetic by nature, at once found material to test his metal. Discovering that Ezekias, a brigand-chief, at the head of a large horde, was ravaging the district on the Syrian frontier, he caught him and put him and many of the brigands to death. This welcome achievement was immensely admired by the Syrians. Up and down the villages and in the towns the praises of Herod were sung, as the restorer of their peace and possessions. This exploit, moreover, brought him to the notice of Sextus Caesar, a kinsman of the great Caesar and governor of Syria. Phasael, on his side, with a generous emulation, vied with his brother's reputation ; he increased his popu-

Youthful exploit of HEROD *in Galilee.*

c. 47 B.C.

His brother Phasael *governor of* Jerusalem.

[a] An incorrect term ; Hyrcanus had only the title of ethnarch, *A.* xiv. 191, etc.

[b] Herod the Great, whose history fills the greater part of the remainder of this book.

νουστέρους καθιστάμενος, καὶ δι᾽ αὐτοῦ μὲν ἔχων
τὴν πόλιν μηδὲν δ᾽ ἀπειροκάλως εἰς τὴν ἐξουσίαν
207 ἐξυβρίζων. ἔνθεν[1] Ἀντιπάτρῳ θεραπεία τε ἦν ἐκ
τοῦ ἔθνους βασιλικὴ καὶ τιμαὶ παρὰ πάντων ὡς
δεσπότῃ τῶν ὅλων· οὐ μὴν αὐτὸς τῆς πρὸς Ὑρκανὸν εὐνοίας ἢ πίστεώς τι μετεκίνησεν.

208 (6) Ἀμήχανον δ᾽ ἐν εὐπραγίαις φθόνον διαφυγεῖν. Ὑρκανὸς γοῦν ἤδη μὲν καὶ καθ᾽ ἑαυτὸν
ἡσυχῇ πρὸς τὸ κλέος τῶν νεανίσκων ἐδάκνετο,
μάλιστα δ᾽ ἐλύπει τὰ Ἡρώδου κατορθώματα καὶ
κήρυκες ἐπάλληλοι τῆς καθ᾽ ἕκαστον εὐδοξίας
προστρέχοντες. πολλοὶ δὲ τῶν ἐν τοῖς βασιλείοις
βασκάνων ἠρέθιζον, οἷς ἢ τὸ τῶν παίδων ἢ τὸ
209 Ἀντιπάτρου σωφρονικὸν προσίστατο, λέγοντες ὡς
Ἀντιπάτρῳ καὶ τοῖς υἱοῖς αὐτοῦ παραχωρήσας
τῶν πραγμάτων καθέζοιτο τοὔνομα μόνον βασιλέως ἔχων ἔρημον ἐξουσίας. καὶ μέχρι τοῦ[2] πλα-
νηθήσεται καθ᾽ ἑαυτοῦ βασιλεῖς ἐπιτρέφων; οὐδὲ
γὰρ εἰρωνεύεσθαι τὴν ἐπιτροπὴν αὐτοὺς ἔτι, φανεροὺς δ᾽ εἶναι δεσπότας παρωσαμένους ἐκεῖνον, εἴ
γε μήτε ἐντολὰς δόντος μήτε ἐπιστείλαντος αὐτοῦ
τοσούτους παρὰ τὸν τῶν Ἰουδαίων νόμον ἀνῄρηκεν
Ἡρώδης· ὅν, εἰ μὴ βασιλεύς ἐστιν ἀλλ᾽ ἔτι ἰδιώτης, δεῖν ἐπὶ δίκην ἥκειν ἀποδώσοντα λόγον αὐτῷ
τε καὶ τοῖς πατρίοις νόμοις, οἳ κτείνειν ἀκρίτους[3]
οὐκ ἐφιᾶσιν.

210 (7) Τούτοις κατὰ μικρὸν Ὑρκανὸς ἐξεκαίετο
καὶ τὴν ὀργὴν τελευταῖον ἐκρήξας ἐκάλει κριθη-
σόμενον τὸν Ἡρώδην. ὁ δὲ καὶ τοῦ πατρὸς παρ-

_____

[1] ἐντεῦθεν P.   [2] Destinon: ποῦ mss.
[3] ἀκρίτους Dindorf: ἀκρίτωσ mss.

larity with the inhabitants of Jerusalem, and kept the city under control without any tactless abuse of authority. Antipater, in consequence,[a] was courted by the nation as if he were king and universally honoured as lord of the realm. Notwithstanding this, his affection for Hyrcanus and his loyalty to him underwent no change.

(6) But it is impossible in prosperity to escape envy. The young men's fame already caused Hyrcanus a secret pang. He was vexed in particular by Herod's successes and by the arrival of messenger after messenger with news of each new honour that he had won. His resentment was further roused by a number of malicious persons at court, who had taken offence at the prudent behaviour either of Antipater or of his sons. Hyrcanus, they said, had abandoned to Antipater and his sons the direction of affairs, and rested content with the mere title, without the authority, of a king. How long would he be so mistaken as to rear kings to his own undoing? No longer masquerading as viceroys, they had now openly declared themselves masters of the state, thrusting him aside; seeing that, without either oral or written instructions from Hyrcanus, Herod, in violation of Jewish law, had put all this large number of people to death. If he is not king but still a commoner, he ought to appear in court and answer for his conduct to his king and to his country's laws, which do not permit anyone to be put to death without trial.

(7) These words gradually inflamed Hyrcanus; until at last, in an explosion of rage, he summoned Herod to trial. Herod, on his father's advice, and

Hyrcanus instigated against Herod and his family.

Herod's trial and acquittal.

[a] Or " thenceforth."

αινοῦντος καὶ τῶν πραγμάτων διδόντων παρρησίαν
ἀνῄει, φρουραῖς διαλαβὼν πρότερον τὴν Γαλιλαίαν. ᾔει δὲ μετὰ καρτεροῦ[1] στίφους, ὡς μήτε
καταλύειν δόξειεν Ὑρκανὸν ἁδρὰν[2] ἄγων δύναμιν
211 μήτε γυμνὸς ἐμπέσοι τῷ φθόνῳ. Σέξτος δὲ Καῖσαρ δείσας περὶ τῷ νεανίᾳ, μή τι παρὰ τοῖς ἐχθροῖς ἀποληφθεὶς πάθῃ, πέμπει πρὸς Ὑρκανὸν
τοὺς παραγγελοῦντας διαρρήδην ἀπολύειν Ἡρώδην τῆς φονικῆς δίκης. ὁ δὲ καὶ ἄλλως ὡρμημένος, ἠγάπα γὰρ Ἡρώδην, ἀποψηφίζεται.

212 (8) Καὶ ὃς ὑπολαμβάνων ἄκοντος τοῦ βασιλέως διαφυγεῖν εἰς Δαμασκὸν ἀνεχώρησεν πρὸς
Σέξτον, παρασκευαζόμενος οὐδ' αὖθις ὑπακοῦσαι
καλοῦντι. καὶ πάλιν οἱ πονηροὶ παρώξυνον τὸν
Ὑρκανὸν κατ' ὀργήν τε οἴχεσθαι τὸν Ἡρώδην
λέγοντες καὶ παρεσκευασμένον κατ' αὐτοῦ· πι-
στεύων δ' ὁ βασιλεὺς οὐκ εἶχεν ὅ τι χρὴ δρᾶν, ὡς
213 ἑώρα μείζονα τὸν διάφορον. ἐπεὶ δὲ ὑπὸ Σέξτου
Καίσαρος καὶ στρατηγὸς ἀνεδείχθη κοίλης Συρίας
καὶ Σαμαρείας, οὐ μόνον τε κατ' εὔνοιαν τὴν ἐκ
τοῦ ἔθνους ἀλλὰ καὶ δυνάμει φοβερὸς ἦν, εἰς
ἔσχατον δέους κατέπεσεν [Ὑρκανός],[3] ὅσον οὔπω
προσδοκῶν ἐπ' αὐτὸν ὁρμήσειν μετὰ στρατιᾶς.

214 (9) Καὶ οὐ διήμαρτεν τῆς οἰήσεως· ὁ γὰρ
Ἡρώδης κατ' ὀργὴν τῆς περὶ τὴν δίκην ἀπειλῆς
στρατιὰν ἀθροίσας ἐπὶ Ἱεροσολύμων ἦγεν κατα-
λύσων τὸν Ὑρκανόν. κἂν ἔφθη τοῦτο ποιήσας,

---

[1] ἀρκετοῦ conj. Destinon (A. ‖ ἀποχρῶντος).
[2] LVRC: λαμπρὰν PAM.   [3] ins. P: om. the rest.

with the confidence which his own conduct inspired, went up to the capital, after posting garrisons throughout Galilee. He went with a strong escort, calculated to avoid, on the one hand, the appearance of wishing to depose Hyrcanus by bringing an overwhelming force, and, on the other, the risk of falling unprotected a prey to envy. Sextus Caesar, however, fearing that the young man might be isolated by his adversaries and meet with misfortune, sent express orders to Hyrcanus to clear Herod of the charge of manslaughter. Hyrcanus, being inclined to take that course on other grounds, for he loved Herod, acquitted him.[a]

(8) Herod, however, imagining that his escape was contrary to the king's wishes, retired to join Sextus at Damascus, and made ready to refuse compliance to a second summons. The knaves at court continued to exasperate Hyrcanus, saying that Herod had departed in anger and was prepared to attack him. The king believed them, but knew not what to do, seeing his adversary to be more than a match for himself. But when Sextus Caesar proceeded to appoint Herod governor of Coele-Syria and Samaria, and he was now doubly formidable owing to his popularity with the nation and his own power, Hyrcanus was reduced to consternation, expecting every moment to see him marching upon him at the head of an army.

(9) Nor was he mistaken in his surmise. Herod, furious at the threat which this trial had held over him, collected an army and advanced upon Jerusalem to depose Hyrcanus. This object he would indeed have

His intended retaliation forestalled.

---

[a] In *A.* xiv. 177 Hyrcanus merely adjourns the trial and advises Herod to escape.

εἰ μὴ προεξελθόντες ὅ τε πατὴρ καὶ ὁ ἀδελφὸς
ἔκλασαν αὐτοῦ τὴν ὁρμὴν παρακαλοῦντες [καὶ]¹
αὐτὸν ἀπειλῇ καὶ ἀνατάσει μόνῃ μετρῆσαι τὴν
ἄμυναν, φείσασθαι δὲ τοῦ βασιλέως, ὑφ' οὗ μέχρι
τοσαύτης δυνάμεως προῆλθεν· δεῖν τε, εἰ κληθεὶς
ἐπὶ δίκην παρώξυνται, καὶ περὶ τῆς ἀφέσεως εὐ-
χαριστεῖν καὶ μὴ πρὸς μὲν τὸ σκυθρωπὸν ἀπαντᾶν,
215 περὶ δὲ τῆς σωτηρίας ἀχάριστον εἶναι. εἰ δὲ δὴ
λογιστέον εἴη καὶ πολέμου ῥοπὰς βραβεύεσθαι
⟨θεῷ⟩, θεωρητέον² εἶναι τῆς στρατείας³ τὸ
ἄδικον. διὸ δὴ καὶ περὶ τῆς νίκης οὐ χρῆναι⁴ καθ'
ἅπαν εὔελπιν εἶναι, μέλλοντά γε⁵ συμβαλεῖν
βασιλεῖ καὶ συντρόφῳ καὶ πολλάκις μὲν εὐεργέτῃ,
χαλεπῷ δὲ οὐδέποτε, πλὴν ὅσον πονηροῖς συμβούλοις χρώμενος ἐπισείσειεν αὐτῷ σκιὰν ἀδική-
ματος. πείθεται τούτοις Ἡρώδης ὑπολαβὼν εἰς
τὰς ἐλπίδας αὔταρκες εἶναι καὶ τὸ τὴν ἰσχὺν
ἐπιδείξασθαι τῷ ἔθνει.

216   (10) Κἀν τούτῳ γίνεται περὶ Ἀπάμειαν ταραχὴ
Ῥωμαίων καὶ πόλεμος ἐμφύλιος, Καικιλίου μὲν
Βάσσου διὰ τὴν εἰς Πομπήιον εὔνοιαν δολοφονή-
σαντος Σέξτον Καίσαρα καὶ τὴν ἐκείνου δύναμιν
παραλαβόντος, τῶν δ' ἄλλων Καίσαρος στρατηγῶν ἐπὶ τιμωρίᾳ τοῦ φόνου Βάσσῳ συμβαλόντων
217 μετὰ πάσης τῆς δυνάμεως. οἷς καὶ διὰ τὸν ἀν-
ῃρημένον καὶ διὰ τὸν περιόντα Καίσαρα, φίλους
ὄντας ἀμφοτέρους, ὁ Ἀντίπατρος διὰ τῶν παίδων
ἔπεμψεν συμμαχίαν. μηκυνομένου δὲ τοῦ πολέ-

---

¹ om. VC.
² θεῷ, θεωρητέον conj. after Aldrich: θεωρητέον PAMLR:
θεῷ, πλεῖον VC (assimilation to A. ‖).
³ Destinon: στρατιᾶς mss.
⁴ χρή PAM.   ⁵ Bekker: τε mss.

speedily achieved, had not his father and brother gone out in time to meet him and mollified his rage. They implored him to restrict his revenge to menaces and intimidation, and to spare the king under whom he had attained to such great power. Indignant as he might be at the summons to trial, he ought on the other hand to be thankful for his acquittal; after facing the black prospect of condemnation,[a] he ought not to be ungrateful for escaping with his life. Moreover, if we are to believe that the fortunes of war are in the hands of God, the injustice of his present campaign ought to be taken into consideration.[b] He should not, therefore, be altogether confident of success, when about to make war on his king and companion, frequently his benefactor, never his oppressor, save that, under the influence of evil counsellors, he had menaced him with a mere shadow of injury. To this advice Herod yielded, thinking that he had satisfied his expectations for the future by this exhibition of his strength before the eyes of the nation.

(10) Meanwhile at Apamea the Romans had trouble on their hands leading to civil war. Caecilius Bassus, out of devotion to Pompey, assassinated Sextus Caesar and took command of his army; whereupon Caesar's other generals, to avenge the murder, attacked Bassus with all their forces. Antipater, for the sake of his two friends, the deceased and the surviving Caesar, sent them reinforcements under his sons. The war dragged

War of Apamea : murder of Sextus Caesar 46 B.C.

---

[a] For τὸ σκυθρωπόν in this sense *cf. A.* ii. 156 (opposed to acquittal), and *B.* i. 542.

[b] Or perhaps, with the other reading, " the injustice [of his case] might outweigh an army."

μου Μοῦρκος μὲν ἀπὸ τῆς Ἰταλίας Ἀντιστίου[1]
παραγίνεται διάδοχος.

218   (xi. 1) Συνίσταται δὲ Ῥωμαίοις κατὰ τοῦτον
τὸν καιρὸν ὁ μέγας πόλεμος, Κασσίου καὶ Βρού-
του[2] κτεινάντων δόλῳ Καίσαρα, κατασχόντα τὴν
ἀρχὴν ἐπ᾽ ἔτη τρία καὶ μῆνας ἑπτά. μεγίστου δ᾽
ἐπὶ τῷ φόνῳ γενομένου κινήματος καὶ διαστα-
σιασθέντων τῶν δυνατῶν ἕκαστος ἐλπίσιν οἰκείαις
ἐχώρει πρὸς ὃ συμφέρειν ὑπελάμβανεν, καὶ δὴ
καὶ Κάσσιος εἰς Συρίαν καταληψόμενος τὰς περὶ
219 Ἀπάμειαν δυνάμεις. ἔνθα Βάσσῳ τε Μοῦρκον
καὶ τὰ διεστῶτα τάγματα διαλλάξας ἐλευθεροῖ
μὲν Ἀπάμειαν τῆς πολιορκίας, ἡγούμενος δ᾽
αὐτὸς τῆς στρατιᾶς ἐπῄει φορολογῶν τὰς πόλεις
καὶ παρὰ δύναμιν τὰς εἰσπράξεις ποιούμενος.

220   (2) Κελευσθὲν δὲ καὶ Ἰουδαίοις εἰσενεγκεῖν
ἑπτακόσια τάλαντα, δείσας Ἀντίπατρος τὴν ἀπειλὴν τοῦ Κασσίου τοῖς τε υἱοῖς διεῖλεν εἰσπράττειν
τὰ χρήματα καί τισιν ἄλλοις τῶν ἐπιτηδείων κατὰ
τάχος, ἐν οἷς καὶ Μαλίχῳ τινὶ τῶν διαφόρων·
221 οὕτως ἤπειγεν ἡ ἀνάγκη. πρῶτος· δ᾽ ἀπεμειλί-
ξατο Κάσσιον Ἡρώδης τὴν ἑαυτοῦ μοῖραν ἐκ τῆς
Γαλιλαίας κομίσας ἑκατὸν τάλαντα, καὶ διὰ
τοῦτο ἐν τοῖς μάλιστα φίλος ἦν. τοὺς δὲ λοιποὺς
εἰς βραδυτῆτα κακίσας αὐταῖς ἐθυμοῦτο ταῖς
222 πόλεσιν. Γόφνα γοῦν καὶ Ἀμμαοῦν καὶ δύο
ἑτέρας τῶν ταπεινοτέρων ἐξανδραποδισάμενος ἐχώ-

---

[1] Lat. (= C. Antistius Vetus, who besieged Bassus in
Apamea before the arrival of Murcus, Dio Cass. xlvii. 27):
ἀντὶ Κασσίου P : ἀντὶ Κεστίου A : Σέξτου the rest (apparently
from A. ‖).   [2] + ἄφνω PAMC.

---

[a] See critical note.

on and Murcus arrived from Italy to succeed
Antistius.[a]

(xi. 1) At this time the great war of the
Romans broke out, arising out of the death of Caesar,
treacherously murdered by Cassius and Brutus after
holding sovereign power for three years and seven
months.[b] This murder produced a tremendous upheaval; leading men split up into factions; each
joined the party which he considered would best
serve his personal ambitions. Cassius, for his part,
went to Syria to take command of the armies concentrated round Apamea. There he effected a reconciliation between Murcus and Bassus and the
opposing legions, raised the siege of Apamea, and,
putting himself at the head of the troops, went
round the towns levying tribute and exacting sums
which it was beyond their ability to pay.

(2) The Jews received orders to contribute seven
hundred talents. Antipater, alarmed at the threats
of Cassius, to expedite payment distributed the task
of collection between his sons and some of his
acquaintance, including—so urgent was the necessity
of the case—one of his enemies named Malichus.
Herod was the first to bring his quota—the sum
of one hundred talents—from Galilee, thereby
appeasing Cassius and being regarded as one of his
best friends. The rest Cassius abused for dilatori-
ness and then vented his wrath on the cities themselves. Gophna, Emmaus and two other places of
less importance [c] he reduced to servitude. He was

Marginal notes:
Civil war
after murder
of Julius
Caesar
44 B.C.

Cassius in
Syria : his
exactions.

---

[b] "3 years and 6 months," *A.* xiv. 270. From the battle
of Pharsalia (9 August 48) to 15 March 44 the period was
just over 3 years and 7 months.

[c] Lydda and Thamna, *A.* xiv. 275.

ρει μὲν ὡς καὶ Μάλιχον ἀναιρήσων, ὅτι μὴ σπεύ-
σας εἰσέπραξεν, ἐπέσχεν δὲ τὴν τούτου καὶ τὴν
τῶν ἄλλων πόλεων ἀπώλειαν Ἀντίπατρος ταχέως
ἑκατὸν ταλάντοις θεραπεύσας Κάσσιον.

223 (3) Οὐ μὴν Μάλιχος ἀναχωρήσαντος Κασσίου
τῆς χάριτος ἀπεμνημόνευσεν Ἀντιπάτρῳ, κατὰ
δὲ τοῦ πολλάκις σωτῆρος ἐπιβουλὴν ἐνεσκευά-
ζετο σπεύδων ἀνελεῖν τὸν ἐμπόδιον αὐτοῦ τοῖς
ἀδικήμασιν ὄντα· Ἀντίπατρος δὲ τήν τε ἰσχὺν
καὶ τὸ πανοῦργον τἀνδρὸς ὑποδείσας διαβαίνει
τὸν Ἰορδάνην, στρατὸν ἀθροίσων εἰς τὴν τῆς
224 ἐπιβουλῆς ἄμυναν. φωραθεὶς δὲ Μάλιχος ἀναιδείᾳ
τῶν Ἀντιπάτρου παίδων περιγίνεται· τόν τε γὰρ
Ἱεροσολύμων φρουρὸν Φασάηλον καὶ Ἡρώδην
πεπιστευμένον τὰ ὅπλα πολλαῖς ἀπολογίαις καὶ
ὅρκοις ἐκγοητεύσας διαλλακτὰς αὐτῷ πρὸς τὸν
πατέρα πείθει γίνεσθαι. πάλιν γοῦν ὑπ᾽ Ἀντιπάτρου σώζεται πείσαντος Μοῦρκον τὸν τότε
στρατηγοῦντα Συρίας, ὃς ὥρμητο κτεῖναι Μάλιχον
ἐφ᾽ οἷς ἐνεωτέρισεν.

225 (4) Συστάντος δὲ τοῦ πρὸς Κάσσιον καὶ Βροῦ-
τον πολέμου Καίσαρί τε τῷ νέῳ καὶ Ἀντωνίῳ
Κάσσιος καὶ Μοῦρκος στρατιὰν ἀθροίσαντες ἐκ
τῆς Συρίας, ἐπειδὴ μέγα μέρος εἰς τὰς χρείας
Ἡρώδης ἔδοξε, τότε μὲν αὐτὸν Συρίας ἁπάσης
ἐπιμελητὴν καθιστᾶσιν δύναμιν πεζήν τε καὶ
ἱππικὴν δόντες, μετὰ δὲ τὴν τοῦ πολέμου κατάλυσιν ἀποδείξειν Κάσσιος ὑπέσχετο καὶ Ἰουδαίας
226 βασιλέα. συνέβη δ᾽ Ἀντιπάτρῳ τήν τε ἰσχὺν τοῦ
παιδὸς καὶ τὴν ἐλπίδα αἰτίαν ἀπωλείας γενέσθαι·

---

[a] Or perhaps "out of consideration for the large part
which H. had played in rendering assistance." The un-

proceeding so far as to put Malichus to death for tardiness in levying the tribute ; but Antipater saved both his life and the other cities from destruction, by hastily propitiating Cassius with a gift of a hundred talents.

(3) However, on the departure of Cassius, Malichus, far from remembering this service of Antipater, concocted a plot against the man who had often saved his life, impatient to remove one who was an obstacle to his malpractices. Antipater, dreading the man's strength and cunning, crossed the Jordan to collect an army to defeat the conspiracy. Malichus, though detected, succeeded by effrontery in outwitting Antipater's sons ; for Phasael, the warden of Jerusalem, and Herod, the custodian of the armoury, cajoled by a multitude of excuses and oaths, consented to act as mediators with their father. Once again Antipater saved Malichus by his influence with Murcus, who when governor of Syria had determined to put him to death as a revolutionary.

(4) When the young Caesar and Antony declared war on Cassius and Brutus, Cassius and Murcus levied an army in Syria, and, regarding Herod's future assistance as a great asset,[a] appointed him then and there prefect [b] of the whole of Syria, putting a force of horse and foot at his disposal ; Cassius further promising on the termination of the war to make him king of Judaea. These powers and brilliant expectations of the son proved in the end the occasion

Antipater assassinated by Malichus.

certainty arises from the absence of a verb (γενήσεσθαι as in *A*. xv. 264, or γενέσθαι as *ib*. 307). The addition, συμβεβλῆσθαι, in cod. C is a gloss, due to misunderstanding of the Latinism *magna pars*.

[b] Or " procurator " ; *A*. says " governor of Coele-Syria," a less considerable and more probable appointment.

ταῦτα γὰρ δείσας ὁ Μάλιχος διαφθείρει τινὰ τῶν
βασιλικῶν οἰνοχόων χρήμασιν δοῦναι φάρμακον
Ἀντιπάτρῳ. καὶ ὁ μὲν ἀγώνισμα τῆς Μαλίχου
παρανομίας γενόμενος μετὰ τὸ συμπόσιον θνήσκει,
τά τε ἄλλα δραστήριος ἀνὴρ ἐν ἀφηγήσει πραγμάτων καὶ τὴν ἀρχὴν ἀνακτησάμενός τε Ὑρκανῷ
καὶ διαφυλάξας.

227   (5) Μάλιχος δὲ καθ' ὑπόνοιαν τῆς φαρμακείας
ὀργιζόμενον τὸ πλῆθος ἀρνούμενος ἔπειθεν καὶ
δυνατώτερον ἑαυτὸν κατεσκεύαζεν ὁπλίτας συγ-
κροτῶν· οὐ γὰρ ἠρεμήσειν Ἡρώδην ὑπελάμβανεν,
ὃς δὴ καὶ παρῆν αὐτίκα στρατὸν ἄγων ἐπὶ
228 τιμωρίᾳ τοῦ πατρός.   Φασαήλου δὲ τἀδελφοῦ
συμβουλεύσαντος αὐτῷ μὴ φανερῶς τὸν ἄνδρα
μετιέναι, διαστασιάσειν γὰρ τὸ πλῆθος, τότε μὲν
ἀπολογούμενόν τε προσίεται τὸν Μάλιχον καὶ τῆς
ὑπονοίας ἀπολύειν ὡμολόγει, λαμπρὰν δὲ πομπὴν
ἐπὶ τῷ πατρὶ κηδείας ἐτέλεσεν.

229   (6) Τραπεὶς δ' ἐπὶ Σαμάρειαν στάσει τεταραγ-
μένην κατεστήσατο τὴν πόλιν· ἔπειτα καθ' ἑορτὴν
ὑπέστρεφεν εἰς Ἱεροσόλυμα τοὺς ὁπλίτας ἄγων.
καὶ πέμπων Ὑρκανός, ἐνῆγεν γὰρ δεδοικὼς τὴν
ἔφοδον Μάλιχος, ἐκώλυεν τοὺς ἀλλοφύλους εἰσαγαγεῖν ἐφ' ἁγνεύοντας τοὺς ἐπιχωρίους. ὁ δὲ
τῆς προφάσεως καταφρονήσας καὶ τοῦ προστάσ-
230 σοντος εἰσέρχεται διὰ νυκτός. καὶ πάλιν Μάλιχος
προσιὼν ἔκλαιεν Ἀντίπατρον· ἀνθυπεκρίνετο δὲ
μόλις Ἡρώδης τὸν θυμὸν ἐπέχων καὶ Κασσίῳ δι'
ἐπιστολῶν τὴν τοῦ πατρὸς ἀναίρεσιν ἀπωδύρετο
μισοῦντι καὶ ἄλλως Μάλιχον. ὁ δ' αὐτῷ μετιέναι

of his father's destruction. For Malichus, taking
alarm, bribed one of the royal butlers to serve poison
to Antipater. Thus, a victim of the villainy of
Malichus, Antipater expired after leaving the ban- 43 B.C.
quet—a man of great energy in the conduct of affairs,
whose crowning merit was that he recovered and
preserved the kingdom for Hyrcanus.

(5) Malichus, being suspected of poisoning him, Herod's
appeased the indignant populace by denial, and revenge on
strengthened his position by mustering troops. For Malichus.
he never supposed that Herod would remain idle, and
in fact the latter appeared forthwith at the head of
an army to avenge his father. Phasael, however,
advised his brother not to proceed to open vengeance
on the scoundrel, for fear of exciting a popular riot.
Herod, accordingly, for the moment accepted
Malichus's defence and professed to clear him from
suspicion. He then celebrated with splendid pomp
the obsequies of his father.

(6) Samaria being distracted by sedition, Herod
betook himself thither, and, after restoring order in
the city, set out on the return journey to Jerusalem,
then keeping festival, at the head of his troops.
Instigated by Malichus, who was alarmed at his
approach, Hyrcanus sent orders forbidding him to
intrude aliens upon the country-folk during their
period of purification. Herod, scorning the subter-
fuge and the man from whom the order came,
entered by night. Malichus again waited on him
and wept over Antipater's fate. Herod, scarce able
to restrain his wrath, dissembled in his turn. At
the same time he sent a letter to Cassius, deploring
the murder of his father. Cassius, who had other
grounds for hating Malichus, replied, " Have your

107

τὸν φονέα τοῦ πατρὸς ἀντεπιστείλας καὶ τοῖς ὑφ'
ἑαυτὸν χιλιάρχοις λάθρα προσέταξεν Ἡρώδῃ βοηθεῖν εἰς πρᾶξιν δικαίαν.

231 (7) Κἀπειδὴ Λαοδίκειαν ἑλόντος αὐτοῦ συνῆσαν
οἱ πανταχόθεν δυνατοὶ δωρεάς τε καὶ στεφάνους
φέροντες, Ἡρώδης μὲν τοῦτον τῇ τιμωρίᾳ τὸν
καιρὸν ἀφώρισεν, Μάλιχος δὲ ὑποπτεύσας, ὡς ἐν
Τύρῳ γίνεται, τόν τε υἱὸν ὁμηρεύοντα παρὰ τοῖς
Τυρίοις ὑπεξαγαγεῖν ἔγνω λάθρα καὶ αὐτὸς εἰς
232 τὴν Ἰουδαίαν ἀποδρᾶναι παρεσκευάζετο. παρώξυνεν δ' αὐτὸν ἡ τῆς σωτηρίας ἀπόγνωσις ἐνθυ-
μεῖσθαι καὶ μείζονα· τό τε γὰρ ἔθνος ἐπαναστή-
σειν Ῥωμαίοις ἤλπισεν, Κασσίου τῷ πρὸς Ἀντώνιον πολέμῳ περισπωμένου, καὶ βασιλεύσειν αὐτὸς
Ὑρκανὸν καταλύσας εὐμαρῶς.

233 (8) Ἐπεγέλα δ' ἄρα τὸ χρεὼν αὐτοῦ ταῖς
ἐλπίσιν. ὁ γοῦν Ἡρώδης προϊδόμενος αὐτοῦ τὴν
ὁρμὴν τόν τε Ὑρκανὸν κἀκεῖνον ἐπὶ δεῖπνον ἐκάλει, παρεστῶτα δ' ἔπειτα τῶν οἰκετῶν τινα πρὸς
αὐτὸν εἰσέπεμψεν ὡς ἐπὶ τὴν τοῦ δείπνου παρα-
σκευήν, τῷ δὲ ὄντι προειπεῖν τοῖς χιλιάρχοις ἐξ-
234 ελθεῖν ἐπὶ τὴν ἐνέδραν. κἀκεῖνοι τῶν Κασσίου
προσταγμάτων ἀναμνησθέντες ἐπὶ τὸν πρὸ τῆς
πόλεως αἰγιαλὸν ἐξῇεσαν ξιφήρεις, ἔνθα περιστάντες τὸν Μάλιχον πολλοῖς τραύμασιν ἀναιροῦσιν.
Ὑρκανὸς δὲ παραχρῆμα μὲν λυθεὶς[1] ὑπ' ἐκπλήξεως ἔπεσεν, μόλις δὲ ἀνενεγκὼν Ἡρώδην διηρώτα
235 τίς ὁ κτείνας εἴη Μάλιχον. ἀποκριναμένου δέ
τινος τῶν χιλιάρχων " τὸ Κασσίου πρόσταγμα,"
" Κάσσιος ἄρα," ἔφη, " κἀμὲ καὶ τὴν πατρίδα
μου σώζει τὸν ἀμφοτέρων ἐπίβουλον ἀνελών."
εἴτε δὲ φρονῶν Ὑρκανὸς οὕτως εἴθ' ὑπὸ δέους

revenge on the murderer," and gave secret orders to the tribunes under his command to lend Herod aid in a righteous deed.

(7) When Cassius took Laodicea, and the grandees from all parts of the country flocked to him with gifts and crowns, Herod fixed on this as the moment for his revenge. Malichus had his suspicions, and on reaching Tyre resolved to effect the secret escape of his son, then a hostage in that city, while he made his own preparations to fly to Judaea. Desperation stimulated him to conceive yet grander schemes ; he had dreams of raising a national revolt against the Romans, while Cassius was preoccupied with the war against Antony, of deposing Hyrcanus without difficulty, and of mounting the throne himself.

(8) But Destiny derided his hopes. Herod, divining his intention, invited him and Hyrcanus to supper, and then dispatched one of his attendant menials to his house, ostensibly to prepare the banquet, in reality to instruct the tribunes to come out for the ambuscade. Remembering the orders of Cassius, they came out, sword in hand, to the sea-shore in front of the city, and there, surrounding Malichus, stabbed him through and through to death. Hyrcanus from sheer fright instantly swooned and fell ; when brought, not without difficulty, to himself,[1] he asked Herod by whom Malichus was killed. One of the tribunes replied " By Cassius's orders." " Then," said Hyrcanus, " Cassius has saved both me and my country, by destroying one who conspired against both." Whether he expressed his real opinion or

---

[1] ἐκλυθεὶς C.

ὁμόσε τῇ πράξει χωρῶν εἶπεν, ἄδηλον ἦν. ἀλλὰ
γὰρ Μάλιχον μὲν οὕτως Ἡρώδης μετῆλθεν.

236   (xii. 1) Κασσίου δὲ ἀναχωρήσαντος ἐκ Συρίας
πάλιν στάσις ἐν Ἱεροσολύμοις γίνεται, Ἕλικος
μετὰ στρατιᾶς ἐπαναστάντος Φασαήλῳ καὶ κατὰ
τὴν ὑπὲρ Μαλίχου τιμωρίαν ἀμύνεσθαι θέλοντος
Ἡρώδην εἰς τὸν ἀδελφόν. Ἡρώδης δὲ ἔτυχεν
μὲν ὢν παρὰ Φαβίῳ τῷ στρατηγῷ κατὰ Δαμασκόν, ὡρμημένος δὲ βοηθεῖν ὑπὸ νόσου κατ-
237 είχετο. κἀν τούτῳ Φασάηλος καθ' ἑαυτὸν Ἕλικος
περιγενόμενος Ὑρκανὸν ὠνείδιζεν εἰς ἀχαριστίαν
ὧν τε Ἕλικι συμπράξειεν, καὶ ὅτι περιορῴη τὸν
ἀδελφὸν τὸν Μαλίχου τὰ φρούρια καταλαμβάνοντα·
πολλὰ γὰρ δὴ[1] κατείληπτο καὶ τὸ πάντων ὀχυ-
ρώτατον Μασάδαν.

238   (2) Οὐ μὴν αὐτῷ τι πρὸς τὴν Ἡρώδου βίαν
ἤρκεσεν, ὃς ἀναρρωσθεὶς τά τε ἄλλα παραλαμβάνει κἀκεῖνον ἐκ τῆς Μασάδας ἱκέτην ἀφῆκεν.
ἐξήλασεν δὲ καὶ ἐκ τῆς Γαλιλαίας Μαρίωνα τὸν
Τυρίων τύραννον ἤδη τρία κατεσχηκότα τῶν ἐρυμάτων, τοὺς δὲ ληφθέντας Τυρίους ἔσωσεν μὲν
πάντας, ἦσαν δ' οὓς καὶ δωρησάμενος ἀπέπεμψεν,
εὔνοιαν ἑαυτῷ παρὰ τῆς πόλεως καὶ τῷ τυράννῳ
239 μῖσος παρασκευαζόμενος. ὁ δὲ Μαρίων ἠξίωτο
μὲν τῆς τυραννίδος ὑπὸ Κασσίου τυραννίσιν πᾶσαν
διαλαβόντος τὴν Συρίαν, κατὰ δὲ τὸ πρὸς Ἡρώδην ἔχθος συγκατήγαγεν Ἀντίγονον τὸν Ἀριστοβούλου, καὶ τὸ πλέον διὰ Φάβιον, ὃν Ἀντίγονος
χρήμασιν προσποιησάμενος βοηθὸν εἶχεν τῆς καθ-
όδου· χορηγὸς δ' ἦν ἁπάντων ὁ κηδεστὴς Πτολεμαῖος Ἀντιγόνῳ.

[1] ἤδη LVRC.

from fear acquiesced in the deed, was uncertain. Be that as it may, thus was Herod avenged on Malichus.

(xii. 1) The exit of Cassius from Syria was followed by a fresh outbreak at Jerusalem. A certain Helix, with a body of troops, attacked Phasael, wishing to punish Herod, through his brother, for the chastisement which he had inflicted on Malichus. Herod at the time was with Fabius the Roman general at Damascus, where, though impatient to lend his aid, he was detained by illness. Meanwhile Phasael, unassisted, defeated Helix and reproached Hyrcanus for ingratitude both in abetting the rebel and in allowing the brother of Malichus to take possession of the fortresses. Quite a large number of these had been taken, including Masada, the strongest of all. *42 B.C. Revolt of Helix.*

(2) But nothing could avail the captor against the might of Herod. Once restored to health, he recovered the other forts and ousted him from Masada, a suppliant for mercy. He likewise expelled from Galilee Marion, the despot of Tyre, already master of three of the strongholds. The Tyrians whom he took prisoners, he spared to a man ; some he even sent away with presents, to procure for himself the favour of the citizens and for the tyrant their hatred. Marion owed his position to Cassius, who had cut up the whole of Syria into principalities. Hatred of Herod had led to his taking part in bringing back the exiled Antigonus,[a] son of Aristobulus ; and in this he was influenced still more by Fabius, whom Antigonus had induced by bribery to assist in his restoration. All the exile's expenses were met by his brother-in-law,[b] Ptolemy. *Herod defeats his adversaries.*

^a *Cf.* § 173.   ^b § 186.

240　(3) Πρὸς οὓς Ἡρώδης ἀντιπαραταξάμενος ἐπὶ τῶν ἐμβολῶν τῆς Ἰουδαίας κρατεῖ τῇ μάχῃ, καὶ τὸν Ἀντίγονον ἐξελάσας ὑπέστρεψεν εἰς Ἱεροσόλυμα πᾶσιν ἀγαπητὸς ὢν ἐπὶ τῷ κατορθώματι· καὶ γὰρ οἱ μὴ προσέχοντες πάλαι τότε ᾠκείωντο

241　διὰ τὴν πρὸς Ὑρκανὸν ἐπιγαμίαν αὐτῷ. πρότερον μὲν γὰρ ἦκτο γυναῖκα τῶν ἐπιχωρίων οὐκ ἄσημον, Δωρὶς ἐκαλεῖτο, ἐξ ἧς ἐγέννησεν Ἀντίπατρον, τότε δὲ γήμας τὴν Ἀλεξάνδρου τοῦ Ἀριστοβούλου θυγατέρα, θυγατριδῆν δὲ Ὑρκανοῦ, Μαριάμμην οἰκεῖος τῷ βασιλεῖ γίνεται.

242　(4) Ἐπεὶ δὲ Κάσσιον περὶ Φιλίππους ἀνελόντες ἀνεχώρησαν εἰς μὲν Ἰταλίαν Καῖσαρ ἐπὶ δὲ τῆς Ἀσίας[1] Ἀντώνιος, πρεσβευομένων τῶν ἄλλων πόλεων πρὸς Ἀντώνιον εἰς Βιθυνίαν ἦκον καὶ Ἰουδαίων οἱ δυνατοὶ κατηγοροῦντες Φασαήλου καὶ Ἡρώδου, βίᾳ μὲν αὐτοὺς κρατεῖν τῶν πραγμάτων, ὄνομα δὲ μόνον περιεῖναι Ὑρκανῷ τίμιον. πρὸς ἃ παρὼν Ἡρώδης καὶ τεθεραπευκὼς οὐκ ὀλίγοις Ἀντώνιον χρήμασιν οὕτως διέθηκεν, ὡς μηδὲ λόγου τῶν ἐχθρῶν ἀνασχέσθαι. καὶ τότε μὲν οὕτως διελύθησαν.

243　(5) Αὖθις δὲ οἱ ἐν τέλει Ἰουδαίων ἑκατὸν ἄνδρες ἦκον εἰς τὴν πρὸς Ἀντιόχειαν Δάφνην ἐπ' Ἀντώνιον ἤδη τῷ Κλεοπάτρας ἔρωτι δεδουλωμένον· οἳ προστησάμενοι τοὺς ἀξιώματι καὶ λόγῳ σφῶν δυνατωτάτους κατηγόρουν τῶν ἀδελφῶν. ὑπήντα δὲ Μεσσάλας ἀπολογούμενος συμπαρ-

244　εστῶτος Ὑρκανοῦ διὰ τὸ κῆδος. καὶ Ἀντώνιος

---

[1] L*VR : τὴν Ἀσίαν the rest.

[a] Or rather, apparently, betrothed : the marriage is recorded later in § 344.

(3) These enemies were opposed by Herod at the entry to the territory of Judaea, where a battle took place in which he was victorious. Antigonus being banished from the country, Herod returned to Jerusalem, where his success won him all men's hearts. Even those who had hitherto stood aloof were now reconciled by his marriage into the family of Hyrcanus. His first wife was a Jewess of some standing, named Doris, by whom he had a son, Antipater ; but now he married[a] Mariamme, daughter of Alexander, the son of Aristobulus, and grand-daughter of Hyrcanus, and thus became kinsman of the king.[b]

His marriage with Mariamme.

(4) After the death of Cassius at Philippi, the victors departed, Caesar going to Italy, Antony to Asia. Embassies from the various states waited upon Antony in Bithynia, and among them came the Jewish leaders, who accused Phasael and Herod of usurping the government and leaving to Hyrcanus merely titular honours. Herod thereupon appeared and by large bribes so wrought upon Antony that he refused his adversaries a hearing. So for the time being these enemies were dispersed.

M. Antony, after hearing Jewish accusations against the brothers, appoints Herod and Phasael tetrarchs of Judaea 42–41 B.C.

(5) But on a later occasion a hundred Jewish officials approached Antony, now a slave to his passion for Cleopatra, at Daphne beside Antioch, and, putting forward the most eminent and eloquent of their number, laid accusations against the brothers. The defence was undertaken by Messala,[c] Hyrcanus supporting him because of his marriage connexion with Herod. After hearing both parties, Antony

[b] Hyrcanus II, incorrectly entitled " king," as in § 203.

[c] M. Valerius Messalla Corvinus, c. 70-3 B.C., attached himself in the civil wars respectively to Cassius, Antony and Augustus; author, orator and patron of literature, a friend of Horace and Tibullus.

113

ἀκούσας ἑκατέρων Ὑρκανοῦ διεπυνθάνετο τοὺς
ἐπιτηδειοτέρους ὄντας ἄρχειν· τοῦ δὲ τοὺς περὶ
τὸν Ἡρώδην προκρίναντος,[1] ἡσθείς, ἣν γὰρ ἤδη
καὶ ξένος αὐτοῖς πατρῷος, δεχθεὶς ὑπ' Ἀντιπάτρου φιλοφρόνως ὅτε εἰς τὴν Ἰουδαίαν σὺν
Γαβινίῳ παρέβαλλεν, τετράρχας ἀποδείκνυσιν τοὺς
ἀδελφοὺς πᾶσαν διοικεῖν τὴν Ἰουδαίαν ἐπιτρέπων.

245 (6) Προσαγανακτούντων δὲ τῶν πρέσβεων πεν-
τεκαίδεκα μὲν συλλαβὼν εἴργνυσιν, οὓς καὶ ἀνελεῖν ὥρμησεν, τοὺς δὲ λοιποὺς μεθ' ὕβρεως ἀπήλασεν. πρὸς ὃ μείζων ἐν τοῖς Ἱεροσολύμοις γίνεται ταραχή· χιλίους γοῦν πάλιν ἔπεμψαν πρέσβεις
εἰς Τύρον, ἔνθα διέτριβεν Ἀντώνιος ἐπὶ Ἱεροσολύμων ὡρμημένος. ἐπὶ τούτους κεκραγότας
ἐκπέμπει τὸν ἄρχοντα τῶν Τυρίων κολάζειν
προστάξας οὓς ἂν λάβῃ, συγκατασκευάζειν τε[2] τὴν
ἀρχὴν τοῖς ὑπ' αὐτοῦ κατασταθεῖσιν τετράρχαις.

246 (7) Πρὸ δὲ τούτου πολλὰ παρῄνει προελθὼν
ἐπὶ τὸν αἰγιαλὸν Ἡρώδης σὺν Ὑρκανῷ μήθ'
ἑαυτοῖς ἀπωλείας αἰτίους μήτε τῇ πατρίδι πολέμου γίνεσθαι φιλονεικοῦντας ἀκρίτως. τῶν δὲ
ἔτι μᾶλλον ἀγανακτούντων Ἀντώνιος ἐκπέμψας
ὁπλίτας πολλοὺς μὲν ἀπέκτεινεν, πολλοὺς δὲ
ἔτρωσεν· ὧν οἵ τε πεσόντες ταφῆς καὶ οἱ τραυ-
247 ματίαι θεραπείας ἠξιώθησαν ὑπὸ Ὑρκανοῦ. οὐ
μὴν οἱ διαφυγόντες ἠρέμουν, ἀλλὰ τὰ κατὰ τὴν
πόλιν συνταράσσοντες παρώξυναν Ἀντώνιον ὥστε
καὶ τοὺς δεσμώτας ἀποκτεῖναι.

248 (xiii. 1) Μετὰ δὲ ἔτη δύο Βαρζαφράνου τοῦ

---

[1] προκρίνοντος PA.   [2] MVC: δὲ the rest.

inquired of Hyrcanus who was the best qualified ruler. Hyrcanus pronouncing in favour of Herod and his brother, Antony was delighted, because he had formerly been their father's guest and had been hospitably entertained by Antipater when he accompanied Gabinius on his Judaean campaign. He, accordingly, created the brothers tetrarchs, entrusting to them the administration of the whole of Judaea.

(6) The deputies giving vent to indignation, and massacres the Jewish deputies. Antony arrested and imprisoned fifteen of them, and was even prepared to put them to death ; the rest he ignominiously dismissed. His action intensified the agitation in Jerusalem. A second embassy, numbering this time a thousand, was sent to Tyre, where Antony had broken the journey to Jerusalem. To check the clamour of this party he dispatched the governor of Tyre, with orders to chastise all whom he caught and to support the authority *a* of the tetrarchs whom he had appointed.

(7) Before these orders were executed, Herod, accompanied by Hyrcanus, came out to the deputies on the shore, and strongly recommended them not to bring ruin upon themselves and war upon their country by injudicious strife. His words only increasing their fury, Antony ordered out troops, who killed or wounded a large number ; burial for the dead and medical attention for the wounded were granted by Hyrcanus. Those who escaped were, even now, not silenced, and by the disturbance which they created in the city so exasperated Antony that he put his prisoners to death.

(xiii. 1) Two years later, Barzapharnes, the Par-

---

a συγκατασκευάζειν τὴν ἀρχήν, after Thuc. i. 93.

Πάρθων σατράπου σὺν Πακόρῳ τῷ βασιλέως υἱῷ
Συρίαν κατασχόντος Λυσανίας διαδεδεγμένος¹ ἤδη
τὴν ἀρχὴν τοῦ πατρὸς τελευτήσαντος, Πτολεμαῖος δ' ἦν οὗτος ὁ Μενναίου, πείθει τὸν σα-
τράπην ὑποσχέσει χιλίων ταλάντων καὶ πεντακοσίων γυναικῶν καταγαγεῖν ἐπὶ τὰ βασίλεια τὸν
249 Ἀντίγονον, καταλῦσαι δὲ τὸν Ὑρκανόν. τούτοις
ὑπαχθεὶς Πάκορος αὐτὸς μὲν ᾔει κατὰ τὴν παράλιον, Βαρζαφράνην δὲ διὰ τῆς μεσογείου προσέταξεν ἐμβαλεῖν. τῶν δ' ἐπιθαλαττίων Τύριοι
Πάκορον οὐκ ἐδέξαντο καίτοι Πτολεμαιῶν καὶ
Σιδωνίων δεδεγμένων. ὁ δ' οἰνοχόῳ τινὶ τῶν
βασιλικῶν ὁμωνύμῳ μοῖραν τῆς ἵππου παραδοὺς
προεμβαλεῖν ἐκέλευσεν εἰς τὴν Ἰουδαίαν, κατα-
σκεψόμενόν τε τὰ τῶν πολεμίων καὶ πρὸς ἃ δέοι
βοηθήσοντα Ἀντιγόνῳ.

250   (2) Τῶν δὲ ληζομένων τὸν Κάρμηλον πολλοὶ
Ἰουδαῖοι συνδραμόντες πρὸς Ἀντίγονον προθύμους ἑαυτοὺς ἐπὶ τὴν εἰσβολὴν παρεῖχον. ὁ
δὲ αὐτοὺς ἐπὶ τὸν καλούμενον Δρυμὸν προέπεμψεν
τὸ χωρίον καταλαβεῖν· ἐν ᾧ γενομένης συμβολῆς
ὠσάμενοι τοὺς πολεμίους καὶ διώξαντες ἐπὶ
Ἱεροσολύμων ἔθεον, γενόμενοί τε πλείους μέχρι
251 τῶν βασιλείων προῆλθον. Ὑρκανοῦ δὲ καὶ Φασαήλου δεξαμένων αὐτοὺς καρτερῷ στίφει μάχη
κατὰ τὴν ἀγορὰν συρρήγνυται, καθ' ἣν τρεψά-
μενοι τοὺς πολεμίους οἱ περὶ Ἡρώδην κατα-
κλείουσιν εἰς τὸ ἱερὸν καὶ φρουροὺς αὐτῶν ἄνδρας
ἑξήκοντα ταῖς πλησίον οἰκίαις ἐγκατέστησαν.
252 τούτους μὲν² ὁ στασιάζων πρὸς τοὺς ἀδελφοὺς
λαὸς ἐπελθὼν ἐμπίπρησιν, Ἡρώδης δὲ τοῦ δήμου

---

¹ ἀναδεδεγμένος PAMC.   ² PA: μὲν οὖν the rest.

thian satrap, with Pacorus, the king's son, occupied Syria. Lysanias, who had inherited the principality of his father Ptolemy, son of Mennaeus, induced the satrap, by the promise [a] of a thousand talents and five hundred women, to bring back Antigonus and raise him to the throne, after deposing Hyrcanus. Lured by this offer, Pacorus followed the coast route, directing Barzapharnes to advance through the interior. Of the maritime towns, Tyre closed its gates to Pacorus, Ptolemais and Sidon admitted him. Entrusting a squadron of horse to one of the royal cup-bearers who bore his own name, the prince ordered him to proceed in advance into Judaea, to reconnoitre the enemy's position and to lend Antigonus such aid as he might require.

(2) While these troops were raiding Carmel, Jews flocked to Antigonus in large numbers and volunteered for the invasion. These he sent forward with orders to capture a place called Drymus.[b] Here they came into action, repulsed the enemy, rushed in pursuit to Jerusalem, and, with growing numbers, actually reached the palace. They were received by Hyrcanus and Phasael with a strong force, and a fierce battle ensued in the market-place. The Herodian party routed their adversaries, shut them up in the temple, and posted sixty men in the adjoining houses to keep guard over them. The section of the populace that was in league against the brothers attacked this garrison and burnt them to death, which so enraged Herod that he turned his

---

[a] In *A.* this promise is given by Antigonus himself; *cf.* § 257 below. [b] "Oak-coppice."

πολλοὺς κατ' ὀργὴν τῶν ἀπολωλότων ἀναιρεῖ
συμβαλών, καὶ καθ' ἡμέραν ἐπεκθεόντων ἀλλήλοις κατὰ λόχους φόνος ἦν ἀδιάλειπτος.

253 (3) Ἐνστάσης δ' ἑορτῆς, ἣ πεντηκοστὴ καλεῖται, τά τε περὶ τὸ ἱερὸν πάντα καὶ ἡ πόλις ὅλη
πλήθους τῶν ἀπὸ τῆς χώρας ἀναπίμπλαται, τὸ
πλέον ὁπλιτῶν. καὶ Φασάηλος μὲν τὸ τεῖχος,
Ἡρώδης δ' οὐ μετὰ πολλῶν ἐφρούρει τὰ βασί-
λεια· καὶ τοῖς πολεμίοις ἐπεκδραμὼν ἀσυντάκτοις
κατὰ τὸ προάστειον¹ πλείστους μὲν ἀναιρεῖ, τρέπεται δὲ πάντας καὶ τοὺς μὲν εἰς τὴν πόλιν, τοὺς
δὲ εἰς τὸ ἱερόν, τοὺς δὲ εἰς τὸ ἔξω χαράκωμα
254 συγκλείει.² κἂν τούτῳ διαλλακτὴν μὲν Ἀντίγονος παρακαλεῖ Πάκορον εἰσαφεῖναι, Φασάηλος
δὲ πεισθεὶς τῇ τε πόλει καὶ ξενίᾳ τὸν Πάρθον
εἰσδέχεται μετὰ πεντακοσίων ἱππέων, προφάσει
μὲν ἥκοντα τοῦ παῦσαι τὴν στάσιν, τὸ δ' ἀληθὲς
255 Ἀντιγόνῳ βοηθόν. τὸν γοῦν Φασάηλον ἐν-
εδρεύων ἀνέπεισεν πρὸς Βαρζαφράνην πρεσβεύ-
σασθαι περὶ καταλύσεως, καίτοι τε³ πολλὰ ἀπο-
τρέποντος Ἡρώδου καὶ παραινοῦντος ἀναιρεῖν τὸν
ἐπίβουλον, ἀλλὰ μὴ ταῖς ἐπιβουλαῖς ἑαυτὸν ἐκ-
διδόναι, φύσει γὰρ ἀπίστους εἶναι τοὺς βαρβάρους,
ἔξεισιν Ὑρκανὸν παραλαβών. καὶ Πάκορος, ὡς
ἧττον ὑποπτεύοιτο, καταλιπὼν παρ' Ἡρώδῃ
τινὰς τῶν καλουμένων Ἐλευθέρων ἱππέων τοῖς
λοιποῖς προέπεμψεν Φασάηλον.

256 (4) Ὡς δ' ἐγένοντο κατὰ τὴν Γαλιλαίαν, τοὺς

---

¹ PA Lat. (so Λ. ‖): προσάρκτιον the rest.
² ἐγκλείει PAM.   ³ τε Niese: γε mss.

ᵃ Probably the cup-bearer, not the prince, for, as Reinach
remarks, the latter would have been in a position to treat

arms against the citizens and slew many of them. Every day small companies sallied out against each other, and slaughter was incessant.

(3) When the feast called Pentecost came round, the whole neighbourhood of the temple and the entire city were crowded with country-folk, for the most part in arms. Phasael defended the walls; Herod, with a small force, the palace. With this he descended upon the enemy's disordered ranks in the suburb, killed large numbers of them, put the rest to flight and shut them up, some in the city, others in the temple, others in the entrenched camp outside the walls. Thereupon, Antigonus petitioned for the admission of Pacorus [a] as mediator. Phasael consented, and received into the city and offered hospitality to the Parthian, who, with five hundred horsemen, had come ostensibly to put an end to strife, in reality to support Antigonus. With this object, Pacorus insidiously induced Phasael to go on an embassy to Barzapharnes with a view to the cessation of hostilities. So, notwithstanding the strong dissuasion of Herod, who urged his brother to kill the schemer and not to abandon himself to his schemes, barbarians being (he said) by nature perfidious, Phasael left the city, accompanied by Hyrcanus. To allay suspicions, Pacorus left with Herod some of the cavalry called by the Parthians " Freemen " ; [b] with the remainder he escorted Phasael on his way.

Phasael and Hyrcanus are induced to leave Jerusalem on an embassy to the satrap

(4) On their arrival in Galilee they found the

directly with Phasael and there would have been no need for the subsequent embassy.

[b] More precisely 200 cavalry and 10 " freemen " (*A.* xiv. 342). Most of the Parthian soldiers were slaves (Justin, xli. 2. 5, quoted by Reinach).

μὲν ἐπιχωρίους ἀφεστῶτας κἂν τοῖς ὅπλοις ὄντας
καταλαμβάνουσιν, τῷ σατράπῃ δ' ἐνετύγχανον
πανούργῳ[1] σφόδρα καὶ ταῖς φιλοφρονήσεσιν τὴν
ἐπιβουλὴν καλύπτοντι· δῶρα γοῦν δοὺς αὐτοῖς
257 ἔπειτ' ἀναχωροῦντας ἐλόχα. τοῖς δ' αἴσθησις
γίνεται τῆς ἐπιβουλῆς καταχθεῖσιν εἴς τι τῶν
παραθαλασσίων χωρίων, ὃ καλεῖται Ἐκδίππων·
ἐκεῖ γὰρ τήν τε ὑπόσχεσιν τῶν χιλίων ἤκουσαν
ταλάντων καὶ ὡς Ἀντίγονος τὰς πλείστας τῶν
παρ' αὐτοῖς γυναικῶν ἐν ταῖς πεντακοσίαις καθ-
258 οσιώσειεν Πάρθοις, ὅτι τε προλοχίζοιντο μὲν
αὐτοῖς αἱ νύκτες ὑπὸ τῶν βαρβάρων ἀεί, πάλαι
δ' ἂν καὶ συνελήφθησαν, εἰ μὴ περιέμενον ἐν Ἱεροσολύμοις Ἡρώδην πρότερον λαβεῖν, ὡς μὴ προ-
πυθόμενος τὰ κατ' αὐτοὺς φυλάξαιτο. ταῦτ'
οὐκέτι λόγος ἦν μόνον, ἀλλὰ καὶ φυλακὰς ἤδη
πόρρωθεν[2] ἑαυτῶν ἔβλεπον.

259   (5) Οὐ μὴν Φασάηλος καίτοι πολλὰ παραινοῦντος Ὀφελλίου φεύγειν, πέπυστο γὰρ οὗτος
παρὰ Σαραμάλλα τοῦ πλουσιωτάτου τότε Σύρων
τὴν σύνταξιν τῆς ἐπιβουλῆς ὅλην, καταλιπεῖν Ὑρκανὸν ὑπέμεινεν, ἀλλὰ τῷ σατράπῃ προσελθὼν ἄντικρυς ὠνείδιζεν τὴν ἐπιβουλήν, καὶ μάλισθ' ὅτι
γένοιτο τοιοῦτος χρημάτων ἕνεκεν· πλείω γε μὴν
αὐτὸς ὑπὲρ σωτηρίας δώσειν ὧν Ἀντίγονος ὑπὲρ
260 βασιλείας ὑπέσχετο. πρὸς ταῦτα πανούργως ὁ
Πάρθος ἀπολογίαις τε καὶ ὅρκοις ἀποσκευα-
σάμενος τὴν ὑποψίαν ᾤχετο πρὸς Πάκορον. εὐθέως δὲ τῶν καταλειφθέντων Πάρθων οἷς προσετέτακτο Φασάηλόν τε καὶ Ὑρκανὸν συνελάμβανον,

---

[1] AM : πανούργως the rest.   [2] haud procul Lat.

inhabitants in revolt and up in arms. The satrap,[a] and are
with whom they had an audience, was a very crafty captured by
individual who disguised his plot under a show of Parthians.
benevolence : he gave them presents, and then laid
an ambush to catch them on their departure. They
discovered the conspiracy at a maritime town, where
they halted, named Ekdippa.[b] There they heard of
the promise of the thousand talents,[c] and that the
five hundred women whom Antigonus had devoted
to the Parthians included most of their own ; that
the barbarians invariably kept a watch upon them
at night ; and that they would long since have been
arrested, had not the conspirators been waiting till
Herod was caught at Jerusalem, fearing that the
news of their capture would put him on his guard.
This was now no mere idle gossip ; for already they
could see the sentries posted in the distance.

(5) Phasael, however, notwithstanding the urgent
exhortations to flee made to him by a certain
Ophellius, who had learnt the whole plan of the
conspiracy from Saramalla, the wealthiest Syrian of
his time, could not bring himself to desert Hyrcanus.
Instead, he went to the satrap and frankly reproached
him for the plot, and in particular for acting as he
had done from mercenary motives ; undertaking, for
his part, to give him a larger sum for his life than
Antigonus had promised for a kingdom. To this the
Parthian made a wily reply, clearing himself of suspicion by protestations and oaths, and went off to
join Pacorus.[d] Immediately after, certain Parthians
who had been left behind, with orders to do so,

[a] Barzapharnes.
[b] Achzib (ez Zib), half way between Tyre and the
promontory of Carmel.
[c] § 248.   [d] Apparently the prince.

πολλὰ[1] πρὸς τὴν ἐπιορκίαν καὶ τὸ ἄπιστον αὐτοῖς
καταρωμένους.

261 (6) Ἐν δὲ τούτῳ καὶ τὸν Ἡρώδην ὁ πεμφθεὶς
οἰνοχόος ἐπεβούλευε συλλαβεῖν, ἔξω τοῦ τείχους
ἀπατήσας προελθεῖν, ὥσπερ ἐντολὰς εἶχεν. ὁ δὲ
ἀπ᾽ ἀρχῆς ὑποπτεύων τοὺς βαρβάρους καὶ τότε
πεπυσμένος εἰς τοὺς πολεμίους ἐμπεπτωκέναι τὰ
μηνύοντα τὴν ἐπιβουλὴν αὐτῷ γράμματα, προελθεῖν οὐκ ἠβούλετο, καίτοι μάλα ἀξιοπίστως τοῦ
Πακόρου φάσκοντος δεῖν αὐτὸν ὑπαντῆσαι τοῖς
τὰς ἐπιστολὰς κομίζουσιν· οὔτε γὰρ ἑαλωκέναι
τοῖς πολεμίοις αὐτὰς καὶ περιέχειν οὐκ ἐπι-
262 βουλήν, ἀλλ᾽ ὁπόσα διεπράξατο Φασάηλος. ἔτυχεν
δὲ παρ᾽ ἄλλων προακηκοὼς τὸν ἀδελφὸν συν-
ειλημμένον, καὶ προσῄει Ὑρκανοῦ θυγάτηρ [Μα-
ριάμμη][2] συνετωτάτη γυναικῶν, καταντιβολοῦσα
μὴ προϊέναι μηδ᾽ ἐμπιστεύειν ἑαυτὸν ἤδη φανερῶς
ἐπιχειροῦσι τοῖς βαρβάροις.

263 (7) Ἔτι δὲ τῶν περὶ Πάκορον σκεπτομένων,
πῶς ἂν κρύφα τὴν ἐπιβουλὴν ἀπαρτίσειαν, οὐ γὰρ
ἐκ φανεροῦ οἷόν τ᾽ ἦν ἀνδρὸς οὕτω δυνατοῦ[3] περιγενέσθαι, προλαβὼν Ἡρώδης μετὰ τῶν οἰκειο-
τάτων προσώπων νύκτωρ ἐπὶ Ἰδουμαίας ἐχώρει
264 λάθρα τῶν πολεμίων. αἰσθόμενοι δ᾽ οἱ Πάρθοι
κατεδίωκον. κἀκεῖνος τὴν μὲν μητέρα καὶ τὰς
ἀδελφὰς[4] καὶ τὴν καθωμολογημένην παῖδα μετὰ

---

[1] πολλὰ Destinon (with *A.* ‖): τά τε ἄλλα MSS.
[2] Perhaps a gloss (Niese), or read Μαριάμμης δὲ μήτηρ
(Destinon), *cf. A.* xiv. 351.   [3] συνετοῦ LVR Lat.
[4] τὰς ἀδελφὰς Niese, *cf. A.* ‖ ἀδελφὴν : τοὺς ἀδελφοὺς MSS.

---

[a] Pacorus (§ 249): *A.* incorrectly has εὐνοῦχος instead of
οἰνοχόος.

arrested Phasael and Hyrcanus, the prisoners cursing them bitterly for their perjury and breach of faith.

(6) Meanwhile a plot to arrest Herod also was in progress, and the cup-bearer [a] who had been sent to execute it was, in accordance with instructions, endeavouring to lure him to come outside the walls. Herod, however, having suspected the barbarians from the first, had now learnt that letters informing him of the conspiracy had fallen into the enemy's hands. He, therefore, refused to come out, notwithstanding the highly plausible assertions of Pacorus that he ought to meet the bearers of the documents, which, he said, had neither been intercepted by his enemies, nor contained any mention of a plot but a full report of Phasael's proceedings. But Herod had already heard from another source of his brother's arrest. Moreover, Mariamme, the daughter [b] of Hyrcanus, most sagacious of women, came and implored him not to venture out or trust himself to the barbarians, who were now openly planning his ruin.

(7) While Pacorus and his accomplices were still deliberating by what stealthy means they might achieve their design, as it was impossible openly to triumph over so powerful an adversary, Herod forestalled them and, unobserved by his enemies, set out by night, with the nearest and dearest of his family, for Idumaea. The Parthians, discovering his flight, started in pursuit. Herod, thereupon, directed his mother and sisters, the young girl who was betrothed

Plot to entrap Herod.

Herod's flight to Arabia.

---

[b] Strictly grand-daughter (§ 241) ; but *A.* xiv. 351 is here probably correct in mentioning " the daughter of Hyrcanus, the *mother* of his betrothed." His bride would hardly be referred to in this way.

τῆς μητρὸς καὶ τοῦ νεωτάτου τῶν ἀδελφῶν προσ
τάξας ὁδεύειν αὐτὸς ἀσφαλῶς μετὰ τῶν θερα
πόντων ἀνέκοπτε τοὺς βαρβάρους· καὶ πολλοὺς
κατὰ πᾶσαν προσβολὴν ἀποκτείνας εἰς Μασάδαν
τὸ φρούριον ἠπείγετο.

265 (8) Βαρυτέρους δὲ κατὰ τὴν φυγὴν Πάρθων
Ἰουδαίους ἐπείρασεν, ἐνοχλήσαντας μὲν διηνεκῶς,
ἀπὸ δ' ἑξήκοντα τῆς πόλεως σταδίων καὶ παρα
ταξαμένους ἐπιεικῶς πολὺν χρόνον. ἔνθα κρατήσας
Ἡρώδης καὶ πολλοὺς αὐτῶν ἀποκτείνας αὖθις
εἰς μνήμην τοῦ κατορθώματος ἔκτισεν τὸ χωρίον
καὶ βασιλείοις πολυτελεστάτοις ἐκόσμησεν, καὶ
ἀκρόπολιν ὀχυρωτάτην ἀνεδείματο, Ἡρώδειόν τε
266 ἐκάλεσεν ἀφ' ἑαυτοῦ. τηνικαῦτά γε μὴν φεύ
γοντι καθ' ἡμέραν αὐτῷ προσεγίνοντο πολλοί, καὶ
κατὰ Ῥῆσαν γενομένῳ[1] τῆς Ἰδουμαίας Ἰώσηπος
ἀδελφὸς ὑπαντήσας συνεβούλευσεν τοὺς πολλοὺς
τῶν ἑπομένων ἀποφορτίσασθαι, μὴ γὰρ ἂν τοσοῦ
τον ὄχλον δέξασθαι τὴν Μασάδαν· ἦσαν δ' ὑπὲρ
267 τοὺς ἐννακισχιλίους. πεισθεὶς [οὖν][2] Ἡρώδης τοὺς
μὲν βαρυτέρους τῆς χρείας διαφῆκεν ἀνὰ τὴν
Ἰδουμαίαν δοὺς ἐφόδια, μετὰ δὲ τῶν ἀναγκαιο
τάτων τοὺς ἀλκιμωτάτους κατασχὼν εἰς τὸ φρού
ριον διασώζεται. καταλιπὼν δ' ἐνταῦθα ταῖς
γυναιξὶν ὀκτακοσίους φύλακας καὶ διαρκῆ τἀπι
τήδεια πρὸς πολιορκίαν αὐτὸς εἰς τὴν Ἀραβικὴν
Πέτραν ἠπείγετο.

268 (9) Πάρθοι δ' ἐν Ἱεροσολύμοις ἐφ' ἁρπαγὴν
τραπόμενοι τῶν φυγόντων εἰς τὰς οἰκίας εἰσ

---

[1] κατὰ Ῥ. γενομένῳ Niese: παρῆσαν γενομένῳ δ' ἐπὶ PAM:
κατὰ (τὴν) Θρῆσαν the rest, cf. A. xiv. 361 (ἐν Θρήσᾳ).
[2] om. PA.

to him, with her mother, and his youngest brother to continue their journey, and then, aided by his attendants, secured their retreat, holding the barbarians at bay. In every encounter he slew large numbers of them, and then pressed on to the fortress of Masada.[a]

(8) But he found in this flight the Jews even more troublesome than the Parthians, for they perpetually harassed him, and at a distance of sixty furlongs from the city brought on a regular action which was prolonged for a considerable time. Here Herod eventually defeated them with great slaughter ; and here subsequently, to commemorate his victory, he founded a city, adorned it with the most costly palaces, erected a citadel of commanding strength, and called it after his own name Herodion.[b] Thenceforward the fugitive was joined daily by many others, and on reaching Rhesa in Idumaea was advised by his brother Joseph, who met him there, to disencumber himself of the bulk of his followers, Masada being unable to accommodate such a crowd, numbering upwards of nine thousand. Herod, acting on his advice, dispersed throughout Idumaea those who were more an encumbrance than an assistance, after supplying them with provisions ; and retaining the most stalwart of them together with his cherished kinsfolk reached the fortress[c] in safety. Leaving there a guard of eight hundred to protect the women, with sufficient supplies to stand a siege, he himself pushed on to Petra in Arabia.

(9) In Jerusalem, meanwhile, the Parthians gave themselves up to pillage, breaking into the houses

[a] Above the west coast of the Dead Sea, near its lower extremity.

[b] A description is given later, §§ 419 ff.

[c] Masada.

ἔπιπτον καὶ τὸ βασίλειον, ἀπεχόμενοι μόνων τῶν
Ὑρκανοῦ χρημάτων· ἦν δ' οὐ πλείω τριακοσίων
ταλάντων. ἐπετύγχανον δὲ καὶ τῶν ἄλλων οὐχ
ὅσοις ἤλπισαν· ὁ γὰρ Ἡρώδης ἐκ πολλοῦ τὴν
ἀπιστίαν τῶν βαρβάρων ὑφορώμενος εἰς τὴν Ἰδουμαίαν τὰ λαμπρότατα τῶν κειμηλίων προαν-
εσκεύαστο, καὶ τῶν αὐτῷ προσεχόντων ὁμοίως
269 ἕκαστος. Πάρθοι δὲ μετὰ τὰς ἁρπαγὰς ἐπὶ τοσοῦτον ὕβρεως ἐχώρησαν ὡς ἐμπλῆσαι μὲν ἀκηρύκτου
πολέμου τὴν χώραν ἅπασαν, ἀνάστατον δὲ ποιῆσαι
τὴν Μαρισαίων πόλιν, μὴ μόνον δὲ καταστῆσαι
βασιλέα Ἀντίγονον, ἀλλὰ καὶ παραδοῦναι αὐτῷ
Φασάηλόν τε καὶ Ὑρκανὸν δεσμώτας αἰκίσασθαι.
270 ὁ δὲ Ὑρκανοῦ μὲν προσπεσόντος[1] αὐτὸς τὰ ὦτα
λωβᾶται τοῖς ὀδοῦσιν, ὡς μηδὲ αὖθις ἐν μεταβολῇ
ποτε δύναιτο τὴν ἀρχιερωσύνην ἀπολαβεῖν· δεῖ
γὰρ ὁλοκλήρους ἀρχιερᾶσθαι.

271   (10) Τῆς Φασαήλου δὲ ἀρετῆς ὑστερίζει φθάσαντος πέτρᾳ προσρῆξαι τὴν κεφαλήν, ὡς καὶ σιδή-
ρου καὶ χειρῶν εἴργετο. κἀκεῖνος μέν, Ἡρώδου
γνήσιον ἑαυτὸν ἀποδείξας ἀδελφὸν καὶ Ὑρκανὸν
ἀγεννέστατον, ἀνδρειότατα θνήσκει, ποιησάμενος
τὴν καταστροφὴν τοῖς κατὰ τὸν βίον ἔργοις
272 πρέπουσαν. κατέχει δὲ καὶ ἄλλος λόγος, ὡς ἀν-
ενέγκαι μὲν ἐκ τῆς τότε πληγῆς, πεμφθεὶς δ' ἰα-
τρὸς ὑπ' Ἀντιγόνου θεραπεῦσαι δῆθεν αὐτὸν ἐμ-
πλήσειεν τὸ τραῦμα δηλητηρίων φαρμάκων καὶ

_____

[1] προσπεσόντος MLVR : om. Lat. : προσπεσὼν the rest, *i.e.*
"Antigonus personally assaulted H."

_____

[a] Whether from sacrilegious scruples, because H. was
high-priest, or more probably as reserved for Antigonus, does
not appear.

of the fugitives and into the palace ; refraining only The Parthians, masters of Jerusalem, place Antigonus on the throne. from the funds of Hyrcanus,[a] which, however, amounted to no more than three hundred talents. Elsewhere they found less than they had expected; for Herod, long since suspecting the barbarians of perfidy, had taken the precaution of removing the most precious of his treasures to Idumaea, and each of his friends had done likewise. After the pillage, the insolence of the Parthians proceeded to extremes. They let loose on the whole country the horrors of implacable [b] war, laid the city of Marisa [c] in ruins, and, not content with raising Antigonus to the throne, delivered up to him Phasael and Hyrcanus, in chains, for torture. Hyrcanus threw himself at the feet of Antigonus, who with his own teeth [d] lacerated his suppliant's ears, in order to disqualify him for ever, under any change of circumstances, from resuming the high priesthood ; since freedom from physical defect is essential to the holder of that office.[e]

(10) Phasael, on the other hand, courageously Death of Phasael. forestalled the king's malice by dashing his head upon a rock, being deprived of the use of hands or steel. Thus showing himself to be a true brother of Herod, and Hyrcanus the most ignoble of men, he died a hero's death—an end in keeping with his life's career. According to another account, Phasael recovered from his self-inflicted blow, and a physician sent by Antigonus, ostensibly to attend him, injected noxious drugs into the wound and so killed him.

[b] Or " undeclared."

[c] Mareshah (*Khurbet Mer'ash*), some 25 miles S.W. of Jerusalem, in Idumaea (§ 63).

[d] *A.* xiv. 366 omits this detail, saying merely " docked his ears."

[e] *Cf.* Lev. xxi. 17-23.

διαφθείρειεν αὐτόν. ὁπότερον δ' ἂν ἀληθὲς ᾖ,
τὴν ἀρχὴν ἔχει λαμπράν. φασὶν γοῦν αὐτὸν καὶ
πρὶν ἐκπνεῦσαι πυθόμενον παρὰ γυναίου τινὸς
ὡς Ἡρώδης διαπεφεύγοι, " νῦν," εἰπεῖν, " εὔθυμος
ἄπειμι τὸν μετελευσόμενον τοὺς ἐχθροὺς καταλιπὼν ζῶντα."

273   (11) Ὁ μὲν οὖν οὕτως τελευτᾷ. Πάρθοι δὲ
καίτοι διημαρτηκότες ὧν μάλιστα ἐπεθύμουν γυναικῶν καθιστᾶσιν μὲν ἐν Ἱεροσολύμοις Ἀντιγόνῳ
τὰ πράγματα, δεσμώτην δ' Ὑρκανὸν ἀνάγουσιν
εἰς τὴν Παρθυηνήν.

274   (xiv. 1) Ἡρώδης δὲ συντονώτερον ἤλαυνεν εἰς
τὴν Ἀραβίαν ὡς ἔτι τἀδελφοῦ ζῶντος ἐπειγόμενος
χρήματα παρὰ τοῦ βασιλέως λαβεῖν, οἷς μόνοις
πείσειν ὑπὲρ Φασαήλου τὴν τῶν βαρβάρων ἤλπιζεν
πλεονεξίαν. ἐλογίζετο γάρ, εἰ τῆς πατρῴας φιλίας
ἀμνημονέστερος ὁ Ἄραψ γένοιτο καὶ τοῦ δοῦναι
δωρεὰν μικρολογώτερος, δανείσασθαι παρ' αὐτοῦ
τὰ λύτρα ῥύσιον θεὶς τὸν τοῦ λυτρουμένου παῖδα·

275 καὶ γὰρ ἐπήγετο τὸν ἀδελφιδοῦν ὄντα ἐτῶν
ἑπτά· τάλαντα δ' ἦν ἕτοιμος τριακόσια δοῦναι προ-
στησάμενος Τυρίους παρακαλοῦντας. τὸ χρεὼν δ'
ἄρα τὴν αὑτοῦ σπουδὴν ἐφθάκει καὶ Φασαήλου
τεθνηκότος εἰς κενὸν Ἡρώδης φιλάδελφος ἦν· οὐ

276 μὴν οὐδὲ παρὰ Ἄραψιν εὑρίσκει φιλίαν οὖσαν.[1] ὁ
γοῦν βασιλεὺς αὐτῶν Μάλχος προπέμψας ἐκ τῆς
χώρας κατὰ τάχος προσέτασσεν ἀναστρέφειν,
προφάσει μὲν χρώμενος Πάρθοις, ἐπικηρυκεύ-
σασθαι γὰρ αὐτοὺς ἐκβαλεῖν Ἡρώδην τῆς Ἀραβίας, τῷ δὲ ὄντι κατασχεῖν προαιρούμενος τὰ παρ'
Ἀντιπάτρου χρέα καὶ μηδὲν εἰς τὰς ἐκείνου δωρεὰς

[1] μένουσαν LVRC (perhaps rightly).

But whichever account be true, the initial act re-
dounds to his glorious credit. It is said, moreover,
that before he expired, being informed by a woman
of Herod's escape, he exclaimed, " Now I shall depart
happy, since I leave one behind me who will have
vengeance on my foes."

(11) Such was Phasael's end. The Parthians,
though disappointed of their most coveted prize,
the women, none the less installed Antigonus as Hyrcanus
master in Jerusalem, and carried off Hyrcanus a a prisoner.
prisoner to Parthia.

(xiv. 1) Herod, in the belief that his brother was Herod,
still alive, was now accelerating his march to Arabia, repulsed by
hastening to obtain from its king the money by king of
which alone he hoped to move the avaricious bar- Arabia,
barians on behalf of Phasael. For, should the Arab
prove unduly forgetful of the ties of friendship with
his (Herod's) father and too mean to make him a
present, he counted on borrowing from him the
amount of the ransom and leaving in pledge the son of
the prisoner whom he wished to redeem ; for he had
with him his nephew, a lad of seven years old. He
was, moreover, prepared to give three hundred
talents, offering as his sureties the Tyrians who had
volunteered their services. Fate, however, proved
to have outstripped his zeal : Phasael was dead and
Herod's fraternal affection was all in vain. He found,
too, that the Arabs were no longer his friends. For
their king, Malchus, forwarded peremptory orders
to him instantly to quit his territory, pretending to
have received formal notice from the Parthians to
expel Herod from Arabia ; in reality, he was determined not to repay his debts to Antipater, nor to be

ἀντιπαρασχεῖν χρήζουσιν τοῖς τέκνοις δυσωπεῖσθαι.
συμβούλοις δ' ἐχρῆτο τῆς ἀναιδείας τοῖς ὁμοίως
ἀποστερεῖν τὰς Ἀντιπάτρου παρακαταθήκας θέλου-
σιν· ἦσαν δὲ τῶν περὶ αὐτὸν οἱ δυνατώτατοι.

277   (2) Ἡρώδης μὲν δὴ πολεμίους τοὺς Ἄραβας
εὑρὼν δι' ἃ φιλτάτους ἤλπισεν καὶ τοῖς ἀγγέλοις
ἀποκρινάμενος¹ ὡς ὑπηγόρευε τὸ πάθος ὑπέστρεψεν
ἐπ' Αἰγύπτου. καὶ τὴν μὲν πρώτην ἑσπέραν κατά
τι τῶν ἐπιχωρίων ἱερὸν αὐλίζεται τοὺς ὑπολειφ-
θέντας ἀναλαβών, τῇ δ' ἐξῆς εἰς Ῥινοκόρουρα
προελθόντι τὰ περὶ τὴν τἀδελφοῦ τελευτὴν ἀπαγ-
278 γέλλεται. προσλαβὼν δὲ πένθους² ὅσον ἀπεθήκατο
φροντίδων ᾔει προσωτέρω. καὶ δὴ βραδέως ὁ
Ἄραψ μετανοήσας ἔπεμψεν διὰ τάχους τοὺς ἀνα-
καλέσοντας τὸν ὑβρισμένον. ἔφθανεν δὲ καὶ τούτους
Ἡρώδης εἰς Πηλούσιον ἀφικόμενος, ἔνθα τῆς
παρόδου μὴ τυγχάνων ὑπὸ τῶν ἐφορμούντων³ τοῖς
ἡγεμόσιν ἐντυγχάνει· κἀκεῖνοι τήν τε φήμην καὶ
τὸ ἀξίωμα τἀνδρὸς αἰδεσθέντες προπέμπουσιν
279 αὐτὸν εἰς Ἀλεξάνδρειαν. ὁ δὲ παρελθὼν εἰς τὴν
πόλιν ἐδέχθη μὲν λαμπρῶς ὑπὸ Κλεοπάτρας στρατηγὸν ἐλπιζούσης ἕξειν εἰς ἃ παρεσκευάζετο·
διακρουσάμενος δὲ τὰς παρακλήσεις τῆς βασιλίδος
καὶ μήτε τὴν ἀκμὴν τοῦ χειμῶνος ὑποδείσας μήτε
τοὺς κατὰ τὴν Ἰταλίαν θορύβους ἐπὶ Ῥώμης
ἔπλει.

¹ ὑποκρινόμενος PLV.   ² πένθος PA.
³ ἐφορμούντων Spanheim: ἐφορμώντων MSS.

ᵃ Or Rhinocolura (el-'Arish), the maritime town on the
frontiers of Egypt and Palestine.
ᵇ Such seems to be the meaning of the text of the best
MSS., literally " Having taken as much of grief as he laid

forced by any sense of shame into making the slightest return, for all he had received from the father, to his children in their hour of need. His advisers in this shameless conduct were the most powerful men at his court, who like himself desired to embezzle the moneys entrusted to them by Antipater.

(2) Herod, finding the Arabs hostile to him for the very reasons which had made him look for their warm friendship, gave the messengers the reply which his feelings dictated and turned back towards Egypt. The first evening he encamped in one of the temples of the country, where he picked up those of his men who had been left in the rear. The next day he advanced to Rhinocorura,[a] where he received the news of his brother's death. His load of anxiety thus replaced by as heavy a burden of grief,[b] he resumed his march. The Arab king, now tardily repenting his conduct, dispatched messengers in haste to recall his insulted suitor ; but Herod outstripped them, having already reached Pelusium. Here, being refused a passage by the fleet stationed in that port, he applied to the authorities, who, out of respect for his fame and rank, escorted him to Alexandria. On entering the city he had a magnificent reception from Cleopatra, who hoped to entrust him with the command of an expedition which she was preparing ; but he eluded the queen's solicitations, and, deterred neither by the perils of mid-winter nor by the disturbances in Italy, set sail for Rome.

makes his way via Egypt

down of care." Traill, following an inferior text, renders " Having indulged such sorrow as became the occasion, he dismissed his grief " ; similarly Whiston and Reinach.

280 (3) Κινδυνεύσας δὲ περὶ Παμφυλίαν καὶ τοῦ
φόρτου τὸ πλεῖον ἐκβαλὼν μόλις εἰς Ῥόδον διασώζεται, σφόδρα τῷ πρὸς Κάσσιον πολέμῳ τετρυ-
χωμένην, δεχθεὶς[1] ὑπὸ Πτολεμαίου καὶ Σαπφινίου
τῶν φίλων. καίπερ δ' ὢν ἐν ἀπορίᾳ χρημάτων
281 ναυπηγεῖται τριήρη μεγίστην, ἐν ᾗ μετὰ τῶν
φίλων εἰς Βρεντέσιον καταπλεύσας, κἀκεῖθεν εἰς
Ῥώμην ἐπειχθείς, πρώτῳ διὰ τὴν πατρῴαν φιλίαν
ἐνετύγχανεν Ἀντωνίῳ, καὶ τάς τε αὐτοῦ καὶ τοῦ
γένους συμφορὰς ἐκδιηγεῖτο, ὅτι τε τοὺς οἰκειο-
τάτους ἐν φρουρίῳ καταλιπὼν πολιορκουμένους διὰ
χειμῶνος πλεύσειεν ἐπ' αὐτὸν ἱκέτης.

282 (4) Ἀντωνίου δὲ ἥπτετο πρὸς τὴν μεταβολὴν
οἶκτος, καὶ κατὰ μνήμην μὲν τῆς Ἀντιπάτρου
ξενίας, τὸ δὲ ὅλον καὶ διὰ τὴν τοῦ παρόντος
ἀρετήν, ἔγνω καὶ τότε βασιλέα καθιστᾶν Ἰουδαίων
ὃν πρότερον αὐτὸς ἐποίησεν τετράρχην. ἐνῆγεν δὲ
οὐκ ἔλαττον τῆς εἰς Ἡρώδην φιλοτιμίας ἡ πρὸς
Ἀντίγονον διαφορά· τοῦτον γὰρ δὴ στασιώδη τε
283 καὶ Ῥωμαίων ἐχθρὸν ὑπελάμβανεν. Καῖσαρ[2] μὲν
οὖν εἶχεν ἑτοιμότερον αὐτοῦ τὰς Ἀντιπάτρου
στρατείας[3] ἀνανεούμενος,[4] ἃς κατ' Αἴγυπτον αὐτοῦ
τῷ πατρὶ συνδιήνεγκεν, τήν τε ξενίαν καὶ τὴν ἐν
ἅπασιν εὔνοιαν, ὁρῶντά γε μὴν καὶ τὸ Ἡρώδου
284 δραστήριον· συνήγαγεν δὲ τὴν βουλήν, ἐν ᾗ Μεσσάλας καὶ μετ' αὐτὸν Ἀτρατῖνος παραστησάμενοι
τὸν Ἡρώδην τάς τε πατρῴας εὐεργεσίας καὶ τὴν
αὐτοῦ πρὸς Ῥωμαίους εὔνοιαν διεξῄεσαν, ἀπο-
δεικνύντες ἅμα καὶ πολέμιον τὸν Ἀντίγονον οὐ

---

[1] + δὲ and om. δ' below MLVR.
[2] Καῖσαρ PAM : Καίσαρα the rest.
[3] στρατηγίας P : στρατιὰς most mss.
[4] PM : ἀνανεούμενον the rest.

(3) Nearly shipwrecked off Pamphylia, after throw- and Rhodes
ing overboard the bulk of the cargo, he with difficulty
came safe to Rhodes, which had suffered severely
from the war with Cassius. Here he was welcomed
by his friends Ptolemy and Sapphinius, and, notwithstanding his lack of funds, procured the construction
of an immense trireme, which carried him and his
friends to Brundisium, whence he sped to Rome.
He waited first on Antony, as his father's friend, and to Rome.
told him the story of his own and his family's misfortunes, and how he had left his nearest relatives
besieged in a fortress and crossed the sea in the depth
of winter to implore his aid.

(4) Antony was moved with compassion at his By Antony's
reverse of fortune ; and influenced by the recollec- influence
the Senate
tion of Antipater's hospitality, but above all by declare
the heroic qualities of the man in front of him, Herod king
of the Jews.
determined then and there to make him king of the
Jews whom he had himself previously appointed
tetrarch.[a] Besides admiration for Herod, he had as
strong an incentive in his aversion for Antigonus,
whom he regarded as a promoter of sedition and an
enemy of Rome. Caesar proved a yet more ready
champion than Antony, as his memory recalled
the part which Antipater had borne with his own
father in the Egyptian campaigns,[b] his hospitality
and invariable loyalty, while his eyes rested on
Herod and read his enterprising character. So he
convened the Senate, to which Messala, seconded by
Atratinus, presented Herod and dwelt on the services
rendered by his father and his own goodwill towards
the Roman people ; demonstrating at the same time
that Antigonus was their enemy, not only from the

<hr>

[a] § 244. [b] §§ 187 ff.

μόνον ἐξ ὧν διηνέχθη τάχιον, ἀλλ' ὅτι καὶ τότε
διὰ Πάρθων λάβοι τὴν ἀρχὴν Ῥωμαίους ὑπεριδών.
τῆς δὲ συγκλήτου πρὸς ταῦτα κεκινημένης, ὡς
παρελθὼν Ἀντώνιος καὶ πρὸς τὸν κατὰ Πάρθων
πόλεμον βασιλεύειν Ἡρώδην συμφέρειν ἔλεγεν,
285 ἐπιψηφίζονται πάντες. λυθείσης δὲ τῆς βουλῆς
Ἀντώνιος μὲν καὶ Καῖσαρ μέσον ἔχοντες Ἡρώδην
ἐξῄεσαν, προῆγον δὲ σὺν ταῖς ἄλλαις ἀρχαῖς οἱ
ὕπατοι θύσοντές τε καὶ τὸ δόγμα ἀναθήσοντες εἰς
τὸ Καπετώλιον. τὴν δὲ πρώτην Ἡρώδῃ τῆς βασιλείας ἡμέραν Ἀντώνιος εἱστία [αὐτὸν].[1]

286 (xv. 1) Παρὰ δὲ τὸν χρόνον τοῦτον Ἀντίγονος
ἐπολιόρκει τοὺς ἐν Μασάδᾳ, τοῖς μὲν ἄλλοις
ἐπιτηδείοις διαρκουμένους, σπανίζοντας δὲ ὕδατος·
διὸ καὶ Ἰώσηπος ἀδελφὸς Ἡρώδου σὺν διακοσίοις
τῶν οἰκείων δρασμὸν ἐβουλεύετο εἰς Ἄραβας,
ἀκηκοὼς τῶν εἰς Ἡρώδην ἁμαρτημάτων Μάλχῳ
287 μεταμέλειν. κἂν ἔφθη καταλιπὼν τὸ φρούριον, εἰ
μὴ περὶ τὴν νύκτα τῆς ἐξόδου συνέβη πλεῖστον
ὗσαι· τῶν γὰρ ἐκδοχείων ὕδατος ἀναπλησθέντων
οὐκέτ' ἔχρῃζεν φυγῆς, ἀλλ' ἐπεξῄεσαν ἤδη τοῖς
περὶ τὸν Ἀντίγονον, καὶ τὰ μὲν φανερῶς συμ-
πλεκόμενοι, τὰ δὲ λοχῶντες συχνοὺς διέφθειρον.
οὐ μὴν ἐν ἅπασιν εὐστόχουν, ἔστιν δ' ὅπη[2] καὶ
αὐτοὶ πταίοντες ἀνέστρεφον.

288 (2) Κἂν τούτῳ Βεντίδιος ὁ Ῥωμαίων στρατηγὸς πεμφθεὶς ἐκ Συρίας Πάρθους ἀνείργειν μετ'
ἐκείνους εἰς Ἰουδαίαν παρέβαλεν, λόγῳ μὲν ὡς
βοηθήσων τοῖς περὶ Ἰώσηπον, ἔργῳ δ' Ἀντίγονον

---

[1] om. Niese with C.   [2] ὅπου PAM.

earlier quarrel which they had had with him, but because he had also just been guilty of contempt of Rome in accepting his crown from Parthian hands. These words stirred the Senate, and when Antony came forward and said that with a view to the war with Parthia it was expedient that Herod should be king, the proposal was carried unanimously. The meeting was dissolved and Antony and Caesar left the senate-house with Herod between them, preceded by the consuls and the other magistrates, as they went to offer sacrifice and to lay up the decree in the Capitol. On this, the first day of his reign, 40 B.C. (end) Herod was given a banquet by Antony.

(xv. 1) All this time Antigonu{ was besieging the Antigonus occupants of Masada, who, though well supplied with besieges Herod's all other necessaries, were in want of water. In family in these straits Joseph, Herod's brother, with two hundred Masada. of his men resolved to escape to Arabia, having heard that Malchus had repented of his criminal treatment of Herod. He was on the point of leaving the fortress, when on the very night fixed for his departure, rain fell in abundance ; the reservoirs were replenished and Joseph saw no further need for flight. Instead, the garrison now began to sally out against the forces of Antigonus and partly in open combat, partly by ambuscades, destroyed a considerable number. They were not, however, uniformly successful, meeting with occasional reverses themselves and being forced to retire.

(2) Meanwhile Ventidius, the Roman general dis- Ventidius patched from Syria to hold the Parthians in check, and Silo in Syria. had in his pursuit of them advanced into Judaea, nominally to relieve Joseph and his friends, but in

289 ἀργυριούμενος. ἔγγιστα γοῦν Ἱεροσολύμων αὐλι-
σάμενος, ὡς ἐνεπλήσθη χρημάτων, αὐτὸς μὲν
ἀνεχώρει μετὰ τῆς πλείστης δυνάμεως, Σίλωνα
δὲ σὺν μέρει κατέλιπεν,[1] ὡς μὴ κατάφωρον τὸ
λῆμμα ποιήσειεν πάντας ἀπαναστήσας. Ἀντίγονος δὲ πάλιν ἐλπίζων Πάρθους ἐπαμυνεῖν καὶ
Σίλωνα τέως ἐθεράπευεν, ὡς μηδὲν ἐνοχλοίη πρὸ
τῆς ἐλπίδος.[2]

290 (3) Ἤδη δὲ Ἡρώδης καταπεπλευκὼς ἀπὸ τῆς
Ἰταλίας εἰς Πτολεμαΐδα καὶ συναγηοχὼς δύναμιν
οὐκ ὀλίγην ξένων τε καὶ ὁμοφύλων ἤλαυνεν διὰ
τῆς Γαλιλαίας ἐπ' Ἀντίγονον, συλλαμβανόντων
Βεντιδίου καὶ Σίλωνος, οὓς Δέλλιος ὑπ' Ἀντωνίου

291 πεμφθεὶς Ἡρώδην συγκαταγαγεῖν ἔπεισεν. ἐτύγ-
χανεν δὲ Βεντίδιος μὲν ἐν ταῖς πόλεσιν τὰς διὰ
Πάρθους ταραχὰς καθιστάμενος, Σίλων δ' ἐν
Ἰουδαίᾳ χρήμασιν ὑπ' Ἀντιγόνου διεφθαρμένος.
οὐ μὴν Ἡρώδης ἰσχύος ἠπόρει, προϊόντι δ' αὐτῷ
καθ' ἡμέραν ηὐξεῖτο τὰ τῆς δυνάμεως, καὶ πλὴν

292 ὀλίγων πᾶσα ἡ Γαλιλαία προσέθετο. προύκειτο
μὲν οὖν τὸ ἀναγκαιότατον ἀγώνισμα Μασάδα καὶ
τὸ ῥύσασθαι πρῶτον τοὺς οἰκείους ἐκ τῆς πολιορκίας, γίνεται δ' ἐμπόδιον Ἰόππη· ταύτην γὰρ ἐχρῆν
πολεμίαν οὖσαν ἐξελεῖν πρότερον, ὡς μὴ χωροῦντος
ἐπὶ Ἱεροσολύμων κατὰ νώτου τι τοῖς ἐχθροῖς
ἔρυμα καταλείποιτο. συνῆπτεν δὲ καὶ Σίλων
ἀσμένως τῆς ἀπαναστάσεως πρόφασιν εὑρών, ᾧ
προσέκειντο Ἰουδαῖοι διώκοντες.[3] ἐπὶ τούτους
Ἡρώδης ἐκδραμὼν μετ' ὀλίγου στίφους τρέπεται
ταχέως καὶ Σίλωνα διασῴζει κακῶς ἀμυνόμενον.

---

[1] Destinon : καταλέλοιπεν MSS.
[2] πρὸς τὰς ἐλπίδας C.   [3] προσήκοντες PA.

reality to extort money from Antigonus. He accordingly encamped in the immediate vicinity of Jerusalem and, after glutting his avarice, retired with the bulk of his troops ; leaving, however, a detachment under the command of Silo, to prevent the detection of his mercenary proceedings which might ensue from the withdrawal of the entire force. Antigonus, on his side, hoping for renewed assistance from the Parthians, meanwhile paid court to Silo, as he had to Ventidius, to prevent any trouble from him before his expectations were realized.

(3) But already Herod, having sailed from Italy to Ptolemais and collected a considerable army of foreign and native troops, was advancing through Galilee upon Antigonus. Ventidius and Silo, induced by Dellius, Antony's emissary, to assist in reinstating Herod, were co-operating. But Ventidius was occupied in quelling local disturbances arising out of the Parthian invasion, while Silo, corrupted by the bribes of Antigonus, lingered in Judaea. Herod, however, had no lack of support : new recruits added daily to his strength as he advanced, and, with few exceptions, all Galilee went over to him. The most urgent task ahead of him was Masada and, above all, the liberation of his relatives from the siege. But Joppa was a preliminary obstacle. For that town being hostile had first to be reduced, in order that there might be no stronghold left in enemy hands in his rear when he marched against Jerusalem. Silo, glad of an excuse for quitting Jerusalem, now proceeded to join him, hotly pursued by the Jews. Herod with a small party flew out upon them and soon routed them, rescuing Silo, who was making but a poor defence.

Herod returns to Palestine 39 B.C.

293 (4) Ἔπειτα Ἰόππην ἑλὼν πρὸς τὴν Μασάδαν
ῥυσόμενος τοὺς οἰκείους ἠπείγετο. καὶ τῶν ἐπιχωρίων οὓς μὲν πατρῷα φιλία προσῆγεν, οὓς δὲ τὸ
αὐτοῦ κλέος, οὓς δὲ τῆς ἐξ ἀμφοῖν εὐεργεσίας
ἀμοιβῇ, πλείστους γε μὴν ἐλπὶς ὡς ἐκ βασιλέως
βεβαίου, δυσνίκητός[1] τε ἤδη δύναμις ἤθροιστο.
294 προϊόντα δ' Ἀντίγονος ἐνήδρευεν τἀπιτήδεια τῶν
παρόδων προλοχίζων, ἐν οἷς οὐδὲν ἢ μικρὰ τοὺς
πολεμίους ἔβλαπτεν. Ἡρώδης δὲ τοὺς ἐκ Μασάδας οἰκείους παραλαβὼν ῥᾳδίως καὶ Ῥῆσαν[2] τὸ
φρούριον ᾔει πρὸς τὰ Ἱεροσόλυμα· συνῆπτε δ'
αὐτῷ τὸ μετὰ Σίλωνος στρατιωτικὸν καὶ πολλοὶ
τῶν ἐκ τῆς πόλεως τὴν ἰσχὺν καταπλαγέντες.
295 (5) Στρατοπεδευσαμένους δὲ κατὰ τὸ πρὸς δύσιν
κλίμα τοῦ ἄστεος οἱ ταύτῃ φύλακες ἐτόξευόν τε
καὶ ἐξηκόντιζον αὐτούς, ἄλλοι δὲ κατὰ στῖφος
ἐκθέοντες ἀπεπειρῶντο τῶν προτεταγμένων.
Ἡρώδης δὲ τὸ μὲν πρῶτον κηρύσσειν περὶ τὸ
τεῖχος ἐκέλευεν ὡς ἐπ' ἀγαθῷ τε παρείη τοῦ δήμου
καὶ ἐπὶ σωτηρίᾳ τῆς πόλεως, μηδὲν μηδὲ[3] τοὺς
φανεροὺς ἐχθροὺς ἀμυνούμενος, δώσων δὲ καὶ τοῖς
296 διαφορωτάτοις ἀμνηστίαν. ἐπεὶ δὲ ἀντιπαρηγο-
ροῦντες οἱ περὶ τὸν Ἀντίγονον οὔτε κατακούειν
τῶν κηρυγμάτων εἴων τινὰς οὔτε μεταβάλλεσθαι,
τὸ λοιπὸν ἀμύνεσθαι τοὺς ἀπὸ τοῦ τείχους ἐπέτρεπεν τοῖς σφετέροις· οἱ δὲ ταχέως ἅπαντας ἀπὸ
τῶν πύργων ἐτρέψαντο τοῖς βέλεσιν.
297 (6) Ἔνθα δὴ καὶ Σίλων ἀπεκαλύψατο τὴν δωρο-
δοκίαν· ἐπισκευασάμενος γὰρ πολλοὺς τῶν στρα-

---

[1] Naber: δυσκίνητος mss.; the same confusion occurs in
A. xviii. 23.

[2] Θρῆσαν MVC; cf. § 266.   [3] Bekker: μήτε mss.

138

(4) Then, after taking Joppa, he hastened to Masada to rescue his friends. The country-folk rallied to him, some drawn by old affection for his father, others by his own renown ; some in return for benefits conferred by both father and son, but the majority attracted by their expectations from one whose claim to the throne seemed assured ; so that by now he had assembled a formidable army. Antigonus sought to obstruct his advance by posting ambuscades in suitable passes, but caused little or no injury to the enemy. Herod without difficulty rescued his friends in Masada, recovered the fortress of Rhesa,[a] and then marched against Jerusalem ; where he was joined by Silo's troops and by many of the citizens, who were alarmed at the strength of his army.

He takes Joppa and relieves Masada.

(5) Having encamped on the west side of the town, his forces were assailed by showers of arrows and javelins from the guards posted at that quarter, while others sallying out in companies made attacks on his outposts. At the outset, Herod ordered heralds to patrol the walls and proclaim that he had come for the good of the people and the salvation of the city, that he had no intention of punishing even avowed enemies and would grant an amnesty to his bitterest foes. But when Antigonus issued counter-exhortations forbidding any to listen to these proclamations or to go over to the enemy, Herod at once gave his men permission to retaliate on their assailants on the ramparts, and with their missiles they soon drove them all out of the towers.

Herod before Jerusalem.

(6) And now Silo's conduct betrayed his corruption. For he induced a large number of his soldiers

---

[a] In Idumaea, § 266.

τιωτῶν σπάνιν ἐπιτηδείων ἀναβοᾶν καὶ χρήματα
εἰς τροφὰς ἀπαιτεῖν, ἀπάγειν τε σφᾶς χειμεριοῦντας
εἰς τοὺς ἐπιτηδείους[1] τόπους, ἐπειδὴ τὰ περὶ τὴν
πόλιν ἦν ἔρημα πάντα τῶν περὶ Ἀντίγονον προαν-
εσκευασμένων, ἐκίνει τε τὸ στρατόπεδον καὶ ἀνα-
298 χωρεῖν ἐπειρᾶτο. Ἡρώδης δ' ἐντυγχάνων τοῖς τε
ὑπὸ τὸν Σίλωνα ἡγεμόσιν καὶ κατὰ πλῆθος τοῖς
στρατιώταις ἐδεῖτο μὴ καταλιπεῖν αὐτὸν ὑπό τε
Καίσαρος καὶ Ἀντωνίου καὶ τῆς συγκλήτου προ-
πεμφθέντα· λύσειν γὰρ αὐθημερὸν αὐτῶν τὰς
299 ἀπορίας. καὶ μετὰ τὴν δέησιν εὐθέως[2] ὁρμήσας
αὐτὸς εἰς τὴν χώραν τοσαύτην αὐτοῖς ἐπιτηδείων
ἀφθονίαν ἐκόμισεν, ὡς πάσας ἀποκόψαι τὰς
Σίλωνος προφάσεις, εἴς τε τὰς ἑξῆς ἡμέρας μὴ
διαλιπεῖν τὴν χορηγίαν προνοούμενος ἐπέστελλεν
τοῖς περὶ Σαμάρειαν, ᾠκείωτο δ' ἡ πόλις αὐτῷ,
σῖτον καὶ οἶνον καὶ ἔλαιον καὶ βοσκήματα κατάγειν
300 εἰς Ἱεριχοῦντα. ταῦτ' ἀκούσας Ἀντίγονος διέπεμψεν περὶ τὴν χώραν εἴργειν καὶ λοχᾶν τοὺς
σιτηγοὺς κελεύων. οἱ δ' ὑπήκουον, καὶ πολὺ
πλῆθος ὁπλιτῶν ὑπὲρ τὴν Ἱεριχοῦντα συνηθροίσθη·
διεκαθέζοντο δὲ ἐπὶ τῶν ὀρῶν παραφυλάσσοντες
301 τοὺς τἀπιτήδεια ἐκκομίζοντας. οὐ μὴν Ἡρώδης
ἠρέμει, δέκα δὲ σπείρας ἀναλαβών, ὧν πέντε μὲν
Ῥωμαίων πέντε δ' Ἰουδαίων ἦσαν, ἔχουσαι καὶ
μισθοφόρους μιγάδας πρὸς οἷς ὀλίγους τῶν ἱππέων,
ἐπὶ τὴν Ἱεριχοῦντα παραγίνεται, καὶ τὴν μὲν
πόλιν καταλελειμμένην εὑρίσκει, πεντακοσίους δὲ
τὰ ἄκρα κατειληφότας σὺν γυναιξὶν καὶ γενεαῖς.
302 αὐτοὺς μὲν οὖν ἀπολύει λαβών, Ῥωμαῖοι δ'

---

[1] ἰδίους PA.

[2] εὐθέως om. PA Lat. Heg., but probably not a gloss from
A. ‖ (εὐθὺς); εὐθέως is the normal form of the adverb in B.

to raise an outcry about a lack of supplies and to
demand money for the purchase of provisions and to
be marched to suitable winter quarters, as the troops
of Antigonus had already completely cleared the
neighbourhood of the city and reduced it to a desert.
He, therefore, broke up his camp and attempted to
retire. Herod, however, interviewed[a] first the
officers of Silo's staff and then the assembled troops,
and besought them not to desert him, holding, as he
did, a commission from Caesar, Antony, and the
senate; "for," said he, "this very day I will relieve
your wants." After making this appeal he instantly
set off in person into the country and brought back
such an abundance of supplies as to cut away all Silo's
excuses; while, to ensure that there should be no
shortage in the immediate future, he instructed the
inhabitants of the district of Samaria, that city having
declared in his favour, to bring corn, wine, oil, and
cattle down to Jericho. Hearing of this, Antigonus
issued orders throughout the country to hold up and
waylay the convoys. Acting on these orders, large
bodies of men in arms assembled above Jericho and
took up positions on the hills, on the look-out for
the conveyors of the supplies. Herod, however, was
on the alert, and with ten cohorts, of which five were
Roman, and five Jewish with mercenaries intermixed,
and a small body of horse, proceeded to Jericho. He
found the city deserted and the heights[b] occupied
by five hundred persons with their wives and children.
These he made prisoners and then released; while

---

[a] Or " interceded with."

[b] τὰ ἄκρα here and in *A*.; not τὴν ἄκραν ("the citadel ")
which might have been expected.

εἰσπεσόντες τὸ λοιπὸν ἄστυ διήρπασαν πλήρεις
καταλαμβάνοντες τὰς οἰκίας παντοίων κειμηλίων.
Ἱεριχοῦντος μὲν οὖν φρουρὰν ὁ βασιλεὺς καταλιπὼν ὑπέστρεψεν, καὶ χειμεριοῦσαν τὴν Ῥωμαίων
στρατιὰν εἰς τὰς προσκεχωρηκυίας[1] διαφῆκεν
Ἰδουμαίαν καὶ Γαλιλαίαν καὶ Σαμάρειαν. ἐπέτυχεν δὲ καὶ Ἀντίγονος παρὰ τῆς Σίλωνος δωρο-
δοκίας ὑποδέξασθαι τοῦ στρατοῦ μοῖραν ἐν Λύδδοις
θεραπεύων Ἀντώνιον.

303 (xvi. 1) Καὶ Ῥωμαῖοι μὲν ἐν ἀφθόνοις διῆγον
ἀνειμένοι τῶν ὅπλων, Ἡρώδης δ' οὐκ ἠρέμει,
ἀλλὰ τὴν μὲν Ἰδουμαίαν δισχιλίοις πεζοῖς καὶ
τετρακοσίοις ἱππεῦσιν διαλαμβάνει πέμψας τὸν
ἀδελφὸν Ἰώσηπον, ὡς μή τι νεωτερισθείη πρὸς
Ἀντίγονον[2]· αὐτὸς δὲ τὴν μητέρα καὶ ὅσους ἐκ
Μασάδας οἰκείους ἐξήγαγεν μεταγαγὼν εἰς Σαμάρειαν καὶ καταστησάμενος ἀσφαλῶς ᾔει τὰ λοιπὰ
τῆς Γαλιλαίας καταστρεψόμενος καὶ τὰς Ἀντιγόνου φρουρὰς ἐξελάσων.

304 (2) Πρὸς δὲ τὴν Σέπφωριν ἐν νιφετῷ σφοδροτάτῳ διανύσας ἀκονιτὶ παραλαμβάνει τὴν πόλιν,
πρὸ τῆς ἐφόδου τῶν φυλάκων ἐκφυγόντων. ἔνθα
τοὺς ἑπομένους ὑπὸ τοῦ χειμῶνος κακωθέντας
ἀναλαβών, πολλὴ δ' ἦν ἀφθονία τῶν ἐπιτηδείων,
ἐπὶ τοὺς ἐν τοῖς σπηλαίοις ὥρμητο λῃστάς, οἳ
πολλὴν τῆς χώρας κατατρέχοντες οὐκ ἐλάττω κακὰ
305 πολέμου διετίθεσαν τοὺς ἐπιχωρίους. προπέμψας
δὲ πεζῶν τρία τέλη καὶ μίαν ἴλην ἱππέων πρὸς

───────

[1] C (adding πόλεις): προκεχ. the rest.
[2] Ἀντιγόνου VC " on the part of A." (perhaps rightly).

the Romans fell upon and rifled the rest of the town, where they found the houses full of treasures of every sort. Leaving a garrison in Jericho, the king returned and dismissed his Roman army to winter quarters in the districts which had joined his standard, Idumaea, Galilee, and Samaria. Antigonus, on his side, to ingratiate himself with Antony, induced Silo by a bribe to billet a division of his troops in Lydda.[a]

Winter of 39-38 B.C.

(xvi. 1) While the Romans were thus living on the fat of the land, at rest from arms, Herod, never idle, occupied Idumaea with two thousand foot and four hundred horse, which he sent thither under his brother Joseph, to prevent any insurrection in favour of Antigonus. His own care was the removal of his mother and other relations, whom he had rescued from Masada, to Samaria ; having safely installed them there, he set out to reduce the remaining strongholds of Galilee and to expel the garrisons of Antigonus.

Herod's winter campaign in Idumaea

and Galilee.

(2) He pushed on to Sepphoris through a very heavy snowstorm and took possession of the city without a contest, the garrison having fled before his assault. Here, provisions being abundant, he refreshed his troops, sorely tried by the tempest, and then started on a campaign against the cave-dwelling brigands, who were infesting a wide area and inflicting on the inhabitants evils no less than those of war. Having sent in advance three battalions of infantry and a squadron of cavalry to the village

He defeats the brigands at Arbela

---

[a] On the west frontier of Judaea ; an action in the enemy's favour apparently intended to weaken the allegiance of the Roman troops.

Ἄρβηλα κώμην, αὐτὸς μετὰ τεσσαράκοντα ἡμέρας
ἐπῆλθεν μετὰ τῆς λοιπῆς δυνάμεως. οὐ μὴν πρὸς
τὴν ἔφοδον ἔδεισαν οἱ πολέμιοι, μετὰ δὲ τῶν
ὅπλων ἀπήντων, ἐμπειρίαν μὲν πολεμικὴν ἔχοντες,
306 τὸ δὲ θράσος ληστρικόν. συμβαλόντες γοῦν τῷ
σφετέρῳ δεξιῷ τὸ εὐώνυμον κέρας τῶν Ἡρώδου
τρέπονται. περιελθὼν δὲ ταχέως Ἡρώδης ἐκ τοῦ
καθ' ἑαυτὸν δεξιοῦ προσεβοήθει, καὶ τὸ μὲν οἰκεῖον
ἐπέστρεφεν ἐκ τῆς φυγῆς, τοῖς δὲ διώκουσιν
ἐμπίπτων ἀνέκοπτεν τὴν ὁρμήν, μέχρι τὰς κατὰ
στόμα προσβολὰς μὴ φέροντες ἐξέκλιναν.

307 (3) Ὁ δὲ ἕως Ἰορδάνου κτείνων εἵπετο καὶ
πολὺ μὲν αὐτῶν μέρος διέφθειρεν, οἱ λοιποὶ δ'
ὑπὲρ τὸν ποταμὸν ἐσκεδάσθησαν, ὥστε τὴν Γαλιλαίαν ἐκκεκαθάρθαι φόβων, πλὴν καθόσον οἱ τοῖς
σπηλαίοις ἐμφωλεύοντες ὑπελείποντο· κἀπὶ τούτοις
308 ἔδει διατριβῆς. διὸ δὴ πρῶτον τοῖς στρατιώταις
τὰς ἐκ τῶν πεπονημένων ἐπικαρπίας ἀπεδίδου,
διανέμων ἑκάστῳ δραχμὰς ἑκατὸν πεντήκοντα
ἀργυρίου καὶ τοῖς ἡγεμόσιν πολυπλασίονα, ⟨καὶ⟩[1]
διέπεμψεν εἰς οὓς ἐχειμέριζον σταθμούς. Φερώρα
δὲ τῷ νεωτάτῳ τῶν ἀδελφῶν ἐπέστελλεν τῆς τε
ἀγορᾶς αὐτοῖς ποιεῖσθαι πρόνοιαν καὶ τειχίζειν
Ἀλεξάνδρειον. κἀκεῖνος ἀμφοτέρων ἐπεμελήθη.

309 (4) Ἐν δὲ τούτῳ περὶ μὲν Ἀθήνας διῆγεν
Ἀντώνιος, Βεντίδιος δ' ἐπὶ τὸν πρὸς Πάρθους
πόλεμον Σίλωνά τε καὶ Ἡρώδην μετεπέμπετο,
καταστήσασθαι πρότερον ἐπιστέλλων τὰ περὶ
Ἰουδαίαν. Ἡρώδης δ' ἀσμένως Σίλωνα πρὸς

---

[1] I have inserted the conjunction which seems necessary.
Without it the sense would be " and sent much larger sums
to the officers in their various winter quarters."

of Arbela,[a] he joined them forty days later with the rest of his army. Nothing daunted by his approach, the enemy, who combined the experience of seasoned warriors with the daring of brigands, went armed to meet him, and, coming into action, routed Herod's left wing with their right. Herod instantly wheeling round his troops from the right wing, where he was in command, came to the relief, and not only checked the flight of his own men, but falling upon their pursuers broke their charge, until, overpowered by his frontal attacks, they in turn gave way.

(3) Herod pursued them, with slaughter, to the Jordan and destroyed large numbers of them; the rest fled across the river and dispersed. Thus was Galilee purged of its terrors, save for the remnant still lurking in the caves, and their extirpation required time. So, before proceeding further, Herod awarded to his soldiers the fruits of their labours, distributing to each man a hundred and fifty drachmas of silver and to their officers much larger sums, and then dismissed them to their various winter quarters. He instructed Pheroras, his youngest brother, to take charge of the commissariat department[b] and to fortify Alexandrion; both tasks received his brother's attention.

(4) At this time Antony was residing in the neighbourhood of Athens, and Silo and Herod were summoned by Ventidius for the war with Parthia, being instructed first to settle affairs in Judaea. Herod gladly dismissed Silo to Ventidius, and set out him-

and exterminates the cavedwellers.

[a] *Irbid*, near the Lake of Gennesaret, N.W. of Tiberias.

[b] In *A.* xiv. 418 it is not Herod's troops which Pheroras is instructed to provision, but Silo and the Romans, whose supplies Antigonus at the end of a month had cut short (see § 302).

Βεντίδιον ἀπολύσας αὐτὸς ἐπὶ τοὺς ἐν τοῖς σπη-
310 λαίοις ἐστράτευσεν. τὰ δὲ σπήλαια ταῦτα πρὸς
ἀποκρήμνοις ὄρεσιν ἦν οὐδαμόθεν προσιτά, πλαγίας
δὲ ἀνόδους μόνον ἔχοντα στενοτάτας. ἡ δὲ κατὰ
μέτωπον αὐτῶν πέτρα κατέτεινεν εἰς βαθυτάτας
φάραγγας ὄρθιος ἐπιρρέπουσα ταῖς χαράδραις,
ὥστε τὸν βασιλέα μέχρι πολλοῦ μὲν ἀπορεῖν πρὸς
τὸ ἀμήχανον τοῦ τόπου, τελευταῖον δ᾽ ἐπινοίᾳ
311 χρήσασθαι σφαλερωτάτῃ. τοὺς γοῦν ἀλκίμους
καθιμῶν ἐν λάρναξιν ἐνίει τοῖς στομίοις, οἱ δὲ
ἀπέσφαττόν τε αὐτοὺς σὺν γενεαῖς καὶ πῦρ ἐνίεσαν
τοῖς ἀμυνομένοις. βουληθεὶς δ᾽ ἐξ αὐτῶν καὶ
περισῶσαί τινας Ἡρώδης ἐκήρυξεν ἀναχωρεῖν[1]
πρὸς αὐτόν. τῶν δὲ ἐθελουσίως μὲν οὐδεὶς προσέθετο, καὶ τῶν βιαζομένων δὲ πολλοὶ τῆς αἰχμα-
312 λωσίας προείλοντο θάνατον. ἔνθα καὶ τῶν γηραιῶν
τις, ἑπτὰ παίδων πατήρ, μετὰ τῆς μητρὸς δεο-
μένους τοὺς παῖδας ἐπιτρέψαι σφίσιν ἐξελθεῖν ἐπὶ
δεξιᾷ κτείνει τρόπῳ τοιῷδε· καθ᾽ ἕνα προϊέναι
κελεύσας αὐτὸς ἵστατο ἐπὶ τὸ στόμιον[2] καὶ τὸν
ἀεὶ προϊόντα τῶν υἱῶν ἀπέσφαττεν. ἐξ ἀπόπτου
δὲ Ἡρώδης ἐπιβλέπων τῷ τε πάθει συνεχεῖτο[3] καὶ
τῷ πρεσβύτῃ δεξιὰν ὤρεγεν φείσασθαι τῶν τέκνων
313 παρακαλῶν. ὁ δὲ πρὸς οὐδὲν ἐνδοὺς τῶν λεγομένων, ἀλλὰ καὶ προσονειδίσας τὸν Ἡρώδην εἰς
ταπεινότητα, ἐπὶ τοῖς παισὶν ἀναιρεῖ καὶ τὴν
γυναῖκα, καὶ καταβαλὼν κατὰ τοῦ κρημνοῦ τοὺς
νεκροὺς τελευταῖον ἑαυτὸν ἔρριψεν.

---

[1] PA : ἀποχωρεῖν the rest.
[2] τοῦ στομίου Niese from the parallel passage in *A*.
[3] So most mss., *cf. B.* vii. 200 : συνείχετο Niese with C.

---

[a] Or " chests."

self on a campaign against the bandits in the caves. These caves, opening on to mountain precipices, were inaccessible from any quarter, except by some tortuous and extremely narrow paths leading up to them ; the cliff in front of them dropped sheer down into ravines far below, with water-courses at the bottom. The king was, consequently, for long baffled by the impracticable nature of the ground, but at length had recourse to a most hazardous scheme. By means of ropes he lowered the most stalwart of his men in cradles[a] and so gave them access to the cavern-mouths ; these then massacred the brigands and their families, hurling in fire-brands upon those who resisted. Anxious to save some of them, Herod, by word of herald, summoned them to his presence. Not one of them voluntarily surrendered,[b] and of those taken by force many preferred death to captivity. It was then that one old man, the father of seven children, being asked by them and their mother permission to leave under Herod's pledge, killed them in the following manner. Ordering them to come forward one by one, he stood at the entrance and slew each son as he advanced. Herod, watching this spectacle from a conspicuous[c] spot, was profoundly affected and, extending his hand to the old man, implored him to spare his children ; but he, unmoved by any word of Herod, and even upbraiding him as a low-born upstart,[d] followed up the slaughter of his sons by that of his wife, and, having flung their corpses down the precipice, finally threw himself over after them.

[b] *Ant.* 427, on the contrary, mentions many cases of surrender. [c] Or " commanding."
[d] *Cf.* § 478 ; perhaps " for his abject spirit."

314 (5) Χειροῦται μὲν οὕτως τὰ σπήλαια καὶ τοὺς
ἐν αὐτοῖς Ἡρώδης· καταλιπὼν δὲ τοῦ στρατοῦ
μοῖραν ὅσην ἀποχρήσειν ὑπελάμβανεν πρὸς τὰς
ἐπαναστάσεις καὶ Θολεμαῖον[1] ἐπ᾽ αὐτῆς ἐπὶ Σαμαρείας ὑπέστρεφεν, ὁπλίτας μὲν τρισχιλίους ἱππεῖς
315 δὲ ἄγων ἑξακοσίους ἐπ᾽ Ἀντίγονον. ἔνθα πρὸς
τὴν ἀποχώρησιν αὐτοῦ λαβόντες ἄδειαν οἷς ἔθος
ἦν θορυβεῖν τὴν Γαλιλαίαν κτείνουσιν μὲν Θολεμαῖον[1] τὸν στρατηγὸν ἀδοκήτως προσπεσόντες,
ἐπόρθουν δὲ τὴν χώραν ποιούμενοι τὰς ἀναφυγὰς
εἰς τὰ ἕλη καὶ τὰ δυσερεύνητα τῶν χωρίων.
316 πυθόμενος δὲ Ἡρώδης τὴν ἐπανάστασιν διὰ τάχους
ἐπεβοήθει καὶ πολὺ μὲν αὐτῶν πλῆθος διαφθείρει,
τὰ φρούρια δὲ πάντα πολιορκίαις ἐξελὼν ἐπιτίμιον
τῆς μεταβολῆς εἰσεπράξατο παρὰ τῶν πόλεων[2]
ἑκατὸν τάλαντα.

317 (6) Ἤδη δὲ Πάρθων μὲν ἐξεληλαμένων, ἀνῃρη-
μένου δὲ Πακόρου, Βεντίδιος ἐπιστείλαντος Ἀντωνίου πέμπει συμμάχους Ἡρώδῃ κατ᾽ Ἀντιγόνου χιλίους ἱππεῖς καὶ δύο τάγματα. τούτων δὲ
τὸν στρατηγὸν Μαχαιρᾶν Ἀντίγονος ἱκέτευσεν δι᾽
ἐπιστολῶν ἑαυτῷ βοηθὸν ἀφικέσθαι, πολλά τε
περὶ[3] τῆς Ἡρώδου βίας [καὶ ἐπηρείας τῆς βασι-
λείας][4] ἀποδυρόμενος καὶ χρήματα δώσειν ὑπισχ-
318 νούμενος. ὁ δέ, οὐ γὰρ κατεφρόνει τοῦ πέμψαντος
ἄλλως τε καὶ πλείον[5] Ἡρώδου διδόντος, εἰς μὲν
τὴν προδοσίαν οὐχ ὑπήκουσεν, ὑποκρινόμενος δὲ
φιλίαν κατάσκοπος ᾔει τῶν Ἀντιγόνου πραγμάτων,

[1] PA: Πτολεμαῖον the rest (as in A.‖).
[2] πολεμίων LVRC. [3] +τε MSS.
[4] The bracketed words only in MVC; omitted, probably
hrough homoioteleuton, by the rest.
[5] P: πλέον the rest.

(5) Herod having thus mastered the caves and their inhabitants, leaving behind him under the command of Ptolemy a contingent sufficient, in his opinion, to repress insurrection, returned towards Samaria, bringing to meet Antigonus a force of three thousand heavy infantry and six hundred cavalry. Thereupon, emboldened by his departure, the usual promoters of disturbance in Galilee made a surprise attack on his general Ptolemy and slew him, and proceeded to ravage the country, finding refuge in the marshes and other places difficult to search. Apprised of the revolt, Herod returned in haste to the relief, killed a large number of the rebels, besieged and destroyed all their fortresses, and imposed on the towns, as the penalty for their defection, a fine of a hundred talents.

(6) The Parthians having now at last been expelled and Pacorus slain, Ventidius, under instructions from Antony, dispatched a thousand horse with two legions to support Herod in opposing Antigonus, the officer in command being Machaeras. To this general Antigonus wrote, imploring him instead to come to his own assistance, complaining bitterly of Herod's high-handed and abusive treatment of the realm,[a] and adding a promise of money. Machaeras, not being prepared for such contempt of his superior's orders, especially as Herod was offering him a larger sum, declined the temptation to treason, but, feigning amity, went off to spy out the position of Antigonus,

---

[a] Or perhaps " the throne."

149

319 Ἡρώδῃ μὴ πεισθεὶς ἀποτρέποντι. προαισθόμενος δ' αὐτοῦ τὴν διάνοιαν Ἀντίγονος τήν τε πόλιν ἀπέκλεισεν καὶ ἀπὸ τῶν τειχῶν ὡς πολέμιον ἠμύνατο, μέχρις αἰδούμενος Μαχαιρᾶς εἰς Ἀμμαοῦντα πρὸς Ἡρώδην ἀναχωρεῖ καὶ πρὸς τὴν διαμαρτίαν θυμούμενος ὅσοις ἐπετύγχανεν Ἰουδαίοις ἀνῄρει, μηδεμίαν τῶν Ἡρωδείων φειδὼ ποιούμενος, ἀλλ' ὡς Ἀντιγονείοις χρώμενος ἅπασιν.

320 (7) Ἐφ' οἷς χαλεπήνας Ἡρώδης ὥρμησεν μὲν ἀμύνασθαι Μαχαιρᾶν ὡς πολέμιον, κρατήσας δὲ τῆς ὀργῆς ἤλαυνεν πρὸς Ἀντώνιον κατηγορήσων τῆς Μαχαιρᾶ παρανομίας. ὁ δ' ἐν διαλογισμῷ τῶν ἡμαρτημένων γενόμενος ταχέως μεταδιώκει τε τὸν βασιλέα καὶ πολλὰ δεηθεὶς ἑαυτῷ διαλλάττει.

321 οὐ μὴν Ἡρώδης ἐπαύσατο τῆς πρὸς Ἀντώνιον ὁρμῆς· ἀκηκοὼς δ' αὐτὸν μετὰ πολλῆς δυνάμεως προσπολεμοῦντα Σαμοσάτοις, πόλις δ' ἐστὶν Εὐφράτου πλησίον καρτερά, θᾶττον ἠπείγετο τὸν καιρὸν ἐπιτήδειον ὁρῶν πρός τε ἐπίδειξιν ἀνδρείας

322 καὶ τοῦ μᾶλλον ἀρέσασθαι τὸν Ἀντώνιον. γίνεται γοῦν ἐπελθὼν τέλος αὐτοῖς τῆς πολιορκίας, πολλοὺς μὲν τῶν βαρβάρων ἀποκτείνας, πολλὴν δὲ ἀποτεμόμενος λείαν, ὥστε τὸν μὲν Ἀντώνιον θαυμάζοντα καὶ πάλαι τῆς ἀρετῆς αὐτὸν τότε μᾶλλον οὕτως ἔχειν καὶ προσθεῖναι πολὺ ταῖς τε ἄλλαις τιμαῖς αὐτοῦ καὶ ταῖς εἰς τὴν βασιλείαν ἐλπίσιν, Ἀντίοχον δὲ τὸν βασιλέα ἀναγκασθῆναι παραδοῦναι τὰ Σαμόσατα.

323 (xvii. 1) Κἀν τούτῳ θραύεται τὰ κατὰ τὴν Ἰουδαίαν Ἡρώδου πράγματα. κατελελοίπει μὲν γὰρ Ἰώσηπον τὸν ἀδελφὸν ἐπὶ τῶν ὅλων παραγγείλας μηδὲν μέχρι τῆς ὑποστροφῆς αὐτοῦ παρα-

without listening to Herod, who tried to dissuade him. Antigonus, divining his intention, refused him admittance to the city, and repulsed him from the walls as an enemy ; until at length Machaeras, for very shame, was forced to retire to Emmaus and rejoin Herod. Infuriated by his discomfiture, he killed all the Jews whom he met on his march, not even sparing the Herodians, but treating all alike as friends of Antigonus.

(7) At this Herod, in indignation, hastened to attack Machaeras as an enemy, but, restraining his anger, set out instead to lay before Antony an accusation of his enormities. Machaeras, reflecting on his errors, pursued after the king and by dint of entreaties succeeded in pacifying him. Herod, notwithstanding, continued his march to join Antony ; the receipt of intelligence that the latter with a large army was assaulting Samosata, a strong city near the Euphrates, quickened his pace, as he saw in this a favourable opportunity for displaying his courage and strengthening his hold upon Antony's affection. His arrival, in fact, brought the siege to a conclusion. He killed numbers of the barbarians and secured booty in abundance, with the result that Antony, who had long admired his valour, now held it in even higher respect, and largely increased both his honours and his high expectations of sovereignty ; while King Antiochus was compelled to surrender Samosata. *Herod assists Antony in the siege of Samosata.*

(xvii. 1) Meanwhile Herod's cause had suffered a grave reverse in Judaea. He had left his brother Joseph in charge of the realm, with injunctions to take no action against Antigonus until his return, *Defeat and death of Herod's brother Joseph.*

κινεῖν πρὸς Ἀντίγονον· οὐ γὰρ δὴ βέβαιον εἶναι
Μαχαιρᾶν σύμμαχον ἐξ ὧν ἔδρασεν. ὁ δὲ ὡς
ἤκουσεν ὄντα πορρωτάτω τὸν ἀδελφόν, ἀμελήσας
τῶν παραγγελμάτων ἐπὶ Ἱεριχοῦντος ἐχώρει μετὰ
πέντε σπειρῶν, ἃς συνέπεμψεν Μαχαιρᾶς· ᾔει δὲ
324 τὸν σῖτον ἁρπάσων ἐν ἀκμῇ τοῦ θέρους. ἐπι-
θεμένων δὲ ἐν τοῖς ὄρεσιν καὶ ταῖς δυσχωρίαις
τῶν ἐναντίων αὐτός τε θνήσκει, μάλα γενναῖος ἐν τῇ
μάχῃ φανείς, καὶ τὸ Ῥωμαϊκὸν πᾶν διαφθείρεται·
νεοσύλλεκτοι γὰρ ἦσαν ἐκ τῆς Συρίας αἱ σπεῖραι,
καὶ οὐδὲν αὐταῖς ἐνεκέκρατο τῶν πάλαι στρατιωτῶν καλουμένων, ἐπαμύνειν τοῖς ἀπείροις
πολέμου δυναμένων.

325 (2) Ἀντιγόνῳ δὲ οὐκ ἀπέχρησεν ἡ νίκη, προῆλθεν δὲ εἰς τοσοῦτον ὀργῆς, ὥστε καὶ νεκρὸν αἰκίσασθαι τὸν Ἰώσηπον· κρατήσας γοῦν τῶν σωμάτων
ἀποτέμνει τὴν κεφαλὴν αὐτοῦ, καίτοι πεντήκοντα
τάλαντα λύτρον αὐτῆς Φερώρα τἀδελφοῦ διδόντος.
326 τὰ δὲ τῆς Γαλιλαίας μετὰ τὴν Ἀντιγόνου νίκην
ἐνεωτερίσθη πρὸς τοσοῦτον, ὥστε τοὺς τὰ Ἡρώδου
φρονοῦντας τῶν δυνατῶν προαγαγόντες[1] εἰς τὴν
λίμνην κατέδυσαν οἱ προσέχοντες Ἀντιγόνῳ.
μετεβάλλετο δὲ πολλὰ καὶ τῆς Ἰδουμαίας, ἔνθα
Μαχαιρᾶς ἀνετείχιζέν τι τῶν ἐρυμάτων· Γιτθὰ
327 καλεῖται. τούτων δὲ οὐδὲν οὔπω[2] πέπυστο Ἡρώ-
δης· μετὰ γὰρ τὴν Σαμοσάτων ἅλωσιν Ἀντώνιος
μὲν καταστήσας ἐπὶ τῆς Συρίας Σόσσιον καὶ
προστάξας Ἡρώδῃ βοηθεῖν ἐπ᾽ Ἀντίγονον αὐτὸς
εἰς Αἴγυπτον ἀνεχώρησεν, Σόσσιος δὲ δύο μὲν

---

[1] Niese, with Lat.: προσαγαγόντες or προσάγοντες MSS.
[2] οὐδὲν οὔπω M: οὐδέπω LVR: οὔπω PA: οὐδέν πω Bekker.

[a] Of Gennesaret.

because the previous conduct of Machaeras proved him to be an untrustworthy ally. No sooner, however, did Joseph hear that his brother was at a safe distance, than, disregarding instructions, he marched towards Jericho with five cohorts sent to him by Machaeras, with the object of carrying off the corn-crop in its midsummer prime. On the way he was attacked by his adversaries on difficult ground in the hills ; after displaying great gallantry in the battle he fell, and the whole Roman force was cut to pieces. For the cohorts had been recently levied in Syria and had no leavening of the so-called " veterans " to support these raw recruits.

Summer of 38 B.C.

(2) Not content with his victory, Antigonus was so far carried away by rage as actually to do outrage to Joseph's corpse. Being in possession of the bodies of the slain, he had his head cut off, notwithstanding the ransom of fifty talents with which Pheroras, the brother of the deceased, offered to redeem it. In Galilee this victory of Antigonus led to so serious a revolution that his partisans dragged out of their houses the men of rank who were in favour of Herod and drowned them in the lake.[a] There was defection also in many parts of Idumaea,[b] where Machaeras was rebuilding the walls of a fortress called Gittha. Of all this Herod as yet knew nothing. For after the capture of Samosata Antony had appointed Sossius governor of Syria, with orders to support Herod in opposing Antigonus, and had then taken his departure for Egypt.[c] Sossius, thereupon, sent on

Further revolt in Galilee and Idumaea.

[b] A. has Judaea ; the position of the fort is uncertain. Smith and Bartholomew (*Hist. Atlas of Holy Land*, map 44) place it S.W. of Hebron.

[c] This, as Reinach points out, is an error. Antony passed the winter of 38–37 B.C. at Athens (Plut. *Ant.* 34).

τάγματα προαπέστειλεν εἰς Ἰουδαίαν Ἡρώδῃ
συμμαχῶν, αὐτὸς δὲ μετὰ τῆς λοιπῆς δυνάμεως
ἠκολούθει σχεδόν.

328 (3) Ὄντι δ' Ἡρώδῃ κατὰ τὴν πρὸς Ἀντιοχείᾳ[1]
Δάφνην ὄνειροι σαφεῖς τὸν τἀδελφοῦ θάνατον
προσημαίνουσιν, καὶ μετὰ ταραχῆς ἐκθορόντι τῆς
κοίτης εἰσῄεσαν ἄγγελοι τῆς συμφορᾶς. ὁ δὲ
ὀλίγον μὲν προσοιμώξας τῷ πάθει, τὸ πλεῖον δὲ
τοῦ πένθους ὑπερθέμενος, ἐπὶ τοὺς ἐχθροὺς ἠπεί-
329 γετο, ποιούμενος[2] τὴν πορείαν ὑπὲρ δύναμιν. καὶ
διανύσας ἐπὶ τὸν Λίβανον ὀκτακοσίους μὲν τῶν
περὶ τὸ ὄρος προσλαμβάνει συμμάχους, Ῥωμαίων
δὲ ἐν τάγμα ταύτῃ συνῆψεν. μεθ' ὧν οὐ περιμείνας
ἡμέραν εἰς τὴν Γαλιλαίαν ἐνέβαλεν, τούς τε πολεμίους ὑπαντιάσαντας εἰς ὃ καταλελοίπεσαν χωρίον
330 τρέπεται, καὶ προσέβαλλεν μὲν συνεχῶς τῷ φρουρίῳ, πρὶν δὲ ἑλεῖν χειμῶνι βιασθεὶς χαλεπωτάτῳ
ταῖς πλησίον ἐνστρατοπεδεύεται κώμαις. ἐπεὶ δ'
αὐτῷ μετ' ὀλίγας ἡμέρας καὶ τὸ δεύτερον παρὰ
Ἀντωνίου[3] τάγμα συνέμιξεν, δείσαντες τὴν ἰσχὺν
οἱ πολέμιοι διὰ νυκτὸς ἐξέλιπον τὸ ἔρυμα.

331 (4) Καὶ τὸ λοιπὸν διὰ Ἱεριχοῦντος ᾔει σπεύδων
ᾗ τάχιστα τοὺς τἀδελφοῦ φονεῖς μετελθεῖν· ἔνθα[4]
καὶ δαιμόνιόν τι αὐτῷ συμβαίνει τέρας, ἐξ οὗ παρ'
ἐλπίδα σωθεὶς ἀνδρὸς θεοφιλεστάτου δόξαν ἀπηνέγ-
κατο. πολλοὶ μὲν γὰρ αὐτῷ τῶν ἐν τέλει συν-
εἱστιάθησαν κατ' ἐκείνην τὴν ἑσπέραν, διαλυθέντος
δὲ τοῦ συμποσίου μετὰ τὸ πάντας ἐξελθεῖν ὁ οἶκος

---

[1] Destinon : Ἀντιόχειαν mss.
[2] +δὲ LVRC.
[3] M : Ἀντωνίῳ the rest.
[4] +δὴ LVRC.

two legions into Judaea to assist Herod, and followed himself close behind with the rest of his troops.

(3) But while Herod was at Daphne, near Antioch, he had a dream distinctly warning him of his brother's death, and springing in horror from his bed was met by the messengers bringing news of the catastrophe. After brief lamentation for his loss, he deferred further mourning for another season and set out in haste to meet his foes. By forced marches he pushed on to Lebanon, where he received a reinforcement of eight hundred of the mountaineers and was joined by one of the Roman legions. With these allies, without waiting for daylight,[a] he invaded Galilee ; he was met by the enemy, but drove them back to the position which they had just left. He made repeated attacks upon their fortress, but before he could capture it was compelled by a terrific storm to encamp in the neighbouring villages. A few days later he was joined by the second of Antony's legions,[b] whereupon the enemy, alarmed at his strength, under cover of night evacuated their stronghold.

(4) His subsequent march, accelerated by the desire for speedy vengeance on his brother's murderers, took him through Jericho. Here he had a providential and miraculous escape, the surprising nature of which won him the reputation of a special favourite of heaven. A large company of magistrates had dined with him that evening, and no sooner had the banquet ended and all the guests departed, than the

Herod returns to Palestine.

His miraculous escape at Jericho.

---

[a] The Greek might mean " without a day's delay " ; but the rendering above seems fixed by the parallel in *A.* xiv. 452 (νυκτὸς ἀναστάς); περιμένειν in Josephus usually means " to wait *for*." But the narrative is here abbreviated ; in *A.* the night march starts not from Lebanon, but from Ptolemais.

[b] § 327.

332 εὐθέως συνέπεσεν. τοῦτο καὶ κινδύνων καὶ σωτηρίας κοινὸν ἐπὶ τῷ μέλλοντι πολέμῳ κρίνας εἶναι σημεῖον ὑπὸ τὴν ἔω διεκίνει τὴν στρατιάν. καὶ τῶν ἐναντίων εἰς ἑξακισχιλίους ἀπὸ τῶν ὀρῶν κατατρέχοντες ἀπεπειρῶντο τῶν προτεταγμένων, κατὰ χεῖρα μὲν συμπλέκεσθαι τοῖς Ῥωμαίοις οὐ σφόδρα θαρροῦντες, πόρρωθεν δὲ χερμάσιν καὶ παλτοῖς[1] ἔβαλλον, ὥστε συχνοὺς κατατιτρώσκειν. ἐν ᾧ καὶ αὐτὸς Ἡρώδης παρελαύνων παλτῷ[2] κατὰ τὴν πλευρὰν ἀκοντίζεται.

333 (5) Βουλόμενος δὲ Ἀντίγονος μὴ μόνον τόλμῃ τῶν σφετέρων ἀλλὰ καὶ πλήθει περιεῖναι δοκεῖν, Πάππον τινὰ τῶν ἑταίρων μετὰ στρατιᾶς ἐπὶ 334 Σαμάρειαν περιπέμπει.[3] τούτῳ[4] μὲν οὖν ἦν Μαχαιρᾶς ἀγώνισμα, Ἡρώδης δὲ τὴν πολεμίαν καταδραμὼν πέντε μὲν πολίχνας καταστρέφεται, δισχιλίους δὲ τῶν ἐν αὐταῖς διαφθείρει, καὶ τὰς οἰκίας ἐμπρήσας ὑπέστρεψεν ἐπὶ τὸ στρατόπεδον· ηὐλίστο δὲ περὶ τὴν καλουμένην Κανᾶ κώμην.

335 (6) Προσεγίνετο δ᾽ αὐτῷ καθ᾽ ἡμέραν πολὺ πλῆθος Ἰουδαίων ἔκ τε τῆς[5] Ἱεριχοῦντος κἀκ τῆς ἄλλης χώρας, οἱ μὲν διὰ μῖσος τὸ πρὸς Ἀντίγονον, οἱ δ᾽ ἐπὶ τοῖς αὐτοῦ κατορθώμασιν κεκινημένοι· τούς γε μὴν πολλοὺς ἐνῆγεν ἐπιθυμία μεταβολῆς ἄλογος. καὶ ὁ μὲν ἠπείγετο συμβαλεῖν, οἱ δὲ περὶ Πάππον οὔτε πρὸς τὸ πλῆθος οὔτε πρὸς τὴν ὁρμὴν ὑποδείσαντες αὐτοῦ προθύμως ἀντεπεξῆλθον. 336 γενομένης δὲ τῆς παρατάξεως τὰ μὲν ἄλλα μέρη πρὸς ὀλίγον ἀντέσχεν, Ἡρώδης δὲ κατὰ μνήμην[6]

---

[1] Hudson : πελτοῖς MSS.   [2] πελτῷ MSS.
[3] PA : ἐπιπέμπει the rest.   [4] Destinon : τούτων MSS.
[5] Niese : αὐτῆς MSS.   [6] μῆνιν LVRC.

156

building collapsed. Seeing in this an omen alike of perils and of preservation during the coming campaign, he at daybreak put his troops in motion. Some six thousand of the enemy rushed down from the hills and assailed his 'vanguard ; they had not the courage to come to close quarters with the Romans, but pelted them from a distance with stones and darts, wounding many of them. On this occasion Herod himself, while riding along the lines, was struck by a javelin in the side.

(5) Antigonus, wishing to create an impression of the superiority of his men, not only in enterprise but in numbers, dispatched an army to Samaria under one of his comrades named Pappus, whose commission was to oppose Machaeras. Herod, meanwhile, ravaged the enemy's territory, subdued five small towns, slew two thousand of their inhabitants, set fire to the houses, and returned to his camp. His present headquarters were in the neighbourhood of a village called Cana.[a]

(6) Multitudes of Jews now joined him daily from He defeats Jericho and elsewhere, some drawn by hatred of Pappus, general of Antigonus, others by his own successes, the majority Antigonus. by a blind love of change. Herod was burning for a fight, and Pappus, undeterred either by the number or the ardour of his adversaries, advanced with alacrity to meet them. On coming into action the enemy made a brief stand in other parts of the line ; but Herod, with his memories of his murdered

---

[a] We should doubtless read, as in the parallel account, *A.* xiv. 458, Isana, a place due north of Jerusalem near the frontier of Judaea and Samaria.

157

τοῦ φονευθέντος ἀδελφοῦ παραβαλλόμενος, ὡς ἂν
τίσαιτο τοὺς αἰτίους τοῦ φόνου, ταχέως τῶν καθ᾽
ἑαυτὸν ἐκράτει καὶ μετ᾽ ἐκείνους ἐπὶ τὸ συνεστὸς
337 αἰεὶ[1] τρεπόμενος ἅπαντας διώκει. φόνος δ᾽ ἦν
πολύς, τῶν μὲν εἰς τὴν κώμην συνεξωθουμένων ἐξ
ἧς ὥρμηντο, τοῦ δὲ προσκειμένου τοῖς ὑστάτοις
καὶ κτείνοντος ἀπείρους. συνεισπίπτει δὲ τοῖς
πολεμίοις εἴσω, καὶ πᾶσα μὲν ὁπλιτῶν οἰκία
νένακτο, τὰ τέγη δ᾽ ἦν ὕπερθεν ἀμυνομένων κατά-
338 πλεα. κἀπειδὴ περιῆν τῶν ἔξωθεν, τὰς οἰκήσεις
σπαράττων εἷλκεν τοὺς ἔνδοθεν. καὶ τοῖς μὲν
πολλοῖς ἐπικατασείων τοὺς ὀρόφους ἀθρόους[2]
ἀνῄρει, τοὺς ὑποφεύγοντας δὲ τῶν ἐρειπίων οἱ
στρατιῶται ξιφήρεις ἀνεδέχοντο, καὶ τοσοῦτον
ἐσωρεύθη νεκρῶν πλῆθος, ὥστε τὰς ὁδοὺς ἀπο-
339 φραγῆναι τοῖς κρατοῦσιν. ταύτην τὴν πληγὴν οὐκ
ἤνεγκαν οἱ πολέμιοι· τὸ γοῦν ἐπισυλλεγόμενον
αὐτῶν πλῆθος ὡς ἐθεάσατο τοὺς ἀνὰ τὴν κώμην
διεφθαρμένους, εἰς φυγὴν διεσκεδάσθη, κἂν εὐθέως
τῇ νίκῃ τεθαρρηκὼς Ἡρώδης ἐπὶ Ἱεροσολύμων
ἤλασεν, εἰ μὴ χειμῶνι διεκωλύθη σφοδροτάτῳ.
τοῦτ᾽ ἐμπόδιον ἐκείνῳ τε παντελοῦς κατορθώματος
καὶ ἥττης Ἀντιγόνῳ κατέστη, βουλευομένῳ καταλιπεῖν ἤδη τὴν πόλιν.

340 (7) Ἡρώδης δὲ πρὸς ἑσπέραν [ἤδη][3] τοὺς
φίλους κεκμηκότας ἐπὶ θεραπείᾳ τοῦ σώματος
διαφεὶς καὶ αὐτὸς ὡς ἦν ἔτι θερμὸς ἐκ τῶν ὅπλων
λουσόμενος ᾔει στρατιωτικώτερον· εἷς γοῦν αὐτῷ
παῖς εἵπετο. καὶ πρὶν εἰς τὸ βαλανεῖον εἰσελθεῖν,
ἐναντίον αὐτοῦ τις ἐκτρέχει τῶν πολεμίων ξιφήρης,

---

[1] αἰεὶ P.   [2] PM: ἀθρόως the rest.
[3] om. PAM Lat.

brother, hazarding all to be avenged on his murderers, quickly overcame the troops in front of him, and then, successively directing his attacks upon any that still held together, routed the whole body. A scene of carnage ensued, the enemy driven pell-mell back into the village from which they had issued, Herod pressing upon their rear and massacring untold numbers. Rushing with his foes into the village, he found every house packed with soldiers and the roofs thronged with others who attacked him from above. After defeating his enemies in the open, he pulled the buildings to pieces and dragged out those within. Many perished in a mass under the roofs which he brought down upon their heads, while those who escaped from beneath the ruins were met by the soldiers with drawn swords ; and there was such a heap of corpses that the streets were impassable to the victors. This blow was too much for the enemy ; those of them who rallied after the battle, when they saw the village strewn with dead, dispersed and fled. With the confidence of his victory, Herod would instantly have marched upon Jerusalem, had he not been detained by a storm of exceptional severity. This accident impeded the completion of his success and the defeat of Antigonus, who was by now meditating the abandonment of the capital.

(7) That evening, Herod having dismissed his companions to refresh themselves after their fatigues, went himself just as he was, yet hot from the fight, to take a bath, like any common soldier, for only a single slave attended him. Before he entered the bath-house one of the enemy ran out in front of him, sword in hand, then a second and a third,

Another miraculous escape.

341 ἔπειτα δεύτερος καὶ τρίτος, ἑξῆς δὲ πλείους. οὗτοι
κατεπεφεύγεσαν μὲν ἐκ τῆς παρατάξεως εἰς τὸ
βαλανεῖον ὡπλισμένοι, τέως δ' ὑποπεπτηχότες καὶ
διαλανθάνοντες, ὡς ἐθεάσαντο τὸν βασιλέα, λυ-
θέντες ὑπ' ἐκπλήξεως αὐτὸν μὲν παρέτρεχον γυμνὸν
ὄντα τρέμοντες, ἐπὶ δὲ τὰς ἐξόδους ἐχώρουν. τῶν
μὲν οὖν ἄλλων οὐδεὶς παρῆν κατὰ τύχην ὁ συλ-
ληψόμενος τοὺς ἄνδρας, Ἡρώδῃ δ' ἀπέχρη τὸ
μηδὲν παθεῖν, ὥστε διαφεύγουσιν πάντες.

342 (8) Τῇ δ' ὑστεραίᾳ Πάππον μὲν τὸν Ἀντιγόνου
στρατηγὸν καρατομήσας, ἀνῄρητο δ' ἐπὶ τῆς
παρατάξεως, πέμπει τὴν κεφαλὴν Φερώρᾳ τἀδελφῷ ποινὴν τοῦ φονευθέντος αὐτῶν ἀδελφοῦ· καὶ
343 γὰρ οὗτος ἦν ὁ τὸν Ἰώσηπον ἀνελών. λωφή-
σαντος δὲ τοῦ χειμῶνος ἤλαυνεν ἐπὶ Ἱεροσολύμων
καὶ μέχρι τοῦ τείχους ἀγαγὼν τὴν δύναμιν, συνήγετο δ' αὐτῷ τρίτον ἔτος ἐξ οὗ βασιλεὺς ἐν Ῥώμῃ
ἀπεδέδεικτο, πρὸ τοῦ ἱεροῦ στρατοπεδεύεται·
ταύτῃ γὰρ ἦν ἐπίμαχον, καθ' ὃ καὶ πρὶν εἷλεν
344 Πομπήιος τὴν πόλιν. διελὼν δὲ εἰς ἔργα τὴν
στρατιὰν καὶ τεμὼν τὰ προάστεια, τρία μὲν
ἐγείρειν χώματα καὶ πύργους ἐποικοδομεῖν αὐτοῖς
κελεύει, καταλιπὼν δὲ τοὺς ἀνυτικωτάτους τῶν
ἑταίρων ἐπὶ τῶν ἔργων αὐτὸς εἰς Σαμάρειαν ᾔει,
τὴν Ἀλεξάνδρου τοῦ Ἀριστοβούλου μετιὼν θυγατέρα καθωμολογημένην, ὡς ἔφαμεν, αὐτῷ καὶ
πάρεργον ποιούμενος[1] τῆς πολιορκίας τὸν γάμον·
ἤδη γὰρ ὑπερηφάνει τοὺς πολεμίους.

345 (9) Γήμας δὲ ὑπέστρεψεν ἐπὶ Ἱεροσολύμων

---

[1] PA: ποιεῖται the rest.

followed by more. These were men who had escaped from the combat and taken refuge, fully armed, in the baths. There for a while they had remained lurking and concealed ; but when they saw the king, they were panic-stricken and ran trembling past him, unarmed though he was, and made for the exits. By chance not a man was there to lay hands on them ; but Herod was content to have come off unscathed, and so they all escaped.

(8) On the following day he cut off the head of Pappus, Antigonus's general, who had been killed in the combat, and sent it to his brother Pheroras in retribution for the murder of their brother ; for it was Pappus who had slain Joseph.[a] When the tempest abated, he advanced upon Jerusalem and marched his army up to the walls, it being now just three years since he had been proclaimed king in Rome.[b] He encamped opposite the Temple, for from that quarter the city was open to attack and had on a previous occasion been captured by Pompey.[c] He then appointed his army their several tasks, cut down the trees in the suburbs, and gave orders to raise three lines of earth-works and to erect towers upon them. Leaving his most efficient lieutenants to superintend these works, he went off himself to Samaria to fetch the daughter of Alexander, son of Aristobulus, who, as we have said, was betrothed to him.[d] Thus, so contemptuous was he already of the enemy, he made his wedding an interlude of the siege.

He besieges Jerusalem, spring of 37 B.C.

His marriage with Mariamme.

(9) After his marriage he returned with a larger

---

a §§ 323 f.   b § 284.   c § 145.   d § 241.

μετὰ μείζονος¹ δυνάμεως· συνῆπτε δ' αὐτῷ καὶ
Σόσσιος μετὰ πλείστης στρατιᾶς ἱππέων τε καὶ
πεζῶν, ἣν προεκπέμψας διὰ τῆς μεσογείου τὴν
346 πορείαν αὐτὸς διὰ Φοινίκης ἐποιήσατο. συν-
αθροισθείσης δὲ τῆς ὅλης δυνάμεως εἰς ἕνδεκα μὲν
τέλη πεζῶν, ἱππεῖς δὲ ἑξακισχιλίους δίχα τῶν ἀπὸ
Συρίας συμμάχων, οἳ μέρος οὐκ ὀλίγον ἦσαν,
καταστρατοπεδεύονται τοῦ βορείου τείχους πλησίον,
αὐτὸς μὲν πεποιθὼς τοῖς τῆς συγκλήτου δόγμασιν,
δι' ὧν βασιλεὺς ἀπεδέδεικτο, Σόσσιος δὲ Ἀντωνίῳ
τῷ πέμψαντι τὴν ὑπ' αὐτῷ στρατιὰν Ἡρώδῃ
σύμμαχον.

347 (xviii. 1) Τῶν δ' ἀνὰ τὴν πόλιν Ἰουδαίων τὸ
πλῆθος ποικίλως ἐτετάρακτο· καὶ γὰρ περὶ τὸν
ναὸν ἀθροιζόμενον τὸ ἀσθενέστερον ἐδαιμονία καὶ
πολλὰ θειωδέστερον πρὸς τοὺς καιροὺς ἐλογοποίει,
καὶ τῶν τολμηροτέρων κατὰ στῖφος ἦσαν λῃστεῖαι
πολύτροποι, μάλιστα τὰ περὶ τὴν πόλιν ἁρπα-
ζόντων ἐπιτήδεια καὶ μήτε ἵπποις μήτε ἀνδράσιν
348 ὑπολειπομένων τροφήν. τοῦ γε μὴν μαχίμου τὸ
εὐτακτότερον ἐτέτακτο πρὸς ἄμυναν τῆς πολιορκίας, τούς τε χωννύντας εἶργον ἀπὸ τοῦ τείχους
καὶ τοῖς ὀργάνοις ἀντιμηχανώμενον ἀεί τι κώλυμα
καινότερον· ἐν οὐδενὶ δ' οὕτως ὡς ἐν ταῖς μεταλ-
λείαις περιῆσαν τῶν πολεμίων.

349 (2) Τῷ δὲ βασιλεῖ πρὸς μὲν τὰς λῃστείας ἀντεπ-
ενοήθησαν λόχοι δι' ὧν ἀνέστελλεν τὰς διεκδρομάς,
πρὸς δὲ τὴν τῶν ἐπιτηδείων ἀπορίαν αἱ πόρρωθεν
συγκομιδαί, τῶν δὲ μαχομένων περιὴν τῇ Ῥωμαίων

¹ πλείστης PAM : πλείονος τῆς Destinon.

ᵃ Cf. § 327.

force to Jerusalem. Here too he was joined by Sossius[a] with an imposing army of horse and foot, which that general had sent on ahead through the interior, while he himself took the route by Phoenicia. The total strength of the united armies amounted to eleven battalions of infantry and six thousand cavalry, not including the Syrian auxiliaries, who formed no inconsiderable contingent. The two generals encamped near the north wall : Herod with the confidence inspired by the senatorial decrees, which had proclaimed him king ; Sossius relying on Antony, who had dispatched the army under his command in support of Herod.

Sossius joins Herod before Jerusalem.

(xviii. 1) Throughout the city the agitation of the Jewish populace showed itself in various forms. The feebler folk, congregating round the Temple, indulged in transports of frenzy and fabricated numerous oracular utterances to fit the crisis. The more daring went out in companies on marauding expeditions of all kinds, their main object being to seize all provisions in the neighbourhood of the city and to leave no sustenance for horse or man. Of the military the more disciplined men were employed in repelling the besiegers, from their position on the ramparts beating off the excavators of the earth-works and constantly contriving some new means of parrying the enemy's engines ; but it was above all in their mining operations that they showed their superiority.

The siege.

(2) To stop the raiders the king arranged ambuscades, by which he succeeded in checking their incursions ; to meet the shortage of provisions he had supplies brought from a distance ; while as for the combatants, the military experience of the

Capture of Jerusalem and wholesale massacre.

ἐμπειρίᾳ, καίτοι τόλμης οὐδεμίαν καταλιπόντων
350 ὑπερβολήν· φανερῶς μέν γε οὐ¹ συνερρήγνυντο τοῖς
Ῥωμαίοις ἐπὶ προύπτῳ τῷ θανεῖν, διὰ δὲ τῶν
ὑπονόμων ἐν μέσοις αὐτοῖς ἐξαπίνης ἐφαίνοντο,
καὶ πρὶν κατασεισθῆναί τι τοῦ τείχους ἕτερον
ἀντῳχύρουν· καθόλου τε [εἰπεῖν]² οὔτε χερσὶν οὔτ᾽
ἐπινοίαις ἔκαμνον εἰς ἔσχατον ἀντισχεῖν δι-
351 εγνωκότες. ἀμέλει τηλικαύτης δυνάμεως περικαθ-
εζομένης πέντε μησὶν διήνεγκαν τὴν πολιορκίαν,
ἕως τῶν Ἡρώδου τινὲς ἐπιλέκτων ἐπιβῆναι τοῦ
τείχους θαρσήσαντες εἰσπίπτουσιν εἰς τὴν πόλιν,
ἐφ᾽ οἷς ἑκατοντάρχαι Σοσσίου. πρῶτα δὲ τὰ περὶ
τὸ ἱερὸν ἡλίσκετο, καὶ τῆς δυνάμεως ἐπεισ-
χυθείσης πανταχοῦ φόνος ἦν μυρίος, τῶν μὲν
Ῥωμαίων τῇ τριβῇ τῆς πολιορκίας διωργισμέ-
νων, τοῦ δὲ περὶ Ἡρώδην Ἰουδαϊκοῦ μηδὲν ὑπο-
352 λιπέσθαι σπουδάζοντος ἀντίπαλον. ἐσφάττοντο δὲ
παμπληθεῖς ἔν τε τοῖς στενωποῖς καὶ κατὰ τὰς
οἰκίας συνωθούμενοι καὶ τῷ ναῷ προσφεύγοντες·
ἦν τε οὔτε νηπίων οὔτε γήρως ἔλεος οὔτε ἀσθενείας
γυναικῶν, ἀλλὰ καίτοι περιπέμποντος τοῦ βασιλέως καὶ φείδεσθαι παρακαλοῦντος οὐδεὶς ἐκράτησεν τῆς δεξιᾶς, ἀλλ᾽ ὥσπερ μεμηνότες πᾶσαν
353 ἡλικίαν ἐπεξῄεσαν. ἔνθα καὶ Ἀντίγονος μήτε τῆς
πάλαι μήτε τῆς τότε τύχης ἔννοιαν λαβὼν κάτεισιν
μὲν ἀπὸ τῆς βάρεως, προσπίπτει δὲ τοῖς Σοσσίου
ποσίν. κἀκεῖνος μηδὲν αὐτὸν οἰκτείρας πρὸς τὴν
μεταβολὴν ἐπεγέλασέν τε ἀκρατῶς καὶ Ἀντιγόνην

¹ μέν γε οὐ M : μέν γε PA : μὲν οὖν οὐ the rest.
² om. PA.

───────────────

[a] Or (omitting the negative with PA) " They openly flung
themselves."

Romans gave him the advantage over them, although their audacity knew no bounds. If they did not openly fling themselves against[a] the Roman lines, to face certain death, they would through their underground passages appear suddenly in the enemy's midst; and before one portion of the wall was overthrown they were erecting another in its stead. In a word, neither in action nor ingenuity did they ever flag, fully resolving to hold out to the last. In fact, notwithstanding the strength of the beleaguering army, they sustained the siege into the fifth month;[b] until some of Herod's picked men ventured to scale the wall and leapt into the city, followed by Sossius's centurions. The environs of the Temple were first secured, and, when the troops poured in, a scene of wholesale massacre ensued; for the Romans were infuriated by the length of the siege, and the Jews of Herod's army were determined to leave none of their opponents alive. Masses were butchered in the alleys, crowded together in the houses, and flying to the sanctuary. No quarter was given to infancy, to age, or to helpless womanhood. Nay, though the king sent messengers in every direction, entreating them to spare, none stayed his hand, but like madmen they wreaked their rage on all ages indiscriminately. In this scene Antigonus, regardless alike of his former fortune and that which now was his, came down from the castle and threw himself at the feet of Sossius. The latter, far from pitying his changed condition, burst into uncontroll-

Summer of
37 B.C.

---

[b] *A.* xiv. 487 appears to state, on the contrary, that Jerusalem was taken " in the third month " or even in less, the first wall being captured in 40 days, the second in 15 (*ib.* 476).

ἐκάλεσεν· οὐ μὴν ὡς γυναῖκά γε καὶ φρουρᾶς
ἐλεύθερον ἀφῆκεν, ἀλλ' ὁ μὲν δεθεὶς ἐφυλάττετο.

354 (3) Πρόνοια δ' ἦν Ἡρώδη κρατοῦντι τῶν
πολεμίων τότε κρατῆσαι καὶ τῶν ἀλλοφύλων
συμμάχων· ὥρμητο γὰρ τὸ ξενικὸν πλῆθος ἐπὶ
θέαν τοῦ τε ἱεροῦ καὶ τῶν κατὰ τὸν ναὸν ἁγίων.
ὁ δὲ βασιλεὺς τοὺς μὲν παρακαλῶν, τοῖς δ' ἀπ-
ειλούμενος, ἔστιν δ' οὓς καὶ τοῖς ὅπλοις ἀνέστειλεν,
ἥττης χαλεπωτέραν τὴν νίκην ὑπολαμβάνων, εἰ
355 τι τῶν ἀθεάτων παρ' αὐτῶν ὀφθείη. διεκώλυσεν
δὲ ἤδη καὶ τὰς κατὰ τὴν πόλιν ἁρπαγάς, πολλὰ
διατεινόμενος πρὸς Σόσσιον, εἰ χρημάτων τε καὶ
ἀνδρῶν τὴν πόλιν Ῥωμαῖοι κενώσαντες κατα-
λείψουσιν αὐτὸν ἐρημίας βασιλέα, καὶ ὡς ἐπὶ
τοσούτων πολιτῶν φόνῳ βραχὺ καὶ τὴν τῆς οἰκου-
356 μένης ἡγεμονίαν ἀντάλλαγμα κρίνοι. τοῦ δὲ ἀντὶ
τῆς πολιορκίας τὰς ἁρπαγὰς δικαίως τοῖς στρατιώταις ἐπιτρέπειν φαμένου, αὐτὸς ἔφη διανεμεῖν
ἐκ τῶν ἰδίων χρημάτων τοὺς μισθοὺς ἑκάστοις·
οὕτως τε τὴν λοιπὴν ἐξωνησάμενος πατρίδα τὰς
ὑποσχέσεις ἐπλήρωσεν· λαμπρῶς μὲν γὰρ ἕκαστον
στρατιώτην, ἀναλόγως δὲ τοὺς ἡγεμόνας, βασιλικώτατα δὲ αὐτὸν ἐδωρήσατο Σόσσιον, ὡς μηδένα
357 χρημάτων ἀπελθεῖν δεόμενον. Σόσσιος δὲ χρυσοῦν
ἀναθεὶς τῷ θεῷ στέφανον ἀνέζευξεν ἀπὸ Ἱεροσολύμων, ἄγων δεσμώτην Ἀντίγονον Ἀντωνίῳ.
τοῦτον μὲν οὖν φιλοψυχήσαντα μέχρις ἐσχάτου διὰ
ψυχρᾶς ἐλπίδος ἄξιος τῆς ἀγεννείας πέλεκυς
ἐκδέχεται.

358 (4) Βασιλεὺς δὲ Ἡρώδης διακρίνας τὸ κατὰ
τὴν πόλιν πλῆθος τοὺς μὲν τὰ αὐτοῦ φρονήσαντας

able laughter and called him Antigone.[a] He did not, however, treat him as a woman and leave him at liberty : no, he was put in irons and kept under strict guard.

(3) Now master of his enemies, Herod's next task was to gain the mastery over his foreign allies ; for this crowd of aliens rushed to see the Temple and the holy contents of the sanctuary. The king expostulated, threatened, sometimes even had recourse to weapons to keep them back, deeming victory more grievous than defeat, if these people should set eyes on any objects not open to public view. Now too he put a stop to the pillage of the town, forcibly representing to Sossius that, if the Romans emptied the city of money and men, they would leave him king of a desert, and that he would count the empire of the world itself too dearly bought with the slaughter of so many citizens. Sossius replying that he was justified in permitting the soldiers to pillage in return for their labours in the siege, Herod promised to distribute rewards to each man out of his private resources. Having thus redeemed what remained of his country, he duly fulfilled his engagement, remunerating each soldier liberally, the officers in proportion, and Sossius himself with truly royal munificence ; so that none went unprovided. Sossius, after dedicating to God a crown of gold, withdrew from Jerusalem, taking with him to Antony Antigonus in chains. This prisoner, to the last clinging with forlorn hope to life, fell beneath the axe, a fitting end to his ignominious career.

(4) King Herod, discriminating between the two classes of the city population, by the award of

Herod checks profanation of Temple and pillage of city.

Antigonus put to death.

---

[a] Or in the general's Latin " Antigona."

εὐνουστέρους ταῖς τιμαῖς καθίστατο, τοὺς δ'
Ἀντιγονείους ἀνῄρει. καὶ κατὰ σπάνιν ἤδη χρημάτων ὅσον εἶχεν κόσμον καταναμιστεύσας Ἀν-
359 τωνίῳ καὶ τοῖς περὶ αὐτὸν ἀνέπεμψεν. οὐ μὴν εἰς
ἅπαν[1] ἐξωνήσατο τὸ μηδὲν παθεῖν· ἤδη γὰρ
Ἀντώνιος τῷ Κλεοπάτρας ἔρωτι διεφθαρμένος
ἥττων ἦν ἐν πᾶσιν τῆς ἐπιθυμίας, Κλεοπάτρα δὲ
διεξελθοῦσα τὴν γενεὰν τὴν ἑαυτῆς ὡς μηδένα
τῶν ἀφ' αἵματος ὑπολείπεσθαι, τὸ λοιπὸν ἐπὶ τοὺς
360 ἔξωθεν ἐφόνα, καὶ τοὺς ἐν τέλει Σύρων διαβάλλουσα
πρὸς τὸν Ἀντώνιον ἀναιρεῖν ἔπειθεν, ὡς ἂν τῶν
κτήσεων ἑκάστου ῥᾳδίως γινομένη δεσπότις, ἔτι
δ' ἐκτείνουσα τὴν πλεονεξίαν ἐπὶ Ἰουδαίους καὶ
Ἄραβας ὑπειργάζετο τοὺς ἑκατέρων βασιλεῖς
Ἡρώδην καὶ Μάλχον ἀναιρεθῆναι.

361   (5) Ἐν μέρει γοῦν τῶν προσταγμάτων ἐπινήψας
Ἀντώνιος τὸ κτεῖναι μὲν ἄνδρας ἀγαθοὺς καὶ
βασιλεῖς τηλικούτους ἀνόσιον ἡγήσατο, τὸ δὲ
τούτων ἔγγιον φίλους[2] διεκρούσατο· πολλὰ δὲ τῆς
χώρας αὐτῶν ἀποτεμόμενος, καὶ δὴ καὶ τὸν ἐν
Ἱεριχοῦντι φοινικῶνα, ἐν ᾧ γεννᾶται τὸ βάλσαμον,
δίδωσιν αὐτῇ πόλεις τε πλὴν Τύρου καὶ Σιδῶνος
362 τὰς ἐντὸς Ἐλευθέρου ποταμοῦ πάσας. ὧν γενο-
μένη κυρία καὶ προπέμψασα μέχρις Εὐφράτου τὸν
Ἀντώνιον ἐπιστρατεύοντα Πάρθοις ἦλθεν εἰς
Ἰουδαίαν δι' Ἀπαμείας καὶ Δαμασκοῦ. κἀνταῦθα

---

[1] εἰς ἅπαξ LVRC.
[2] φίλους PA Exc. Lat. : φίλος εἶναι the rest.   Text and
meaning uncertain.   I follow the Latin "quod autem his
morte propius est, inter amicos non habuit."   Perhaps
(reading φίλος εἶναι) "But of any closer friendship he showed
no sign."

honours attached more closely to himself those who
had espoused his cause, while he exterminated the
partisans of Antigonus. Finding his funds now reduced, he converted all the valuables in his possession
into money, which he then transmitted to Antony
and his staff. Yet even at this price he failed to
secure for himself complete exemption from injury ;
for Antony, already demoralized by his love for
Cleopatra, was becoming wholly enslaved to his
passion, and Cleopatra, after killing off her own *Cleopatra's*
family, one after another, till not a single relative *plots against*
remained, was now thirsting for the blood of for- *Herod*
eigners. Laying before Antony calumnious charges
against high officials in Syria, she urged him to put
them to death, in the belief that she would have no
difficulty in appropriating their possessions ; and
now, her ambitions extending to Judaea and Arabia,
she was secretly contriving the ruin of their respective
kings, Herod and Malchus.

(5) One part, at any rate, of her orders brought *and*
Antony to his sober senses : he held it sacrilege to *exactions*
take the lives of innocent men and kings of such *realm.* *from his*
eminence. But—what touched them more nearly—
he threw over his friends. He cut off large tracts of
their territory—including, in particular, the palm- *34 B.C.*
grove of Jericho where the balsam grows—and pre- *(Schürer).*
sented them to Cleopatra, together with all the towns
to the south of [a] the river Eleutherus,[b] Tyre and
Sidon excepted. Now mistress of all this land, she
escorted Antony, who was starting on a campaign
against the Parthians, as far as the Euphrates, and
then, by way of Apamea and Damascus, came into

---

[a] Greek " within," *i.e.* " on this side of."
[b] North of Tyre.

μεγάλαις μὲν αὐτῆς τὴν δυσμένειαν δωρεαῖς
Ἡρώδης ἐκμειλίσσεται, μισθοῦται δὲ καὶ τὰ τῆς
βασιλείας ἀπορραγέντα χωρία διακοσίων ταλάντων
εἰς ἕκαστον ἐνιαυτόν, προπέμπει δ' αὐτὴν μέχρι
363 Πηλουσίου πάσῃ θεραπείᾳ καταχρώμενος. καὶ
μετ' οὐ πολὺ παρῆν ἐκ Πάρθων Ἀντώνιος ἄγων
αἰχμάλωτον Ἀρταβάζην τὸν Τιγράνου παῖδα δῶρον
Κλεοπάτρᾳ· μετὰ γὰρ τῶν χρημάτων καὶ τῆς
λείας ἁπάσης ὁ Πάρθος εὐθὺς ἐχαρίσθη.

364   (xix. 1) Τοῦ δ' Ἀκτιακοῦ πολέμου συνερρω-
γότος παρεσκεύαστο μὲν Ἡρώδης Ἀντωνίῳ συνεξ-
ορμᾶν, ἤδη τῶν τε ἄλλων τῶν κατὰ Ἰουδαίαν
ἀπηλλαγμένος θορύβων καὶ κεκρατηκὼς Ὑρκα-
νίας, ὃ δὴ χωρίον ἡ Ἀντιγόνου κατεῖχεν ἀδελφή.
365 διεκλείσθη γε μὴν πανούργως ὑπὸ τῆς Κλεοπάτρας συμμετασχεῖν τῶν κινδύνων Ἀντωνίῳ· τοῖς
γὰρ βασιλεῦσιν, ὡς ἔφαμεν, ἐπιβουλεύουσα πείθει
τὸν Ἀντώνιον Ἡρώδῃ διαπιστεῦσαι τὸν πρὸς
Ἄραβας πόλεμον, ἵν' ἢ κρατήσαντος Ἀραβίας ἢ
κρατηθέντος Ἰουδαίας γένηται δεσπότις καὶ θατέ-
ρῳ τῶν δυναστῶν καταλύσῃ τὸν ἕτερον.

366   (2) Ἔρρεψεν μέντοι καθ' Ἡρώδην τὸ βού-
λευμα· πρῶτον μὲν γὰρ ῥύσια [κατὰ]¹ τῶν πολεμίων ἄγων καὶ πολὺ συγκροτήσας ἱππικὸν ἐπαφίησιν αὐτοῖς περὶ Διόσπολιν, ἐκράτησέν τε καίτοι

¹ om. P.

ᵃ This Artabazes (Artavasdes) was not a Parthian, but
king of Armenia, who, having joined Antony in an attack
on his namesake Artavasdes, king of Media, deserted him
and was subsequently taken captive by Antony (Plut. *Ant.*
50). Josephus or his source appears to have confused the

Judaea. There, by large bounties, Herod appeased her ill will, and agreed to take on lease for an annual sum of two hundred talents the lands which had been detached from his realm. He then escorted her to Pelusium, treating her with every mark of respect. Not long after Antony returned from Parthia bringing, as a present for Cleopatra, his prisoner Artabazes, son of Tigranes ; for upon her, together with the money and all the spoils of war, the Parthian [a] was instantly bestowed.

(xix. 1) On the outbreak of the war of Actium Herod prepared to join forces with Antony ; for he was now rid of disturbances in Judaea and had captured the fortress of Hyrcania, hitherto held by the sister of Antigonus. The craft of Cleopatra, however, precluded him from sharing Antony's perils. For, as we have stated,[b] she had designs on the kings, in pursuance of which she now induced Antony to entrust the war against the Arabs to Herod, hoping, if he were successful, to become mistress of Arabia, if unsuccessful, of Judaea, and by means of one of the two potentates to overthrow the other.

(2) Her scheme, however, turned to Herod's advantage. For, beginning with raids[c] upon the enemy's territory, he mustered a large body of cavalry, flung them at the foe in the neighbourhood of Diospolis[d] and, though he met with a stubborn

Herod's war with the Arabs 32 B.C.

Victor at Diospolis

two namesakes (Reinach). In the parallel account, *A.* xv. 104, he is not called a Parthian.

    [b] § 360.   [c] Or " reprisals."

    [d] In Coele-Syria, not (as stated in Shilleto's Whiston) Lydda, which only received the name Diospolis at a later date ; it has been mentioned in § 132.

καρτερῶς ἀντιπαραταξαμένων. πρὸς δὲ τὴν ἧτταν
μέγα γίνεται κίνημα τῶν Ἀράβων, καὶ συναθροισθέντες εἰς Κάναθα τῆς κοίλης Συρίας ἄπειροι
367 τὸ πλῆθος τοὺς Ἰουδαίους ἔμενον. ἔνθα μετὰ
τῆς δυνάμεως Ἡρώδης ἐπελθὼν ἐπειρᾶτο προ-
μηθέστερον ἀφηγεῖσθαι τοῦ πολέμου καὶ στρατόπεδον ἐκέλευε τειχίζειν. οὐ μὴν ὑπήκουσεν τὸ
πλῆθος, ἀλλὰ τῇ προτέρᾳ νίκῃ τεθαρρηκότες
ὥρμησαν ἐπὶ τοὺς Ἄραβας. καὶ πρὸς μὲν τὴν
πρώτην ἐμβολὴν τραπέντας ἐδίωκον, ἐπιβουλεύε-
ται δὲ Ἡρώδης ἐν τῇ διώξει, τοὺς ἐκ τῶν Κανά-
θων ἐπιχωρίους ἀνέντος Ἀθηνίωνος, ὃς ἦν αὐτῷ
368 τῶν Κλεοπάτρας στρατηγῶν ἀεὶ διάφορος· πρὸς
γὰρ τὴν τούτων ἐπίθεσιν ἀναθαρρήσαντες οἱ Ἄραβες ἐπιστρέφονται καὶ συνάψαντες τὸ πλῆθος περὶ
πετρώδη καὶ δύσβατα χωρία τοὺς Ἡρώδου τρέπονται πλεῖστόν τε αὐτῶν φόνον εἰργάσαντο. οἱ
δὲ διασωθέντες ἐκ τῆς μάχης εἰς Ὅρμιζα καταφεύγουσιν, ὅπου καὶ τὸ στρατόπεδον αὐτῶν περισχόντες αὔτανδρον εἷλον οἱ Ἄραβες.
369   (3) Μετ' οὐ πολὺ δὲ τῆς συμφορᾶς βοήθειαν
ἄγων Ἡρώδης παρῆν τῆς χρείας ὑστέραν. ταύτης τῆς πληγῆς αἴτιον αὐτῷ τὸ τῶν ταξιάρχων
ἀπειθὲς κατέστη· μὴ γὰρ ἐξαπιναίου τῆς συμβολῆς γενομένης οὐδ' ἂν Ἀθηνίων εὗρεν καιρὸν
ἐπιβουλῆς. ἐτιμωρήσατο μέντοι τοὺς Ἄραβας
αὖθις ἀεὶ τὴν χώραν κατατρέχων, ὡς ἀνακαλέ-
370 σασθαι τὴν μίαν αὐτοῖς νίκην πολλάκις. ἀμυνο-
μένῳ δὲ τοὺς ἐχθροὺς ἐπιπίπτει συμφορὰ δαι-
μόνιος ἄλλη, κατ' ἔτος μὲν τῆς βασιλείας ἕβδομον,

---

[a] Canata or Cana in A. xv. 112.
[b] Unidentified ; the name is not mentioned in A.

resistance, defeated them. This defeat occasioned a great commotion among the Arabs, who assembled in vast numbers at Canatha [a] in Coele-Syria and there awaited the Jews. Herod, arriving with his troops, endeavoured to conduct operations with due caution and ordered the camp to be fortified. His orders, however, were defied by the rank and file, who, flushed with their recent victory, rushed upon the Arabs. With their first charge they routed them and followed at their heels ; but during the pursuit a snare was laid for Herod by Athenion, one of Cleopatra's generals, who had always been hostile to him, and now let loose upon him the natives of Canatha. Encouraged by their allies' attack, the Arabs faced about and, after uniting their forces on rocky and difficult ground, routed Herod's troops with immense slaughter. Those who escaped from the battle took refuge in Ormiza,[b] where, however, the Arabs surrounded and captured their camp with all its defenders.

(3) Shortly after this disaster Herod arrived with reinforcements, too late to be of use. This calamity was brought upon him by the insubordination of the divisional officers ; for, had they not precipitated an engagement, Athenion would have found no opportunity for a ruse. However, Herod subsequently avenged himself on the Arabs by constantly raiding their territory, so that they had frequent occasion to rue [c] their single victory. But while he was punishing his foes, he was visited by another calamity—an act of God which occurred in the seventh [d] year of

he is defeated at Canatha.

[c] Such, or " regretfully recall," seems to be the meaning.
[d] Reckoning from the year of the taking of Jerusalem, 37 B.C., as the effective beginning of Herod's reign.

173

ἀκμάζοντος δὲ τοῦ περὶ "Ακτιον πολέμου. ἀρχομένου γὰρ[1] ἔαρος ἡ γῆ σεισθεῖσα βοσκημάτων μὲν ἄπειρον πλῆθος ἀνθρώπων δὲ τρεῖς διέφθειρεν μυριάδας, τὸ δὲ στρατιωτικὸν ἔμεινεν ἀβλαβές·
371 ὕπαιθρον γὰρ ηὐλίζετο. κἂν τούτῳ τοὺς "Αραβας ἐπὶ μεῖζον θράσος ἦρεν ἡ φήμη προσλογοποιοῦσα τοῖς σκυθρωποῖς ἀεί τι χαλεπώτερον· ὡς γοῦν ἁπάσης 'Ιουδαίας κατερριμμένης οἰηθέντες ἐρήμου τῆς χώρας κρατήσειν ὥρμησαν εἰς αὐτήν, προθυσάμενοι τοὺς πρέσβεις οἳ παρὰ 'Ιουδαίων ἔτυχον
372 ἥκοντες πρὸς αὐτούς. πρὸς δὲ τὴν ἐμβολὴν καταπλαγὲν τὸ πλῆθος[2] καὶ μεγέθει συμφορῶν ἐπαλλήλων ἔκλυτον συναγαγὼν 'Ηρώδης ἐπειρᾶτο παρορμᾶν ἐπὶ τὴν ἄμυναν λέγων τοιάδε·

373 (4) " Παραλογώτατά μοι δοκεῖ τὸ παρὸν ὑμῶν καθάπτεσθαι δέος· πρὸς μέν γε τὰς δαιμονίους πληγὰς ἀθυμεῖν εἰκὸς ἦν, τὸ δ' αὐτὸ καὶ πρὸς ἀνθρωπίνην ἔφοδον πάσχειν ἀνάνδρων.[3] ἐγὼ γὰρ τοσοῦτον ἀποδέω κατεπτηχέναι τοὺς πολεμίους μετὰ τὸν σεισμόν, ὥσθ' ὑπολαμβάνειν τὸν θεὸν "Αραψιν δέλεαρ τοῦτο καθεικέναι τοῦ δοῦναι δίκας ἡμῖν· οὐ γὰρ τοσοῦτον ὅπλοις ἢ χερσὶν πεποιθότες ὅσον ταῖς αὐτομάτοις ἡμῶν συμφοραῖς ἧκον· σφαλερὰ δ' ἐλπὶς οὐκ ἐξ οἰκείας ἰσχύος ἀλλ' ἐξ ἀλλο
374 τρίας ἠρτημένη κακοπραγίας. οὔτε δὲ τὸ δυστυχεῖν οὔτε τοὐναντίον ἐν ἀνθρώποις βέβαιον, ἀλλ' ἔστιν ἰδεῖν ἐπαμειβομένην εἰς ἑκάτερα τὴν τύχην.

[1] ἀρχ. γὰρ C: κατὰ γὰρ ἀρχομένου the rest: καὶ γὰρ ἀρχ. Destinon.
[2] ἔθνος LVRC.   [3] ἄνανδρον PAM Lat.

  [a] Cf. B. iii. 433; Josephus may have known Virgil's description of rumour (Fama), Aen. iv. 173 ff.
  [b] This speech is quite independent of that contained in
174

his reign, when the war of Actium was at its height. In the early spring an earthquake destroyed cattle innumerable and thirty thousand souls; but the army, being quartered in the open, escaped injury. At the same moment the confidence of the Arabs rose, stimulated by rumour which always exaggerates the horrors of a tragedy.[a] Imagining that the whole of Judaea was in ruins and that they had only to take possession of an abandoned country, they hastened to invade it, after massacring the envoys whom the Jews had sent to them. So dismayed were the people at this invasion, and so demoralized by the magnitude of these successive disasters, that Herod called them together and endeavoured to rouse them to resistance by the following speech.[b] Earthquake in Palestine, spring of 31 B.C.

(4) " This alarm which has now laid hold of you seems to me most unreasonable. To be disheartened by the visitations of heaven was natural ; but to be similarly despondent at the attack of a human foe is unmanly. For my part, far from being intimidated by the enemy's invasion following the earthquake, I regard that catastrophe as a snare which God has laid to decoy the Arabs and deliver them up to our vengeance. It is not because they have confidence in their weapons or their might that they are here, but because they count on our accidental calamities ; but hopes are fallacious which are dependent not on one's own strength, but on the misadventures of another. Moreover, with mankind fortune is never permanently either adverse or favourable ; one sees her veering from one mood to the other. Of this you Herod's address to his disconsolate troops.

$\varLambda$. xv. 127. It in some respects recalls that of Pericles in Thuc. ii. 60 ff. (the earthquake is here a " visitation of heaven," as the plague is there).

καὶ τοῦτο μάθοιτ' ἂν ἐξ οἰκείων ὑποδειγμάτων·
τῇ γοῦν προτέρᾳ μάχῃ κρατούντων ἐκράτησαν
ἡμῶν οἱ πολέμιοι, καὶ κατὰ τὸ εἰκὸς νῦν ἁλώ-
σονται κρατήσειν δοκοῦντες. τὸ μὲν γὰρ ἄγαν πεποιθὸς ἀφύλακτον, οἱ φόβοι δὲ διδάσκουσιν προ-
μήθειαν· ὥστε ἔμοιγε κἀκ τοῦ δεδοικότος ὑμῶν[1]
375 παρίσταται θαρρεῖν. ὅτε γὰρ ἐθρασύνεσθε πέρα
τοῦ δέοντος καὶ κατὰ τῶν ἐχθρῶν παρὰ τὴν ἐμὴν
γνώμην ἐξωρμήσατε, καιρὸν ἔσχεν ἡ Ἀθηνίωνος
ἐνέδρα· νυνὶ δὲ ὁ ὄκνος ὑμῶν καὶ τὸ δοκοῦν ἄθυμον
376 ἀσφάλειαν ἐμοὶ νίκης ἐγγυᾶται. χρὴ μέντοι γε
μέχρι τοῦ μέλλειν[2] οὕτως ἔχειν, ἐν δὲ τοῖς ἔργοις
ἐγεῖραι τὰ φρονήματα καὶ πεῖσαι τοὺς ἀσεβεστά-
τους, ὡς οὔτ' ἀνθρώπειόν τι κακὸν οὔτε δαιμόνιον ταπεινώσει ποτὲ τὴν Ἰουδαίων ἀνδραγαθίαν,
ἐφ' ὅσον τὰς ψυχὰς ἔχουσιν, οὐδὲ περιόψεταί τις
Ἄραβα τῶν ἑαυτοῦ ἀγαθῶν δεσπότην γενόμενον,
ὃν παρ' ὀλίγον[3] πολλάκις αἰχμάλωτον ἔλαβεν.
377 μηδ' ὑμᾶς ταρασσέτω τὰ τῶν ἀψύχων κινήματα,
μηδ' ὑπολαμβάνετε τὸν σεισμὸν ἑτέρας συμφορᾶς
τέρας γεγονέναι· φυσικὰ γὰρ τὰ τῶν στοιχείων
πάθη καὶ οὐδὲν ἀνθρώποις πλέον ἢ τὴν ἐν ἑαυτοῖς
βλάβην ἐπιφέρεται. λοιμοῦ μὲν γὰρ καὶ λιμοῦ καὶ
τῶν χθονίων βρασμῶν προγένοιτ' ἄν τι σημεῖον
βραχύτερον, αὐτὰ δὲ ταῦτα περιγραφὴν ἔχει τὸ
μέγεθος. ἐπεὶ τί δύναται μεῖζον ἡμᾶς τοῦ σει-
378 σμοῦ βλάψαι καὶ κρατήσας ὁ πόλεμος[4]; τέρας

---

[1] δεδοικέναι ὑμᾶς PAM.
[2] ante proelium Lat., reading μέχρι τοῦ πολεμεῖν.
[3] παρὰ λόγον LVR.   [4] πόλεμιος Cocceius.

---

[a] " During the period of waiting " seems to be the meaning if the text is right.
[b] Cf. Aristot. Meteor. ii. 8 for premonitions of earthquakes.

might find an illustration in your own experiences : conquerors in the first battle you were then conquered by our enemies, who in all probability, expecting a victory, will now be defeated. For excessive confidence throws men off their guard, whereas fear teaches precaution ; so that your very timidity is to me reassuring. When you displayed uncalled for temerity and, disdaining my advice, dashed out upon the foe, Athenion had his opportunity for a ruse ; but now your hesitation and apparent despondency are to me a sure pledge of victory. Appropriate, however, as are such feelings before an impending battle,[a] when once in action your spirits must be roused and you must teach these scoundrels that no disaster, whether inflicted by God or man, will ever reduce the valour of Jews, so long as they have breath in their bodies, and that not one of them will consent to see his property pass into the hands of an Arab, who has often so narrowly escaped becoming his prisoner.

" Do not let the convulsions of inanimate nature disturb you or imagine that the earthquake is a portent of a further disaster. These accidents to which the elements are subject have physical causes, and beyond the immediate injury inflicted bring no further consequences to mankind. A pestilence, a famine, subterranean commotions may possibly be preceded by some slighter premonition,[b] but these catastrophes themselves are limited by their very magnitude to their instant effects. I ask you, can war,[c] even if we are defeated, do us more harm than the earthquake ?

" Our adversaries, on the other hand, have one

[c] Or, with the conjectural reading, " the enemy."

μέντοι μέγιστον ἁλώσεως γέγονεν τοῖς ἐχθροῖς
οὐκ αὐτομάτως οὐδὲ διὰ χειρὸς ἀλλοτρίας, οἳ
πρέσβεις ἡμετέρους παρὰ τὸν πάντων ἀνθρώπων
νόμον ὠμῶς ἀπέκτειναν καὶ τοιαῦτα τῷ θεῷ
θύματα περὶ τοῦ πολέμου κατέστεψαν.[1] ἀλλ' οὐ
διαφεύξονται τὸν μέγαν ὀφθαλμὸν αὐτοῦ καὶ τὴν
ἀνίκητον δεξιάν, δώσουσιν δ' ἡμῖν αὐτίκα δίκας,
ἂν τοῦ πατρίου φρονήματος ἤδη σπάσαντες τιμω-
379 ροὶ τῶν παρεσπονδημένων ἀναστῶμεν. ἴτω τις
οὐχ ὑπὲρ γυναικὸς οὐδ' ὑπὲρ τέκνων οὐδ' ὑπὲρ
κινδυνευούσης πατρίδος, ἀλλ' ὑπὲρ τῶν πρέσβεων
ἀμυνόμενος· ἐκεῖνοι στρατηγήσουσιν τοῦ πολέμου
τῶν ζώντων [ἡμῶν][2] ἄμεινον. προκινδυνεύσω δὲ
κἀγὼ χρώμενος ὑμῖν πειθηνίοις· εὖ γὰρ ἴστε τὴν
ἑαυτῶν ἀνδρείαν ἀνυπόστατον, ἐὰν μὴ προπετείᾳ
τινι βλαβῆτε.''

380 (5) Τούτοις παρακροτήσας τὸν στρατὸν ὡς
ἑώρα προθύμους, ἔθυεν τῷ θεῷ καὶ μετὰ τὴν
θυσίαν διέβαινεν τὸν Ἰορδάνην ποταμὸν μετὰ τῆς
δυνάμεως. στρατοπεδευσάμενος δὲ περὶ Φιλαδέλφειαν ἐγγὺς τῶν πολεμίων περὶ τοῦ μεταξὺ
φρουρίου πρὸς αὐτοὺς ἠκροβολίζετο βουλόμενος
ἐν τάχει συμβαλεῖν· ἔτυχον γὰρ κἀκεῖνοί τινας
προπεπομφότες τοὺς καταληψομένους τὸ ἔρυμα.
381 τούτους μὲν οὖν ἀπεκρούσαντο ταχέως οἱ πεμφθέντες ὑπὸ τοῦ βασιλέως καὶ τὸν λόφον κατέσχον,
αὐτὸς δὲ καθ' ἡμέραν προάγων τὴν δύναμιν εἰς
μάχην παρετάσσετο καὶ προυκαλεῖτο τοὺς Ἄραβας. ὡς δ' οὐδεὶς ἐπεξῄει, δεινὴ γάρ τις αὐτοὺς
κατάπληξις εἶχε καὶ πρὸ τοῦ πλήθους ὁ στρατηγὸς

[1] C: κατέστρεψαν the rest.　　　　[2] om. PA.

[a] Rabbath Ammon, the ancient capital of the Ammonites.

grave portent of impending disaster in a recent incident, due neither to natural causes nor to the action of others. Contrary to the universal law of mankind they have brutally murdered our ambassadors; such are the garlanded victims which they have offered to God to obtain success! But they will not escape his mighty eye, his invincible right hand; and to us they will soon answer for their crimes if, with some vestige of the spirit of our fathers, we now arise to avenge this violation of treaties. Let us each go into action not to defend wife or children or country at stake, but to avenge our envoys. They will conduct the campaign better than we who are alive. I myself will bear the brunt of the battle, if I have you obedient at my back; for, be assured, your courage is irresistible, if you do not by some reckless action bring injury upon yourselves."

(5) Having by this speech reanimated his army, Herod, observing their ardour, offered sacrifice to God, and then proceeded to cross the Jordan with his troops. Encamping in the neighbourhood of Philadelphia,[a] close to the enemy, and anxious to force on an engagement, he began skirmishing with them for the possession of a fort which lay between the opposing lines. The enemy on their side had sent forward a detachment to occupy this post; the party sent by the king promptly beat them off and secured the hill. Daily Herod marched out his troops, formed them in battle array, and challenged the Arabs to combat. But when none came out to oppose him—for a dire consternation had seized them and, even more than the rank and file,[b] their

Herod defeats the Arabs at Philadelphia,

___

[b] Or perhaps "in presence of his troops."

JOSEPHUS

"Ελθεμος αὖος ἦν τῷ δέει, προσελθὼν ἐσπάραττεν
382 αὐτῶν τὸ χαράκωμα. κἀν τούτῳ συναναγκα-
σθέντες ἐξίασιν ἐπὶ τὴν μάχην ἄτακτοι καὶ πε-
φυρμένοι τοῖς ἱππεῦσιν οἱ πεζοί. πλήθει μὲν οὖν
τῶν Ἰουδαίων περιῆσαν, ἐλείποντο δὲ ταῖς προθυμίαις, καίτοι διὰ τὴν ἀπόγνωσιν τῆς νίκης
ὄντες καὶ αὐτοὶ παράβολοι.

383   (6) Διὸ μέχρι μὲν ἀντεῖχον οὐ πολὺς ἦν αὐτῶν
φόνος, ὡς δ' ὑπέδειξαν τὰ νῶτα, πολλοὶ μὲν ὑπὸ
τῶν Ἰουδαίων πολλοὶ δὲ ὑπὸ σφῶν αὐτῶν συμ-
πατούμενοι διεφθείροντο· πεντακισχίλιοι γοῦν ἔπεσον ἐν τῇ τροπῇ, τὸ δὲ λοιπὸν πλῆθος ἔφθη συν-
ωσθὲν εἰς τὸ χαράκωμα. τούτους περισχὼν ἐπολιόρκει, καὶ μέλλοντας ἁλώσεσθαι τοῖς ὅπλοις προ-
κατήπειγεν ἡ δίψα τῶν ὑδάτων ἐπιλειπόντων.
384 ὑπερηφάνει δὲ πρεσβευομένους ὁ βασιλεὺς καὶ
λύτρα διδόντων πεντακόσια τάλαντα μᾶλλον ἐνέκειτο. τοῦ δὲ δίψους ἐκκαίοντος ἐξιόντες κατὰ
πλῆθος ἐνεχείριζον σφᾶς αὐτοὺς τοῖς Ἰουδαίοις
ἑκόντες, ὡς πέντε μὲν ἡμέραις τετρακισχιλίους
δεθῆναι, τῇ δ' ἕκτῃ τὸ λειπόμενον πλῆθος ὑπ'
ἀπογνώσεως ἐξελθεῖν ἐπὶ μάχην· οἷς συμβαλὼν
385 Ἡρώδης πάλιν εἰς ἑπτακισχιλίους κτείνει. τηλι-
καύτῃ πληγῇ τὴν Ἀραβίαν ἀμυνάμενος[1] καὶ
σβέσας τῶν ἀνδρῶν τὰ φρονήματα προύκοψεν
ὥστε καὶ προστάτης ὑπὸ τοῦ ἔθνους αἱρεθῆναι.

386   (XX. 1) Μεταλαμβάνει δὲ αὐτὸν εὐθέως ἡ
περὶ τῶν ὅλων πραγμάτων φροντὶς διὰ τὴν πρὸς
Ἀντώνιον φιλίαν, Καίσαρος περὶ Ἄκτιον νενικη-

[1] Bekker: ἀμυνόμενος MSS.

180

general Elthemus was paralysed[a] with fright—the
king advanced and proceeded to tear up their
palisades. Thereupon, impelled by necessity, the
enemy at length emerged for action, in disorder,
infantry and cavalry intermingled. Superior in
numbers to the Jews, they had less stomach for a
fight, though despair of success rendered even them
reckless.

(6) Consequently, so long as they held out, their
casualties were slight ; but when they turned their
backs multitudes were slain by the Jews, and many
others were trodden to death by their own men.
Five thousand fell in the rout ; the rest of the crowd
succeeded in forcing their way into their entrenched
camp. There Herod surrounded and besieged them,
and they must have succumbed to an assault, had
not the failure of their water-supply and thirst precipitated their capitulation. The king treated their
envoys with scorn, and, although they offered a
ransom of five hundred talents, only pressed his
attack the harder. Parched with thirst, the Arabs
came out in crowds and willingly surrendered to the
Jews, so that in five days four thousand were made
prisoners. On the sixth the remnant in desperation
came forth to battle ; these Herod engaged, killing
some seven thousand more. Having, by this crushing
blow, punished Arabia and broken the spirit of its
people, he gained such a reputation with them that
the nation chose him for its Protector.

and becomes
Protector of
the Arab
nation.

(xx. 1) But, this peril surmounted, Herod was instantly plunged into anxiety about the security of
his position. He was Antony's friend, and Antony
had been defeated by Caesar[b] at Actium. (In reality,

[a] Literally " dry."　　　　　　[b] Octavius.

κότος. παρεῖχεν μέντοι δέους πλέον ἢ ἔπασχεν·
οὔπω γὰρ ἑαλωκέναι Καῖσαρ Ἀντώνιον ἔκρινεν
387 Ἡρώδου συμμένοντος. ὅ γε μὴν βασιλεὺς ὁμόσε
χωρῆσαι τῷ κινδύνῳ διέγνω, καὶ πλεύσας εἰς
Ῥόδον, ἔνθα διέτριβεν Καῖσαρ, πρόσεισιν αὐτῷ
δίχα διαδήματος, τὴν μὲν ἐσθῆτα καὶ τὸ σχῆμα
ἰδιώτης, τὸ δὲ φρόνημα βασιλεύς. μηδὲν γοῦν
τῆς ἀληθείας ὑποστειλάμενος ἄντικρυς εἶπεν
388 " ἐγώ, Καῖσαρ, ὑπὸ Ἀντωνίου βασιλεὺς[1] γενόμενος ἐν πᾶσιν ὁμολογῶ γεγονέναι χρήσιμος
Ἀντωνίῳ. καὶ οὐδὲ τοῦτ' ἂν ὑποστειλαίμην
εἰπεῖν, ὅτι πάντως ἄν με μετὰ τῶν ὅπλων ἐπεί-
ρασας ἀχώριστον,[2] εἰ μὴ διεκώλυσαν Ἄραβες.
καὶ συμμαχίαν μέντοι γε αὐτῷ κατὰ τὸ δυνατὸν
καὶ σίτου πολλὰς ἔπεμψα μυριάδας, ἀλλ' οὐδὲ
μετὰ τὴν ἐν Ἀκτίῳ πληγὴν κατέλιπον τὸν εὐ-
389 εργέτην, ἐγενόμην δὲ σύμβουλος ἄριστος, ὡς οὐκέτ'
χρήσιμος ἤμην σύμμαχος, μίαν εἶναι λέγων τῶν
πταισθέντων διόρθωσιν τὸν Κλεοπάτρας θάνατον
ἦν ἀνελόντι καὶ χρήματα καὶ τείχη πρὸς ἀσφάλειαν καὶ στρατιὰν καὶ ἐμαυτὸν ὑπισχνούμην
390 κοινωνὸν τοῦ πρὸς σὲ πολέμου. τοῦ δ' ἄρα τὰς
ἀκοὰς ἀπέφραξαν οἱ Κλεοπατρας ἵμεροι καὶ θεὸς
ὁ σοὶ τὸ κρατεῖν χαριζόμενος. συνήττημαι δ
Ἀντωνίῳ καὶ τέθεικα μετὰ τῆς ἐκείνου τύχης τὸ
διάδημα. πρὸς σὲ δὲ ἦλθον ἔχων τὴν ἀρετὴν τῆς
σωτηρίας ἐλπίδα καὶ προλαβὼν ἐξετασθήσεσθαι
ποταπὸς φίλος, οὐ τίνος, ἐγενόμην."
391 (2) Πρὸς ταῦτα Καῖσαρ " ἀλλὰ σώζου γε,'

---

[1] βασιλεὺς P Lat.: τῶν Ἰουδαίων βασιλεὺς the rest.
[2] ἀχώριστον Havercamp from a Leyden ms.: εὐχάριστον
(" a grateful ally ") PAM Lat.: om. the rest.

he inspired more fear than he felt himself ; for Caesar considered his victory to be incomplete so long as Herod remained Antony's ally).[a] The king, nevertheless, resolved to confront the danger and, having sailed to Rhodes, where Caesar was sojourning, presented himself before him without a diadem, a commoner in dress and demeanour, but with the proud spirit of a king. His speech was direct ; he told the truth without reserve.

Battle of Actium September 31 B.C.

Herod makes his peace with Octavius 30 B.C.

"Caesar," he said, "I was made king by Antony, and I acknowledge that I have in all things devoted my services to him. Nor will I shrink from saying that, had not the Arabs detained me, you would assuredly have found me in arms inseparable from his side. I sent him, however, such auxiliary troops as I could and many thousand measures of corn ; nor even after his defeat at Actium did I desert my benefactor. When no longer useful as an ally, I became his best counsellor ; I told him the one remedy for his disasters—the death of Cleopatra. Would he but kill her, I promised him money, walls to protect him, an army, and myself as his brother in arms in the war against you. But his ears, it seems, were stopped by his infatuation for Cleopatra and by God who has granted you the mastery. I share Antony's defeat and with his downfall lay down my diadem. I am come to you resting my hope of safety upon my integrity, and presuming that the subject of inquiry will be not whose friend, but how loyal a friend, I have been."

(2) To this Caesar replied : "Nay, be assured of

---

[a] An exaggerated statement, absent from *A*.

ἔφη, " καὶ βασίλευε νῦν βεβαιότερον· ἄξιος γὰρ
εἶ πολλῶν ἄρχειν οὕτω φιλίας προϊστάμενος.
πειρῶ δὲ καὶ τοῖς εὐτυχεστέροις διαμένειν πιστός,
ὡς ἔγωγε λαμπροτάτας ὑπὲρ τοῦ σοῦ φρονήματος
ἐλπίδας ἔχω. καλῶς μέντοι γε ἐποίησεν Ἀντώνιος Κλεοπάτρᾳ πεισθεὶς μᾶλλον ἢ σοί· καὶ
392 γὰρ σὲ κεκερδήκαμεν ἐκ τῆς ἀνοίας αὐτοῦ. κατ-
άρχεις δ', ὡς ἔοικεν, εὐποιίας δι' ὧν μοι γράφει
Κύντος Δίδιος[1] συμμαχίαν σε πεπομφέναι πρὸς
τοὺς μονομάχους αὐτῷ. νῦν μὲν οὖν δόγματι τὸ
βέβαιόν σοι τῆς βασιλείας ἐξαγγέλλω, πειρά-
σομαι δὲ καὶ αὖθις ἀγαθόν τί σε ποιεῖν, ὡς μὴ
ζητοίης Ἀντώνιον."

393   (3) Τούτοις φιλοφρονησάμενος τὸν βασιλέα καὶ
περιθεὶς αὐτῷ τὸ διάδημα δόγματι διεσήμαινεν
τὴν δωρεάν, ἐν ᾧ πολλὰ μεγαλοφρόνως εἰς ἔπαινον
τἀνδρὸς ἐφθέγξατο. ὁ δὲ δώροις ἐπιμειλιξάμενος
αὐτὸν ἐξῃτεῖτό τινα τῶν Ἀντωνίου φίλων Ἀλεξᾶν ἱκέτην γενόμενον· ἐνίκα δὲ ἡ Καίσαρος ὀργὴ
πολλὰ καὶ χαλεπὰ μεμφομένου τὸν ἐξαιτούμενον
394 οἷς διεκρούσατο τὴν δέησιν. μετὰ δὲ ταῦτα πο-
ρευόμενον ἐπ' Αἰγύπτου διὰ Συρίας Καίσαρα παντὶ
τῷ βασιλικῷ πλούτῳ δεξάμενος Ἡρώδης †τότε
πρῶτον καὶ συνιππάσατο ποιουμένῳ περὶ Πτολεμαΐδα τῆς δυνάμεως ἐξέτασιν εἱστίασέν τε σὺν
ἅπασιν τοῖς φίλοις· μεθ' οὓς καὶ τῇ λοιπῇ στρα-
395 τιᾷ πρὸς εὐωχίαν πάντα διέδωκεν. προυνόησεν

---

[1] Κύντος Δίδιος conj. Hudson from Dio Cass. li. 7: καὶ
Δίδιος Niese: καὶ Βεντίδιος or Βεντίδιος mss.

[a] After the battle of Actium Cleopatra, seeking aid in all
directions, sent for some gladiators who were being trained
for Antony at Trapezus; the gladiators started but were
intercepted.

your safety, and reign henceforth more securely than and is confirmed king. before. So staunch a champion of the claims of friendship deserves to be ruler over many subjects. Endeavour to remain as loyal to those who have been more fortunate ; since, for my part, I entertain the most brilliant hopes for your high spirit. Antony, however, did well in obeying Cleopatra's behests rather than yours ; for through his folly we have gained you. But you have already, it seems, done me a service ; for Quintus Didius writes to me that you have sent a force to assist him against the gladiators.ᵃ I therefore now confirm your kingdom to you by decree ; and hereafter I shall endeavour to confer upon you some further benefit, that you may not feel the loss of Antony."

(3) Having thus graciously addressed the king, he placed the diadem on his head, and publicly notified this award by a decree, in which he expressed his commendation of the honoured man in ample and generous terms. Herod, after propitiating Caesar with presents, then sought to obtain pardon for Alexas, one of Antony's friends, who had come to sue for mercy ; but here Caesar's resentment was too strong for him, and with many bitter complaints against Herod's client the emperor rejected his petition. Subsequently, when Caesar passed through Herod's services to Octavius Syria on his way to Egypt, Herod entertained him in his Egyptian campaign 30 B.C. for the first time with all the resources of his realm ; he accompanied the emperor on horseback when he reviewed his troops at Ptolemais ; he entertained him and all his friends at a banquet ; and he followed this up by making ample provision for the good cheer of the rest of the army. Then, for the march

δὲ καὶ διὰ τῆς ἀνύδρου πορευομένοις μέχρι Πη
λουσίου παρασχεῖν ὕδωρ ἄφθονον ἐπανιοῦσί τ•
ὁμοίως, οὐδὲ ἔστιν ὅ τι τῶν ἐπιτηδείων ἐνεδέησε•
τῇ δυνάμει. δόξα γοῦν αὐτῷ τε Καίσαρι καὶ τοῖ•
στρατιώταις παρέστη πολλῷ βραχυτέραν Ἡρώδη
396 περιεῖναι βασιλείαν πρὸς ἃ παρέσχεν. διὰ τοῦτο
ὡς ἧκεν εἰς Αἴγυπτον, ἤδη Κλεοπάτρας κα•
Ἀντωνίου τεθνεώτων, οὐ μόνον αὐτοῦ ταῖς ἄλ•
λαις τιμαῖς, ἀλλὰ καὶ τῇ βασιλείᾳ προσέθηκε•
τήν τε ὑπὸ Κλεοπάτρας ἀποτμηθεῖσαν χώραν κα•
ἔξωθεν Γάδαρα καὶ Ἵππον καὶ Σαμάρειαν, πρὸς
δὲ τούτοις τῶν παραλίων Γάζαν καὶ Ἀνθηδόνα
397 καὶ Ἰόππην καὶ Στράτωνος πύργον· ἐδωρήσατο
δ᾽ αὐτῷ καὶ πρὸς φυλακὴν τοῦ σώματος τετρακοσίους Γαλάτας, οἳ πρότερον ἐδορυφόρουν Κλεο-
πάτραν. οὐδὲν δὲ οὕτως ἐνῆγεν αὐτὸν εἰς τὰς
δωρεὰς ὡς τὸ μεγαλόφρον τοῦ λαμβάνοντος.

398   (4) Μετὰ δὲ τὴν πρώτην Ἀκτιάδα προστίθησι
αὐτοῦ τῇ βασιλείᾳ τόν τε Τράχωνα καλούμενοι
καὶ τὴν προσεχῆ Βαταναίαν τε καὶ τὴν Αὐρανῖτι
χώραν ἐξ αἰτίας τοιᾶσδε· Ζηνόδωρος ὁ τὸν Λυσανίου μεμισθωμένος οἶκον οὐ διέλειπεν ἐπαφεὶς
τοὺς ἐκ τοῦ Τράχωνος λῃστὰς Δαμασκηνοῖς. οἱ
δ᾽ ἐπὶ Οὐάρρωνα τὸν ἡγεμόνα τῆς Συρίας καταφυγόντες ἐδεήθησαν δηλῶσαι τὴν συμφορὰν αὐτῶι
Καίσαρι· Καῖσαρ δὲ γνοὺς ἀντεπέστειλεν ἐξ-
399 αιρεθῆναι τὸ λῃστήριον. στρατεύσας οὖν Οὐάρρων

---

[a] §§ 361 f.   [b] The later Caesarea.
[c] "The games at Actium were celebrated for the first
186

to Pelusium across the arid desert, and likewise for
the return, he took care to furnish the troops with
abundance of water ; in short, there were no necessaries which the army lacked. The thought could
not but occur both to Caesar himself and to his
soldiers that Herod's realm was far too restricted, in
comparison with the services which he had rendered
them. Accordingly, when Caesar reached Egypt,
after the death of Cleopatra and Antony, he not
only conferred new honours upon him, but also
annexed to his kingdom the territory which Cleopatra   Annexations
had appropriated,[a] with the addition of Gadara,   to Herod's
Hippos and Samaria and the maritime towns of   kingdom.
Gaza, Anthedon, Joppa, and Strato's Tower.[b] He
further presented him, as a bodyguard, with four
hundred Gauls, who had formerly served Cleopatra
in the same capacity. And nothing so strongly
moved the emperor to this liberality as the generous
spirit of him who was the object of it.

(4) After the first period of the Actian era,[c]   Subsequent
Caesar added to Herod's realm the country called   additions
Trachonitis, with the adjacent districts of Batanaea   (Trachonitis
and Auranitis. The occasion of this grant was as   etc.)
follows. Zenodorus, who had taken on lease the   c. 23 B.C.
domain of Lysanias, was perpetually setting the
brigands of Trachonitis to molest the inhabitants of
Damascus. The latter fled for protection to Varro,
the governor of Syria, and besought him to report
their sufferings to Caesar ; on learning the facts
Caesar sent back orders to exterminate the bandits.
Varro, accordingly, led out his troops, cleared the
time in 28 B.C., then in the years 24, 20, 16 B.C., etc. That
enlargement of territory therefore took place ' after the
course of the first Actiad had run,' *i.e.* in the end of 24 B.C.
or beginning of 23 B.C. " (Schürer).

καθαίρει τε τῶν ἀνδρῶν τὴν γῆν καὶ ἀφαιρεῖται
Ζηνόδωρον· ἦν ὕστερον Καῖσαρ, ὡς μὴ γένοιτο
πάλιν ὁρμητήριον τοῖς λῃσταῖς ἐπὶ τὴν Δαμασκόν,
Ἡρώδῃ δίδωσιν. κατέστησεν δὲ αὐτὸν καὶ Συρίας ὅλης ἐπίτροπον ἔτει δεκάτῳ πάλιν ἐλθὼν εἰς
τὴν ἐπαρχίαν, ὡς μηδὲν ἐξεῖναι δίχα τῆς ἐκείνου
400 συμβουλίας τοῖς ἐπιτρόποις διοικεῖν. ἐπεὶ δὲ
τελευτᾷ Ζηνόδωρος, προσένειμεν αὐτῷ καὶ τὴν
μεταξὺ Τράχωνος καὶ τῆς Γαλιλαίας γῆν ἅπασαν.
ὃ δὲ τούτων Ἡρώδῃ μεῖζον ἦν, ὑπὸ μὲν Καίσαρος
ἐφιλεῖτο μετ' Ἀγρίππαν, ὑπ' Ἀγρίππα δὲ μετὰ
Καίσαρα. ἔνθεν ἐπὶ πλεῖστον μὲν εὐδαιμονίας
προύκοψεν, εἰς μεῖζον δ' ἐξήρθη φρόνημα καὶ τὸ
πλέον τῆς μεγαλονοίας ἐπέτεινεν εἰς εὐσέβειαν.

401 (xxi. 1) Πεντεκαιδεκάτῳ γοῦν ἔτει τῆς βασιλείας αὐτόν τε τὸν ναὸν ἐπεσκεύασεν καὶ περὶ
αὐτὸν ἀνετειχίσατο χώραν τῆς οὔσης διπλασίονα,
ἀμέτροις μὲν χρησάμενος τοῖς ἀναλώμασιν ἀν-
υπερβλήτῳ δὲ τῇ πολυτελείᾳ. τεκμήριον δὲ ἦσαν
αἱ μεγάλαι στοαὶ περὶ τὸ ἱερὸν καὶ τὸ βόρειον ἐπ'
αὐτῷ φρούριον· ἃς μὲν γὰρ ἀνῳκοδόμησεν ἐκ
θεμελίων, ὃ δ' ἐπισκευάσας πλούτῳ δαψιλεῖ κατ'
οὐδὲν τῶν βασιλείων ἔλαττον Ἀντωνίαν ἐκάλεσεν
402 εἰς τὴν Ἀντωνίου τιμήν. τό γε μὴν ἑαυτοῦ
βασίλειον κατὰ τὴν ἄνω δειμάμενος πόλιν, δύο
τοὺς μεγίστους καὶ περικαλλεστάτους οἴκους, οἷς

---

[a] M. Vipsanius Agrippa (63–12 B.C.), the devoted friend,
minister and presumptive successor to Augustus, builder of
the Pantheon and organizer of the Roman navy.

[b] " Or thanks to this favoured position."

[c] According to A. xv. 380 " the eighteenth year "; the

district of these pests and deprived Zenodorus of his
tenure. This was the territory which Caesar subsequently presented to Herod, to prevent it from again
being used by the brigands as a base for raids upon
Damascus. When ten years after his first visit *c.* 20 B.C.
Caesar returned to the province, he, moreover,
gave Herod the position of procurator of all Syria,
for the (Roman) procurators were forbidden to take
any measures without his concurrence. Finally, on
the death of Zenodorus, he further assigned to him
all the territory between Trachonitis and Galilee.
But what Herod valued more than all these privileges
was that in Caesar's affection he stood next after
Agrippa,[a] in Agrippa's next after Caesar. Thenceforth [b] he advanced to the utmost prosperity ; his
noble spirit rose to greater heights, and his lofty
ambition was mainly directed to works of piety.

(XXI. 1) Thus, in the fifteenth year[c] of his reign, Herod's
he restored the Temple and, by erecting new founda- buildings :
reconstruc-
tion-walls, enlarged the surrounding area to double tion of the
its former extent. The expenditure devoted to this Temple
begun
work was incalculable, its magnificence never sur- *c.* 20–19 B.C.
passed ; as evidence one would have pointed to the
great colonnades around the Temple courts and to
the fortress which dominated it on the north. The
colonnades Herod reconstructed from the founda-
tions ; the fortress he restored at a lavish cost in a The fortress
style no way inferior to that of a palace, and called of Antonia.
it Antonia in honour of Antony. His own palace, The royal
which he erected in the upper city, comprised two palace.
most spacious and beautiful buildings, with which
latter appears to be the correct date of the beginning of the
work (Schürer), which was not completed till *c.* A.D. 28
(Gospel of S. John ii. 20).

οὐδ' ὁ[1] ναός πῃ συνεκρίνετο, προσηγόρευσεν ἀπὸ
τῶν φίλων τὸν μὲν Καισάρειον τὸν δὲ Ἀγρίππειον.

403　(2) Ἀλλὰ γὰρ οὐκ οἴκοις μόνον αὐτῶν τὴν
μνήμην καὶ τὰς ἐπικλήσεις περιέγραψεν, διέβη δὲ
εἰς ὅλας πόλεις αὐτῷ τὸ φιλότιμον. ἐν μέν γε τῇ
Σαμαρείτιδι πόλιν καλλίστῳ περιβόλῳ τειχισά-
μενος ἐπὶ σταδίους εἴκοσι καὶ καταγαγὼν ἑξακισχιλίους εἰς αὐτὴν οἰκήτορας, γῆν δὲ τούτοις προσ-
νείμας λιπαρωτάτην, καὶ ἐν μέσῳ τῷ κτίσματι
ναόν τε ἐνιδρυσάμενος μέγιστον καὶ περὶ αὐτὸν
τέμενος ἀποδείξας τῷ Καίσαρι τριῶν ἡμισταδίων,
τὸ ἄστυ Σεβαστὴν ἐκάλεσεν· ἐξαίρετον δὲ τοῖς ἐν
αὐτῷ παρέσχεν εὐνομίαν.

404　(3) Ἐπὶ τούτοις δωρησαμένου τοῦ Καίσαρος
αὐτὸν ἑτέρας προσθέσει χώρας, ὁ δὲ κἀνταῦθα
ναὸν αὐτῷ λευκῆς μαρμάρου καθιδρύσατο παρὰ
τὰς Ἰορδάνου πηγάς· καλεῖται δὲ Πάνειον ὁ
405 τόπος. ἔνθα κορυφὴ μέν τις ὄρους εἰς ἄπειρον
ὕψος ἀνατείνεται, παρὰ δὲ τὴν ὑπόρειον λαγόνα
συνηρεφὲς ἄντρον ὑπανοίγει, δι' οὗ βαραθρώδης
κρημνὸς εἰς ἀμέτρητον ἀπορρῶγα βαθύνεται,
πλήθει τε ὕδατος ἀσαλεύτου καὶ τοῖς καθιμῶσίν
406 τι πρὸς ἔρευναν γῆς οὐδὲν μῆκος ἐξαρκεῖ. τοῦ
δὲ ἄντρου κατὰ τὰς ἔξωθεν ῥίζας ἀνατέλλουσιν αἱ
πηγαί· καὶ γένεσις μέν, ὡς ἔνιοι δοκοῦσιν, ἔνθεν
Ἰορδάνου, τὸ δ' ἀκριβὲς ἐν τοῖς ἑξῆς δηλώσομεν.

407　(4) Ὁ δὲ βασιλεὺς καὶ ἐν Ἱεριχοῖ μεταξὺ
Κύπρου τοῦ φρουρίου καὶ τῶν προτέρων βασι-

---

[1] οὐδ' ὁ Bekker from a Leyden ms. : οὐδὲ the rest.

[a] Mount Hermon. For a description of Paneion or

the Temple itself bore no comparison ; these he named after his friends, the one Caesareum, the other Agrippeum.

(2) He was not content, however, to commemorate his patrons' names by palaces only ; his munificence extended to the creation of whole cities. In the district of Samaria he built a town enclosed within magnificent walls twenty furlongs in length, introduced into it six thousand colonists, and gave them allotments of highly productive land. In the centre of this settlement he erected a massive temple, enclosed in ground, a furlong and a half in length, consecrated to Caesar ; while he named the town itself Sebaste. The inhabitants were given a privileged constitution. *Foundation of Sebaste in Samaria.*

(3) When, later on, through Caesar's bounty he received additional territory, Herod there too dedicated to him a temple of white marble near the sources of the Jordan, at a place called Paneion. At this spot a mountain [a] rears its summit to an immense height aloft ; at the base of the cliff is an opening into an overgrown cavern ; within this, plunging down to an immeasurable depth, is a yawning chasm, enclosing a volume of still water, the bottom of which no sounding-line has been found long enough to reach. Outside and from beneath the cavern well up the springs from which, as some think, the Jordan takes its rise ; but we will tell the true story of this in the sequel.[b] *The Temple of Augustus at Paneion.*

(4) At Jericho, again, between the fortress of Cypros [c] and the former palace, the king constructed

[a] Paneas, later Caesarea Philippi, mod. *Banias*, see G. A. Smith, *Hist. Geog. of Holy Land*, 473.

[b] See iii. 509 ff.

[c] Built by Herod in honour of his mother, § 417.

λείων ἄλλα κατασκευάσας ἀμείνω καὶ χρησιμώτερα πρὸς τὰς ἐπιδημίας ἀπὸ τῶν αὐτῶν ὠνόμασεν φίλων. καθόλου δὲ οὐκ ἔστιν εἰπεῖν ὅντινα
τῆς βασιλείας ἐπιτήδειον τόπον τῆς πρὸς Καίσαρα
τιμῆς γυμνὸν εἴασεν. ἐπεὶ δὲ τὴν ἰδίαν χώραν
ἐπλήρωσεν ναῶν, εἰς τὴν ἐπαρχίαν αὐτοῦ τὰς
τιμὰς ὑπερεξέχεεν καὶ πολλαῖς πόλεσιν ἐνιδρύσατο Καισάρεια.

408   (5) Κατιδὼν δὲ κἂν τοῖς παραλίοις πόλιν ἤδη
μὲν κάμνουσαν, Στράτωνος ἐκαλεῖτο πύργος, διὰ
δὲ εὐφυΐαν τοῦ χωρίου δέξασθαι δυναμένην τὸ
φιλότιμον αὐτοῦ, πᾶσαν ἀνέκτισεν λευκῷ λίθῳ
καὶ λαμπροτάτοις ἐκόσμησεν βασιλείοις, ἐν ᾗ
409 μάλιστα τὸ φύσει μεγαλόνουν ἐπεδείξατο. μεταξὺ
γὰρ Δώρων καὶ Ἰόππης, ὧν ἡ πόλις μέση κεῖται,
πᾶσαν εἶναι συμβέβηκεν τὴν παράλιον ἀλίμενον,
ὡς πάντα τὸν τὴν Φοινίκην ἐπ' Αἰγύπτου παρα-
πλέοντα σαλεύειν ἐν πελάγει διὰ τὴν ἐκ λιβὸς
ἀπειλήν, ᾧ καὶ μετρίως ἐπαυρίζοντι τηλικοῦτον
ἐπεγείρεται[1] κῦμα πρὸς ταῖς πέτραις, ὥστε τὴν
ὑποστροφὴν τοῦ κύματος ἐπὶ πλεῖστον ἐξαγριοῦν
410 τὴν θάλασσαν. ἀλλ' ὁ βασιλεὺς τοῖς ἀναλώμασιν
καὶ τῇ φιλοτιμίᾳ νικήσας τὴν φύσιν μείζονα μὲν
τοῦ Πειραιῶς λιμένα κατεσκεύασεν, ἐν δὲ τοῖς
μυχοῖς αὐτοῦ βαθεῖς ὅρμους ἑτέρους.

411   (6) Καθάπαν δ' ἔχων ἀντιπράσσοντα τὸν τόπον
ἐφιλονείκησεν πρὸς τὴν δυσχέρειαν, ὡς τὴν μὲν
ὀχυρότητα τῆς δομήσεως δυσάλωτον εἶναι τῇ
θαλάσσῃ, τὸ δὲ κάλλος ὡς ἐπὶ μηδενὶ δυσκόλῳ
κεκοσμῆσθαι. συμμετρησάμενος γὰρ ὅσον εἰρή-

---

[1] ἐπεγείρετο PM : ἐγείρεται the rest.

new buildings, finer and more commodious for the reception of guests, and named them after the same friends.[a] In short, one can mention no suitable spot within his realm, which he left destitute of some mark of homage to Caesar. And then, after filling his own territory with temples, he let the memorials of his esteem overflow into the province and erected in numerous cities monuments to Caesar.

(5) His notice was attracted by a town on the coast, called Strato's Tower, which, though then dilapidated, was, from its advantageous situation, suited for the exercise of his liberality. This he entirely rebuilt with white stone, and adorned with the most magnificent palaces, displaying here, as nowhere else, the innate grandeur of his character. For the whole sea-board from Dora to Joppa, midway between which the city lies, was without a harbour, so that vessels bound for Egypt along the coast of Phoenicia had to ride at anchor in the open when menaced by the south-west wind; for even a moderate breeze from this quarter dashes the waves to such a height against the cliffs, that their reflux spreads a wild commotion far out to sea. However, by dint of expenditure and enterprise, the king triumphed over nature and constructed a harbour larger than the Piraeus, including other deep roadsteads within its recesses.

(6) Notwithstanding the totally recalcitrant nature of the site, he grappled with the difficulties so successfully, that the solidity of his masonry defied the sea, while its beauty was such as if no obstacle had existed. Having determined upon the comparative size[b] of

Marginal notes: Other buildings in honour of Augustus. / Caesarea and its harbour.

---

[a] Augustus and Agrippa.
[b] *i.e.* "larger than the Piraeus" (§ 410),

καμὲν τῷ λιμένι μέγεθος καθίει λίθους ἐπ' ὀργυιὰς
εἴκοσιν εἰς τὸ πέλαγος, ὧν ἦσαν οἱ πλεῖστοι μῆκος
ποδῶν πεντήκοντα, βάθος ἐννέα, εὖρος δέκα, τινὲς
412 δὲ καὶ μείζους. ἐπεὶ δὲ ἀνεπληρώθη τὸ ὕφαλον,[1]
οὕτως ἤδη τὸ ὑπερέχον τοῦ πελάγους τεῖχος ἐπὶ
διακοσίους πόδας ηὐρύνετο· ὧν οἱ μὲν ἑκατὸν
προδεδόμηντο πρὸς τὴν ἀνακοπὴν τοῦ κύματος,
προκυμία γοῦν ἐκλήθη, τὸ δὲ λοιπὸν ὑπόκειται
τῷ περιθέοντι λιθίνῳ τείχει. τοῦτο δὲ πύργοις
τε διείληπται μεγίστοις, ὧν ὁ προύχων καὶ περι-
καλλέστατος ἀπὸ τοῦ Καίσαρος προγόνου Δρού-
σιον κέκληται.

413 (7) Ψαλίδες τε πυκναὶ πρὸς καταγωγὴν τῶν
ἐνορμιζομένων, καὶ τὸ πρὸ αὐτῶν πᾶν κύκλῳ
νάγμα τοῖς ἀποβαίνουσιν πλατὺς περίπατος. ὁ δ'
εἴσπλους βόρειος, αἰθριώτατος γὰρ ἀνέμων τῷ
τόπῳ βορέας, καὶ ἐπὶ τοῦ στόματος κολοσσοὶ
τρεῖς ἑκατέρωθεν ὑπεστηριγμένοι κίοσιν, ὧν τοὺς
μὲν ἐκ λαιᾶς χειρὸς εἰσπλεόντων πύργος ναστὸς
ἀνέχει, τοὺς δὲ ἐκ δεξιοῦ δύο ὀρθοὶ λίθοι συν-
εζευγμένοι τοῦ κατὰ θάτερον χεῖλος πύργου μεί-
414 ζονες. προσεχεῖς δ' οἰκίαι τῷ λιμένι, λευκοῦ καὶ
αὐταὶ λίθου, καὶ κατατείνοντες ἐπ' αὐτὸν οἱ
στενωποὶ τοῦ ἄστεος πρὸς ἓν διάστημα μεμε-
τρημένοι. καὶ τοῦ στόματος ἀντικρὺ ναὸς Καίσαρος ἐπὶ γηλόφου κάλλει καὶ μεγέθει διάφορος·

---

[1] Destinon from Lat.: ὑψηλὸν PA: βάθος the rest.

[a] " not less than eighteen," A.
[b] A. adds " who died young." Nero Claudius Drusus
(38–9 B.C.), son of Livia, afterwards wife of Augustus, and
father of Germanicus.
[c] Or "vaulted chambers," "crypts."
[d] Strictly a temple of Rome and Augustus, as Reinach

the harbour as we have stated, he had blocks of stone
let down into twenty fathoms of water, most of
them measuring fifty feet in length by nine in depth
and ten [a] in breadth, some being even larger. Upon
the submarine foundation thus laid he constructed
above the surface a mole two hundred feet broad ;
of which one hundred were built out to break the
surge, whence this portion was called the break-
water, while the remainder supported a stone wall
encircling the harbour. From this wall arose, at
intervals, massive towers, the loftiest and most
magnificent of which was called Drusion after the
step-son of Caesar.[b]

(7) Numerous inlets [c] in the wall provided landing-
places for mariners putting in to harbour, while the
whole circular terrace fronting these channels served
as a broad promenade for disembarking passengers.
The entrance to the port faced northwards, because
in these latitudes the north wind is the most favourable of all. At the harbour-mouth stood colossal
statues, three on either side, resting on columns ;
the columns on the left of vessels entering port were
supported by a massive tower, those on the right by
two upright blocks of stone clamped together, whose
height exceeded that of the tower on the opposite
side. Abutting on the harbour were houses, also
of white stone, and upon it converged the streets
of the town, laid at equal distances apart. On an
eminence facing the harbour-mouth stood Caesar's
temple,[d] remarkable for its beauty and grand pro-

remarks, referring to Suet. *Aug.* 52 " templa . . . in nulla
provincia nisi communi suo Romaeque nomine recepit."
This is indicated in Josephus by the mention of the two
statues.

ἐν δ' αὐτῷ κολοσσὸς Καίσαρος οὐκ ἀποδέων τοῦ
Ὀλυμπίασιν Διός, ᾧ καὶ προσείκασται, Ῥώμης
δὲ ἴσος Ἥρᾳ τῇ κατ' Ἄργος. ἀνέθηκεν δὲ τῇ
μὲν ἐπαρχίᾳ τὴν πόλιν, τοῖς ταύτῃ δὲ πλοϊζο-
μένοις τὸν λιμένα, Καίσαρι δὲ τὴν τιμὴν τοῦ
κτίσματος· Καισάρειαν γοῦν ὠνόμασεν αὐτήν.

415 (8) Τά γε μὴν λοιπὰ τῶν ἔργων, ἀμφιθέατρον
καὶ θέατρον καὶ ἀγοράς, ἄξια τῆς προσηγορίας
ἐνιδρύσατο. καὶ πενταετηρικοὺς ἀγῶνας καταστησάμενος ὁμοίως ἐκάλεσεν ἀπὸ τοῦ Καίσαρος,
πρῶτος αὐτὸς ἆθλα μέγιστα προθεὶς ἐπὶ τῆς
ἑκατοστῆς ἐνενηκοστῆς δευτέρας ὀλυμπιάδος, ἐν
οἷς οὐ μόνον οἱ νικῶντες, ἀλλὰ καὶ οἱ μετ' αὐτοὺς
καὶ οἱ τρίτοι τοῦ βασιλικοῦ πλούτου μετελάμ-
416 βανον. ἀνακτίσας δὲ καὶ Ἀνθηδόνα τὴν παράλιον καταρριφθεῖσαν ἐν πολέμῳ Ἀγρίππειον προσ-
ηγόρευσε· τοῦ δ' αὐτοῦ φίλου δι' ὑπερβολὴν
εὐνοίας καὶ ἐπὶ τῆς πύλης ἐχάραξεν τὸ ὄνομα, ἣν
αὐτὸς ἐν τῷ ναῷ κατεσκεύασεν.

417 (9) Φιλοπάτωρ γε μήν, εἰ καί τις ἕτερος· καὶ
γὰρ τῷ πατρὶ μνημεῖον κατέθηκεν πόλιν, ἣν ἐν
τῷ καλλίστῳ τῆς βασιλείας πεδίῳ κτίσας ποταμοῖς
τε καὶ δένδρεσιν πλουσίαν ὠνόμασεν Ἀντιπατρίδα,
καὶ τὸ ὑπὲρ Ἱεριχοῦντος φρούριον ὀχυρότητι
καὶ κάλλει διάφορον τειχίσας ἀνέθηκεν τῇ μητρὶ
418 προσειπὼν Κύπρον. Φασαήλῳ δὲ τἀδελφῷ τὸν
ἐν Ἱεροσολύμοις ὁμώνυμον πύργον, οὗ τό τε
σχῆμα καὶ τὴν ἐν τῷ μεγέθει πολυτέλειαν διὰ
τῶν ἑξῆς δηλώσομεν. καὶ πόλιν ἄλλην κτίσας

ᵃ Or Agrippias, A. xiii. 357 ; the town was close to Gaza.
ᵇ At Jerusalem ; the particular gate so called is unknown.

portions ; it contained a colossal statue of the emperor, not inferior to the Olympian Zeus, which served for its model, and another of Rome, rivalling that of Hera at Argos. The city Herod dedicated to the province, the harbour to navigators in these waters, to Caesar the glory of this new foundation, to which he accordingly gave the name of Caesarea.

(8) The rest of the buildings—amphitheatre, theatre, public places—were constructed in a style worthy of the name which the city bore. He further instituted quinquennial games, likewise named after Caesar, and inaugurated them himself, in the hundred and ninety-second Olympiad, offering prizes of the highest value ; at these games not the victors only, but also those who obtained second and third places, participated in the royal bounty.

Quin-
quennial
games at
Caesarea.

10-9 B.C.
(3rd year
of the
Olympiad).

Another maritime town, which had been destroyed in war-time, namely Anthedon, he rebuilt and renamed Agrippium[a] ; and so great was his affection for this same friend Agrippa, that he engraved his name upon the gate which he erected in the Temple.[b]

Foundation
of Anthedon
(Agrip-
pium);

(9) No man ever showed greater filial affection. As a memorial to his father he founded a city in the fairest plain in his realm, rich in rivers and trees, and named it Antipatris.[c] Above Jericho he built the walls of a fortress, remarkable alike for solidity and beauty, which he dedicated to his mother under the name of Cypros. To his brother Phasael he erected the tower in Jerusalem called by his name, the appearance and splendid proportions of which we shall describe in the sequel.[d] He also gave the

of Anti-
patris,
Cypros and
Phasaelis.

[c] *Ras el ʿAin*, some 10 miles inland from and N.E. of Joppa, on the road from Jerusalem to Caesarea.
[d] v. 166-169.

κατὰ τὸν ἀπὸ Ἱεριχοῦς ἰόντων αὐλῶνα πρὸς
βορέαν Φασαηλίδα ὠνόμασεν.

419 (10) Παραδοὺς δ' αἰῶνι τούς τε οἰκείους καὶ
φίλους οὐδὲ τῆς ἑαυτοῦ μνήμης ἠμέλησεν, ἀλλὰ
φρούριον μὲν ἐπιτειχίσας τῷ πρὸς Ἀραβίαν ὄρει
προσηγόρευσεν Ἡρώδειον ἀφ' ἑαυτοῦ, τὸν δὲ
μαστοειδῆ κολωνὸν ὄντα χειροποίητον, ἑξήκοντα
σταδίων ἄπωθεν Ἱεροσολύμων, ἐκάλεσεν μὲν
420 ὁμοίως, ἐξήσκησεν δὲ φιλοτιμότερον. στρογγύ-
λοις μὲν γὰρ τὴν ἄκραν πύργοις περιέσχεν, ἐπλήρωσεν δὲ τὸν περίβολον βασιλείοις πολυτελεστάτοις, ὡς μὴ μόνον τὴν ἔνδον τῶν οἰκημάτων ὄψιν
εἶναι λαμπράν, ἀλλὰ καὶ τοῖς ἔξωθεν τοίχοις καὶ
θριγκοῖς καὶ στέγαις περικεχύσθαι τὸν πλοῦτον
δαψιλῆ. πόρρωθεν δὲ μεγίστοις ἀναλώμασιν ὑδάτων πλῆθος εἰσήγαγεν καὶ βαθμοῖς διακοσίοις
λευκοτάτης μαρμάρου τὴν ἄνοδον διέλαβεν· ἦν γὰρ
δὴ τὸ γήλοφον ἐπιεικῶς ὑψηλὸν καὶ πᾶν χειρο-
421 ποίητον. κατεσκεύασεν δὲ καὶ περὶ τὰς ῥίζας
ἄλλα βασίλεια τήν τε ἀποσκευὴν καὶ τοὺς φίλους
δέξασθαι δυνάμενα, ὥστε τῷ μὲν πάντα ἔχειν
πόλιν εἶναι δοκεῖν τὸ ἔρυμα, τῇ περιγραφῇ δὲ
βασίλειον.

422 (11) Τοσαῦτα συγκτίσας πλείσταις καὶ τῶν
ἔξω πόλεων τὸ μεγαλόψυχον ἐπεδείξατο, Τρι-
πόλει μὲν [γὰρ][1] καὶ Δαμασκῷ καὶ Πτολεμαΐδι
γυμνάσια, Βύβλῳ δὲ τεῖχος, ἐξέδρας δὲ καὶ στοὰς
καὶ ναοὺς καὶ ἀγορὰς Βηρυτῷ κατασκευάσας καὶ
Τύρῳ, Σιδῶνί γε μὴν καὶ Δαμασκῷ θέατρα, Λαο-

[1] om. Bekker.

---

a Literally " in the form of a breast."

name of Phasaelis to another city which he built in the valley to the north of Jericho.

(10) But while he thus perpetuated the memory of his family and his friends, he did not neglect to leave memorials of himself. Thus he built a fortress in the hills on the Arabian frontier and called it after himself Herodium. An artificial rounded [a] hill, sixty furlongs from Jerusalem, was given the same name, but more elaborate embellishment.[b] The crest he crowned with a ring of round towers ; the enclosure was filled with gorgeous palaces, the magnificent appearance of which was not confined to the interior of the apartments, but outer walls, battlements, and roofs, all had wealth lavished upon them in profusion. He had, at immense expense, an abundant supply of water brought into it from a distance, and provided an easy ascent by two hundred steps of the purest white marble ; the mound, though entirely artificial, being of a considerable height. Around the base he erected other palaces for the accommodation of his furniture and his friends. Thus, in the amplitude of its resources this stronghold resembled a town, in its restricted area a simple palace.

(11) After founding all these places, he proceeded to display his generosity to numerous cities outside his realm. Thus, he provided gymnasia for Tripolis, Damascus and Ptolemais, a wall for Byblus, halls, porticoes, temples, and market-places for Berytus and Tyre, theatres for Sidon and Damascus, an aqueduct

The two buildings called Herodium.

Herod's various bounties to foreign cities.

[b] Built in memory of his victory over the Jewish allies of the Parthians, § 265 ; modern *Jebel Fereidis* (" Hill of Paradise " or Frank mountain), some 4 miles S.E. of Bethlehem. The site of the other Herodium is unidentified.

δικεῦσι δὲ τοῖς παραλίοις ὑδάτων εἰσαγωγήν,
᾿Ασκαλωνίταις δὲ βαλανεῖα καὶ κρήνας πολυτελεῖς, πρὸς δὲ περίστυλα θαυμαστὰ τήν τε ἐργασίαν καὶ τὸ μέγεθος· εἰσὶ δ᾽ οἷς ἄλση καὶ λειμῶ-
423 νας ἀνέθηκεν. πολλαὶ δὲ πόλεις ὥσπερ κοινωνοὶ
τῆς βασιλείας καὶ χώραν ἔλαβον παρ᾽ αὐτοῦ·
γυμνασιαρχίαις δ᾽ ἄλλας ἐπετησίοις τε καὶ δι-
ηνεκέσιν ἐδωρήσατο προσόδους κατατάξας, ὥσπερ
424 Κῴοις, ἵνα μηδέποτε ἐκλείπῃ τὸ γέρας. σῖτόν γε
μὴν πᾶσιν ἐχορήγησεν τοῖς δεομένοις, καὶ τῇ
῾Ρόδῳ χρήματα μὲν εἰς ναυτικοῦ κατασκευὴν
παρέσχεν πολλαχοῦ[1] καὶ πολλάκις, ἐμπρησθὲν δὲ
τὸ Πύθιον ἰδίοις ἀναλώμασιν ἄμεινον ἀνεδείματο.
425 καὶ τί δεῖ λέγειν τὰς εἰς Λυκίους ἢ Σαμίους δωρεὰς
ἢ τὴν δι᾽ ὅλης τῆς ᾿Ιωνίας, ἐν οἷς ἐδεήθησαν ἕκαστοι, δαψίλειαν; ἀλλ᾽ ᾿Αθηναῖοι καὶ Λακεδαιμόνιοι Νικοπολῖταί τε καὶ τὸ κατὰ Μυσίαν Πέργα-
μον οὐ τῶν ῾Ηρώδου γέμουσιν ἀναθημάτων; τὴν
δ᾽ ᾿Αντιοχέων τῶν ἐν Συρίᾳ πλατεῖαν οὐ φευκτὴν
οὖσαν ὑπὸ βορβόρου κατέστρωσέν τε, σταδίων
εἴκοσι τὸ μῆκος οὖσαν, ξεστῇ μαρμάρῳ καὶ πρὸς
τὰς τῶν ὑετῶν ἀποφυγὰς ἐκόσμησεν ἰσομήκει
στοᾷ;
426 (12) Ταῦτα μὲν ἄν τις εἴποι ἴδια τῶν εὖ πα-
θόντων[2] δήμων ἑκάστου, τὸ δὲ ᾿Ηλείοις χαρισθὲν
οὐ μόνον κοινὸν τῆς ῾Ελλάδος, ἀλλ᾽ ὅλης τῆς
οἰκουμένης δῶρον, εἰς ἣν ἡ δόξα τῶν ᾿Ολυμπίασιν[3]
427 ἀγώνων δικνεῖται. τούτους γὰρ δὴ καταλυο-

---

[1] πολλὰ Destinon : ? πολλαχῇ (cf. Plato, Rep. 538 D).
[2] εὐπαθούντων PLV and a Leipzig ms.
[3] Bekker: τῶν ἐν ᾿Ολυμπιᾶσιν mss.

---

[a] Keeper of the gymnasium, responsible for the conduct

for Laodicea on sea, baths, sumptuous fountains and colonnades, admirable alike for their architecture and their proportions, for Ascalon ; to other communities he dedicated groves and meadow-land. Many cities, as though they had been associated with his realm, received from him grants of land ; others, like Cos, were endowed with revenues to maintain the annual office of gymnasiarch *a* to perpetuity, to ensure that this honourable post should never lapse. Corn he supplied to all applicants *b* ; to the people of Rhodes he made contributions again and again for shipbuilding,*c* and when their *d* Pythian temple was burnt down he rebuilt it on a grander scale at his own expense. Need I allude to his donations to the people of Lycia or Samos, or to his liberality, extended to every district of Ionia, to meet its needs ? Nay, are not Athenians and Lacedaemonians, the inhabitants of Nicopolis and of Pergamum in Mysia, laden with Herod's offerings ? And that broad street in Syrian Antioch, once shunned on account of the mud—was it not he who paved its twenty furlongs with polished marble, and, as a protection from the rain, adorned it with a colonnade of equal length ?

(12) In these cases, it may be said, the individual communities concerned were the sole beneficiaries ; his bounty to the people of Elis, on the other hand, was a gift not only to Hellas at large but to the whole world, wherever the fame of the Olympic games penetrates. For, observing that these were

His endowment of the Olympic games.

of festal games and for the maintenance and payment of trainers and training-masters.

b Or " to all in need of it."

c Cf. § 280 for his shipbuilding at Rhodes in humbler circumstances.　　　　　　*d* Cf. A. xvi. 147.

μένους ἀπορίᾳ χρημάτων ὁρῶν καὶ τὸ μόνον λεί-
ψανον τῆς ἀρχαίας Ἑλλάδος ὑπορρέον, οὐ μόνον
ἀγωνοθέτης ἧς ἐπέτυχεν πενταετηρίδος εἰς Ῥώμην παραπλέων ἐγένετο, ἀλλὰ καὶ πρὸς τὸ δι-
ηνεκὲς πόρους χρημάτων ἀπέδειξεν, ὡς μηδέποτε
428 ἀγωνοθετοῦσαν αὐτοῦ τὴν μνήμην ἐπιλιπεῖν. ἀνήνυτον ἂν εἴη χρεῶν διαλύσεις ἢ φόρων ἐπεξιέναι,
καθάπερ Φασηλίταις καὶ Βαλανεώταις καὶ τοῖς
περὶ τὴν Κιλικίαν πολιχνίοις τὰς ἐτησίους εἰσ-
φορὰς ἐπεξεκούφισεν. πλεῖστόν γε μὴν αὐτοῦ
τῆς μεγαλονοίας ἔθραυσεν ὁ φόβος, ὡς μὴ δόξειεν
ἐπίφθονος ἤ τι θηρᾶσθαι μεῖζον, εὐεργετῶν τὰς
πόλεις πλέον τῶν ἐχόντων.

429   (13) Ἐχρήσατο δὲ καὶ σώματι πρὸς τὴν ψυχὴν
ἀναλόγῳ, κυνηγέτης μὲν ἄριστος ἀεὶ γενόμενος,
ἐν ᾧ μάλιστα δι' ἐμπειρίαν ἱππικῆς ἐπετύγχανεν·
μιᾷ γοῦν ἡμέρᾳ ποτὲ τεσσαράκοντα θηρίων ἐκράτησεν, ἔστι δὲ καὶ συοτρόφος μὲν ἡ χώρα, τὸ
πλέον δ' ἐλάφων καὶ ὀνάγρων εὔπορος· πολε-
430 μιστὴς δ' ἀνυπόστατος. πολλοὶ γοῦν κἂν ταῖς
γυμνασίαις αὐτὸν κατεπλάγησαν ἀκοντιστήν τε
ἰθυβολώτατον[1] καὶ τοξότην εὐστοχώτατον ἰδόντες.
πρὸς δὲ τοῖς ψυχικοῖς καὶ τοῖς σωματικοῖς προ-
τερήμασιν ἐχρήσατο καὶ δεξιᾷ τύχῃ· καὶ γὰρ
σπάνιον ἔπταισεν ἐν πολέμῳ, καὶ τῶν πταισμά-
των οὐκ αὐτὸς αἴτιος, ἀλλ' ἢ προδοσίᾳ τινῶν ἢ
προπετείᾳ στρατιωτῶν ἐγένετο.

[1] εὐθυβολώτατον PAM Exc.

---

[a] Either his second visit to Rome (12 B.C.) or his third
(c. 8 B.C.) (Schürer).

[b] A maritime town of Lycia.

[c] On the Syrian coast opposite Cyprus, between Laodicea
and Aradus.

declining for want of funds and that this solitary relic of ancient Greece was sinking into decay, he not only accepted the post of president for the quadrennial celebration which coincided with his visit [a] on his voyage to Rome, but he endowed them for all time with revenues, which should preserve an unfading memory of his term as president. The enumeration of the debts and taxes discharged by himself would be endless; it was thus, for instance, that he lightened the burden of their annual taxes for the inhabitants of Phaselis,[b] Balanea [c] and various minor towns in Cilicia. Often, however, his noble generosity was thwarted by the fear of exciting either jealousy or the suspicion of entertaining some higher ambition, in conferring upon states greater benefits than they received from their own masters.

(13) [d] Herod's genius was matched by his physical constitution. Always foremost in the chase, in which he distinguished himself above all by his skill in horsemanship, he on one occasion brought down forty wild beasts in a single day; for the country breeds boars and, in greater abundance, stags and wild asses. As a fighter he was irresistible; and at practice spectators were often struck with astonishment at the precision with which he threw the javelin, the unerring aim with which he bent the bow. But besides these pre-eminent gifts of soul and body, he was blessed by good fortune; [e] he rarely met with a reverse in war, and, when he did, this was due not to his own fault, but either to treachery or to the recklessness of his troops.

His physical prowess.

[d] This paragraph has no parallel in *A*.
[e] *Cf.* and contrast the estimate in *A*. xvii. 191 f.

431 (xxii. 1) Τάς γε μὴν ὑπαίθρους εὐπραγίας ἡ
τύχη τοῖς κατ' οἶκον ἀνιαροῖς ἐνεμέσησεν, καὶ
κακοδαιμονεῖν ἐκ γυναικὸς ἤρξατο περὶ ἣν μάλι-
432 στα ἐσπούδασεν. ἐπειδὴ γὰρ εἰς τὴν ἀρχὴν παρ-
ῆλθεν, ἀποπεμψάμενος ἣν ἰδιώτης ἦκτο γαμετήν,
γένος ἦν ἐξ Ἱεροσολύμων Δωρὶς ὄνομα, γαμεῖ
Μαριάμμην τὴν Ἀλεξάνδρου τοῦ Ἀριστοβούλου
θυγατέρα, δι' ἣν αὐτῷ στασιασθῆναι συνέβη τὸν
οἶκον, καὶ τάχιον μέν, μάλιστα δὲ μετὰ τὴν ἐκ
433 Ῥώμης ἄφιξιν. πρῶτον μὲν γὰρ τὸν ἐκ τῆς
Δωρίδος υἱὸν Ἀντίπατρον διὰ τοὺς ἐκ Μαριάμμης ἐφυγάδευσεν τῆς πόλεως, μόναις ταῖς ἑορταῖς
ἐφεὶς[1] κατιέναι· ἔπειτα τὸν πάππον τῆς γυναικὸς
Ὑρκανὸν ἐκ Πάρθων πρὸς αὐτὸν ἐλθόντα δι'
ὑπόνοιαν ἐπιβουλῆς ἀνεῖλεν, ὃν ᾐχμαλωτίσατο μὲν
Βαρζαφράνης καταδραμὼν Συρίαν, ἐξῃτήσαντο δὲ
434 κατ' οἶκτον οἱ ὑπὲρ Εὐφράτην ὁμοεθνεῖς. καὶ εἴ
γε τούτοις ἐπείσθη παραινοῦσιν μὴ διαβῆναι πρὸς
Ἡρώδην, οὐκ ἂν παραπώλετο· δέλεαρ δ' αὐτῷ
θανάτου τῆς υἱωνῆς ὁ γάμος κατέστη· τούτῳ γὰρ
πεποιθὼς καὶ περισσόν τι τῆς πατρίδος ἐφιέμενος
ἧκεν. παρώξυνεν δὲ Ἡρώδην οὐκ αὐτὸς ἀντι-
ποιούμενος βασιλείας, ἀλλ' ἐπεὶ τὸ βασιλεύειν
ἐπέβαλλεν αὐτῷ.

435 (2) Τῶν δὲ ἐκ Μαριάμμης πέντε τέκνων αὐτῷ
γενομένων δύο μὲν θυγατέρες, τρεῖς δ' ἦσαν υἱεῖς.
καὶ τούτων ὁ νεώτατος μὲν ἐν Ῥώμῃ παιδευό-
μενος τελευτᾷ, δύο δὲ τοὺς πρεσβυτάτους βασι-

---

[1] ἐφεὶς Exc. (the usual verb in Josephus): ἀφεὶς the rest.

^a Cf. § 241.   ^b § 260.
^c For his resignation of the throne see B. i. 120 ff.
^d Salampsio and Cypros.

(xxii. 1) But, in revenge for his public prosperity, fortune visited Herod with troubles at home ; his ill-fated career originated with a woman to whom he was passionately attached. For, on ascending the throne, he had dismissed the wife whom he had taken when he was still a commoner, a native of Jerusalem named Doris, and married Mariamme, daughter of Alexander, the son of Aristobulus.[a] It was she who brought into his house the discord, which, beginning at an earlier date, was greatly aggravated after his return from Rome. For, in the first place, in the interests of his children by Mariamme, he banished from the capital the son whom he had had by Doris, namely Antipater, allowing him to visit it on the festivals only. Next he put to death, on suspicion of conspiracy, Hyrcanus, Mariamme's grandfather, who had come back from Parthia to Herod's court. Hyrcanus had been taken prisoner by Barzapharnes when the latter overran Syria,[b] but had been liberated through the intercession of his compassionate countrymen living beyond the Euphrates. And had he but followed their advice not to cross the river to join Herod, he would have escaped his tragic fate ; but the marriage of his grand-daughter lured him to his death. He came relying upon that and impelled by an ardent longing for his native land, and roused Herod's resentment not by making any claim to the throne, but because it actually belonged to him by right.[c]

(2) Herod had five children by Mariamme, two daughters[d] and three sons. The youngest son died in the course of his training in Rome ; to the two elder sons[e] he gave a princely education, both out

Marginal notes: Herod's domestic tragedies. — Banishment of his son Antipater. — Execution of Hyrcanus *c.* 30 B.C. — Herod's children by Mariamme.

[e] Alexander and Aristobulus.

λικῶς ἦγεν διά τε τὴν μητρῴαν εὐγένειαν καὶ ὅτι
436 βασιλεύοντι ἐγεγόνεισαν αὐτῷ. τὸ δὲ τούτων
ἰσχυρότερον ὁ Μαριάμμης ἔρως συνήργει, καθ᾽
ἡμέραν ἐκκαίων Ἡρώδην λαβρότερος, ὡς μηδενὸς
τῶν διὰ τὴν στεργομένην λυπηρῶν αἰσθάνεσθαι·
τοσοῦτον γὰρ ἦν μῖσος εἰς αὐτὸν τῆς Μαριάμμης,
437 ὅσος ἐκείνου πρὸς αὐτὴν ἔρως. ἔχουσα δὲ τὴν
μὲν ἀπέχθειαν ἐκ τῶν πραγμάτων εὔλογον, τὴν
δὲ παρρησίαν ἐκ τοῦ φιλεῖσθαι, φανερῶς ὠνείδιζεν
αὐτῷ τὰ κατὰ τὸν πάππον Ὑρκανὸν καὶ τὸν
ἀδελφὸν Ἰωνάθην· οὐδὲ γὰρ τούτου καίπερ ὄντος
παιδὸς ἐφείσατο, δοὺς μὲν αὐτῷ τὴν ἀρχιερωσύνην ἑπτακαιδεκέτει, μετὰ δὲ τὴν τιμὴν κτείνας
εὐθέως, ἐπειδὴ τὴν ἱερὰν ἐσθῆτα λαβόντι καὶ
τῷ βωμῷ προσελθόντι καθ᾽ ἑορτὴν ἄθρουν ἐπ-
εδάκρυσεν τὸ πλῆθος. πέμπεται μὲν οὖν ὁ παῖς
διὰ νυκτὸς εἰς Ἱεριχοῦντα, ἐκεῖ δὲ κατ᾽ ἐντολὴν
ὑπὸ τῶν Γαλατῶν βαπτιζόμενος ἐν κολυμβήθρᾳ
τελευτᾷ.
438   (3) Διὰ ταῦθ᾽ Ἡρώδην μὲν ὠνείδιζεν ἡ Μαριάμμη, καὶ τὴν ἀδελφὴν αὐτοῦ καὶ τὴν μητέρα
δειναῖς ἐξύβριζεν λοιδορίαις. ἀλλ᾽ ὁ μὲν πεφί-
μωτο τοῖς ἱμέροις, δεινὴ δὲ τὰς γυναῖκας ἀγανάκτησις εἰσήει, καὶ πρὸς ὃ μάλιστα κινήσειν τὸν
Ἡρώδην ἔμελλον, εἰς μοιχείαν διέβαλλον αὐτήν,
439 ἄλλα τε πολλὰ πρὸς τὸ πιθανὸν ἐνσκευαζόμεναι,
καὶ κατηγοροῦσαι διότι τὴν εἰκόνα τὴν ἑαυτῆς

───

ᵃ Called Aristobulus (probably his second name) in the
narrative in A. (xv. 51, etc.).
ᵇ A detail not in A. and, as Reinach points out, an
anachronism, as Herod only received his guard of Gauls

of respect for their mother's illustrious parentage, and because they had been born after his accession to the throne. But a still stronger influence in their favour was Herod's passion for Mariamme, the consuming ardour of which increased from day to day, so that he was insensible to the troubles of which his beloved one was the cause ; for Mariamme's hatred of him was as great as was his love for her. As the events of the past gave her just reason for aversion, and her husband's love enabled her to speak plainly, she openly upbraided him with the fate of her grandfather Hyrcanus and her brother Jonathan.[a] For Herod had not spared even this poor lad ; he had bestowed upon him in his seventeenth year the office of high-priest, and then immediately after conferring this honour had put him to death, because, on the occasion of a festival, when the lad approached the altar, clad in the priestly vestments, the multitude with one accord burst into tears. He was, consequently, sent by night to Jericho, and there, in accordance with instructions, plunged into a swimming-bath by the Gauls [b] and drowned.

His passion for Mariamme.

He murders his brother-in-law Jonathan (Aristobulus) 35 B.C.

(3) It was on these grounds that Mariamme upbraided Herod, and then proceeded violently to abuse his mother and sister. He was paralyzed by his infatuation ; but the women, seething with indignation, brought against her the charge which was bound in their opinion to touch Herod most nearly, that of adultery. Among much else which they invented to convince him, they accused Mariamme of having sent her portrait to Antony in

and his wife Mariamme.

after the death of Cleopatra in 30 B.C. (*A.* xv. 217 ‖ ; *B.* i. 397). Aristobulus was murdered five years earlier.

πέμψειεν εἰς Αἴγυπτον Ἀντωνίῳ καὶ δι' ὑπερβολὴν ἀσελγείας ἀποῦσαν δείξειεν ἑαυτὴν ἀνθρώπῳ
440 γυναικομανοῦντι καὶ βιάζεσθαι δυναμένῳ. τοῦθ'
ὥσπερ σκηπτὸς ἐμπεσὼν ἐτάραξεν Ἡρώδην,
μάλιστα μὲν διὰ τὸν ἔρωτα ζηλοτύπως ἔχοντα,
λογιζόμενον δὲ καὶ τὴν Κλεοπάτρας δεινότητα, δι'
ἣν Λυσανίας τε ὁ βασιλεὺς ἀνῄρητο καὶ Μάλχος
ὁ Ἄραψ· οὐ γὰρ ἀφαιρέσει γαμετῆς ἐμέτρει τὸν
κίνδυνον, ἀλλὰ θανάτῳ.

441   (4) Μέλλων οὖν ἀποδημήσειν Ἰωσήπῳ τῷ
ἀνδρὶ Σαλώμης τῆς ἀδελφῆς αὐτοῦ, πιστὸς δὲ ἦν
καὶ διὰ τὸ κῆδος εὔνους, παρατίθεται τὴν γυναῖκα,
κρύφα δοὺς ἐντολὰς ἀναιρεῖν αὐτήν, εἰ κἀκεῖνον
Ἀντώνιος. ὁ δὲ Ἰώσηπος οὔτι κακοήθως, ἀλλὰ
τὸν ἔρωτα τοῦ βασιλέως παραστῆσαι τῇ γυναικὶ
βουλόμενος, ὡς οὐδὲ ἀποθανὼν αὐτῆς ὑπομένοι
442 διαζευχθῆναι, τὸ ἀπόρρητον ἐκφαίνει. κἀκείνη
πρὸς ἐπανήκοντα τὸν Ἡρώδην πολλά τε περὶ τοῦ
πρὸς αὐτὴν συμπαθοῦς ἐν ταῖς ὁμιλίαις ἐπομνύ-
μενον,[1] ὡς οὐδ' ἐρασθείη ποτὲ γυναικὸς ἄλλης,
" πάνυ γοῦν," εἶπεν, " ταῖς πρὸς [τὸν]² Ἰώσηπον
ἐντολαῖς ἐπεδείξω τὸν πρὸς ἡμᾶς ἔρωτα κτεῖναί
με προστάξας."

443   (5) Ἔκφρων εὐθέως ἀκούσας τὸ ἀπόρρητον ἦν,
καὶ οὐκ ἄν ποτε τὸν Ἰώσηπον ἐξαγγεῖλαι τὴν
ἐντολὴν φάμενος εἰ μὴ διαφθείρειεν αὐτήν, ἐνε-
θουσία τῷ πάθει καὶ τῆς κοίτης ἐξαλόμενος³
ἀνέδην ἐν τοῖς βασιλείοις ἀνειλεῖτο. καὶ τοῦτον
Σαλώμη ἡ ἀδελφὴ τὸν καιρὸν εἰς τὰς διαβολὰς
ἁρπάσασα τὴν εἰς τὸν Ἰώσηπον ἐπεβεβαίωσεν

---

¹ +καὶ C Lat.   ² P: om. the rest.
³ Destinon: ἐξαλλόμενος MSS.

Egypt and of carrying wantonness so far as to exhibit herself, though at a distance, to a man with a madness for her sex and powerful enough to resort to violence. This accusation struck Herod like a thunderbolt. His love intensified his jealousy; he reflected on Cleopatra's craft which had brought both King Lysanias [a] and the Arab Malchus to their end; he was menaced, he reckoned, with the loss not merely of his consort but of his life.

(4) So, being on the eve of departure from his realm, he entrusted his wife to Joseph, the husband of his sister Salome, a faithful friend whose loyalty was assured by this marriage connexion, giving him private injunctions to kill her, should Antony kill him. Joseph, not with any malicious intention, but from a desire to convince her of the love which the king bore her, since even in death he could not bear to be separated from her, betrayed the secret. When Herod, on his return, in familiar intercourse was *c. 29 B.C.* protesting with many oaths his affection for her and that he had never loved any other woman, " A fine exhibition you gave," she replied, " of your love for me by your orders to Joseph to put me to death ! "

(5) He was beside himself, the moment he heard the secret was out. Joseph, he exclaimed, would never have disclosed his orders, had he not seduced her; and, frenzied with passion, he leapt from the bed and paced the palace to and fro in his distraction. His sister Salome, seizing this opportunity to slander Mariamme, confirmed his suspicion of Joseph.

[a] King of Chalcis; his murder at Cleopatra's instigation is mentioned in *A.* xv. 92; he is not named in the general reference to plots against high officials in Syria in *B.* i. 360. Malchus is named in the last passage as an intended victim of Cleopatra, but there is no further allusion to his end.

ὑποψίαν. ὁ δ' ὑπ' ἀκράτου ζηλοτυπίας ἐκμανεὶς
444 παραχρῆμα κτείνειν προσέταξεν ἀμφοτέρους. μετά-
νοια δ' εὐθέως εἵπετο τῷ πάθει, καὶ τοῦ θυμοῦ
πεσόντος ὁ ἔρως πάλιν ἀνεζωπυρεῖτο. τοσαύτη
δ' ἦν φλεγμονὴ τῆς ἐπιθυμίας, ὡς μηδὲ τεθνάναι
δοκεῖν αὐτήν, ὑπὸ δὲ κακώσεως ὡς ζώσῃ προσ-
λαλεῖν, μέχρι τῷ χρόνῳ διδαχθεὶς τὸ πάθος[1]
ἀνάλογον τὴν λύπην ἔσχεν τῇ πρὸς περιοῦσαν[2]
διαθέσει.

445 (xxiii. 1) Κληρονομοῦσι δὲ τῆς μητρῴας οἱ
παῖδες ὀργῆς καὶ τοῦ μύσους ἔννοιαν λαμβάνοντες
ὡς πολέμιον ὑφεώρων τὸν πατέρα, καὶ τὸ πρότερον μὲν ἐπὶ 'Ρώμης παιδευόμενοι, πλέον δ'
ὡς εἰς Ἰουδαίαν ὑπέστρεψαν· συνηνδροῦτο δ'
446 αὐτῶν ταῖς ἡλικίαις ἡ διάθεσις. καὶ ἐπειδὴ γάμων
ἔχοντες ὥραν ὁ μὲν τῆς τηθίδος Σαλώμης, ἣ τῆς
μητρὸς αὐτῶν κατηγόρησεν, ὁ δ' ἔγημεν Ἀρχελάου τοῦ Καππαδόκων βασιλέως θυγατέρα, προσ-
447 ελάμβανον ἤδη τῷ μίσει καὶ παρρησίαν. ἐκ δὲ
τοῦ θράσους αὐτῶν ἀφορμὰς οἱ διαβάλλοντες
ἐλάμβανον, καὶ φανερώτερον ἤδη τῷ βασιλεῖ δι-
ελέγοντό τινες ὡς ἐπιβουλεύοιτο μὲν ὑπ' ἀμφοτέρων τῶν υἱῶν, ὁ δὲ Ἀρχελάῳ κηδεύσας καὶ
φυγὴν παρασκευάζοιτο τῷ πενθερῷ πεποιθώς, ἵν'
448 ἐπὶ Καίσαρος αὐτοῦ κατηγορήσειεν. ἀναπλησ-
θεὶς δὲ τῶν διαβολῶν 'Ηρώδης ὥσπερ ἐπιτεί-
χισμα τοῖς υἱοῖς κατάγει τὸν ἐκ τῆς Δωρίδος
Ἀντίπατρον καὶ πάντα τρόπον προτιμᾶν ἄρχεται.

---

[1] Conj. from Lat. "funere cognito": πένθος mss.
[2] Hudson from Lat.: περιουσίαν mss.

---

[a] The narrative of Mariamme's death in *A.* xv. is differ-
ently told. There are there two episodes, curiously similar.

Mad with sheer jealousy, he ordered that both should instantly be put to death. But remorse followed hard upon rage ; his wrath subsided, his love revived. So consuming, indeed, was the flame of his passion that he believed she was not dead, and in his affliction would address her as though she were alive ; until time taught him the reality of his loss, when his grief was as profound as the love which he bore her while she was alive.[a]

(xxiii. 1) The sons inherited their mother's resentment, and, reflecting on their father's abominable crimes, eyed him as an enemy, even in the early days of their education in Rome, and still more on their return to Judaea. The antagonism grew with their years ; and when, on reaching an age to marry, one [b] espoused the daughter of his aunt Salome, their mother's accuser, and the other [c] the daughter of Archelaus, king of Cappadocia, their hatred found vent in open speech. Their rashness lent a handle to slanderers, and from this time certain persons threw out plainer hints to the king that both his sons were conspiring against him, and that the son-in-law of Archelaus, counting on his father-in-law's influence, was preparing to fly, in order to lay an accusation against his father before the emperor. Herod, drugged with these calumnies, recalled Antipater, his son by Doris, to serve as a bulwark against his other sons, and began to honour him with every mark of his special esteem.

Hostility to Herod of his sons by Mariamme, Alexander, and Aristobulus c. 18 B.C.

Recall of Antipater c. 14 B.C.

An indiscretion of Joseph during a voyage of Herod to Antony (c. 34 B.C.) leads to the execution of Joseph and the imprisonment of Mariamme. A similar indiscretion of Soemus during a voyage of Herod to Augustus (c. 29 B.C.) leads to her trial, condemnation, and death.

[b] Aristobulus.   [c] Alexander.

449 (2) Τοῖς δ' ἀφόρητος ἦν ἡ μεταβολή, καὶ τὸν
ἐξ ἰδιώτιδος μητρὸς ὁρῶντες προκόπτοντα, διὰ
τὴν ἑαυτῶν εὐγένειαν οὐκ ἐκράτουν τῆς ἀγανακτήσεως, ἐφ' ἑκάστου[1] δὲ τῶν ἀνιαρῶν τὴν ὀργὴν
ἐξέφαινον· ὥσθ'[2] οἱ μὲν καθ' ἡμέραν προσίσταντο
450 μᾶλλον, ὁ δ' Ἀντίπατρος ἤδη καὶ δι' αὐτὸν ἐσπου-
δάζετο, δεινότατος μὲν ὢν ἐν ταῖς πρὸς τὸν πατέρα
κολακείαις, διαβολὰς δὲ κατὰ τῶν ἀδελφῶν ποικίλας ἐνσκευαζόμενος καὶ τὰ μὲν αὐτὸς λογο-
ποιῶν, τὰ δὲ τοὺς ἐπιτηδείους φημίζειν καθιείς,
μέχρι παντάπασιν τοὺς ἀδελφοὺς ἀπέρρηξεν τῆς
451 βασιλικῆς ἐλπίδος. καὶ γὰρ ἐν ταῖς διαθήκαις
καὶ φανερῶς αὐτὸς ἦν ἤδη διάδοχος· ὡς βασιλεὺς
γοῦν ἐπέμφθη καὶ πρὸς Καίσαρα τῷ τε κόσμῳ καὶ
ταῖς ἄλλαις θεραπείαις πλὴν διαδήματος χρώμενος. χρόνῳ δ' ἐξίσχυσεν εἰσαγαγεῖν ἐπὶ τὴν
Μαριάμμης κοίτην τὴν μητέρα. δυσὶ δ' ὅπλοις
κατὰ τῶν ἀδελφῶν χρώμενος, κολακείᾳ καὶ δια-
βολῇ, τὸν βασιλέα καὶ περὶ θανάτου τῶν υἱῶν ὑπ-
ειργάσατο.

452 (3) Τὸν γοῦν Ἀλέξανδρον σύρας μέχρι Ῥώμης
ὁ πατὴρ τῆς ἐφ' ἑαυτῷ φαρμακείας ἔκρινεν ἐπὶ
Καίσαρος. ὁ δ' εὑρὼν μόλις ὀλοφυρμοῦ παρρησίαν καὶ δικαστὴν ἐμπειρότατον Ἀντιπάτρου καὶ
Ἡρώδου φρονιμώτερον, τὰ μὲν ἁμαρτήματα τοῦ
πατρὸς αἰδημόνως ὑπεστείλατο, τὰς δ' αὐτοῦ
453 διαβολὰς ἰσχυρῶς ἀπελύσατο.[3] καθαρὸν δὲ καὶ

---

[1] ἕκαστον PAMV.   [2] Bekker: ὡς δ(ὲ) MSS.
[3] Niese and Naber: ἀπεδύσατο MSS. ; cf. B. ii. 92.

---

[a] From the narrative in A. xvi. it appears that both the
sons were taken to Italy and that the case was heard not at
Rome but at Aquileia (xvi. 91).

(2) To the young men this new departure was intolerable. At the sight of the promotion of this son of a woman of no standing, they in their pride of birth could not restrain their indignation, and on every fresh occasion for annoyance openly displayed their wrath. The result was that, while each succeeding day saw them in greater disfavour, Antipater was now gaining respect on his own merits. Showing remarkable adroitness in flattering his father, he concocted various calumnies upon his half-brothers, some of which he set in motion himself, while others were, at his instigation, circulated by his confidants, until he completely wrecked his brothers' prospects of the throne. For both in his father's will and by public acts he was now declared to be the heir : thus, when he was sent on an embassy to Caesar, he went as a prince, with the robes and all the ceremonial of royalty except the diadem. Eventually his influence was strong enough to bring back his mother to Mariamme's bed ; and by employing against his brothers the two weapons of flattery and slander, he stealthily so wrought upon the king's mind as to make him even contemplate putting his sons to death.

Antipater's intrigues.

He is declared heir to the throne c. 13 B.C.

(3) One of them, at any rate, namely Alexander, was dragged by his father to Rome and there accused at Caesar's tribunal of attempting to poison him.*a* The young man, finding himself at last at liberty to vent his grievances and in the presence of a judge with far more experience than Antipater, more sagacity than Herod, modestly threw a veil over his father's faults, but forcibly exposed the calumnies directed against himself. He next proved that his

Alexander tried before Augustus, who effects a reconciliation c. 12 B.C.

τὸν ἀδελφὸν ἀποδείξας κοινωνοῦντα τῶν κινδύνων,
οὕτως ἤδη τό τε Ἀντιπάτρου πανοῦργον καὶ τὴν
αὑτῶν ἀτιμίαν ἀπωδύρετο. συνήργει δ᾽ αὐτῷ
μετὰ καθαροῦ τοῦ συνειδότος ἡ περὶ λόγους ἰσχύς·
454 ἦν γὰρ δὴ δεινότατος εἰπεῖν. κτὶ τὸ τελευταῖον
φάμενος ὡς τῷ πατρὶ κτείνειν αὐτοὺς ἔστιν †εἰ δὴ¹
καὶ προσίεται†² τὸ ἔγκλημα, προήγαγεν μὲν εἰς
δάκρυα πάντας, τὸν δὲ Καίσαρα διέθηκεν οὕτως,
ὡς ἀπογνῶναι μὲν αὐτῶν τὰ κατηγορημένα, δι-
αλλάξαι δὲ Ἡρώδην εὐθέως. αἱ διαλλαγαὶ δ᾽ ἐπὶ
τούτοις ἦσαν, ὥστε ἐκείνους μὲν τῷ πατρὶ πάντα
πειθαρχεῖν, τὸν δὲ τὴν βασιλείαν καταλιπεῖν ᾧ
βούλεται.

455 (4) Μετὰ ταῦτα δ᾽ ἀπὸ Ῥώμης ὑπέστρεφεν ὁ
βασιλεύς, τῶν μὲν ἐγκλημάτων ἀφιέναι³ τοὺς
υἱοὺς δοκῶν, τῆς δ᾽ ὑπονοίας οὐκ ἀπηλλαγμένος·
παρηκολούθει γὰρ Ἀντίπατρος ἡ τοῦ μίσους
ὑπόθεσις, ἀλλ᾽ εἴς γε τὸ φανερὸν τὴν ἀπέχθειαν
456 οὐκ ἐξέφερεν τὸν διαλλακτὴν αἰδούμενος. ὡς δὲ
τὴν Κιλικίαν παραπλέων κατῆρεν εἰς Ἐλαιοῦσαν,⁴
ἑστιᾷ μὲν αὐτὸν φιλοφρόνως Ἀρχέλαος, ὑπὲρ τῆς
τοῦ γαμβροῦ σωτηρίας εὐχαριστῶν καὶ ταῖς δι-
αλλαγαῖς ἐφηδόμενος, ὡς ἂν καὶ τάχιον γεγραφὼς
τοῖς ἐπὶ Ῥώμης φίλοις συλλαμβάνεσθαι περὶ τὴν
δίκην Ἀλεξάνδρῳ· προπέμπει δὲ μέχρι Ζεφυρίου
δῶρα δοὺς μέχρι τριάκοντα ταλάντων.

457 (5) Ὡς δ᾽ εἰς Ἱεροσόλυμα Ἡρώδης ἀφικνεῖται, συναγαγὼν τὸν λαὸν καὶ τοὺς τρεῖς υἱοὺς
παραστησάμενος ἀπελογεῖτο περὶ τῆς ἀποδημίας,

¹ εἰ δὴ conj. after Aldrich (εἰ δὲ) : ἠδὺ mss.
² προσίεται Holwerda : προστίθεται MVR : προτίθεται the rest.
³ ἀφεικέναι (-ηκέναι) VRC : soluisse Lat.
⁴ Ἐλιοῦσαν or Ἐλεοῦσαν mss.

brother, his partner in peril, was equally innocent, and then proceeded bitterly to complain of Antipater's villainy and of the ignominy to which he and his brother were exposed. He was assisted not only by a clear conscience but by his powerful oratory, for he was an extremely able speaker. Concluding with the remark that it was open to their father to put them to death, if he really believed the charge to be true, he reduced all his hearers to tears, and so deeply affected Caesar that he acquitted the accused and brought Herod to a reconciliation on the spot. The conditions of the agreement were that the sons should render implicit obedience to their father, and that he should be at liberty to bequeath the kingdom to whom he would.

(4) After this the king left Rome on his homeward journey, apparently dismissing his charges against his sons, though not abandoning his suspicions. For he was accompanied by Antipater, the cause of all this hatred, who, however, was withheld by awe of the author of the reconciliation from openly displaying his animosity. Skirting the coast of Cilicia, Herod put in at Elaeusa and received friendly entertainment at the table of Archelaus, who congratulated him on his son-in-law's acquittal and was delighted at the reconciliation; for he had previously written to his friends in Rome to assist Alexander on his trial. He accompanied his guests as far as Zephyrion and made them presents amounting in value to thirty talents. *Herod visits Archelaus of Cappadocia.*

(5) On reaching Jerusalem, Herod assembled the people, presented to them his three sons, made his excuses for his absence, and rendered profuse thanks *Herod's address to the people of Jerusalem.*

καὶ πολλὰ μὲν εὐχαρίστει τῷ θεῷ, πολλὰ δὲ Καίσαρι καταστησαμένῳ τὸν οἶκον αὐτοῦ τεταραγμένον καὶ μεῖζόν τι τοῖς υἱοῖς βασιλείας παρα-
458 σχόντι τὴν ὁμόνοιαν, "ἣν αὐτός," ἔφη, "συναρμόσω μᾶλλον· ὁ μὲν γὰρ ἐμὲ κύριον τῆς ἀρχῆς καὶ δικαστὴν διαδόχου κατέστησεν, ἐγὼ δὲ μετὰ τοῦ συμφέροντος ἐμαυτῷ κἀκεῖνον ἀμείβομαι.¹ τούσδε τοὺς τρεῖς παῖδας ἀποδείκνυμι βασιλεῖς, καὶ τῆς γνώμης πρῶτον τὸν θεὸν σύμψηφον, ἔπειτα καὶ ὑμᾶς παρακαλῶ γενέσθαι· τῷ μὲν γὰρ ἡλικία, τοῖς δ' εὐγένεια τὴν διαδοχὴν προξενεῖ· τό γε μὴν μέγεθος τῆς βασιλείας ἀρκεῖ καὶ πλείο-
459 σιν. οὓς δὲ Καῖσαρ μὲν ἥνωσεν, καθίστησιν δὲ πατήρ, ὑμεῖς τηρήσατε μήτε ἀδίκους μήτε ἀνωμάλουςᵃ τὰς τιμὰς διδόντες, ἑκάστῳ δὲ κατὰ τὸ πρεσβεῖον· οὐ γὰρ τοσοῦτον εὐφρανεῖ τις τὸν παρ' ἡλικίαν θεραπευόμενον, ὅσον ὀδυνήσει τὸν
460 ἀτιμούμενον. οὕς γε μὴν ἑκάστῳ συνεῖναι δεήσει συγγενεῖς καὶ φίλους, ἐγὼ διανεμῶ καὶ τῆς ὁμονοίας ἐγγυητὰς ἐκείνους καταστήσομαι, σαφῶς ἐπιστάμενος ὅτι τὰς στάσεις καὶ τὰς φιλονεικίας γεννῶσιν αἱ τῶν συνδιατριβόντων κακοήθειαι, κἂν
461 ὦσιν οὗτοι χρηστοί, τηροῦσιν τὰς στοργάς. ἀξιῶ δ' οὐ μόνον τούτους ἀλλὰ καὶ τοὺς ἐν τῇ στρατιᾷ μου ταξιάρχους ἐν ἐμοὶ μόνον τὰς ἐλπίδας ἔχειν ἐπὶ τοῦ παρόντος· οὐ γὰρ βασιλείαν, ἀλλὰ τιμὴν βασιλείας τοῖς υἱοῖς παραδίδωμι, καὶ τῶν μὲν ἡδέων ὡς ἄρχοντες ἀπολαύσουσιν, τὸ βάρος δὲ

¹ ἀμειβόμενος Havercamp on ᴍꜱ. authority.

ᵃ Greek "uneven."

to God, and no less to Caesar, who had re-established his disordered household and had given his sons a greater boon than a kingdom, namely concord.

"The ties of that concord," he continued, "I shall bind more closely myself; for Caesar has appointed me lord of the realm and arbiter of the succession, and I, in consulting my own advantage, also repay my debt to him. I now declare these my three sons kings, and I beseech first God, and then you, to ratify my decision. They are entitled to the succession, this one by his age, the others by their noble birth; indeed the extent of my kingdom would suffice for even a greater number. Those, therefore, whom Caesar has united and their father now nominates, do you uphold; let the honours you award them be neither undeserved nor unequal,[a] but proportioned to the rank of each; for in paying deference to any beyond the deserts of his age, you gratify him less than you grieve the one whom you slight. I myself shall select the advisers and attendants[b] who are to consort with each of my sons, and shall hold them responsible for keeping the peace, being well aware that factions and rivalries among princes are produced by the malign influence of associates, while virtuous companions promote natural affection.

"I must require these persons, however, and not them only but also the officers of my army, for the present to rest their hopes on me alone; for it is not the kingdom, but the mere honours of royalty, which I am now delivering over to my sons. They will enjoy the pleasures of power, as if actual rulers,

He declares his three sons heirs to the throne.

---

[b] συγγενεῖς and φίλοι are, as Reinach points out, technical terms in the hierarchy of a Hellenistic court.

462 τῶν πραγμάτων ἐμόν ἐστιν, κἂν μὴ θέλω. σκεπ-
τέσθω δ' ἕκαστος τήν τε ἡλικίαν μου καὶ τὴν
ἀγωγὴν τοῦ βίου καὶ τὴν εὐσέβειαν· οὔτε γὰρ
οὕτως εἰμὶ γέρων, ὥστ' ἂν ἀπελπισθῆναι ταχέως,
οὔτε εἰς τρυφὴν ἐκδιαιτώμενος, ἢ καὶ νέους ἐπι-
τέμνεται, τὸ δὲ θεῖον οὕτως τεθεραπεύκαμεν, ὥστ'
463 ἂν ἐπὶ μήκιστον βίου προελθεῖν. ὁ δὴ τοὺς ἐμοὺς
παῖδας θεραπεύων ἐπὶ τῇ ἐμῇ καταλύσει δώσει
μοι καὶ περὶ ἐκείνων δίκας· οὐ γὰρ ἐγὼ φθονῶν
τοῖς ἐξ ἐμοῦ γεγενημένοις ἀνακόπτω τὴν εἰς
αὐτοὺς φιλοτιμίαν, ἐπιστάμενος δὲ τοῖς νέοις
464 γίνεσθαι τὰς σπουδὰς θράσους ἐφόδιον. εἴ γε
μὴν ἕκαστος ἐνθυμηθείη τῶν προσιόντων, ὅτι χρη-
στὸς μὲν ὢν παρ' ἐμοῦ λήψεται τὴν ἀμοιβήν, στασιάζων δὲ καὶ παρὰ τῷ θεραπευομένῳ τὸ κακό-
ηθες ἀνόνητον ἕξει, πάντας οἶμαι τὰ ἐμὰ φρονή-
σειν, τουτέστιν τὰ τῶν ἐμῶν υἱῶν· καὶ γὰρ τούτοις συμφέρει κρατεῖν ἐμὲ κἀμοὶ τούτους[1] ὁμο-
465 νοεῖν. ὑμεῖς δέ, ὦ παῖδες ἀγαθοί, πρῶτον μὲν
ἐνθυμούμενοι τὴν ἱερὰν φύσιν, ἧς καὶ παρὰ θηρίοις
αἱ στοργαὶ μένουσιν, ἔπειτα τὸν ποιησάμενον
ἡμῶν τὰς διαλλαγὰς Καίσαρα, τρίτον ἐμὲ τὸν ἐν
οἷς ἔξεστιν ἐπιτάσσειν παρακαλοῦντα, μείνατε
ἀδελφοί. δίδωμι δὲ ὑμῖν ἐσθῆτα [τε][2] ἤδη καὶ
θεραπείαν βασιλικήν· ἐπεύχομαι δὲ καὶ τῷ θεῷ
466 τηρῆσαι τὴν ἐμὴν κρίσιν, ἂν ὁμονοῆτε.'' ταῦτ'
εἰπὼν καὶ φιλοφρόνως ἕκαστον τῶν υἱῶν κατα-
σπασάμενος διέλυσεν τὸ πλῆθος, τοὺς μὲν συν-

---

[1] So the corrector of A: τούτοις the rest.
[2] LRC: om. the rest.

but upon me, however unwilling, will fall the burden of office. Consider, each one of you, my age, my manner of life, my piety. I am not so old that my life may soon be past praying for, nor given over to the pleasures of luxury, which cut short the lives even of the young : I have served the deity so faithfully that I may hope for the longest term of life. Whoever, then, pays court to my sons to bring about my downfall shall be punished by me for their sakes as well as my own. For it is not jealousy of my offspring which causes me to restrict the homage to be paid them ; it is the knowledge that such flattering attentions foster recklessness in the young. If everyone who is brought into contact with my sons will but remember that, if he acts honourably he will win his reward from me, whereas if he promotes discord his malicious conduct will bring him no benefit even from the object of his flattery, then I think that all will have my interests, in other words my sons' interest, at heart ; for it is to their advantage that I should govern, and to mine that they should live in harmony.

" As for you, my good children, think first of the sacred ties of nature and the constancy of affection which she instils even into the beasts ; think of Caesar, who brought about our reconciliation ; think, lastly, of me, who entreat you, when I might command, and continue as brothers. I present you, from this moment, with the robes and retinue of royalty ; and I pray God to uphold my decision, if you live in unity."

With these words he tenderly embraced each of his sons and then dismissed the multitude. Of these

εὐχομένους τοῖς εἰρημένοις, ὅσοι δ' ἐπεθύμουν μεταβολῆς, μηδ' ἀκηκοέναι προσποιουμένους.

467 (xxiv. 1) Συναπῄει δὲ τοῖς ἀδελφοῖς ἡ στάσις, καὶ χείρους τὰς ἐπ' ἀλλήλοις ὑπονοίας ἔχοντες ἀπηλλάγησαν, Ἀλέξανδρος μὲν καὶ Ἀριστόβουλος ὀδυνώμενοι κεκυρωμένου Ἀντιπάτρῳ τοῦ πρεσβείου, Ἀντίπατρος δὲ καὶ τοῦ δευτερεύειν

468 νεμεσῶν τοῖς ἀδελφοῖς. ἀλλ' ὁ μὲν ποικιλώτατος ὢν τὸ ἦθος ἐχεμυθεῖν τε ᾔδει καὶ πολλῷ τῷ πανούργῳ τὸ πρὸς αὐτοὺς ἐκάλυπτε μῖσος, τοῖς δὲ δι' εὐγένειαν πᾶν τὸ νοηθὲν ἦν ἐπὶ γλώσσης· καὶ παροξύνοντες μὲν ἐνέκειντο πολλοί, πλείους δὲ

469 τῶν φίλων παρεδύοντο κατάσκοποι. πᾶν δὲ τὸ παρ' Ἀλεξάνδρῳ λαληθὲν εὐθέως ἦν παρ' Ἀντιπάτρῳ, καὶ μετὰ προσθήκης μετέβαινεν ἀπὸ Ἀντιπάτρου πρὸς Ἡρώδην· οὔτε γὰρ ἁπλῶς φθεγξάμενος ὁ νεανίας ἀνυπεύθυνος ἦν, ἀλλὰ εἰς διαβολὴν τὸ ῥηθὲν ἐστρέφετο, καὶ μετρίως παρρησιασαμένου μέγιστα τοῖς ἐλαχίστοις προσ-

470 επλάττετο. καθίει δ' Ἀντίπατρος ἀεὶ τοὺς ἐρεθίσοντας, ὅπως αὐτῷ τὸ ψεῦδος ἔχοι τὰς ἀφορμὰς ἀληθεῖς· καὶ τῶν φημιζομένων ἕν τι διελεγχθὲν ἅπασιν πίστιν ἐπετίθει. καὶ τῶν μὲν αὐτοῦ φίλων ἢ φύσει στεγανώτατος ἦν ἕκαστος, ἢ κατεσκευάζετο δωρεαῖς, ὡς μηδὲν ἐκφέρεσθαι τῶν ἀπορρήτων, καὶ τὸν Ἀντιπάτρου βίον οὐκ ἂν ἥμαρτέν τις εἰπὼν κακίας μυστήριον·[a] τοὺς δὲ Ἀλεξάνδρῳ συνόντας χρήμασι διαφθείρων ἢ κολακείαις ὑπιών,

---

[a] Cf. the N.T. phrase " mystery of lawlessness " (μυστήριον τῆς ἀνομίας) in 2 Thess. ii. 7.

some joined in his prayer ; while those who hankered for change pretended that they had not even heard him.

(xxiv. 1) But the brothers on parting carried with them discord in their hearts. They separated more suspicious of each other than before : Alexander and Aristobulus aggrieved at the confirmation of Antipater's right of primogeniture, Antipater resenting the rank accorded to his brothers, even though second to his own. The latter, however, with the extreme subtlety of his character, knew how to hold his tongue and, with much adroitness, dissembled his hatred of his brothers ; while they, from their pride of birth, had all their thoughts upon their lips. They were, moreover, beset by many persons trying to excite them, while a still larger number insinuated themselves into their friendship to spy upon them. Every word spoken in Alexander's circle was instantly in the possession of Antipater and passed from Antipater to Herod, with amplifications. The young man could not make the simplest remark without becoming incriminated, so distorted were his words for the purposes of slander ; if he spoke with a little freedom, the merest trifles were magnified into enormities. Antipater was constantly setting his agents on to irritate him, in order that his lies might have some basis of truth ; and if among the speeches reported one item was established, that was sufficient warrant for the rest. His own friends were all either of a very secretive nature or were induced by presents to divulge no secrets ; so that Antipater's life might have been not incorrectly described as a mystery of iniquity.[a] Alexander's associates, on the other hand, either by bribery or by that seductive

221

αἷς πάντα κατειργάσατο, πεποιήκει προδότας καὶ
471 τῶν πραττομένων ἢ λαλουμένων φῶρας. πάντα
δὲ περιεσκεμμένως δραματουργῶν τὰς πρὸς Ἡρώδην ὁδοὺς ταῖς διαβολαῖς ἐποιεῖτο τεχνικωτάτας,
αὐτὸς μὲν ἀδελφοῦ προσωπεῖον ἐπικείμενος, καθ-
ιεὶς δὲ μηνυτὰς ἑτέρους. κἀπειδὰν ἀπαγγελθείη
τι κατ' Ἀλεξάνδρου, παρελθὼν ὑπεκρίνετο καὶ
διασύρειν τὸ ῥηθὲν ἀρξάμενος, ἔπειτα κατεσκεύαζεν ἡσυχῆ καὶ πρὸς ἀγανάκτησιν ἐξεκαλεῖτο τὸν
472 βασιλέα. πάντα δ' εἰς ἐπιβουλὴν ἀνήγετο καὶ τὸ
δοκεῖν τῇ σφαγῇ τοῦ πατρὸς ἐφεδρεύειν Ἀλέξ-
ανδρον· οὐδὲν γὰρ οὕτως πίστιν ἐχορήγει ταῖς διαβολαῖς, ὡς ἀπολογούμενος Ἀντίπατρος ὑπὲρ αὐτοῦ.
473   (2) Τούτοις Ἡρώδης ἐξαγριούμενος ὅσον ὑφ-
ήρει καθ' ἡμέραν τῆς πρὸς τὰ μειράκια στοργῆς,
τοσοῦτον Ἀντιπάτρῳ προσετίθει. συναπέκλιναν
δὲ καὶ τῶν κατὰ τὸ βασίλειον οἱ μὲν ἑκόντες, οἱ
δ' ἐξ ἐπιτάγματος, ὥσπερ Πτολεμαῖος ὁ τιμιώ-
τατος τῶν φίλων, οἵ τε ἀδελφοὶ τοῦ βασιλέως καὶ
πᾶσα ἡ γενεά· πάντα γὰρ Ἀντίπατρος ἦν, καὶ τὸ
πικρότατον Ἀλεξάνδρῳ, πάντα ἦν ἡ Ἀντιπάτρου μήτηρ, σύμβουλος κατ' αὐτῶν μητρυιᾶς χα-
λεπωτέρα καὶ πλεῖόν τι προγόνων μισοῦσα τοὺς ἐκ
474 βασιλίδος. πάντες μὲν οὖν ἐπὶ ταῖς ἐλπίσιν ἐθερά-
πευον Ἀντίπατρον ἤδη, συναφίστα δ' ἕκαστον τὰ

---

[a] Mentioned as entertaining Herod at Rhodes (i. 280), as
his executor (i. 667), as befriending Archelaus (ii. 14), etc.
[b] Doris.

flattery, which Antipater invariably found effective, had been converted by the latter into traitors and detectives to report all that was said or done by his brother. With a careful eye to every detail in the staging of the play, he would plan with consummate art the modes of bringing these calumnies to the ears of Herod, himself assuming the rôle of a devoted brother, and leaving that of informer to others. Then, when any word was spoken against Alexander, he would come forward and play his part, and, beginning by ridiculing the allegation, would afterwards quietly proceed to confirm it and so call forth the king's indignation. Everything was interpreted as a plot and made to produce the impression that Alexander was watching his opportunity to murder his father ; and nothing lent more credit to these calumnies than Antipater's pleading in his brother's defence.

(2) These insinuations exasperating Herod, his affection for the young princes diminished daily, while his regard for Antipater proportionately increased. The king's alienation from the lads was shared by people at court, some acting of their own accord, others under orders, such as Ptolemy,[a] the most honoured of his friends, the king's brothers and all his family. For Antipater was all-powerful, and —this was Alexander's bitterest blow—all-powerful too was Antipater's mother,[b] who was in league with him against the two and harsher than a stepmother, with a hatred for these sons of a princess greater than for ordinary stepchildren. All persons, accordingly, now paid court to Antipater, because of the expectations which he inspired ; everyone was further instigated to desert his rivals by the orders

Antipater all-powerful.

τοῦ βασιλέως προστάγματα, παραγγείλαντος τοῖς
τιμιωτάτοις μήτε προσιέναι μήτε προσέχειν τοῖς
περὶ Ἀλέξανδρον. φοβερὸς δ' ἦν οὐ μόνον τοῖς
ἐκ τῆς βασιλείας, ἀλλὰ καὶ τοῖς ἔξωθεν φίλοις·
οὐδενὶ γὰρ βασιλέων Καῖσαρ τοσαύτην ἔδωκεν
ἐξουσίαν, ὥστε τὸν ἀπ' αὐτοῦ φυγόντα καὶ μὴ
475 προσηκούσης πόλεως ἐξαγαγεῖν. τὰ δὲ μειράκια
τὰς μὲν διαβολὰς ἠγνόουν,[1] παρὸ καὶ μᾶλλον ἀφυ-
λάκτως ἐνέπιπτον αὐταῖς· οὐδὲν[2] γὰρ ὁ πατὴρ
φανερῶς ἀπεμέμφετο· συνίει δὲ κατὰ μικρὸν ἀπὸ
τοῦ ψύγματος καὶ ⟨ὅτι⟩[3] πρὸς τὸ λυποῦν μᾶλλον
ἐτραχύνετο. διέθηκεν δὲ πρὸς αὐτὰ καὶ τὸν θεῖον
Φερώραν Ἀντίπατρος ἐχθρωδῶς καὶ τὴν τηθίδα
Σαλώμην, ὡς ἂν γαμετὴν[4] οὖσαν, καθομιλῶν ἀεὶ
476 καὶ παροξύνων. συνήργει δὲ καὶ πρὸς τὴν ταύτης
ἀπέχθειαν ἡ Ἀλεξάνδρου γυνὴ Γλαφύρα γενεα-
λογοῦσα τὴν ἑαυτῆς εὐγένειαν, καὶ ὡς πασῶν τῶν
κατὰ τὸ βασίλειον εἴη δεσπότις, κατὰ πατέρα μὲν
ἀπὸ Τημένου, κατὰ μητέρα δὲ ἀπὸ Δαρείου τοῦ
477 Ὑστάσπεως οὖσα. πολλὰ δὲ ὠνείδιζεν εἰς ἀγένειαν
τήν τε ἀδελφὴν τὴν Ἡρώδου καὶ τὰς γυναῖκας,
ὧν ἑκάστη δι' εὐμορφίαν οὐκ ἀπὸ γένους ᾑρέθη.
πολλαὶ δ' ἦσαν, ὡς ἂν ἐφειμένου τε πατρίως Ἰουδαίοις γαμεῖν πλείους καὶ τοῦ βασιλέως ἡδομένου
πλείοσιν, αἳ πᾶσαι διὰ τὸ μεγάλαυχον τὸ Γλαφύρας καὶ τὰς λοιδορίας ἐμίσουν Ἀλέξανδρον.

[1] PAM: ἠγνόει the rest.
[2] PA: οὐδενὶ the rest.   [3] Ins. Casaubon.
[4] Text suspected; Naber reads συνετὴν, Destinon χαλεπὴν.

of the king, who had forbidden those highest in his favour to approach or pay any attention to Alexander or his brother. Herod's formidable influence extended, moreover, beyond his realm to his friends abroad ; for no other sovereign had been empowered by Caesar, as he had, to reclaim a fugitive subject even from a state outside his jurisdiction. The young men, meanwhile, as their father had never openly reproached them, were ignorant of these calumnies, and being, consequently, off their guard, laid themselves still more open to them ; but little by little their eyes were opened by his coldness and increased asperity whenever anything annoyed him. Antipater further roused against them the enmity of their uncle Pheroras and their aunt Salome, perpetually coaxing and working upon his aunt's feelings, as though she had been his wife. Salome's hostility was aggravated by Glaphyra, Alexander's wife,[a] who boasted of her noble ancestry and claimed to be mistress of all the ladies at court, because she was descended on her father's side from Temenus,[b] on her mother's from Darius, son of Hystaspes. On the other hand, she was constantly taunting with their low birth Herod's sister and his wives, all of whom had been chosen for their beauty and not for their family. His wives were numerous, since polygamy was permitted by Jewish custom and the king gladly availed himself of the privilege. All these, on account of Glaphyra's arrogance and abuse, hated Alexander.

Arrogance of Glaphyra provokes the ladies of Herod's court.

---

[a] And daughter of Archelaus, king of Cappadocia (§ 446).
[b] One of the Heracleidae, who gave his name to the Temenid kings of Macedonia (Thuc. ii. 99), from whom Archelaus claimed to be descended.

478 (3) Τὴν δὲ δὴ Σαλώμην, καίτοι πενθερὰν
οὖσαν, αὐτὸς Ἀριστόβουλος ἑαυτῷ διεστασίασεν,
ὠργισμένην καὶ πρόσθεν ἐπὶ ταῖς ἐκ Γλαφύρας
βλασφημίαις· ὠνείδιζεν γὰρ τῇ γυναικὶ συνεχῶς
τὴν ταπεινότητα, καὶ ὡς αὐτὸς μὲν ἰδιῶτιν, ὁ δ'

479 ἀδελφὸς αὐτοῦ Ἀλέξανδρος γήμαι βασιλίδα. τοῦτο κλαίουσα τῇ Σαλώμῃ διήγγειλεν ἡ θυγάτηρ,
προσετίθει δ' ὅτι καὶ τῶν ἄλλων ἀδελφῶν τὰς μὲν
μητέρας ἀπειλοῖεν οἱ περὶ Ἀλέξανδρον, ἐπειδὰν
παραλάβωσιν τὴν βασιλείαν, ἱστουργοὺς ἅμα ταῖς
δούλαις ποιήσειν, αὐτοὺς δὲ κωμῶν γραμματεῖς,
ἐπισκώπτοντες ὡς πεπαιδευμένους[1] ἐπιμελῶς.
πρὸς ἃ τὴν ὀργὴν οὐ κατασχοῦσα Σαλώμη πάντα
διήγγειλεν Ἡρώδῃ· σφόδρα δ' ἦν ἀξιόπιστος κατὰ

480 γαμβροῦ λέγουσα. καί τις ἑτέρα διαβολὴ συνέδραμεν ἡ τὸν θυμὸν ὑπεκκαύσασα τοῦ βασιλέως·
ἤκουσεν γὰρ αὐτοὺς ἀνακαλεῖσθαι μὲν συνεχῶς
τὴν μητέρα καὶ κατοιμώζειν ἐπαρωμένους αὐτῷ,
πολλάκις δ' αὐτοῦ διαδιδόντος τῶν Μαριάμμης ἐσθήτων τινὰ ταῖς μεταγενεστέραις γυναιξὶν ἀπειλεῖν,
ὡς ἀντὶ τῶν βασιλικῶν ἐν τάχει περιθήσουσιν
αὐταῖς ἐκ τρυχῶν[2] πεποιημένας.

481 (4) Διὰ ταῦτα καίτοι τὸ φρόνημα τῶν νεανίσκων ὑποδείσας, ὅμως οὐκ ἀπέκοπτε τὴν ἐλπίδα
τῆς διορθώσεως, ἀλλὰ προσκαλεσάμενος αὐτούς,
καὶ γὰρ εἰς Ῥώμην ἐκπλεύσειν ἔμελλε, βραχέα
μὲν ἠπείλησεν ὡς βασιλεύς, τὰ πολλὰ δ' ἐνου-
θέτησεν ὡς πατήρ, καὶ φιλεῖν τοὺς ἀδελφοὺς παρεκάλει διδοὺς τῶν προημαρτημένων ἄφεσιν, εἰ

482 πρὸς τὸ μέλλον ἀμείνους γένοιντο. οἱ δὲ τὰς μὲν

[1] M: παιδευομένους the rest.
[2] Niese: τριχῶν " hair-cloth " mss. The parallel passage

(3) Aristobulus himself alienated Salome, his own mother-in-law, furious as she was already at Glaphyra's scurrility; for he was continually upbraiding his wife for her low origin, saying that he had married a woman of the people and his brother Alexander a princess. Salome's daughter reported this, with tears, to her mother; she added that Alexander and Aristobulus had threatened, when they came to the throne, to set the mothers of their other brothers to work at the loom along with the slave-girls, and to make the princes themselves village clerks, sarcastically referring to the careful education which they had received. At that Salome, unable to control her indignation, reported the whole to Herod; as she was accusing her own son-in-law, her evidence carried very great weight. Another calumny came simultaneously to inflame the king's wrath. He was told that the young princes had their mother's name perpetually on their lips, cursing him while they bemoaned her, and that when he distributed, as he often did, some of Mariamme's apparel to his more recent wives, they would threaten that they would ere long strip them of these royal robes and clothe them in rags.

Salome denounces the princes to Herod.

(4) Herod, though he had learnt through such reports to fear these high-spirited young men, did not abandon hopes of their reformation. Just before setting sail for Rome he sent for them, and delivered some curt threats as sovereign, followed by a long paternal admonition, exhorting them to love their brothers and promising to pardon their past offences if they would amend their ways for the

Herod admonishes them.

A. xvi. 204 has τρίχεσιν which appears to be a corruption of τρύχεσιν.

διαβολὰς ἀπεσκευάζοντο ψευδεῖς εἶναι λέγοντες,
πιστώσεσθαι δὲ τὴν ἀπολογίαν τοῖς ἔργοις ἔφα-
σκον· δεῖν μέντοι κἀκεῖνον ἀποφράττειν τὰς λογο-
ποιίας τῷ μὴ πιστεύειν ῥᾳδίως· οὐ γὰρ ἐπι-
λείψειν τοὺς καταψευσομένους αὐτῶν, ἕως ἂν ὁ
πειθόμενος ᾖ.

483   (5) Τούτοις ὡς πατέρα πείσαντες ταχέως τὸν
μὲν ἐν χερσὶν φόβον διεκρούσαντο, τὴν δ' εἰς τὰ
μέλλοντα λύπην προσέλαβον· ἔγνωσαν γὰρ τήν τε
Σαλώμην ἐχθρὰν καὶ τὸν θεῖον Φερώραν. ἦσαν
δὲ βαρεῖς [μὲν][1] ἀμφότεροι καὶ χαλεποί, Φερώρας
δὲ μείζων,[2] ὃς πάσης μὲν ἐκοινώνει τῆς βασιλείας
πλὴν διαδήματος, προσόδους[3] δὲ ἰδίας εἶχεν ἑκατὸν τάλαντα, τὴν δὲ πέραν Ἰορδάνου πᾶσαν ἐκαρ-
ποῦτο χώραν λαβὼν παρὰ τἀδελφοῦ δῶρον, ὃς
αὐτὸν ἐποίησεν καὶ τετράρχην αἰτησάμενος παρὰ
Καίσαρος, βασιλικῶν τε γάμων ἠξίωσεν συνοι-
κίσας ἀδελφὴν τῆς ἰδίας γυναικός· μετὰ δὲ τὴν
ἐκείνης τελευτὴν καθωσίωσε τὴν πρεσβυτάτην
τῶν ἑαυτοῦ θυγατέρων ἐπὶ προικὶ τριακοσίοις
484 ταλάντοις. ἀλλ' ἀπέδρα Φερώρας τὸν βασιλικὸν
γάμον πρὸς ἔρωτα δούλης, ἐφ' ᾧ χαλεπήνας
Ἡρώδης τὴν μὲν θυγατέρα τῷ πρὸς Πάρθων
ὕστερον ἀναιρεθέντι συνέζευξεν ἀδελφιδῷ· Φερώρᾳ

---

[1] om. PAM.
[2] μεῖζον ML : amplius Lat. : μειζόνως Destinon.
[3] προσόδου PVC.

---

[a] Name unknown.
[b] Salampsio, daughter of Mariamme I.
[c] i.e. to the son of his brother Phasael (A. xvi. 196), also
called Phasael (A. xvii. 22). Nothing is known of the fate
228

future. For their part, they repudiated the charges, declaring that they were false, and assured their father that their actions would vindicate their statement; he ought, however (they added), on his side to stop the mouths of these tale-bearers by refusing so readily to believe them; for there would never be wanting persons ready to calumniate them, so long as they found anyone to listen to them.

(5) The father's heart was quickly reassured by their words; but if the youths thus dispelled their immediate anxiety, the thought of the future brought them new apprehensions, knowing, as they did, the hostility of Salome and their uncle Pheroras. Both were formidable and dangerous, but the more redoubtable was Pheroras, who shared with Herod all the honours of royalty, except the diadem. He had a private income of a hundred talents, exclusive of the revenue derived from the whole of the trans-Jordanic region, a gift from his brother, who had also, after requesting Caesar's permission, appointed him tetrarch. Herod had conferred upon him the further honour of marrying one of the royal family, by uniting him to the sister of his own wife.[a] On her death, he had pledged to him the eldest of his own daughters,[b] with a dowry of three hundred talents; but Pheroras rejected the royal wedding to run after a slave-girl of whom he was enamoured. Herod, indignant at this slight, married his daughter to one of his nephews,[c] who was subsequently killed by the Parthians; his resentment, however, subsided

Pheroras in disfavour with Herod

of this youth, and Reinach suggests that in the following words there has been some confusion or corruption of text, and that Josephus intended to say " son of Phasael who had been *previously* killed by the Parthians " (see B. i. 271).

δὲ μετ' οὐ πολὺ τὴν ὀργὴν ἀνίει διδοὺς συγγνώμην τῇ νόσῳ.

485 (6) Διεβάλλετο δὲ καὶ πάλαι μὲν ἔτι ζώσης τῆς
βασιλίδος ἐπιβουλεύειν αὐτῷ φαρμάκοις, τότε δὲ
πλεῖστοι μηνυταὶ προσῄεσαν, ὡς καίπερ φιλ-
αδελφότατον ὄντα τὸν Ἡρώδην εἰς πίστιν ὑπ-
αχθῆναι τῶν λεγομένων καὶ δέος. πολλοὺς δὲ τῶν
ἐν ὑπονοίᾳ βασανίσας τελευταῖον ἦλθεν ἐπὶ τοὺς
486 Φερώρου φίλους. ὧν ἐπιβουλὴν μὲν ἄντικρυς
ὡμολόγησεν οὐδείς, ὅτι δὲ τὴν ἐρωμένην ἁρπα-
σάμενος εἰς Πάρθους ἀποδρᾶναι παρεσκευάζετο,
συμμετέχοι[1] δὲ τοῦ σκέμματος αὐτῷ καὶ τῆς
φυγῆς Κοστόβαρος ὁ Σαλώμης ἀνήρ, ᾧ συνῴκισεν αὐτὴν ὁ βασιλεὺς ἐπὶ μοιχείᾳ τοῦ προτέρου
487 διαφθαρέντος. ἦν δ' ἐλευθέρα διαβολῆς οὐδὲ Σα-
λώμη· καὶ γὰρ αὐτῆς Φερώρας ἀδελφὸς κατηγόρει συνθήκας περὶ γάμου πρὸς Συλλαῖον τὸν
Ὀβάδα τοῦ Ἀράβων βασιλέως ἐπίτροπον, ὃς ἦν
ἐχθρότατος Ἡρώδῃ. διελεγχθεῖσα δὲ καὶ τοῦτο
καὶ πάνθ' ὅσα Φερώρας ἐνεκάλει συγγινώσκεται,
καὶ αὐτὸν δὲ Φερώραν ὁ βασιλεὺς ἀπέλυσεν τῶν
ἐγκλημάτων.

488 (7) Μετέβαινεν δὲ ἐπ' Ἀλέξανδρον ὁ χειμὼν
τῆς οἰκίας καὶ περὶ τὴν ἐκείνου κεφαλὴν ὅλος
ἀπηρείσατο. τρεῖς ἦσαν εὐνοῦχοι τιμιώτατοι τῷ
βασιλεῖ, καὶ δῆλον ἐξ ὧν ἐλειτούργουν· τῷ μὲν
γὰρ οἰνοχοεῖν προσετέτακτο, τῷ δὲ δεῖπνον προσ-
φέρειν, ὁ δ' αὐτὸν κατεκοίμιζέν τε καὶ συγκατ-

---

[1] Destinon : συμμέτοχοι MSS.

[a] Mariamme I.

ere long and he made allowance for his love-sick brother.

(6) Long before, while the queen [a] was still alive, Pheroras had been accused of a plot to poison Herod ; but at the period now reached informers came forward in such numbers that Herod, though the most affectionate of brothers, was led to believe their statements and to take alarm. After putting many suspected persons to the torture he came last of all to the friends of Pheroras. None of these admitted outright that there was such a plot, though they said that Pheroras was preparing to fly to Parthia, carrying off his mistress with him, and that his accomplice in this design and partner in his intended flight was Costobarus, Salome's husband, to whom the king had given his sister, when her former husband was put to death on a charge of adultery. Even Salome herself did not escape calumny : she was accused by her brother Pheroras of signing a contract to marry Syllaeus, the procurator [b] of Obadas, king of Arabia, and Herod's bitterest enemy. However, though convicted of this and of everything else of which she was accused by Pheroras, she was pardoned ; while Pheroras himself was acquitted by the king of the charges against him.

and suspected of plotting against him c. 10 B.C.

Herod pardons him and Salome.

(7) The tempest lowering over Herod's house thus veered round to Alexander and burst in full force about his devoted head. There were three eunuchs who held a special place in the king's esteem, as is indicated by the services with which they were charged : one poured out his wine, another served him his supper, and the third put him to bed and

Alexander is denounced by Herod's eunuchs

[b] Or " viceroy " ; see *A.* xvi. 220 (Syllaeus administers the realm of the indolent Obadas).

231

489 ἐκλίνετο. τούτους εἰς τὰ παιδικὰ δώροις μεγάλοις
ὑπηγάγετο ὁ Ἀλέξανδρος. μηνυθὲν δὲ τῷ βασιλεῖ διηλέγχοντο βασάνοις, καὶ τὴν μὲν συνουσίαν
εὐθέως ὡμολόγουν, ἐξέφερον δὲ καὶ τὰς εἰς αὐτὴν
ὑποσχέσεις, ὃν τρόπον ἀπατηθεῖεν ὑπὸ Ἀλεξάν-
490 δρου λέγοντος, ὡς οὐκ ἐν Ἡρώδῃ δέοι τὰς ἐλπίδας
ἔχειν, ἀναιδεῖ γέροντι καὶ βαπτομένῳ τὰς κόμας,
εἰ μὴ διὰ τοῦτ' αὐτὸν οἴονται καὶ νέον, αὑτῷ δὲ
προσέχειν, ὃς καὶ παρὰ ἄκοντος διαδέξεται τὴν
βασιλείαν, οὐκ εἰς μακράν τε τοὺς μὲν ἐχθροὺς
ἀμυνεῖται, τοὺς φίλους δ' εὐδαίμονας ποιήσει καὶ
491 μακαρίους, πρὸ πάντων δὲ αὑτούς· εἶναι δὲ καὶ
θεραπαίαν τῶν δυνατῶν περὶ τὸν Ἀλέξανδρον
λαθραίαν, τούς τε ἡγεμόνας τοῦ στρατιωτικοῦ
καὶ τοὺς ταξιάρχους κρύφα πρὸς αὐτὸν συνιέναι.

492 (8) Ταῦτα τὸν Ἡρώδην οὕτως ἐξεφόβησεν, ὡς
μηδὲ παραχρῆμα τολμῆσαι τὰς μηνύσεις ἐκ-
φέρειν, ἀλλὰ κατασκόπους ὑποπέμπων νύκτωρ καὶ
μεθ' ἡμέραν ἕκαστα τῶν πραττομένων ἢ λεγομένων διηρεύνα καὶ τοὺς ἐν ταῖς ὑποψίαις εὐθέως
493 ἀνῄρει. δεινῆς δὲ[1] ἀνομίας ἐνεπλήσθη τὸ βασί-
λειον· κατὰ γὰρ ἔχθραν ἢ μῖσος ἴδιον ἕκαστος
ἔπλασσεν τὰς διαβολάς, καὶ πολλοὶ πρὸς τοὺς διαφόρους φονῶντι τῷ βασιλικῷ θυμῷ κατεχρῶντο.
καὶ τὸ μὲν ψεῦδος εἶχεν παραχρῆμα πίστιν, αἱ
κολάσεις δὲ τῶν διαβολῶν ἦσαν ὠκύτεραι· κατ-
ηγορεῖτο γοῦν τις ἄρτι κατηγορήσας καὶ τῷ
πρὸς αὐτοῦ διελεγχθέντι συναπήγετο, τὰς γὰρ
ἐξετάσεις τοῦ βασιλέως ὁ περὶ τῆς ψυχῆς κίν-
494 δυνος ὑπετέμνετο.[2] προύβη δ' εἰς τοσοῦτον πι-
κρίας, ὡς μηδὲ τῶν ἀκαταιτιάτων τινὶ προσβλέ-

[1] δὴ A : itaque Lat.   [2] ἐπετέμνετο AM.

slept in his chamber. Alexander by large presents corrupted these menials for criminal ends ; on being informed of which the king submitted them to trial by torture. They at once confessed their relations with Alexander, and then went on to reveal the promises which had brought them about. Alexander, they said, had inveigled them by saying : " You ought not to place your hopes on Herod, a shameless old man who dyes his hair, unless this disguise has actually made you take him for a youngster ; it is to me, Alexander, that you should look, to me, who am to inherit the throne, whether he will or no, and shall ere long be avenged on my enemies and bring fortune and bliss to my friends, and above all to you." They added that persons of rank secretly paid court to Alexander and that the generals and officers of the army had clandestine interviews with him.

(8) These disclosures so terrified Herod that at the time he did not even dare to divulge them ; but, sending out spies night and day, he scrutinized all that was done or said, and at once put to death any who fell under suspicion. The palace was given over to frightful anarchy. Everyone, to gratify some personal enmity or hatred, invented calumnies ; many turned to base account against their adversaries the murderous mood of wrathful royalty. Lies found instant credit, but chastisement was even swifter than calumny : the accuser of a moment ago found himself accused and led off to death with him whose conviction he had obtained ; for the grave peril to his life cut short the king's inquiries. He grew so embittered that he had no gentle looks even for

and arrested.

πειν ἡμέρως, εἶναι δὲ καὶ τοῖς φίλοις ἀπηνέστατος·
πολλοῖς γοῦν αὐτῶν ἀπεῖπεν τὸ βασίλειον καὶ πρὸς
οὓς οὐκ εἶχεν χειρὸς ἐξουσίαν τῷ λόγῳ χαλεπὸς
495 ἦν. συνεπέβη δὲ Ἀντίπατρος ἐν ταῖς συμφοραῖς
Ἀλεξάνδρῳ καὶ στῖφος ποιήσας τῶν συγγενῶν
οὐκ ἔστιν ἥντινα διαβολὴν παρέλιπεν. προήχθη
γέ τοι πρὸς τοσοῦτον δέος ὁ βασιλεὺς ὑπὸ τῆς
τερατείας αὐτοῦ καὶ τῶν συνταγμάτων, ὡς ἐφ-
εστάναι δοκεῖν αὐτῷ τὸν Ἀλέξανδρον ξιφήρη.
496 συλλαβὼν οὖν[1] αὐτὸν ἐξαπίνης ἔδησεν καὶ πρὸς
βάσανον ἐχώρει τῶν φίλων αὐτοῦ. σιγῶντες δὲ
ἀπέθνησκον πολλοὶ καὶ μηδὲν ὑπὲρ τὸ συνειδὸς
εἰπόντες· οἱ δ' ὑπὸ τῶν ἀλγηδόνων ψεύσασθαι
βιασθέντες ἔλεγον, ὡς ἐπιβουλεύοι τε αὐτῷ μετὰ
Ἀριστοβούλου τοῦ ἀδελφοῦ καὶ παραφυλάττει
497 κυνηγοῦντα κτείνας εἰς Ῥώμην ἀποδρᾶναι. τούτοις καίπερ οὐ πιθανοῖς οὖσιν ἀλλ' ὑπὸ τῆς ἀνάγκης ἐσχεδιασμένοις ὁ βασιλεὺς ἐπίστευσεν ἡδέως,
παραμυθίαν λαμβάνων τοῦ δῆσαι τὸν υἱὸν τὸ μὴ
δοκεῖν ἀδίκως.
498 (xxv. 1) Ὁ δ' Ἀλέξανδρος ἐπεὶ τὸν πατέρα
μεταπείθειν ἀμήχανον ἑώρα, τοῖς δεινοῖς ὁμόσε
χωρεῖν διέγνω, καὶ τέσσαρας κατὰ τῶν ἐχθρῶν
βίβλους συνταξάμενος προσωμολόγει μὲν τὴν ἐπιβουλήν, κοινωνοὺς δ' ἀπεδείκνυεν τοὺς πλείστους
αὐτῶν, πρὸ δὲ πάντων Φερώραν καὶ Σαλώμην·
ταύτην γὰρ δὴ καὶ μιγῆναί ποτε αὐτῷ μὴ θέλοντι
499 νύκτωρ εἰσβιασαμένην. αἵ τε οὖν βίβλοι παρῆσαν
Ἡρώδῃ εἰς χεῖρας πολλὰ καὶ δεινὰ κατὰ τῶν

[1] γοῦν LTRC.

234

those who were not accused and treated his own friends with the utmost harshness : many of these he refused to admit to court, while those who were beyond the reach of his arm came under the lash of his tongue. To add to Alexander's misfortunes, Antipater returned to the charge and, raising a band of kindred spirits, had recourse to every conceivable form of calumny. By his portentous fictions and fabrications the king was, in fact, reduced to such a state of alarm, that he fancied he saw Alexander coming upon him sword in hand. He, accordingly, had the prince suddenly arrested and imprisoned, and then proceeded to put his friends to the torture. Many died silent, without saying anything beyond what they knew ; but some were driven by their sufferings to falsehood and declared that Alexander and his brother Aristobulus were conspiring against him and were watching for an opportunity to kill him, while out hunting, meaning then to escape to Rome. This statement, improbable as it was and invented off-hand under the pressure of torment, the king nevertheless found satisfaction in believing, consoling himself for having imprisoned his son with the thought that his action had been justified.

(xxv. 1) Alexander, perceiving the impossibility of shaking his father's belief, resolved boldly to confront the perils that menaced him. He, therefore, composed four books directed against his enemies, in which he avowed the conspiracy, but denounced most of them as accomplices, above all Pheroras and Salome ; the latter, he declared, had one night even forced her way into his chamber and, against his will, had immoral relations with him. These documents —a mass of shocking accusations incriminating per-

Alexander's written statement.

235

δυνατωτάτων βοῶσαι, καὶ διὰ τάχους εἰς Ἰουδαίαν Ἀρχέλαος ἀφικνεῖται περὶ τῷ γαμβρῷ καὶ
τῇ θυγατρὶ δείσας. γίνεται δὲ βοηθὸς αὐτοῖς
μάλα προμηθὴς καὶ τέχνῃ τὴν τοῦ βασιλέως
500 ἀπειλὴν διεκρούσατο. συμβαλὼν γὰρ εὐθέως αὐτῷ
" ποῦ ποτέ ἐστιν ὁ ἀλιτήριός μου γαμβρός; "
ἐβόα, " ποῦ δὲ τὴν πατροκτόνον ὄψομαι κεφαλήν,
ἣν ταῖς ἐμαυτοῦ χερσὶν διασπαράξω; προσθήσω
δὲ καὶ τὴν θυγατέρα μου τῷ καλῷ νυμφίῳ· καὶ
γὰρ εἰ μὴ κεκοινώνηκεν τοῦ σκέμματος, ὅτι
501 τοιούτου γυνὴ γέγονεν, μεμίανται. θαυμάζω δὲ
καὶ σὲ τὸν ἐπιβουλευθέντα τῆς ἀνεξικακίας, εἰ ζῇ
μέχρι νῦν Ἀλέξανδρος· ἐγὼ γὰρ ἠπειγόμην ἀπὸ
Καππαδοκίας ὡς τὸν μὲν εὑρήσων πάλαι δεδω-
κότα δίκας, μετὰ δὲ σοῦ περὶ τῆς θυγατρὸς ἐξετά-
σων, ἣν ἐκείνῳ γε πρὸς τὸ σὸν ἀξίωμα βλέπων
ἐνεγύησα.[1] νῦν δὲ περὶ ἀμφοῖν ἡμῖν βουλευτέον,
κἂν ᾖς πατὴρ λίαν ἢ[2] τοῦ κολάζειν υἱὸν ἀτονώτε-
ρος ἐπίβουλον, ἀμείψωμεν τὰς δεξιὰς καὶ γενώ-
μεθα τῆς ἀλλήλων ὀργῆς διάδοχοι."

502   (2) Τούτοις περικομπήσας καίπερ παρατεταγ-
μένον Ἡρώδην ὑπάγεται· δίδωσι γοῦν αὐτῷ τὰς
συνταχθείσας ὑπ' Ἀλεξάνδρου βίβλους ἀναγνῶ-
ναι καὶ καθ' ἕκαστον ἐφιστὰς κεφάλαιον συν-
εσκέπτετο. λαμβάνει δ' ὁ Ἀρχέλαος ἀφορμὴν τοῦ
στρατηγήματος καὶ κατὰ μικρὸν εἰς τοὺς ἐγγε-
γραμμένους καὶ Φερώραν μετήγαγεν τὰς αἰτίας.
503 ὡς δ' ἑώρα πιστεύοντα τὸν βασιλέα, " σκεπτέον, "

---

[1] ἐνεγγύησα most mss.
[2] ἢ PA : et Lat. : om. the rest.

sons of the highest rank—had passed into Herod's hands, when Archelaus, alarmed for his son-in-law and daughter, arrived in haste in Judaea. Coming with singular sagacity to their aid, he succeeded by stratagem in diverting the king's threats in another direction. For, the moment he met him, he exclaimed : " Where is my scoundrel of a son-in-law ? Where shall I set eyes on the person of this parricide, that I may tear him in pieces with my own hands ? My daughter, too, shall share the fate of her fine spouse ; for even if she has had no part in his schemes, as the wife of such a miscreant she is polluted. But you too, the intended victim of the plot, astonish me by your forbearance, in leaving, as it seems, Alexander still alive ! For my part, I hurried hither from Cappadocia expecting to find that the culprit had long since paid his penalty and to hold an inquiry with you upon my daughter, whom, out of regard for your exalted rank, I gave away to that wretch. But now, I find, we have to deliberate about the pair of them. If, then, the fondness of a father's heart unnerves you for punishing a rebellious son, let us each lend the other his hand, each take the other's place in visiting our wrath upon our children."

(2) With this blustering oration he deluded Herod, notwithstanding the latter's attitude of defiance. Herod, at any rate, handed him for perusal the documents composed by Alexander and examined chapter after chapter with him, dwelling upon each. Archelaus, finding here an opportunity for furthering his ruse, little by little shifted the blame on to the persons whose names appeared in the volumes, particularly Pheroras. When he observed that he was

ἔφη, "μή ποτε τὸ μειράκιον ὑπὸ τοσούτων εἴη
πονηρῶν ἐπιβουλευόμενον, οὐχ ὑπὸ τοῦ μειρακίου
σύ· καὶ γὰρ οὐχ ὁρᾶν αἰτίαν, ἐξ ἧς ἂν εἰς τηλικοῦτον μύσος προέπεσεν, ἀπολαύων μὲν ἤδη βασιλείας, ἐλπίζων δὲ καὶ διαδοχήν, εἰ μή τινες ἦσαν
ἀναπείθοντες καὶ τὸ τῆς ἡλικίας εὔκολον ἐπὶ
κακῷ μεταχειριζόμενοι. διὰ γὰρ τῶν τοιούτων
ἐξαπατᾶσθαι μὲν οὐκ ἐφήβους μόνον ἀλλὰ καὶ
γέροντας, οἴκους δὲ λαμπροτάτους καὶ βασιλείας
ὅλας ἀνατρέπεσθαι."

504   (3) Συνῄνει τοῖς λεγομένοις Ἡρώδης, καὶ τὴν
μὲν πρὸς Ἀλέξανδρον ὀργὴν ἐπανίει πρὸς ὀλίγον,
πρὸς δὲ Φερώραν παρωξύνετο· τῶν γὰρ τεσσάρων
βίβλων οὗτος ἦν ὑπόθεσις. ὃς κατιδὼν τό τε τοῦ
βασιλέως ὀξύρροπον καὶ τὴν Ἀρχελάου φιλίαν
παρ' αὐτῷ πάντων κρατοῦσαν, ὡς οὐκ ἐνῆν εὐ-
σχήμων σωτηρία, τὴν δι' ἀναιδείας ἐπορίζετο·
καταλείψας γοῦν Ἀλέξανδρον προσέφυγεν Ἀρχε-
505 λάῳ. κἀκεῖνος οὐχ ὁρᾶν ἔφη, πῶς ἂν αὐτὸν
ἐξαιτήσαιτο τοσούτοις ἐνεχόμενον ἐγκλήμασιν, ἐξ
ὧν σαφῶς ἀποδείκνυται τοῦ βασιλέως ἐπίβουλος
καὶ τῶν παρόντων τῷ μειρακίῳ κακῶν αἴτιος
γεγονώς, εἰ μὴ βούλεται τὸ πανοῦργον καὶ τὰς
ἀρνήσεις ἀφεὶς προσομολογῆσαι μὲν τὰ κατηγορημένα, συγγνώμην δ' αἰτήσασθαι παρὰ τἀδελφοῦ[1]
καὶ φιλοῦντος· εἰς γὰρ τοῦτο πάντα τρόπον αὐτῷ[2]
συνεργήσειν.

506   (4) Πείθεται Φερώρας, καὶ κατασκευάσας ἑαυτόν, ὡς ἂν οἰκτρότατος φανείη, μελαίνῃ τε ἐσθῆτι
καὶ δακρύοις προσπίπτει τοῖς Ἡρώδου ποσίν, ὡς[3]

[1] παρά τ' ἀδελφοῦ Cobet.
[2] αὐτὸς PA.   [3] ἧς Niese.

238

gaining the king's confidence, he remarked : " We must be careful to see that all these villains have not been conspiring against this young man, and not the young man against you. For I can see no reason why he should have plunged into such heinous crime, when he already enjoyed the honours of royalty and expected to succeed to the throne, unless there were others seducing him and misguiding the tractable spirit of youth. Such persons, indeed, have been known to impose not only on the young, but on old men as well ; by them the most illustrious houses and entire kingdoms have been overturned."

(3) Herod assented to this speech ; and for a while relaxed his wrath with Alexander and vented it upon Pheroras, as he was the main theme of the four documents. Pheroras, observing this quick change in the king's feelings and the paramount influence exercised on him by his friend Archelaus, despairing of saving himself by honourable means sought protection in effrontery : he abandoned Alexander and threw himself on the mercy of Archelaus. The latter replied that he did not see how he could sue for pardon for a man involved in such grave charges, which clearly proved that he had plotted against the king and been the cause of the young prince's present misfortunes, unless he were prepared to renounce his villainy and his denials, to own up to the crimes of which he was accused, and to ask pardon of his brother, who indeed loved him ; for that object, said Archelaus, he would render him every possible assistance.

(4) Pheroras took his advice, and assuming an attitude calculated to arouse the deepest compassion, in black raiment and in tears, threw himself at

πολλάκις ἔτυχεν συγγνώμης αἰτούμενος καὶ μιαρὸν
μὲν ἑαυτὸν ὁμολογῶν, δεδρακέναι γὰρ πάντα, ὅσα
κατηγοροῖτο, παρακοπὴν δὲ φρενῶν καὶ μανίαν
ὀδυρόμενος, ἧς αἴτιον εἶναι τὸν ἔρωτα τῆς γυναι-
507 κὸς ἔλεγεν. παραστήσας δὴ κατήγορον καὶ μάρ-
τυν ἑαυτοῦ Φερώραν Ἀρχέλαος οὕτως ἤδη παρ-
ῃτεῖτο καὶ τὴν Ἡρώδου κατέστελλεν ὀργὴν χρώμενος οἰκείοις ὑποδείγμασιν· καὶ γὰρ αὐτὸς πολλῷ
χαλεπώτερα πάσχων ὑπὸ τἀδελφοῦ τῆς ἀμύνης
ἐπίπροσθεν τίθεσθαι τὸ τῆς φύσεως δίκαιον· ἐν
γὰρ ταῖς βασιλείαις ὥσπερ ἐν μεγάλοις σώμασιν
ἀεί τι μέρος φλεγμαίνειν ὑπὸ τοῦ βάρους, ὅπερ
ἀποκόπτειν μὲν οὐ χρῆναι, θεραπεύειν δὲ πρᾳό-
τερον.

508   (5) Πολλὰ τοιαῦτα λέγων Ἡρώδην μὲν ἐπὶ
Φερώρᾳ μειλίσσεται, διέμενε δ' αὐτὸς ἀγανακτῶν
πρὸς Ἀλέξανδρον καὶ τὴν θυγατέρα διαζεύξας
ἀπάξειν ἔφασκεν, ἕως περιέστησεν Ἡρώδην ἀντι-
παρακαλεῖν ὑπὲρ τοῦ μειρακίου καὶ πάλιν αὐτῷ
μνηστεύεσθαι τὴν θυγατέρα. σφόδρα δὲ ἀξιοπίστως Ἀρχέλαος ᾧ βούλεται συνοικίζειν αὐτὴν
ἐπέτρεπεν πλὴν Ἀλεξάνδρου· περὶ πλείστου γὰρ
ποιεῖσθαι τηρεῖν πρὸς αὐτὸν τὰ τῆς ἐπιγαμίας
509 δίκαια. φαμένου δὲ τοῦ βασιλέως δῶρον ἕξειν
παρ' αὐτοῦ τὸν υἱόν, εἰ μὴ λύσειεν τὸν γάμον,
ὄντων μὲν αὐτοῖς ἤδη καὶ τέκνων, στεργομένης δ'
οὕτως ὑπὸ τοῦ μειρακίου τῆς γυναικός, ἣν παρα-

Herod's feet and craved his pardon as he had often successfully done before. He confessed himself a polluted wretch, guilty of all that was laid to his charge, but deplored his mental derangement and madness, which he attributed to his passion for his wife. Archelaus, after thus inducing Pheroras to appear as his own accuser and to bear witness against himself, now proceeded to plead for him and sought to appease Herod's wrath, citing parallel cases in his own family history. He had himself, he said, suffered much worse injury from his brother, but had preferred the claims of natural affection to revenge ; for in kingdoms, as in corpulent individuals, there was always some member becoming inflamed from the weight which it supported ; yet what it needed was not amputation but some milder method of cure.

pleads for Pheroras,

(5) By many such representations Archelaus succeeded in soothing Herod's anger against Pheroras. He himself, however, affected to be still indignant with Alexander, protesting that he would divorce his daughter and carry her off with him, until he brought Herod round into the position of a suppliant on the young man's behalf and a suitor, once more, for the hand of Archelaus's daughter for his son. With an air of complete sincerity, Archelaus said that he had his permission to unite her to whom he would, save only Alexander ; for his dearest desire was to maintain the marriage ties which linked him to Herod. To this the king replied that Archelaus, by consenting not to break the marriage, would really be giving his son back to him, seeing that they already had children and that the young man was so deeply attached to his wife ; if she

and brings about a general reconciliation.

241

μένουσαν μὲν ἔσεσθαι δυσώπημα τῶν ἁμαρτημάτων, ἀπορραγεῖσαν δὲ αἰτίαν τῆς εἰς ἅπαντα
ἀπογνώσεως· μαλακωτέρας γὰρ γίνεσθαι τὰς
510 τόλμας πάθεσιν οἰκείοις περισπωμένας· κατανεύει
μόλις Ἀρχέλαος διαλλάσσεταί τε καὶ διαλλάσσει
τῷ νεανίσκῳ τὸν πατέρα. δεῖν μέντοι πάντως
ἔφη πέμπειν αὐτὸν εἰς Ῥώμην Καίσαρι διαλεξό-
μενον· γεγραφέναι γὰρ αὐτὸς ἐκείνῳ περὶ πάντων.

511   (6) Τὸ μὲν οὖν Ἀρχελάου στρατήγημα, δι' οὗ
τὸν γαμβρὸν ἐρρύσατο, πέρας εἶχεν· μετὰ δὲ τὰς
διαλλαγὰς ἐν εὐωχίαις καὶ φιλοφρονήσεσιν διῆγον.
ἀπιόντα δ' αὐτὸν Ἡρώδης δωρεῖται ταλάντων
ἑβδομήκοντα δώροις θρόνῳ τε χρυσῷ διαλίθῳ καὶ
εὐνούχοις καὶ παλλακίδι, ἥτις ἐκαλεῖτο Παννυχίς,
τῶν τε φίλων ἐτίμησεν ἕκαστον κατ' ἀξίαν.
512 ὁμοίως τε καὶ οἱ συγγενεῖς, προστάξαντος τοῦ
βασιλέως, πάντες Ἀρχελάῳ δῶρα λαμπρὰ ἔδοσαν,
προεπέμφθη τε ὑπό τε Ἡρώδου καὶ τῶν δυνατῶν
ἕως[1] Ἀντιοχείας.

513   (xxvi. 1) Μετ' οὐ πολὺ δὲ εἰς τὴν Ἰουδαίαν
παρέβαλεν ἀνὴρ πολὺ τῶν Ἀρχελάου στρατηγη-
μάτων δυνατώτερος, ὃς οὐ μόνον τὰς ὑπ' ἐκείνου
πολιτευθείσας Ἀλεξάνδρῳ διαλλαγὰς ἀνέτρεψεν,
ἀλλὰ καὶ ἀπωλείας αἴτιος αὐτῷ κατέστη. γένος
ἦν Λάκων, Εὐρυκλῆς τοὔνομα, πόθῳ χρημάτων
εἰς τὴν βασιλείαν εἰσφθαρείς· οὐ γὰρ ἀντεῖχεν
514 ἔτι ἡ Ἑλλὰς αὐτοῦ τῇ πολυτελείᾳ. λαμπρὰ δ'
Ἡρώδῃ δῶρα προσενεγκών, δέλεαρ ὧν ἐθηρᾶτο,

***

[1] P: μέχρι(s) the rest.

***

[a] In A. xvi. 270 it is Herod who undertakes to go to Rome.
[b] Mentioned by Pausanias (ii. 3. 5) as the builder of the
finest baths at Corinth.

remained with him, her very presence would make him ashamed of his errors, whereas, were she torn from him, he would be driven to utter desperation ; for the domestic affections exercised a chastening and diverting influence on reckless characters. Archelaus was induced, not without difficulty, to assent, was reconciled to the youthful offender, and reconciled him to his father ; he added, however, that it was absolutely essential that the latter should be sent to Rome for an interview with Caesar, as he himself had forwarded a full report of the matter to the emperor.[a]

(6) Such was the end of the ruse by which Arche- Herod's laus rescued his son-in-law. After the reconciliation presents to Archelaus. the time was passed in festivity and interchange of courtesies. On his departure Herod presented him with seventy talents, a throne of gold set with precious stones, some eunuchs, and a concubine, named Pannychis ; he conferred other favours upon each of his friends, proportionate to their rank. Magnificent presents were, likewise, by order of royalty, made to Archelaus by all the high officials at court. Herod and his nobles then escorted him as far as Antioch.

(xxvi. 1) Not long after, however, there arrived in Visit of Judaea a man whose influence far outmatched the Eurycles the Laconian artifices of Archelaus, and who not only broke up the villain: his reconciliation which the latter had negotiated in the flattery of Herod. interest of Alexander, but also proved the cause of that prince's ruin. He was a Lacedaemonian, named Eurycles,[b] whose accursed visit to the realm arose from a craving for money, when Greece could no longer meet his extravagant requirements. He brought with him magnificent presents for Herod, as

καὶ παραχρῆμα πολλαπλασίῳ λαβὼν οὐδὲν ἡγεῖτο
τὴν καθαρὰν δόσιν, εἰ μὴ δι' αἵματος ἐμπορεύ-
515 σεται τὴν βασιλείαν. περιέρχεται γοῦν τὸν βασιλέα κολακείᾳ καὶ δεινότητι λόγων καὶ περὶ
αὑτοῦ ψευδέσιν ἐγκωμίοις. ταχέως δὲ συνιδὼν
τὸν Ἡρώδου τρόπον καὶ πάντα λέγων τε καὶ
πράττων τὰ πρὸς ἡδονὴν αὐτῷ, φίλος ἐν τοῖς
πρώτοις γίνεται· καὶ γὰρ ὁ βασιλεὺς διὰ τὴν
πατρίδα καὶ πάντες οἱ περὶ αὐτὸν ἡδέως προ-
ετίμων τὸν Σπαρτιάτην.

516 (2) Ὁ δ' ἐπεὶ τὰ σαθρὰ τῆς οἰκίας κατέμαθεν,
τάς τε τῶν ἀδελφῶν διαφορὰς καὶ ὅπως διέκειτο
πρὸς ἕκαστον ὁ πατήρ, Ἀντιπάτρου μὲν ξενίᾳ
προκατείληπτο, †φιλίᾳ δὲ Ἀλέξανδρον†[1] ὑποκρίνε-
ται ψευσάμενος ἑταῖρον ἑαυτὸν εἶναι καὶ Ἀρχελάου πάλαι· διὸ δὴ καὶ ταχέως ὡς δεδοκι-
μασμένος ἐδέχθη, συνίστησιν δ' αὐτὸν[2] εὐθέως
517 καὶ Ἀριστοβούλῳ τῷ ἀδελφῷ. πάντων δ' ἀπο-
πειραθεὶς τῶν προσώπων ἄλλον ἄλλως ὑπῄει,
γίνεται δὲ προηγουμένως μισθωτὸς Ἀντιπάτρου καὶ
προδότης Ἀλεξάνδρου, τῷ μὲν ὀνειδίζων, εἰ πρεσβύτατος ὢν περιόψεται τοὺς ἐφεδρεύοντας αὐτοῦ
ταῖς ἐλπίσιν, Ἀλεξάνδρῳ δέ, εἰ γεγεννημένος[3] ἐκ
βασιλίδος καὶ βασιλίδι συνοικῶν ἐάσει διαδέχεσθαι
τὴν ἀρχὴν τὸν ἐξ ἰδιώτιδος, καὶ ταῦτα μεγίστην
518 ἀφορμὴν ἔχων Ἀρχέλαον. ἦν δὲ πιστὸς τῷ μει-

---

[1] Text corrupt: φιλίαν δὲ Ἀλεξάνδρου Bekker.
[2] ἑαυτὸν LTRC.   [3] γεγενημένος AL.

---

[a] Perhaps, as Reinach suggests, because of the pretended
relationship of Spartans and Jews, 1 Macc. xii. 21 ; Jos.
A. xii. 226.

a bait to secure his quarry, and instantly found them returned with interest ; but he accounted a pure and simple gift as nothing, if he failed to make merchandise out of the realm at the price of blood. So he proceeded to impose on the king by flattery, clever talk, and lying encomiums upon his merits. Quickly reading Herod's character and studying in all he said or did to please him, he was soon numbered among his principal friends ; indeed the king and the whole court were delighted to show special honour to this Spartan, out of regard for his country.[a]

(2) When he had learnt everything about the rottenness that was sapping the royal house, the quarrel between the brothers and their father's disposition towards each of them, Eurycles, although under a prior obligation to Antipater for the latter's hospitality, nevertheless feigned a friendship for Alexander, falsely claiming to be an old comrade of Archelaus. With this recommendation he was quickly received as a proved friend and was at once introduced by Alexander to his brother Aristobulus. Exploiting in turn all the various personages,[b] he insinuated himself into favour with each by a different method ; but he chiefly acted as a hireling of Antipater and a traitor to Alexander. To the former he represented how disgraceful it was that he, the eldest son, should overlook the intrigues of persons who had an eye upon his prospects ; to Alexander, that he, the son of one princess and husband of another, should suffer the son of a woman of no station to succeed to the throne, especially when he had in Archelaus such powerful support behind him. The fiction of his being a friend of

He denounces Alexander to Herod.

[b] Or possibly " Trying in turn all the parts in the play."

ρακίῳ σύμβουλος τὴν Ἀρχελάου φιλίαν πλασά-
μενος· διὸ μηδὲν ὑποστελλόμενος Ἀλέξανδρος τά
τε κατ' Ἀντίπατρον ἀπωδύρετο πρὸς αὐτὸν καὶ
ὡς Ἡρώδης αὐτῶν τὴν μητέρα κτείνας οὐ παρά-
δοξον εἰ καὶ αὐτοὺς ἀφαιρεῖται τὴν ἐκείνης βασι-
λείαν· ἐφ' οἷς ὁ Εὐρυκλῆς οἰκτείρειν τε καὶ συν-
519 αλγεῖν ὑπεκρίνετο. τὰ δ' αὐτὰ καὶ τὸν Ἀριστόβουλον εἰπεῖν δελεάσας καὶ ταῖς κατὰ τοῦ πατρὸς
μέμψεσιν ἐνδησάμενος ἀμφοτέρους ᾤχετο φέρων
Ἀντιπάτρῳ τὰ ἀπόρρητα· προσεπιψεύδεται δ'
ἐπιβουλὴν ὡς ἐνεδρευόντων αὐτὸν τῶν ἀδελφῶν
καὶ μόνον οὐκ ἐπιφερόντων ἤδη τὰ ξίφη. λαβὼν
δ' ἐπὶ τούτοις χρημάτων πλῆθος ἐπαινέτης ἦν
520 Ἀντιπάτρου[1] πρὸς τὸν πατέρα. τὸ δὲ τελευταῖον
ἐργολαβήσας τὸν Ἀριστοβούλου καὶ Ἀλεξάνδρου
θάνατον κατήγορος αὐτῶν ἐπὶ τοῦ πατρὸς γίνεται,
καὶ προσελθὼν ἀντιδιδόναι τὸ ζῆν ἔφασκεν Ἡρώδῃ
τῶν εἰς αὐτὸν εὐεργεσιῶν καὶ τὸ φῶς ἀμοιβὴν τῆς
ξενίας ἀντιπαρέχειν· πάλαι γὰρ ἐπ' αὐτὸν ἠκονῆ-
σθαι ξίφος καὶ τὴν Ἀλεξάνδρου τετονῶσθαι δεξιάν,
ἐμποδὼν δ' αὐτὸς γεγονέναι τῷ τάχει συνεργεῖν
521 ὑποκριθείς· φάναι γὰρ τὸν Ἀλέξανδρον, ὡς οὐκ
ἀγαπᾷ βασιλεύσας αὐτὸς Ἡρώδης ἐν ἀλλοτρίοις[a]
καὶ μετὰ τὸν τῆς μητρὸς αὐτῶν φόνον τὴν ἐκείνης
ἀρχὴν σπαθήσας, ἀλλ' ἔτι καὶ νόθον εἰσάγεται
διάδοχον Ἀντιπάτρῳ τῷ φθόρῳ τὴν παππῴαν
αὐτῶν βασιλείαν προτείνων. τιμωρήσειν γε μὴν
αὐτὸς τοῖς Ὑρκανοῦ καὶ [τοῖς][2] Μαριάμμης
δαίμοσιν· οὐδὲ γὰρ πρέπειν αὐτὸν διαδέξασθαι

---

[1] + καὶ PA.　　　　　　　[2] P: τῆς AM : om. the rest.

---

[a] Or " in which he was an alien."

Archelaus made the young prince regard him as a counsellor to be trusted ; and so, without any reserve, Alexander poured out to him his grievances against Antipater, adding that it would not be surprising if Herod, after murdering their mother, should rob him and his brother of her kingdom. Thereupon Eurycles pretended to pity and condole with him. He then inveigled Aristobulus into using similar language, and having implicated both brothers in complaints against their father, went off with these confidences to Antipater ; with the addition of his own invention, that the brothers were plotting against him, watching their opportunity, and even then were almost upon him sword in hand. Richly rewarded for his intelligence, he proceeded to sing the praises of Antipater to his father. Finally, having undertaken at a price to bring about the death of Aristobulus and Alexander, he came to lay his indictment of them before their parent.

Visiting Herod, he declared that he came to bring him life in return for his benefactions to himself, the light of day in repayment for his hospitality. " For," he said, " a sword has long since been sharpened for your destruction and Alexander's right arm braced to wield it. It is I who have retarded the blow by pretending to assist him." Alexander, he continued, had said that Herod, not content with reigning himself over an empire which belonged to others,[a] not content, after murdering their mother, with squandering her realm, was now proceeding to foist in a bastard as his successor and to offer their grandfather's kingdom to that pest, Antipater. But he, Alexander (so Eurycles reported him), would avenge the spirits of Hyrcanus and Mariamme ; for it would

παρὰ τοιούτου πατρὸς τὴν ἀρχὴν δίχα φόνου.
522 πολλὰ δ᾽ εἶναι τὰ παροξύνοντα καθ᾽ ἡμέραν, ὥστε
μηδὲ λαλιᾶς τινα τρόπον ἀσυκοφάντητον κατα-
λελεῖφθαι· περὶ μὲν γὰρ εὐγενείας ἑτέρων μνείας
γενομένης αὐτὸς ἀλόγως ὑβρίζεσθαι, τοῦ πατρὸς
λέγοντος " ὁ μόνος εὐγενὴς Ἀλέξανδρος καὶ τὸν
πατέρα δι᾽ ἀγένειαν ἀδοξῶν"· κατὰ δὲ τὰς θήρας
προσκρούειν μὲν σιωπῶν, ἐπαινέσας δὲ προσ-
523 ακούειν εἴρων. πανταχοῦ δ᾽ ἀμείλικτον εὑρίσκειν
τὸν πατέρα καὶ μόνῳ φιλόστοργον Ἀντιπάτρῳ, δι᾽
ὃν[1] ἡδέως καὶ τεθνήξεσθαι μὴ κρατήσας τῆς ἐπι-
βολῆς.[2] κτείναντι δὲ εἶναι σωτηρίας ἀφορμὴν
πρῶτον μὲν Ἀρχέλαον ὄντα κηδεστήν, πρὸς ὃν
διαφεύξεσθαι ῥᾳδίως, ἔπειτα Καίσαρα μέχρι νῦν
524 ἀγνοοῦντα τὸν Ἡρώδου τρόπον· οὐ γὰρ ὡς πρότερον αὐτῷ παραστήσεσθαι πεφρικὼς τὸν ἐφ-
εστῶτα πατέρα, οὐδὲ φθέγξεσθαι[3] περὶ τῶν ἑαυτοῦ
μόνον ἐγκλημάτων, ἀλλὰ πρῶτον μὲν κηρύξειν τὰς
τοῦ ἔθνους συμφορὰς καὶ τοὺς μέχρι ψυχῆς φορο-
λογουμένους, ἔπειτ᾽ εἰς οἵας τρυφὰς καὶ πράξεις
τὰ δι᾽ αἵματος πορισθέντα χρήματα ἀνηλώθη,
τούς τε ἐξ ἡμῶν πλουτήσαντας οἷοι, καὶ τὰς
525 θεραπευθείσας πόλεις ἐπὶ τίσιν. ζητήσειν δὲ καὶ
τὸν πάππον ἐκεῖ καὶ τὴν μητέρα καὶ τὰ τῆς
βασιλείας μύση πάντα κηρύξειν, ἐφ᾽ οἷς οὐ κριθή-
σεσθαι πατροκτόνος.

---

[1] δ Destinon : quae Lat.
[2] Destinon : ἐπιβουλῆς mss. ; cf. B. vi. 64 (some mss.).
[3] Bekker with Lat. : φθέγξασθαι mss.

---

[a] Rather his great-grandfather, Hyrcanus, who was the
father of Alexandra, the mother of Mariamme.

ill become him to inherit the throne from such a
father without bloodshed. Then there were the
constant daily provocations to which he was subjected, insomuch that he could not utter a single
word which escaped calumny. Were allusion made
to other persons' noble lineage, his father gratuitously
insulted him by remarking, " Nobody is noble but
Alexander here, who scorns his father for the base-
ness of his birth ! " On the hunting-field, were he
silent, he gave offence ; did he express commendation, he was pronounced ironical to boot. On all
occasions, in fact, he found his father implacable,
reserving all his affection for Antipater. He would,
therefore, willingly die, if his enterprise miscarried.
If, on the other hand, he struck the fatal blow, he
had protectors to fall back upon : first Archelaus,
his father-in-law, to whom he could easily make his
escape ; and then Caesar, who to that very day was
ignorant of Herod's true character. For he would
not, as once before, stand before the emperor, overawed by his father's presence, nor would he confine
his observations to his personal grievances. No ; he
would first proclaim to the world the sufferings of his
nation, bled to death by taxation, and then go on to
describe the luxury and malpractices on which the
money obtained by its blood was lavished, the characters of the men who had grown rich at his and his
brother's expense, and the motives which had led to
the favouritism shown to particular cities. There,
too, he would bring up for inquiry the fate of his
grandfather [a] and his mother, and make public all
the abominations of the realm.[b] Under such conditions he could not be condemned as a parricide.

[b] Or " reign."

526 (3) Τοιαῦτα κατ' Ἀλεξάνδρου τερατευσάμενος Εὐρυκλῆς ἐπῄνει πολλὰ τὸν Ἀντίπατρον, ὡς ἄρα μόνος τε εἴη φιλοπάτωρ καὶ διὰ τοῦτο μέχρι νῦν τῆς ἐπιβουλῆς ἐμπόδιος. μήπω δὲ καλῶς ἐπὶ τοῖς πρώτοις ὁ βασιλεὺς κατεσταλμένος εἰς ἀνήκεστον

527 ὀργὴν ἐξαγριοῦται. καὶ πάλιν λαβὼν καιρὸν Ἀντίπατρος ἑτέρους κατὰ τῶν ἀδελφῶν ὑπέπεμπεν κατηγόρους λέγειν ὅτι Ἰουκούνδῳ καὶ Τυράννῳ λάθρα διαλέγοιντο, τοῖς ἱππάρχοις μέν ποτε τοῦ βασιλέως γενομένοις, τότε δ' ἔκ τινων προσκρουσμάτων ἀποπεπτωκόσι τῆς τάξεως. ἐφ' οἷς Ἡρώδης ὑπεραγανακτήσας εὐθέως ἐβασάνισεν

528 τοὺς ἄνδρας. ἀλλ' οἱ μὲν οὐδὲν τῶν διαβληθέντων ὡμολόγουν, προεκομίσθη δέ τις πρὸς τὸν Ἀλεξανδρείου[1] φρούραρχον ἐπιστολὴ παρὰ Ἀλεξάνδρου παρακαλοῦντος ἵνα αὐτὸν δέξηται τῷ φρουρίῳ μετὰ Ἀριστοβούλου τοῦ ἀδελφοῦ κτείναντα τὸν πατέρα, καὶ παράσχῃ τοῖς ὅπλοις χρήσασθαι καὶ

529 ταῖς ἄλλαις ἀφορμαῖς. ταύτην Ἀλέξανδρος μὲν εἶναι ἔλεγεν τέχνασμα Διοφάντου· γραμματεὺς δ' ἦν ὁ Διόφαντος τοῦ βασιλέως, τολμηρὸς ἀνὴρ καὶ δεινὸς μιμήσασθαι πάσης χειρὸς γράμματα· πολλὰ γοῦν παραχαράξας τελευταῖον ἐπὶ τούτῳ [καὶ][2] κτείνεται. βασανίσας δὲ τὸν φρούραρχον Ἡρώδης οὐδὲν ἤκουσεν οὐδὲ παρ' ἐκείνου τῶν διαβεβλημένων.

530 (4) Ἀλλὰ καίτοι τοὺς ἐλέγχους εὑρίσκων ἀσθενεῖς τοὺς υἱοὺς ἐκέλευσεν τηρεῖν, ἔτι μέντοι λελυμένους, τὸν δὲ λυμεῶνα τῆς οἰκίας καὶ δραματουργὸν ὅλου τοῦ μύσους Εὐρυκλέα, σωτῆρα καὶ

---

[1] Destinon from Lat.: Ἀλεξάνδρου PA: Ἡρώδου the rest.
[2] om. PAM Lat.

(3) Having delivered this monstrous tirade against Alexander, Eurycles proceeded to extol Antipater to the skies, as the only son who had any filial affection, an affection which had so far enabled him to thwart the plot. The king, who had scarcely recovered his composure after previous shocks, burst into ungovernable fury. Antipater, seizing this new opportunity, privily sent in others to accuse his brothers of holding clandestine interviews with Jucundus and Tyrannus, at one time commanders of the king's cavalry, but now, owing to some misdemeanours, degraded. This report brought Herod's indignation to a climax, and he instantly had the two men put to the torture. They made no confession of the crimes imputed to them ; but a letter was produced, addressed by Alexander to the governor of Alexandrion, requesting him to admit him and his brother Aristobulus to that fortress after they had slain their father, and to grant them the use of the arms and the other resources of the place. This letter Alexander declared to be the handiwork of Diophantus, a secretary of the king, an audacious fellow who had a clever knack of imitating any handwriting, and who, after numerous forgeries, was eventually put to death for a crime of that nature. Herod had the keeper of the fortress put to the torture, but from him too failed to elicit anything bearing on the alleged facts.

Officers put to the torture.

(4) Notwithstanding the weakness of the obtainable evidence, Herod gave orders for a watch to be kept on his sons, though still leaving them their liberty. As for Eurycles, the bane of his house and stage-manager of the whole abominable business,

The end of Eurycles.

251

εὐεργέτην καλῶν, πεντήκοντα δωρεῖται ταλάντοις.
ὁ δὲ τὴν ἀκριβῆ φήμην φθάσας εἰς Καππαδοκίαν
ἀργυρίζεται καὶ παρὰ Ἀρχελάου, τολμήσας εἰπεῖν
531 ὅτι καὶ διαλλάξειεν Ἡρώδην Ἀλεξάνδρῳ. διάρας
δ' εἰς τὴν Ἑλλάδα τοῖς ἐκ κακῶν κτηθεῖσιν εἰς
ὅμοια κατεχρήσατο· δὶς γοῦν ἐπὶ Καίσαρος κατ-
ηγορηθεὶς ἐπὶ τῷ στάσεως ἐμπλῆσαι τὴν Ἀχαΐαν
καὶ περιδύειν τὰς πόλεις φυγαδεύεται. κἀκεῖνον
μὲν οὕτως ἡ Ἀλεξάνδρου καὶ Ἀριστοβούλου
ποινὴ περιῆλθεν.

532   (5) Ἄξιον δὲ ἀντιθεῖναι τὸν Κῷον Εὐάρεστον[1]
τῷ Σπαρτιάτῃ· καὶ γὰρ οὗτος ὢν ἐν τοῖς μάλιστα
φίλος[2] Ἀλεξάνδρῳ καὶ κατὰ τὸν αὐτὸν Εὐρυκλεῖ
καιρὸν ἐπιδημήσας πυνθανομένῳ τῷ βασιλεῖ περὶ
ὧν ἐκεῖνος διέβαλλεν ὅρκοις τὸ μηδὲν ἀκηκοέναι
533 [παρὰ][3] τῶν μειρακίων ἐπιστώσατο. οὐ μὴν
ὤνησέν γέ τι τοὺς ἀθλίους· μόνων γὰρ ἦν τῶν
κακῶν ἀκροατὴς ἑτοιμότατος Ἡρώδης καὶ κε-
χαρισμένος αὐτῷ πᾶς ὁ συμπιστεύων καὶ συν-
αγανακτῶν.

534   (xxvii. 1) Παρώξυνεν δ' αὐτοῦ καὶ Σαλώμη
τὴν ἐπὶ τοῖς τέκνοις ὠμότητα. ταύτην γὰρ συν-
δήσασθαι τοῖς κινδύνοις ὁ Ἀριστόβουλος θέλων,
οὖσαν ἑκυρὰν καὶ τηθίδα, διαπέμπεται σώζειν
ἑαυτὴν παραινῶν· παρεσκευάσθαι γὰρ βασιλέα
κτείνειν αὐτὴν διαβληθεῖσαν ἐφ' οἷς καὶ πρότερον,
ὅτι Συλλαίῳ τῷ Ἄραβι γήμασθαι σπουδάζουσα
λάθρα τὰ τοῦ βασιλέως ἀπόρρητα διαγγέλλοι πρὸς
535 αὐτὸν ἐχθρὸν ὄντα. τοῦθ' ὥσπερ τελευταία θύελλα

---

[1] Εὐάρατον RC (through assimilation to Α.‖).
[2] Niese: φίλοις mss.   [3] om. PA.

[a] Cf. § 487.

the king called him his saviour and benefactor, and presented him with fifty talents. That villain then, before the true story of the affair got abroad, made off to Cappadocia, where he extorted more money from Archelaus, having the impudence to assert that he had reconciled Herod to Alexander. Thence he crossed to Greece, where he employed the proceeds of his crimes on equally criminal objects. Twice arraigned before Caesar for spreading sedition throughout Achaia and fleecing the cities of that province, he was condemned to exile. Thus did retribution overtake him for his betrayal of Alexander and Aristobulus.

(5) As a contrast to the conduct of this Spartan may fitly be mentioned that of Euarestus of Cos. The latter, who was one of Alexander's most intimate friends, paid a visit to Judaea at the same time as Eurycles, and on being questioned by the king upon the allegations made by his other guest, affirmed on oath that he had heard nothing of the kind from the young men. His testimony, however, was of no avail to the unfortunate wretches ; for Herod had a ready ear only for slander, and all stood high in his favour who shared his credulity and his indignation. *Contrasted conduct of another visitor.*

(xxvii. 1) A further stimulus to Herod's cruelty to his sons was given by Salome. For Aristobulus, wishing to involve her, who was at once his mother-in-law and aunt, in the perils threatening himself, sent her a warning to look to her own safety, as the king was prepared to kill her on the charge previously brought against her [a] : namely that, in her anxiety to marry the Arab Syllaeus, she had privately communicated to him the secrets of the king, whose enemy he was. This was, as it were, the final hurricane *Salome's denunciation.*

253

χειμαζομένους τοὺς νεανίσκους ἐπεβάπτισεν· ἡ
γὰρ Σαλώμη δραμοῦσα πρὸς βασιλέα τὴν παραίνεσιν ἐμήνυσεν. κἀκεῖνος οὐκέτι καρτερήσας
δεσμεῖ μὲν ἀμφοτέρους τοὺς υἱεῖς καὶ διεχώρισεν
ἀπ' ἀλλήλων, πέμπει δὲ πρὸς Καίσαρα διὰ τάχους
Οὐολούμνιόν τε τὸν στρατοπεδάρχην καὶ τῶν φίλων[1] Ὄλυμπον ἐγγράφους[2] τὰς μηνύσεις φέροντας.
536 οἱ δ' ὡς εἰς Ῥώμην πλεύσαντες ἀπέδοσαν τὰ ἀπὸ
τοῦ βασιλέως γράμματα, σφόδρα μὲν ἠχθέσθη
Καῖσαρ ἐπὶ τοῖς νεανίσκοις, οὐ μὴν ᾤετο δεῖν
ἀφελέσθαι τὸν πατέρα τὴν περὶ[3] τῶν υἱῶν ἐξουσίαν.
537 ἀντιγράφει γοῦν κύριον μὲν αὐτὸν καθιστάς, εὖ
μέντοι ποιήσειν λέγων, εἰ μετὰ κοινοῦ συνεδρίου
τῶν τε ἰδίων συγγενῶν καὶ τῶν κατὰ τὴν ἐπαρχίαν
ἡγεμόνων ἐξετάσειεν τὴν ἐπιβουλήν· κἂν μὲν
ἐνέχωνται, κτείνειν, ἐὰν δὲ μόνον ὦσιν δρασμὸν
βεβουλευμένοι, κολάζειν μετριώτερον.
538   (2) Τούτοις Ἡρώδης πείθεται, καὶ παραγενόμενος εἰς Βηρυτόν, ἔνθα προσέταξεν Καῖσαρ,
συνῆγε τὸ δικαστήριον. προκαθίζουσίν[4] τε οἱ
ἡγεμόνες[5] γραφὲν αὐτοῖς ὑπὸ Καίσαρος, Σατορ-
νῖνός τε καὶ οἱ περὶ Πεδάνιον πρέσβεις, σὺν οἷς
καὶ Οὐολούμνιος [ὁ][6] ἐπίτροπος, ἔπειθ' οἱ τοῦ
βασιλέως συγγενεῖς καὶ φίλοι, Σαλώμη τε καὶ
Φερώρας, μεθ' οὓς οἱ πάσης Συρίας ἄριστοι πλὴν
Ἀρχελάου τοῦ βασιλέως· τοῦτον γὰρ ὄντα κηδεστὴν Ἀλεξάνδρου δι' ὑποψίας εἶχεν Ἡρώδης.

---

[1] Destinon from Lat.: τὸν φίλον mss.
[2] ἐγγράφως LTRC.   [3] PA: κατὰ the rest.
[4] PA: προκαθέζονταί the rest.
[5] +κατὰ τὸ PAM.   [6] om. PA.

---

[a] Beirut.

which submerged the tempest-tossed youths. For Salome ran off to the king and reported the warning which she had received. Herod, his patience exhausted, put both his sons in irons and in separate confinement ; he then hastily dispatched Volumnius, the military tribune, and Olympus, one of his friends, with all the information in writing, to Caesar. Taking ship to Rome they delivered the king's dispatches to the emperor, who, while deeply distressed for the young men, did not think it right to deprive the father of his authority over his sons. He replied accordingly, leaving Herod complete liberty of action, but adding a recommendation to him to hold an inquiry into the plot before a joint council of his own relatives and the provincial governors ; then, if his sons were convicted, to put them to death, but if they had merely meditated flight, to be content with a milder penalty.

Herod imprisons the princes and reports the case to Augustus.

Augustus gives Herod a free hand.

(2) Acting on this advice, Herod repaired to Berytus,[a] the place appointed by Caesar, and there assembled the court. In accordance with written instructions received from Caesar, the Roman officers presided, namely Saturninus[b] and his legates, Pedanius and others ; with them was associated Volumnius[c] the procurator. Next came the king's relatives and friends, including Salome and Pheroras, and after these all the aristocracy of Syria, with the exception of King Archelaus ;[d] for, as Alexander's father-in-law, he was regarded by Herod with distrust. His

Trial held at Berytus c. 7-6 B.C.

[b] C. Sentius Saturninus, governor of Syria, previously consul in 19 B.C.

[c] It is uncertain whether he is identical with Herod's friend and ambassador (§ 535).

[d] Cappadocia, it appears, must at this time have been under the superintendence of the governor of Syria.

539 τούς γε μὴν υἱοὺς οὐ προήγαγεν εἰς τὴν δίκην
μάλα προμηθῶς· ἤδει γὰρ ὅτι καὶ μόνον ὀφθέντες
ἐλεηθήσονται πάντως· εἰ δὲ δὴ καὶ λόγου μετα-
λάβοιεν, ῥᾳδίως Ἀλέξανδρον ἀπολύσεσθαι τὰς
αἰτίας. ἀλλ' οἱ μὲν ἐν Πλατάνῃ κώμῃ Σιδωνίων
ἐφρουροῦντο.

540 (3) Καταστὰς δ' ὁ βασιλεὺς ὡς πρὸς παρόντας
διετείνετο, κατηγόρει τε τὴν μὲν ἐπιβουλὴν
ἀσθενῶς, ὡς ἂν ἀπορούμενος εἰς αὐτὴν ἐλέγχων,
λοιδορίας δὲ καὶ σκώμματα καὶ ὕβρεις καὶ πλημμελείας μυρίας εἰς αὐτόν, ἃ καὶ θανάτου χαλεπώτερα τοῖς συνέδροις ἀπέφηνεν. ἔπειτα μηδενὸς
ἀντιλέγοντος ἐποικτισάμενος, ὡς αὐτὸς ἁλίσκοιτο
καὶ νικῶν¹ νίκην πικρὰν κατὰ τῶν τέκνων, ἐπηρώτα

541 τὴν γνώμην ἑκάστου. καὶ πρῶτος Σατορνῖνος
ἀπεφήνατο κατακρίνειν μὲν τῶν νεανίσκων, ἀλλ'
οὐ θάνατον· οὐ γὰρ εἶναι θεμιτὸν αὐτῷ, τριῶν
παρεστώτων τέκνων, ἑτέρου τέκνοις ἀπώλειαν
ἐπιψηφίσασθαι. σύμψηφοι δ' αὐτῷ καὶ οἱ δύο
πρεσβευταὶ γίνονται, καὶ τούτοις ἕτεροί τινες

542 ἠκολούθησαν. Οὐολούμνιος δὲ τῆς σκυθρωπῆς
ἀποφάσεως ἤρξατο, καὶ μετ' αὐτὸν πάντες θάνατον
κατακρίνουσιν τῶν μειρακίων, οἱ μὲν κολακεύοντες,
οἱ δὲ μισοῦντες Ἡρώδην, καὶ οὐδεὶς δι' ἀγανάκτη-

543 σιν. ἔνθα δὴ μετέωρος ἦ τε Συρία πᾶσα καὶ τὸ
Ἰουδαϊκὸν ἦν ἐκδεχομένων τὸ τέλος τοῦ δράματος·
οὐδεὶς μέντοι ὑπελάμβανεν ἔσεσθαι μέχρι τεκνο-
κτονίας ὠμὸν Ἡρώδην. ὁ δὲ σύρας τοὺς υἱοὺς

¹ νικῴη M and apparently Lat.

sons were not produced by Herod in court—a very wise precaution, for he knew that their mere appearance would be sure to arouse compassion, while, if they were further permitted to speak, Alexander would have no difficulty in rebutting the charges. So they were detained in custody at Platana,[a] a village in the territory of Sidon.

(3) The king, on rising, nevertheless inveighed against them as though they had been present. His accusation of a plot was, for lack of proofs, weak ; but he dwelt on the affronts, mockeries, insults, and offences innumerable of which he had been the victim, and which, he declared to the court, were more cruel than death itself. After that, none contradicting him, he commiserated his hard fate that even in winning his case against his sons his triumph would be bitter and himself the loser, and then asked them all to express their opinions. Saturninus first delivered his opinion, which was to condemn the young men, but not to death ; as the father of three children present in court, it would not be right for him, he said, to vote for the destruction of the children of another. His two legates voted in the same sense and their example was followed by some others. Volumnius was the first to pronounce a pitiless sentence ; and all who followed him condemned the lads to death, some from flattery, others from hatred of Herod, none from indignation against the prisoners. From that moment all Syria and Jewry were in suspense, anxiously awaiting the last act of the drama ; yet none supposed that Herod would carry his cruelty to the length of murdering his children. He, mean-

Condemnation of the princes.

---

[a] *Ras Damur*, on the coast, S. of Beirut and about halfway between it and Sidon.

εἰς Τύρον κἀκεῖθεν διαπλεύσας εἰς Καισάρειαν τρόπον ἀναιρέσεως τοῖς μειρακίοις ἐσκέπτετο.

544 (4) Παλαιὸς δέ τις τοῦ βασιλέως στρατιώτης, ὄνομα Τίρων, ἔχων υἱὸν σφόδρα συνήθη καὶ φίλον Ἀλεξάνδρῳ καὶ αὐτὸς ἠγαπηκὼς ἰδίᾳ τὰ μειράκια, δι' ὑπερβολὴν ἀγανακτήσεως ἔκφρων ἐγίνετο,[1] καὶ τὸ μὲν πρῶτον ἐβόα περιιὼν πεπατῆσθαι τὸ δίκαιον, ἀπολωλέναι τὴν ἀλήθειαν, συγκεχύσθαι τὴν φύσιν, ἀνομίας γέμειν τὸν βίον, καὶ πάνθ' ὅσα

545 μὴ φειδομένῳ τοῦ ζῆν ὑπηγόρευε τὸ πάθος. τέλος δὲ καὶ τῷ βασιλεῖ τολμήσας προσελθεῖν " ἀλλ' ἐμοὶ μέν," ἔφη, " κακοδαιμονέστατος εἶναι δοκεῖς, ὅστις κατὰ τῶν φιλτάτων πείθῃ τοῖς πονηροτάτοις, εἴ γε Φερώρᾳ καὶ Σαλώμῃ καταγνοὺς πολλάκις θάνατον πιστεύεις τούτοις κατὰ τῶν τέκνων, οἵ σε τῶν γνησίων περικόπτοντες διαδόχων ἐπ' Ἀντιπάτρῳ καταλείπουσι μόνῳ, τὸν ἑαυτοῖς εὐ-

546 μεταχείριστον αἱρούμενοι βασιλέα. σκέψαι μέντοι γε, μή ποτε κἀκείνῳ γένηται μῖσος ἐν τοῖς στρατιώταις ὁ τῶν ἀδελφῶν θάνατος· οὐ γὰρ ἔστιν ὅστις οὐκ ἐλεεῖ τὰ μειράκια, τῶν δὲ ἡγεμόνων καὶ φανερῶς ἀγανακτοῦσιν πολλοί." ταῦθ' ἅμα λέγων ὠνόμαζεν τοὺς ἀγανακτοῦντας. ὁ δὲ βασιλεὺς εὐθέως ἐκείνους τε καὶ αὐτὸν καὶ τὸν υἱὸν αὐτοῦ συνελάμβανεν.

547 (5) Ἐφ' ᾧ τῶν ἐκ τῆς αὐλῆς τις κουρέων, Τρύφων ὄνομα, προεκπηδήσας ἔκ τινος θεο-βλαβείας[2] ἑαυτοῦ μηνυτὴς γίνεται. " κἀμέ," γὰρ ἔφη, " Τίρων οὗτος ἀνέπειθεν, ὅταν θεραπεύω

---

[1] PA : ἐγένετο the rest.
[2] PA : φρενοβλαβείας the rest.

while, dragged his sons to Tyre, and, taking ship thence to Caesarea, pondered in his mind over the manner of their execution.

(4) Now there was an old soldier in the king's army, named Tiro, whose son was on very intimate and friendly terms with Alexander, and who had a personal affection himself for the young princes. This man, in the excess of his indignation, lost his reason. At first he went about shouting that justice had been trampled under foot, truth was dead, the laws of nature confounded, the world full of iniquity, and whatever else his emotion suggested to one who was careless of his life. At length he boldly presented himself to the king and thus addressed him : " Most god-forsaken of men, that is my opinion of you, you who to the injury of your nearest and dearest trust the word of the basest of scoundrels, if it be true that Pheroras and Salome, whom you have so often sentenced to death, have now made you believe their slanders upon your children. They are cutting off your legitimate heirs, leaving you none but Antipater, choosing him for king as the most manageable in their leading-strings. But take care that the death of his brothers does not one day rouse against him the hatred of the army ; for there is not a man there who does not pity the lads, and many of the officers are freely expressing their indignation." He forthwith named these malcontents ; and they were promptly arrested by the king, together with Tiro and his son.

(5) Thereupon, one of the court barbers, named Trypho, possessed by some strange frenzy, rushed forward and turned informer against himself. " Me too," he cried, " this Tiro tried to induce to cut your

JOSEPHUS

τῷ ξυρῷ σε διαχειρίσασθαι, μεγάλας τέ μοι παρ'
548 Ἀλεξάνδρου δωρεὰς ὑπισχνεῖτο." ταῦτ' ἀκούσας
Ἡρώδης τόν τε Τίρωνα σὺν τῷ παιδὶ καὶ τὸν
κουρέα βασάνοις διήλεγχεν, καὶ τῶν μὲν ἀρνου-
μένων, τοῦ δὲ μηδὲν πλέον λέγοντος, στρεβλοῦν
549 ἐκέλευσεν τὸν Τίρωνα σφοδρότερον. ὁ δ' υἱὸς
οἰκτείρας ὑπέσχετο τῷ βασιλεῖ πάντα μηνύσειν,
εἰ χαρίσαιτο τὸν πατέρα αὐτῷ. κἀκείνου δόντος
εἶπεν ὡς ὁ πατὴρ αὐτοῦ πεισθεὶς Ἀλεξάνδρῳ
θελήσειεν αὐτὸν ἀνελεῖν. τοῦθ' οἱ μὲν εἰς ἀπαλλαγὴν τῆς τοῦ πατρὸς αἰκίας πεπλάσθαι, τινὲς
δὲ ἀληθὲς ἔλεγον.

550 (6) Ἡρώδης γε μὴν ἐν ἐκκλησίᾳ τῶν τε ἡγεμόνων καὶ Τίρωνος κατηγορήσας τὸν λαὸν ἐπ'
αὐτοὺς ἐστρατολόγησεν· αὐτόθι γοῦν ἀναιροῦνται
μετὰ τοῦ κουρέως ξύλοις βαλλόμενοι καὶ λίθοις.
551 πέμψας δὲ καὶ τοὺς υἱεῖς εἰς Σεβαστήν, οὖσαν οὐ
πόρρω τῆς Καισαρείας, προσέταξεν ἀποπνῖξαι.
καὶ τελεσθέντος αὐτῷ ταχέως τοῦ προστάγματος
τοὺς νεκροὺς εἰς Ἀλεξάνδρειον ἐκέλευσεν ἀνα-
κομισθῆναι τὸ φρούριον, συνταφησομένους Ἀλεξάνδρῳ τῷ μητροπάτορι. τὸ μὲν οὖν Ἀλεξάνδρου
καὶ Ἀριστοβούλου τέλος τοιοῦτον [ἦν].¹

552 (xxviii. 1) Ἀντιπάτρῳ δὲ ἀδήριτον ἔχοντι
τὴν διαδοχὴν μῖσος μὲν ἀφόρητον ἐκ τοῦ ἔθνους
ἐπεγείρεται, πάντων ἐπισταμένων ὅτι τὰς διαβολὰς τοῖς ἀδελφοῖς πάσας ἐπισυντάξειεν οὗτος,
ὑποικούρει δὲ καὶ δέος οὐ μέτριον αὐξανομένην
ὁρῶντι τὴν τῶν ἀνῃρημένων γενεάν· ἦσαν γὰρ
Ἀλεξάνδρῳ μὲν ἐκ Γλαφύρας υἱεῖς δύο, Τιγράνης

¹ om. LTRC.

throat with my razor when in attendance upon you, promising me a large reward from Alexander." On hearing this, Herod put Tiro, his son and the barber under the torture, and when father and son denied all and the other would add nothing more, gave orders to rack Tiro still more severely. The son, thereupon, moved with compassion, promised to tell the king everything if he would spare him his father. Herod granting his request, he stated that his father, at the instigation of Alexander, intended to kill him. This statement, according to some, was a fabrication to end his father's sufferings, while others maintained that it was true.

(6) Herod summoned a public assembly, formally accused the officers concerned and Tiro, and enlisted the aid of the populace to dispatch them ; they and the barber were beaten to death on the spot with cudgels and stones. He then sent his sons to Sebaste,[a] a town not far from Caesarea, and ordered them to be strangled. The order was promptly executed, and direction was given to convey the bodies to the fortress of Alexandrion, for burial there with Alexander, their maternal grandfather. Such was the end of Alexander and Aristobulus.

Execution of Alexander and Aristobulus.

7-6 B.C.

(xxviii. 1) Antipater, having now an indisputable claim to the succession, became an object of intolerable abhorrence to the nation ; for all knew that it was he who had contrived all the calumnies against his brothers. He was, moreover, haunted with grave alarm at the sight of the children of his victims growing to maturity. For Alexander had by Glaphyra two sons, Tigranes and Alexander ; and by his

Unpopularity and fears of Antipater.

---

[a] Samaria.

καὶ 'Αλέξανδρος, 'Αριστοβούλῳ δ' ἐκ Βερνίκης
τῆς Σαλώμης Ἡρώδης μὲν καὶ 'Αγρίππας καὶ
'Αριστόβουλος υἱοί, θυγατέρες δὲ Ἡρωδιὰς καὶ
553 Μαριάμμη. τὴν μὲν οὖν Γλαφύραν μετὰ τῆς
προικὸς Ἡρώδης ἀπέπεμψεν[1] εἰς Καππαδοκίαν,
ὡς ἀνεῖλεν 'Αλέξανδρον, τὴν 'Αριστοβούλου δὲ
Βερνίκην συνῴκισεν θείῳ πρὸς μητρὸς 'Αντι-
πάτρου· τὴν γὰρ Σαλώμην οὖσαν διάφορον ἐξ-
οικειούμενος ὁ 'Αντίπατρος τοῦτον ἐπραγματεύσατο
554 τὸν γάμον. περιῄει δὲ καὶ τὸν Φερώραν δώροις
τε καὶ ταῖς ἄλλαις θεραπείαις καὶ τοὺς Καίσαρος
φίλους οὐκ ὀλίγα πέμπων εἰς τὴν Ῥώμην[2] χρήματα. οἵ γε μὴν περὶ Σατορνῖνον ἐν Συρίᾳ πάντες
ἐνεπλήσθησαν τῶν ἀπ' αὐτοῦ δωρεῶν. ἐμισεῖτο
δὲ διδοὺς πλεῖον, ὡς ἂν οὐκ ἐκ τοῦ μεγαλοψύχου
555 χαριζόμενος ἀλλ' ἀναλίσκων κατὰ δέος. συνέβαινεν
δὲ[3] τοὺς μὲν λαμβάνοντας οὐδὲν μᾶλλον εὔνους
γίνεσθαι, χαλεπωτέρους δ' ἐχθροὺς οἷς μὴ διδοίη.
λαμπροτέρας δὲ καθ' ἡμέραν ἐποιεῖτο τὰς δια-
δόσεις, ὁρῶν τὸν βασιλέα παρ' ἃς αὐτὸς ἐλπίδας
εἶχεν ἐπιμελούμενον τῶν ὀρφανῶν καὶ τὴν ἐπὶ
τοῖς ἀνῃρημένοις μετάνοιαν ἐμφαίνοντα δι' ὧν
ἠλέει τοὺς ἐξ ἐκείνων.
556   (2) Συναγαγὼν γάρ ποτε Ἡρώδης συγγενεῖς
τε καὶ φίλους παραστησάμενός τε τὰ παιδία καὶ
δακρύων ἐμπλήσας τοὺς ὀφθαλμοὺς εἶπεν· "ἐμὲ
τοὺς μὲν τούτων πατέρας σκυθρωπὸς ἀφείλετο
δαίμων, ταῦτα δέ μοι μετὰ τῆς φύσεως συνίστησιν
ἔλεος ὀρφανίας. πειρῶμαι δ', εἰ καὶ πατὴρ
ἐγενόμην ἀτυχέστατος, πάππος γοῦν γενέσθαι

---

[1] ἀνέπεμψεν M.   [2] ἐπὶ Ῥώμης P.
[3] δὴ LRC : τε Niese.

marriage with Bernice, Salome's daughter, Aristobulus had three, Herod, Agrippa, and Aristobulus, besides two daughters, Herodias and Mariamme. After the execution of Alexander, Herod had sent back Glaphyra to Cappadocia with her dowry ; Bernice, the widow of Aristobulus, he gave in marriage to Antipater's maternal uncle,[a] this match being arranged by Antipater in order to conciliate his enemy Salome. Antipater further sought to ingratiate himself with Pheroras by presents and other attentions, and with Caesar's friends by sending considerable sums to Rome. Saturninus and all his staff in Syria were glutted with his gifts. Yet the more he gave, the more he was hated, as it was felt that his bounties were not the outcome of generosity but extorted from him by fear. The result was that the recipients were no better disposed to him than before, while those whom he overlooked became more implacable enemies. The presents distributed, nevertheless, became daily more magnificent, when he saw the king, to the undoing of his own expectations, taking care of the orphans and showing his remorse for the murder of his sons by his compassion for their offspring.

(2) For Herod, one day, assembled his relatives and friends,[b] set the young children before them, and said, with tears in his eyes : " I have been bereaved by some evil genius of the sires of these infants, but pity for the orphans and nature alike commend them to my care. If I have been the most unfortunate of fathers, I will try at any rate to prove

Herod's pity and marriage arrangements for the children of the murdered princes.

---

[a] Theudion, *A.* xvii. 70.
[b] Reinach regards these words as having the technical meaning of high officials at court, *cf.* § 460.

κηδεμονικώτερος καὶ μετ' ἐμὲ ἡγεμόνας αὐτοῖς[1]
557 καταλιπεῖν τοὺς ἐμοὶ φιλτάτους. ἐγγυῶ δὲ τὴν
μὲν σήν, ὦ Φερώρα, θυγατέρα τῷ πρεσβυτέρῳ
τῶν ἀδελφῶν Ἀλεξάνδρου παίδων, ἵνα ᾖς αὐτῷ
κηδεμὼν ἀναγκαῖος, τῷ δὲ σῷ παιδί, Ἀντίπατρε,
τὴν Ἀριστοβούλου θυγατέρα· γένοιο γὰρ ἂν οὕτω
πατὴρ τῆς ὀρφανῆς. καὶ τὴν ἀδελφὴν αὐτῆς ὁ
ἐμὸς Ἡρώδης λήψεται, πρὸς μητρὸς ὢν ἀρχιερέως
558 πάππου. τὰ μὲν οὖν ἐμὰ ταύτην ἐχέτω τὴν
κρίσιν, ἣν διακόψῃ[2] μηδεὶς τῶν ἐμὲ φιλούντων·
ἐπεύχομαι δὲ καὶ τῷ θεῷ συναρμόσαι τοὺς γάμους
ἐπὶ συμφέροντι τῆς ἐμῆς βασιλείας καὶ τῶν ἐμῶν
ἐκγόνων, τά τε παιδία ταυτὶ γαληνοτέροις ἐπιδεῖν
ὄμμασιν ἢ τοὺς πατέρας αὐτῶν."
559   (3) [Ἐπειδὴ][3] ταῦτα εἰπὼν ἀπεδάκρυσέν τε καὶ
τῶν παίδων συνήρμοσεν τὰς δεξιάς, ἔπειτα κατα-
σπασάμενος ἕκαστον φιλοφρόνως διέλυσεν τὸ
συνέδριον. ἐπαχνώθη δ' εὐθὺς Ἀντίπατρος καὶ
δῆλος ἦν ἅπασιν ὀδυνώμενος· ὑπελάμβανεν γὰρ
εἶναι παρὰ τῷ πατρὶ τὴν τῶν ὀρφανῶν τιμὴν
ἑαυτοῦ κατάλυσιν, αὖθίς τε κινδυνεύσειν περὶ τῶν
ὅλων, εἰ πρὸς Ἀρχελάῳ καὶ Φερώραν ὄντα
τετράρχην βοηθὸν ἔχοιεν οἱ Ἀλεξάνδρου παῖδες.
560 συνελογίζετο δὲ τὸ ἑαυτοῦ μῖσος καὶ τὸν τῶν
ὀρφανῶν ἔλεον ἐκ τοῦ ἔθνους, ὅση τε σπουδὴ
ζώντων καὶ ὅση μνήμη παρὰ Ἰουδαίοις τῶν δι'

---

[1] ἡγεμόνας αὐτοὺς PA : κηδεμόνας αὐτοῖς the rest.
[2] M : διακόψει the rest.
[3] Corrupt text: Destinon proposes ἐπεῖδε, to be joined to the preceding sentence.

---

[a] Names unknown.
[b] Tigranes (§ 552) or perhaps Alexander (*A.* xviii. 139, where the order of names is reversed).

myself a more considerate grandfather and to leave their tutelage, after my death, to those most dear to me. I affiance your daughter,[a] Pheroras, to the elder of these brothers,[b] Alexander's sons, in order that this alliance may make you his natural guardian. To your son,[a] Antipater, I betroth the daughter of Aristobulus[c]; so may you become a father to this orphan girl. Her sister[d] my own Herod shall take, for on his mother's[e] side he is grandson of a high-priest. Let then effect be given to my wishes, and let no friend of mine frustrate them. And I pray God to bless these unions, to the benefit of my realm and of my descendants, and to look with serener eyes upon these children here than those with which he beheld their fathers."

(3) Having thus spoken he gave way to tears and joined the children's hands, and then fondly embracing one after the other dismissed the assembly. At that Antipater's blood ran cold[f] and his chagrin was evident to all. For he imagined that the honour bestowed by his father on the orphans was his own ruin and that his claims to the throne would be again endangered, if Alexander's children were to have, in addition to the support of Archelaus, that of Pheroras, a tetrarch. He reflected on the hatred which the nation bore him and their pity for the orphans, the enthusiasm which the Jews had shown for his brothers in their lifetime and their fond memory of them now that, in his interest, they were

[c] Mariamme.
[d] The celebrated Herodias mentioned in the New Testament.
[e] Mariamme II, daughter of the high priest Simon, son of Boethus (*A.* xv. 320).
[f] Or " Antipater instantly shuddered."

αὐτὸν ἀπολωλότων ἦν ἀδελφῶν. ἔγνω δὴ πάντα
τρόπον διακόπτειν τὰς ἐγγύας.

561 (4) Καὶ τὸ μὲν ὑπιέναι πανούργως ἔδεισε τὸν
πατέρα χαλεπὸν ὄντα καὶ πρὸς τὰς ὑποψίας
κινούμενον ὀξέως, ἐτόλμησεν δὲ προσελθὼν ἱκε-
τεύειν ἄντικρυς μὴ στερίσκειν αὐτὸν ἧς ἠξίωσεν
τιμῆς, μηδὲ αὐτῷ μὲν ὄνομα βασιλείας, δύναμιν
δὲ ὑπάρχειν ἄλλοις· οὐ γὰρ κρατήσειν τῶν πραγμάτων, εἰ πρὸς Ἀρχελάῳ πάππῳ καὶ Φερώραν
562 κηδεστὴν ὁ Ἀλεξάνδρου παῖς προσλάβοι. κατηντιβόλει δὲ πολλῆς οὔσης γενεᾶς κατὰ τὸ βασίλειον
μεταθεῖναι τοὺς γάμους. ἦσαν γὰρ τῷ βασιλεῖ
γυναῖκες μὲν ἐννέα, τέκνα δ' ἐκ τῶν[1] ἑπτά, αὐτὸς
μὲν Ἀντίπατρος ἐκ Δωρίδος, Ἡρώδης δ' ἐκ
Μαριάμμης τῆς τοῦ ἀρχιερέως θυγατρός, Ἀντίπας
δὲ καὶ Ἀρχέλαος ἐκ Μαλθάκης τῆς Σαμαρείτιδος,
καὶ θυγάτηρ Ὀλυμπιάς, ἣν ὁ ἀδελφιδοῦς αὐτοῦ
Ἰώσηπος εἶχεν, ἐκ δὲ τῆς Ἱεροσολυμίτιδος Κλεοπάτρας Ἡρώδης καὶ Φίλιππος, ἐκ δὲ Παλλάδος
563 Φασάηλος. ἐγένοντο δ' αὐτῷ καὶ ἄλλαι θυγατέρες,
Ῥωξάνη τε καὶ Σαλώμη, ἡ μὲν ἐκ Φαίδρας, ἡ
δὲ ἐξ Ἐλπίδος. δύο δ' εἶχεν ἀτέκνους, ἀνεψιάν
τε καὶ ἀδελφιδῆν· χωρὶς δὲ τούτων δύο ἀδελφὰς
Ἀλεξάνδρου καὶ Ἀριστοβούλου τὰς ἐκ Μαριάμμης.
οὔσης δὲ πολυπροσώπου τῆς γενεᾶς ὁ Ἀντίπατρος
ἐδεῖτο μετατεθῆναι τοὺς γάμους.

564 (5) Χαλεπῶς δ' ὁ βασιλεὺς ἠγανάκτησεν καταμαθὼν αὐτοῦ τὸ πρὸς τοὺς ὀρφανοὺς ἦθος, ἔννοιά

---

[1] τῶν of LTRC must surely be right: τούτων PAM.

[a] Not including the deceased Mariamme I, who raises
the total to ten. See chart, "The Herodian Family."

dead. He resolved accordingly at all costs to break off these betrothals.

(4) Afraid of practising a ruse upon so harsh a father, whose suspicions were easily aroused, he boldly ventured into his presence and besought him outright not to deprive him of the honour which he had deigned to confer on him, nor to leave him the mere title of king while others enjoyed the power ; for he would never be master of affairs, should Alexander's son, with Archelaus as his grandfather, also have Pheroras as his father-in-law. He therefore earnestly entreated him, as the palace contained a numerous family, to modify these matrimonial arrangements. The king, in fact, had nine [a] wives and issue by seven of them. Antipater himself was son of Doris, Herod (II) of Mariamme (II), the high-priest's daughter, Antipater and Archelaus were sons of Malthace, the Samaritan ; Olympias, a daughter by this last wife had married Joseph,[b] the king's nephew. By Cleopatra, a native of Jerusalem, he had Herod and Philip ; by Pallas, Phasael. He had besides other daughters, Roxane and Salome, one by Phaedra, the other by Elpis. Two of his wives, one a cousin, the other a niece, were childless. In addition there were two daughters [c] by Mariamme (I), sisters of Alexander and Aristobulus. In view of this large family Antipater begged for an alteration in the projected marriages.

Herod's wives and children.

(5) The king, on discovering Antipater's attitude to the orphans, was highly indignant, and the thought

[b] Son of Herod's brother Joseph, who was killed at the battle of Jericho (§§ 323 f.).
[c] Salampsio and Cypros.

τε αὐτῷ παρέστη περὶ τῶν ἀνῃρημένων, μή ποτε
κἀκεῖνοι γένοιντο τῶν Ἀντιπάτρου διαβολῶν
565 ἀγώνισμα. τότε μὲν οὖν πολλὰ πρὸς ὀργὴν ἀπο-
κρινάμενος ἀπελαύνει τὸν Ἀντίπατρον, αὖθις δ'
ὑπαχθεὶς αὐτοῦ ταῖς κολακείαις μεθηρμόσατο, καὶ
αὐτῷ μὲν τὴν Ἀριστοβούλου συνῴκισεν θυγατέρα,
τὸν δὲ υἱὸν αὐτοῦ τῇ Φερώρα θυγατρί.
566 (6) Καταμάθοι δ' ἄν τις, ὅσον ἴσχυσεν ἐν
τούτοις κολακεύων Ἀντίπατρος, ἐκ τοῦ Σαλώμην
ἐν ὁμοίοις ἀποτυχεῖν. ταύτην γὰρ δὴ καίπερ
οὖσαν ἀδελφὴν καὶ πολλὰ διὰ Λιουίας[1] τῆς γυναικὸς
Καίσαρος ἱκετεύουσαν γαμηθῆναι τῷ Ἄραβι Συλλαίῳ, διωμόσατο μὲν ἐχθροτάτην ἕξειν, εἰ μὴ
παύσαιτο τῆς σπουδῆς, τὸ δὲ τελευταῖον ἄκουσαν
Ἀλεξᾷ τινι τῶν φίλων συνῴκισεν, καὶ τῶν θυγατέρων αὐτῆς τὴν μὲν τῷ Ἀλεξᾷ παιδί, τὴν δ'
ἑτέραν τῷ πρὸς μητρὸς Ἀντιπάτρου θείῳ.[2] τῶν
δ' ἐκ Μαριάμμης θυγατέρων ἡ μὲν ἀδελφῆς υἱὸν
Ἀντίπατρον εἶχεν, ἡ δὲ ἀδελφοῦ Φασάηλον.

567 (xxix. 1) Διακόψας δὲ τὰς τῶν ὀρφανῶν
ἐλπίδας ὁ Ἀντίπατρος καὶ πρὸς τὸ συμφέρον
αὑτῷ τὰς ἐπιγαμίας ποιησάμενος, ὡς ἐπὶ βεβαίοις
μὲν ὤρμει ταῖς ἐλπίσιν, προσλαβὼν δὲ τῇ κακίᾳ
τὸ πεποιθὸς ἀφόρητος ἦν· τὸ γὰρ παρ' ἑκάστῳ
μῖσος ἀποσκευάσασθαι μὴ δυνάμενος ἐκ τοῦ
φοβερὸς εἶναι τὴν ἀσφάλειαν ἐπορίζετο. συνήργει
δὲ καὶ Φερώρας ὡς ἂν ἤδη [καὶ][3] βασιλεῖ βεβαίῳ.

---

[1] Niese with Heg.: Λευίας PA (as in § 641): Ἰουλίας the rest.
[2] +σπουδάσαντος ὡς ἔφαμεν Ἀντιπάτρου PAM (doubtless a gloss).
[3] P: om. the rest.

crossed his mind—might not his murdered sons also
have been the victims of this man's slanders ? He,
accordingly, at the moment replied in a long and
angry speech, and dismissed Antipater from his
presence. Subsequently, however, seduced by his
flatteries, he made other arrangements, and gave the
daughter of Aristobulus to Antipater himself, and
the daughter of Pheroras to his son.

(6) How powerful was the effect of Antipater's
adulation on this occasion may be gauged from
Salome's ill success in a similar suit. For, although
she was Herod's sister and had recourse to the intercession of the Empress Livia to plead with him for
permission to marry the Arab Syllaeus,[a] Herod swore
that he would regard her as his bitterest enemy if
she did not renounce this passion ; and, in the end,
he married her, against her will, to one of his friends,
named Alexas, and one of her daughters [b] to the son [b]
of Alexas, the other [c] to Antipater's maternal uncle.[d]
Of his daughters by Mariamme, one [e] was given to
Antipater, his sister's, the other [f] to Phasael, his
brother's son.

(xxix. 1) Antipater, having cut off the orphans'
expectations and arranged the marriages to his own
advantage, regarded his prospects as securely an-
chored, and, with assurance now added to villainy,
became insufferable. For, unable to avert the hatred
which he inspired in all, he sought security in
intimidation. He was assisted by Pheroras, who

---

[a] §§ 487, 534. In *A.* xvii. 10 it is stated that the empress
(Julia) took Herod's side and sought to break off Salome's
proposed match with Syllaeus.
 [b] Names unknown. [c] Berenice, widow of Aristobulus.
 [d] Theudion (§ 553 note). [e] Cypros. [f] Salampsio.

568 γίνεται δὲ καὶ γυναικῶν σύνταγμα κατὰ τὴν αὐλήν,
ὃ νεωτέρους ἐκίνησεν θορύβους. ἡ γὰρ Φερώρα
γυνὴ μετὰ τῆς μητρὸς καὶ τῆς ἀδελφῆς προσ-
λαβοῦσα καὶ τὴν ᾿Αντιπάτρου μητέρα πολλὰ μὲν
ἠσέλγαινεν κατὰ τὸ βασίλειον, ἐτόλμησεν δὲ καὶ
τοῦ βασιλέως ὑβρίσαι δύο θυγατέρας, δι᾽ ἃ δὴ
μάλιστα ταύτην ἐκεῖνος προβέβλητο· μισούμεναί
569 γε μὴν ὑπ᾽ αὐτοῦ τῶν ἄλλων ἐπεκράτουν. μόνη
δὲ τῆς ὁμονοίας αὐτῶν ἀντίπαλος ἦν Σαλώμη καὶ
βασιλεῖ διέβαλλεν τὴν σύνοδον, ὡς οὐκ ἐπ᾽ ἀγαθῷ
τῶν αὐτοῦ πραγμάτων εἴη. γνοῦσαι δ᾽ ἐκεῖναι
τὴν διαβολὴν καὶ ὡς ἀγανακτήσειεν Ἡρώδης, τῆς
μὲν φανερᾶς συνόδου καὶ τῶν φιλοφρονήσεων
ἐπαύσαντο, τοὐναντίον δ᾽ ὑπεκρίνοντο καὶ δια-
φέρεσθαι πρὸς ἀλλήλας ἀκούοντος βασιλέως· αἷς
συνυπεκρίνετο καὶ ᾿Αντίπατρος, ἐν τῷ φανερῷ
570 προσκρούων Φερώρᾳ. συνουσίαι δὲ ἦσαν αὐτῶν
λάθρα καὶ κῶμοι νυκτερινοί, τήν τε ὁμόνοιαν ἡ
παρατήρησις ἐπέτεινεν. ἠγνόει δὲ οὐδὲν Σαλώμη
τῶν πραττομένων καὶ πάνθ᾽ Ἡρώδῃ διήγγελλεν.

571 (2) Ἐξεκαίετο δ᾽ ἐκεῖνος εἰς ὀργὴν καὶ μάλιστα
ἐπὶ τὴν Φερώρου γυναῖκα· ταύτην γὰρ πλέον ἡ
Σαλώμη διέβαλλεν. ἀθροίσας οὖν συνέδριον τῶν
τε φίλων καὶ συγγενῶν ἄλλα τε πολλὰ τῆς ἀνθρώπου κατηγόρει καὶ τὴν εἰς τὰς ἑαυτοῦ θυγατέρας
ὕβριν, ὅτι τε Φαρισαίοις μὲν χορηγήσειεν μισθοὺς
κατ᾽ αὐτοῦ καὶ τὸν ἀδελφὸν αὐτῷ κατασκευάσειεν
572 πολέμιον ἐνδησαμένη φαρμάκοις. τελευταῖον δ᾽
εἰς Φερώραν ἀπέστρεφεν τὸν λόγον, δυοῖν θάτερον

---

[a] Salome and Roxana.
[b] She had paid the fine imposed upon them for refusing
270

looked on Antipater's claim to the throne as already
assured. There was, moreover, a gang of women at A cabal of women at court.
court who created new disturbances. The wife of
Pheroras, in league with her mother and sister and
the mother of Antipater, displayed constant effrontery
in the palace, and even ventured to insult two young
daughters of the king.[a] She became, in consequence,
the object of Herod's special aversion ; yet, notwithstanding the king's hatred, these women domineered
over the rest. The sole opponent of their league was Salome reports their proceedings to Herod.
Salome, who reported it to the king as a conclave
not conducive to the interests of his realm. Informed
of this denunciation and of Herod's wrath, they
abandoned their public meetings and all signs of
friendly recognition, and on the contrary pretended
to quarrel with one another in the king's hearing ;
Antipater joined in their dissimulation by taking
offence, in public, at Pheroras. But they continued
to hold clandestine meetings and nocturnal carousals,
and the knowledge that they were watched only
bound them closer together. Salome, however, was
ignorant of none of their proceedings and reported
everything to Herod.

(2) The king was furiously indignant, particularly Pheroras refuses to divorce his wife.
at the wife of Pheroras, the principal object of
Salome's charges. He, accordingly, assembled a
council of his friends and relations and accused the
wretched woman of numerous misdeeds, among
others of insulting his own daughters, of subsidizing
the Pharisees to oppose him,[b] and of alienating his
brother, after bewitching him with drugs. In conclusion, he addressed Pheroras and told him that he

to take the oath of allegiance to Herod on his accession
(A. xvii. 42).

271

ἐλέσθαι λέγων, ἢ ἑαυτὸν ἀδελφὸν ἢ τὴν γυναῖκα.
τοῦ δὲ θᾶττον ἀπολείψειν τὸ ζῆν ἢ τὴν γυναῖκα
φήσαντος, οὐκ ἔχων ὅ τι χρὴ δρᾶν μετέβαινεν ἐπ'
Ἀντίπατρον, ᾧ παρήγγειλεν μήτε τῇ Φερώρα
γυναικὶ μήτε αὐτῷ μήτ' ἄλλῳ τινὶ τῶν ἐκείνης
διαλέγεσθαι. ὁ δὲ φανερῶς μὲν οὐ παρέβαινεν[1] τὸ
πρόσταγμα, λάθρα δὲ διενυκτέρευεν σὺν ἐκείνοις.
573 καὶ δεδοικὼς τὴν ἐπιτηροῦσαν Σαλώμην πραγ-
ματεύεται διὰ τῶν ἐπὶ τῆς Ἰταλίας φίλων τὴν εἰς
Ῥώμην ἀποδημίαν αὐτῷ· γραψάντων γὰρ ἐκείνων
δεῖν Ἀντίπατρον διὰ χρόνου πεμφθῆναι πρὸς
Καίσαρα, ὁ δὲ οὔ τι μελλήσας ἐξέπεμψεν θεραπείαν
τε λαμπρὰν καὶ πλεῖστα δοὺς χρήματα τήν τε
διαθήκην κομίζειν, ἐν ᾗ βασιλεὺς μὲν Ἀντίπατρος
ἐγέγραπτο, Ἀντιπάτρου δὲ Ἡρώδης διάδοχος ὁ ἐκ
Μαριάμμης τῆς τοῦ ἀρχιερέως θυγατρὸς γεγονώς.
574 (3) Ἔπλευσεν δὲ καὶ Συλλαῖος ὁ Ἄραψ ἐπὶ
Ῥώμης, ἠμεληκὼς μὲν τῶν Καίσαρος προσταγμάτων, ἀνταγωνιούμενος δὲ πρὸς Ἀντίπατρον
περὶ ὧν ἐδεδίκαστο Νικολάῳ τάχιον. οὐ μικρὸς
δ' αὐτῷ καὶ πρὸς Ἀρέταν ἦν ἀγὼν τὸν ἑαυτοῦ
βασιλέα· τούτου γὰρ ἄλλους τε φίλους ἀνῃρήκει
575 καὶ Σόαιμον τῶν ἐν Πέτρᾳ δυνατωτάτων.[2] πείσας
δὲ πολλοῖς χρήμασιν Φάβατον τὸν Καίσαρος διοικητὴν ἐχρῆτο βοηθῷ καὶ καθ' Ἡρώδου. πλείονα
δὲ δοὺς Ἡρώδης ἀφίστησίν τε ἀπὸ Συλλαίου
Φάβατον καὶ δι' αὐτοῦ τὰ κελευσθέντα ὑπὸ Καίσαρος εἰσέπραττεν. ὁ δὲ μηδὲν ἀποδοὺς ἔτι καὶ

[1] Niese: μετέβαινεν mss.
[2] Niese: τὸν ἐν Π. δυνατώτατον PAM, τῶν ἐν Π. τὸν δυνατώτατον the rest.

---

[a] Mariamme II, daughter of Simon the high priest.

must choose one or the other, either his brother or his wife. Pheroras replying that he would sooner part with his existence than with his wife, Herod, in perplexity, turned to Antipater and ordered him to have no further intercourse either with the wife of Pheroras, or with her husband, or with any of her set. Antipater, while not openly violating this injunction, continued secretly and at night to associate with them; but fearing the vigilance of Salome he contrived, with the help of friends in Italy, a visit to Rome. A letter arriving from them, suggesting that Antipater ought to be sent before long to Caesar's court, Herod without a moment's delay sent him off with a brilliant retinue, a large sum of money and his will, in which Antipater was named as heir to the throne, and Herod, the king's son by Mariamme, the high-priest's daughter,[a] as Antipater's successor.

Antipater's visit to Rome. c. 6 B.C.

(3) Syllaeus the Arab also set sail for Rome; he had disregarded Caesar's orders and went to maintain against Antipater the case which he had previously pleaded against Nicolas.[b] There was also a grave matter at issue between him and his own sovereign, Aretas, for he had put to death a number of that prince's friends, including Soaemus, one of the most powerful personages in Petra. By a large bribe he secured the services of Fabatus, Caesar's treasurer, whom he also employed to assist him against Herod. The latter, however, by even larger bribes, detached Fabatus from Syllaeus and endeavoured, through him, to exact from Syllaeus the penalty imposed by Caesar.[c] But Syllaeus still refused to pay anything,

Intrigues of Syllaeus the Arab.

[b] Nicolas of Damascus had, in the course of an attempted mediation between Herod and Augustus (*c.* 7 B.C.), accused Syllaeus of treasonable designs (*A.* xvi. 335 ff., no parallel in *B.*).   [c] *A.* xvi. 352 f.

κατηγόρει Φαβάτου παρὰ Καίσαρι, διοικητὴν εἶναι
λέγων οὐ τῶν ἐκείνῳ, τῶν δὲ Ἡρώδῃ συμ-
576 φερόντων. ἐφ' οἷς ὀργισθεὶς Φάβατος, ἦν δ' ἔτι
παρὰ Ἡρώδῃ μάλιστα τιμώμενος, γίνεται προδότης Συλλαίου τῶν ἀπορρήτων, τῷ τε βασιλεῖ
φησιν ὅτι Σύλλαιος διαφθείρειεν αὐτοῦ τὸν σωματο-
φύλακα Κόρινθον χρήμασιν, ὃν δεῖ φυλάττεσθαι.
πείθεται δ' ὁ βασιλεύς· καὶ γὰρ τέθραπτο μὲν ὁ
Κόρινθος ἐν τῇ βασιλείᾳ, γένος δ' ἦν Ἄραψ.
577 συλλαμβάνει δ' εὐθέως οὐκ αὐτὸν μόνον ἀλλὰ καὶ
δύο ἑτέρους Ἄραβας εὑρὼν παρ' αὐτῷ, τὸν μὲν
φίλον Συλλαίου τὸν δὲ φύλαρχον. οἱ δὲ βασανιζόμενοι πεῖσαι Κόρινθον ὡμολόγησαν ἐπὶ πολλοῖς
χρήμασιν Ἡρώδην ἀνελεῖν. οὗτοι μὲν οὖν ἀνα-
κριθέντες καὶ παρὰ Σατορνίνῳ τῷ διέποντι τὴν
Συρίαν ἀνεπέμφθησαν εἰς Ῥώμην.

578   (4) Ἡρώδης δ' οὐκ ἀνίει Φερώραν βιαζόμενος
ἀπαλλαγῆναι τῆς γυναικός, οὐδ'[1] ἐπενόει μηχανὴν
δι' ἧς ἂν τιμωρήσαιτο τὴν ἄνθρωπον, πολλὰς τοῦ
μίσους ἔχων αἰτίας, ἕως ὑπεραγανακτήσας σὺν
579 αὐτῇ καὶ τὸν ἀδελφὸν ἐκβάλλει. Φερώρας δὲ
ἀγαπήσας τὴν ὕβριν ἀπαλλάσσεται μὲν εἰς τὴν
ἑαυτοῦ τετραρχίαν ὀμόσας ὅρον ἕξειν ἕνα τῆς
φυγῆς τὸν Ἡρώδου θάνατον καὶ μηδέποτε πρὸς
ζῶντα ὑποστρέψειν, ἐπανῆλθεν δὲ οὐδὲ πρὸς
νοσοῦντα τὸν ἀδελφὸν καίτοι λιπαρῶς μεταπεμ-
πόμενον· ἐβούλετο γὰρ αὐτῷ τινας ἐντολὰς κατα-
580 λείψειν ὡς τεθνηξόμενος. ἀλλ' ὁ μὲν παρ' ἐλπίδα
σώζεται, μετ' οὐ πολὺ δὲ νοσεῖ Φερώρας, εὑρίσκετο

[1] ὁ δ' or ὁ δὲ PAM.

and furthermore accused Fabatus to Caesar, asserting that the emperor's agent was acting not for his but for Herod's interests. Indignant at this and still highly paid by Herod, Fabatus betrayed the secrets of Syllaeus, informing the king that he had by bribery corrupted Corinthus, one of his bodyguard, and warning him to be on his guard against this man. The king acted on this advice, knowing that this Corinthus, though brought up within his dominion, was an Arab by birth. He straightway had him arrested and with him two other Arabs, whom he discovered in his company, one a friend of Syllaeus, the other the chief of a tribe. Being put to the torture, these men confessed that Corinthus had by large bribes induced them to kill Herod. They were, accordingly, after being further examined by Saturninus, the governor of Syria, sent up for trial to Rome.

Discovery of a plot of another Arab against Herod.

(4) Herod, meanwhile, never relaxed his efforts to compel Pheroras to divorce his wife. But, notwithstanding the abundant cause which he had for his hatred of the creature, he could devise no means of punishing her, until finally, in extreme indignation, he banished both her and his brother from the realm. Pheroras, accepting this affront with equanimity, departed to his own tetrarchy,[a] swearing that the only limit to his exile should be Herod's death, and that never, so long as his brother lived, would he return to him. Nor, in fact, would he revisit his brother, even during his illness, though urgently pressed to do so; for Herod, believing that he was dying, desired to leave him certain instructions. Herod, however, unexpectedly recovered, and not long after, Pheroras himself fell sick; Herod thereupon dis-

Exile and death of Pheroras 5 B.C.

---

[a] Peraea (§ 483).

δὲ Ἡρώδης μετριώτερος· καὶ γὰρ ἥκει πρὸς αὐτὸν
καὶ συμπαθῶς ἐθεράπευεν. οὐ μὴν ὑπερίσχυσεν
τοῦ πάθους· μετὰ γὰρ ἡμέρας ὀλίγας ἀποθνήσκει
581 Φερώρας. ὃν καίπερ ἀγαπήσας Ἡρώδης μέχρι
τελευταίας ἡμέρας ὅμως καὶ αὐτὸν ἀνελεῖν ἐφη-
μίσθη φαρμάκῳ. τόν γε μὴν νεκρὸν εἰς Ἱεροσόλυμα κομίσας πένθος τε μέγιστον ὅλῳ τῷ ἔθνει
κατήγγειλεν καὶ κηδείας ἠξίωσεν λαμπροτάτης.
ἕνα μὲν δὴ τῶν Ἀλεξάνδρου καὶ Ἀριστοβούλου
φονέων τοιοῦτον περιέρχεται τέλος.

582 (xxx. 1) Μετέβαινεν δ' ἐπὶ τὸν αὐθέντην
Ἀντίπατρον ἡ ποινὴ τὸν Φερώρα θάνατον ἀρχὴν
λαβοῦσα. τῶν τούτου γάρ τινες ἀπελευθέρων
κατηφεῖς τῷ βασιλεῖ προσελθόντες τὸν ἀδελφὸν
αὐτοῦ διεφθάρθαι φαρμάκοις ἔλεγον· προσενεγκεῖν
μὲν γὰρ αὐτῷ τι τὴν γυναῖκα τῶν οὐ συνήθως
ἐσκευασμένων, φαγόντα δ' εὐθέως εἰς τὴν νόσον
583 καταπεσεῖν. ἀγηοχέναι τε πρὸ δυοῖν ἡμερῶν τὴν
μητέρα ταύτης[1] καὶ τὴν ἀδελφὴν γύναιον ἐκ τῆς
Ἀραβίας φαρμάκων ἔμπειρον, ὅπως φίλτρον
σκευάσῃ τῷ Φερώρᾳ, δεδωκέναι δ' ἀντὶ τούτου
θανάσιμον Συλλαίου πραγματευσαμένου· τούτῳ
γὰρ ἦν γνώριμον.

584 (2) Πληγεὶς οὖν ὁ βασιλεὺς ὑποψίαις πλείοσιν
θεραπαίνας τε καί τινας τῶν ἐλευθέρων ἐβασάνιζεν.
ἐβόα δέ τις ἐν ταῖς ἀλγηδόσιν " θεὸς ὁ γῆν καὶ
οὐρανὸν διέπων μετέλθοι τὴν τούτων ἡμῖν τῶν
κακῶν αἰτίαν, τὴν Ἀντιπάτρου μητέρα." ταύτης
τῆς ἀρχῆς ὁ βασιλεὺς λαβόμενος ἐπεξήει πρόσω
585 τὴν ἀλήθειαν.[2] ἡ δὲ γυνὴ τήν τε φιλίαν τῆς

___
[1] αὐτῆς PM. [2] +ἐπιζητῶν LTRC.

played greater humanity, for he went to him and
affectionately tended him. But he could not cope
with the malady, and a few days later Pheroras
expired. Notwithstanding the love which Herod had
for his brother to his dying day, a report was spread
that he had poisoned even him. Anyhow, he had the
corpse conveyed to Jerusalem, gave orders for a
solemn national mourning, and honoured him with
the most imposing funeral. Such was the end to
which came one of the murderers of Alexander and
Aristobulus.

(xxx. 1) But retribution was now, in turn, descend-
ing upon the real perpetrator of that crime, Antipater; this retribution arose out of the death of
Pheroras. For certain freedmen of the deceased
came, in dejection, to the king and informed him
that his brother had been carried off by poison; his
wife, they said, had served up to him some extraordinary concoction, after eating which he was immediately taken ill. They added that, two days
before, her mother and sister had brought from
Arabia a woman who was an expert in drugs, to
make up a love-potion for Pheroras; but, instead of
this, she had given him a deadly poison, at the
instigation of Syllaeus, who knew her. Herod discovers that Pheroras has been poisoned.

(2) Beset with all sorts of suspicions, the king put
the women-servants and some ladies above that rank
to the torture. One victim in her agonies exclaimed,
" May God who governs earth and heaven punish
the author of our present miseries, Antipater's
mother ! "[a] Clutching at this clue, the king pushed
his search for the facts yet further. The woman Revelations of the women concerning Antipater.

[a] Doris.

᾿Αντιπάτρου μητρὸς πρὸς Φερώραν καὶ τὰς ἐκείνου
γυναῖκας ἐδήλου καὶ τὰς λαθραίας αὐτῶν συνόδους,
ὅτι τε Φερώρας καὶ ᾿Αντίπατρος σὺν ἐκείναις
πίνοιεν, ὑποστρέφοντες ἀπὸ τοῦ βασιλέως, δι'
ὅλης[1] νυκτός, μηδένα μήτε οἰκέτην μήτε θερά-
παιναν ἐῶντες παρατυγχάνειν. μία δὴ τῶν ἐλευθέρων ταῦτα μηνύει.

586 (3) Τὰς δὲ δούλας χωρὶς ἑκάστην Ἡρώδης
ἐβασάνιζεν. ἐρρήθη δὲ παρὰ πάσαις τὰ προ-
ειρημένα σύμφωνα, καὶ διότι κατὰ συνθήκην ᾿Αντί-
πατρος μὲν εἰς Ῥώμην, Φερώρας δ' ὑποχωρήσειεν
εἰς τὴν Περαίαν· πολλάκις γὰρ αὐτοὺς διαλαλεῖν,
ὡς μετ' ᾿Αλέξανδρον καὶ ᾿Αριστόβουλον ἐπ' αὐτοὺς
Ἡρώδης μεταβήσεται καὶ τὰς ἑαυτῶν γυναῖκας·
οὐ γὰρ φείσεσθαι[2] μετὰ Μαριάμμην καὶ τοὺς ἐξ
ἐκείνης ἑτέρου τινός, ὥστε ἄμεινον εἶναι φεύγειν
587 ὡς πορρωτάτω τοῦ θηρίου. πολλάκις δὲ ἀπ-
οδυρόμενον πρὸς τὴν μητέρα τὸν ᾿Αντίπατρον εἰπεῖν
ὡς αὐτὸς μὲν εἴη πολιὸς ἤδη, νεάζοι δὲ καθ'
ἡμέραν ὁ πατήρ, φθάσαι δ' ἂν τάχα καὶ τελευτήσας πρὶν ἄρξασθαι βασιλείας ἀληθοῦς. εἰ δὲ
καί ποτε ἐκεῖνος τελευτήσειεν, (πότε δ' ἂν γένοιτο
τοῦτο;) παντάπασιν αὐτῷ τὴν ἀπόλαυσιν τῆς
588 διαδοχῆς γίνεσθαι σύντομον. ὑποβλαστάνειν δὲ
τὰς τῆς ὕδρας κεφαλάς, τοὺς ᾿Αριστοβούλου καὶ
᾿Αλεξάνδρου παῖδας. ἀφηρῆσθαι δ' αὐτὸν ὑπὸ
τοῦ πατρὸς καὶ τὴν ἐπὶ τέκνοις ἐλπίδα· διάδοχον
γὰρ οὐ τῶν αὐτοῦ τινα παίδων μετὰ τὴν τελευτήν,
ἀλλὰ τὸν ἐκ Μαριάμμης Ἡρώδην γεγραφέναι.
καὶ κατὰ τοῦτό γε παντάπασιν παραγηρᾶν οἰόμενον
αὐτοῦ καὶ διαθήκας μενεῖν κυρίας· αὐτὸν γὰρ
589 προνοήσειν μηδένα τῆς γενεᾶς ἀπολιπεῖν. ὄντα

then revealed the intimacy of Antipater's mother with Pheroras and the ladies of his family, and their clandestine meetings ; she added that Pheroras and Antipater, on their return from the king, would pass the whole night drinking with those women, without allowing a single servant, male or female, to be present. This information was given by one of the ladies of rank.

(3) Herod had each of the slave girls separately tortured. All their evidence agreed with that already stated ; they added that it was by a mutual arrangement that Antipater had withdrawn to Rome and Pheroras to Peraea ; for they were constantly saying to each other, " After Alexander and Aristobulus, we and our wives will be Herod's next victims. Having slain Mariamme and her offspring, he will spare none ; so it will be better to flee as far as possible from the ferocious beast." Antipater, they continued, would often complain to his mother that he was already grey-headed, while his father grew younger every day ; he would perhaps be the first to die, before he began to be really king. Even supposing his father ever did die (and when would that be ?) his enjoyment of his heritage must be extremely short. Then there were these hydra heads, the sons of Aristobulus and Alexander, shooting up. His father had robbed him of his hopes for his children, by nominating as the next heir to the throne not one of his own children, but Herod, the son of Mariamme. In that at least he betrayed his extreme senility, if he supposed that that part of his will would stand ; for he, Antipater, would take good care to leave none of the family alive. Never had

---

¹ +τῆς AM. ² Bekker: φείσασθαι mss.

γε μὴν τῶν πώποτε πατέρων μισοτεκνότατον
Ἡρώδην πολὺ μᾶλλον εἶναι μισάδελφον· δοῦναι
γοῦν αὐτῷ πρῴην ἑκατὸν τάλαντα ἐπὶ τῷ μὴ διαλέγεσθαι Φερώρᾳ. τοῦ δὲ εἰπόντος "τί γὰρ
αὐτὸν ἐβλάπτομεν;" ἀποκρίνασθαι τὸν Ἀντίπατρον "εἴθε πάνθ' ἡμᾶς ἀφελόμενος γυμνοὺς
ἐάσειεν¹ ζῶντας. ἀλλ' ἀμήχανον ἐκφυγεῖν οὕτω
φονικὸν θηρίον, παρ' ᾧ μηδὲ φιλεῖν τινας ἔξεστι
φανερῶς. λάθρα γοῦν νῦν ἀλλήλοις σύνεσμεν,
ἐξέσται δὲ φανερῶς, ἐὰν σχῶμέν ποτ' ἀνδρῶν
φρόνημα καὶ χεῖρας."

590   (4) Ταῦτ' ἔλεγον αἱ βασανιζόμεναι, καὶ ὅτι
Φερώρας βουλεύσαιτο φυγεῖν μετ' αὐτῶν εἰς
Πέτραν. ἐπίστευσεν δ' Ἡρώδης πᾶσιν τοῖς λεγομένοις ἐκ τῶν ἑκατὸν ταλάντων· μόνῳ γὰρ Ἀντιπάτρῳ διείλεκτο περὶ αὐτῶν. ἀποσκήπτει δ' εἰς
πρώτην ὁ θυμὸς Δωρίδα τὴν Ἀντιπάτρου μητέρα·
καὶ γυμνώσας αὐτὴν παντὸς οὗ δεδώρητο κόσμου,
591 πολλῶν δ' ἦν ταλάντων, ἐκβάλλει δεύτερον. τὰς
δὲ Φερώρου γυναῖκας ἀπὸ τῶν βασάνων ἐτημέλει
διηλλαγμένος. ἐπτόητο δὲ τῷ φόβῳ καὶ πρὸς
πᾶσαν ὑπόνοιαν ἐξερριπίζετο, πολλούς τε τῶν οὐκ
αἰτίων εἷλκεν εἰς βασάνους, δεδοικὼς μή τινα τῶν
αἰτίων παραλίπῃ.

592   (5) Κἀν τούτῳ τρέπεται πρὸς τὸν Σαμαρείτην
Ἀντίπατρον, ὃς ἦν ἐπίτροπος Ἀντιπάτρου. βα-
σανίζων δὲ αὐτὸν ἤκουσεν ὅτι μετεπέμψατο μὲν
Ἀντίπατρος ἐξ Αἰγύπτου δηλητήριον φάρμακον
ἐπ' αὐτὸν διά τινος τῶν ἑταίρων Ἀντιφίλου, λάβοι
δὲ παρ' ἐκείνου Θευδίων ὁ θεῖος² Ἀντιπάτρου καὶ

¹ Dindorf: ἐάσει γε or ἐάσει mss.
² φίλος PAM Heg.: for text cf. A. xvii. 70.

father so hated his children, yet Herod hated his brother far more ; only the other day he had given him (Antipater) a hundred talents to break off all intercourse with Pheroras. And when Pheroras remarked, " Why, what harm were we doing him ? " he had replied : " Would to heaven he would rob us of everything and leave us to live in nakedness. But it is impossible to escape so blood-thirsty a beast, who will not even allow us to show affection for anyone. Now we must meet in secret ; we shall be able to do so openly, if ever we possess the courage and arms of men."

(4) To these revelations the tortured women added that Pheroras had had designs of flying with them to Petra. Herod believed all these statements because of the detail of the hundred talents, which he had mentioned to none but Antipater. The first to feel the explosion of his wrath was Doris, Antipater's mother ; he stripped her of all the finery which he had bestowed on her and for the second time dismissed her from court. With the ladies of Pheroras's household he made his peace and showed them special attentions after their tortures. But he was scared with fright and flared up at the least suspicion, and many innocent persons were haled by him to torture, for fear that a single culprit should escape him. _{Repudiation of Doris, Antipater's mother.}

(5) His attention was now directed to Antipater the Samaritan, agent to his son Antipater. From him, under torture, he learnt that Antipater had procured from Egypt, through Antiphilus, one of his companions, a deadly poison intended for the king ; that from Antiphilus it had passed into the hands of Theudion, Antipater's uncle, who had delivered it _{Discovery of a plot of Antipater and Pheroras to poison Herod.}

παραδοίη Φερώρα· τούτῳ γὰρ ἐντείλασθαι τὸν
Ἀντίπατρον Ἡρώδην ἀνελεῖν ἕως αὐτός ἐστιν
ἐν Ῥώμῃ τῆς ὑπονοίας κεχωρισμένος· Φερώραν
593 δὲ τῇ γυναικὶ παραθέσθαι τὸ φάρμακον. ταύτην
[οὖν]¹ ὁ βασιλεὺς μεταπεμψάμενος αὐτίκα τὸ
ληφθὲν ἐκέλευσεν κομίζειν. ἡ δ᾽ ἔξεισι μὲν ὡς
κομιοῦσα, ῥίπτει δ᾽ ἑαυτὴν ἀπὸ τοῦ τέγους τόν τε
ἔλεγχον καὶ τὴν ἐκ τοῦ βασιλέως αἰκίαν φθάνουσα·
προνοίᾳ δ᾽, ὡς ἔοικεν, θεοῦ μετιόντος Ἀντίπατρον
οὐκ ἐπὶ κεφαλὴν ἀλλ᾽ ἐπὶ θάτερα πεσοῦσα δια-
594 σῴζεται. κομισθεῖσαν δ᾽ αὐτὴν ὁ βασιλεὺς ἀνα-
κτησάμενος, κεκάρωτο γὰρ ἀπὸ τοῦ πτώματος,
ἠρώτα δι᾽ ἣν αἰτίαν ῥίψειεν ἑαυτήν, εἰ μὲν εἴποι
τἀληθές, ἀφήσειν πάσης τιμωρίας ἐπομνύμενος, εἰ
δ᾽ ὑποστείλαιτο, δαπανήσειν αὐτῆς ἐν βασάνοις τὸ
σῶμα καὶ μηδὲ τάφῳ καταλείψειν.

595   (6) Πρὸς ταῦθ᾽ ἡ γυνὴ μικρὸν διαλιποῦσα "καὶ
τί γάρ," εἶπεν, "ἔτι φείδομαι τῶν ἀπορρήτων,
Φερώρα τεθνεῶτος; ἢ² σώζουσα τὸν ἀπολέσαντα
πάντας ἡμᾶς Ἀντίπατρον; ἄκουε, βασιλεῦ, καὶ
μετὰ σοῦ θεὸς ὁ μάρτυς ἐμοὶ τῆς ἀληθείας πλανη-
596 θῆναι μὴ δυνάμενος. ὅτε ἀποθνήσκοντι Φερώρᾳ
παρεκαθέζου δεδακρυμένος, τότε με προσκαλεσάμενος ἐκεῖνος 'ἦ πολύ γε,' ἔφη, 'ὦ γύναι, τῆς
εἰς ἐμαυτὸν διανοίας τοῦ ἀδελφοῦ διήμαρτον, τὸν
οὕτως στέργοντα μισήσας καὶ κτεῖναι βουλευσάμενος τὸν οὕτως ἐπ᾽ ἐμοὶ μηδὲ τεθνεῶτί πω
συγχεόμενον. ἀλλ᾽ ἐγὼ μὲν ἀπέχω τῆς ἀσεβείας
τὸ ἐπιτίμιον, σὺ δ᾽ ὃ φυλάσσεις κατ᾽ αὐτοῦ φάρμακον ὑπ᾽ Ἀντιπάτρου καταλειφθὲν ἡμῖν φέρε καὶ
βλέποντός μου ταχέως ἀφάνισον, ἵνα μὴ καὶ καθ᾽

¹ AM Lat.: om. the rest.   ² ἢ conj.: ἦ mss.

to Pheroras, since it was he whom Antipater had commissioned to kill Herod while he himself was at Rome and out of the way of suspicion ; and that Pheroras had entrusted the poison to his wife. The king sent for her and ordered her instantly to produce what she had received. She went out, as though to fetch it, and then flung herself from the roof, in order to evade conviction and the king's rack. However, by the providence, it seems, of God, whose vengeance was pursuing Antipater, she fell not on her head, but on another part of her body, and was not killed. She was carried to the king, who had restoratives applied, as she was stunned by the fall ; he then asked her why she had thrown herself from the roof, and swore that, if she told the truth, he would exempt her from all punishment, but, if she prevaricated, he would tear her body to pieces with tortures and leave not a limb for burial.

(6) At this the woman hesitated an instant and then replied : " After all, why should I longer guard these secrets, now that Pheroras is dead ? Merely to save Antipater who has been the ruin of us all ? Listen to me, O king, and may God hear me too, a witness to the truth of my words who cannot be deceived ! At the time when you were sitting weeping beside the dying Pheroras, he called me to him and said, ' Much have I been mistaken, my wife, in my brother's feelings towards me ; I hated him who loves me so tenderly ; I plotted to kill him who is so overwhelmed with grief for me even before my death. I am but receiving the reward of my impiety ; as for you, bring that poison which Antipater left us, and you are keeping for his destruction, and promptly destroy it under my eyes, lest I carry away

Confession of the widow of Pheroras.

597 ᾅδου φέροιμι τὸν ἀλάστορα.' καὶ κελεύσαντος
ἐκόμισα καὶ πλεῖστον μὲν εἰς τὸ πῦρ ὁρῶντος
αὐτοῦ κατεκένωσα, βραχὺ δὲ ἐμαυτῇ πρὸς τὰ
ἄδηλα καὶ τὸν ἐκ σοῦ φόβον ἐτήρησα.''

598 (7) Ταῦτ' εἰποῦσα προκομίζει τὴν πυξίδα παντάπασιν ἔχουσαν τοῦ φαρμάκου βραχύ. βασιλεὺς
δ' ἐπὶ τὴν μητέρα τὴν Ἀντιφίλου καὶ τὸν ἀδελφὸν
τὰς βασάνους μετέφερεν, κἀκεῖνοι τὸν Ἀντίφιλον
κομίσαι τε ἀπ' Αἰγύπτου τὴν πυξίδα ὡμολόγουν
καὶ λαβεῖν παρ' ἀδελφοῦ τὸ φάρμακον ἔφασκον

599 ἰατρεύοντος ἐν Ἀλεξανδρείᾳ. περιόντες δὲ οἱ
Ἀλεξάνδρου καὶ Ἀριστοβούλου δαίμονες ἅπαν τὸ
βασίλειον ἐρευνηταί τε καὶ μηνυταὶ τῶν ἀδήλων
ἐγίνοντο, τούς τε πορρωτάτω τῆς ὑποψίας ὄντας
ἔσυρον εἰς τοὺς ἐλέγχους. εὑρίσκεται γοῦν καὶ ἡ
τοῦ ἀρχιερέως θυγάτηρ Μαριάμμη τῆς ἐπιβουλῆς
συνίστωρ· βασανιζόμενοι γὰρ τοῦτ' ἀπέδειξαν

600 αὐτῆς οἱ ἀδελφοί. βασιλεὺς δὲ τῆς μητρῴας τόλμης καὶ τὸν υἱὸν ἠμύνατο· τὸν γοῦν ἐξ αὐτῆς
Ἡρώδην, ὄντα διάδοχον Ἀντιπάτρου, τῆς δια-
θήκης ἐξήλειψεν.

601 (xxxi. 1) Ἐπὶ τούτοις καὶ Βάθυλλος εἰς τοὺς
ἐλέγχους συνέδραμεν, ἡ τελευταία πίστις τῶν
Ἀντιπάτρῳ βεβουλευμένων· ἦν μὲν γὰρ ἀπελεύ-
θερος αὐτοῦ, κομίζων δ' ἧκεν ἄλλο δηλητήριον,
ἰοὺς ἀσπίδων καὶ χυλοὺς ἑτέρων ἑρπετῶν, ἵνα εἰ
τὸ πρῶτον ἀσθενήσει[1] φάρμακον, τούτῳ Φερώρας
μετὰ τῆς γυναικὸς ὁπλίσαιτο κατὰ τοῦ βασιλέως.

602 πάρεργον δὲ τῆς ἐπὶ τὸν πατέρα τόλμης ἐκόμιζεν
τὰς κατὰ τῶν ἀδελφῶν ἐσκευωρημένας ἐπιστολὰς
ὑπ' Ἀντιπάτρου· ἦσαν γὰρ Ἀρχέλαος καὶ Φίλ-

---

[1] ἀσθενήσειε Dindorf.

with me an avenging demon even to the world below.' So I brought it, as he bade me, and emptied most of it into the fire beneath his eyes, but reserved a little for myself against the uncertainties of the future and my terror of you."

(7) After this declaration she produced the box containing a mere scrap of the poison. The king then applied torture to the mother and brother of Antiphilus, who both confessed that Antiphilus had brought the box from Egypt and asserted that he had procured the drug from another brother, a doctor in Alexandria. The ghosts of Alexander and Aristobulus [a] were indeed patrolling the palace from end to end, detecting and disclosing all the mysteries, and dragging to judgement persons who seemed farthest removed from suspicion. Thus, even Mariamme, the high-priest's daughter, was discovered to be privy to the plot; for her brothers, when put upon the rack, denounced her. The king's punishment for the mother's audacity fell upon her son: her Herod, whom he had appointed successor to Antipater, was struck out of the will.

(xxxi. 1) Corroborative evidence of Antipater's designs, the last link in the chain, was now furnished by Bathyllus, his freedman. This man arrived with another noxious drug, composed of the poison of asps and the secretions of other reptiles, in order that Pheroras and his wife might be armed with this against the king, should the first poison fail to take effect. A further object of his visit, subsidiary to the audacious attempt on the father's life, was the conveyance of letters fabricated by Antipater to injure his brothers, Archelaus and Philip. These

Antipater denounced by his freedman Bathyllus.

---

[a] For this image, in the vein of Greek tragedy, cf. § 607.

ιππος βασιλέως παῖδες ἐπὶ Ῥώμης παιδευόμενοι,
603 μειράκιά τε ἤδη καὶ φρονήματος μεστοί. τούτους
ἐπανακύπτοντας αὐτοῦ ταῖς ἐλπίσιν ἀποσκευάσασθαι σπεύδων Ἀντίπατρος ἃς μὲν πλάττεται κατ᾽
αὐτῶν ἐπιστολὰς ἐξ ὀνόματος τῶν ἐπὶ Ῥώμης
φίλων, οὓς δὲ ἔπειθεν γράψαι διαφθείρας χρήμασιν,
ὡς πολλὰ μὲν βλασφημοῖεν τὸν πατέρα, φανερῶς
δὲ Ἀλέξανδρον καὶ Ἀριστόβουλον ὀδύροιντο, πρὸς
δὲ τὴν μετάκλησιν ἀγανακτοῖεν· ἤδη γὰρ¹ αὐτοὺς
ὁ πατὴρ μετεπέμπετο, καὶ τοῦτο ἦν τὸ μάλιστα
ταράσσον Ἀντίπατρον.

604   (2) Ἔτι δὲ καὶ πρὸ τῆς ἀποδημίας ἐν Ἰουδαίᾳ
μένων τοιαύτας κατ᾽ αὐτῶν ἐπὶ Ῥώμης ἠγόραζεν
ἐπιστολάς, προσιών τε ὡς ἀνύποπτος εἴη τῷ πατρὶ
περὶ τῶν ἀδελφῶν² ἀπελογεῖτο, τὰ μὲν ψευδῆ
λέγων εἶναι τῶν γραφομένων, ἃ δὲ νεότητος ἁμαρ-
605 τήματα. τηνικαῦτά γε μὴν τοῖς γράφουσιν κατὰ
τῶν ἀδελφῶν πλεῖστα δοὺς χρήματα συμφύρειν
ἐπειρᾶτο τὸν ἔλεγχον, ἐσθῆτάς τε πολυτελεῖς καὶ
στρωμνὰς ποικίλας ἐκπώματά τε ἀργυρᾶ καὶ
χρυσᾶ συνωνούμενος ἄλλα τε πολλὰ τῶν κειμηλίων,
ἵνα τῷ πλήθει τῆς εἰς ταῦτα δαπάνης τοὺς εἰς
ἐκεῖνα μισθοὺς ἐγκατακρύψῃ³· διακόσια γοῦν ἀνα-
λώματος ἀνήνεγκεν τάλαντα, καὶ τούτων μεγίστη
606 πρόφασις ἦν ἡ πρὸς Συλλαῖον δίκη. πάντων δ᾽
αὐτοῦ τότε καὶ τῶν βραχυτέρων ἐν τῷ μείζονι
κακῷ διακαλυφθέντων, ὅθ᾽ αἱ μὲν βάσανοι πᾶσαι

¹ γὰρ Niese from Lat.: δ᾽ or δὲ mss.
² The alternative reading of LTRC καὶ προσιὼν τέως
ἀνύποπτος ἦν τῷ πατρὶ περὶ τῶν ἀδελφῶν δὲ (" and then, while
as yet his father had no suspicion of him, would go to him
and " etc.) is specious.
³ LTRC Lat.: ἐγκαταγράψῃ PAM (perhaps rightly).

sons of the king, now growing lads and full of manly spirit, were receiving their education in Rome. Anxious to rid himself of these scions springing up to dash his hopes, Antipater forged several letters to their injury in the name of their friends in Rome, while he prevailed on others by bribery to write that the young princes were constantly railing at their father, publicly deploring the fate of Alexander and Aristobulus, and indignant at their own recall ; for their father was now summoning them back, and it was this fact which caused Antipater the greatest uneasiness.

His forgery of letters to injure his half-brothers.

(2) Even before his departure abroad, Antipater, while still in Judaea, used to procure, at a price, the sending of such letters of abuse of his brothers written in Rome, and then, in order to avoid suspicion, would go to his father and make excuses for his brothers, urging that such and such statements were false, while other matters mentioned were mere youthful indiscretions. Now, in Rome, having to pay immense sums to the writers of these letters against his brothers, his efforts were directed to confusing the evidence of such outlay. To this end he bought up costly apparel, embroidered carpets, cups of silver and gold, and many other precious objects, in order to conceal under the enormous total of these outgoings the wages paid for the other affair. His returns showed an expenditure of 200 talents, of which the greater part was put down to his suit with Syllaeus. But now, though even all these petty knaveries were exposed with the larger crime, now when every fresh torture was loudly

τὴν πατροκτονίαν, αἱ δ' ἐπιστολαὶ δευτέρας
ἀδελφοκτονίας κεκράγεσαν, ὅμως οὐδεὶς τῶν
εἰς Ῥώμην ἀφικνουμένων ἀπήγγειλεν αὐτῷ τὰς
ἐν Ἰουδαίᾳ τύχας, καίτοι μεταξὺ τῶν ἐλέγχων καὶ
τῆς ἐπανόδου διελθόντων ἑπτὰ μηνῶν· τοσοῦτον
607 πρὸς αὐτὸν ἐκ πάντων μῖσος ἦν. τάχα καὶ τοὺς
ἀπαγγέλλειν προῃρημένους οἱ τῶν ἀνῃρημένων
δαίμονες ἀδελφῶν ἐφίμουν. γράφει γοῦν ἀπὸ
Ῥώμης ἄφιξιν ἑαυτοῦ ταχεῖαν εὐαγγελιζόμενος,
καὶ ὡς ὑπὸ Καίσαρος μετὰ τιμῆς ἀπολυθείη.

608 (3) Ὁ βασιλεὺς δὲ εἰς χεῖρας λαβεῖν σπεύδων
τὸν ἐπίβουλον καὶ δεδοικὼς μή ποτε προγνοὺς
φυλάξηται, δι' ἐπιστολῆς ἀνθυπεκρίνετο, τά τε
ἄλλα φιλοφρονούμενος καὶ σπεύδειν παρακαλῶν·
θήσεσθαι γὰρ αὐτοῦ καὶ τὰς πρὸς τὴν μητέρα
μέμψεις ἐπειχθέντος· οὐ γὰρ ἠγνόει τὴν ἐκβολὴν
609 τῆς μητρὸς Ἀντίπατρος. πρότερον μὲν οὖν εἰλή-
φει τὴν περὶ τῆς Φερώρα τελευτῆς ἐπιστολὴν ἐν
Τάραντι καὶ μέγιστον ἐποιήσατο πένθος, ὅ τινες
ὡς ἐπὶ θείῳ καθύμνουν, ἦν δ', ὡς ἔοικεν, ἐπὶ
διαμαρτίᾳ τῆς ἐπιβουλῆς ἡ σύγχυσις καὶ οὐ
Φερώραν κλαίοντος, ἀλλὰ τὸν ὑπηρέτην· ἤδη δὲ
καὶ φόβος ἐπῄει τις αὐτὸν τῶν τετελεσμένων, μή
610 ποτε φωραθείη τὸ φάρμακον. τότε δ' ἐν Κιλικίᾳ
λαβὼν ἦν προειρήκαμεν παρὰ τοῦ πατρὸς ἐπιστολὴν παραχρῆμα μὲν ἔσπευδεν, ὡς δὲ εἰς Κελέν-
δεριν κατέπλει, λαμβάνει τις αὐτὸν ἔννοια τῶν
περὶ τὴν μητέρα κακῶν, προμαντευομένης ἤδη καὶ

[a] On the borders of Pamphylia and Cilicia. Reinach
suspects some confusion as Celenderis was the first port in
Cilicia which he would reach.

proclaiming him a parricide, when the letters were revealing him as once more a fratricide, none the less not one of the visitors to Rome told him of the turn of his fortunes in Judaea, although seven months elapsed between his conviction and his return ; so intense was the hatred which all bore him. Perhaps, moreover, the lips of those who were minded to speak were sealed by the spirits of his murdered brothers. However that may be, he wrote from Rome to announce the good news of his early return and of the honours paid to him by Caesar in taking leave of him.

(3) The king, impatient to lay hands on the conspirator and fearing that he might be forewarned and on his guard, replied in an equally dissembling letter, couched in affectionate terms and bidding him hasten his return ; because, if he made speed, added Herod, he would be prepared to relinquish his complaints against his mother. For Antipater was not ignorant of her dismissal from court. He had previously received at Tarentum a letter announcing the death of Pheroras and had displayed the profoundest grief, for which some applauded him, attributing it to the loss of an uncle ; but his emotion, it seems, was due to the failure of the plot : he wept not for Pheroras but for his accomplice. He was, moreover, already alarmed at the thought of his past proceedings : had the poison been discovered? But now, when he received in Cilicia the above mentioned letter from his father, he instantly pressed on. However, as he was entering the harbour of Celenderis,[a] the thought of his mother's disgrace came over him, and even without such prompting [b] his soul had already

Return of Antipater in ignorance of his detection.

___

[b] Perhaps " involuntarily," *proprio motu.*

611 καθ' ἑαυτὴν τῆς ψυχῆς. οἱ μὲν οὖν προμηθέστεροι
τῶν φίλων συνεβούλευον μὴ πρότερον ἐμπίπτειν
τῷ πατρὶ πρὶν πυθέσθαι σαφῶς δι' ἃς αἰτίας
ἐξέβαλεν αὐτοῦ τὴν μητέρα· δεδιέναι γάρ, μή ποτε
612 προσθήκη γένοιτο τῶν κατ' ἐκείνης διαβολῶν. οἱ
δὲ ἀσκεπτότεροι καὶ τὴν πατρίδα σπεύδοντες ἰδεῖν
μᾶλλον ἢ τὸ συμφέρον Ἀντιπάτρῳ σκοποῦντες,
ἐπείγεσθαι παρῄνουν καὶ μὴ τῇ μελλήσει παρασχεῖν τῷ πατρὶ μὲν ὑποψίαν φαύλην, τοῖς δια-
βάλλουσι δὲ ἀφορμήν· καὶ γὰρ νῦν, εἴ τι κεκίνηται
κατ' αὐτοῦ, παρὰ τὴν ἀπουσίαν γέγονεν· μηδὲ γὰρ
ἂν τολμῆσαι παρόντος· ἄτοπον δ' εἶναι δι' ἀδήλους
ὑποψίας προδήλων ἀγαθῶν στερίσκεσθαι, καὶ μὴ
θᾶττον ἀποδοῦναι μὲν ἑαυτὸν τῷ πατρί, κομίσασθαι
δὲ τὴν βασιλείαν ἐπ' αὐτῷ μόνῳ σαλεύουσαν.
613 πείθεται τούτοις, ἐνῆγεν γὰρ τὸ δαιμόνιον, καὶ
διαπεράσας εἰς τὸν Σεβαστὸν λιμένα τῆς Καισαρείας κατάγεται.

614 (4) Παρυπήντησεν δ' αὐτῷ παρὰ δόξαν ἐρημία
πολλή, πάντων ἐκτρεπομένων καὶ μηδενὸς προσιέναι τολμῶντος· ἐμισεῖτο μὲν γὰρ ἐπίσης, καὶ
τότε φανῆναι τὸ μῖσος ἔσχεν παρρησίαν, πολλοὺς
δὲ ὁ ἐκ τοῦ βασιλέως φόβος ἀπέστρεψεν,[1] ἐπειδὴ
πᾶσα πόλις ἤδη τῆς κατ' Ἀντιπάτρου φήμης
πεπλήρωτο καὶ μόνος ἠγνόει τὰ κατ' αὐτὸν[2] Ἀντί-
πατρος· οὔτε δὲ προεπέμφθη λαμπρότερόν τις
ἐκείνου πλέοντος ἐπὶ Ῥώμης οὔτε ἀτιμότερον
615 ὑπεδέχθη. ὁ δὲ ἤδη μὲν ἐνενόει τὰς οἴκοι συμφοράς, ἔτι δὲ ἐκ πανουργίας ὑπεκρύπτετο καὶ τῷ

---

[1] PA: ἀπέστρεφεν the rest.   [2] καθ' ἑαυτὸν LTR.

a premonition of the future. The more far-sighted
of his friends advised him not to put himself into his
father's clutches until he had clearly ascertained the
reasons for his mother's dismissal, as they feared
that his arrival might only serve to swell the charges [a]
against her. But the less reflective, anxious rather
to see their native country than to serve Antipater's
interests, urged him to push on and not by pro-
crastinating to afford his father ground for sinister
suspicions and his traducers a handle for calumny.
" Even supposing," they said, " any intrigue against
you is now on foot, it is because of your absence ;
none would have ventured on such a thing had you
been there. It is absurd to let vague suspicions rob
you of certain happiness, and not to run to your
father's arms to receive the kingdom which is totter-
ing on his unaided shoulders." Antipater, under the
impulse of his evil genius, followed their advice, and
sailing across landed at the port of Augustus, at
Caesarea.

(4) Here he found a solitude, unlooked for, pro- His
found, and ominous ; all avoided him, none ventured reception
to approach him. For, equally hated though he had in Judaea,
always been,[b] this hatred was now at liberty to show
itself. Moreover, fear of the king kept many aloof,
for every city by now was full of the Antipater
scandal, and the only person ignorant how he stood
was Antipater himself. No man ever had a more
brilliant escort than his when he sailed for Rome,
none on return a more ignominious reception.
Divining now the disasters which had befallen at
home, he still maintained a crafty dissimulation and,

---

[a] Or perhaps " feared that there might have been some
addition to the charges." [b] Or " as he was by all."

δέει τεθνηκὼς ἔνδοθεν σοβαρὸς εἶναι τὸ πρόσωπον
616 ἐβιάζετο. φυγὴ δ' οὐκέτι ἦν οὐδ' ἐκ τῶν περι-
εχόντων ἀνάδυσις, καὶ σαφὲς μὲν οὐδέν[1] τι τῶν
οἴκοθεν ἀπηγγέλλετο διὰ τὴν ἐκ τοῦ βασιλέως
ἀπειλήν, ὑπελείπετο δὲ ἐλπὶς ἱλαρωτέρα, τάχα
μὲν μηδὲν πεφωρᾶσθαι, τάχα δ', εἴ τι καὶ πεφώραται, διασκευάσειν ἀναιδείᾳ καὶ δόλοις, ἅπερ
ἦν αὐτῷ μόνα τὰ τῆς σωτηρίας ἐφόδια.

617 (5) Φραξάμενος οὖν αὐτοῖς ἧκεν εἰς τὸ βασίλειον
δίχα τῶν φίλων· οὗτοι γὰρ ὑβρισθέντες ἐπὶ τοῦ
πρώτου πυλῶνος εἴρχθησαν· ἔτυχεν δ' ἔνδον ὢν
Οὔαρος ὁ τῆς Συρίας ἡγεμών. ὁ δὲ εἴσεισι πρὸς
τὸν πατέρα καὶ τῇ τόλμῃ παρακροτήσας ἑαυτὸν
618 ἤγγιζεν ὡς ἀσπασόμενος. κἀκεῖνος τὰς χεῖρας
προβαλὼν καὶ τὴν κεφαλὴν παρακλίνας, " ἔστιν,"
ἐξεβόησεν, " καὶ τοῦτο πατροκτόνου τὸ περι-
πλέκεσθαί μοι θέλειν ἐν τηλικαύταις αἰτίαις ὄντα.
φθείρου, δυσσεβεστάτη κεφαλή, μηδέ μου ψαύσῃς
πρὶν ἀποσκευάσασθαι τὰ ἐγκλήματα. δίδωμι δέ
σοι δικαστήριον καὶ δικαστὴν εὐκαίρως ἥκοντα
Οὔαρον. ἴθι καὶ σκέπτου τὴν ἀπολογίαν εἰς αὔριον·
παρέχω γάρ σου[2] καιρὸν τοῖς πανουργεύμασιν.[3]"
619 πρὸς ταῦτα μηδὲν ὑπ' ἐκπλήξεως ἀποκρίνασθαι
δυνηθεὶς αὐτὸς ὑπέστρεψεν, παραγενόμεναι δὲ πρὸς
αὐτὸν ἐκδιηγήσαντο πάντας τοὺς ἐλέγχους ἥ τε
μήτηρ καὶ ἡ γυνή. καὶ τότε μὲν ἀνανήψας ἐν
σκέψει τῆς ἀπολογίας ἦν.

---

[1] οὐδὲ ἐκεῖ LTRC Lat.   [2] σοι Naber.
[3] πανουργήμασιν AMLR.

though dead with fright at the bottom of his heart, contrived to preserve an imposing exterior. There was no longer any possibility of flight or retreat from the perils encompassing him. However, he had received no definite tidings of events at the palace—owing to the king's threats against informers—and he still cherished a ray of hope : perhaps nothing had been discovered, perhaps, even if anything had been discovered, he might mend matters by effrontery and guile, his sole means of salvation.

(5) Armed, then, with these weapons he entered the palace, without his friends, for they had been insolently stopped at the outer gate. At the time there was a visitor within—Varus,[a] the governor of Syria. Antipater proceeded to his father's presence and, seeking courage in audacity, approached as though to kiss him. Herod, with arms extended and head averted, cried out : " That too betrays the parricide : he would embrace me, with such accusations against him ! Perdition take thee, most impious wretch, and touch me not until you have cleared yourself of the charges. I offer you a tribunal and for judge this timely visitor, Varus. Go and prepare your defence for to-morrow ; I leave you that interval for your artifices." Unable through consternation to utter a word in reply, Antipater withdrew, and his mother and his wife [b] came to him and told him in detail of all the evidence against him. Then he collected himself and applied himself to preparing his defence.

and at Herod's court.

[a] P. Quintilius Varus, *legatus* of Syria *c.* 6–4 B.C., afterwards slain by Arminius and the Germans at the battle of Teutoburg.

[b] The daughter of Herod's predecessor Antigonus, *A.* xvii. 92, not his other wife, the daughter of Aristobulus (§ 565).

620 (xxxii. 1) Τῇ δ' ἐπιούσῃ συνέδριον μὲν ὁ βασιλεὺς ἀθροίζει τῶν συγγενῶν καὶ φίλων, εἰσκαλεῖ δὲ καὶ τοὺς Ἀντιπάτρου φίλους. προκαθέζεται δὲ αὐτὸς ἅμα Οὐάρῳ καὶ τοὺς μηνυτὰς πάντας ἐκέλευσεν εἰσαγαγεῖν, ἐν οἷς εἰσήχθησαν καὶ τῆς Ἀντιπάτρου μητρὸς οἰκέται τινὲς οὐ πρὸ πολλοῦ συνειλημμένοι, κομίζοντες γράμματα παρ' αὐτῆς πρὸς τὸν υἱὸν τοιάδε· " ἐπεὶ[1] πεφώραται πάντα ἐκεῖνα τῷ πατρί σου, μὴ παραγίνου πρὸς αὐτόν, ἂν μή τινα πορίσῃ παρὰ τοῦ Καίσαρος
621 δύναμιν." τούτων σὺν τοῖς ἄλλοις εἰσηγμένων Ἀντίπατρος εἰσέρχεται καὶ πεσὼν πρηνὴς πρὸ τῶν ποδῶν τοῦ πατρός, " ἱκετεύω, πάτερ," ἔφη, " μηδέν μου προκατεγνωκέναι, παρασχεῖν δέ μοι τὰς ἀκοὰς ἀκεραίους εἰς τὴν ἀπολογίαν· ἀποδείξω γὰρ ἐμαυτὸν καθαρόν, ἂν σὺ θέλῃς."[2]
622 (2) Ὁ δ' αὐτῷ σιγᾶν ἐγκραγὼν[2] πρὸς τὸν Οὐάρον εἶπεν· " ἀλλ' ὅτι μὲν καὶ σύ, Οὐάρε, καὶ πᾶς δικαστὴς ὅσιος Ἀντίπατρον ἐξώλη κρινεῖ, πέπεισμαι. δέδοικα δὲ μὴ κἀμοῦ μισήσῃς τὴν τύχην, κἀμὲ κρίνῃς πάσης ἄξιον συμφορᾶς τοιούτους υἱοὺς γεγεννηκότα. χρὴ δέ με διὰ τοῦτο ἐλεεῖσθαι πλέον, ὅτι πρὸς οὕτω μιαροὺς καὶ φιλο-
623 στοργότατος πατὴρ ἐγενόμην. τοὺς μὲν γὰρ προτέρους βασιλείας τε ἔτι νέους ἀξιώσας καὶ πρὸς τοῖς ἐν Ῥώμῃ τροφείοις φίλους Καίσαρος, ζηλωτοὺς δὲ ποιήσας βασιλεῦσιν ἑτέροις, εὗρον ἐπιβούλους, οἳ τεθνήκασι τὸ πλέον Ἀντιπάτρῳ· νέῳ γὰρ ὄντι καὶ διαδόχῳ τούτῳ μάλιστα τὴν ἀσφά-
624 λειαν ἐποριζόμην. τὸ δὲ μιαρὸν τοῦτο θηρίον τῆς ἐμῆς ὑπερεμπλησθὲν ἀνεξικακίας ἤνεγκεν κατ' ἐμοῦ

---

[1] ἐπείπερ LTRC. [2] κεκραγὼς (sic) PA.

(xxxii. 1) On the following day the king assembled a council of his relatives and friends, inviting Antipater's friends to attend as well. He himself presided, with Varus, and ordered all the informers to be produced. Among these were some domestics of Antipater's mother, recently arrested in the act of carrying a letter from her to her son in these terms : " As your father has discovered all, do not come near him, unless you have obtained support from Caesar." When these witnesses had been brought in with the rest, Antipater entered and, falling prostrate at his father's feet, said : " I beseech you, father, do not condemn me in advance, but lend an unprejudiced ear to my defence ; for I shall, if you permit, establish my innocence."

Trial of Antipater.

(2) Herod burst out upon him to be silent and then addressed Varus : " That you, Varus, and every honest judge will condemn Antipater as an abandoned criminal, I am fully persuaded. What I fear is that *my* fate may also appear hateful to you and that you may judge me deserving of every calamity for having begotten such sons. And yet you ought rather to pity me for having been the most devoted of fathers to such abominable wretches. My late sons, whom when they were quite young I thought fit to destine for the throne, whom I not only expensively educated in Rome, but introduced to Caesar's friendship, and made an object of envy to other sovereigns, these I found to be conspirators. They have died, mainly to further Antipater's interests : he was young, he was the heir, and to secure him was the object which I had most at heart. And now this foul monster, gorged with the benefits of my for-

Herod's indictment.

295

τὸν κόρον· ἔδοξα γὰρ αὐτῷ πολὺν ζῆν χρόνον,
καὶ τὸ ἐμὸν γῆρας ἐβαρύνθη, βασιλεύς τ' οὐχ
ὑπέμεινεν εἰ μὴ διὰ πατροκτονίας γενέσθαι, δίκαια
γοῦν βουλευσάμενος, ὅτι καταγαγὼν αὐτὸν ἀπὸ
τῆς χώρας ἀπερριμμένον καὶ παρωσάμενος τοὺς
ἐκ βασιλίδος μοι γεγεννημένους ἀπέδειξα τῆς
625 ἀρχῆς διάδοχον. ἐξομολογοῦμαί σοι, Οὔαρε, τὴν
ἐμαυτοῦ φρενοβλάβειαν· ἐγὼ [γὰρ]¹ τοὺς υἱοὺς
ἐκείνους κατ' ἐμαυτοῦ παρώξυνα, δικαίας αὐτῶν
ἀποκόψας ἐλπίδας δι' Ἀντίπατρον. καὶ τί μὲν
ἐκείνους εὐεργέτησα τηλικοῦτον, ἡλίκον τοῦτον;
ᾧ γε ζῶν μὲν ὀλίγου δεῖν παρεχώρησα τῆς ἐξουσίας, φανερῶς δὲ ταῖς διαθήκαις ἐνέγραψα τῆς
ἀρχῆς διάδοχον καὶ πρόσοδον μὲν ἰδίᾳ πεντήκοντα
ταλάντων ἔνειμα, τῶν δ' ἐμῶν ἐχορήγησα χρημάτων ἀνέδην, πλέοντι δὲ νῦν εἰς Ῥώμην ἔδωκα
τριακόσια τάλαντα, Καίσαρι δ' ἐξ ὅλης τῆς γενεᾶς
626 μόνον ὡς σωτῆρα τοῦ πατρὸς παρεθέμην. τί δ'
ἐκεῖνοι τοιοῦτον ἠσέβησαν, οἷον Ἀντίπατρος; ἢ
τίς ἔλεγχος ἠνέχθη κατ' αὐτῶν, ἡλίκος ἀπο-
627 δείκνυσιν τοῦτον ἐπίβουλον; ἀλλὰ φθέγγεσθαί τι
τετόλμηκεν ὁ πατροκτόνος καὶ πάλιν δόλοις τὴν
ἀλήθειαν ἐπικαλύψειν ἐλπίζει. Οὔαρε, σοὶ φυλακ-
τέον· ἐγὼ [μὲν]³ γὰρ οἶδα τὸ θηρίον καὶ προ-
ορῶμαι τὴν μέλλουσαν ἀξιοπιστίαν καὶ τὸν ἐπί-
πλαστον ὀλοφυρμόν. οὗτός ἐστιν ὁ παραινῶν ἐμοί
ποτε φυλάττεσθαι ζῶντα Ἀλέξανδρον καὶ μὴ
πᾶσιν πιστεύειν τὸ σῶμα· οὗτος ὁ μέχρι τῆς
κοίτης εἰσάγων καὶ μή μέ τις ἐνεδρεύοι περι-
βλέπων· οὗτος ὁ ταμίας τῶν ὕπνων καὶ χορηγὸς
τῆς ἀμεριμνίας, ὁ παραμυθούμενος τὴν ἐπὶ τοῖς

¹ P: om. the rest.

bearance, has turned his bloated insolence upon me. He thought me too long-lived ; my old age oppressed him ; he could not endure the idea of becoming king by other means than parricide. Justly indeed has he served me for bringing him back, a castaway, from the country, ousting the sons whom a princess bore me and declaring him heir to the throne ! I admit, Varus, my own infatuation. It was I who exasperated those sons against me by cutting off their just expectations in the interests of Antipater. When did I ever indulge them as I have this scoundrel ? To him in my own lifetime I well nigh resigned my power ; I nominated him in my will, in the public eye, heir to the throne ; I assigned him a private income of fifty talents, apart from liberal contributions from my personal revenues ; recently, when he set sail for Rome, I presented him with three hundred talents, and recommended him to Caesar, alone of all my children, as his father's pre-server. What crime did those others commit comparable to that of Antipater ? Or what proof was brought against them so convincing as that which establishes this traitor's guilt ?

" However, this parricide has presumed to open his mouth, hoping once more to smother the truth under his wiles. Varus, you must be on your guard. *I* know the creature and foresee the plausible pleading, the hypocritical lamentations, that are to follow. This is the man who, in former days, when Alexander was alive, advised me to beware of him and not to trust my life to all men's hands ; this is he who conducted me to my couch and looked round to see that no assassin was concealed ; this is he who dispensed my hours of slumber, ensured my freedom from care,

ἀνῃρημένοις λύπην καὶ διακρίνων τὴν τῶν ζώντων
εὔνοιαν ἀδελφῶν, ὁ ὑπερασπιστὴς ὁ ἐμός, ὁ σωματο-
628 φύλαξ. ὅταν ἀναμνησθῶ, Οὔαρε, τὸ πανοῦργον
ἐν ἑκάστῳ καὶ τὴν ὑπόκρισιν, ἀπιστία με τοῦ
ζῆν εἰσέρχεται καὶ θαυμάζω πῶς βαθὺν[1] οὕτως
ἐπίβουλον διέφυγον. ἀλλ' ἐπεὶ δαίμων τις ἐξερημοῖ
τὸν ἐμὸν οἶκον καί μοι τοὺς φιλτάτους ἐπανίστησιν
ἀεί, κλαύσομαι μὲν ἐγὼ τὴν ἄδικον εἱμαρμένην καὶ
κατ' ἐμαυτὸν στενάξω τὴν ἐρημίαν, διαφεύξεται
δ' οὐδεὶς διψήσας τοὐμὸν αἷμα, κἂν διὰ πάντων
μου τῶν τέκνων ὁ ἔλεγχος ἔλθῃ."

629 (3) Τοιαῦτα λέγων αὐτὸς μὲν ὑπὸ συγχύσεως
ἐνεκόπη, Νικολάῳ δ' ἑνὶ τῶν φίλων λέγειν τὰς
ἀποδείξεις ἔνευσεν. μεταξὺ δ' ὁ Ἀντίπατρος
ἐπάρας τὴν κεφαλήν, ἔμενεν γὰρ δὴ βεβλημένος
630 πρὸ τῶν ποδῶν τοῦ πατρός, ἐκβοᾷ· "σύ, πάτερ,
ὑπὲρ ἐμοῦ πεποίηκας[2] τὴν ἀπολογίαν· πῶς γὰρ
ἐγὼ πατροκτόνος, ὃν ὁμολογεῖς φύλακα διὰ παντὸς
ἐσχηκέναι; τερατείαν δέ μου καὶ ὑπόκρισιν λέγεις
τὴν εὐσέβειαν. πῶς ὁ πανοῦργος ἐν τοῖς ἄλλοις
οὕτως ἄφρων ἐγενόμην, ὡς μὴ νοεῖν, ὅτι λαθεῖν
οὐδ' ἀνθρώπους ῥάδιον τηλικοῦτον μύσος ἐνσκευα-
ζόμενον, τὸν δ' ἀπ' οὐρανοῦ δικαστὴν ἀμήχανον,
631 ὃς ἐφορᾷ πάντα καὶ πανταχοῦ πάρεστιν; ἢ τὸ
τῶν ἀδελφῶν τέλος ἠγνόουν, οὓς ὁ θεὸς οὕτως
μετῆλθε τῆς εἰς σὲ κακοβουλίας; τί δέ με καὶ
παρώξυνεν κατὰ σοῦ; βασιλείας ἐλπίς; ἀλλ' ἐβα-
σίλευον. ὑπόνοια μίσους; οὐ γὰρ ἐστεργόμην;
φόβος ἐκ σοῦ τις ἄλλος; ἀλλὰ μὴν σὲ τηρῶν

___
[1] βαρὺν PA Lat. [2] πεποίησαι LVRC.

298

consoled me in my sorrow for my victims, and sounded the feelings of his surviving brothers ; this is my buckler, my bodyguard ! When I recall, Varus, his knavery and hypocrisy on each occasion, I can scarce believe I am alive and marvel how I escaped so deep a schemer. But since some evil genius is bent on desolating my house and raising up against me one after another those who are nearest to my heart, I may weep over my unjust destiny, I may groan in spirit over my forlorn state, but not one shall escape who thirsts for my blood, no, not though conviction should extend to all my children."

(3) Here his emotion rendered further speech im- Speech of possible, and he signalled to Nicolas, one of his Antipater. friends, to state the evidence. But now Antipater, who still lay prostrate at his father's feet, raised his head and cried out : " You, father, have made my defence yourself. For, how could I be a parricide, I who, as you admit, have ever served as your protector ? You call my filial piety imposture and hypocrisy. How could I, cunning in all else, have been so senseless as not to perceive that, while it was difficult to conceal from man the concoction of so atrocious a crime, it was impossible to hide it from the Judge in heaven, who sees all, who is present everywhere ? Was I ignorant of my brothers' fate, whom God so relentlessly punished for their wicked designs upon you ? And then, what motive could have instigated me against you ? Aspiration to the throne ? But I reigned already ! Suspicion of your hatred ? But was I not beloved ? Had I other reason to fear you ?[a] Nay, by preserving you I

---

[a] Possibly for ἐκ σοῦ we should read ἔξω σου: " Had I reason to fear others beside you ? "

JOSEPHUS

632 ἑτέροις φοβερὸς ἤμην. ἔνδεια χρημάτων; καὶ τίνι
μᾶλλον ἐξῆν ἀναλίσκειν; εἰ γὰρ ἐξωλέστατος
πάντων ἀνθρώπων ἐγενόμην καὶ θηρίου ψυχὴν
εἶχον ἀνημέρου, πάτερ, οὐκ ἂν ταῖς σαῖς εὐεργε-
σίαις ἐνικήθην, ὃν κατήγαγες μέν, ὡς ἔφης αὐτός,
προέκρινας δὲ τοσούτων τέκνων, ἀπέδειξας δὲ ζῶν
βασιλέα, δι᾽ ὑπερβολὴν δὲ τῶν ἄλλων ἀγαθῶν
633 ἐποίησας ἐπίφθονον; ὢ τάλας ἐγὼ τῆς πικρᾶς
ἀποδημίας, ὡς πολὺν ἔδωκα καιρὸν τῷ φθόνῳ καὶ
μακρὰν τοῖς ἐπιβουλεύουσι διωρίαν. σοὶ δέ, πάτερ,
καὶ τοῖς σοῖς ἀγῶσιν ἀπεδήμουν, ἵνα μὴ Συλλαῖος
τοῦ σοῦ γήρως καταφρονήσῃ. Ῥώμη μοι μάρτυς
τῆς εὐσεβείας καὶ ὁ τῆς οἰκουμένης προστάτης
Καῖσαρ, ὁ φιλοπάτορα πολλάκις με εἰπών. λάβε,
πάτερ, τὰ παρ᾽ αὐτοῦ γράμματα. ταῦτα τῶν
ἐνθάδε διαβολῶν πιστότερα, ταῦτα ἀπολογία μοι
μόνη, τούτοις τῆς εἰς σὲ φιλοστοργίας τεκμηρίοις
634 χρῶμαι. μέμνησο δὲ ὡς οὐχ ἑκὼν ἔπλεον, ἐπιστάμενος τὴν ἐμφωλεύουσαν τῇ βασιλείᾳ κατ᾽ ἐμοῦ
δυσμένειαν. σὺ δέ με, πάτερ, ἄκων ἀπώλεσας,
ἀναγκάσας καιρὸν διαβολῆς δοῦναι τῷ φθόνῳ.
πάρειμι δὲ ἐπὶ τοὺς ἐλέγχους, πάρειμι διὰ γῆς καὶ
θαλάσσης οὐδὲν οὐδαμοῦ παθὼν ὁ πατροκτόνος.
635 ἀλλὰ μήπω με τούτῳ φίλει[1] τῷ τεκμηρίῳ· κατ-
έγνωσμαι γὰρ καὶ παρὰ θεῷ καὶ παρὰ σοί, πάτερ.
κατεγνωσμένος δὲ δέομαι μὴ ταῖς ἄλλων βασάνοις
πιστεύειν, ἀλλὰ κατ᾽ ἐμοῦ φερέσθω τὸ πῦρ,

---

[1] μήπω . . . φίλει PAM Lat.: μήπω τούτῳ ὠφέλημαι the
rest ; text apparently corrupt.

---

[a] " Lover of his father."
[b] Text doubtful ; perhaps "I do not ask to be given the
benefit of this evidence."

inspired fear in others. Was it lack of money ? Who had more at his disposal than I ? Even had I been the most abandoned of men, with the heart of a ferocious beast, must I not have been reclaimed, father, by your benefactions ? For, as you have said yourself, you recalled me from exile, you gave me preference over such a number of sons, you proclaimed me king in your own lifetime, and by loading me with other favours made me the envy of all. Ah me ! that fatal journey ! What an opportunity I gave to jealousy, what an ample period to those who were intriguing against me ! Yet it was for you, father, and to fight your battles that I took that journey, to prevent Syllaeus from treating your old age with contempt. Rome is witness to my filial piety and Caesar, the lord of the universe, who has often called me ' Philopator.' [a] Take, father, these letters from him. These are more trustworthy than the calumnies against me here ; these are my sole vindication ; here are the proofs which I offer of my tender feelings for you. Remember how reluctantly I embarked, knowing the lurking hostility to me within this realm. It was you, father, who involuntarily brought about my ruin, by compelling me to give my envious foes an opportunity for calumny. But here I am to meet my accusers ; here I am, the ' parricide,' who has traversed sea and land, and nowhere been molested ! But I do not ask for your love on the strength of the evidence so far given of my innocence ; [b] for I stand condemned before God and before you, father. But, condemned though I am, I entreat you not to rely on admissions extracted by the torture of others. Let the fire be

ὁδευέτω διὰ τῶν ἐμῶν σπλάγχνων τὰ ὄργανα,
μὴ φειδέσθω¹ τοῦ μιαροῦ σώματος· εἰ γὰρ εἰμὶ
πατροκτόνος, οὐκ ὀφείλω θνήσκειν ἀβασάνιστος.²''
636 τοιαῦτα μετ' ὀλοφυρμοῦ καὶ δακρύων ἐκβοῶν τούς
τε ἄλλους ἅπαντας καὶ τὸν Οὔαρον εἰς οἶκτον
προυκαλέσατο, μόνον δὲ ὁ θυμὸς Ἡρώδην ἄδακρυν
διεκράτει τοὺς ἐλέγχους ἀληθεῖς ἐπιστάμενον.

637 (4) Ἐν τούτῳ Νικόλαος τοῦ βασιλέως κελεύσαντος πολλὰ πρὸς τὸ πανοῦργον τὸ Ἀντιπάτρου
προειπὼν καὶ τὸν ἐπ' αὐτῷ διαχέας ἔλεον, ἔπειτα
πικρὰν κατηγορίαν κατετείνατο, πάντα μὲν τὰ
κατὰ τὴν βασιλείαν κακουργήματα περιτιθεὶς αὐτῷ,
μάλιστα δὲ τὴν ἀναίρεσιν τῶν ἀδελφῶν, ἀποδεικνὺς
ταῖς ἐκείνου διαβολαῖς ἀπολωλότας. ἐπιβουλεύειν
δὲ αὐτὸν ἔλεγεν καὶ τοῖς περιοῦσιν ὡς ἐφέδροις
τῆς διαδοχῆς· τὸν γὰρ παρασκευάσαντα πατρὶ
φάρμακον ἦ πού γ' ἂν ἀδελφῶν ἀποσχέσθαι;
638 προελθὼν δ' ἐπὶ τὸν ἔλεγχον τῆς φαρμακείας τάς
τε μηνύσεις [ἐξῆς]³ ἐπεδείκνυεν καὶ περὶ Φερώρα
κατεσχετλίαζεν, ὅτι κἀκεῖνον Ἀντίπατρος ποιήσειεν ἀδελφοκτόνον καὶ τοὺς φιλτάτους τῷ βασιλεῖ
διαφθείρας ὅλον τοῦ μύσους ἀναπλήσειεν τὸν οἶκον,
ἄλλα τε πολλὰ πρὸς τούτοις εἰπὼν καὶ ἀποδείξας
καταπαύει τὸν λόγον.

639 (5) Οὔαρος δὲ ἀπολογεῖσθαι κελεύσας τὸν Ἀντίπατρον, ὡς οὐδὲν πλέον εἰπὼν ἢ '' θεός ἐστίν μοι
τοῦ μηδὲν ἀδικεῖν μάρτυς '' ἔκειτο σιγῶν, αἰτήσας

---

¹ The мss. add ὀλοφυρμὸς (or -οῦ), an obvious gloss, absent
from Lat.
² Bekker: ἀβασανίστως mss.   ³ om. PAM.

applied to me! Let the instruments of torment course through my frame nor spare this polluted body! For, if I am a parricide, I ought not to die without being put upon the rack."

These ejaculations, accompanied by moaning and tears, moved all to compassion, including Varus. Herod alone remained dry-eyed, furious and knowing that the evidence was true.[a]

(4) Thereupon Nicolas, as ordered by the king, addressed the assembly. He began with a full exposure of Antipater's knavery, dissipating the commiseration which his speech had aroused. He then launched out into a severe indictment, attributing to him all the crimes which had been committed throughout the realm, and in particular the execution of his brothers, demonstrating that they owed their death to Antipater's calumnies. He added that he had further designs on the survivors as presumptive heirs to the throne; "Would one who had prepared to poison his father have stopped short at his brothers?" Passing on to the evidence for the poisoning plot, he brought forward in succession all the information extracted; being roused to indignation on the subject of Pheroras, at the idea of Antipater converting even him into a fratricide and, by corrupting the king's nearest of kin, infecting the whole palace with pollution. With many more observations, supported by proofs, Nicolas concluded his speech. *Speech of Nicolas.*

(5) Varus then called on Antipater for his defence. But he would say no more than "God is witness of my innocence" and remained prostrate and silent. *Outcome of the trial: Antipater imprisoned.*

---

[a] According to *A.* xvii. 106 even Herod was not unmoved, though he sought to conceal his emotion.

τὸ φάρμακον δίδωσί τινι τῶν ἐπὶ θανάτῳ κατα-
640 κρίτων δεσμώτῃ πιεῖν. τοῦ δὲ παραχρῆμα τελευτήσαντος, ὁ μὲν ἀπορρήτους ποιήσας τὰς πρὸς
Ἡρώδην ὁμιλίας καὶ τὰ περὶ τὸ συνέδριον Καίσαρι
γράψας μετὰ μίαν ἡμέραν χωρίζεται· δεσμεῖ δὲ
ὁ βασιλεὺς Ἀντίπατρον καὶ πρὸς Καίσαρα τοὺς
δηλώσοντας τὴν συμφορὰν ἐξέπεμψεν.

641   (6) Μετὰ δὲ ταῦτα καὶ κατὰ Σαλώμης ἐπίβουλος Ἀντίπατρος εὑρίσκεται¹· τῶν γὰρ Ἀντιφίλου τις οἰκετῶν ἧκεν ἐπιστολὰς κομίζων ἀπὸ
Ῥώμης παρὰ Λιουίας² θεραπαινίδος, Ἀκμῆς τοὔνομα. καὶ παρὰ μὲν ταύτης ἐπέσταλτο βασιλεῖ
τὰς παρὰ Σαλώμης ἐπιστολὰς ἐν τοῖς Λιουίας²
εὑρηκέναι γράμμασιν, πεπομφέναι δὲ αὐτῷ λάθρα
642 δι' εὔνοιαν. αἱ δὲ τῆς Σαλώμης λοιδορίας τε τοῦ
βασιλέως περιεῖχον πικροτάτας καὶ κατηγορίαν
μεγίστην. ταύτας δὲ πλάσας Ἀντίπατρος καὶ τὴν
643 Ἀκμὴν διαφθείρας ἔπεισεν Ἡρώδῃ πέμψαι. δι-
ηλέγχθη δὲ ἐκ τῆς πρὸς αὐτὸν ἐπιστολῆς· καὶ
γὰρ ἐκείνῳ τὸ γύναιον ἔγραψεν· " ὡς ἐβουλήθης,
ἔγραψά σου τῷ πατρὶ καὶ τὰς ἐπιστολὰς ἐκείνας
ἔπεμψα, πεπεισμένη τὸν βασιλέα μὴ φείσεσθαι τῆς
ἀδελφῆς, ὅταν ἀναγνῷ. καλῶς δὲ ποιήσεις, ἐπειδὰν ἀπαρτισθῇ πάντα, μνημονεύσας ὧν ὑπέσχου."
644   (7) Ταύτης φωραθείσης τῆς ἐπιστολῆς καὶ τῶν
κατὰ Σαλώμης ἐνσκευασθεισῶν, ἔννοια μὲν ἐμπίπτει τῷ βασιλεῖ τάχα καὶ ⟨τὰ⟩³ κατ' Ἀλεξάνδρου
πλασθῆναι γράμματα, περιαλγὴς δ' ἦν ὑπὸ τοῦ
πάθους ὡς παρ' ὀλίγον καὶ τὴν ἀδελφὴν ἀπο-

¹ ἐπιβουλὰς Ἀντ. εὑρίσκ. πεποιηκὼς PAM.
² Λευίας PA : Ἰουλίας the rest ; cf. § 566.
³ καὶ τὰ Destinon : καὶ mss.

304

The governor, thereupon, called for the poison and had it applied to a prisoner under sentence of death, who drank it and instantly expired. Then, after a private interview with Herod, Varus drafted his report of the meeting for Caesar, and a day later took his departure. The king had Antipater put in irons and dispatched messengers to the emperor to inform him of the catastrophe.

(6) It was subsequently discovered that Antipater had also plotted against Salome. For a domestic of Antiphilus arrived from Rome with letters from a maid-servant of Livia,[a] named Acme ; she wrote to the king to say that she had found among Livia's papers some letters from Salome, which, as his well-wisher, she had privately transmitted to him. These letters of Salome, containing the most cruel abuse of the king and the most scathing condemnation of his conduct, were forgeries of Antipater, who had bribed Acme to send them to Herod. He was convicted by the letter which the woman addressed at the same time to him, in these terms : " As you desired, I have written to your father and forwarded those letters, and feel sure that, when he has read them, he will not spare his sister. Be good enough, when all is over, to remember what you promised." *Discovery of Antipater's plot against Salome.*

(7) When this letter was brought to light, with those concocted to injure Salome, a suspicion crossed the king's mind that perhaps the letters incriminating Alexander were also forgeries.[b] He was, moreover, deeply distressed at the thought that he had almost killed his sister also, owing to Antipater's intrigues. *Herod's illness and new will, naming Antipas heir.*

[a] Livia Drusilla, the wife of Augustus, and after his death known as Julia Augusta ; by her former husband she was mother of the emperor Tiberius.

[b] Cf. § 528.

κτείνας δι’ Ἀντίπατρον· οὐκέτι οὖν ἀνεβάλλετο
645 λαβεῖν τιμωρίαν ὑπὲρ ἁπάντων. ὡρμημένος δ’
ἐπὶ τὸν Ἀντίπατρον ἐπεσχέθη νόσῳ χαλεπῇ· περὶ
μέντοι τῆς Ἀκμῆς καὶ τῶν κατὰ Σαλώμης ἐσκευ-
646 ωρημένων ἐπέστειλεν Καίσαρι. τήν τε διαθήκην
αἰτήσας μετέγραφεν, καὶ βασιλέα μὲν ἀπεδείκνυεν
Ἀντίπαν ἀμελῶν τῶν πρεσβυτάτων, Ἀρχελάου
καὶ Φιλίππου· διαβεβλήκει γὰρ καὶ τούτους
Ἀντίπατρος· Καίσαρι δὲ σὺν τοῖς δίχα[1] χρημάτων
δώροις χίλια τάλαντα, τῇ δὲ γυναικὶ καὶ τέκνοις
αὐτοῦ καὶ φίλοις καὶ ἀπελευθέροις περὶ πεντακόσια,
ἀπένειμεν δὲ καὶ τοῖς ἄλλοις παισὶν[2] τῆς τε χώρας
οὐκ ὀλίγα καὶ τῶν χρημάτων· λαμπροτάταις δὲ
δωρεαῖς ἐτίμα Σαλώμην τὴν ἀδελφήν. ἐν μὲν οὖν
ταῖς διαθήκαις ταῦτα διωρθώσατο.

647 (xxxiii. 1) Προῄει δ’ αὐτῷ πρὸς τὸ χαλεπώτερον ἡ νόσος, ἅτε δὴ τῶν ἀρρωστημάτων ἐν
γήρᾳ καὶ ἀθυμίᾳ ἐπιπεσόντων· ἦν μὲν γὰρ ἤδη
σχεδὸν ἐτῶν ἑβδομήκοντα, τεταπείνωτο δὲ τὴν
ψυχὴν ταῖς περὶ τῶν τέκνων συμφοραῖς, ὡς μηδ’
ἐν ὑγιείᾳ[3] τι τῶν ἡδέων προσίεσθαι. τῆς νόσου
δ’ ἦν ἐπίτασις ζῶν Ἀντίπατρος, ὃν οὐκ ἐν παρέργῳ,
ῥαΐσας δὲ προῄρητο ἀνελεῖν.

648 (2) Γίνεται δ’ ἐν ταῖς συμφοραῖς αὐτῷ καὶ
δημοτική τις ἐπανάστασις. δύο ἦσαν σοφισταὶ
κατὰ τὴν πόλιν μάλιστα δοκοῦντες ἀκριβοῦν τὰ

---

[1] Havercamp on ms. authority: διὰ most mss.; cf. B. i.
104 for the same error.
[2] Destinon (after A. xvii. 147 υἱέσιν): ἅπασιν mss.
[3] ὑγείᾳ mss.

---

[a] Literally “without money.”
[b] Greek “sophists.” The Greek term, originally free
from any sinister associations, for a paid professor of

He determined, therefore, to delay no longer to punish him for all his crimes. But when proceeding to extreme measures against Antipater, he was arrested by a serious illness. He wrote, however, to Caesar on the subject of Acme and the fraud which had been practised on Salome ; he also called for his will and modified it. He now named Antipas king, passing over his eldest sons, Archelaus and Philip, who had also been the objects of Antipater's calumnies. To Augustus he bequeathed, besides gifts in kind,[a] one thousand talents ; to the empress, to the children, friends and freedmen of the emperor about five hundred ; to the other members of his own family he assigned large tracts of territory and considerable sums of money, honouring his sister Salome with the most magnificent presents of all. Such were the corrections which Herod made in his will.

(xxxiii. 1) His illness steadily grew worse, aggravated as were the attacks of disease by age and despondency. For he was now nearly seventy years old, and his tragic experiences with his children had so broken his spirit, that even in good health he no longer enjoyed any of the pleasures of life. His malady was further increased by the thought that Antipater was still alive ; for he had determined that his execution should be no casual affair, but seriously undertaken on his recovery.

Herod's increasing illness.

(2) To his other troubles was now added an insurrection of the populace. There were in the capital two doctors[b] with a reputation as profound experts in the laws of their country, who con-

A seditious attempt to pull down the golden eagle from the Temple 4 B.C.

rhetoric etc. is employed by Josephus as the equivalent of the Jewish " Rabbi."

πάτρια καὶ διὰ τοῦτο ἐν παντὶ τῷ ἔθνει μεγίστης
ἠξιωμένοι δόξης, Ἰούδας τε υἱὸς Σεπφωραίου[1] καὶ
649 Ματθίας ἕτερος Μαργάλου. τούτοις οὐκ ὀλίγοι
προσῄεσαν τῶν νέων ἐξηγουμένοις τοὺς νόμους,
καὶ συχνὸν συνεῖχον[2] ὁσημέραι τῶν ἡβώντων στρατόπεδον. οἳ τότε τὸν βασιλέα πυνθανόμενοι ταῖς
ἀθυμίαις ὑπεκρέοντα[3] καὶ τῇ νόσῳ λόγον καθίεσαν
εἰς τοὺς γνωρίμους, ὡς ἄρα καιρὸς ἐπιτηδειότατος
εἴη τιμωρεῖν ἤδη τῷ θεῷ καὶ τὰ κατασκευασθέντα
650 παρὰ τοὺς πατρίους νόμους ἔργα κατασπᾶν. ἀ-
θέμιτον γὰρ εἶναι κατὰ τὸν ναὸν ἢ εἰκόνας ἢ προ-
τομὰς ἢ ζῴου τινὸς ἐπώνυμον ἔργον εἶναι· κατ-
εσκευάκει δ᾽ ὁ βασιλεὺς ὑπὲρ τὴν μεγάλην πύλην
ἀετὸν χρυσοῦν· ὃν δὴ τότε παρῄνουν ἐκκόπτειν οἱ
σοφισταί, καλὸν εἶναι λέγοντες, εἰ καί τις γένοιτο
κίνδυνος, ὑπὲρ τοῦ πατρίου νόμου θνήσκειν· τοῖς
γὰρ οὕτω τελευτῶσιν ἀθάνατόν τε τὴν ψυχὴν καὶ
τὴν ἐν ἀγαθοῖς αἴσθησιν αἰώνιον παραμένειν, τοὺς
δὲ ἀγεννεῖς[4] καὶ τῆς ἑαυτῶν σοφίας ἀπείρους
ἀγνοοῦντας φιλοψυχεῖν καὶ πρὸ τοῦ δι᾽ ἀρετῆς τὸν
ἐκ νόσου θάνατον αἱρεῖσθαι.

651   (3) Ἅμα δὲ τοῖς ἐκείνων λόγοις διεφημίσθη
καὶ θνήσκειν ὁ βασιλεύς, ὥστε θαρραλεώτερον
ἥπτοντο τῆς ἐπιχειρήσεως οἱ νέοι. μέσης γοῦν
ἡμέρας καὶ πολλῶν κατὰ τὸ ἱερὸν ἀναστρεφομένων
σχοίνοις παχείαις καθιμήσαντες σφᾶς αὐτοὺς ἀπὸ
τοῦ τέγους τὸν χρυσοῦν ἀετὸν ἐξέκοπτον πελέκεσιν.

---

[1] Variant readings Σεπφεραίου, Σεπφαιρέου : A. ‖ has
Σαριφαίου.   [2] συχνὸν συνεῖχον P : συνῆγον the rest.
[3] LVRC : ὑπορ(ρ)έοντα the rest.   [4] ἀγενεῖς PC.

---

[a] Perhaps in imitation of the pediments of Greek temples.
In the early temples of Zeus the flat surface of the pediment

sequently enjoyed the highest esteem of the whole
nation ; their names were Judas, son of Sepphoraeus,
and Matthias, son of Margalus. Their lectures on
the laws were attended by a large youthful audience,
and day after day they drew together quite an army
of men in their prime. Hearing now that the king
was gradually sinking under despondency and disease, these doctors threw out hints to their friends
that this was the fitting moment to avenge God's
honour and to pull down those structures which had
been erected in defiance of their fathers' laws. It
was, in fact, unlawful to place in the temple either
images or busts or any representation whatsoever of
a living creature ; notwithstanding this, the king
had erected over the great gate a golden eagle.[a]
This it was which these doctors now exhorted their
disciples to cut down, telling them that, even if the
action proved hazardous, it was a noble deed to die
for the law of one's country ; for the souls of those
who came to such an end attained immortality and
an eternally abiding sense of felicity ; it was only
the ignoble, uninitiated in their philosophy, who
clung in their ignorance to life and preferred death
on a sick-bed to that of a hero.

(3) While they were discoursing in this strain, a
rumour spread that the king was dying ; the news
caused the young men to throw themselves more
boldly into the enterprise. At mid-day, accordingly,
when numbers of people were perambulating the
temple, they let themselves down from the roof by
stout cords and began chopping off the golden eagle

Punishment of the culprits.

was ornamented with an eagle as a symbol of the god,
whence the whole pediment derived its name (ἀετός or
ἀέτωμα).

JOSEPHUS

652 ἠγγέλθη δ' εὐθέως τῷ βασιλέως στρατηγῷ, κἀκεῖνος μετὰ χειρὸς οὐκ ὀλίγης ἀναδραμὼν περὶ τεσσαράκοντα νεανίας συλλαμβάνει καὶ κατήγαγεν πρὸς
653 βασιλέα. πυνθανομένῳ δ' αὐτῷ πρῶτον, εἰ τολμή-
σειαν τὸν χρυσοῦν ἀετὸν ἐκκόπτειν, ὡμολόγουν.
ἔπειτα, τίνος κελεύσαντος, ἀπεκρίναντο τοῦ πατρίου
νόμου. τί δ' οὕτως γεγήθασιν διερωτήσαντος,
ἀναιρεῖσθαι μέλλοντες, ἔλεγον ὅτι πλειόνων ἀγαθῶν
ἀπολαύσουσιν μετὰ τὴν τελευτήν.

654 (4) Ἐπὶ τούτοις ὁ βασιλεὺς δι' ὑπερβολὴν
ὀργῆς κρείττων τῆς νόσου γενόμενος πρόεισιν εἰς
ἐκκλησίαν, καὶ πολλὰ τῶν ἀνδρῶν κατηγορήσας
ὡς ἱεροσύλων καὶ προφάσει τοῦ νόμου πειραζόντων
655 τι μεῖζον ἠξίου κολάζειν ὡς ἀσεβεῖς. ὁ δὲ δῆμος
δείσας, μὴ διὰ πολλῶν ὁ ἔλεγχος ἔλθῃ, παρεκάλει
πρῶτον μὲν τοὺς ὑποθεμένους τὴν πρᾶξιν, ἔπειτα
τοὺς ἐν αὐτῇ συλληφθέντας κολάσαντα τοῖς λοιποῖς τὴν ὀργὴν ἀφιέναι. πείθεται μόλις ὁ βασιλεύς, καὶ τοὺς μὲν καθιμήσαντας ἑαυτοὺς ἅμα
τοῖς σοφισταῖς κατέκαυσε ζῶντας, τοὺς λοιποὺς
δὲ τῶν συλληφθέντων παρέδωκεν τοῖς ὑπηρέταις
ἀνελεῖν.

656 (5) Ἔνθεν αὐτοῦ τὸ σῶμα πᾶν ἡ νόσος δια-
λαβοῦσα ποικίλοις πάθεσιν ἐμερίζετο· πυρετὸς μὲν
γὰρ ἦν οὐ λάβρος, κνησμὸς δὲ ἀφόρητος τῆς ἐπι-
φανείας ὅλης καὶ κόλου συνεχεῖς ἀλγηδόνες, περί
τε τοὺς πόδας ὥσπερ ὑδρωπιῶντος οἰδήματα, τοῦ
τε ἤτρου φλεγμονὴ καὶ δὴ[1] αἰδοίου σηπεδὼν σκώ-

---

[1] δὴ Niese : δι' mss.

---

[a] Perhaps " the captain of the Temple " is intended (cf.
Acts iv. 1, v. 24).

with hatchets. The king's captain,[a] to whom the matter was immediately reported, hastened to the scene with a considerable force, arrested about forty of the young men and conducted them to the king. Herod first asked them whether they had dared to cut down the golden eagle; they admitted it. "Who ordered you to do so?" he continued. "The law of our fathers." "And why so exultant, when you will shortly be put to death?" "Because, after our death, we shall enjoy greater felicity."

(4) These proceedings provoked the king to such fury that he forgot his disease and had himself carried to a public assembly,[b] where at great length he denounced the men as sacrilegious persons who, under the pretext of zeal for the law, had some more ambitious aim in view, and demanded that they should be punished for impiety. The people, apprehensive of wholesale prosecutions, besought him to confine the punishment to the instigators of the deed and to those who had been arrested in the perpetration of it, and to forgo his anger against the rest. The king grudgingly consented; those who had let themselves down from the roof together with the doctors he had burnt alive; the remainder of those arrested he handed over to his executioners.

(5) From this time onwards Herod's malady began to spread to his whole body and his sufferings took a variety of forms. He had fever, though not a raging fever, an intolerable itching of the whole skin, continuous pains in the intestines, tumours in the feet as in dropsy, inflammation of the abdomen and

Herod's last illness.

[b] A meeting of the magistrates in the theatre at Jericho, according to *A.* xvii. 160 f.

ληκας γεννῶσα, πρὸς τούτοις ὀρθόπνοια καὶ δύσπνοια καὶ σπασμοὶ πάντων τῶν μελῶν, ὥστε τοὺς ἐπιθειάζοντας ποινὴν εἶναι τῶν σοφιστῶν τὰ
657 νοσήματα λέγειν. ὁ δὲ παλαίων τοσούτοις πάθεσιν ὅμως τοῦ ζῆν ἀντείχετο, σωτηρίαν τε ἤλπιζεν καὶ θεραπείας ἐπενόει· διαβὰς γοῦν τὸν Ἰορδάνην τοῖς κατὰ Καλλιρρόην ἐχρῆτο θερμοῖς· ταῦτα δ' ἔξεισι μὲν εἰς τὴν Ἀσφαλτῖτιν λίμνην, ὑπὸ γλυκύτητος δ' ἐστὶ [καὶ]¹ πότιμα. δόξαν δὲ ἐνταῦθα τοῖς ἰατροῖς ἐλαίῳ θερμῷ πᾶν ἀναθάλψαι τὸ σῶμα χαλασθὲν εἰς πλήρη πύελον, ἐκλύει καὶ τοὺς
658 ὀφθαλμοὺς ὡς τεθνεὼς ἀνέστρεψεν. θορύβου δὲ τῶν θεραπευόντων γενομένου πρὸς μὲν τὴν φωνὴν ἀνήνεγκεν, εἰς δὲ τὸ λοιπὸν ἀπογνοὺς τὴν σωτηρίαν τοῖς τε στρατιώταις ἀνὰ πεντήκοντα δραχμὰς ἐκέλευσεν διανεῖμαι καὶ πολλὰ χρήματα τοῖς ἡγεμόσι καὶ τοῖς φίλοις.

659   (6) Αὐτὸς δὲ ὑποστρέφων εἰς Ἱεριχοῦντα παραγίνεται μελαγχολῶν ἤδη, καὶ μόνον οὐκ ἀπειλῶν αὐτῷ τῷ θανάτῳ προέκοπτεν εἰς ἐπιβολὴν² ἀθεμίτου πράξεως· τοὺς γὰρ ἀφ' ἑκάστης κώμης ἐπισήμους ἄνδρας ἐξ ὅλης Ἰουδαίας συναγαγὼν εἰς τὸν καλούμενον ἱππόδρομον ἐκέλευσεν συγ-
660 κλεῖσαι. προσκαλεσάμενος δὲ Σαλώμην τὴν ἀδελφὴν καὶ τὸν ἄνδρα ταύτης Ἀλεξᾶν " οἶδα," ἔφη, " Ἰουδαίους τὸν ἐμὸν ἑορτάσοντας θάνατον, δύνα-

¹ om. PAM Lat.
² Hudson : ἐπιβουλὴν MSS.

gangrene of the privy parts, engendering worms,[a] in addition to asthma,[b] with great difficulty in breathing, and convulsions in all his limbs. His condition led diviners to pronounce his maladies a judgement on him for his treatment of the professors. Yet, struggling as he was with such numerous sufferings, he clung to life, hoped for recovery, and devised one remedy after another. Thus he crossed the Jordan to take the warm baths at Callirrhoe, the waters of which descend into the Lake Asphaltitis[c] and from their sweetness are also used for drink. There, the physicians deciding to raise the temperature of his whole body with hot oil, he was lowered into a bath full of that liquid, whereupon he fainted and turned up his eyes as though he were dead. His attendants raising an uproar, their cries brought him to himself, but, now despairing of recovery, he gave orders to distribute fifty drachmas per head to the soldiers and considerable sums to their officers and to his friends.

Herod at Callirrhoe.

(6) He started on his return journey and reached Jericho in an atrabilious condition, in which, hurling defiance as it were at death itself, he proceeded to devise an outrageous scheme. Having assembled the distinguished men from every village from one end of Judaea to the other, he ordered them to be locked into the hippodrome. He then summoned his sister Salome and her husband Alexas and said : " I know that the Jews will celebrate my death by

Herod at Jericho : arrest of the notables.

---

[a] *Cf.* the description of the death of his grandson, Herod Agrippa I, " eaten of worms," in Acts xii. 23.

[b] The Greek word means inability to breathe except in an upright posture.

[c] The Dead Sea. Callirrhoe (" Baths of Herod ") was near the N.E. end of it.

μαι δὲ πενθεῖσθαι δι' ἑτέρων καὶ λαμπρὸν ἐπιτάφιον
ἔχειν, ἂν ὑμεῖς θελήσητε ταῖς ἐμαῖς ἐντολαῖς
ὑπουργῆσαι. τούσδε τοὺς φρουρουμένους ἄνδρας
ἐπειδὰν ἐκπνεύσω τάχιστα κτείνατε, περιστήσαν-
τες τοὺς στρατιώτας, ἵνα πᾶσα Ἰουδαία καὶ πᾶς
οἶκος ἄκων ἐπ' ἐμοὶ δακρύσῃ."

661   (7) Ταῦτα ἐνετέλλετο, καὶ παρὰ τῶν ἐν Ῥώμῃ
πρέσβεων ἧκον ἐπιστολαί, δι' ὧν Ἀκμὴ μὲν ἀν-
ῃρημένη κελεύσαντος Καίσαρος ἐδηλοῦτο, θανάτῳ
δ' Ἀντίπατρος κατάκριτος· ἔγραφόν γε μὴν ὡς,
εἰ καὶ φυγαδεύειν αὐτὸν ἐθελήσειεν ὁ πατήρ,
662 ἐπιτρέποι Καῖσαρ. ὁ δὲ βραχὺ μὲν πρὸς τὴν
εὐθυμίαν ἀνήνεγκεν, αὖθις δέ, καὶ γὰρ ἐνδείᾳ
τροφῆς καὶ βηχὶ σπασμώδει διετείνετο, τῶν ἀλγηδόνων ἡσσηθεὶς φθάσαι τὴν εἱμαρμένην ἐπεβάλετο.
λαβὼν δὲ μῆλον ᾔτησεν καὶ μαχαίριον, εἰώθει γὰρ
ἀποτέμνων ἐσθίειν, ἔπειτα περιαθρήσας μή τις ὁ
κωλύων εἴη, ἐπῆρεν τὴν δεξιὰν ὡς πλήξων ἑαυτόν.
προσδραμὼν δὲ ἐκώλυσεν Ἀχίαβος ὁ ἀνεψιὸς
663 αὐτοῦ τὴν χεῖρα κατασχών. οἰμωγὴ δ' εὐθέως
ἤρθη μεγίστη κατὰ τὸ βασίλειον ὡς οἰχομένου
βασιλέως, καὶ ταχέως ἀκούσας Ἀντίπατρος ἀνα-
θαρρεῖ τε καὶ γεγηθὼς τοὺς φύλακας ἱκέτευεν ἐπὶ
χρήμασιν ἐξαφεῖναι λύσαντας αὐτόν. ὁ δὲ ἡγεμὼν
οὐ μόνον ἐκώλυσεν ἀλλὰ καὶ βασιλεῖ δραμὼν

---

[a] *A.* xvii. 176, " He was not blind to the feelings of the
Jews and knew what relief and intense delight his death
would bring them." A Jewish festival on the seventh of
the month Kislev (December), of which the occasion is unrecorded in the Jewish calendar known as *Megillath Taanith*,
is said by a late Scholiast to commemorate Herod's death;

a festival ;[a] yet I can obtain a vicarious mourning and a magnificent funeral, if you consent to follow my instructions. You know these men here in custody ; the moment I expire have them surrounded by the soldiers and massacred ; so shall all Judaea and every household weep for me, whether they will or no.''

(7) At the moment when he was giving these instructions, he received letters from his ambassadors at Rome, informing him that Acme[b] had been executed by Caesar's orders and Antipater condemned to death ; but, the letter continued, if his father were content with banishing him, he had Caesar's permission to do so. At this news he for a while recovered his spirits, but later, under the strain of lack of nourishment and a convulsive cough, overpowered by his tortures, he endeavoured to anticipate the hour of destiny. He took an apple and called for a knife, as it was his custom to cut up this fruit when eating it, and then, looking round to see that there was no one to prevent him, raised his hand to strike himself. However, his cousin Achiab rushed up and seizing his hand arrested the blow. Instantly there arose loud lamentations throughout the palace, in the belief that the king had passed away. Antipater, quick to catch the sound, took heart again and, radiant with joy, besought his jailers, for a remuneration, to loose him and let him go. The head jailer, however, not only prevented this, but hastened to the king and reported his prisoner's

Execution of Acme.

Herod attempts suicide.

Execution of Antipater.

but the tradition is untrustworthy. It appears from the sequel (*B.* ii. 10) that Herod died a little before Passover. See Zeitlin, *Megillat Taanit*, pp. 100 f., Schürer, *G.J.V.* (ed. 3) i. 416 f.   [b] § 641.

664 ἀνήγγειλεν τὴν ἐπιβολήν.[1] ἀνέκραγεν δ' ἐκεῖνος
ἰσχυρότερον τῆς νόσου καὶ παραχρῆμα πέμψας
τοὺς δορυφόρους ἀποκτείνει τὸν Ἀντίπατρον.
θάψαι δὲ τὸν νεκρὸν αὐτοῦ προστάξας ἐν Ὑρκανίᾳ
πάλιν τὰς διαθήκας ἐπανορθοῦται, καὶ διάδοχον
μὲν Ἀρχέλαον τὸν πρεσβύτατον υἱόν, ἀδελφὸν δὲ
Ἀντίπα, γράφει, τετράρχην δὲ Ἀντίπαν.

665 (8) Μετὰ δὲ τὴν ἀναίρεσιν τοῦ παιδὸς ἐπιβιοὺς
πέντε ἡμέρας τελευτᾷ, βασιλεύσας ἀφ' οὗ μὲν
ἀποκτείνας Ἀντίγονον ἐκράτησεν τῶν πραγμάτων
ἔτη τέσσαρα καὶ τριάκοντα, ἀφ' οὗ δὲ ὑπὸ Ῥωμαίων ἀπεδείχθη βασιλεὺς ἑπτὰ καὶ τριάκοντα,
καὶ κατὰ μὲν τὰ ἄλλα πάντα τύχῃ δεξιᾷ χρησάμενος, εἰ καί τις ἄλλος, ὅστις κατεκτήσατο βασιλείαν ἰδιώτης ὢν καὶ τοσούτῳ χρόνῳ φυλάξας
ἰδίοις τέκνοις κατέλιπεν, ἐν δὲ τοῖς κατ' οἶκον

666 ἀτυχέστατος. πρὶν δὲ γνῶναι τὴν τελευτὴν αὐτοῦ
τὸ στρατιωτικόν, προελθοῦσα μετὰ τἀνδρὸς[2] ἡ
Σαλώμη διαφῆκεν τοὺς δεσμώτας, οὓς κτείνειν ὁ
βασιλεὺς ἐνετείλατο, μεταπεισθῆναι τὸν βασιλέα
λέγουσα καὶ πάλιν ἀναπέμπειν ἕκαστον εἰς τὰ
ἴδια. τούτων δ' οἰχομένων ἐδήλουν ἤδη τοῖς
στρατιώταις καὶ συνῆγον αὐτοὺς εἰς ἐκκλησίαν
μετὰ τοῦ λοιποῦ πλήθους ἐν τῷ κατὰ Ἱεριχοῦντα

667 ἀμφιθεάτρῳ. ἔνθα παρελθὼν Πτολεμαῖος ὁ καὶ
τὸν σημαντῆρα δακτύλιον παρὰ τοῦ βασιλέως
πεπιστευμένος τόν τε βασιλέα κατευδαιμονίζει καὶ
τὸ πλῆθος παρακαλεῖ, καὶ τὴν ἀπολειφθεῖσαν τοῖς

---

[1] Niese: ἐπιβουλήν mss.   [2] Destinon: μετ' ἀνδρὸς mss.

design. Herod, with a shout which might have seemed beyond a sick man's strength, instantly sent his guards and had Antipater executed. He ordered his body to be buried at Hyrcanium.[a] After that he again amended his will, nominating Archelaus, his eldest son and brother of Antipas, heir to the throne, and Antipas tetrarch.[b]

Herod's last will in favour of Archelaus.

(8) Herod survived the execution of his son but five days. He expired after a reign of thirty-four years, reckoning from the date[c] when, after putting Antigonus to death, he assumed control of the state ; of thirty-seven years, from the date[d] when he was proclaimed king by the Romans. In his life as a whole he was blessed, if ever man was, by fortune : a commoner, he mounted to a throne, retained it for all those years and bequeathed it to his own children ; in his family life, on the contrary, no man was more unfortunate. Before the army had learnt of his decease, Salome left the palace with her husband and released the prisoners whom Herod had ordered to be put to death, telling them that the king had changed his mind and now dismissed them all to their homes. Not until after their departure did she and her husband announce the news to the soldiers, summoning them and the rest of the people to a public assembly in the amphitheatre at Jericho. Here Ptolemy, to whom the king had entrusted his signet-ring, came forward, pronounced a benediction on the deceased king, delivered an exhortation to the people, and read a letter which Herod had left

Herod's death 4 B.C. (about March).

Reading of his will.

---

[a] Greek here " Hyrcania."
[b] Both sons of the Samaritan Malthace.   [c] 37 B.C.
[d] 40 B.C. (end). Josephus reckons the short portions of a Roman calendar year at the beginning and end of the reign as complete years (Schürer, *G.J.V.* i. 416).

στρατιώταις ἀνεγίνωσκεν ἐπιστολήν, ἐν ᾗ πολλὰ
περὶ τῆς εἰς τὸν διάδοχον εὐνοίας παρεκάλει.
668 μετὰ δὲ τὴν ἐπιστολὴν λύσας τὰς ἐπιδιαθήκας
ἀνεγίνωσκεν, ἐν αἷς Φίλιππος μὲν τοῦ Τράχωνος
καὶ τῶν γειτνιώντων χωρίων κληρονόμος, τετράρ-
χης δ', ὡς προείπαμεν, Ἀντίπας, βασιλεὺς δ'
669 Ἀρχέλαος ἀπεδείκνυτο. τούτῳ [δὲ]¹ τόν τε δακτύλιον τὸν ἑαυτοῦ Καίσαρι φέρειν ἐνετέλλετο καὶ
τὰς διοικήσεις τῆς βασιλείας σεσημασμένας· κύριον
γὰρ ἀπάντων ὧν διατάξειεν καὶ βεβαιωτὴν τῶν
διαθηκῶν εἶναι Καίσαρα· τά γε μὴν λοιπὰ κατὰ
τὰς προτέρας διαθήκας φυλάττειν.

670   (9) Βοὴ δ' εὐθὺς ἐγένετο τῶν Ἀρχελάῳ συν-
ηδομένων, καὶ κατὰ στῖφος οἱ στρατιῶται μετὰ
τοῦ πλήθους προσιόντες ὑπισχνοῦντο μὲν τὴν
ἑαυτῶν εὔνοιαν, συνηύχοντο δὲ καὶ τὴν παρὰ τοῦ
θεοῦ, [καὶ]² μετὰ ταῦτα πρὸς ταφὴν ἐτρέποντο
671 τοῦ βασιλέως. παρέλιπεν δ' οὐδὲν Ἀρχέλαος εἰς
πολυτέλειαν, ἀλλὰ πάντα τὸν βασιλικὸν κόσμον
προήνεγκεν συμπομπεύσοντα τῷ νεκρῷ· κλίνη μὲν
γὰρ ὁλόχρυσος ἦν διάλιθος, στρωμνὴ δὲ ἁλουργὶς
ποικίλη, τὸ σῶμα δ' ἐπ' αὐτῆς πορφύρα κεκα-
λυμμένον, καὶ διάδημα μὲν ἐπέκειτο τῇ κεφαλῇ,
στέφανος δ' ὑπὲρ αὐτοῦ χρυσοῦς, τὸ δὲ σκῆπτρον
672 παρὰ τὴν δεξιάν. καὶ περὶ τὴν κλίνην οἵ τε υἱεῖς
καὶ τὸ πλῆθος τῶν συγγενῶν, ἐφ' οἷς οἱ δορυφόροι
καὶ τὸ Θράκιον στῖφος, Γερμανοί τε καὶ Γαλάται,
673 διεσκευασμένοι πάντες ὡς εἰς πόλεμον. προῆγεν
δ' ἡ λοιπὴ δύναμις ὡπλισμένη τοῖς ἡγεμόσιν καὶ

¹ om. P.   ² P: om. the rest.

for the troops, in which he earnestly appealed to them to be loyal to his successor. After this letter, he opened and read the codicils : under these Philip [a] inherited Trachonitis and the neighbouring districts, Antipas, as we have already mentioned,[b] was appointed tetrarch,[c] and Archelaus king. The last-named received a charge from Herod to carry his ring to Caesar, with the documents relating to the administration of the realm, under seal, because he had vested in Caesar the control of all his dispositions and the ratification of the will ; in the remaining particulars the directions of the previous will were to hold good.

(9) Archelaus was instantly hailed with acclamations and congratulations ; and the troops advancing by companies, with the people, made promises of allegiance on their own part, and invoked upon him the blessing of God. The king's funeral next occupied attention. Archelaus, omitting nothing that could contribute to its magnificence, brought forth all the royal ornaments to accompany the procession in honour of the deceased. The bier was of solid gold, studded with precious stones, and had a covering of purple, embroidered with various colours ; on this lay the body enveloped in a purple robe, a diadem encircling the head and surmounted by a crown of gold, the sceptre beside his right hand. Around the bier were Herod's sons and a large group of his relations ; these were followed by the guards, the Thracian contingent, Germans and Gauls, all equipped as for war. The remainder of the troops marched in front, armed and in orderly array, led by

His funeral.

[a] Son of Cleopatra.   [b] § 664.
[c] Of Galilee and Peraea (*A*. xvii. 188).

ταξιάρχοις ἀκολουθοῦντες ἐν κόσμῳ, πεντακόσιοι
δὲ ἐπ᾽ αὐτοῖς τῶν οἰκετῶν καὶ ἀπελευθέρων ἀρω-
ματοφόροι. σταδίους δ᾽ ἐκομίσθη τὸ σῶμα δια-
κοσίους¹ εἰς Ἡρώδειον, ὅπου κατὰ τὰς ἐντολὰς
ἐτάφη. καὶ τὰ μὲν περὶ Ἡρώδην τοιοῦτον ἔσχεν
πέρας.

¹ LVRC Lat. Heg.: ἑβδομήκοντα PAM (reading οʹ for cʹ).
The procession starts from Jericho which was 150 stades
(N.E.) from Jerusalem (B. iv. 474); Herodion was 60 stades
south of Jerusalem (B. i. 265, 419).

their commanders and subordinate officers ; behind these came five hundred of Herod's servants and freedmen, carrying spices. The body was thus conveyed for a distance of two hundred furlongs to Herodion, where, in accordance with the directions of the deceased, it was interred. So ended Herod's reign.

1 (i. 1) Ἀρχελάῳ δὲ νέων ἦρξε θορύβων ἡ τῆς
ἐπὶ Ῥώμην ἀποδημίας ἀνάγκη. πενθήσας γὰρ
ἡμέρας ἑπτὰ τὸν πατέρα καὶ τὴν ἐπιτάφιον ἑστίασιν
πολυτελῆ τῷ πλήθει παρασχών· ἔθος δὲ τοῦτο παρὰ
Ἰουδαίοις πολλοῖς πενίας αἴτιον, διὰ τὸ πλῆθος
ἑστιᾶν οὐκ ἄνευ ἀνάγκης,[1] εἰ γὰρ παραλείποι τις,
οὐχ ὅσιος· μεταλαμβάνει μὲν ἐσθῆτα λευκήν,
πρόεισι δὲ εἰς τὸ ἱερόν, ἔνθα ποικίλαις αὐτὸν
2 εὐφημίαις ὁ λαὸς ἐκδέχεται. κἀκεῖνος τὸ πλῆθος
ἀφ' ὑψηλοῦ βήματος καὶ χρυσοῦ θρόνου δεξιωσά-
μενος τῆς τε σπουδῆς, ἣν ἐνεδείξαντο περὶ τὴν
κηδείαν τοῦ πατρός, εὐχαριστεῖ καὶ τῆς πρὸς αὐτὸν
θεραπείας ὡς πρὸς βέβαιον ἤδη βασιλέα· φείδεσθαί
γε μὴν οὐ μόνον ἔφη τῆς ἐξουσίας ἐπὶ τοῦ παρόντος,
ἀλλὰ καὶ τῶν ὀνομάτων, ἕως ἂν αὐτῷ Καῖσαρ
ἐπικυρώσῃ τὴν διαδοχήν, ὁ καὶ κατὰ τὰς διαθήκας
3 τῶν ὅλων δεσπότης· οὐδὲ γὰρ ἐν Ἱεριχοῦντι τῆς
στρατιᾶς τὸ διάδημα περιαπτούσης αὐτῷ δεδέχθαι·
τοῦ μέντοι προθύμου καὶ τῆς εὐνοίας, ὥσπερ τοῖς
στρατιώταις, οὕτω καὶ τῷ δήμῳ πλήρεις ἀπο-

---

[1] διά . . . ἀνάγκης om. Lat.

BOOK II

(i. 1) [a] The necessity under which Archelaus found himself of undertaking a journey to Rome was the signal for fresh disturbances. After keeping seven days' mourning for his father and providing the usual funeral banquet for the populace on a sumptuous scale—a Jewish custom which reduces many to poverty, such entertainment of the people being considered obligatory and its omission an act of impiety—he changed into white raiment and went forth to the Temple, where the people received him with varied acclamations. Speaking from a golden throne on a raised platform he greeted the multitude. He thanked them for the zeal which they had displayed over his father's funeral and for the marks of homage shown to himself, as to a king whose claim to the throne was already confirmed. He would, however, he said, for the present abstain not only from the exercise of the authority, but even from the assumption of the titles, of royalty, until his right to the succession had been ratified by Caesar, to whose ruling everything had been submitted under the terms of the will. Even when, as he reminded them, the army at Jericho had desired to place the diadem on his head, he had declined it. He would, none the less, make an ample return alike to the soldiers and to the citizens for their devotion and

[a] §§ 1-3 = A. xvii. 200-203.

δώσειν τὰς ἀμοιβάς, ὁπόταν ὑπὸ τῶν κρατούντων
βασιλεὺς ἀποδειχθῇ βέβαιος· σπουδάσειν γὰρ ἐν
πᾶσιν πρὸς αὐτοὺς φανῆναι τοῦ πατρὸς ἀμείνων.
4 (2) Ἐπὶ τούτοις ἡδόμενον τὸ πλῆθος εὐθέως
ἀπεπειρᾶτο τῆς διανοίας αὐτοῦ μεγάλοις αἰτή-
μασιν· οἱ μὲν γὰρ ἐβόων ἐπικουφίζειν τὰς εἰσφοράς, οἱ δὲ ἀναιρεῖν τὰ τέλη, τινὲς δὲ ἀπολύειν
τοὺς δεσμώτας. ἐπένευσε δ᾽ ἑτοίμως ἅπασι θεραπεύων τὸ πλῆθος. ἔπειτα θύσας ἐν εὐωχίᾳ μετὰ
5 τῶν φίλων ἦν. ἔνθα δὴ περὶ δείλην ἀθροισθέντες
οὐκ ὀλίγοι τῶν νεωτερίζειν προῃρημένων ἤρξαντο
ἰδίου πένθους, ὅτε τὸ κοινὸν ἐπὶ τῷ βασιλεῖ
πέπαυτο, κατολοφυρόμενοι τοὺς κολασθέντας ὑπὸ
Ἡρώδου διὰ τὸν ἐκκοπέντα χρυσοῦν ἀετὸν τῆς
6 πύλης τοῦ ναοῦ. ἦν δὲ τὸ πένθος οὐχ ὑπ-
εσταλμένον, ἀλλ᾽ οἰμωγαὶ διαπρύσιοι καὶ θρῆνος
ἐγκέλευστος κοπετοί τε περιηχοῦντες ὅλην τὴν
πόλιν, ὡς ἂν ἐπ᾽ ἀνδράσιν οὓς ἔφασκον ὑπὲρ τῶν
πατρίων νόμων καὶ τοῦ ναοῦ [πυρὶ][1] παραπολέσθαι.
7 τιμωρεῖν δ᾽ αὐτοῖς ἀνεβόων ἐκ τῶν ὑφ᾽ Ἡρώδου
τετιμημένων χρῆναι[2] καὶ πρῶτον τὸν ὑπ᾽ ἐκείνου
κατα- σταθέντα παύειν ἀρχιερέα· προσήκειν γὰρ
αὐτοῖς εὐσεβέστερον αἱρεῖσθαι καὶ καθαρώτερον.
8 (3) Πρὸς ἃ παρωξύνετο μὲν Ἀρχέλαος, ἐπεῖχε
δὲ τὴν ἄμυναν ὑπὸ τῆς περὶ τὴν ἔξοδον ἐπείξεως,
δεδοικὼς μήποτε τὸ πλῆθος ἐκπολεμώσας κατα-
σχεθείη τῷ κινήματι. διὸ πειθοῖ μᾶλλον ἢ βίᾳ

---

[1] om. LVRC Lat. ; cf. i. 655.
[2] VC: χρήμασι the rest with Lat.

[a] Duties on sales, A. xvii. 205.
[b] Judas, Matthias and their followers, B. i. 648-655.
[c] Joazar, A. xvii. 164.

goodwill, as soon as the supreme authorities had definitely declared him king ; for it would be his earnest and constant endeavour to treat them better than they had been treated by his father.

(2) Delighted at these professions, the multitude at once proceeded to test his intentions by making large demands. One party clamoured for a reduction of the taxes, another for the abolition of the duties,[a] a third for the liberation of the prisoners. To all these requests, in his desire to ingratiate himself with the people, he readily assented. Then, after offering a sacrifice, he regaled himself with his friends. Towards evening, however, a large number of those who were bent on revolution assembled on the same spot, and, now that the public mourning for the king was ended, began a lamentation on their own account, bewailing the fate of those whom Herod had punished for cutting down the golden eagle from the gate of the Temple.[b] This mourning was in no subdued tones : there were piercing shrieks, a dirge directed by a conductor, and lamentations with beating of the breast which resounded throughout the city ; all this in honour of the unfortunate men who, they asserted, had in defence of their country's laws and the Temple perished on the pyre. These martyrs ought, they clamoured, to be avenged by the punishment of Herod's favourites, and the first step was the deposition of the high-priest whom he had appointed,[c] as they had a right to select a man of greater piety and purer morals.

(3) Archelaus, exasperated by these proceedings, but in haste to depart, wished to defer retaliation, from fear that, if he provoked the hostility of the people, he would be detained by a general rising.

Demands of the Jews.

Their sedition on the occasion of the obsequies of the martyred doctors

325

καταστέλλειν ἐπειρᾶτο τοὺς νεωτερίζοντας καὶ τὸν
9 στρατηγὸν ὑποπέμψας παύσασθαι παρεκάλει. τοῦτον εἰς τὸ ἱερὸν παρελθόντα, πρὶν φθέγξασθαί τι,
λίθοις ἀπήλαυνον οἱ στασιασταὶ καὶ τοὺς μετ᾽
αὐτὸν ἐπὶ σωφρονισμῷ προσιόντας, ἐνίει δὲ πολλοὺς ὁ Ἀρχέλαος, καὶ πάντα πρὸς ὀργὴν ἀπεκρίναντο, δῆλοί τε ἦσαν οὐκ ἠρεμήσοντες, εἰ
10 πλήθους ἐπιλάβοιντο. καὶ δὴ τῆς τῶν ἀζύμων ἐνστάσης ἑορτῆς, ἣ πάσχα παρὰ Ἰουδαίοις καλεῖται,
πολύ τι θυμάτων πλῆθος ἐκδεχομένη, κάτεισι μὲν
ἐκ τῆς χώρας λαὸς ἄπειρος ἐπὶ τὴν θρησκείαν,
οἱ δὲ τοὺς σοφιστὰς πενθοῦντες ἐν τῷ ἱερῷ συν-
11 ειστήκεσαν τροφὴν τῇ στάσει πορίζομενοι. πρὸς
ὃ δείσας Ἀρχέλαος, πρὶν δι᾽ ὅλου τοῦ πλήθους
διαδραμεῖν τὴν νόσον, ὑποπέμπει μετὰ σπείρας
χιλίαρχον προστάξας βίᾳ τοὺς ἐξάρχοντας τῆς
στάσεως κατασχεῖν. πρὸς οὓς τὸ πλῆθος ἅπαν
παροξύνεται καὶ τοὺς μὲν πολλοὺς τῆς σπείρας
βάλλοντες λίθοις διέφθειρον, ὁ δὲ χιλίαρχος ἐκ-
12 φεύγει τραυματίας μόλις. ἔπειθ᾽ οἱ μὲν ὡς μηδενὸς
δεινοῦ γεγονότος ἐτρέποντο πρὸς θυσίαν· οὐ μὴν
Ἀρχελάῳ δίχα φόνου καθεκτὸν ἔτι τὸ πλῆθος
ἐφαίνετο, τὴν δὲ στρατιὰν ἐπαφίησιν αὐτοῖς ὅλην,
τοὺς μὲν πεζοὺς διὰ τῆς πόλεως ἀθρόους, τοὺς δὲ
13 ἱππεῖς ἀνὰ τὸ πεδίον· οἳ θύουσιν ἑκάστοις ἐξαίφνης

---

[a] Or perhaps the " captain of the Temple " (*Sagan*),
Acts iv. 1.

[b] Greek " sustenance." In the parallel *A.* xvii. 214 the
writer (an assistant of Josephus), using the same source,
appears to have taken the word τροφή literally : " they had no
lack of food for the rebels, not being ashamed to beg for it."

[c] Apparently rounding the N.W. side of the city outside

He, accordingly, endeavoured to appease the rebels by persuasion, without resort to force, and quietly sent his general [a] to entreat them to desist. This officer on entering the Temple and before he had even opened his mouth, was driven off by the rioters with a shower of stones ; many others whom Archelaus sent in after him to call them to reason were similarly treated. To all remonstrances they replied with anger, and it was evident that, given any accession to their numbers, they had no intention of remaining inactive. And now the feast of unleavened bread, which the Jews call Passover, came round ; it is an occasion for the contribution of a multitude of sacrifices, and a vast crowd streamed in from the country for the ceremony. The promoters of the mourning for the doctors stood in a body in the temple, procuring recruits [b] for their faction. This alarmed Archelaus, who, wishing to prevent the contagion from spreading to the whole crowd, sent in a tribune in command of a cohort, with orders to restrain by force the ringleaders of the sedition. Indignant at the appearance of the troops, the whole crowd pelted them with stones ; most of the cohort were killed, while their commander was wounded and escaped with difficulty. Then, as if nothing serious had happened, the rioters returned to their sacrifices. Archelaus, however, now felt that it would be impossible to restrain the mob without bloodshed, and let loose upon them his entire army, the infantry advancing in close order through the city, the cavalry by way of the plain.[c] The soldiers falling unexpectedly upon the

is quelled with bloodshed, April, 4 B.C.

the walls, while the infantry struck straight across from the palace which lay on the S.W. of the city to the Temple on the N.E.

προσπεσόντες διαφθείρουσι μὲν περὶ τρισχιλίους,
τὸ δὲ λοιπὸν πλῆθος εἰς τὰ πλησίον ὄρη διεσκέδασαν. εἵποντο δὲ Ἀρχελάου κήρυκες κε-
λεύοντες ἕκαστον ἀναχωρεῖν ἐπ᾽ οἴκου, καὶ
πάντες ᾤχοντο τὴν ἑορτὴν ἀπολιπόντες.

14 (ii. 1) Αὐτὸς δὲ μετὰ τῆς μητρὸς καὶ τῶν
φίλων Ποπλᾶ καὶ Πτολεμαίου καὶ Νικολάου
κατῄει πρὸς θάλασσαν καταλιπὼν ἐπίτροπόν τε
τῶν βασιλείων καὶ κηδεμόνα τῶν οἰκείων Φίλ-
15 ιππον. συνεξῄει δ᾽ ἅμα τοῖς τέκνοις Σαλώμη καὶ
τοῦ βασιλέως ἀδελφιδοῖ τε καὶ γαμβροί, τῷ
μὲν δοκεῖν συναγωνιούμενοι περὶ τῆς διαδοχῆς
Ἀρχελάῳ, τὸ δ᾽ ἀληθὲς κατηγορήσοντες περὶ
τῶν κατὰ τὸ ἱερὸν παρανομηθέντων.

16 (2) Συναντᾷ δ᾽ αὐτοῖς κατὰ τὴν Καισάρειαν
Σαβῖνος ὁ τῆς Συρίας ἐπίτροπος εἰς Ἰουδαίαν
ἀνιὼν ἐπὶ φυλακῇ τῶν Ἡρώδου χρημάτων. τοῦτον ἐπέσχεν προσωτέρω χωρεῖν ἐπελθὼν Οὔαρος,
ὃν διὰ Πτολεμαίου πολλὰ δεηθεὶς Ἀρχέλαος μετ-
17 επέμψατο. τότε μὲν οὖν Σαβῖνος Οὐάρῳ χαριζόμενος οὔτ᾽ ἐπὶ τὰς ἄκρας ἔσπευσεν οὔτε τὰ ταμιεῖα
τῶν πατρῴων χρημάτων ἀπέκλεισεν Ἀρχελάῳ,
μέχρι δὲ τῆς Καίσαρος διαγνώσεως ἠρεμήσειν
18 ὑπέσχετο καὶ διέτριβεν ἐπὶ τῆς Καισαρείας. ὡς
δὲ τῶν ἐμποδιζόντων ὁ μὲν εἰς Ἀντιόχειαν
ἀπῆρεν, Ἀρχέλαος δὲ εἰς Ῥώμην ἀνήχθη, διὰ
τάχους ἐπὶ Ἱεροσολύμων ὁρμήσας παραλαμβάνει
τὰ βασίλεια, καὶ μεταπεμπόμενος τούς τε φρουρ-

---

[a] Malthace. [b] Called Ptollas in A. xvii. 219.
[c] Herod's chief friend and executor, B. i. 473, 667, ii. 21.
[d] Of Damascus, another friend of Herod, and the historian
on whose work Josephus is here probably dependent.

328

various parties busy with their sacrifices slew about three thousand of them and dispersed the remainder among the neighbouring hills. The heralds of Archelaus followed and ordered everyone to return home ; so they all abandoned the festival and departed.

(ii. 1) Archelaus himself with his mother [a] and his friends, Poplas,[b] Ptolemy,[c] and Nicolas,[d] now descended to the coast, leaving Philip to take charge of the palace [e] and to protect his private interests. Salome,[f] with her children, also accompanied him, and the nephews and sons-in-law of the late king, ostensibly to support the claims of Archelaus to the succession, but in reality to accuse him of the recent illegal proceedings in the Temple.

Archelaus departs for Rome.

(2) At Caesarea the party were met by Sabinus, procurator of Syria,[g] on his way up to Judaea to take charge of Herod's estate. He was prevented from continuing his journey by the arrival of Varus,[h] whose presence Archelaus had, through Ptolemy, urgently solicited. Sabinus, in deference to Varus, abandoned for the moment his intention of rushing to the castles and excluding Archelaus from access to his father's treasuries, and, promising to take no action until Caesar had given his decision, remained at Caesarea. But as soon as those who had obstructed his designs had left, Varus for Antioch,[i] Archelaus for Rome, he sped to Jerusalem and took possession of the palace ; and then, summoning the

Mercenary designs of Sabinus the procurator.

---

[e] Or perhaps " the realm."   [f] Herod's sister.

[g] More accurately described in A. xvii. 221 as Καίσαρος ἐπίτροπος τῶν ἐν Συρίᾳ πραγμάτων, i.e. imperial finance officer for the province.

[h] Quintilius Varus, governor (legatus) of Syria (B. i. 617).

[i] Before returning to Antioch he visited Jerusalem and left a legion there to keep order (§ 40).

ἄρχους καὶ διοικητὰς ἐπειρᾶτο διερευνᾶν τοὺς
τῶν χρημάτων ἀναλογισμοὺς τάς τε ἄκρας παρα-
19 λαμβάνειν. οὐ μὴν οἱ φύλακες τῶν Ἀρχελάου
κατημέλουν ἐντολῶν, ἔμενον δὲ φρουροῦντες
ἕκαστα καὶ τὴν φρουρὰν ἀνατιθέντες Καίσαρι
μᾶλλον ἢ Ἀρχελάῳ.
20   (3) Κἂν τούτῳ πάλιν Ἀντίπας ἀμφισβητῶν
περὶ τῆς βασιλείας ἐπέξεισιν ἀξιῶν τῆς ἐπιδιαθή-
κης κυριωτέραν εἶναι τὴν διαθήκην, ἐν ᾗ βασιλεὺς
αὐτὸς ἐγέγραπτο. συλλήψεσθαι δ' αὐτῷ προϋπ-
έσχετο Σαλώμη καὶ πολλοὶ τῶν σὺν Ἀρχελάῳ
21 πλεόντων συγγενῶν. ἐπήγετο δὲ τὴν μητέρα καὶ
τὸν ἀδελφὸν Νικολάου Πτολεμαῖον, ῥοπὴν εἶναι
δοκοῦντα διὰ τὴν παρὰ Ἡρώδῃ πίστιν· γεγόνει
γὰρ δὴ τῶν φίλων ἐκείνου τιμιώτατος· πλεῖστον
μέντοι πεποίθει διὰ δεινότητα λόγων Εἰρηναίῳ τῷ
ῥήτορι, διὸ καὶ τοὺς νουθετοῦντας εἴκειν Ἀρχελάῳ
κατὰ τὸ πρεσβεῖον καὶ τὰς ἐπιδιαθήκας διεκρού-
22 σατο. μεθίστατο δὲ ἐν Ῥώμῃ πάντων πρὸς αὐτὸν
ἡ σπουδὴ τῶν συγγενῶν, οἷς διὰ μίσους ἦν Ἀρχέλαος, καὶ προηγουμένως ἕκαστος αὐτονομίας
ἐπεθύμει στρατηγῷ Ῥωμαίων διοικουμένης, εἰ δὲ
τοῦτο[1] διαμαρτάνοι, βασιλεύειν Ἀντίπαν ἤθελεν.
23   (4) Συνήργει δ' αὐτοῖς εἰς τοῦτο καὶ Σαβῖνος δι'
ἐπιστολῶν, κατηγορήσας μὲν Ἀρχελάου παρὰ
24 Καίσαρι, πολλὰ δ' ἐπαινέσας Ἀντίπαν. συν-
τάξαντες δὲ τὰ ἐγκλήματα οἱ περὶ Σαλώμην ἐν-
εχείρισαν Καίσαρι, καὶ μετὰ τούτους Ἀρχέλαος τά
τε[2] κεφάλαια τῶν ἑαυτοῦ δικαίων γράψας καὶ τὸν

[1] τούτου LVRC.   [2] +ἄλλα PAM.

[a] B. i. 646. [b] Malthace who had sailed with her other son, § 14.
330

governors of the forts and the controllers of the treasury, endeavoured to search into the accounts and to take possession of the castles. These officers, however, mindful of the injunctions of Archelaus, continued to guard their respective trusts, for which they professed to hold themselves responsible to Caesar, rather than to Archelaus.

(3) Meanwhile another claimant to the throne had set out for Rome, namely, Antipas, who maintained that the will in which he had been named king had greater validity than the codicil.[a] He had received previous promises of support from Salome and from many of his relations who had sailed with Archelaus. He had won over his mother[b] and Ptolemy, brother of Nicolas, from whose influence much was expected, owing to the confidence reposed in him by Herod, who had honoured him above all his friends. But what Antipas mainly relied on was the brilliant eloquence of his advocate Irenaeus ; on the strength of this he refused to listen to those who advised him to give way to Archelaus, in consideration of his rights of seniority and the terms of the codicil. At Rome, all the relations, who detested Archelaus, transferred their support to him ; the object that was uppermost in the minds of every one of these was autonomy under the administration of a Roman governor, but, in default of that, they preferred to have Antipas for king. *Antipas, a rival claimant to the throne.*

(4) They were aided in this design by Sabinus, who, in dispatches to Caesar, accused Archelaus and highly commended Antipas. Salome and her friends now drew up their indictment and placed it in Caesar's hands ; Archelaus responded by drafting a summary statement of his rights and sending in his father's *The rivals at Rome.*

δακτύλιον τοῦ πατρὸς καὶ τοὺς λόγους[1] εἰσπέμπει
25 διὰ Πτολεμαίου. προσκεψάμενος δὲ ὁ Καῖσαρ τὰ
παρ' ἀμφοῖν κατ' ἰδίαν, τό τε μέγεθος τῆς βασιλείας καὶ τὸ πλῆθος τῆς προσόδου, πρὸς οἷς τὸν
ἀριθμὸν τῆς Ἡρώδου γενεᾶς, προαναγνοὺς[2] δὲ
καὶ τὰ παρὰ Οὐάρου καὶ Σαβίνου περὶ τούτων
ἐπεσταλμένα, συνέδριον μὲν ἀθροίζει τῶν ἐν τέλει
Ῥωμαίων, ἐν ᾧ καὶ τὸν ἐξ Ἀγρίππα καὶ Ἰουλίας
τῆς θυγατρὸς θετὸν παῖδα Γάιον πρώτως ἐκάθισεν,
ἀποδίδωσι δὲ λόγον αὐτοῖς.
26   (5) Ἔνθα καταστὰς ὁ Σαλώμης υἱὸς Ἀντίπατρος, ἦν δὲ τῶν ἐναντιουμένων Ἀρχελάῳ δεινότατος εἰπεῖν, κατηγόρει φάσκων τοῖς μὲν λόγοις
ἀμφισβητεῖν ἄρτι βασιλείας Ἀρχέλαον, τοῖς δ'
ἔργοις πάλαι γεγονέναι βασιλέα, κατειρωνεύεσθαι
δὲ νῦν τῶν Καίσαρος ἀκοῶν, ὃν δικαστὴν τῆς
27 διαδοχῆς οὐ περιέμεινεν, εἴ γε μετὰ τὴν Ἡρώδου
τελευτὴν ἐγκαθέτους μὲν ὑποπέμψας τοὺς περι-
θήσοντας αὐτῷ τὸ διάδημα, προκαθίσας δ' ἐπὶ
τοῦ θρόνου καὶ χρηματίσας[3] βασιλεύς, τάξεις τε
τῆς στρατιᾶς ἀμείψας καὶ προκοπὰς χαρισάμενος,
28 ἔτι δὲ τῷ δήμῳ πάντα κατανεύσας ὅσων ὡς παρὰ
βασιλέως τυχεῖν ἠξίουν, καὶ τοὺς ἐπὶ μεγίσταις
αἰτίαις παρὰ τοῦ πατρὸς δεδεμένους λύσας, νῦν
ἥκει παρὰ τοῦ δεσπότου σκιὰν αἰτησόμενος
βασιλείας, ἧς ἥρπασεν ἑαυτῷ τὸ σῶμα, καὶ ποιῶν
οὐ τῶν πραγμάτων ἀλλὰ τῶν ὀνομάτων κύριον
29 Καίσαρα. προσωνείδιζεν δ' ὡς καὶ τὸ πένθος

---

[1] rationes administrationis Lat. (apparently reading
λογισμούς, as in A. ‖).
[2] PAV*: προσαναγνοὺς the rest (perhaps rightly).
[3] + ὡς MLVRC.

ring and papers[a] by Ptolemy to the emperor. Caesar, after reflecting in private on the allegations of both parties, the extent of the kingdom, the amount of the revenue, as well as the number of Herod's children, and after perusing the letters on the subject which he had received from Varus and Sabinus, summoned a council of leading Romans, at which for the first time he gave a seat to Gaius, the son of Agrippa and his daughter Julia, whom he had adopted himself ; he then called upon the parties to speak. *Council held by Augustus.*

(5) Thereupon Antipater, son of Salome, the ablest orator among the opponents of Archelaus, rose as his accuser. Archelaus, he stated, although at the moment ostensibly suing for a crown, had in reality long since acted as king. He was now merely playing upon the patient ears of Caesar, whose sentence upon the subject of the succession he had not awaited. For, after Herod's death, had he not suborned persons to place the diadem on his head, sat in state upon the throne and given audience as a king, made changes in the ranks of the army and conferred promotions, assented to all the favours which the people had claimed from him as sovereign, and liberated those whom his father had imprisoned for the gravest crimes ? And after all this he had now come to beg from his lord for the shadow of royalty, of which he had already appropriated the substance, thus making Caesar a dispenser not of realities, but of mere titles ! A further charge which Antipater brought against *Antipater, son of Salome, accuses Archelaus.*

---

[a] Or, with the other reading λογισμούς, " (public) accounts."

κατειρωνεύσατο τοῦ πατρός, μεθ' ἡμέραν μὲν
ἐπισχηματίζων τὸ πρόσωπον εἰς λύπην, νύκτωρ
δὲ μέχρις κώμων μεθυσκόμενος, ἐν ᾧ καὶ τὴν
ταραχὴν τοῦ πλήθους ἐκ τῆς ἐπὶ τούτοις ἀγα-
30 νακτήσεως ἔλεγεν γεγονέναι. καὶ τὸν ἀγῶνα τοῦ
λόγου παντὸς ἐναπηρείσατο τῷ πλήθει τῶν περὶ
τὸν ναὸν φονευθέντων, οὓς ἐληλυθέναι μὲν ἐφ'
ἑορτήν, παρὰ δὲ ταῖς ἰδίαις θυσίαις ὠμῶς ἀπ-
εσφάχθαι· καὶ τοσοῦτον ἐν τῷ ἱερῷ σεσωρεῦσθαι
νεκρῶν πλῆθος, ὅσον οὐδ' [ἂν]¹ ἀλλόφυλος ἐσώ-
31 ρευσεν πόλεμος ἐπελθὼν ἀκήρυκτος. ταύτην μέντοι
τὴν ὠμότητα προσκεψάμενον αὐτοῦ καὶ τὸν πατέρα
μηδ' ἐλπίδος αὐτόν ποτε ἀξιῶσαι βασιλικῆς, ἢ
ὅτε χεῖρον τὴν ψυχὴν κάμνων τοῦ σώματος
ἀκρατὴς ἦν ὑγιαίνοντος λογισμοῦ καὶ οὐδ' ὃν
ἔγραφεν ἐν ταῖς ἐπιδιαθήκαις ᾔδει διάδοχον, καὶ
ταῦτα μηδὲν τὸν ἐν ταῖς διαθήκαις μέμψασθαι
δυνάμενος, ἃς ἔγραψεν ὑγιαίνων μὲν τὸ σῶμα,
32 καθαρὰν δὲ τὴν ψυχὴν ἔχων πάθους παντός. εἰ
μέντοι καὶ κυριωτέραν τιθείη τις τὴν τοῦ κάμνον-
τος κρίσιν, ἀποκεχειροτονῆσθαι βασιλείας Ἀρχέλαον ὑφ' ἑαυτοῦ τοῖς εἰς αὐτὴν παρανομηθεῖσιν·
ποταπὸν γὰρ ἂν γενέσθαι λαβόντα τὴν ἀρχὴν
παρὰ Καίσαρος τὸν πρὶν λαβεῖν τοσούτους ἀν-
ῃρηκότα;
33 (6) Πολλὰ τοιαῦτα διεξελθὼν Ἀντίπατρος καὶ
τοὺς πλείστους τῶν συγγενῶν παραστησάμενος
ἐφ' ἑκάστῳ τῶν κατηγορημένων μάρτυρας κατα-

¹ om. PA.

Archelaus was that even in his mourning for his father he had played the hypocrite, in the day-time assuming a pose of grief, at night drinking to riotous excess. In this connexion, he added that the recent outbreak of the populace was attributable to their indignation at such conduct. Proceeding to the main contention of his speech, he laid great stress on the multitude of Jews who had been massacred around the sanctuary, poor people who had come for a festival and, while offering their sacrifices, had themselves been brutally immolated.[a] There had been, he said, such a pile of corpses in the temple as would never have been raised even by the ruthless inroad of a foreign foe. It was, indeed, because he foresaw this ferocity of Archelaus that his father had never deigned to hold out to him even a hope of ascending the throne, until the day when, more stricken in mind than in body, and incapable of sound reasoning, he did not even know whose name he was inscribing in the codicil as that of his successor ; when, moreover, he had no fault to find with the heir named in the will which he had drafted while he possessed health of body and a mind quite unclouded by affliction. But, he continued, even if greater weight were attached by any to the decision of an invalid, Archelaus had pronounced his own deposition from the kingdom by his outrages upon it. What would he become, once invested with authority by Caesar, who before receiving it had massacred such multitudes !

(6) After dilating at length in this strain, and producing most of the relatives as witnesses to each item in his accusation, Antipater concluded his speech.

[a] Cf. the charge against Pilate of mingling the blood of Galilaeans with their sacrifices, Luke xiii. 1.

34 παύει τὸν λόγον. ἀνίσταται δὲ Νικόλαος ὑπὲρ
Ἀρχελάου, καὶ τὸν μὲν ἐν τῷ ἱερῷ φόνον ἀναγ-
καῖον ἀπέφηνεν· πολεμίους γὰρ γεγονέναι τοὺς ἀν-
ῃρημένους οὐ τῆς βασιλείας μόνον ἀλλὰ καὶ τοῦ
35 δικάζοντος αὐτὴν Καίσαρος. τῶν δ' ἄλλων ἐγκλημάτων συμβούλους ἀπεδείκνυεν αὐτοὺς τοὺς κατηγόρους γεγονέναι. τήν γε μὴν ἐπιδιαθήκην ἠξίου
διὰ τοῦτο μάλιστα εἶναι κυρίαν, ὅτι βεβαιωτὴν ἐν
36 αὐτῇ Καίσαρα καθίστατο τοῦ διαδόχου· ὁ γὰρ
σωφρονῶν ὥστε τῷ δεσπότῃ τῶν ὅλων παραχωρεῖν
τῆς ἐξουσίας οὐ δήπου περὶ κληρονόμου κρίσιν
ἐσφάλλετο, σωφρονῶν δ' ᾑρεῖτο καὶ τὸν καθ-
ιστάμενον ὁ γινώσκων τὸν καθιστάντα.

37 (7) Διεξελθόντος δὲ πάντα καὶ Νικολάου παρελθὼν Ἀρχέλαος προπίπτει[1] τῶν Καίσαρος γονάτων
ἡσυχῇ. κἀκεῖνος αὐτὸν μάλα φιλοφρόνως ἀνα-
στήσας ἐνέφηνεν μὲν ὡς ἄξιος εἴη τῆς πατρῴας
38 διαδοχῆς, οὐ μήν τι βέβαιον ἀπεφήνατο. διαλύσας
δὲ τοὺς συνέδρους ἐκείνης τῆς ἡμέρας καθ' ἑαυτὸν
περὶ ὧν διήκουσεν ἐσκέπτετο, εἴτε χρὴ τῶν ἐν
ταῖς διαθήκαις καταστῆσαί τινα διάδοχον, εἴτε καὶ
πάσῃ τῇ γενεᾷ διανεῖμαι τὴν ἀρχήν· ἐδόκει γὰρ
ἐπικουρίας χρήζειν τὸ πλῆθος τῶν προσώπων.

39 (iii. 1) Πρὶν δὲ ὁρίσαι τι περὶ τούτων Καίσαρα
τελευτᾷ μὲν ἡ Ἀρχελάου μήτηρ Μαλθακὴ νοσή-
σασα, παρὰ Οὐάρου δ' ἐκομίσθησαν ἐκ Συρίας
40 ἐπιστολαὶ περὶ τῆς Ἰουδαίων ἀποστάσεως, ἣν
προϊδόμενος ὁ Οὔαρος, ἀνέβη γὰρ μετὰ τὸν Ἀρχελάου πλοῦν εἰς Ἱεροσόλυμα τοὺς παρακινοῦντας
καθέξων, ἐπειδὴ πρόδηλον ἦν τὸ πλῆθος οὐκ

---

[1] προσπίπτει most mss.

Nicolas then rose in defence of Archelaus. He main- Nicolas of
Damascus
for the
defence.
tained that the slaughter in the Temple had been
rendered necessary, because the victims had shown
themselves enemies not only of the kingdom, but
also of Caesar, the arbiter of the kingdom. As
for the other charges made against Archelaus, he
showed that his accusers themselves had advised
him to act as he did. The validity of the codicil, he
claimed, was proved by this fact above all, that in it
Caesar was constituted surety for the succession ;
one who was sane enough to cede his authority to
the master of the world was surely not mistaken in
his selection of an heir. The sagacity shown in his
choice of the donor was a guarantee of his sanity in
the choice of the recipient.

(7) Nicolas on his side having fully stated his case, Perplexity
of
Augustus.
Archelaus came forward and fell, in silence, at the
knees of Caesar. The emperor very graciously
raised him up, intimating that he thought him worthy
to succeed his father, but pronouncing no final decision. After dismissing his council, he passed the
day in reflection on what he had heard, considering
whether he ought to appoint as successor one of
those named in the wills or to divide the dominion
among all the children ; for the numerous members
of this family all seemed in need of support.

(iii. 1) But before Caesar had come to any de- Further
sedition at
Pentecost
provoked
by the
conduct of
Sabinus at
Jerusalem.
cision on these matters, Malthace, the mother of
Archelaus, was taken ill and died, and dispatches
arrived from Varus in Syria concerning the revolt
of the Jews. This outbreak had been foreseen by
Varus, who, after the sailing of Archelaus, had gone
up to Jerusalem to repress its promoters, and, as it
was evident that the people would not remain quiet,

ἠρεμῆσον, ἓν τῶν τριῶν ἀπὸ Συρίας ταγμάτων,
41 ὅπερ ἄγων ἧκεν, ἐν τῇ πόλει καταλείπει. καὶ
αὐτὸς μὲν ὑπέστρεψεν εἰς Ἀντιόχειαν, ἐπελθὼν
δὲ ὁ Σαβῖνος ἀφορμὴν αὐτοῖς παρέσχεν νεωτερο-
ποιίας· τούς τε γὰρ φρουροὺς παραδιδόναι τὰς
ἄκρας ἐβιάζετο καὶ πικρῶς τὰ βασιλικὰ χρήματα
διηρεύνα, πεποιθὼς οὐ μόνον τοῖς ὑπὸ Οὐάρου
καταλειφθεῖσι στρατιώταις, ἀλλὰ καὶ πλήθει δούλων ἰδίων, οὓς ἅπαντας ὁπλίσας ὑπηρέταις ἐχρῆτο
42 τῆς πλεονεξίας. ἐνστάσης δὲ τῆς πεντηκοστῆς,
οὕτω καλοῦσίν τινα ἑορτὴν Ἰουδαῖοι παρ' ἑπτὰ
γινομένην ἑβδομάδας καὶ[1] τὸν ἀριθμὸν τῶν ἡμερῶν
προσηγορίαν ἔχουσαν, οὐχ ἡ συνήθης θρησκεία
43 συνήγαγεν τὸν δῆμον, ἀλλ' ἡ ἀγανάκτησις. συνέδραμεν γοῦν πλῆθος ἄπειρον ἔκ τε τῆς Γαλιλαίας
καὶ ἐκ τῆς Ἰδουμαίας, Ἱεριχοῦντός τε καὶ τῆς
ὑπὲρ Ἰορδάνην Περαίας, ὑπερεῖχεν δὲ πλήθει καὶ
προθυμίαις ἀνδρῶν ὁ γνήσιος ἐξ αὐτῆς Ἰουδαίας
44 λαός. διανείμαντες δὲ σφᾶς αὐτοὺς εἰς τρία μέρη
τριχῇ στρατοπεδεύονται, πρός τε τῷ βορείῳ τοῦ
ἱεροῦ κλίματι καὶ πρὸς τῷ μεσημβρινῷ κατὰ τὸν
ἱππόδρομον, ἡ δὲ τρίτη μοῖρα πρὸς τοῖς βασιλείοις
κατὰ δύσιν. περικαθεζόμενοι δὲ πανταχόθεν τοὺς
Ῥωμαίους ἐπολιόρκουν.

45   (2) Ὁ δὲ Σαβῖνος πρός τε τὸ πλῆθος αὐτῶν
ὑποδείσας καὶ τὰ φρονήματα, συνεχεῖς μὲν ἀγγέλους ἔπεμπεν πρὸς Οὐάρον ἐπαμύνειν ἐν τάχει
δεόμενος, ὡς εἰ βραδύνοι κατακοπησομένου τοῦ
46 τάγματος· αὐτὸς δὲ ἐπὶ τὸν ὑψηλότατον τοῦ φρουρίου πύργον ἀναβάς, ὃς ἐκαλεῖτο Φασάηλος ἐπ-

_____
[1] κατὰ Hudson (after Lat.).

[a] § 16.

had left in the city one of the three legions from Syria which he had brought with him ; he himself then returned to Antioch. It was the arrival of Sabinus [a] which gave the Jews an occasion for insurrection. For this officer endeavoured to force the guardians of the citadels to hand them over to him and instituted an exacting search for the royal treasures, relying for this task not only on the soldiers left by Varus, but on a crowd of his own slaves, all of whom he armed and employed as instruments of his avarice. So, on the arrival of Pentecost—thus the Jews call a feast which occurs seven weeks after (Passover),[b] and takes its name from the number of intervening days—it was not the customary ritual so much as indignation which drew the people in crowds to the capital. A countless multitude flocked in from Galilee, from Idumaea, from Jericho, and from Peraea beyond the Jordan, but it was the native population of Judaea itself which, both in numbers and ardour, was pre-eminent. Distributing themselves into three divisions, they formed three camps, one on the north of the Temple, another on the south, adjoining the hippodrome,[c] and the third near the palace, on the west. Thus investing the Romans on all sides, they held them under siege.

(2) Sabinus, terrified at their numbers and determination, dispatched messenger after messenger to Varus, begging for his prompt support and assuring him that, if he delayed, the legion would be cut to pieces. He himself mounted to the highest tower in

Margin notes: End of May 4 B.C. | A fight in the Temple.

[b] Such must be the meaning, but this sense of παρά is unusual.

[c] Mentioned here only and in the parallel in *A.* xvii. 255 ; its exact position is unknown. It was probably built by Herod.

ώνυμον ἔχων ἀδελφὸν Ἡρώδου διαφθαρέντα ὑπὸ
Πάρθων, ἐντεῦθεν κατέσειεν τοῖς ἐν τῷ τάγματι
στρατιώταις ἐπιχειρεῖν τοῖς πολεμίοις· δι᾽ ἔκπληξιν
γὰρ οὐδ᾽ εἰς τοὺς σφετέρους καταβαίνειν ἐθάρρει.
47 παραπεισθέντες δὲ οἱ στρατιῶται προπηδῶσιν εἰς
τὸ ἱερὸν καὶ μάχην καρτερὰν τοῖς Ἰουδαίοις
συνάπτουσιν, ἐν ᾗ μέχρι μὲν οὐδεὶς καθύπερθεν
ἐπήμυνεν περιῆσαν ἐμπειρίᾳ πολέμου τῶν ἀπείρων·
48 ἐπεὶ δὲ πολλοὶ Ἰουδαίων ἀναβάντες ἐπὶ τὰς στοὰς
κατὰ κεφαλῆς αὐτῶν ἠφίεσαν τὰ βέλη, συνετρίβοντο
πολλοὶ καὶ οὔτε τοὺς ἄνωθεν βάλλοντας ἀμύνεσθαι
ῥᾴδιον ἦν, οὔτε τοὺς συστάδην μαχομένους ὑπο-
μένειν.

49 (3) Καταπονούμενοι δὲ[1] πρὸς ἀμφοτέρων ὑποπιμπρᾶσιν τὰς στοάς, ἔργα θαυμάσια μεγέθους τε
καὶ πολυτελείας ἕνεκεν· οἱ δ᾽ ἐπ᾽ αὐτῶν ἐξαίφνης
ὑπὸ τῆς φλογὸς περισχεθέντες πολλοὶ μὲν ἐν αὐτῇ
διεφθάρησαν, πολλοὶ δὲ ὑπὸ τῶν πολεμίων πη-
δῶντες εἰς αὐτούς, τινὲς δ᾽ εἰς τοὐπίσω κατὰ τοῦ
τείχους ἐκρημνίζοντο, ἔνιοι δ᾽ ὑπ᾽ ἀμηχανίας τοῖς
50 ἰδίοις ξίφεσιν τὸ πῦρ ἔφθανον· ὅσοι δὲ καθερπύ-
σαντες ἀπὸ τῶν τειχῶν ᾖξαν εἰς τοὺς Ῥωμαίους
εὐμεταχείριστοι διὰ τὴν ἔκπληξιν ἦσαν. καὶ[2] τῶν
μὲν ἀπολωλότων, τῶν δ᾽ ὑπὸ τοῦ δέους σκεδα-
σθέντων, ἐρήμῳ τῷ τοῦ θεοῦ θησαυρῷ προσ-

---

[1] μὲν PA, which Destinon retains, writing συνετρίβοντό ⟨τε⟩
above and making the apodosis begin at καταπονούμενοι.
[2] μέχρι LVRC Lat.

the fortress—called Phasael, after Herod's brother, who was slain by the Parthians[a]—and thence signalled to the legionaries to attack the enemy, for he was in such a panic that he had not even the courage to descend to his own men. The soldiers, obedient to this poltroon, leapt into the Temple and engaged in a stubborn contest with the Jews. So long as they remained unassailed from above, their military experience gave them the advantage over the novices opposed to them; but when a large body of Jews mounted the porticoes and poured their missiles down upon their heads, many fell, and the Romans found it no easy task either to defend themselves against those attacking them from above or to hold their ground against their other opponents in hand-to-hand fight.

(3) Harassed by these two foes, the legionaries set fire to the porticoes, which for massive grandeur and magnificence were wonderful works of art. Of the Jews who occupied them, many, suddenly enveloped, perished in the flames; many leapt down among their enemies and were slain by them; some flung themselves over the precipitous wall in their rear; others, in despair, threw themselves on their own swords to avoid becoming victims of the flames; while any who successfully crept down from the wall and dashed at the Romans fell an easy prey, owing to their dazed condition. Then, their enemies either slain or dispersed in panic, the soldiers fell upon God's treasury, now reft of defenders, and plundered it to the amount of some

Burning of the portioes and pillage of the treasury.

---

[a] *Cf. B.* i. 271 f., and for the tower of Phasael i. 418, v. 166.

πεσόντες οἱ στρατιῶται περὶ τετρακόσια τάλαντα
διήρπασαν, ὧν ὅσα μὴ διεκλάπη Σαβῖνος ἤθροισεν.
51 (4) Ἰουδαίους δὲ ἥ τε τῶν ἔργων καὶ ἀνδρῶν
φθορὰ πολὺ πλείους καὶ μαχιμωτέρους ἐπισυν-
έστησεν Ῥωμαίοις, καὶ περισχόντες τὰ βασίλεια
πάντας ἠπείλουν διαφθείρειν, εἰ μὴ θᾶττον ἀπίοιεν·
ὑπισχνοῦντο γὰρ ἄδειαν τῷ Σαβίνῳ βουλομένῳ
52 μετὰ τοῦ τάγματος ἐξιέναι. συνελάμβανον δ'
αὐτοῖς[1] οἱ πλείους τῶν βασιλικῶν αὐτομολήσαντες.
τὸ μέντοι πολεμικώτατον μέρος, Σεβαστηνοὶ
τρισχίλιοι, Ῥοῦφός τε καὶ Γρᾶτος ἐπὶ τούτοις, ὁ
μὲν τοὺς πεζοὺς τῶν βασιλικῶν ὑπ' αὐτὸν ἔχων,
Ῥοῦφος δὲ τοὺς ἱππεῖς, ὧν ἑκάτερος καὶ χωρὶς
ὑπηκόου δυνάμεως δι' ἀλκὴν καὶ σύνεσιν ἦν
53 πολέμου ῥοπή,[2] προσέθεντο Ῥωμαίοις. Ἰουδαῖοι
μὲν οὖν ἐνέκειντο τῇ πολιορκίᾳ, τῶν τειχῶν ἅμα
πειρώμενοι τοῦ φρουρίου καὶ τοῖς περὶ τὸν Σαβῖνον
ἐμβοῶντες ἀπιέναι, μηδ' ἐμποδὼν αὐτοῖς γενέσθαι
διὰ χρόνου πολλοῦ κομιζομένοις τὴν πάτριον
54 αὐτονομίαν. Σαβίνῳ δ' ἀγαπητὸν μὲν ἦν ὑπεξ-
ελθεῖν, ἠπίστει δὲ ταῖς ὑποσχέσεσιν καὶ τὸ πρᾷον
αὐτῶν δέλεαρ εἰς ἐνέδραν ὑπώπτευεν· ἅμα δὲ καὶ
τὴν ἀπὸ Οὐάρου βοήθειαν ἐλπίζων διέτριβεν τὴν
πολιορκίαν.
55 (iv. 1) Ἐν δὲ τούτῳ καὶ τὰ κατὰ τὴν χώραν

---

[1] ed. pr. : αὐτοὺς mss.
[2] ἦν πολέμου ῥοπή Naber : ἢ πολέμου ῥοπήν most mss.

[a] According to *A.* xvii. 264 Sabinus secured 400 talents
apart from the sums stolen by the soldiers. The writer of *A.*
is clearly imitating Thuc. vii. 85 τὸ μὲν οὖν ἀθροισθὲν τοῦ
στρατεύματος ἐς τὸ κοινὸν οὐ πολὺ ἐγένετο, τὸ δὲ διακλαπὲν πολύ,
a passage of which there may be a faint reminiscence here.
[b] *i.e.* troops drafted in the region of Sebaste = Samaria.

four hundred talents ; of this sum all that was not stolen by them was collected by Sabinus.[a]

(4) However, the effect of this loss of buildings and of lives was only to rally the Jews in far greater strength and efficiency against the Romans. Surrounding the palace, they threatened to kill them to a man unless they promptly withdrew ; if Sabinus were prepared to retire with his legion, they guaranteed him a safe conduct. The rebels now had with them the bulk of the royal troops which had deserted to their side. The most efficient division, however, of those troops still adhered to the Romans, namely, three thousand Sebastenians,[b] under Rufus and Gratus, the latter commanding the royal infantry, the former the cavalry ;—a pair, either of whom, even without any force under him, was worth an army,[c] owing to their bravery and acumen. So the Jews pressed the siege, making assaults on the fortress, while at the same time they loudly called on Sabinus and his followers to depart and not to stand in the way of men who after such a lapse of time were on the road to recovering their national independence. Sabinus would have been quite content to slink away, but he mistrusted their promises, and suspected that their mildness was a bait to ensnare him ; he was, moreover, hoping for succour from Varus and so let the siege drag on.

(iv. 1) Meanwhile, the country also, in various

Sabinus besieged in the palace.

These cohorts of *Sebasteni* are often mentioned in inscriptions, and elsewhere in Josephus, *e.g. B.* ii. 58, 63, 74, 236. The σπεῖρα Σεβαστή mentioned in Acts xxvii. 1 as quartered at Caesarea was probably one of them, though Σεβαστή = *Augusta*, not Sebastenian ; its full title was probably *cohors Augusta Sebastenorum* (Schürer).

[c] Literally " sufficient to turn the scale of war."

πολλαχόθεν ἐταράσσετο, καὶ συχνοὺς βασιλειᾶν ὁ
καιρὸς ἀνέπειθεν. κατὰ μέν γε τὴν Ἰδουμαίαν
δισχίλιοι τῶν ὑπὸ Ἡρώδῃ πάλαι στρατευσαμένων
συστάντες ἔνοπλοι διεμάχοντο τοῖς βασιλικοῖς, οἷς
Ἀχίαβος ἀνεψιὸς βασιλέως ἀπὸ τῶν ἐρυμνοτάτων
χωρίων ἐπολέμει, ὑποφεύγων τὴν ἐν τοῖς πεδίοις
56 συμπλοκήν· ἐν δὲ Σεπφώρει τῆς Γαλιλαίας Ἰούδας,
υἱὸς Ἐζεκία τοῦ κατατρέχοντός ποτε τὴν χώραν
ἀρχιλῃστοῦ καὶ χειρωθέντος ὑφ' Ἡρώδου βασιλέως, συστήσας πλῆθος οὐκ ὀλίγον ἀναρρήγνυσιν
τὰς βασιλικὰς ὁπλοθήκας καὶ τοὺς περὶ αὐτὸν
ὁπλίσας τοῖς τὴν δυναστείαν ζηλοῦσιν ἐπεχείρει.

57 (2) Κατὰ δὲ τὴν Περαίαν Σίμων τις τῶν βασιλικῶν δούλων, εὐμορφίᾳ σώματος καὶ μεγέθει
πεποιθώς, περιτίθησιν μὲν ἑαυτῷ διάδημα, περιιὼν
δὲ μεθ' ὧν συνήθροισεν λῃστῶν τά τε ἐν Ἱεριχοῖ
βασίλεια καταπίμπρησιν καὶ πολλὰς ἑτέρας. τῶν
πολυτελῶν ἐπαύλεις, ἁρπαγὰς ῥᾳδίως ἐκ τοῦ
58 πυρὸς αὐτῷ ποριζόμενος. κἂν ἔφθη πᾶσαν οἴκησιν
εὐπρεπῆ καταφλέξας, εἰ μὴ Γρᾶτος ὁ τῶν βασιλικῶν πεζῶν ἡγεμὼν τούς τε Τραχωνίτας[1] τοξότας
καὶ τὸ μαχιμώτατον τῶν Σεβαστηνῶν ἀναλαβὼν
59 ὑπαντιάζει τὸν ἄνδρα. τῶν μὲν οὖν Περαίων[2]
συχνοὶ διεφθάρησαν ἐν τῇ μάχῃ, τὸν Σίμωνα δ'
αὐτὸν ἀναφεύγοντα δι' ὀρθίου φάραγγος ὁ Γρᾶτος
ὑποτέμνεται καὶ φεύγοντος ἐκ πλαγίου τὸν αὐχένα
πλήξας ἀπέρραξεν.[3] κατεφλέγη δὲ καὶ τὰ πλησίον

---

[1] Hudson from Lat.: Τραχαιῶτας etc. mss.
[2] Destinon from A. ‖: παίων, παίδων or πεζῶν mss.
[3] ἀπέρρηξεν PA.

---

[a] i.e. Herod, whom he had once saved from suicide,
B. i. 662 ; cf. ii. 77. [b] B. i. 204.

districts, was a prey to disorder, and the opportunity Anarchy in Palestine. induced numbers of persons to aspire to sovereignty. In Idumaea, two thousand of Herod's veterans formed Revolt of Herod's veterans in Idumaea up in arms and took the field against the royal troops. They were opposed by Achiab, the king's [a] cousin, who, avoiding an engagement in the plain, fell back on the strongest positions. At Sepphoris in Galilee and of Judas in Galilee. Judas, son of Ezechias, the brigand-chief who in former days infested the country and was subdued by King Herod,[b] raised a considerable body of followers, broke open the royal arsenals, and, having armed his companions, attacked the other aspirants to power.

(2) In Peraea Simon,[c] one of the royal slaves, proud The usurper Simon in Peraea. of his tall and handsome figure, assumed the diadem. Perambulating the country with the brigands whom he had collected, he burnt down the royal palace at Jericho and many other stately mansions, such incendiarism providing him with an easy opportunity for plunder. Not a house of any respectability would have escaped the flames, had not Gratus, the commander of the royal infantry, with the archers of Trachonitis and the finest troops of the Sebastenians, gone out to encounter this rascal. In the ensuing engagement numbers of the Peraeans fell. Simon himself, endeavouring to escape up a steep ravine, was intercepted by Gratus, who struck the fugitive from the side a blow on the neck, which severed his head from his body. The palace at Betharamatha,[d]

[c] Mentioned by Tacitus, *Hist.* v. 9 " post mortem Herodis ... Simo quidam regium nomen inuaserat " (Reinach).

[d] Beth-haram of the Old Test. (Jos. xiii. 27), Beth-ramtha of the Talmud, rebuilt by Herod Antipas and renamed Julias (*A.* xviii. 27) or Livias ; some six miles north of the head of the Dead Sea and east of the Jordan.

Ἰορδάνου βασίλεια κατὰ Βηθαράμαθα[1] συστάντων
ἑτέρων τινῶν ἐκ τῆς Περαίας.

60 (3) Τότε καὶ ποιμήν τις ἀντιποιηθῆναι βασιλείας ἐτόλμησεν. Ἀθρογγαῖος ἐκαλεῖτο, πρου-
ξένει δ' αὐτῷ τὴν ἐλπίδα σώματος ἰσχὺς καὶ ψυχὴ
θανάτου καταφρονοῦσα, πρὸς δὲ τούτοις ἀδελφοὶ
61 τέσσαρες ὅμοιοι. τούτων ἑκάστῳ λόχον ὑποζεύξας
ἔνοπλον ὥσπερ στρατηγοῖς ἐχρῆτο καὶ σατράπαις
ἐπὶ τὰς καταδρομάς, αὐτὸς δὲ καθάπερ βασιλεὺς
62 τῶν σεμνοτέρων ἥπτετο πραγμάτων. τότε μὲν
οὖν ἑαυτῷ περιτίθησιν διάδημα, διέμεινεν δ'
ὕστερον οὐκ ὀλίγον χρόνον τὴν χώραν κατατρέχων
σὺν τοῖς ἀδελφοῖς· καὶ τὸ κτείνειν αὐτοῖς προ-
ηγούμενον ἦν Ῥωμαίους τε καὶ τοὺς βασιλικούς,
διέφευγεν δ' οὐδὲ Ἰουδαίων εἴ τις εἰς χεῖρας ἔλθοι
63 φέρων κέρδος. ἐτόλμησαν δέ ποτε Ῥωμαίων
λόχον ἄθρουν περισχεῖν κατ' Ἀμμαοῦντα· σῖτα δ'
οὗτοι καὶ ὅπλα διεκόμιζον τῷ τάγματι. τὸν μὲν
οὖν ἑκατοντάρχην αὐτῶν Ἄρειον καὶ τεσσαράκοντα
τοὺς γενναιοτάτους κατηκόντισαν, οἱ δὲ λοιποὶ
κινδυνεύοντες ταὐτὸ παθεῖν, Γράτου σὺν τοῖς
64 Σεβαστηνοῖς ἐπιβοηθήσαντος, ἐξέφυγον. πολλὰ
τοιαῦτα τοὺς ἐπιχωρίους καὶ τοὺς ἀλλοφύλους
παρ' ὅλον τὸν πόλεμον ἐργασάμενοι μετὰ χρόνον
οἱ μὲν τρεῖς ἐχειρώθησαν, ὑπ' Ἀρχελάου μὲν ὁ
πρεσβύτατος, οἱ δ' ἑξῆς δύο Γράτῳ καὶ Πτολεμαίῳ περιπεσόντες· ὁ δὲ τέταρτος Ἀρχελάῳ
65 προσεχώρησεν κατὰ δεξιάν. τοῦτο μὲν δὴ τὸ
τέλος ὕστερον αὐτοὺς ἐξεδέχετο, τότε δὲ ληστρικοῦ
πολέμου τὴν Ἰουδαίαν πᾶσαν ἐνεπίμπλασαν.

---

[1] Niese: Βηθαράμιν ἔνθα or Βηθαραμάθου mss.: ἐν Ἀμμάθοις
A. ‖, Βηθαραμφθᾶ Λ. xviii. 27.

near the Jordan, was likewise burnt to the ground by another body of Peraean insurgents.

(3) Now, too, a mere shepherd had the temerity to aspire to the throne. He was called Athrongaeus, and his sole recommendations, to raise such hopes, were vigour of body, a soul contemptuous of death, and four brothers resembling himself. To each of these he entrusted an armed band and employed them as generals and satraps for his raids, while he himself, like a king, handled matters of graver moment. It was now that he donned the diadem, but his raiding expeditions throughout the country with his brothers continued long afterwards. Their principal object was to kill Romans and royalists, but no Jew, from whom they had anything to gain, escaped, if he fell into their hands. On one occasion they ventured to surround, near Emmaus,[a] an entire Roman company,[b] engaged in convoying corn and arms to the legion. Their centurion Arius and forty of his bravest men were shot down by the brigands; the remainder, in danger of a like fate, were rescued through the intervention of Gratus with his Sebastenians. After perpetrating throughout the war many such outrages upon compatriot and foreigner alike, three of them were eventually captured, the eldest by Archelaus, the two next by Gratus and Ptolemy; the fourth made terms with Archelaus and surrendered.[c] Such was the end to which they ultimately came; but at the period of which we are speaking, these men were making the whole of Judaea one scene of guerilla warfare.

The usurper Athrongaeus the shepherd.

[a] See § 71 note. [b] *Centuria.*
[c] There were five in all (§ 60); the fate of the fifth is unrecorded.

66 (v. 1) Οὐάρῳ δὲ δεξαμένῳ τὰ παρὰ Σαβίνου
καὶ τῶν ἡγεμόνων γράμματα δεῖσαί τε περὶ τοῦ
τάγματος ὅλου παρέστη καὶ σπεύδειν ἐπὶ τὴν
67 βοήθειαν. ἀναλαβὼν δὴ τὰ λοιπὰ δύο τάγματα
καὶ τὰς σὺν αὐτοῖς τέσσαρας ἴλας ἱππέων ἐπὶ
Πτολεμαΐδος ᾔει, προστάξας ἐκεῖ καὶ τοὺς παρὰ
τῶν βασιλέων καὶ δυναστῶν ἐπικούρους συνελθεῖν·
προσέλαβεν δὲ καὶ παρὰ Βηρυτίων διερχόμενος
68 τὴν πόλιν χιλίους καὶ πεντακοσίους ὁπλίτας. ἐπεὶ
δ' εἰς τὴν Πτολεμαΐδα τό τε ἄλλο συμμαχικὸν
πλῆθος αὐτῷ παρῆν καὶ κατὰ τὸ πρὸς Ἡρώδην
ἔχθος Ἀρέτας ὁ Ἄραψ οὐκ ὀλίγην ἄγων δύναμιν
ἱππικήν τε καὶ πεζικήν, μέρος τῆς στρατιᾶς εὐθέως
ἔπεμπεν εἰς τὴν Γαλιλαίαν γειτνιῶσαν τῇ Πτολεμαΐδι καὶ Γάιον[1] ἡγεμόνα τῶν αὐτοῦ φίλων, ὃς
τούς τε ὑπαντιάσαντας τρέπεται καὶ Σέπφωριν
πόλιν ἑλὼν αὐτὴν μὲν ἐμπίπρησι, τοὺς δ' ἐν-
69 οικοῦντας ἀνδραποδίζεται. μετὰ δὲ τῆς ὅλης δυνάμεως αὐτὸς Οὔαρος εἰς Σαμάρειαν ἐλάσας τῆς μὲν
πόλεως ἀπέσχετο, μηδὲν ἐν τοῖς τῶν ἄλλων θορύβοις παρακεκινηκυῖαν εὑρών, αὐλίζεται δὲ περί
τινα κώμην Ἀροῦν καλουμένην· κτῆμα δὲ ἦν
Πτολεμαίου καὶ διὰ τοῦτο ὑπὸ τῶν Ἀράβων
διηρπάσθη μηνιόντων καὶ τοῖς Ἡρώδου φίλοις.
70 ἔνθεν εἰς Σαπφὼ πρόεισιν, κώμην ἑτέραν ἐρυμνήν,
ἣν ὁμοίως διήρπασαν τάς τε προσόρους[2] πάσας
ὅσαις ἐπετύγχανον. πυρὸς δὲ καὶ φόνου πεπλήρωτο πάντα καὶ πρὸς τὰς ἁρπαγὰς τῶν Ἀράβων

---

[1] Γάιον] Galli filio Lat.: τῷ υἱῷ A. ‖.
[2] Destinon and Niese: προσόδους mss.

(v. 1) On receiving the dispatches from Sabinus and his officers, Varus was alarmed for the whole legion and resolved to hasten to its relief. Accordingly, mobilizing the two remaining legions with the four regiments[a] of horse which were attached to them, he marched for Ptolemais, having ordered the auxiliary troops furnished by the kings and chieftains to assemble at that place. On his way through Berytus,[b] his army was further increased by 1500 armed recruits from that city. When the other contingent of allies had joined him at Ptolemais, as well as Aretas the Arab who, in memory of his hatred of Herod, brought a considerable body of cavalry and infantry, Varus at once sent a detachment of his army into the region of Galilee adjoining Ptolemais, under the command of his friend Gaius ; the latter routed all who opposed him, captured and burnt the city of Sepphoris and reduced its inhabitants to slavery. Varus himself with the main body pursued his march into the country of Samaria ; he spared the city, finding that it had taken no part in the general tumult, and encamped near a village called Arous[c] ; this belonged to Ptolemy and for that reason was sacked by the Arabs, who were infuriated even against the friends of Herod. Thence he advanced to Sappho,[d] another fortified village, which they likewise sacked, as well as all the neighbouring villages which they encountered on their march. The whole district became a scene of fire and blood, and nothing was safe against the ravages of the

consisting of 500 horse, as distinct from the strictly " legionary " squadrons of cavalry, consisting of only 120 horse, *B.* iii. 120 (Reinach).

[b] Beirut. [c] Position unknown.

[d] Unknown ; Sampho in *A.* xvii. 290.

71 οὐδὲν ἀντεῖχεν. κατεφλέγη δὲ καὶ ᾿Αμμαοῦς
φυγόντων τῶν οἰκητόρων, Οὐάρου δι' ὀργὴν τῶν
περὶ ῎Αρειον ἀποσφαγέντων κελεύσαντος.

72 (2) ᾿Ενθένδε[1] εἰς ῾Ιεροσόλυμα προελθὼν ὀφθείς
τε μόνον μετὰ τῆς δυνάμεως τὰ στρατόπεδα τῶν

73 ᾿Ιουδαίων διεσκέδασεν. καὶ οἱ μὲν ᾤχοντο φυγόντες ἀνὰ τὴν χώραν· δεξάμενοι δὲ αὐτὸν οἱ κατὰ
τὴν πόλιν ἀπεσκευάζοντο τὰς αἰτίας τῆς ἀποστάσεως, αὐτοὶ μὲν οὐδὲν παρακινῆσαι λέγοντες, διὰ δὲ τὴν ἑορτὴν ἀναγκαίως δεξάμενοι τὸ
πλῆθος συμπολιορκηθῆναι μᾶλλον ῾Ρωμαίοις ἢ συμ-

74 πολεμῆσαι τοῖς ἀποστᾶσιν. προϋπηντήκεισαν δὲ
αὐτῷ ᾿Ιώσηπός [τε][2] ὁ ἀνεψιὸς ᾿Αρχελάου καὶ
σὺν Γράτῳ ῾Ροῦφος, ἄγοντες ἅμα τῷ βασιλικῷ
στρατῷ καὶ τοὺς Σεβαστηνούς, οἵ τε ἀπὸ τοῦ
῾Ρωμαϊκοῦ τάγματος τὸν συνήθη τρόπον κεκοσμη-
μένοι· Σαβῖνος μὲν γὰρ οὐδ' εἰς ὄψιν ὑπομείνας
ἐλθεῖν Οὐάρῳ προεξῆλθεν τῆς πόλεως ἐπὶ θάλασ-

75 σαν. Οὔαρος δὲ [κατὰ][3] μοῖραν τῆς στρατιᾶς ἐπὶ
τοὺς αἰτίους τοῦ κινήματος ἔπεμψεν περὶ[4] τὴν
χώραν, καὶ πολλῶν ἀγομένων τοὺς μὲν ἧττον
θορυβώδεις φανέντας ἐφρούρει, τοὺς δ' αἰτιωτάτους
ἀνεσταύρωσεν περὶ δισχιλίους.

76 (3) ᾿Ηγγέλθη δ' αὐτῷ κατὰ τὴν ᾿Ιδουμαίαν ἔτι
συμμένειν μυρίους ὁπλίτας. ὁ δὲ τοὺς μὲν ῎Αραβας
εὑρὼν οὐ συμμάχων ἦθος ἔχοντας, ἀλλ' ἰδίῳ πάθει
στρατευομένους καὶ πέρα τῆς ἑαυτοῦ προαιρέσεως
τὴν χώραν κακοῦντας ἔχθει τῷ πρὸς ῾Ηρώδην
ἀποπέμπεται, μετὰ δὲ τῶν ἰδίων ταγμάτων ἐπὶ

_____

[1] P : ἔνθεν δὲ ΑΜ : ἔνθεν the rest.   [2] om. PAM.
[3] om. LVRC.   [4] ἐπὶ PAM.

_____

[a] § 63.   The Emmaus intended is doubtless the town S.E.

Arabs. Emmaus, the inhabitants of which had fled, was burnt to the ground by the orders of Varus, in revenge for the slaughter of Arius and his men.[a]

(2) Proceeding thence to Jerusalem, he had only to show himself at the head of his troops to disperse the Jewish camps. Their occupants fled up country; but the Jews in the city received him and disclaimed all responsibility for the revolt, asserting that they themselves had never stirred, that the festival had compelled them to admit the crowd, and that they had been rather besieged with the Romans than in league with the rebels. Prior to this, Varus had been met outside the city by Joseph, the cousin of Archelaus,[b] with Rufus and Gratus, at the head of the royal army and the Sebastenians, and by the Roman legionaries, in their customary equipment; for Sabinus, not venturing to face Varus, had previously left the city for the coast. Varus now detached part of his army to scour the country in search of the authors of the insurrection, many of whom were brought in. Those who appeared to be the less turbulent individuals he imprisoned; the most culpable, in number about two thousand, he crucified.

He quells the insurrection in Jerusalem

(3) He was informed that in Idumaea ten thousand still held together in arms. Finding that the Arabs were not properly conducting themselves as allies, but were rather making war to gratify their private resentment, and, from hatred of Herod, were doing more injury to the country than he had intended, he dismissed them, and with his own legions marched

and in Idumaea.

of Lydda at the foot of the Judaean hills, mod. *Amwas*, at one time Nicopolis, not the village much nearer to Jerusalem mentioned in Luke xxiv. 13.

[b] Joseph, son of Herod's brother Joseph, who was killed at Jericho (*A*. xviii. 134, *B*. i. 323 f.).

351

77 τοὺς ἀφεστῶτας ἠπείγετο. κἀκεῖνοι πρὶν εἰς
χεῖρας ἐλθεῖν Ἀχιάβου συμβουλεύσαντος σφᾶς
αὐτοὺς παρέδοσαν, Οὔαρος δὲ τῷ πλήθει μὲν ἠφίει
τὰς αἰτίας, τοὺς δὲ ἡγεμόνας ἐξετασθησομένους
78 ἔπεμπεν ἐπὶ Καίσαρα. Καῖσαρ δὲ τοῖς μὲν ἄλλοις
συνέγνω, τινὰς δὲ τῶν τοῦ βασιλέως συγγενῶν,
ἦσαν γὰρ ἐν αὐτοῖς ἔνιοι προσήκοντες Ἡρώδῃ
κατὰ γένος, κολάσαι προσέταξεν, ὅτι κατ' οἰκείου
79 βασιλέως ἐστρατεύσαντο. Οὔαρος μὲν οὖν τοῦτον
τὸν τρόπον καταστησάμενος τὰ ἐν Ἱεροσολύμοις
καὶ φρουρὰν καταλιπὼν τὸ καὶ πρότερον τάγμα
εἰς Ἀντιόχειαν ἐπάνεισιν.

80 (vi. 1) Ἀρχελάῳ δ' ἐπὶ Ῥώμης πάλιν ἄλλη
συνίσταται δίκη πρὸς Ἰουδαίους, οἳ πρὸ τῆς ἀποστάσεως ἐπιτρέψαντος Οὔαρου πρέσβεις ἐξελη-
λύθεσαν περὶ τῆς τοῦ ἔθνους αὐτονομίας· ἦσαν δὲ
πεντήκοντα μὲν οἱ παρόντες, συμπαρίσταντο δὲ
αὐτοῖς τῶν ἐπὶ Ῥώμης Ἰουδαίων ὑπὲρ ὀκτακισ-
81 χιλίους. ἀθροίσαντος δὲ Καίσαρος συνέδριον τῶν
ἐν τέλει Ῥωμαίων καὶ τῶν φίλων ἐν τῷ κατὰ τὸ
Παλάτιον Ἀπόλλωνος ἱερῷ, κτίσμα δ' ἦν ἴδιον
αὐτοῦ θαυμασίῳ πολυτελείᾳ κεκοσμημένον, μετὰ
μὲν τῶν πρεσβευτῶν τὸ Ἰουδαϊκὸν πλῆθος ἔστη,
82 σὺν δὲ τοῖς φίλοις ἄντικρυς Ἀρχέλαος, τῶν δὲ
τούτου συγγενῶν οἱ φίλοι παρ' οὐδετέροις, συμπαρ-
ίστασθαι μὲν Ἀρχελάῳ διὰ μῖσος καὶ φθόνον οὐχ
ὑπομένοντες, ὀφθῆναι δὲ μετὰ τῶν κατηγόρων
83 ὑπὸ Καίσαρος αἰδούμενοι. τούτοις συμπαρῆν[1] καὶ
Φίλιππος ἀδελφὸς Ἀρχελάου, προπεμφθεὶς κατ'
εὔνοιαν ὑπὸ Οὐάρου δυοῖν ἕνεκα, Ἀρχελάῳ τε
συναγωνίσασθαι, κἂν διανέμῃ τὸν Ἡρώδου Καῖσαρ
οἶκον πᾶσι τοῖς ἐγγόνοις, κλήρου τινὸς ἀξιωθῆναι.

in haste to meet the rebels. They, before any action took place, on the advice of Achiab,[a] surrendered ; Varus discharged the rank and file and sent the leaders to Caesar for trial. Caesar pardoned all with the exception of certain individuals of royal blood, for their number included some relatives of Herod ; these he ordered to be punished for taking up arms against a sovereign who was of their own family. Having thus restored order in Jerusalem, Varus left as garrison the legion previously quartered there and returned to Antioch.

(vi. 1) Meanwhile, Archelaus in Rome had to defend himself in a new suit against certain Jewish deputies who, before the revolt, had set out with the permission of Varus to plead for the autonomy of their nation. Fifty deputies appeared, but more than eight thousand of the Jews in Rome espoused their cause. Caesar assembled a council, composed of the Roman magistrates and his friends, in the temple of the Palatine Apollo, a building erected by himself with astonishingly rich ornamentation. The Jewish crowd took up a position with the deputies ; opposite them was Archelaus with his friends ; the friends of his relatives appeared neither on the one side nor on the other, scorning through hatred and envy to join Archelaus, yet ashamed to let Caesar see them among his accusers. Another person present was Philip, brother of Archelaus, whom Varus, out of friendliness, had sent off under escort with two objects : primarily to support Archelaus, but also to come in for a share of Herod's estate in case Caesar should distribute it among all his descendants.

A Jewish embassy to Rome asks for autonomy.

Augustus summons a fresh council.

---

[a] § 55.

¹ M : τούτοις παρῆν PA : ἐπὶ τούτοις παρῆν the rest.

84 (2) Ἐπιτραπὲν δὲ λέγειν τοῖς κατηγόροις τὰς Ἡρώδου παρανομίας πρῶτον διεξήεσαν, οὐ βασιλέα λέγοντες, ἀλλὰ τῶν πώποτε τυραννησάντων ὠμότατον ἐνηνοχέναι τύραννον· πλείστων γοῦν ἀνηρημένων ὑπ' αὐτοῦ τοιαῦτα πεπονθέναι τοὺς καταλειφθέντας, ὥστε μακαρίζεσθαι τοὺς ἀπολωλότας·

85 βεβασανικέναι γὰρ οὐ μόνον τὰ σώματα τῶν ὑποτεταγμένων, ἀλλὰ καὶ τὰς πόλεις· τὰς μὲν γὰρ ἰδίας λελωβῆσθαι, τὰς δὲ τῶν ἀλλοφύλων κεκοσμηκέναι καὶ τὸ τῆς Ἰουδαίας αἷμα κεχαρίσθαι

86 τοῖς ἔξωθεν δήμοις. ἀντὶ δὲ τῆς παλαιᾶς εὐδαιμονίας καὶ τῶν πατρίων νόμων πενίας τὸ ἔθνος καὶ παρανομίας ἐσχάτης πεπληρωκέναι, καθόλου δὲ πλείους ὑπομεμενηκέναι τὰς ἐξ Ἡρώδου συμφορὰς ἐν ὀλίγοις ἔτεσιν Ἰουδαίους ὧν ἐν παντὶ τῷ χρόνῳ μετὰ τὴν ἐκ Βαβυλῶνος ἀναχώρησιν ἔπαθον οἱ πρόγονοι, Ξέρξου βασιλεύοντος ἀπανα-

87 στάντες. εἰς τοσοῦτον μέντοι μετριότητος[1] καὶ[2] τοῦ δυστυχεῖν ἔθους προελθεῖν, ὥστε ὑπομεῖναι τῆς πικρᾶς δουλείας καὶ διαδοχὴν αὐθαίρετον·

88 Ἀρχέλαον γοῦν τὸν τηλικούτου τυράννου παῖδα μετὰ τὴν τοῦ πατρὸς τελευτὴν βασιλέα τε προσειπεῖν ἑτοίμως καὶ συμπενθῆσαι τὸν Ἡρώδου θάνατον αὐτῷ καὶ συνεύξασθαι περὶ τῆς διαδοχῆς.

89 τὸν δ' ὥσπερ ἀγωνιάσαντα, μὴ νόθος υἱὸς εἶναι δόξειεν Ἡρώδου, προοιμιάσασθαι τὴν βασιλείαν τρισχιλίων πολιτῶν φόνῳ, καὶ τοσαῦτα μὲν παρεστακέναι θύματα περὶ τῆς ἀρχῆς τῷ θεῷ, τοσούτοις

---

[1] PAM Lat.: ταπεινότητος the rest.
[2] ἐκ Hudson, Bekker.

(2) The plaintiffs, being given permission to state their case, began by enumerating Herod's enormities. " It was not a king," they said, " whom they had had to tolerate, but the most cruel tyrant that ever existed. Numerous had been his victims, but the survivors had suffered so much that they envied the fate of the dead. For he had tortured not only the persons of his subjects, but also their cities; and while he crippled the towns in his own dominion, he embellished those of other nations, lavishing the life-blood of Judaea on foreign communities. In place of their ancient prosperity and ancestral laws, he had sunk the nation to poverty and the last degree of iniquity. In short, the miseries which Herod in the course of a few years had inflicted on the Jews surpassed all that their forefathers had suffered during all the time since they left Babylon to return to their country in the reign of Xerxes.[a] And yet so chastened and habituated to misfortune had they become, that they had consented to this bitter servitude being made hereditary and had actually chosen the heir themselves! This Archelaus, son of such a tyrant, they had, on his father's decease, promptly acclaimed king; they had joined in his mourning for Herod's death, in his prayers for the prosperity of his own reign. But he, anxious apparently not to be taken for a bastard son of Herod, had ushered in his reign with the massacre of three thousand citizens; that was the grand total of the victims which he had offered to God on behalf of his throne, that was the number of corpses with which he had filled the

[a] *i.e.* the return under Ezra, which Josephus (*A.* xi. 120) places in the reign of Xerxes, not as in the O.T. in that of Artaxerxes.

90 δ' ἐμπεπληκέναι νεκροῖς τὸ ἱερὸν ἐν ἑορτῇ. τοὺς
μέντοι περιλειφθέντας ἐκ τοσούτων κακῶν εἰκότως
ἐπεστράφθαι ποτὲ ἤδη[1] πρὸς τὰς συμφορὰς καὶ
πολέμου νόμῳ τὰς πληγὰς ἐθέλειν κατὰ πρόσωπον
δέχεσθαι, δεῖσθαι δὲ Ῥωμαίων ἐλεῆσαι τά τε[2]
τῆς Ἰουδαίας λείψανα καὶ μὴ τὸ περισσὸν αὐτῆς
91 ὑπορρῖψαι τοῖς ὠμῶς σπαράττουσιν, συνάψαντας
δὲ τῇ Συρίᾳ τὴν χώραν αὐτῶν διοικεῖν ἐπ' ἰδίοις
ἡγεμόσιν· ἐπιδείξεσθαι γάρ, ὡς οἱ νῦν στασιώδεις
διαβαλλόμενοι καὶ πολεμικοὶ φέρειν οἴδασιν με-
92 τρίους ἡγεμόνας. Ἰουδαῖοι μὲν οὖν ἐκ τῆς κατηγορίας κατέληξαν εἰς τοιαύτην ἀξίωσιν, ἀναστὰς
δὲ Νικόλαος ἀπελύσατο[3] μὲν τὰς εἰς τοὺς βασιλεῖς
αἰτίας, κατηγόρει δὲ τοῦ ἔθνους τό τε δύσαρκτον
καὶ τὸ δυσπειθὲς φύσει πρὸς τοὺς βασιλεῖς.
συνδιέβαλλε δὲ καὶ τοὺς Ἀρχελάου συγγενεῖς,
ὅσοι πρὸς τοὺς κατηγόρους ἀφεισ τήκεσαν.

93 (3) Τότε μὲν οὖν Καῖσαρ ἀκούσας ἑκατέρων
διέλυσε τὸ συνέδριον, μετὰ δ' ἡμέρας ὀλίγας
τὸ μὲν ἥμισυ τῆς βασιλείας Ἀρχελάῳ δίδωσιν
ἐθνάρχην προσειπών, ὑποσχόμενος δὲ καὶ βασιλέα
94 ποιήσειν, εἰ ἄξιον ἑαυτὸν παράσχοι,[4] τὸ δὲ λοιπὸν
ἥμισυ διελὼν εἰς δύο τετραρχίας δυσὶν ἑτέροις
παισὶν Ἡρώδου δίδωσιν, τὴν μὲν Φιλίππῳ, τὴν
δὲ Ἀντίπᾳ τῷ πρὸς Ἀρχέλαον ἀμφισβητοῦντι
95 περὶ τῆς βασιλείας. ἐγένετο δὲ ὑπὸ τούτῳ μὲν ἥ
τε Περαία καὶ Γαλιλαία, πρόσοδος διακοσίων
ταλάντων, Βατανέα δὲ καὶ Τράχων Αὐρανῖτίς τε

---

[1] ἤδη πότε LVRC.   [2] trs. τε τὰ ed. pr.
[3] Niese and others from Lat.: ἀπεδύσατο mss.; cf. B. i. 452.
[4] Niese: παράσχῃ mss.

Temple at a festival ! It was, however, but natural that those who had survived such disasters should now at length turn and confront their calamities and desire to face their blows, in accordance with the laws of war. They implored the Romans to take pity on the relics of Judaea and not to fling what remained of it to those who were savagely rending it in pieces, but to unite their country to Syria and to entrust the administration to governors from among themselves. The Jews would then show that, calumniated though they now were as factious and always at war, they knew how to obey equitable rulers." With this petition the Jews brought their accusation to a close. Nicolas then rose and, after refuting the charges ^{and of} ^{Nicolas.} brought against the occupants of the throne, retorted by an accusation of the national character, impatient of all authority and insubordinate towards their sovereigns. The relatives of Archelaus who had gone over to his accusers also came in for a share of his strictures.

(3) Caesar, after hearing both parties, dismissed the assembly. His decision was announced a few days later : he gave half the kingdom to Archelaus, with the title of ethnarch, promising, moreover, to make him king, should he prove his deserts ; the other half he divided into two tetrarchies, which he presented to two other sons of Herod, one to Philip, the other to Antipas, who had disputed the throne with Archelaus. Antipas had for his province Peraea and Galilee, with a revenue of two hundred talents. Batanaea, Trachonitis, Auranitis and certain portions

Augustus divides Herod's kingdom between his three sons, Archelaus (as ethnarch), Antipas and Philip (as tetrarchs).

καὶ μέρη τινὰ τοῦ Ζήνωνος οἴκου τὰ περὶ Πανιάδα,[1]
πρόσοδον ἔχοντα ταλάντων ἑκατόν, ὑπὸ Φιλίππῳ
96 τέτακτο. τῆς Ἀρχελάου δ᾽ ἐθναρχίας Ἰδουμαία
τε καὶ Ἰουδαία πᾶσα καὶ Σαμαρεῖτις ἦν, κεκου-
φισμένη τετάρτῳ μέρει τῶν φόρων εἰς τιμὴν τοῦ
97 μὴ μετὰ τῶν ἄλλων ἀποστῆναι. πόλεις δ᾽ ὑπ-
ηκόους παρέλαβεν Στράτωνος πύργον καὶ Σεβαστὴν
καὶ Ἰόππην καὶ Ἱεροσόλυμα· τὰς γὰρ Ἑλληνίδας
Γάζαν καὶ Γάδαρα καὶ Ἵππον ἀποτεμόμενος τῆς
βασιλείας προσέθηκεν Συρίᾳ. πρόσοδος [δ᾽][2] ἦν
τῆς Ἀρχελάῳ δοθείσης χώρας τετρακοσίων ταλάν-
98 των. Σαλώμῃ. δὲ πρὸς οἷς ὁ βασιλεὺς ἐν ταῖς
διαθήκαις κατέλιπεν Ἰαμνείας τε καὶ Ἀζώτου καὶ
Φασαηλίδος ἀποδείκνυται δεσπότις, χαρίζεται δ᾽
αὐτῇ Καῖσαρ καὶ τὰ ἐν Ἀσκάλωνι βασίλεια·
συνήγετο δ᾽ ἐκ πάντων ἑξήκοντα προσόδου τάλαντα·
τὸν δὲ οἶκον αὐτῆς ὑπὸ τὴν Ἀρχελάου τοπαρχίαν
99 ἔταξεν. τῆς δ᾽ ἄλλης Ἡρώδου γενεᾶς ἕκαστος τὸ
καταλειφθὲν ἐν ταῖς διαθήκαις ἐκομίζετο. δυσὶ
δ᾽ αὐτοῦ θυγατράσι παρθένοις Καῖσαρ ἔξωθεν
χαρίζεται πεντήκοντα μυριάδας ἀργυρίου καὶ
100 συνῴκισεν αὐτὰς τοῖς Φερώρα παισίν. μετὰ δὲ
τὸν οἶκον ἐπιδιένειμεν αὐτοῖς τὴν ἑαυτῷ κατα-
λειφθεῖσαν ὑφ᾽ Ἡρώδου δωρεάν, οὖσαν χιλίων

---

[1] So Reinach after Graetz and Schürer, cf. A. xvii. 189:
the mss. have Ἰννάνω, Ἵναν or Ἰάμνειαν, the last a worthless
conjecture, conflicting with § 98.   [2] om. P.

---

[a] Called in the parallel passage (A. xvii. 319) and elsewhere (e.g. B. i. 398) Zenodorus.

of the domain of Zeno [a] in the neighbourhood of
Panias,[b] producing a revenue of a hundred talents,
were allotted to Philip. The ethnarchy of Archelaus
comprised the whole of Idumaea and Judaea, besides
the district of Samaria, which had a quarter of its
tribute remitted in consideration of its having taken
no part in the insurrection. The cities subjected to
Archelaus were Strato's Tower,[c] Sebaste,[d] Joppa and
Jerusalem ; the Greek towns of Gaza, Gadara, and
Hippos were, on the other hand, detached from his
principality and annexed to Syria. The territory
given to Archelaus produced a revenue of four
hundred [e] talents. Salome, besides the legacy which
the king had left her in his will, was declared mistress
of Jamnia, Azotus and Phasaelis ; Caesar also made
her a present of the palace of Ascalon, her revenue
from all sources amounting to sixty talents ; her
estates, however, were placed under the jurisdiction [f]
of Archelaus. Each of the other members of Herod's
family received the legacy named in the will. To the
king's two unmarried daughters [g] Caesar presented,
in addition, 500,000 (drachms) of silver and gave
them in marriage to the sons of Pheroras. After
this division of the estate, he further distributed
among the family Herod's legacy to himself, amount-

[b] The region to the south and east of Caesarea Philippi and
referred to as " Ituraea " in Luke iii. 1 (" Philip, tetrarch of
the region of Ituraea and Trachonitis ").
[c] Caesarea-on-sea.
[d] Samaria.
[e] 600 according to *A*. xvii. 320.
[f] Greek " toparchy."
[g] Roxane and Salome (i. 563).

ταλάντων, εὐτελῆ τινα τῶν κειμηλίων εἰς τὴν τοῦ κατοιχομένου τιμὴν ἐξελόμενος.

101 (vii. 1) Κἀν τούτῳ νεανίας τις Ἰουδαῖος μὲν τὸ γένος, τραφεὶς δ' ἐν Σιδῶνι παρά τῳ τῶν Ῥωμαίων ἀπελευθέρῳ,[1] δι' ὁμοιότητα μορφῆς ψευδόμενος ἑαυτὸν Ἀλέξανδρον τὸν ἀναιρεθέντα ὑφ' Ἡρώδου, κατ' ἐλπίδα τοῦ λήσειν ἧκεν εἰς

102 Ῥώμην. συνεργὸς δ' ἦν τις ὁμόφυλος αὐτῷ πάντα τὰ κατὰ τὴν βασιλείαν ἐπιστάμενος, ὑφ' οὗ διδαχθεὶς ἔλεγεν, ὡς οἱ πεμφθέντες ἐπὶ τὴν ἀναίρεσιν αὐτοῦ τε καὶ Ἀριστοβούλου δι' οἶκτον ἐκκλέψειαν αὐτοὺς ὁμοίως ὑποβολῇ σωμάτων.

103 τούτοις γοῦν τοὺς ἐν Κρήτῃ Ἰουδαίους ἐξαπατήσας καὶ λαμπρῶς ἐφοδιασθεὶς διέπλευσεν εἰς Μῆλον· ἔνθα συναγείρας πολλῷ πλέον δι' ὑπερβολὴν ἀξιοπιστίας ἀνέπεισεν καὶ τοὺς ἰδιοξένους

104 εἰς Ῥώμην αὐτῷ συνεκπλεῦσαι. καταχθεὶς δὲ εἰς Δικαιάρχειαν δῶρά τε παμπληθῆ παρὰ τῶν ἐκεῖ Ἰουδαίων λαμβάνει καὶ καθάπερ βασιλεὺς ὑπὸ τῶν πατρῴων προεπέμφθη φίλων. προεληλύθει δ' εἰς τοσοῦτον πίστεως τὸ τῆς μορφῆς ὅμοιον, ὥστε τοὺς ἑωρακότας Ἀλέξανδρον καὶ

105 σαφῶς ἐπισταμένους διόμνυσθαι τοῦτον εἶναι. τό γε μὴν Ἰουδαϊκὸν ἐν τῇ Ῥώμῃ ἅπαν ἐξεχύθη πρὸς τὴν θέαν αὐτοῦ, καὶ πλῆθος ἄπειρον ἦν περὶ τοὺς στενωποὺς δι' ὧν ἐκομίζετο· καὶ γὰρ [δὴ][2] προῆλθον εἰς τοσοῦτον φρενοβλαβείας οἱ Μήλιοι,

---

[1] Ῥωμαϊκῶν ἀπελευθέρων many mss.
[2] om. P.

---

ing to a thousand [a] talents, reserving only some trifling works of art which he kept in honour of the deceased.

(vii. 1) At this time a young man who, though by birth a Jew, had been brought up at Sidon at the house of a Roman freedman, on the strength of a certain physical resemblance passed himself off as the prince Alexander, whom Herod had put to death,[b] and came to Rome in the hope of imposing upon others. He had as his assistant a compatriot, perfectly acquainted with the affairs of the realm, acting upon whose instructions he gave out that the executioners sent to kill him and Aristobulus had, out of compassion, stolen them away, substituting in their stead the corpses of individuals who resembled them. With this tale he completely deceived the Jews of Crete, and, being handsomely furnished with supplies, sailed across to Melos, where, through the extreme plausibility of his story, he collected a much larger sum and even induced his hosts to embark with him for Rome. Landing at Dicaearchia,[c] he was loaded with presents by the Jewish colony there and was escorted on his way like a king by the friends of his supposed father. The resemblance was so convincing that those who had seen Alexander and known him well swore that this was he. At Rome all Jewry poured forth to see him, and vast crowds thronged the narrow streets through which he was borne ; for the crazy Melians went so far as to carry

The pseudo-Alexander.

given in *B.* is probably right ; we are told in *B.* i. 646 (as in the parallel passage in *A.*) that Herod left 1000 talents to Augustus and 500 to his wife, children, and friends. A drachm was "the ordinary day wage of a labourer"; a talent was 6000 drachms.

[b] i. 551.　　　[c] The Greek name for Puteoli (*Vita* 16).

ὥστε φορείῳ τε αὐτὸν κομίζειν καὶ θεραπείαν
βασιλικὴν ἰδίοις παρασχεῖν ἀναλώμασιν.

106 (2) Καῖσαρ δὲ γινώσκων [ἀκριβῶς]¹ τοὺς Ἀλεξάνδρου χαρακτῆρας, κατηγόρητο γὰρ ὑφ' Ἡρώδου
παρ' αὐτῷ, συνεώρα μὲν καὶ πρὶν ἰδεῖν τὸν
ἄνθρωπον τὴν τῆς ὁμοιότητος ἀπάτην, διδοὺς
δέ τι καὶ [πίστεως]² ταῖς ἱλαρωτέραις ἐλπίσιν
Κέλαδόν τινα πέμπει τῶν σαφῶς ἐπισταμένων
Ἀλέξανδρον, κελεύσας ἀγαγεῖν αὐτῷ τὸν νεανί-
107 σκον. ὁ δὲ ὡς εἶδεν, ἐτεκμήρατο μὲν τάχιστα καὶ
τὰς διαφορὰς τοῦ προσώπου, τὸ δὲ ὅλον σῶμα
σκληρότερόν τε καὶ δουλοφανὲς καταμαθὼν ἐνόησεν
108 πᾶν τὸ σύνταγμα. πάνυ δὲ αὐτὸν παρώξυνεν ἡ
τόλμα τῶν παρ' αὐτοῦ λεγομένων· τοῖς γὰρ
πυνθανομένοις περὶ Ἀριστοβούλου σῴζεσθαι μὲν
κἀκεῖνον ἔλεγεν, ἀπολελεῖφθαι δ' ἐπίτηδες ἐν
Κύπρῳ τὰς ἐπιβουλὰς φυλασσόμενον· ἧττον γὰρ
109 ἐπιχειρεῖσθαι διεζευγμένους. ἀπολαβόμενος οὖν
αὐτὸν κατ' ἰδίαν '' μισθόν,'' ἔφη, '' παρὰ Καίσαρος
ἔχεις τὸ ζῆν τοῦ μηνῦσαι τὸν ἀναπείσαντά σε
πλανᾶσθαι³ τηλικαῦτα.'' κἀκεῖνος αὐτῷ δηλώ-
σειν εἰπὼν ἕπεται πρὸς Καίσαρα καὶ τὸν Ἰουδαῖον
ἐνδείκνυται καταχρησάμενον αὐτοῦ τῇ ὁμοιότητι
πρὸς ἐργασίαν· τοσαῦτα γὰρ εἰληφέναι δῶρα καθ'
ἑκάστην πόλιν ὅσα ζῶν Ἀλέξανδρος οὐκ⁴ ἔλαβεν.
110 γελάσας δὲ Καῖσαρ ἐπὶ τούτοις τὸν μὲν ψευδαλέξ-
ανδρον δι' εὐεξίαν σώματος ἐγκατέταξεν τοῖς ἐρέ-
ταις, τὸν ἀναπείσαντα δὲ ἐκέλευσεν ἀναιρεθῆναι·
Μηλίοις δ' ἤρκεσεν ἐπιτίμιον τῆς ἀνοίας τὰ ἀνα-
λώματα.

¹ om. PAM.   ² om. Lat., perhaps rightly ; cf. A. ‖.
³ πλάσασθαι LVRC.   ⁴ om. οὐκ PAM.

him in a litter and to provide a royal retinue at their own expense.

(2) Caesar, who had an exact recollection of Alexander's features, as he had been arraigned by Herod at his tribunal,[a] divined, even before he had seen the fellow, that the affair was an imposture, based on resemblance ; however, to give a chance to a more favourable hope, he sent Celadus, one of those who knew Alexander best, with orders to bring the young man to him. Celadus had no sooner set eyes on him than he detected the points of difference in the face, and noting that his whole person had a coarser and servile appearance, penetrated the whole plot. The audacity of the fellow's statements quite exasperated him. For, when questioned about Aristobulus, he was in the habit of replying that he, too, was alive, but had been purposely left behind in Cyprus as a precaution against treachery, as they were less exposed to assault when separated. Celadus, therefore, took him aside and said, " Caesar will reward you by sparing your life, if you will inform him who induced you to play such a trick." Promising Celadus to give the required information, he accompanied him to Caesar and denounced the Jew who had thus traded upon his resemblance to Alexander ; for, as he said, he had in every town received more presents than Alexander ever received in his lifetime. Caesar laughed at these words and enrolled the pseudo-Alexander, as an able-bodied man, among the oarsmen of his galleys ; his inspiring genius he ordered to execution. As for the Melians he considered them sufficiently punished for their folly by their lavish extravagance.

The impostor detected by Augustus.

[a] i. 452.

111 (3) Παραλαβὼν δὲ τὴν ἐθναρχίαν Ἀρχέλαος
καὶ κατὰ μνήμην τῶν πάλαι διαφορῶν οὐ μόνον
Ἰουδαίοις ἀλλὰ καὶ Σαμαρεῦσι χρησάμενος ὠμῶς,
πρεσβευσαμένων ἑκατέρων κατ' αὐτοῦ πρὸς Καίσαρα ἔτει τῆς ἀρχῆς ἐνάτῳ φυγαδεύεται μὲν αὐτὸς
εἰς Βίενναν πόλιν τῆς Γαλλίας, ἡ οὐσία δ' αὐτοῦ
112 τοῖς Καίσαρος θησαυροῖς ἐγκατατάσσεται. πρὶν
κληθῆναι δ' αὐτὸν ὑπὸ τοῦ Καίσαρος ὄναρ ἰδεῖν
φασιν τοιόνδε· ἔδοξεν ὁρᾶν στάχυς ἐννέα πλήρεις
καὶ μεγάλους ὑπὸ βοῶν καταβιβρωσκομένους.
μεταπεμψάμενος δὲ τοὺς μάντεις καὶ τῶν Χαλ-
δαίων τινὰς ἐπυνθάνετο, τί σημαίνειν δοκοῖεν.
113 ἄλλων δ' ἄλλως ἐξηγουμένων Σίμων τις Ἐσσαῖος
τὸ γένος ἔφη τοὺς μὲν στάχυς ἐνιαυτοὺς νομίζειν,
βόας δὲ μεταβολὴν πραγμάτων διὰ τὸ τὴν χώραν
ἀροτριῶντας ἀλλάσσειν, ὥστε βασιλεύσειν μὲν
αὐτὸν τὸν τῶν σταχύων ἀριθμόν, ἐν ποικίλαις
δὲ πραγμάτων μεταβολαῖς γενόμενον τελευτήσειν.
ταῦτα ἀκούσας Ἀρχέλαος μετὰ πέντε ἡμέρας ἐπὶ
τὴν δίκην μετεκλήθη.[1]
114 (4) Ἄξιον δὲ μνήμης ἡγησάμην καὶ τὸ τῆς
γυναικὸς αὐτοῦ Γλαφύρας ὄναρ, ἥπερ ἦν θυγάτηρ
μὲν Ἀρχελάου τοῦ Καππαδόκων βασιλέως, γυνὴ
δ' Ἀλεξάνδρου γεγονυῖα τὸ πρῶτον, ὃς ἦν ἀδελφὸς
Ἀρχελάου περὶ οὗ διέξιμεν, υἱὸς δ' Ἡρώδου τοῦ

[1] ἐκλήθη P.

---

[a] From this point until the outbreak of the war the narrative becomes much more condensed.   Probably the work
of Nicolas of Damascus, the source hitherto followed, ended
here.
   [b] "The tenth" *A.* xvii. 342 ; so Dio Cass. lv. 27, and *cf.* the
allusion to the 10th year of Archelaus in *Vita* 5 (Reinach).

(3) Archelaus,[a] on taking possession of his ethnarchy, did not forget old feuds, but treated not
only the Jews but even the Samaritans with great
brutality. Both parties sent deputies to Caesar to
denounce him, and in the ninth [b] year of his rule he
was banished to Vienna,[c] a town in Gaul, and his
property confiscated to the imperial treasury. It is
said that, before he received his summons from
Caesar, he had this dream : he thought he saw nine
tall and full-grown ears of corn on which oxen were
browsing. He sent for the soothsayers and some
Chaldaeans and asked them their opinion of its
meaning. Various interpretations being given, a
certain Simon, of the sect [d] of the Essenes, said that
in his view the ears of corn denoted years and the
oxen a revolution, because in ploughing they turn
over the soil ; he would therefore reign for as many
years as there were ears of corn and would die after
a chequered experience of revolutionary changes.[e]
Five days later Archelaus was summoned to his trial.

(4) I think mention may also fitly be made of the
dream of his wife Glaphyra. Daughter of Archelaus,
king of Cappadocia, she had for her first husband
Alexander,[f] the brother of Archelaus, of whom we
have been speaking, and son of King Herod, who

Marginal notes: Cruelty and deposition of Archelaus. 6 A.D. His prophetic dream. History of his wife Glaphyra.

---

[c] A city of the Allobroges in Gallia Narbonensis, on the
east bank of the Rhone, mod. *Vienne.*

[d] Greek " race."

[e] Reinach suggests that the dream of Archelaus, modelled
on Pharaoh's dream in Genesis, is a piece of Essene *Haggadah*
which Josephus learnt during his stay with the hermit
Bannus (*Vita* 11). The historian claims to be an interpreter
of dreams himself (*B.* iii. 352).

[f] i. 446. After Alexander's death Herod sent her back
to her father with her dowry but without her children
(i. 553).

βασιλέως, ὑφ᾿ οὗ καὶ ἀνῃρέθη, καθάπερ δεδηλώ-
115 καμεν. μετὰ δὲ τὸν ἐκείνου θάνατον συνῴκησεν
Ἰόβᾳ τῷ βασιλεύοντι Λιβύης, οὗ τελευτήσαντος
ἐπανελθοῦσαν αὐτὴν καὶ χηρεύουσαν παρὰ τῷ
πατρὶ θεασάμενος ὁ ἐθνάρχης Ἀρχέλαος ἐπὶ τοσοῦτον ἔρωτος ἦλθεν, ὥστε παραχρῆμα τὴν συν-
οικοῦσαν αὐτῷ Μαριάμμην ἀποπεμψάμενος ἐκείνην
116 ἀγαγέσθαι. παραγενομένη τοίνυν εἰς Ἰουδαίαν
μετ᾿ ὀλίγον τῆς ἀφίξεως χρόνον ἔδοξεν ἐπιστάντα
τὸν Ἀλέξανδρον αὐτῇ λέγειν " ἀπέχρη μὲν ὁ κατὰ
Λιβύην σοι γάμος, σὺ δὲ οὐκ ἀρκεσθεῖσα τούτῳ
πάλιν ἐπὶ τὴν ἐμὴν ἀνακάμπτεις ἑστίαν, τρίτον
ἄνδρα, καὶ ταῦτα τὸν ἀδελφόν, ὦ τολμηρά, τὸν
ἐμὸν ᾑρημένη. πλὴν οὐ περιόψομαι τὴν ὕβριν,
ἀπολήψομαι δέ σε καὶ μὴ θέλουσαν." τοῦτο
διηγησαμένη τὸ ὄναρ μόλις δύο ἡμέρας ἐβίω.

117 (viii. 1) Τῆς δὲ Ἀρχελάου χώρας εἰς ἐπαρχίαν περιγραφείσης ἐπίτροπος τῆς ἱππικῆς παρὰ
Ῥωμαίοις τάξεως Κωπώνιος πέμπεται, μέχρι τοῦ
118 κτείνειν λαβὼν παρὰ Καίσαρος ἐξουσίαν. ἐπὶ
τούτου τις ἀνὴρ Γαλιλαῖος Ἰούδας ὄνομα εἰς
ἀπόστασιν ἐνῆγε τοὺς ἐπιχωρίους, κακίζων εἰ

---

^a Juba II, an author and a friend of Augustus, who gave
him first in 29 B.C. the kingdom of Numidia, and afterwards
in 25 B.C., in exchange, that of Mauretania. His first wife
was Cleopatra Selene, daughter of Antony and Cleopatra.

^b This statement is erroneous. The coins of Juba (one
dated in the 48th year of his reign) and Strabo's allusion to
his recent death (xvii. p. 828) prove that he lived till 23 A.D.
It is supposed that he divorced Glaphyra.

^c Only mentioned here and in the parallel passage in
A. xvii. 350.

^d Marriage with a brother's widow was forbidden by
Lev. xviii. 16, xx. 21, except when the first husband died

put him to death, as we have already related. After his death she married Juba, king of Libya,[a] on whose decease[b] she returned home and lived in widowhood with her father. There Archelaus, the ethnarch, saw her and fell so passionately in love with her that he instantly divorced his wife Mariamme[c] and married her. So she came back to Judaea, where, not long after her arrival, she imagined that Alexander stood beside her and said : " Your Libyan marriage might have sufficed you, but, not content with that, you now return to my hearth and home, having taken to yourself a third husband, and him, audacious woman, my own brother.[d] But I will not brook this outrage and shall reclaim you whether you will or no." After relating this dream she survived barely two days.

(viii. 1) The territory of Archelaus was now reduced to a province, and Coponius, a Roman of the equestrian order, was sent out as procurator, entrusted by Augustus with full powers, including the infliction of capital punishment. Under his administration, a Galilaean, named Judas,[e] incited his countrymen to revolt, upbraiding them as cowards

Judaea, a Roman province under the procurator Coponius c. 6–9 A.D.

Rising of Judas the Galilaean.

childless, when it was obligatory, Deut. xxv. 5 (Mark xii. 19). Glaphyra had two children by Alexander ; *A.* xvii. 341 emphasizes this fact.

[e] Judas of Galilee (as he is called here and in Gamaliel's speech in Acts v. 37) or of Gamala in Gaulanitis (*A.* xviii. 4) was the founder of the Zealots, whose fanaticism and violence under Florus, the last of the procurators, hastened the war with Rome. Of the issue of the revolt we learn only from Acts *loc. cit.* : Judas was killed and his followers dispersed. There is no sufficient reason for identifying this fanatic doctor, as Schürer does, with the brigand Judas, son of Ezechias, who raised an insurrection in Galilee after the death of Herod (*B.* ii. 56).

φόρον τε 'Ρωμαίοις τελεῖν ὑπομενοῦσιν καὶ μετὰ
τὸν θεὸν οἴσουσι θνητοὺς δεσπότας. ἦν δ' οὗτος
σοφιστὴς ἰδίας αἱρέσεως οὐδὲν τοῖς ἄλλοις προσ-
εοικώς.

119   (2) Τρία γὰρ παρὰ 'Ιουδαίοις εἴδη φιλοσοφεῖται,
καὶ τοῦ μὲν αἱρετισταὶ Φαρισαῖοι, τοῦ δὲ Σαδδουκαῖοι, τρίτον δέ, ὃ δὴ καὶ δοκεῖ σεμνότητα
ἀσκεῖν, 'Εσσηνοὶ καλοῦνται, 'Ιουδαῖοι μὲν γένος
120 ὄντες, φιλάλληλοι δὲ καὶ τῶν ἄλλων πλέον. οὗτοι
τὰς μὲν ἡδονὰς ὡς κακίαν ἀποστρέφονται, τὴν δὲ
ἐγκράτειαν καὶ τὸ μὴ τοῖς πάθεσιν ὑποπίπτειν
ἀρετὴν ὑπολαμβάνουσιν. καὶ γάμου μὲν παρ'
αὐτοῖς ὑπεροψία, τοὺς δ' ἀλλοτρίους παῖδας ἐκ-
λαμβάνοντες ἁπαλοὺς ἔτι πρὸς τὰ μαθήματα συγγενεῖς ἡγοῦνται καὶ τοῖς ἤθεσιν αὐτῶν ἐντυποῦσι,
121 τὸν μὲν γάμον καὶ τὴν ἐξ αὐτοῦ διαδοχὴν οὐκ
ἀναιροῦντες, τὰς δὲ τῶν γυναικῶν ἀσελγείας
φυλαττόμενοι καὶ μηδεμίαν τηρεῖν πεπεισμένοι
τὴν πρὸς ἕνα πίστιν.

122   (3) Καταφρονηταὶ δὲ πλούτου, καὶ θαυμάσιον
[παρ']¹ αὐτοῖς τὸ κοινωνικόν, οὐδὲ ἔστιν εὑρεῖν
κτήσει τινὰ παρ' αὐτοῖς ὑπερέχοντα· νόμος γὰρ
τοὺς εἰς τὴν αἵρεσιν εἰσιόντας δημεύειν τῷ τάγματι

¹ om. P.

ᵃ An exaggerated statement, corrected in A. xviii. 23
(" while they agree in all other respects with the Pharisees,
they have an invincible passion for liberty and take God for
their only leader and lord ").
ᵇ A shorter sketch of the three sects is given in A. xviii.
11-22, where the author refers to the fuller statement in the

for consenting to pay tribute to the Romans and tolerating mortal masters, after having God for their lord. This man was a sophist who founded a sect of his own, having nothing in common with the others.[a]

(2) Jewish philosophy, in fact, takes three forms. The followers of the first school are called Pharisees, of the second Sadducees, of the third Essenes.[b]

The three Jewish sects.

The Essenes have a reputation for cultivating peculiar sanctity.[c] Of Jewish birth, they show a greater attachment to each other than do the other sects. They shun pleasures as a vice and regard temperance and the control of the passions as a special virtue. Marriage they disdain, but they adopt other men's children, while yet pliable and docile, and regard them as their kin and mould them in accordance with their own principles. They do not, indeed, on principle, condemn wedlock and the propagation thereby of the race, but they wish to protect themselves against women's wantonness, being persuaded that none of the sex keeps her plighted troth to one man.

(i.) The Essenes. Their asceticism, simple life and community of goods.

(3) Riches they despise, and their community of goods is truly admirable ; you will not find one among them distinguished by greater opulence than another. They have a law that new members on admission to the sect shall confiscate their property

present passage. He has first-hand knowledge, having " passed through the three courses " himself (*Vita* 11).

[c] Or " solemnity." The name Essene probably means " pious " (Aram. *ḥaṣa*) ; Philo connected it with the Greek ὅσιος: 'Εσσαῖοι . . . παρώνυμοι ὁσιότητος (*Quod omnis probus liber*, § 12) ; καλοῦνται μὲν 'Εσσαῖοι παρὰ τὴν ὁσιότητα μοὶ δοκῶ τῆς προσηγορίας ἀξιωθέντες (*ap.* Eus. *Praep. Ev.* viii. 11). Philo, Pliny (*Nat. Hist.* v. 17), and Josephus are our three authorities on the sect.

τὴν οὐσίαν, ὥστε ἐν ἅπασιν μήτε πενίας ταπεινότητα φαίνεσθαι μήθ᾽ ὑπεροχὴν πλούτου, τῶν δ᾽
ἑκάστου κτημάτων ἀναμεμιγμένων μίαν ὥσπερ
123 ἀδελφοῖς ἅπασιν οὐσίαν εἶναι. κηλίδα δ᾽ ὑπολαμ-
βάνουσι τοὔλαιον, κἂν ἀλειφθῇ τις ἄκων, σμήχεται
τὸ σῶμα· τὸ γὰρ αὐχμεῖν ἐν καλῷ τίθενται,
λευχειμονεῖν τε διαπαντός. χειροτονητοὶ δ᾽ οἱ τῶν
κοινῶν ἐπιμεληταὶ καὶ αἱρετοί[1] πρὸς ἁπάντων εἰς
τὰς χρείας ἕκαστοι.

124 (4) Μία δ᾽ οὐκ ἔστιν αὐτῶν πόλις, ἀλλ᾽ ἐν
ἑκάστῃ μετοικοῦσιν πολλοί. καὶ τοῖς ἑτέρωθεν
ἥκουσιν αἱρετισταῖς πάντ᾽ ἀναπέπταται τὰ παρ᾽
αὐτοῖς ὁμοίως ὥσπερ ἴδια, καὶ πρὸς οὓς οὐ πρό-
125 τερον εἶδον εἰσίασιν ὡς συνηθεστάτους· διὸ καὶ
ποιοῦνται τὰς ἀποδημίας οὐδὲν μὲν ὅλως ἐπι-
κομιζόμενοι, διὰ δὲ τοὺς λῃστὰς ἔνοπλοι. κηδεμὼν δ᾽ ἐν ἑκάστῃ πόλει τοῦ τάγματος ἐξαιρέτως
τῶν ξένων ἀποδείκνυται, ταμιεύων ἐσθῆτα καὶ τὰ
126 ἐπιτήδεια. καταστολὴ δὲ καὶ σχῆμα σώματος
ὅμοιον τοῖς μετὰ φόβου παιδαγωγουμένοις παισίν.
οὔτε δὲ ἐσθῆτας οὔτε ὑποδήματα ἀμείβουσι πρὶν
διαρραγῆναι τὸ πρότερον παντάπασιν ἢ δαπα-
127 νηθῆναι τῷ χρόνῳ. οὐδὲν δ᾽ ἐν ἀλλήλοις οὔτ᾽
ἀγοράζουσιν οὔτε πωλοῦσιν, ἀλλὰ τῷ χρῄζοντι
διδοὺς ἕκαστος τὰ παρ᾽ αὐτῷ τὸ [παρ᾽ ἐκείνου][2]
χρήσιμον ἀντικομίζεται· καὶ χωρὶς δὲ τῆς ἀντι-
δόσεως ἀκώλυτος ἡ μετάληψις αὐτοῖς παρ᾽[3] ὧν ἂν
θέλωσιν.

128 (5) Πρός γε μὴν τὸ θεῖον εὐσεβεῖς ἰδίως· πρὶν

---

[1] Bekker on ms. authority: ἀδιαίρετοι the rest.   [2] om. P.
[3] om. παρ᾽ Bekker, Naber, "to take whatever they
choose."

to the order, with the result that you will nowhere
see either abject poverty or inordinate wealth ; the
individual's possessions join the common stock and all,
like brothers, enjoy a single patrimony. Oil they
consider defiling, and anyone who accidentally comes
in contact with it scours his person ; for they make
a point of keeping a dry skin and of always being
dressed in white. They elect officers to attend to the
interests of the community, the special services of
each officer being determined by the whole body.

(4) They occupy no one city, but settle in large *Their*
numbers in every town. On the arrival of any of the *settlements.*
sect from elsewhere, all the resources of the community are put at their disposal, just as if they were
their own ; and they enter the houses of men whom
they have never seen before as though they were
their most intimate friends. Consequently, they
carry nothing whatever with them on their journeys,
except arms as a protection against brigands. In
every city there is one of the order expressly appointed to attend to strangers, who provides them
with raiment and other necessaries. In their dress
and deportment they resemble children under rigorous
discipline. They do not change their garments or
shoes until they are torn to shreds or worn thread-
bare with age. There is no buying or selling among
themselves, but each gives what he has to any in need
and receives from him in exchange something useful
to himself ; they are, moreover, freely permitted
to take anything from any of their brothers without
making any return.

(5) Their piety towards the Deity takes a peculiar

371

γὰρ ἀνασχεῖν τὸν ἥλιον οὐδὲν φθέγγονται τῶν
βεβήλων, πατρίους δέ τινας εἰς αὐτὸν εὐχάς,
129 ὥσπερ ἱκετεύοντες ἀνατεῖλαι. καὶ μετὰ ταῦτα
πρὸς ἃς ἕκαστοι τέχνας ἴσασιν ὑπὸ τῶν ἐπιμελητῶν διαφίενται, καὶ μέχρι πέμπτης ὥρας ἐργασάμενοι συντόνως πάλιν εἰς ἓν συναθροίζονται
χωρίον, ζωσάμενοί τε σκεπάσμασιν λινοῖς οὕτως
ἀπολούονται τὸ σῶμα ψυχροῖς ὕδασιν, καὶ μετὰ
ταύτην τὴν ἁγνείαν εἰς ἴδιον οἴκημα συνίασιν,
ἔνθα μηδενὶ τῶν ἑτεροδόξων ἐπιτέτραπται παρελθεῖν, αὐτοί τε καθαροὶ καθάπερ εἰς ἅγιόν τι
130 τέμενος παραγίνονται τὸ δειπνητήριον. καὶ καθ-
ισάντων μεθ' ἡσυχίας ὁ μὲν σιτοποιὸς ἐν τάξει
παρατίθησι τοὺς ἄρτους, ὁ δὲ μάγειρος ἓν ἀγγεῖον
131 ἐξ ἑνὸς ἐδέσματος ἑκάστῳ παρατίθησιν. προ-
κατεύχεται δ' ὁ ἱερεὺς τῆς τροφῆς, καὶ γεύσασθαί
τινα πρὶν τῆς εὐχῆς ἀθέμιτον· ἀριστοποιησαμένοις[1]
δ' ἐπεύχεται πάλιν· ἀρχόμενοί τε καὶ παυόμενοι
γεραίρουσι θεὸν ὡς χορηγὸν τῆς ζωῆς. ἔπειθ'
ὡς ἱερὰς καταθέμενοι τὰς ἐσθῆτας πάλιν ἐπ' ἔργα
132 μέχρι δείλης τρέπονται. δειπνοῦσι δ' ὁμοίως
ὑποστρέψαντες συγκαθεζομένων τῶν ξένων, εἰ
τύχοιεν αὐτοῖς παρόντες. οὔτε δὲ κραυγή ποτε
τὸν οἶκον οὔτε θόρυβος μιαίνει, τὰς δὲ λαλιὰς ἐν
133 τάξει παραχωροῦσιν ἀλλήλοις. καὶ τοῖς ἔξωθεν ὡς
μυστήριόν τι φρικτὸν ἡ τῶν ἔνδον σιωπὴ κατα-
φαίνεται, τούτου δ' αἴτιον ἡ διηνεκὴς νῆψις καὶ

---

[1] Some mss. of Porphyry: ἀριστοποιησάμενος mss. of
Josephus.

---

[a] Cf. § 148, " the rays of the God." How far the Essenes,
with their affinities to Judaism, can be regarded as sun-
worshippers is doubtful. But, un-Jewish as this custom

form. Before the sun is up they utter no word on Their
prayers to
the sun.
mundane matters, but offer to him certain prayers,
which have been handed down from their forefathers,
as though entreating him to rise.[a] They are then
dismissed by their superiors to the various crafts in
which they are severally proficient and are strenu- Their
handicrafts.
ously employed until the fifth hour, when they again
assemble in one place and, after girding their loins
with linen cloths, bathe their bodies in cold water.
After this purification, they assemble in a private
apartment which none of the uninitiated is permitted
to enter ; pure now themselves, they repair to the
refectory, as to some sacred shrine. When they have Their
refectory.
taken their seats in silence, the baker serves out the
loaves to them in order, and the cook sets before
each one plate with a single course. Before meat
the priest says a grace, and none may partake until
after the prayer. When breakfast is ended, he pro-
nounces a further grace ; thus at the beginning and
at the close they do homage to God as the bountiful
giver of life. Then laying aside their raiment, as
holy vestments, they again betake themselves to
their labours until the evening. On their return
they sup in like manner, and any guests who may
have arrived sit down with them. No clamour or
disturbance ever pollutes their dwelling ; they speak
in turn, each making way for his neighbour. To
persons outside the silence of those within appears
like some awful mystery ; it is in fact due to their
invariable sobriety and to the limitation of their

seems, there was a time when even Jews at Jerusalem
" turned their backs on the Temple and their faces towards
the east and worshipped the sun towards the east " (Mishnah,
Sukkah, v. 2-4 ; Ezek. viii. 16).

τὸ μετρεῖσθαι παρ' αὐτοῖς τροφὴν καὶ ποτὸν
μέχρι κόρου.

134 (6) Τῶν μὲν οὖν ἄλλων οὐκ ἔστιν ὅ τι μὴ τῶν
ἐπιμελητῶν προσταξάντων ἐνεργοῦσι, δύο δὲ ταῦτα
παρ' αὐτοῖς αὐτεξούσια, ἐπικουρία καὶ ἔλεος·
βοηθεῖν τε γὰρ τοῖς ἀξίοις, ὁπόταν δέωνται, καὶ
καθ' ἑαυτοὺς ἐφίεται καὶ τροφὰς ἀπορουμένοις
ὀρέγειν. τὰς δὲ εἰς τοὺς συγγενεῖς μεταδόσεις
135 οὐκ ἔξεστι ποιεῖσθαι δίχα τῶν ἐπιτρόπων. ὀργῆς
ταμίαι δίκαιοι, θυμοῦ καθεκτικοί, πίστεως προ-
στάται, εἰρήνης ὑπουργοί. καὶ πᾶν μὲν τὸ ῥηθὲν
ὑπ' αὐτῶν ἰσχυρότερον ὅρκου, τὸ δὲ ὀμνύειν
[αὐτοῖς]¹ περιίστανται χεῖρον τῆς ἐπιορκίας ὑπο-
λαμβάνοντες· ἤδη γὰρ κατεγνῶσθαί φασιν τὸν
136 ἀπιστούμενον δίχα θεοῦ. σπουδάζουσι δ' ἐκτόπως
περὶ τὰ τῶν παλαιῶν συντάγματα, μάλιστα τὰ
πρὸς ὠφέλειαν ψυχῆς καὶ σώματος ἐκλέγοντες·
ἔνθεν αὐτοῖς πρὸς θεραπείαν παθῶν ῥίζαι τε
ἀλεξητήριοι καὶ λίθων ἰδιότητες ἀνερευνῶνται.

137 (7) Τοῖς δὲ ζηλοῦσιν τὴν αἵρεσιν αὐτῶν οὐκ
εὐθὺς ἡ πάροδος, ἀλλ' ἐπὶ ἐνιαυτὸν ἔξω μένοντι
τὴν αὐτὴν ὑποτίθενται δίαιταν, ἀξινάριόν τε καὶ
τὸ προειρημένον περίζωμα καὶ λευκὴν ἐσθῆτα
138 δόντες. ἐπειδὰν δὲ τούτῳ τῷ χρόνῳ πεῖραν ἐγ-
κρατείας δῷ, πρόσεισιν μὲν ἔγγιον τῇ διαίτῃ καὶ

---

¹ om. Dindorf with one ms.: the incorrect reading περι-
ίσταται has probably caused the insertion of the pronoun.

ᵃ Or " when they ask an alms."
ᵇ Herod himself excused them from taking the oath of
allegiance (A. xv. 371). The " tremendous oaths " sworn
on admission to the order (§ 139) form a curious exception.
ᶜ i.e. probably charms or amulets. Lightfoot, Colossians

allotted portions of meat and drink to the demands
of nature.

(6) In all other matters they do nothing without
orders from their superiors ; two things only are left
to individual discretion, the rendering of assistance
and compassion. Members may of their own motion
help the deserving, when in need,[a] and supply food to
the destitute ; but presents to relatives are pro-
hibited, without leave from the managers. Holding
righteous indignation in reserve, they are masters of
their temper, champions of fidelity, very ministers
of peace. Any word of theirs has more force than
an oath ; swearing they avoid, regarding it as worse
than perjury, for they say that one who is not believed
without an appeal to God stands condemned already.[b]
They display an extraordinary interest in the writings
of the ancients, singling out in particular those which
make for the welfare of soul and body ; with the
help of these, and with a view to the treatment of
diseases, they make investigations into medicinal
roots and the properties of stones.[c]

(7) A candidate anxious to join their sect is not
immediately admitted. For one year, during which
he remains outside the fraternity, they prescribe for
him their own rule of life, presenting him with a
small hatchet,[d] the loin-cloth already mentioned,[e]
and white raiment. Having given proof of his
temperance during this probationary period, he is
brought into closer touch with the rule and is allowed

*Their
charity ;*

*and
avoidance
of oaths.*

*Their
studies.*

*Admission
to the
order. The
novice's
probation
and oath.*

(ed. 8), pp. 89 f. note, connecting this passage with *Ant.* viii.
44 ff. (on Solomon's power over demons), regards the " writings " as Solomonian books and the Essenes as primarily
dealers in charms, rather than physicians.
    [d] The object of this is explained below (§ 148).
    [e] § 129.

καθαρωτέρων τῶν πρὸς ἁγνείαν ὑδάτων μεταλαμβάνει, παραλαμβάνεται δὲ εἰς τὰς συμβιώσεις
οὐδέπω. μετὰ γὰρ τὴν τῆς καρτερίας ἐπίδειξιν
δυσὶν ἄλλοις ἔτεσιν τὸ ἦθος δοκιμάζεται καὶ φανεὶς
139 ἄξιος οὕτως εἰς τὸν ὅμιλον ἐγκρίνεται. πρὶν δὲ
τῆς κοινῆς ἅψασθαι τροφῆς ὅρκους αὐτοῖς ὄμνυσι
φρικώδεις, πρῶτον μὲν εὐσεβήσειν τὸ θεῖον,
ἔπειτα τὰ πρὸς ἀνθρώπους δίκαια φυλάξειν καὶ
μήτε κατὰ γνώμην βλάψειν τινὰ μήτε ἐξ ἐπιτάγματος, μισήσειν δ' ἀεὶ τοὺς ἀδίκους καὶ συν-
140 αγωνιεῖσθαι τοῖς δικαίοις· τὸ πιστὸν ἀεὶ πᾶσιν παρ-
έξειν, μάλιστα δὲ τοῖς κρατοῦσιν· οὐ γὰρ δίχα θεοῦ
περιγενέσθαι[1] τινὶ τὸ ἄρχειν· κἂν αὐτὸς ἄρχῃ,
μηδέποτε ἐξυβρίσειν εἰς τὴν ἐξουσίαν, μηδ' ἐσθῆτι
ἤ τινι πλείονι κόσμῳ τοὺς ὑποτεταγμένους ὑπερ-
141 λαμπρυνεῖσθαι[2]· τὴν ἀλήθειαν ἀγαπᾶν ἀεὶ καὶ τοὺς
ψευδομένους προβάλλεσθαι[3]· χεῖρας κλοπῆς καὶ
ψυχὴν ἀνοσίου κέρδους καθαρὰν φυλάξειν, καὶ
μήτε κρύψειν τι τοὺς αἱρετιστὰς μήθ' ἑτέροις
αὐτῶν τι μηνύσειν, κἂν μέχρι θανάτου τις βιάζηται.
142 πρὸς τούτοις ὄμνυσιν μηδενὶ μὲν μεταδοῦναι τῶν
δογμάτων ἑτέρως ἢ ὡς αὐτὸς μετέλαβεν, ἀφέξεσθαι
δὲ λῃστείας καὶ συντηρήσειν ὁμοίως τά τε τῆς
αἱρέσεως αὐτῶν βιβλία καὶ τὰ τῶν ἀγγέλων ὀνό-
ματα. τοιούτοις μὲν ὅρκοις τοὺς προσιόντας
ἐξασφαλίζονται.
143 (8) Τοὺς δ' ἐπ' ἀξιοχρέοις ἁμαρτήμασιν ἁλόντας
ἐκβάλλουσι τοῦ τάγματος. ὁ δ' ἐκκριθεὶς οἰκτίστῳ

---

[1] περιγίνεσθαι LVR Porph.
[2] Herwerden : ὑπερλαμπρύνεσθαι mss.
[3] Porph. : ἐλέγχειν προβάλλεσθαι mss.

to share the purer kind of holy water, but is not yet received into the meetings of the community. For after this exhibition of endurance, his character is tested for two years more, and only then, if found worthy, is he enrolled in the society. But, before he may touch the common food, he is made to swear tremendous oaths : first that he will practise piety towards the Deity, next that he will observe justice towards men : that he will wrong none whether of his own mind or under another's orders ; that he will for ever hate the unjust and fight the battle of the just ; that he will for ever keep faith with all men, especially with the powers that be, since no ruler attains his office save by the will of God ; [a] that, should he himself bear rule, he will never abuse his authority nor, either in dress or by other outward marks of superiority, outshine his subjects ; to be for ever a lover of truth and to expose liars ; to keep his hands from stealing and his soul pure from unholy gain ; to conceal nothing from the members of the sect and to report none of their secrets to others, even though tortured to death. He swears, moreover, to transmit their rules exactly as he himself received them ; to abstain from robbery ; and in like manner carefully to preserve the books of the sect and the names of the angels.[b] Such are the oaths by which they secure their proselytes.

(8) Those who are convicted of serious crimes they expel from the order ; and the ejected individual

Expulsion from the order.

---

[a] Reinach compares *A*. xv. 374, where the Essene Menahem says to Herod : " You will reign, for God has deemed you worthy." *Cf.* also Rom. xiii. 1.

[b] Reinach conjectures that the developed angelology of Rabbinic Judaism was partly of Essene origin. Lightfoot finds in this esoteric doctrine a link with Zoroastrianism.

πολλάκις μόρῳ διαφθείρεται· τοῖς γὰρ ὅρκοις καὶ
τοῖς ἔθεσιν ἐνδεδεμένος οὐδὲ τῆς παρὰ τοῖς ἄλλοις
τροφῆς δύναται μεταλαμβάνειν, ποηφαγῶν δὲ καὶ
144 λιμῷ τὸ σῶμα τηκόμενος διαφθείρεται. διὸ δὴ
πολλοὺς ἐλεήσαντες ἐν ταῖς ἐσχάταις ἀναπνοαῖς
ἀνέλαβον, ἱκανὴν ἐπὶ τοῖς ἁμαρτήμασιν αὐτῶν
τὴν μέχρι θανάτου βάσανον ἡγούμενοι.

145 (9) Περὶ δὲ τὰς κρίσεις ἀκριβέστατοι καὶ
δίκαιοι, καὶ δικάζουσι μὲν οὐκ ἐλάττους τῶν
ἑκατὸν συνελθόντες, τὸ δ' ὁρισθὲν ὑπ' αὐτῶν
ἀκίνητον. σέβας δὲ μέγα παρ' αὐτοῖς μετὰ τὸν
θεὸν τοὔνομα τοῦ νομοθέτου, κἂν βλασφημήσῃ
146 τις εἰς τοῦτον, κολάζεται θανάτῳ. τοῖς δὲ πρε-
σβυτέροις ὑπακούειν καὶ τοῖς πλείοσιν ἐν καλῷ
τίθενται· δέκα γοῦν συγκαθεζομένων οὐκ ἂν λαλή-
147 σειέν τις ἀκόντων τῶν ἐννέα. καὶ τὸ πτύσαι δὲ
εἰς μέσους ἢ τὸ δεξιὸν μέρος φυλάσσονται, καὶ
ταῖς ἑβδομάσιν ἔργων ἐφάπτεσθαι διαφορώτατα
Ἰουδαίων ἁπάντων· οὐ μόνον γὰρ τροφὰς ἑαυτοῖς
πρὸ μιᾶς ἡμέρας παρασκευάζουσιν, ὡς μὴ πῦρ
ἐναύοιεν[1] ἐκείνην τὴν ἡμέραν, ἀλλ' οὐδὲ σκεῦός
148 τι μετακινῆσαι θαρροῦσιν οὐδὲ ἀποπατεῖν. ταῖς
δ' ἄλλαις ἡμέραις βόθρον ὀρύσσοντες βάθος πο-
διαῖον τῇ σκαλίδι, τοιοῦτον γάρ ἐστιν τὸ διδόμενον
ὑπ' αὐτῶν ἀξινίδιον τοῖς νεοσυστάτοις, καὶ περι-
καλύψαντες θοιμάτιον,[2] ὡς μὴ τὰς αὐγὰς ὑβρίζοιεν
149 τοῦ θεοῦ, θακεύουσιν εἰς αὐτόν. ἔπειτα τὴν ἀν-
ορυχθεῖσαν γῆν ἐφέλκουσιν εἰς τὸν βόθρον· καὶ

---

[1] ἐναφθεῖεν PA*: ἐναφθῇ A (corrector): ἐνάπτοιεν correctors
of LR.
[2] ἱμάτιον PAM: θοιματίῳ Porph.

---

[a] Moses.

often comes to a most miserable end. For, being
bound by their oaths and usages, he is not at liberty
to partake of other men's food, and so falls to eating
grass and wastes away and dies of starvation. This
has led them in compassion to receive many back in
the last stage of exhaustion, deeming that torments
which have brought them to the verge of death are a
sufficient penalty for their misdoings.

(9) They are just and scrupulously careful in their
trial of cases, never passing sentence in a court of
less than a hundred members ; the decision thus
reached is irrevocable. After God they hold most
in awe the name of their lawgiver,[a] any blasphemer
of whom is punished with death. It is a point of
honour with them to obey their elders, and a majority ;
for instance, if ten sit together, one will not speak if
the nine desire silence. They are careful not to spit
into the midst of the company or to the right,[b] and
are stricter than all Jews in abstaining from work on
the seventh day ; for not only do they prepare their
food on the day before, to avoid kindling a fire on
that one, but they do not venture to remove any
vessel or even to go to stool. On other days they
dig a trench a foot deep with a mattock—such is the
nature of the hatchet which they present to the
neophytes [c]—and wrapping their mantle about them,
that they may not offend the rays of the deity,[d] sit
above it. They then replace the excavated soil in

_Their
law-courts,
reverence
for Moses,
Sabbatar-
ianism and
other
customs._

---

[b] Reinach refers to a similar prohibition, applying only to
prayer-time, in the Jerusalem Talmud (*Berachoth*, iii. 5).

[c] § 137.

[d] The sun, *cf.* § 128. Schürer contrasts the *Testaments of
the XII Patriarchs, Benj.* 8 (the sun is not defiled by the
sight of ordure, but purifies it).

τοῦτο ποιοῦσι τοὺς ἐρημοτέρους τόπους ἐκλεγόμε-
νοι. καίπερ δὲ[1] φυσικῆς οὔσης τῆς τῶν[2] λυμάτων
ἐκκρίσεως ἀπολούεσθαι μετ' αὐτὴν καθάπερ μεμια-
σμένοις ἔθιμον.

150 (10) Διῄρηνται δὲ κατὰ χρόνον τῆς ἀσκήσεως
εἰς μοίρας τέσσαρας, καὶ τοσοῦτον οἱ μετα-
γενέστεροι τῶν προγενεστέρων ἐλαττοῦνται ὥστ',
εἰ ψαύσειαν αὐτῶν, ἐκείνους ἀπολούεσθαι καθάπερ

151 ἀλλοφύλῳ συμφυρέντας. καὶ μακρόβιοι μέν, ὡς
τοὺς πολλοὺς ὑπὲρ ἑκατὸν παρατείνειν ἔτη, διὰ
τὴν ἁπλότητα τῆς διαίτης, ἔμοιγε δοκεῖν, καὶ τὴν
εὐταξίαν, καταφρονηταὶ δὲ τῶν δεινῶν, καὶ τὰς
μὲν ἀλγηδόνας νικῶντες τοῖς φρονήμασιν, τὸν δὲ
θάνατον, εἰ μετ' εὐκλείας προσίοι,[3] νομίζοντες

152 ἀθανασίας ἀμείνονα. διήλεγξεν δὲ αὐτῶν ἐν ἅπασιν τὰς ψυχὰς ὁ πρὸς Ῥωμαίους πόλεμος, ἐν ᾧ
στρεβλούμενοί τε καὶ λυγιζόμενοι, καιόμενοί τε
καὶ κλώμενοι καὶ διὰ πάντων ὁδεύοντες τῶν βασα-
νιστηρίων ὀργάνων, ἵν' ἢ βλασφημήσωσιν τὸν
νομοθέτην ἢ φάγωσίν τι τῶν ἀσυνήθων, οὐδέτερον
ὑπέμειναν παθεῖν, ἀλλ' οὐδὲ κολακεῦσαί ποτε τοὺς

153 αἰκιζομένους ἢ δακρῦσαι. μειδιῶντες δὲ ἐν ταῖς
ἀλγηδόσιν καὶ κατειρωνευόμενοι τῶν τὰς βασάνους
προσφερόντων εὔθυμοι τὰς ψυχὰς ἠφίεσαν ὡς
πάλιν κομιούμενοι.

154 (11) Καὶ γὰρ ἔρρωται παρ' αὐτοῖς ἥδε ἡ δόξα,
φθαρτὰ μὲν εἶναι τὰ σώματα καὶ τὴν ὕλην οὐ

---

[1] Most mss. δὴ : οὖν M : om. PA.
[2] + σωματικῶν MLVRC.　　　　[3] πρόσεισι PAM.

---

[a] As Reinach remarks, the whole procedure, except the
final ablution, follows the directions given in Deut. xxiii. 12-
14.

the trench. For this purpose they select the more retired spots. And though this discharge of the excrements is a natural function, they make it a rule to wash themselves after it, as if defiled.[a]

(10) They are divided, according to the duration of their discipline, into four grades; [b] and so far are the junior members inferior to the seniors, that a senior if but touched by a junior, must take a bath, as after contact with an alien. They live to a great age— most of them to upwards of a century—in consequence, I imagine, of the simplicity and regularity of their mode of life. They make light of danger, and triumph over pain by their resolute will ; death, if it come with honour, they consider better than immortality. The war with the Romans tried their souls through and through by every variety of test. Racked and twisted, burnt and broken, and made to pass through every instrument of torture, in order to induce them to blaspheme their lawgiver or to eat some forbidden thing, they refused to yield to either demand, nor ever once did they cringe to their persecutors or shed a tear. Smiling in their agonies and mildly deriding their tormentors, they cheerfully resigned their souls, confident that they would receive them back again.

The four grades of Essenes.

Their endurance of persecution.

(11) For it is a fixed belief of theirs that the body is corruptible and its constituent matter impermanent,

Their belief in the immortality of the soul.

[b] Lightfoot (*Col.* p. 363, note) remarks that the passage must be read in connexion with the account of the admission to the order (§§ 137 f.). The three lowest grades are the novices in their first, second, and third years of probation. " After passing through these three stages in three successive years, [the Essene] enters upon the fourth and highest grade, thus becoming a perfect member."

μόνιμον αὐτῶν, τὰς δὲ ψυχὰς ἀθανάτους ἀεὶ διαμένειν, καὶ συμπλέκεσθαι μὲν ἐκ τοῦ λεπτοτάτου
φοιτώσας αἰθέρος ὥσπερ εἰρκταῖς τοῖς σώμασιν
155 ἴυγγί τινι φυσικῇ κατασπωμένας, ἐπειδὰν δὲ ἀν-
εθῶσι τῶν κατὰ σάρκα δεσμῶν, οἷα δὴ μακρᾶς
δουλείας ἀπηλλαγμένας, τότε χαίρειν καὶ μετεώρους φέρεσθαι. καὶ ταῖς μὲν ἀγαθαῖς, ὁμο-
δοξοῦντες παισὶν Ἑλλήνων, ἀποφαίνονται τὴν
ὑπὲρ ὠκεανὸν δίαιταν ἀποκεῖσθαι καὶ χῶρον οὔτε
ὄμβροις οὔτε νιφετοῖς οὔτε καύμασι βαρυνόμενον,
ἀλλ' ὃν ἐξ ὠκεανοῦ πραῢς ἀεὶ ζέφυρος ἐπιπνέων
ἀναψύχει· ταῖς δὲ φαύλαις ζοφώδη καὶ χειμέριον
ἀφορίζονται μυχόν, γέμοντα τιμωριῶν ἀδιαλείπ-
156 των. δοκοῦσι δέ μοι κατὰ τὴν αὐτὴν ἔννοιαν
Ἕλληνες τοῖς τε ἀνδρείοις αὐτῶν, οὓς ἥρωας καὶ
ἡμιθέους καλοῦσιν, τὰς μακάρων νήσους ἀνα-
τεθεικέναι, ταῖς δὲ τῶν πονηρῶν ψυχαῖς καθ' ᾅδου
τὸν[1] ἀσεβῶν χῶρον, ἔνθα καὶ κολαζομένους τινὰς
μυθολογοῦσιν, Σισύφους καὶ Ταντάλους Ἰξίονάς
τε καὶ Τιτυούς, πρῶτον μὲν ἀιδίους ὑφιστάμενοι
τὰς ψυχάς, ἔπειτα εἰς προτροπὴν ἀρετῆς καὶ
157 κακίας ἀποτροπήν. τούς τε γὰρ ἀγαθοὺς γίνεσθαι
κατὰ τὸν βίον ἀμείνους ἐλπίδι τιμῆς καὶ μετὰ τὴν
τελευτήν, τῶν τε κακῶν ἐμποδίζεσθαι τὰς ὁρμὰς
δέει προσδοκώντων, εἰ καὶ λάθοιεν ἐν τῷ ζῆν,
μετὰ τὴν διάλυσιν ἀθάνατον τιμωρίαν ὑφέξειν.
158 ταῦτα μὲν οὖν Ἐσσηνοὶ περὶ ψυχῆς θεολογοῦσιν,
ἄφυκτον δέλεαρ τοῖς ἅπαξ γευσαμένοις τῆς σοφίας
αὐτῶν καθιέντες.[2]

[1] τῶν PLV: τὸν τῶν M.
[2] PAM (cf. i. 373): ἐγκαθιέντες the rest.

but that the soul is immortal and imperishable.[a]
Emanating from the finest ether, these souls become
entangled, as it were, in the prison-house of the body,
to which they are dragged down by a sort of natural
spell ; but when once they are released from the
bonds of the flesh, then, as though liberated from a
long servitude, they rejoice and are borne aloft.
Sharing the belief of the sons of Greece, they maintain that for virtuous souls there is reserved an abode
beyond the ocean, a place which is not oppressed by
rain or snow or heat, but is refreshed by the ever
gentle breath of the west wind coming in from ocean ;
while they relegate base souls to a murky and
tempestuous dungeon, big with never-ending punishments. The Greeks, I imagine, had the same conception when they set apart the isles of the blessed [b]
for their brave men, whom they call heroes and demi-
gods, and the region of the impious for the souls of
the wicked down in Hades, where, as their mytho-
logists tell, persons such as Sisyphus, Tantalus, Ixion,
and Tityus are undergoing punishment. Their aim
was first to establish the doctrine of the immortality
of the soul, and secondly to promote virtue and to
deter from vice ; for the good are made better in
their lifetime by the hope of a reward after death, and
the passions of the wicked are restrained by the fear
that, even though they escape detection while alive,
they will undergo never-ending punishment after their
decease. Such are the theological views of the Essenes
concerning the soul, whereby they irresistibly attract
all who have once tasted their philosophy.

[a] Cf. A. xviii. 18.
[b] First mentioned in Hesiod, *Works and Days*, 170 ff.
" they dwell with care-free hearts in the isles of the blessed
beside the deep-eddying ocean, those happy heroes," etc.

159 (12) Εἰσὶν δ' ἐν αὐτοῖς οἳ καὶ τὰ μέλλοντα
προγινώσκειν ὑπισχνοῦνται, βίβλοις ἱεραῖς καὶ
διαφόροις ἁγνείαις καὶ προφητῶν ἀποφθέγμασιν
ἐμπαιδοτριβούμενοι· σπάνιον δ' εἴ ποτε ἐν ταῖς
προαγορεύσεσιν ἀστοχοῦσιν.

160 (13) Ἔστιν δὲ καὶ ἕτερον Ἐσσηνῶν τάγμα,
δίαιταν μὲν καὶ ἔθη καὶ νόμιμα τοῖς ἄλλοις ὁμο-
φρονοῦν, διεστὼς δὲ τῇ κατὰ γάμον δόξῃ· μέγιστον
γὰρ ἀποκόπτειν οἴονται τοῦ βίου μέρος, τὴν διαδοχήν, τοὺς μὴ γαμοῦντας, μᾶλλον δέ, εἰ πάντες
τὸ αὐτὸ φρονήσειαν, ἐκλιπεῖν ἂν τὸ γένος τάχιστα.

161 δοκιμάζοντες μέντοι τριετίᾳ τὰς γαμετάς, ἐπειδὰν
τρὶς καθαρθῶσιν εἰς πεῖραν τοῦ δύνασθαι τίκτειν,
οὕτως ἄγονται. ταῖς δ' ἐγκύμοσιν οὐχ ὁμιλοῦσιν,
ἐνδεικνύμενοι τὸ μὴ δι' ἡδονὴν ἀλλὰ τέκνων
χρείαν γαμεῖν. λουτρὰ δὲ ταῖς γυναιξὶν ἀμπεχο-
μέναις ἐνδύματα, καθάπερ τοῖς ἀνδράσιν ἐν περι-
ζώματι. τοιαῦτα μὲν ἔθη τοῦδε τοῦ τάγματος.

162 (14) Δύο δὲ τῶν προτέρων Φαρισαῖοι μὲν οἱ
μετ' ἀκριβείας δοκοῦντες ἐξηγεῖσθαι τὰ νόμιμα
καὶ τὴν πρώτην ἀπάγοντες αἵρεσιν εἱμαρμένῃ τε
163 καὶ θεῷ προσάπτουσι πάντα, καὶ τὸ μὲν πράττειν
τὰ δίκαια καὶ μὴ κατὰ τὸ πλεῖστον ἐπὶ τοῖς
ἀνθρώποις κεῖσθαι, βοηθεῖν δὲ εἰς ἕκαστον καὶ τὴν
εἱμαρμένην· ψυχήν τε πᾶσαν μὲν ἄφθαρτον, μετα-

ᵃ Josephus quotes three instances of Essene predictions
which were fulfilled, those of Judas (B. i. 78), Simon (ii. 113)
and Menahem (A. xv. 373 ff.). They taught their art to
disciples (A. xiii. 311). This gift of fortune-telling was
perhaps connected with magic or astrology; it is not treated
as inspired (Lightfoot, Col. p. 89, note 1).

(12) There are some among them who profess to foretell the future, being versed from their early years in holy books, various forms of purification and apophthegms of prophets ; and seldom, if ever, do they err in their predictions.[a]

Their gift of prophecy.

(13) There is yet another order of Essenes, which, while at one with the rest in its mode of life, customs, and regulations, differs from them in its views on marriage. They think that those who decline to marry cut off the chief function of life, the propaga-tion of the race, and, what is more, that, were all to adopt the same view, the whole race would very quickly die out. They give their wives, however, a three years' probation, and only marry them after they have by three [b] periods of purification given proof of fecundity. They have no intercourse with them during pregnancy, thus showing that their motive in marrying is not self-indulgence but the procreation of children. In the bath the women wear a dress, the men a loin-cloth. Such are the usages of this order.

Essene schismatics who practise marriage.

(14) Of the two first-named [c] schools, the Pharisees, who are considered the most accurate interpreters of the laws, and hold the position of the leading sect, attribute everything to Fate and to God ; they hold that to act rightly or otherwise rests, indeed, for the most part with men, but that in each action Fate co-operates.[d] Every soul, they maintain, is im-

(ii.) The Pharisees.

[b] The text can hardly be right ; the Lat. has " *constanti purgatione.*"

[c] " more ancient," Reinach.

[d] *Cf.* the saying of R. Akiba : " Everything is foreseen and freewill is given," *Sayings of Jewish Fathers*, iii. 22 (24). Josephus, as Reinach remarks, substitutes " Fate " for " Providence " for his Gentile readers.

βαίνειν δὲ εἰς ἕτερον σῶμα τὴν τῶν ἀγαθῶν μόνην,
τὰς δὲ τῶν φαύλων ἀιδίῳ τιμωρίᾳ κολάζεσθαι.
164 Σαδδουκαῖοι δέ, τὸ δεύτερον τάγμα, τὴν μὲν
εἱμαρμένην παντάπασιν ἀναιροῦσιν καὶ τὸν θεὸν
165 ἔξω τοῦ δρᾶν τι κακὸν ἢ ἐφορᾶν τίθενται· φασὶν
δ' ἐπ' ἀνθρώπων ἐκλογῇ τό τε καλὸν καὶ τὸ κακὸν
προκεῖσθαι καὶ κατὰ γνώμην ἑκάστου τούτων
ἑκάτερον[1] προσιέναι. ψυχῆς τε τὴν διαμονὴν καὶ
τὰς καθ' ᾅδου[2] τιμωρίας καὶ τιμὰς ἀναιροῦσιν.
166 καὶ Φαρισαῖοι μὲν φιλάλληλοί τε καὶ τὴν εἰς τὸ
κοινὸν ὁμόνοιαν ἀσκοῦντες, Σαδδουκαίων δὲ καὶ
πρὸς ἀλλήλους τὸ ἦθος ἀγριώτερον, αἵ τε ἐπιμιξίαι
πρὸς τοὺς ὁμοίους ἀπηνεῖς ὡς πρὸς ἀλλοτρίους.
τοιαῦτα μὲν περὶ τῶν ἐν Ἰουδαίοις φιλοσοφούντων
εἶχον εἰπεῖν.

167 (ix. 1) Τῆς Ἀρχελάου δ' ἐθναρχίας μετα-
πεσούσης εἰς ἐπαρχίαν οἱ λοιποί, Φίλιππος καὶ
Ἡρώδης ὁ κληθεὶς Ἀντίπας, διῴκουν τὰς ἑαυτῶν
τετραρχίας· Σαλώμη γὰρ τελευτῶσα Ἰουλίᾳ τῇ
τοῦ Σεβαστοῦ γυναικὶ τήν τε αὑτῆς τοπαρχίαν
καὶ Ἰάμνειαν καὶ τοὺς ἐν Φασαηλίδι φοινικῶνας
168 κατέλιπεν. μεταβάσης δὲ εἰς Τιβέριον τὸν Ἰουλίας υἱὸν τῆς Ῥωμαίων ἡγεμονίας μετὰ τὴν
Αὐγούστου τελευτήν, ἀφηγησαμένου τῶν πραγ-

---

[1] Herwerden: ἑκατέρων V : ἑκατέρῳ the rest.
[2] καθ' ᾅδου C : καθόλου the rest.

---

[a] The doctrine of the reincarnation of the soul is expressed
in rather similar terms in B. iii. 374 (cf. Ap. ii. 218).

perishable, but the soul of the good alone passes into another body,[a] while the souls of the wicked suffer eternal punishment.

The Sadducees, the second of the orders, do away with Fate altogether, and remove God beyond, not merely the commission, but the very sight, of evil. They maintain that man has the free choice of good or evil, and that it rests with each man's will whether he follows the one or the other. As for the persistence of the soul after death, penalties in the underworld, and rewards, they will have none of them. (iii.) The Sadducees.

The Pharisees are affectionate to each other and cultivate harmonious relations with the community. The Sadducees, on the contrary, are, even among themselves, rather boorish in their behaviour, and in their intercourse with their peers[b] are as rude as to aliens. Such is what I have to say on the Jewish philosophical schools.

(ix. 1) When the ethnarchy of Archelaus was converted into a province, the other princes, Philip and Herod surnamed Antipas, continued to govern their respective tetrarchies; as for Salome, she at her death[c] bequeathed her toparchy to Julia, the wife of Augustus, together with Jamnia and the palm-groves of Phasaelis. On the death of Augustus, who had directed the state for fifty-seven years six months The tetrarchs Philip and Herod Antipas.

---

[b] *i.e.* with the other sects or generally with their compatriots.

[c] Which took place under the second of the procurators, M. Ambivius (*c.* 9–12 A.D.): *A.* xviii. 31. For her share in the division of Herod's kingdom see § 98. Jamnia was in the lowlands of Philistia, Phasaelis in the Jordan valley, as also was Archelais which is added to the list of Julia's legacies in *A. loc. cit.*

μάτων ἔτεσιν ἑπτὰ καὶ πεντήκοντα, πρὸς δὲ μησὶν
ἓξ καὶ ἡμέραις δύο, διαμείναντες ἐν ταῖς τετραρ-
χίαις ὅ τε Ἡρώδης καὶ ὁ Φίλιππος, ὁ μὲν πρὸς
ταῖς τοῦ Ἰορδάνου πηγαῖς ἐν Πανεάδι πόλιν
κτίζει Καισάρειαν, κἂν τῇ κάτω Γαυλανιτικῇ
Ἰουλιάδα, Ἡρώδης δ᾽ ἐν μὲν τῇ Γαλιλαίᾳ Τιβεριάδα, ἐν δὲ τῇ Περαίᾳ φερώνυμον Ἰουλίας.

169   (2) Πεμφθεὶς δὲ εἰς Ἰουδαίαν ἐπίτροπος ὑπὸ
Τιβερίου Πιλᾶτος νύκτωρ κεκαλυμμένας εἰς Ἱεροσόλυμα παρεισκομίζει τὰς Καίσαρος εἰκόνας, αἳ
170 σημαῖαι καλοῦνται. τοῦτο μεθ᾽ ἡμέραν μεγίστην
ταραχὴν ἤγειρεν Ἰουδαίοις· οἵ τε γὰρ ἐγγὺς πρὸς
τὴν ὄψιν ἐξεπλάγησαν ὡς πεπατημένων αὐτοῖς
τῶν νόμων, οὐδὲν γὰρ ἀξιοῦσιν ἐν τῇ πόλει δείκηλον τίθεσθαι, καὶ πρὸς τὴν ἀγανάκτησιν τῶν
κατὰ τὴν πόλιν ἄθρους ὁ ἐκ τῆς χώρας λαὸς
171 συνέρρευσεν. ὁρμήσαντες δὲ πρὸς Πιλᾶτον εἰς
Καισάρειαν ἱκέτευον ἐξενεγκεῖν ἐξ Ἱεροσολύμων
τὰς σημαίας καὶ τηρεῖν αὐτοῖς τὰ πάτρια. Πιλάτου
δ᾽ ἀρνουμένου περὶ τὴν οἰκίαν πρηνεῖς κατα-

ᵃ This figure, repeated in *A.* xviii. 32, is about a month
too long. From the death of Caesar (15 March 44 B.C.) to
the death of Augustus (19 Aug. A.D. 14, Suet. *Aug.* 100) is 57
years 5 months and 4 days. The four days may be reduced
to two by reckoning from the opening of Caesar's will (17
March) as proposed by Gardthausen, quoted by Reinach ; the
latter accounts for the error in the number of months by a
confusion of the figures for 5 (ε′) and 6 (ϛ′).

ᵇ By her former husband, Tiberius Claudius Nero.

ᶜ Caesarea Philippi of the N.T., mod. *Banias.*

ᵈ Bethsaida Julias (*et-Tell*) east of the Jordan a little to

and two days,[a] the empire of the Romans passed to
Tiberius, son of Julia.[b] On his accession, Herod
(Antipas) and Philip continued to hold their tet-
rarchies and respectively founded cities : Philip built
Caesarea[c] near the sources of the Jordan, in the
district of Paneas, and Julias[d] in lower Gaulanitis ;
Herod built Tiberias in Galilee and a city which also
took the name of Julia, in Peraea.[e]

(2) Pilate, being sent by Tiberius as procurator
to Judaea, introduced into Jerusalem by night and
under cover the effigies of Caesar which are called
standards.[f] This proceeding, when day broke,
aroused immense excitement among the Jews ; those
on the spot were in consternation, considering their
laws to have been trampled under foot, as those laws
permit no image to be erected in the city ; while the
indignation of the townspeople stirred the country-
folk, who flocked together in crowds. Hastening
after Pilate to Caesarea, the Jews implored him to
remove the standards from Jerusalem and to uphold
the laws of their ancestors. When Pilate refused,
they fell prostrate around his house and for five

the north of the head of the Sea of Galilee. It was called
after Julia, daughter of Augustus, *A.* xviii. 28 ; as she was
banished in 2 B.C., Schürer infers that the refoundation of the
town by Philip must have been earlier than that date.

[e] The Peraean Julias (formerly Betharamatha, *B.* ii. 59
note) opposite Jericho was called after the Empress Julia =
Livia (*A.* xviii. 27) ; other writers call it Livias and that,
rather than Julias, was probably the name given by the
founder.

[f] More correctly described in *A.* xviii. 55, " The busts (or
" medallions ") of Caesar which were attached to the
standards." Tacitus (*Hist.* iv. 62) records how these *impera-
torum imagines* were torn down by Civilis and his victorious
Gauls.

πεσόντες ἐπὶ πέντε ἡμέρας καὶ νύκτας ἴσας
ἀκίνητοι διεκαρτέρουν.

172 (3) Τῇ δ' ἑξῆς ὁ Πιλᾶτος καθίσας ἐπὶ βήματος
ἐν τῷ μεγάλῳ σταδίῳ καὶ προσκαλεσάμενος τὸ
πλῆθος ὡς ἀποκρίνασθαι δῆθεν αὐτοῖς θέλων,
δίδωσιν τοῖς στρατιώταις σημεῖον ἐκ συντάγματος
κυκλώσασθαι τοὺς Ἰουδαίους ἐν τοῖς ὅπλοις.

173 περιστάσης δὲ τριστιχεὶ τῆς φάλαγγος Ἰουδαῖοι
μὲν ἀχανεῖς ἦσαν πρὸς τὸ ἀδόκητον τῆς ὄψεως,
Πιλᾶτος δὲ κατακόψειν εἰπὼν αὐτούς, εἰ μὴ
προσδέξαιντο τὰς Καίσαρος εἰκόνας, γυμνοῦν τὰ

174 ξίφη τοῖς στρατιώταις ἔνευσεν. οἱ δὲ Ἰουδαῖοι
καθάπερ ἐκ συνθήματος ἀθρόοι καταπεσόντες καὶ
τοὺς αὐχένας παρακλίναντες ἑτοίμους ἀναιρεῖν[1]
σφᾶς ἐβόων μᾶλλον ἢ τὸν νόμον παραβῆναι.
ὑπερθαυμάσας δὲ ὁ Πιλᾶτος τὸ τῆς δεισιδαιμονίας
ἄκρατον ἐκκομίσαι μὲν αὐτίκα τὰς σημαίας
Ἱεροσολύμων κελεύει.

175 (4) Μετὰ δὲ ταῦτα ταραχὴν ἑτέραν ἐκίνει τὸν
ἱερὸν θησαυρόν, καλεῖται δὲ κορβωνᾶς,[2] εἰς καταγωγὴν ὑδάτων ἐξαναλίσκων· κατῆγεν δὲ ἀπὸ
τετρακοσίων[3] σταδίων. πρὸς τοῦτο τοῦ πλήθους
ἀγανάκτησις ἦν, καὶ τοῦ Πιλάτου παρόντος εἰς
Ἱεροσόλυμα περιστάντες τὸ βῆμα κατεβόων.

176 ὁ δέ, προῄδει γὰρ αὐτῶν τὴν ταραχήν, τῷ πλήθει
τοὺς στρατιώτας ἐνόπλους [ἐν][4] ἐσθῆσιν ἰδιωτικαῖς
κεκαλυμμένους ἐγκαταμίξας καὶ ξίφει μὲν χρήσασθαι κωλύσας, ξύλοις δὲ παίειν τοὺς κεκραγότας ἐγκελευσάμενος, σύνθημα δίδωσιν ἀπὸ τοῦ βή-

---

[1] PA : εἰς ἀναίρεσιν the rest.
[2] P and correctors of A and L : κορβανᾶς the rest.
[3] τριακοσίων Lat. Eus. : διακοσίων A. ‖.

whole days and nights remained motionless in that position.

(3) On the ensuing day Pilate took his seat on his tribunal in the great stadium and summoning the multitude, with the apparent intention of answering them, gave the arranged signal to his armed soldiers to surround the Jews. Finding themselves in a ring of troops, three deep, the Jews were struck dumb at this unexpected sight. Pilate, after threatening to cut them down, if they refused to admit Caesar's images, signalled to the soldiers to draw their swords. Thereupon the Jews, as by concerted action, flung themselves in a body on the ground, extended their necks, and exclaimed that they were ready rather to die than to transgress the law. Overcome with astonishment at such intense religious zeal, Pilate gave orders for the immediate removal of the standards from Jerusalem.

(4) On a later occasion he provoked a fresh uproar (ii.) the by expending upon the construction of an aqueduct ^{affair of the aqueduct.} the sacred treasure known as *Corbonas* [a]; the water was brought from a distance of 400 furlongs. Indignant at this proceeding, the populace formed a ring round the tribunal of Pilate, then on a visit to Jerusalem, and besieged him with angry clamour. He, foreseeing the tumult, had interspersed among the crowd a troop of his soldiers, armed but disguised in civilian dress, with orders not to use their swords, but to beat any rioters with cudgels. He now from

---

[a] *Cf.* Matt. xxvii. 6, τὸν κορβανᾶν (*v.l.* κορβωνᾶν) = " the sacred treasury," the only parallel for this use of the word. *Corban* = " devoted," " taboo " (*cf. Ap.* i. 167).

---

[4] PAM: om. the rest.

177 ματος. τυπτόμενοι δὲ οἱ Ἰουδαῖοι πολλοὶ μὲν ὑπὸ
τῶν πληγῶν, πολλοὶ δὲ ὑπὸ σφῶν αὐτῶν ἐν τῇ φυγῇ
καταπατηθέντες ἀπώλοντο. πρὸς δὲ τὴν συμφορὰν
τῶν ἀνηρημένων καταπλαγὲν τὸ πλῆθος ἐσιώπησεν.
178 (5) Κἂν τούτῳ κατήγορος Ἡρώδου τοῦ τε-
τραρχοῦντος Ἀγρίππας υἱὸς Ἀριστοβούλου, ὃν
ὁ πατὴρ Ἡρώδης ἀπέκτεινεν, παραγίνεται πρὸς
Τιβέριον. τοῦ δὲ μὴ προσδεξαμένου τὴν κατηγορίαν μένων ἐπὶ Ῥώμης τούς τε ἄλλους τῶν
γνωρίμων ἐθεράπευεν καὶ μάλιστα τὸν Γερμανικοῦ
179 παῖδα Γάιον, ἰδιώτην ἔτι ὄντα. καὶ δή ποτε
ἑστιῶν αὐτὸν τά τε ἄλλα ποικίλως ἐφιλοφρονεῖτο,
καὶ τελευταῖον τὰς χεῖρας ἀνατείνας φανερῶς
ηὔξατο θᾶττον αὐτὸν θεάσασθαι τῶν ὅλων δεσπό-
180 την ἀποθανόντος Τιβερίου. τοῦτό τις τῶν οἰκετῶν
αὐτοῦ διαγγέλλει τῷ Τιβερίῳ, καὶ ὃς ἀγανακτήσας
εἴργνυσιν τὸν Ἀγρίππαν καὶ μετ᾽ αἰκίας εἶχεν
αὐτὸν ἐπὶ μῆνας ἓξ ἐν δεσμωτηρίῳ, μέχρις αὐτὸς
ἐτελεύτησεν ἡγεμονεύσας ἔτη δύο πρὸς τοῖς εἴκοσι
καὶ τρεῖς ἡμέρας ἐπὶ μησὶν ἕξ.
181 (6) Ἀποδειχθεὶς δὲ Γάιος Καῖσαρ ἀνίησίν τε
τῶν δεσμῶν τὸν Ἀγρίππαν καὶ τῆς Φιλίππου
τετραρχίας, θνήσκει[1] γὰρ οὗτος, καθίστησι βασιλέα.
παραγενόμενος δὲ εἰς τὴν ἀρχὴν Ἀγρίππας φθόνῳ

---

[1] P: τεθνήκει the rest.

[a] i. 551.
[b] The whole story is told in much greater detail in Α.
xviii. (? from some Roman source), where, however, there is
no mention of this object of his visit. The visit was made
" in the year before Tiberius died " (Α. xviii. 126).
[c] Eutychus, his freedman and charioteer, Α. xviii. 168 ;
according to the account there given the words were spoken
during a drive, not at dinner.

his tribunal gave the agreed signal. Large numbers of the Jews perished, some from the blows which they received, others trodden to death by their companions in the ensuing flight. Cowed by the fate of the victims, the multitude was reduced to silence.

(5) At this time Agrippa, son of the Aristobulus who was put to death by his father Herod,[a] came to Tiberius to accuse Herod the tetrarch.[b] The emperor having declined to countenance the charge, Agrippa remained in Rome, paying court to various notabilities and in particular to Gaius, son of Germanicus, who was still a private citizen. On one occasion when he was entertaining him at dinner, Agrippa, after paying him all kinds of compliments, finally raised his hands to heaven and openly prayed that he might soon see Gaius master of the world, through the decease of Tiberius. This was reported by one of Agrippa's domestics [c] to Tiberius; whereupon the emperor, in indignation, threw Agrippa into prison, where he kept him under rigorous treatment for six months until his own death, which closed a reign of twenty-two years, six months and three days.[d]

(6) Gaius, on being proclaimed emperor, liberated Agrippa and gave him, with the title of king, the tetrarchy of Philip, now deceased.[e] Agrippa's arrival to take possession of his kingdom [f] aroused

Marginal notes:

Herod Agrippa in Rome 36 A.D.

is imprisoned by Tiberius

March 37 A.D.

Accession of GAIUS (CALIGULA). Agrippa liberated and made king.

---

[d] 22 years 5 months and 3 days according to *A.* xviii. 224 (*cf.* § 168 for confusion of the numbers 5 and 6). But neither statement quite agrees with our secular authorities: the reign lasted from 19 Aug. 14 (death of Augustus) to 16 March (Tac.; or 26 March, Dio), *i.e.* 22 years 6 months and 28 days (or 22 years 7 months 7 days).

[e] He had died in the twentieth year of the reign of Tiberius (*A.* xviii. 106), *i.e.* in A.D. 33–4.

[f] A.D. 38–39.

τὰς Ἡρώδου τοῦ τετράρχου διήγειρεν ἐπιθυμίας.
182 ἐνῆγε δὲ μάλιστα τοῦτον εἰς ἐλπίδα βασιλείας
Ἡρωδιὰς ἡ γυνή, κατονειδίζουσα τὴν ἀργίαν καὶ
φαμένη παρὰ τὸ μὴ βούλεσθαι πλεῖν ἐπὶ Καίσαρα
στερίσκεσθαι μείζονος ἀρχῆς· ὅπου γὰρ Ἀγρίππαν ἐξ ἰδιώτου βασιλέα πεποίηκεν, ἦπου γ' ἂν
183 ἐκεῖνον διστάσειεν ἐκ τετράρχου; τούτοις ἀνα-
πεισθεὶς Ἡρώδης ἧκεν πρὸς Γάιον, ὑφ' οὗ τῆς
πλεονεξίας ἐπιτιμᾶται φυγῇ εἰς Σπανίαν¹· ἠκο-
λούθησεν γὰρ αὐτῷ κατήγορος Ἀγρίππας, ᾧ καὶ
τὴν τετραρχίαν τὴν ἐκείνου προσέθηκεν Γάιος.
καὶ Ἡρώδης μὲν ἐν Σπανίᾳ συμφυγούσης αὐτῷ
καὶ τῆς γυναικὸς τελευτᾷ.
184   (x. 1) Γάιος δὲ Καῖσαρ ἐπὶ τοσοῦτον ἐξύβρι-
σεν εἰς τὴν τύχην, ὥστε θεὸν ἑαυτὸν καὶ δοκεῖν²
βούλεσθαι καὶ καλεῖσθαι, τῶν τε εὐγενεστάτων
ἀνδρῶν ἀκροτομῆσαι τὴν πατρίδα, ἐκτεῖναι δὲ τὴν
185 ἀσέβειαν καὶ ἐπὶ Ἰουδαίαν. Πετρώνιον μὲν οὖν
μετὰ στρατιᾶς ἐπὶ Ἱεροσολύμων ἔπεμψεν ἐγ-
καθιδρύσοντα τῷ ναῷ τοὺς ἀνδριάντας αὐτοῦ,
προστάξας, εἰ μὴ δέχοιντο Ἰουδαῖοι, τούς τε
κωλύοντας ἀνελεῖν καὶ πᾶν τὸ λοιπὸν ἔθνος
186 ἐξανδραποδίσασθαι. θεῷ δ' ἄρα τῶν προσταγμάτων ἔμελεν. καὶ Πετρώνιος μὲν σὺν τρισὶ
τάγμασι καὶ πολλοῖς ἐκ τῆς Συρίας συμμάχοις εἰς
187 τὴν Ἰουδαίαν ἤλαυνεν ἐκ τῆς Ἀντιοχείας, Ἰουδαίων δὲ οἱ μὲν ἠπίστουν ἐπὶ ταῖς τοῦ πολέμου

¹ So (or Ἰσπανίαν) all mss.: Γαλλίαν Niese and Γαλλία
below, to conform to A. xviii. 252.
² καὶ δοκεῖν Niese: δοκεῖν καὶ PAM Exc.: καὶ δοκεῖν καὶ the
rest.

ᵃ According to A. xviii. 252 to Lyons in Gaul.

the envy and ambition of Herod the tetrarch. But it
was above all his wife Herodias who instigated the
tetrarch to aspire to a throne ; she reproached him
for his indolence and told him that it was only his
reluctance to set sail and wait upon Caesar which
kept him out of promotion. " Now that he has made
a king of Agrippa, a mere commoner, " she said,
" surely he could not hesitate to confer the same title
on a tetrarch." Yielding to these solicitations,
Herod presented himself to Gaius, who punished him
for his cupidity by banishing him to Spain.[a] For an
accuser had followed him in the person of Agrippa,[b]
to whose kingdom Gaius annexed his rival's tetrarchy.
Herod died in Spain, whither his wife had accompanied him into exile.

The end of Philip and of Herod Antipas.

(x. 1) The insolence with which the emperor
Gaius defied fortune surpassed all bounds : he wished
to be considered a god and to be hailed as such, he
cut off the flower of the nobility of his country, and
his impiety extended even to Judaea. In fact, he
sent Petronius with an army to Jerusalem to instal in
the sanctuary statues of himself ; in the event of the
Jews refusing to admit them, his orders were to put
the recalcitrants to death and to reduce the whole
nation to slavery. But these orders, as the sequel
showed, were under God's care. Petronius, accordingly, with three legions [c] and a large contingent of
Syrian auxiliaries, left Antioch on the march for
Judaea. Among the Jews, some put no belief in the

Gaius orders the erection of his statue in the Temple.

Arrival of Petronius at Ptolemais to execute the order 40 A.D.

[b] In *A.* xviii. 247 Agrippa sends his freedman Fortunatus
to accuse Antipas.

[c] Two only, according to *A.* xviii. 262 (and so Philo, *Leg.
ad Gaium* 31, § 207 " half his army " ; there were four legions
in Syria at this time).

φήμαις, οἱ δὲ πιστεύοντες ἦσαν ἐν ἀμηχάνῳ πρὸς
τὴν ἄμυναν· ταχὺ δ' ἐχώρει διὰ πάντων τὸ δέος
ἤδη παρούσης[1] εἰς Πτολεμαΐδα τῆς στρατιᾶς.

188 (2) Πόλις δ' ἐστὶν αὕτη τῆς Γαλιλαίας παρά-
λιος κατὰ τὸ μέγα πεδίον ἐκτισμένη, περιέχεται
δὲ ὄρεσιν ἐκ μὲν τοῦ πρὸς ἀνατολὴν κλίματος ἀπὸ
σταδίων ἑξήκοντα τῷ τῆς Γαλιλαίας, ἀπὸ δὲ
τοῦ μεσημβρινοῦ τῷ Καρμήλῳ διέχοντι σταδίους
ἑκατὸν εἴκοσι, τῷ δ' ὑψηλοτάτῳ κατ' ἄρκτον, ὃ
καλοῦσιν κλίμακα Τυρίων οἱ ἐπιχώριοι· καὶ τοῦτο
189 δὲ σταδίους ἀφέστηκεν ἑκατόν. τοῦ δ' ἄστεος
ὅσον ἀπὸ δύο σταδίων ὁ καλούμενος Βήλεος
ποταμὸς παραρρεῖ παντάπασιν ὀλίγος, παρ' ᾧ τὸ
Μέμνονος μνημεῖόν ἐστιν ἔχον ἐγγὺς αὐτοῦ τόπον
190 ἑκατονταπήχη θαύματος ἄξιον· κυκλοτερὴς μὲν
γάρ ἐστιν καὶ κοῖλος, ἀναδίδωσιν δὲ τὴν ὑελίνην
ψάμμον, ἣν ὅταν ἐκκενώσῃ πολλὰ πλοῖα προσ-
σχόντα,[2] πάλιν ἀντιπληροῦται τὸ χωρίον, κατα-
συρόντων μὲν ὥσπερ ἐπίτηδες τότε τῶν ἀνέμων
εἰς αὐτὸ τὴν ἔξωθεν ἀργὴν ψάμμον, τοῦ δὲ μετάλ-
191 λου πᾶσαν εὐθέως μεταβάλλοντος εἰς ὕελον. θαυ-
μασιώτερον [δὲ][3] τούτου μοι δοκεῖ τὸ τὴν ὑπερ-
χυθεῖσαν ὕελον ἐκ τοῦ τόπου πάλιν ψάμμον γίνεσθαι εἰκαίαν. τὸ μὲν οὖν χωρίον τοῦτο τοιαύτην
εἴληχεν φύσιν.

192 (3) Ἰουδαῖοι δὲ μετὰ γυναικῶν καὶ τέκνων
ἀθροισθέντες εἰς τὸ πεδίον τὸ πρὸς Πτολεμαΐδι
καθικέτευον τὸν Πετρώνιον ὑπὲρ τῶν πατρίων
νόμων πρῶτον, ἔπειτα ὑπὲρ αὐτῶν. ὁ δὲ πρός
τε τὸ πλῆθος καὶ τὰς δεήσεις ἐνδοὺς τοὺς μὲν

---

[1] Dindorf: γὰρ οὔσης MSS.
[2] Dindorf: προσχόντα MSS.   [3] om. most MSS.

rumours of war, others believed, but saw no means of defence ; alarm, however, soon became universal, the army having already reached Ptolemais.

(2) Ptolemais is a maritime town in Galilee, built at the entrance to the Great Plain, and encompassed with mountains. To the east, at a distance of 60 furlongs, is the Galilaean range ; to the south, 120 furlongs off, lies Carmel ; to the north is the highest chain of all, called by the natives the " Ladder of the Tyrians," 100 furlongs away. At a distance of about two furlongs from the town runs the diminutive river Beleus [a] ; on its bank stands the tomb of Memnon, and close to it is a very remarkable region, a hundred cubits in extent. It consists of a circular basin which produces vitreous sand. Numerous boats put in to this spot and empty the basin of its sand, whereupon it is filled up again by the action of the winds, which, as if by design, drift into it the common sand outside, the latter being all promptly converted by this mine into vitreous matter. But the phenomenon which, to my mind, is even more remarkable, is that the excess particles of glass which overflow from the cavity become ordinary sand as before. Such are the curious properties of this spot.

Digression on Ptolemais and its vitreous sand.

(3) The Jews assembled with their wives and children in the plain of Ptolemais and implored Petronius to have regard first for the laws of their fathers, and next for themselves. Yielding so far to this vast multitude and their entreaties, he left the

Petronius and his Jewish petitioners.

[a] Belus in Tac. *Hist.* v. 7 and Pliny, *N.H.* xxxvi. 190, modern *Nahr Na'man.*

ἀνδριάντας καὶ τὰς στρατιὰς¹ ἐν Πτολεμαΐδι λείπει,
193 προελθὼν² δὲ εἰς τὴν Γαλιλαίαν καὶ συγκαλέσας
τό τε πλῆθος καὶ τοὺς γνωρίμους πάντας εἰς
Τιβεριάδα τήν τε Ῥωμαίων διεξῄει δύναμιν καὶ
τὰς Καίσαρος ἀπειλάς, ἔτι δὲ τὴν ἀξίωσιν ἀπ-
194 έφαινεν ἀγνώμονα· πάντων γὰρ τῶν ὑποτεταγμένων ἐθνῶν κατὰ πόλιν συγκαθιδρυκότων τοῖς
ἄλλοις θεοῖς καὶ τὰς Καίσαρος εἰκόνας, τὸ μόνους
ἐκείνους ἀντιτάσσεσθαι πρὸς τοῦτο σχεδὸν ἀφισταμένων εἶναι καὶ μεθ' ὕβρεως.

195 (4) Τῶν δὲ τὸν νόμον καὶ τὸ πάτριον ἔθος
προτεινομένων καὶ ὡς οὐδὲ θεοῦ τι δείκηλον, οὐχ
ὅπως ἀνδρός, οὐ κατὰ τὸν ναὸν μόνον ἀλλ' οὐδὲ
ἐν εἰκαίῳ τινὶ τόπῳ τῆς χώρας θέσθαι θεμιτὸν
εἴη, ὑπολαβὼν ὁ Πετρώνιος " ἀλλὰ μὴν καὶ ἐμοὶ
φυλακτέος ὁ τοὐμοῦ δεσπότου νόμος," ἔφη·
" παραβὰς γὰρ αὐτὸν καὶ φεισάμενος ὑμῶν
ἀπολοῦμαι δικαίως. πολεμήσει δ' ὑμᾶς ὁ πέμψας
με καὶ οὐκ ἐγώ· καὶ γὰρ αὐτός, ὥσπερ ὑμεῖς,
196 ἐπιτάσσομαι." πρὸς ταῦτα τὸ πλῆθος πάντ'
ἐβόα πρὸ τοῦ νόμου πάσχειν ἑτοίμως ἔχειν.
καταστείλας δ' αὐτῶν ὁ Πετρώνιος τὴν βοήν,
197 " πολεμήσετε," εἶπεν, " ἄρα Καίσαρι; " καὶ Ἰουδαῖοι περὶ μὲν Καίσαρος καὶ τοῦ δήμου τῶν
Ῥωμαίων δὶς τῆς ἡμέρας θύειν ἔφασαν, εἰ δὲ
βούλεται τὰς εἰκόνας ἐγκαθιδρύειν, πρότερον αὐτὸν
δεῖν ἅπαν τὸ Ἰουδαίων ἔθνος προθύσασθαι·
παρέχειν δὲ σφᾶς αὐτοὺς ἑτοίμους εἰς τὴν σφαγὴν
198 ἅμα τέκνοις καὶ γυναιξίν. ἐπὶ τούτοις θαῦμα καὶ
οἶκτος εἰσῄει τὸν Πετρώνιον τῆς τε ἀνυπερβλήτου

¹ So PAM : τὴν μὲν στρατιὰν καὶ τοὺς ἀνδριάντας the rest.
² C : προσελθὼν the rest.

398

statues and his troops at Ptolemais and advanced into
Galilee, where he summoned the people, with all
persons of distinction, to Tiberias. There he dwelt
upon the power of the Romans and the emperor's
menaces, and, moreover, pointed out the recklessness
of their request ; all the subject nations, he urged,
had erected in each of their cities statues of Caesar,
along with those of their other gods, and that they
alone should oppose this practice amounted almost to
rebellion, aggravated by insult.

(4) When the Jews appealed to their law and the
custom of their ancestors, and pleaded that they were
forbidden to place an image of God, much more of a
man, not only in their sanctuary but even in any un-
consecrated spot throughout the country, Petronius
replied, " But I too must obey the law of my master ;
if I transgress it and spare you, I shall be put to
death, with justice. War will be made on you by
him who sent me, not by me ; for I too, like you, am
under orders." At this the multitude cried out that
they were ready to endure everything for the law.
Petronius, having checked their clamour, said, " Will
you then go to war with Caesar ? " The Jews
replied that they offered sacrifice twice daily for
Caesar [a] and the Roman people, but that if he wished
to set up these statues, he must first sacrifice the
entire Jewish nation ; and that they presented themselves, their wives and their children, ready for the
slaughter. These words filled Petronius with astonishment and pity at the spectacle of the incomparable

[a] *Cf. Ap.* ii. 77 with note. From the present passage we
may infer that the daily sacrifice for the Emperor was offered
partly at the morning, partly at the evening service.

θρησκείας τῶν ἀνδρῶν καὶ τοῦ πρὸς θάνατον
ἑτοίμου παραστήματος. καὶ τότε μὲν ἄπρακτοι
διελύθησαν.

199 (5) Ταῖς δ' ἑξῆς ἀθρόους τε τοὺς δυνατοὺς κατ'
ἰδίαν καὶ τὸ πλῆθος ἐν κοινῷ συλλέγων[1] ποτὲ μὲν
παρεκάλει, ποτὲ δὲ συνεβούλευεν, τὸ πλέον μέντοι
διηπείλει, τήν τε Ῥωμαίων ἐπανατεινόμενος ἰσχὺν
καὶ τοὺς Γαΐου θυμοὺς τήν τε ἰδίαν πρὸς τούτοις
200 ἀνάγκην. πρὸς δὲ μηδεμίαν πεῖραν ἐνδιδόντων,
ὡς ἑώρα καὶ τὴν χώραν κινδυνεύουσαν ἄσπορον
μεῖναι, κατὰ γὰρ ὥραν σπόρου πεντήκοντα ἡμέρας
ἀργὰ προσδιέτριβεν αὐτῷ τὰ πλήθη, τελευταῖον
201 ἀθροίσας αὐτοὺς καὶ "παρακινδυνευτέον ἐμοὶ
μᾶλλον," εἰπών, "ἢ γὰρ τοῦ θεοῦ συνεργοῦντος
πείσας Καίσαρα σωθήσομαι μεθ' ὑμῶν ἡδέως,
ἢ παροξυνθέντος ὑπὲρ τοσούτων ἑτοίμως ἐπιδώσω
τὴν ἐμαυτοῦ ψυχήν," διαφῆκεν τὸ πλῆθος πολλὰ
κατευχόμενον[2] αὐτῷ, καὶ παραλαβὼν τὴν στρατιὰν
ἐκ τῆς Πτολεμαΐδος ὑπέστρεψεν εἰς τὴν Ἀντιό-
202 χειαν. ἔνθεν εὐθέως ἐπέστελλεν Καίσαρι τήν τε
ἐμβολὴν τὴν εἰς Ἰουδαίαν ἑαυτοῦ καὶ τὰς ἱκεσίας
τοῦ ἔθνους, ὅτι τε, εἰ μὴ βούλεται πρὸς τοῖς
ἀνδράσιν καὶ τὴν χώραν ἀπολέσαι, δέοι φυλάττειν
τε αὐτοῖς[3] τὸν νόμον καὶ παριέναι τὸ πρόσταγμα.
203 ταύταις ταῖς ἐπιστολαῖς οὐ σφόδρα μετρίως ἀντ-
έγραψεν ὁ Γάιος, ἀπειλῶν Πετρωνίῳ θάνατον, ὅτι
τῶν προσταγμάτων αὐτοῦ βραδὺς ὑπηρέτης ἐγίνετο.[4] ἀλλὰ τοὺς μὲν τούτων γραμματοφόρους
συνέβη χειμασθῆναι τρεῖς μῆνας ἐν τῇ θαλάσσῃ,

---

[1] συλλεγέντων PA, whence συλλεγὲν Destinon.
[2] κατευχομένων PA*.　　　[3] Niese: αὐτοὺς mss.
[4] PA: ἐγένετο the rest.

devotion of this people to their religion and their unflinching resignation to death. So for the time he dismissed them, nothing being decided.

(5) During the ensuing days he held crowded private conferences[a] with the aristocracy, and public meetings with the people ; at these he had recourse alternatively to entreaty, to advice, most often, however, to threats, holding over their heads the might of the Romans, the fury of Gaius, and the necessity which circumstances imposed upon himself. As, however, none of these efforts would induce them to yield, and as he saw that the country was in danger of remaining unsown—for it was seed-time and the people had spent fifty[b] days idly waiting upon him —he finally called them together and said : " It is better that I should take the risk. Either, God aiding me, I shall prevail with Caesar and have the satisfaction of saving myself as well as you, or, if his indignation is roused, I am ready on behalf of the lives of so many to surrender my own." With that he dismissed the multitude, who rained blessings on his head, and collecting his troops left Ptolemais and returned to Antioch. From that city he hastened to report to Caesar his expedition into Judaea and the entreaties of the nation, adding that, unless he wished to destroy the country as well as its inhabitants, he ought to respect their law and revoke the order. To this dispatch Gaius replied in no measured terms, threatening to put Petronius to death for his tardiness in executing his orders. However, it so happened that the bearers of this message were weather-bound for three months at sea, while others, who brought

---

[a] These later conferences were held at Tiberias, *A.* xviii. 269 ff.   [b] 40 according to *A.* xviii. 272.

τὸν δὲ Γαΐου θάνατον ἄλλοι καταγγέλλοντες
εὐπλόουν. ἔφθη γοῦν τὰς περὶ τούτων Πετρώνιος λαβὼν ἐπιστολὰς ἑπτὰ καὶ εἴκοσιν ἡμέραις
ἢ τὰς καθ' ἑαυτοῦ.

204 xi. (1) Γαΐου δὲ ἡγεμονεύσαντος ἔτη τρία καὶ
μῆνας ὀκτὼ καὶ δολοφονηθέντος ἁρπάζεται μὲν
ὑπὸ τῶν ἐν Ῥώμῃ στρατευμάτων [εἰς τὴν ἀρχὴν]¹
205 Κλαύδιος, ἡ δὲ σύγκλητος, ἐξηγουμένων τῶν
ὑπάτων Σεντίου Σατορνίνου καὶ Πομπωνίου Σε-
κούνδου, τρισὶν ταῖς συμμενούσαις σπείραις ἐπι-
τρέψασα φυλάττειν τὴν πόλιν εἰς τὸ Καπετώλιον
ἠθροίσθη, καὶ διὰ τὴν ὠμότητα τὴν Γαΐου Κλαυδίῳ πολεμεῖν ἐψηφίζετο· καταστήσεσθαι γὰρ δι'
ἀριστοκρατίας, ὥσπερ οὖν πάλαι διῳκεῖτο, τὴν
ἀρχὴν ἢ κρινεῖν ψήφῳ τὸν ἄξιον τῆς ἡγεμονίας.

206 (2) Συνέβη [δὲ]² τηνικαῦτα πρὸς ἐπιδημοῦντα
τὸν Ἀγρίππαν τήν τε σύγκλητον καλοῦσαν εἰς
συμβουλίαν πέμψαι καὶ Κλαύδιον ἐκ τῆς παρεμ-
βολῆς, ὅπως πρὸς ἃ δέοι χρήσιμος αὐτοῖς γένοιτο.
[κἀκεῖνος]² συνιδὼν τὸν ἤδη τῇ δυνάμει Καίσαρα
207 πρὸς Κλαύδιον ἄπεισιν. ὁ δ' αὐτὸν πρεσβευτὴν
πρὸς τὴν σύγκλητον ἀναπέμπει δηλοῦντα τὴν
ἑαυτοῦ προαίρεσιν, ὅτι πρῶτον μὲν ἄκων ὑπὸ τῶν
στρατιωτῶν ἁρπαγείη, καὶ οὔτε τὴν ἐκείνων

¹ om. P.　　　² om. PA.

ᵃ In the account of this affair of Petronius Λ. xviii. again
enters much more into detail than Β. ii. ; outstanding additions are the providential rainfall and the intercession of
Agrippa with Gaius at Rome on behalf of the Jews.

ᵇ So Λ. xix. 201 ; in reality just over 3 years and 10
months (16 March 37 to 24 January 41 A.D.)

ᶜ The story of the assassination is told at length from some

402

the news of the death of Gaius, had a fortunate ^{The temple} passage. So Petronius received this last information ^{saved by the death} twenty-seven days earlier than the letter conveying ^{of Gaius} his own death-warrant.^a ^{Jan. 41 A.D.}

(xi. 1) When Gaius, after a reign of three years and ^{Accession of} eight months,^b was assassinated,^c the troops in Rome^d ^{CLAUDIUS.} carried off Claudius by force to make him emperor. But the senate, on the motion of the consuls, Sentius Saturninus and Pomponius Secundus, after entrusting the protection of the city to the three ^e cohorts that remained loyal to them, assembled in the Capitol and, on the ground of the savagery of Gaius, decreed war on Claudius ; they were determined either to revert to their former constitution as an aristocracy, or to elect by suffrage a leader worthy of the empire.

(2) Agrippa was at the time in Rome, and, as ^{Important} chance would have it, he received a summons alike ^{part played by Agrippa} from the senate, calling him into consultation, and ^{as mediator} from Claudius in the camp^f; both parties solicited ^{between Claudius} his services in this pressing emergency. Agrippa, ^{and the} reflecting that Claudius was already virtually em- ^{Senate.} peror with the power at his back, repaired to him. Claudius, thereupon, sent him off as his envoy to inform the senate of his sentiments. He was to state, in the first place, that it was against his will that he had been carried off by the soldiers ; at the same time he considered it both unjust to betray

---

first-hand authority in *A.* xix., where it fills more than half the book. In the accession of Claudius, Agrippa plays a larger part in *B.* than in *A.*

^d The praetorian guard.   ^e Four according to *A.* xix. 188.
^f The praetorian camp established by Sejanus in A.D. 23 on the N.E. of Rome, outside the ancient city, but afterwards included within the Aurelian walls.

σπουδὴν ἐγκαταλιπεῖν δίκαιον οὔτε ἀσφαλὲς τὴν
ἑαυτοῦ τύχην κρίνοι· καὶ γὰρ τὸ τυχεῖν τῆς
208 ἡγεμονικῆς κλήσεως ἐπικίνδυνον εἶναι· ἔπειθ' ὅτι
διοικήσει¹ τὴν ἀρχὴν ὥσπερ ἀγαθὸς προστάτης,
οὐχ ὡς τύραννος· ἀρκεῖσθαι γὰρ τῇ τιμῇ τῆς
προσηγορίας, τὴν δ' ἐφ' ἑκάστῳ τῶν πραγμάτων
βουλὴν πᾶσιν ἀποδώσειν· καὶ γὰρ εἰ μὴ φύσει
μέτριος ἦν, ἱκανὸν ὑπόδειγμα σωφροσύνης αὐτῷ
προκεῖσθαι τὸν Γαΐου θάνατον.

209   (3) Ταῦτ' ἀπήγγειλεν Ἀγρίππας. ἡ δὲ βουλὴ
ἀπεκρίνατο καὶ στρατῷ καὶ γνώμαις ἀγαθαῖς
πεποιθυῖα δουλείαν ἑκούσιον οὐχ ὑπομενεῖν. καὶ
Κλαύδιος ὡς ἤκουσεν τὰ παρὰ τῆς βουλῆς, πάλιν
ἔπεμψεν τὸν Ἀγρίππαν ἀπαγγελοῦντα αὐτοῖς ὅτι
προδοῦναι μὲν τοὺς εἰς αὐτὸν ὁμονοήσαντας² οὐχ
ὑπομένοι, πολεμήσειν δ' ἄκων πρὸς οὓς ἥκιστα
210 βούλοιτο. δεῖν μέντοι προαποδειχθῆναι τῷ πολέμῳ χωρίον ἔξω τῆς πόλεως· οὐ γὰρ ὅσιον διὰ
τὴν αὐτῶν κακοβουλίαν ὁμοφύλῳ φόνῳ μιαίνεσθαι
τὰ τεμένη τῆς πατρίδος. ὁ μὲν οὖν ἀκούσας
ταῦτα τοῖς βουλευταῖς ἀπήγγειλεν.

211   (4) Μεταξὺ δὲ τῶν μετὰ τῆς συγκλήτου στρατιωτῶν τις σπασάμενος τὸ ξίφος " ἄνδρες,"
ἐβόησεν, " συστρατιῶται, τί παθόντες ἀδελφο-
κτονεῖν βουλόμεθα καὶ κατὰ τῶν μετὰ Κλαυδίου
συγγενῶν ὁρμᾶν, ἔχοντες μὲν αὐτοκράτορα μηδὲν
μεμφθῆναι δυνάμενον, τοσαῦτα δὲ τὰ δίκαια πρὸς
212 οὓς μετὰ τῶν ὅπλων χωρεῖν μέλλομεν; " ταῦτα

¹ διοικήσοι LVR.   ² ὁμόσαντας LVRC.

ᵃ There is no verb in the Greek : Reinach suspects the
text.
ᵇ Or, with the other reading, " had sworn fidelity to him."

such devoted supporters and unsafe (to abandon)[a] the fortune which had befallen him, for the mere fact of having received the imperial title entailed risks. Agrippa was further to state that he would govern the empire as a virtuous ruler and not as a tyrant ; he would be content with the honour of the title, and on all public affairs would consult the whole people ; indeed, were he not by nature inclined to moderation, the fate of Gaius would serve as a sufficient warning to him to act with discretion.

(3) To this message, delivered by Agrippa, the senate replied that, relying on the army and the wisdom of their own resolutions, they would not submit to voluntary servitude. When Claudius heard this answer of the senate, he again sent Agrippa to tell them that he would not consent to betray those who had unanimously elected him,[b] and must therefore reluctantly fight those who were the last persons in the world he wished to have as his enemies. It would, however, he said, be necessary to select for the conflict some spot outside the city, as it would be monstrous that their obstinate perversity should cause the sacred precincts of their country to be polluted with her children's blood. Agrippa noted and delivered this message to the senators.

(4) In the midst of these negotiations one of the soldiers who had adhered to the senate, drawing his sword, cried out : " Comrades in arms, what has possessed us that we should wish to murder our brothers and to rush upon our kinsmen in the ranks of Claudius, when we have an emperor with whom no fault can be found and are united by such close ties with those against whom we propose to take the

405

εἰπὼν διὰ μέσης ὥρμησεν τῆς βουλῆς πάντας
τοὺς συστρατιώτας ἐφελκόμενος. οἱ δ' εὐπατρίδαι
παραχρῆμα μὲν πρὸς τὴν ἀπόλειψιν περιδεῶς
ἔσχον, αὖθις δ' ὡς ἀποστροφὴ σωτήριος οὐ
κατεφαίνετο, τὴν τῶν στρατιωτῶν ὁδὸν ἠπείγοντο
213 πρὸς Κλαύδιον. ὑπήντων δ' αὐτοῖς πρὸ τοῦ
τείχους γυμνοῖς τοῖς ξίφεσιν οἱ σφοδρότερον
κολακεύοντες τὴν τύχην· κἂν συνέβη κινδυνεῦσαι
τοὺς προάγοντας πρὶν γνῶναι τὴν ὁρμὴν τῶν
στρατιωτῶν Κλαύδιον, εἰ μὴ προσδραμὼν Ἀγρίππας αὐτῷ τὸ κινδύνευμα τῆς πράξεως ἐδήλωσεν,
ὅτι τε εἰ μὴ κατάσχοι τὴν ὁρμὴν τῶν ἐπὶ τοὺς
εὐπατρίδας λελυσσηκότων, ἀπολέσας δι' οὓς τὸ
κρατεῖν ἐστι περίοπτον ἐρημίας ἔσοιτο βασιλεύς.

214   (5) Ταῦτ' ἀκούσας Κλαύδιος κατέσχεν τὰς
ὁρμὰς τοῦ στρατιωτικοῦ, προσδέχεταί τε τὴν
σύγκλητον εἰς τὸ στρατόπεδον καὶ φιλοφρονησάμενος ἐξῄει σὺν αὐτοῖς αὐτίκα θύσων τῷ θεῷ
215 τὰ περὶ. τῆς ἡγεμονίας χαριστήρια.   καὶ τὸν
Ἀγρίππαν εὐθέως ἐδωρεῖτο τῇ πατρῴᾳ βασιλείᾳ
πάσῃ, προστιθεὶς ἔξωθεν καὶ τὰς ὑπ' Αὐγούστου
δοθείσας Ἡρώδῃ Τραχωνῖτιν καὶ Αὐρανῖτιν,
χωρὶς δὲ τούτων ἑτέραν βασιλείαν τὴν Λυσανίου
216 καλουμένην. καὶ τῷ μὲν δήμῳ διατάγματι τὴν
δωρεὰν ἐδήλου, τοῖς ἄρχουσιν δὲ προσέταξεν
ἐγχαράξαντας δέλτοις χαλκαῖς τὴν δόσιν εἰς τὸ
217 Καπετώλιον ἀναθεῖναι.   δωρεῖται δ' αὐτοῦ καὶ

field ? " With those words he rushed through the midst of the senate, with all his fellow-soldiers at his heels. At this desertion the patricians were momentarily struck with dismay ; then, perceiving no other refuge to which to turn, they followed the soldiers and hastened to Claudius. Outside the walls they found themselves faced by the more hot-headed courtiers of fortune, with bared swords, and the lives of the leaders of the party would have been imperilled before Claudius even knew of the fury of the soldiers, had not Agrippa run to him and told him of the perilous situation and that unless he checked the impetuosity of the troops, who were mad against the patricians, he would lose the very men who lent lustre to his sovereignty and be left monarch of a wilderness.

(5) On receiving this message, Claudius repressed the fury of the soldiers, admitted the senators to his camp, and, after warmly greeting them, went off with them without delay to sacrifice thank-offerings to God on his accession to the empire. Upon Agrippa he forthwith conferred the whole of his grandfather's kingdom, annexing to it from over the border not only the districts of Trachonitis and Auranitis of which Augustus had made a present to Herod,[a] but a further principality known as the kingdom of Lysanias.[b] This donation he announced to the people by an edict, and ordered the magistrates to have it engraved on brazen tablets to be deposited in the Capitol. He, moreover, presented Herod,

Agrippa made king of Judaea

---

[a] *B.* i. 398.

[b] *i.e.* Abila (north-west of Damascus) and parts of Lebanon (*A.* xix. 275). Caligula had already given Agrippa " the tetrarchy of Lysanias " (*A.* xviii. 237); Claudius merely confirms this gift.

τὸν ἀδελφὸν Ἡρώδην, ὁ δ' αὐτὸς καὶ γαμβρὸς
ἦν Βερνίκῃ συνοικῶν, βασιλείᾳ τῇ Χαλκίδι.
218 (6) Ταχέως δ', ὡς ἂν ἐκ τοσαύτης ἀρχῆς,
πλοῦτος Ἀγρίππᾳ συνέρρει, καὶ τοῖς χρήμασιν
αὐτὸς οὐκ εἰς μακρὰν[1] κατεχρήσατο· τηλικοῦτον
γὰρ τοῖς Ἱεροσολύμοις περιβαλεῖν ἤρξατο τεῖχος,
ἡλίκον ἂν τελεσθὲν ἀνήνυτον Ῥωμαίοις ἐποίησεν
219 τὴν πολιορκίαν. ἀλλ' ἔφθη πρὶν ὑψῶσαι τὸ ἔργον
τελευτήσας ἐν Καισαρείᾳ, βεβασιλευκὼς μὲν ἔτη
τρία, πρότερον δὲ τῶν τετραρχιῶν τρισὶν ἑτέροις
220 ἔτεσιν ἀφηγησάμενος. καταλείπει δὲ τρεῖς μὲν
θυγατέρας ἐκ Κύπρου γεγεννημένας, Βερνίκην καὶ
Μαριάμμην καὶ Δρουσίλλαν, υἱὸν δὲ ἐκ τῆς αὐτῆς
Ἀγρίππαν. οὗ παντάπασιν ὄντος νηπίου πάλιν
τὰς βασιλείας Κλαύδιος ἐπαρχίαν ποιήσας ἐπίτροπον πέμπει Κούσπιον Φᾶδον, ἔπειτα Τιβέριον
Ἀλέξανδρον, οἳ μηδὲν παρακινοῦντες τῶν ἐπι-
221 χωρίων ἐθῶν ἐν εἰρήνῃ τὸ ἔθνος διεφύλαξαν. μετὰ
ταῦτα καὶ ὁ βασιλεύων τῆς Χαλκίδος Ἡρώδης
τελευτᾷ, καταλιπὼν ἐκ μὲν τῆς ἀδελφιδῆς Βερνίκης δύο παῖδας Βερνικιανόν τε καὶ Ὑρκανόν, ἐκ
δὲ τῆς προτέρας Μαριάμμης Ἀριστόβουλον. τε-

---

[1] μικρὰ Hudson from Lat. " in rebus exiguis."

[a] Bernice was Herod's second wife ; he had previously
married Mariamme, grand-daughter of Herod the Great
(A. xviii. 134).

[b] On the north of the city, to enclose the suburb Bezetha
or " new city " (B. v. 151 ff., A. xix. 326).

[c] The work was stopped, before Agrippa's death, by
Marsus, the governor of Syria, under orders from Claudius
(B. v. 152, A. xix. 326 f.)

[d] A more precise statement is given in A. xix. 351. He
reigned four years in all under Gaius (37–41) and three under
Claudius (41–44) ; for the first three years under Gaius he

who was at once the brother and, by his marriage with Bernice, the son-in-law of Agrippa,[a] with the kingdom of Chalcis.

(6) From so extensive a realm wealth soon flowed in to Agrippa, nor was he long in expending his riches. For he began to surround Jerusalem with a wall[b] on such a scale as, had it been completed, would have rendered ineffectual all the efforts of the Romans in the subsequent siege. But before the work had reached the projected height, he died[c] at Caesarea, after a reign of three years, to which must be added his previous three years' tenure of his tetrarchies.[d] He left issue by his wife Cypros,[e] three daughters—Bernice, Mariamme, and Drusilla —and one son, Agrippa. As the last was a minor,[f] Claudius again reduced the kingdoms to a province and sent as procurators, first Cuspius Fadus,[g] and then Tiberius Alexander,[h] who by abstaining from all interference with the customs of the country kept the nation at peace. Subsequently Herod, king of Chalcis, died; he left by his marriage with his niece Bernice, two sons, Bernicianus and Hyrcanus, and by his previous wife, Mariamme, a third, Aristobulus.

and his brother Herod, king of Chalcis.

Reign and death of Agrippa I

A.D. 44.

Judaea again put under procurators

Death of Herod king of Chalcis, A.D. 48.

held the tetrarchies of Philip and Lysanias, for the fourth he held that of Herod Antipas as well. His " reign " in the present passage is limited to his tenure of the whole kingdom of Herod the Great.

  [e] Daughter of Phasael, the nephew, and of Salampsio, the daughter of Herod the Great (*A.* xviii. 130 f.)

  [f] He was seventeen years old (*A.* xix. 354).

  [g] *c.* A.D. 44–45.

  [h] *c.* A.D. 46–48. Of a distinguished Jewish family of Alexandria, son of the Alabarch Alexander and nephew of Philo; renounced Judaism to take service under the Romans, as procurator of Judaea, as prefect of Egypt (ii. 309), and as chief of the general staff of Titus at the siege of Jerusalem (vi. 237).

θνήκει δ' αὐτῷ καὶ ἕτερος ἀδελφὸς Ἀριστόβουλος
222 ἰδιώτης καταλιπὼν Ἰωτάπην θυγατέρα. οὗτοι
μὲν οὖν ἦσαν, ὡς προεῖπον, Ἀριστοβούλου τοῦ
Ἡρώδου παῖδες, Ἀριστόβουλος δὲ καὶ Ἀλέξανδρος ἐκ Μαριάμμης Ἡρώδῃ γεγόνεισαν υἱεῖς,
οὓς ὁ πατὴρ ἀνεῖλεν· ἡ δὲ Ἀλεξάνδρου γενεὰ τῆς
μεγάλης Ἀρμενίας ἐβασίλευσεν.

223 (xii. 1) Μετὰ δὲ τὴν Ἡρώδου τελευτήν, ὃς
ἦρχε τῆς Χαλκίδος, καθίστησιν Κλαύδιος εἰς
τὴν βασιλείαν τοῦ θείου τὸν Ἀγρίππαν υἱὸν
Ἀγρίππα· τῆς δ' ἄλλης ἐπαρχίας διαδέχεται τὴν
ἐπιτροπὴν ἀπὸ Ἀλεξάνδρου Κουμανός, ἐφ' οὗ
θόρυβοί τε ἤρξαντο καὶ φθορὰ πάλιν Ἰουδαίων
224 ἐγένετο. συνεληλυθότος γὰρ τοῦ πλήθους ἐπὶ
τὴν ἑορτὴν τῶν ἀζύμων εἰς Ἱεροσόλυμα καὶ τῆς
Ῥωμαϊκῆς σπείρας ὑπὲρ τὴν τοῦ ἱεροῦ στοὰν
ἐφεστώσης, ἔνοπλοι δ' ἀεὶ τὰς ἑορτὰς παραφυλάτ-
τουσιν, ὡς μή τι νεωτερίζοι τὸ πλῆθος ἠθροι-
σμένον, εἷς τις τῶν στρατιωτῶν ἀνασυράμενος τὴν
ἐσθῆτα καὶ κατακύψας ἀσχημόνως προσαπέστρε-
225 ψεν τοῖς Ἰουδαίοις τὴν ἕδραν καὶ τῷ σχήματι
φωνὴν ὁμοίαν ἐπεφθέγγατο. πρὸς τοῦτο ἅπαν
μὲν τὸ πλῆθος ἠγανάκτησεν, καὶ κατεβόων τοῦ
Κουμανοῦ κολάζειν τὸν στρατιώτην, οἱ δὲ ἧττον
νήφοντες τῶν νέων καὶ τὸ φύσει στασιῶδες ἐκ
τοῦ ἔθνους ἐχώρουν ἐπὶ μάχην, λίθους τε ἁρπά-
226 σαντες ἐπὶ τοὺς στρατιώτας ἔβαλλον. καὶ Κου-

---

[a] i.e. of Agrippa.

[b] Called after her mother, a princess of Emesa (A. xviii. 135).

[c] Agrippa, Herod of Chalcis, Aristobulus.

[d] Alexander II and Tigranes. Tigranes was made king of Armenia by Augustus, but was soon deposed; ar ther

Another brother,[a] Aristobulus, died in private station, leaving a daughter Jotape.[b] These three,[c] as I have previously stated, were the children of Aristobulus, son of Herod ; Aristobulus and Alexander were the issue of Herod's marriage with Mariamme and were put to death by their father. The posterity of Alexander became kings of Greater Armenia.[d]

(xii. 1) After the death of Herod, sovereign of Chalcis, Claudius presented his kingdom to his nephew Agrippa, son of Agrippa. As procurator of the rest of the province (Tiberius) Alexander was succeeded by Cumanus[e] ; under his administration disturbances broke out, resulting in another[f] large loss of Jewish lives. The usual crowd had assembled at Jerusalem for the feast of unleavened bread, and the Roman cohort had taken up its position on the roof of the portico of the temple ; for a body of men in arms invariably mounts guard[g] at the feasts, to prevent disorders arising from such a concourse of people. Thereupon one of the soldiers, raising his robe, stooped in an indecent attitude, so as to turn his backside to the Jews, and made a noise in keeping with his posture.[h] Enraged at this insult, the whole multitude with loud cries called upon Cumanus to punish the soldier ; some of the more hot-headed young men and seditious persons in the crowd started a fight, and, picking up stones, hurled them at the

Marginal notes:
Agrippa II king of Chalcis.

Cumanus, procurator, A.D. 48–52.

Sedition at Jerusalem at Passover caused by lewdness of a Roman soldier.

Tigranes, son of Alexander II, was given the same kingdom by Nero (A. xviii. 139 f., cf. Tac. Ann. ii. 3).

[e] Ventidius Cumanus (Tac. Ann. xii. 54).

[f] Cf. B. ii. 51.

[g] We cannot infer from the present tense, as Reinach does, the use of a source anterior to A.D. 70 ; cf. the similar use of this tense in Ap. ii. 193 (note).

[h] Reinach appositely quotes Horace, Sat. i. 9. 69 "hodie tricesima sabbata : vin tu | curtis Iudaeis oppedere ? "

411

μανὸς δείσας, μὴ τοῦ λαοῦ παντὸς ἐπ᾽ αὐτὸν
ὁρμὴ γένοιτο, πλείους ὁπλίτας μεταπέμπεται.
τῶν δὲ ταῖς στοαῖς ἐπιχεομένων φόβος ἐμπίπτει
τοῖς Ἰουδαίοις ἀκατάσχετος, καὶ τραπέντες ἐκ
227 τοῦ ἱεροῦ διέφευγον εἰς τὴν πόλιν. τοσαύτη δὲ
περὶ τὰς ἐξόδους βία συνωθουμένων ἐγένετο,
ὥστε πατηθέντας ὑπ᾽ ἀλλήλων καὶ συντριβέντας
ὑπὲρ τρισμυρίους[1] ἀποθανεῖν, γενέσθαι δὲ τὴν
ἑορτὴν πένθος μὲν ὅλῳ τῷ ἔθνει, θρῆνον δὲ καθ᾽
ἑκάστην οἰκίαν.
228 (2) Μετελάμβανεν δὲ ταύτην τὴν συμφορὰν
[ἄλλος][2] ληστρικὸς θόρυβος. κατὰ γὰρ τὴν Βαι-
θωρὼ δημοσίαν ἄνοδον[3] Στεφάνου τινὸς δούλου
Καίσαρος ἀποσκευὴν κομιζομένην διήρπασαν λη-
229 σταὶ προσπεσόντες. Κουμανὸς δὲ περιπέμψας τοὺς
ἐκ τῶν πλησίον κωμῶν δεσμώτας ἐκέλευσεν
ἀνάγεσθαι πρὸς αὐτόν, ἐπικαλῶν ὅτι μὴ διώξαντες
τοὺς λῃστὰς συλλάβοιεν. ἔνθα τῶν στρατιωτῶν
τις εὑρὼν ἔν τινι κώμῃ τὸν ἱερὸν νόμον διέρρηξέν
230 τε τὸ βιβλίον καὶ εἰς πῦρ κατέβαλεν. Ἰουδαῖοι
δὲ ὡς ὅλης αὐτοῖς τῆς χώρας καταφλεγείσης
συνεχύθησαν, καὶ καθάπερ ὀργάνῳ τινὶ τῇ δεισι-
δαιμονίᾳ συνελκόμενοι πρὸς ἓν κήρυγμα πάντες
εἰς Καισάρειαν ἐπὶ Κουμανὸν συνέδραμον, ἱκετεύοντες τὸν οὕτως εἰς τὸν θεὸν καὶ τὸν νόμον αὐτῶν
231 ἐξυβρίσαντα μὴ περιδεῖν ἀτιμώρητον. ὁ δέ,
οὐ γὰρ ἠρέμει τὸ πλῆθος, εἰ μὴ τύχοι παρα-

---

[1] PAM Lat. (Eus.): τοὺς μυρίους the rest: δύο μυριάδες A. ‖.
[2] om. M Lat.   [3] PA Lat.: ὁδὸν the rest.

---

[a] 20,000 according to A. xx. 112.
[b] The two Bethhorons (Upper and Lower), some ten and
twelve miles respectively north-west of Jerusalem, on the
412

troops. Cumanus, fearing a general attack upon himself, sent for reinforcements. These troops pouring into the porticoes, the Jews were seized with irresistible panic and turned to fly from the temple and make their escape into the town. But such violence was used as they pressed round the exits that they were trodden under foot and crushed to death by one another ; upwards of thirty thousand [a] perished, and the feast was turned into mourning for the whole nation and for every household into lamentation.

(2) This calamity was followed by other disorders, originating with brigands. On the public road leading up to Bethhoron [b] some brigands attacked one Stephen, a slave of Caesar, and robbed him of his baggage. Cumanus, thereupon, sent troops round the neighbouring villages, with orders to bring up the inhabitants [c] to him in chains, reprimanding them for not having pursued and arrested the robbers. On this occasion a soldier, finding in one village a copy of the sacred law, tore the book in pieces and flung it into the fire. [d] At that the Jews were roused as though it were their whole country which had been consumed in the flames; and, their religion acting like some instrument [e] to draw them together, all on the first announcement of the news hurried in a body to Cumanus at Caesarea, and implored him not to leave unpunished the author of such an outrage on God and on their law. The procurator, seeing that the multitude would not be pacified unless they obtained

The affair of the profanation of Scripture.

main road to Joppa, famous in history ; the defile was the scene of the defeat of Cestius described below (*B*. ii. 546 ff.).

[c] *A*. xx. 114, " the notables."

[d] The burning of the book is not mentioned in *A*.

[e] Or, as we should say, a magnet.

413

μυθίας, ἠξίου τε προάγειν τὸν στρατιώτην καὶ
διὰ μέσων τῶν αἰτιωμένων ἀπαχθῆναι τὴν ἐπὶ
θανάτῳ κελεύει. καὶ Ἰουδαῖοι μὲν ἀνεχώρουν.

232   (3) Αὖθις δὲ Γαλιλαίων καὶ Σαμαρέων γίνεται
συμβολή. κατὰ γὰρ Γῆμαν καλουμένην κώμην,
ἥτις ἐν τῷ μεγάλῳ πεδίῳ κεῖται τῆς Σαμαρείτιδος,
πολλῶν ἀναβαινόντων Ἰουδαίων ἐπὶ τὴν ἑορτὴν
233 ἀναιρεῖταί τις Γαλιλαῖος.¹ πρὸς τοῦτο πλεῖστοι
μὲν ἐκ τῆς Γαλιλαίας συνέδραμον ὡς πολεμήσοντες
τοῖς Σαμαρεῦσιν, οἱ γνώριμοι δ' αὐτῶν ἐλθόντες
πρὸς Κουμανὸν ἠντιβόλουν, πρὶν ἀνηκέστου πάθους
εἰς τὴν Γαλιλαίαν διαβάντα τιμωρήσασθαι τοὺς
αἰτίους τοῦ φόνου· μόνως γὰρ ἂν οὕτως διαλυθῆναι
πρὸ πολέμου τὸ πλῆθος. Κουμανὸς μὲν οὖν ἐν
δευτέρῳ τὰς ἐκείνων ἱκεσίας τῶν ἐν χερσὶ² πραγμάτων θέμενος ἀπράκτους ἀπέπεμψεν τοὺς ἱκέτας.

234   (4) Ἀγγελθὲν δὲ εἰς Ἱεροσόλυμα τὸ πάθος τοῦ
πεφονευμένου τὰ πλήθη συνετάραξεν καὶ τῆς ἑορτῆς
ἀφέμενοι πρὸς τὴν Σαμάρειαν ἐξώρμων ἀστρατή-
γητοι καὶ μηδενὶ τῶν ἀρχόντων κατέχοντι πειθό-
235 μενοι. τοῦ ληστρικοῦ δ' αὐτῶν καὶ στασιώδους
Δειναίου τις υἱὸς Ἐλεάζαρος καὶ Ἀλέξανδρος
ἐξῆρχον, οἳ τοῖς ὁμόροις τῆς Ἀκραβατηνῆς τοπαρχίας προσπεσόντες αὐτούς τε ἀνήρουν μηδεμιᾶς
ἡλικίας φειδὼ ποιούμενοι καὶ τὰς κώμας ἐνεπίμπρασαν.

¹ For πολλῶν . . . ἀναιρ. τις Γαλιλαῖος PAM have πολλοὶ
τῶν . . . ἀναιροῦνται (accommodation to A. xx. 118?).
² χειρὶ PAM.

ᵃ Tacitus, Ann. xii. 54, gives a different account of the
events recorded in (3)-(7) (Reinach). According to him
Cumanus was governor of Galilee and Felix of Samaria.
  ᵇ Ginae (A. xx. 118), Ginaea (B. iii. 48), where it is named

satisfaction, thought fit to call out the soldier and ordered him to be led to execution through the ranks of his accusers. On this the Jews withdrew.

(3) Next came a conflict between the Galilaeans and the Samaritans.[a] At a village called Gema,[b] situate in the great plain of Samaria, a Galilaean, one of a large company of Jews on their way up to the festival, was murdered.[c] Thereupon, a considerable crowd assembled in haste from Galilee with the intention of making war on the Samaritans; meanwhile, the notables of the country went off to Cumanus, and entreated him, ere any irreparable mischief was done, to repair to Galilee and punish the perpetrators of the murder, as that was the only means of dispersing the crowd before they came to blows. Cumanus, however, treating their request as less important than other affairs on his hands,[d] dismissed the petitioners without any satisfaction.

(4) When the news of the murder reached Jerusalem, the masses were profoundly stirred, and, abandoning the festival, they dashed off to Samaria, without generals and without listening to any of the magistrates who sought to hold them back. The brigands and rioters among the party had as their leaders Eleazar, son of Deinaeus, and Alexander,[e] who, falling upon the borderers of the toparchy of Acrabatene,[f] massacred the inhabitants without distinction of age and burnt the villages.

Battle between Jews and Samaritans arising out of murder of a Galilaean.

as the northern frontier of Samaria, En-gannim of the Old Testament (Jos. xix. 21), mod. *Jenin*; at the head of the Great Plain of Esdraelon. With the incident *cf.* Luke ix. 52 f.

   [c] According to *A*. xx. 118 several pilgrims were murdered.
   [d] *A*. says " bribed by the Samaritans."
   [e] Alexander is not mentioned in *A*.
   [f] South-east of Shechem.

415

236 (5) Κουμανὸς δὲ ἀναλαβὼν ἀπὸ τῆς Καισαρείας
μίαν ἴλην ἱππέων καλουμένην Σεβαστηνῶν ἐξε-
βοήθει τοῖς πορθουμένοις, καὶ τῶν περὶ τὸν Ἐλεάζαρον πολλοὺς μὲν συνέλαβεν, πλείστους δ' ἀπ-
237 έκτεινεν. πρὸς δὲ τὸ λοιπὸν πλῆθος τῶν πολεμεῖν
τοῖς Σαμαρεῦσιν ὡρμημένων οἱ ἄρχοντες τῶν
Ἱεροσολύμων ἐκδραμόντες σάκκους ἀμπεχόμενοι
καὶ τέφραν τῶν κεφαλῶν καταχέοντες ἱκέτευον
ἀναχωρεῖν, καὶ μὴ διὰ τὴν εἰς Σαμαρεῖς ἄμυναν
ἐπὶ Ἱεροσόλυμα Ῥωμαίους παροξύνειν, ἐλεῆσαί τε
τὴν πατρίδα καὶ τὸν ναόν, τέκνα τε καὶ γυναῖκας
ἰδίας, ἃ πάντα κινδυνεύειν δι' ἑνὸς ἐκδικίαν Γαλι-
238 λαίου παραπολέσθαι. τούτοις πεισθέντες Ἰουδαῖοι
διελύθησαν. ἐτράποντο δὲ πολλοὶ πρὸς λῃστείαν
διὰ τὴν ἄδειαν, καὶ κατὰ πᾶσαν τὴν χώραν ἁρπαγαί
239 τε ἦσαν καὶ τῶν θρασυτέρων ἐπαναστάσεις. καὶ
τῶν Σαμαρέων οἱ δυνατοὶ πρὸς Οὐμμίδιον Κουα-
δρᾶτον, ὃς ἦν ἡγεμὼν τῆς Συρίας, εἰς Τύρον παραγενόμενοι δίκην τινὰ παρὰ τῶν πορθησάντων τὴν
240 χώραν ἠξίουν λαβεῖν. παρόντες δὲ καὶ οἱ γνώριμοι τῶν Ἰουδαίων καὶ ὁ ἀρχιερεὺς Ἰωνάθης
υἱὸς Ἀνάνου κατάρξαι μὲν ἔλεγον τῆς ταραχῆς
Σαμαρέας διὰ τὸν φόνον, αἴτιον δὲ τῶν ἀποβεβη-
κότων Κουμανὸν γεγονέναι, μὴ θελήσαντα τοὺς
αὐθέντας τοῦ σφαγέντος ἐπεξελθεῖν.
241 (6) Κουαδρᾶτος δὲ τότε μὲν ἑκατέρους ὑπερ-
τίθεται φήσας, ἐπειδὰν εἰς τοὺς τόπους παραγένηται, διερευνήσειν ἕκαστα, αὖθις δὲ παρελθὼν

---

^a Lat. *ala.*
^b See ii. 52 (note); *A.* adds " and four companies (τάγ-
ματα, ? cohorts) of infantry."
^c Later the first victim of the *sicarii*, § 256.

(5) Cumanus, taking with him from Caesarea a troop[a] of cavalry known as " Sebastenians,"[b] now set off to the assistance of the victims of these ravages ; he made prisoners of many of Eleazar's companions and killed a yet larger number. As for the rest of the party who had rushed to war with the Samaritans, the magistrates of Jerusalem hastened after them, clad in sackcloth and with ashes strewn upon their heads, and implored them to return home and not, by their desire for reprisals on the Samaritans, to bring down the wrath of the Romans on Jerusalem, but to take pity on their country and sanctuary, on their own wives and children ; all these were threatened with destruction merely for the object of avenging the blood of a single Galilaean. Yielding to these remonstrances the Jews dispersed. Many of them, however, emboldened by impunity, had recourse to robbery, and raids and insurrections, fostered by the more reckless, broke out all over the country. The leading Samaritans, accordingly, went off to Tyre to see Ummidius Quadratus, the governor of Syria, and urged him to punish the authors of these depredations. The Jewish notables, including the high-priest Jonathan,[c] son of Ananus, also presented themselves, and maintained that it was the Samaritans, by the murder in question, who had originated the disturbance, but that the responsibility for all that ensued lay with Cumanus for refusing to take proceedings against the assassins.

(6) Quadratus, at the moment, deferred giving a reply to either party, telling them that when he visited the district he would investigate the particulars ; subsequently he proceeded to Caesarea,[d]

Interven-
tion of
Quadratus,
governor
of Syria.

---

[d] " To Samaria " (*A.* xx. 129).

εἰς Καισάρειαν τοὺς ὑπὸ Κουμανοῦ ζωγρηθέντας
242 ἀνεσταύρωσεν πάντας. ἐκεῖθεν εἰς Λύδδα παραγενόμενος πάλιν διήκουσεν τῶν Σαμαρέων, καὶ
μεταπεμψάμενος ὀκτωκαίδεκα τῶν Ἰουδαίων, οὓς
ἐπέπυστο μετεσχηκέναι τῆς μάχης, πελέκει δι-
243 εχειρίσατο. δύο δ᾽ ἑτέρους τῶν δυνατωτάτων καὶ
τοὺς ἀρχιερεῖς Ἰωνάθην καὶ Ἀνανίαν, τόν τε
τούτου παῖδα Ἄνανον καί τινας ἄλλους Ἰουδαίων
γνωρίμους ἀνέπεμψεν ἐπὶ Καίσαρα, ὁμοίως δὲ
244 καὶ Σαμαρέων τοὺς ἐπιφανεστάτους. παρήγγειλεν
δὲ καὶ Κουμανῷ καὶ Κέλερι τῷ χιλιάρχῳ πλεῖν
ἐπὶ Ῥώμης δώσοντας Κλαυδίῳ λόγον ὑπὲρ τῶν
γεγενημένων. ταῦτα διαπραξάμενος ἀπὸ Λύδδων
ἀνέβαινεν εἰς Ἱεροσόλυμα, καὶ καταλαβὼν τὸ
πλῆθος ἄγον τὴν τῶν ἀζύμων ἑορτὴν ἀθορύβως
εἰς Ἀντιόχειαν ἐπανῄει.
245 (7) Κατὰ δὲ τὴν Ῥώμην Καῖσαρ ἀκούσας
Κουμανοῦ καὶ Σαμαρέων, παρῆν δὲ καὶ Ἀγρίππας
ἐκθύμως ὑπεραγωνιζόμενος Ἰουδαίων, ἐπειδὴ καὶ
Κουμανῷ πολλοὶ τῶν δυνατῶν παρίσταντο, Σαμαρέων μὲν καταγνοὺς τρεῖς ἀνελεῖν προσέταξεν τοὺς
246 δυνατωτάτους, Κουμανὸν δὲ ἐφυγάδευσεν. Κέλερα
δὲ δεσμώτην ἀναπέμψας εἰς Ἱεροσόλυμα παρα-
δοθῆναι Ἰουδαίοις πρὸς αἰκίαν ἐκέλευσεν καὶ
περισυρέντα τὴν πόλιν οὕτω τὴν κεφαλὴν ἀπο-
κοπῆναι.
247 (8) Μετὰ ταῦτα Ἰουδαίας μὲν ἐπίτροπον Φήλικα
τὸν Πάλλαντος ἀδελφὸν ἐκπέμπει τῆς τε Σαμαρείας καὶ Γαλιλαίας καὶ Περαίας, ἐκ δὲ τῆς

where he crucified all the prisoners taken by Cumanus. From there he went on to Lydda, where he gave another hearing to the Samaritans. He then sent for eighteen [a] Jews, who, as he was informed, had taken part in the combat, and had them beheaded. He sent up to Caesar, along with two other persons of the highest eminence, the high-priests Jonathan and Ananias, Ananus,[b] the son of the latter, and some other Jewish notables, together with the most distinguished of the Samaritans. He also directed Cumanus and Celer, the tribune, to take ship for Rome and to render an account of their conduct to Claudius. Having taken these measures, he left Lydda and went up to Jerusalem ; and, finding the people peaceably celebrating the feast of unleavened bread,[c] he returned to Antioch.

(7) At Rome Caesar gave his hearing to Cumanus and the Samaritans in the presence of Agrippa, who made a spirited defence on behalf of the Jews, while Cumanus on his side was supported by many eminent persons. The emperor condemned the Samaritans, ordered three of their most prominent men to be executed, and banished Cumanus. Celer he sent back in chains to Jerusalem, with orders that he was to be delivered over to Jewish outrage : after being dragged round the city, he was then to be beheaded.

Claudius gives judgement for Jews and banishes Cumanus.

(8) After this Claudius sent out Felix, the brother of Pallas, as procurator of Judaea, Samaria, Galilee,

Felix, procurator A.D. 52-60.

---

[a] A certain Doetus with four others (*A.* xx. 130).

[b] " Ananus the captain " (? of the temple) in *A.* xx. 131, where Jonathan's name is omitted.

[c] " A national feast "(unspecified), *A.* xx. 133. According to *B.* the disturbances described in this chapter must have extended over a whole year from one Passover (§ 224) to the next.

Χαλκίδος Ἀγρίππαν εἰς μείζονα βασιλείαν μετα-
τίθησιν, δοὺς αὐτῷ τήν τε Φιλίππου γενομένην
ἐπαρχίαν, αὕτη δ' ἦν Τραχωνῖτις καὶ Βατανέα καὶ
Γαυλανῖτις, προσέθηκεν δὲ τήν τε Λυσανίου βασιλείαν καὶ τὴν Οὐάρου γενομένην τετραρχίαν.

248 αὐτὸς δὲ διοικήσας τὴν ἡγεμονίαν ἔτεσι τρισ-
καίδεκα, πρὸς δὲ μησὶν ὀκτὼ καὶ εἴκοσιν ἡμέραις,
τελευτᾷ καταλιπὼν Νέρωνα τῆς ἀρχῆς διάδοχον,
249 ὃν ταῖς Ἀγριππίνης τῆς γυναικὸς ἀπάταις ἐπὶ
κληρονομίᾳ τῆς ἀρχῆς εἰσεποιήσατο, καίπερ υἱὸν
ἔχων γνήσιον Βρεττανικὸν ἐκ Μεσσαλίνης τῆς
προτέρας γυναικὸς καὶ Ὀκταουίαν θυγατέρα τὴν
ὑπ' αὐτοῦ ζευχθεῖσαν Νέρωνι· γεγόνει δ' αὐτῷ
καὶ ἐκ Πετίνης Ἀντωνία.

250 (xiii. 1) Ὅσα μὲν οὖν Νέρων δι' ὑπερβολὴν
εὐδαιμονίας τε καὶ πλούτου παραφρονήσας ἐξ-
ύβρισεν εἰς τὴν τύχην, ἢ τίνα τρόπον τόν τε ἀδελφὸν καὶ τὴν γυναῖκα καὶ τὴν μητέρα διεξῆλθεν,
ἀφ' ὧν ἐπὶ τοὺς εὐγενεστάτους μετήνεγκεν τὴν
251 ὠμότητα, καὶ ὡς τελευταῖον ὑπὸ φρενοβλαβείας
ἐξώκειλεν εἰς σκηνὴν καὶ θέατρον, ἐπειδὴ δι'
ὄχλου πᾶσίν ἐστιν, παραλείψω, τρέψομαι δὲ ἐπὶ
τὰ Ἰουδαίοις κατ' αὐτὸν γενόμενα.

252 (2) Τὴν μὲν οὖν μικρὰν Ἀρμενίαν δίδωσιν
βασιλεύειν Ἀριστοβούλῳ τῷ Ἡρώδου, τῇ δ'
Ἀγρίππᾳ βασιλείᾳ τέσσαρας πόλεις προστίθησιν
σὺν ταῖς τοπαρχίαις, Ἄβελα μὲν καὶ Ἰουλιάδα

ᵃ Antonius Felix (Tac. *Hist.* v. 9 ; the reading Κλαύδιον
Φήλικα in *A.* xx. 137 is doubtful) was probably, like his
influential brother Pallas, a freedman of Antonia, mother of
Claudius. According to Tacitus (here probably untrustworthy) he had already been procurator of Samaria (§ 232
note).

and Peraea.^{a} Agrippa he transferred from Chalcis Agrippa II king of Trachonitis etc., A.D. 53.
to a larger kingdom, assigning to him Philip's former
province, namely Trachonitis, Batanaea, and Gaulanitis ; to this he added the kingdom of Lysanias
and the old tetrarchy of Varus.^{b} After governing
the empire for thirteen years eight months and
twenty days,^{c} Claudius died, leaving Nero as his Death of Claudius, A.D. 54.
successor. Yielding to the artifices of his wife
Agrippina, he had adopted this prince as heir to the
throne, although he had by his former wife, Messalina,
a legitimate son, Britannicus, besides a daughter,
Octavia, whom he had given in marriage to Nero ;
he had also, by Petina, another daughter, Antonia.

(xiii. 1) All the outrageous acts in defiance of Accession and character of NERO.
fortune of which Nero was guilty, when excess of
prosperity and riches drove him mad ; how he
successively made away with his brother, wife, and
mother ; how his cruelty then found fresh victims in
the highest of the nobility ; how his infatuation
finally landed him on the stage and the boards of the
theatre—all these subjects, being so hackneyed, I
propose to pass over and to turn to the events of
Jewish history under his reign.

(2) He presented the kingdom of the lesser Agrippa's kingdom enlarged.
Armenia to Aristobulus, son of Herod ^{d} ; he annexed
to Agrippa's kingdom four cities with their districts,^{e}

^{b} Varus is identified by Schürer with the minister of
Agrippa II, mentioned in *Vita* 48 ff., where he is described
as a descendant of Soemus who had been a tetrarch in the
Lebanon district (*ib.* 52) ; it is assumed that he inherited
for a time a part of this tetrarchy.

^{c} The calculation, repeated in *A.* xx. 148, is here correct :
Claudius reigned from 24th January 41 to 13th October 54.

^{d} Of Chalcis, grandson of Herod the Great.

^{e} Greek " toparchies."

κατὰ τὴν Περαίαν, Ταριχαίας δὲ καὶ Τιβεριάδα
τῆς Γαλιλαίας, εἰς δὲ τὴν λοιπὴν Ἰουδαίαν Φήλικα
253 κατέστησεν ἐπίτροπον. οὗτος τόν τε ἀρχιληστὴν
Ἐλεάζαρον ἔτεσιν εἴκοσι τὴν χώραν λησάμενον
καὶ πολλοὺς τῶν σὺν αὐτῷ ζωγρήσας ἀνέπεμψεν
εἰς Ῥώμην· τῶν δ' ἀνασταυρωθέντων ὑπ' αὐτοῦ
ληστῶν καὶ τῶν ἐπὶ κοινωνίᾳ φωραθέντων δημο-
τῶν, οὓς ἐκόλασεν, ἄπειρόν τι πλῆθος ἦν.

254 (3) Καθαρθείσης δὲ τῆς χώρας ἕτερον εἶδος
ληστῶν ἐν Ἱεροσολύμοις ἐπεφύετο, οἱ καλούμενοι
σικάριοι, μεθ' ἡμέραν καὶ ἐν μέσῃ τῇ πόλει
255 φονεύοντες ἀνθρώπους. μάλιστα [δὲ][1] ἐν ταῖς
ἑορταῖς μισγόμενοι τῷ πλήθει καὶ ταῖς ἐσθῆσιν
ὑποκρύπτοντες μικρὰ ξιφίδια, τούτοις ἔνυττον
τοὺς διαφόρους, ἔπειτα πεσόντων μέρος ἐγίνοντο
τῶν ἐπαγανακτούντων οἱ πεφονευκότες, διὸ καὶ
παντάπασιν ὑπὸ ἀξιοπιστίας ἦσαν ἀνεύρετοι.
256 πρῶτος μὲν οὖν ὑπ' αὐτῶν Ἰωνάθης ὁ ἀρχιερεὺς
ἀποσφάττεται, μετὰ δ' αὐτὸν καθ' ἡμέραν ἀν-
ῃροῦντο πολλοί· καὶ τῶν συμφορῶν ὁ φόβος ἦν
χαλεπώτερος, ἑκάστου καθάπερ ἐν πολέμῳ καθ'
257 ὥραν τὸν θάνατον προσδεχομένου. προεσκοποῦντο
δὲ πόρρωθεν τοὺς διαφόρους, καὶ οὐδὲ τοῖς φίλοις
προσιοῦσιν[2] πίστις ἦν, ἐν μέσαις δὲ ταῖς ὑπονοίαις
καὶ ταῖς φυλακαῖς ἀνῃροῦντο· τοσοῦτον τῶν ἐπι-
βουλευόντων τὸ τάχος ἦν καὶ τοῦ λαθεῖν ἡ τέχνη.
258 (4) Συνέστη δὲ πρὸς τούτοις στῖφος ἕτερον
πονηρῶν, χειρὶ μὲν καθαρώτερον, ταῖς γνώμαις

---

[1] om. PALV : γὰρ Eus.   [2] + ἔτι LVRC.

[a] Abila is not mentioned in A. xx. 159 ; there were several
places of the name and the exact position of this one is doubtful.   For Julias = Livias see § 168 (note).

namely, Abila and Julias in Peraea,[a] and Tarichaeae and Tiberias in Galilee ; he appointed [b] Felix to be procurator of the rest of Judaea. Felix took prisoner Eleazar,[c] the brigand chief, who for twenty years had ravaged the country, with many of his associates, and sent them for trial to Rome. Of the brigands whom he crucified, and of the common people who were convicted of complicity with them and punished by him, the number was incalculable. Felix quells the brigands.

(3) But while the country was thus cleared of these pests, a new species of banditti was springing up in Jerusalem, the so-called *sicarii*,[d] who committed murders in broad daylight in the heart of the city. The festivals were their special seasons, when they would mingle with the crowd, carrying short daggers concealed under their clothing, with which they stabbed their enemies. Then, when they fell, the murderers joined in the cries of indignation and, through this plausible behaviour, were never discovered. The first to be assassinated by them was Jonathan the high-priest ; after his death there were numerous daily murders. The panic created was more alarming than the calamity itself ; every one, as on the battlefield, hourly expecting death. Men kept watch at a distance on their enemies and would not trust even their friends when they approached. Yet, even while their suspicions were aroused and they were on their guard, they fell ; so swift were the conspirators and so crafty in eluding detection. Rise of the *Sicarii*,

(4) Besides these there arose another body of villains, with purer hands but more impious intentions, and of false prophets.

---

[b] *i.e.* confirmed his previous appointment (§ 247).

[c] Son of Deinaeus, § 235.

[d] " Assassins," from Lat. *sica*, a curved dagger.

δὲ ἀσεβέστερον, ὅπερ οὐδὲν ἧττον τῶν σφαγέων
259 τὴν εὐδαιμονίαν τῆς πόλεως ἐλυμήνατο. πλάνοι
γὰρ ἄνθρωποι καὶ ἀπατεῶνες, [ὑπὸ]¹ προσχήματι
θειασμοῦ νεωτερισμοὺς καὶ μεταβολὰς πραγ-
ματευόμενοι, δαιμονᾶν τὸ πλῆθος ἔπειθον² καὶ
προῆγον εἰς τὴν ἐρημίαν, ὡς ἐκεῖ τοῦ θεοῦ δείξοντος
260 αὐτοῖς σημεῖα ἐλευθερίας. ἐπὶ τούτοις Φῆλιξ,
ἐδόκει γὰρ ἀποστάσεως εἶναι καταβολή, πέμψας
ἱππεῖς καὶ πεζοὺς ὁπλίτας πολὺ πλῆθος διέφθειρεν.
261 (5) Μείζονι δὲ [τούτου]³ πληγῇ Ἰουδαίους
ἐκάκωσεν ὁ Αἰγύπτιος ψευδοπροφήτης. παραγενόμενος γὰρ εἰς τὴν χώραν ἄνθρωπος γόης καὶ
προφήτου πίστιν ἐπιθεὶς ἑαυτῷ περὶ τρισμυρίους
262 μὲν ἀθροίζει τῶν ἠπατημένων, περιαγαγὼν δὲ
αὐτοὺς ἐκ τῆς ἐρημίας εἰς τὸ ἐλαιῶν καλούμενον
ὄρος, ἐκεῖθεν οἷός τε ἦν εἰς Ἱεροσόλυμα παρελθεῖν
βιάζεσθαι καὶ κρατήσας τῆς [τε]⁴ Ῥωμαϊκῆς
φρουρᾶς [καὶ]⁵ τοῦ δήμου τυραννεῖν, χρώμενος
263 τοῖς συνεισπεσοῦσιν δορυφόροις. φθάνει δ' αὐτοῦ
τὴν ὁρμὴν Φῆλιξ ὑπαντήσας⁶ μετὰ τῶν Ῥωμαϊκῶν
ὁπλιτῶν, καὶ πᾶς ὁ δῆμος συνεφήψατο τῆς ἀμύνης,
ὥστε συμβολῆς γενομένης τὸν μὲν Αἰγύπτιον
φυγεῖν μετ' ὀλίγων, διαφθαρῆναι δὲ καὶ ζωγρη-
θῆναι πλείστους τῶν σὺν αὐτῷ, τὸ δὲ λοιπὸν
πλῆθος σκεδασθὲν ἐπὶ τὴν ἑαυτῶν ἕκαστον διαλαθεῖν.

¹ om. VRC.　　　　² ἀνέπειθον VRC.
³ om. Lat.: τούτων Eus. : ταύτης VRC.
⁴ om. PAM.　　　　⁵ om. Lat.
⁶ PA Eus.: ὑπαντιάσας the rest.

ᵃ Cf. Matt. xxiv. 24 ff. " There shall arise . . . false

424

who no less than the assassins ruined the peace of the city. Deceivers and impostors, under the pretence of divine inspiration fostering revolutionary changes, they persuaded the multitude to act like madmen, and led them out into the desert under the belief that God would there give them tokens of deliverance.[a] Against them Felix, regarding this as but the preliminary to insurrection, sent a body of cavalry and heavy-armed infantry, and put a large number to the sword.

(5) A still worse blow was dealt at the Jews by the Egyptian false prophet. A charlatan, who had gained for himself the reputation of a prophet, this man appeared in the country, collected a following of about thirty thousand[b] dupes, and led them by a circuitous route from the desert to the mount called the mount of Olives. From there he proposed to force an entrance into Jerusalem and, after overpowering the Roman garrison, to set himself up as tyrant of the people, employing those who poured in with him as his bodyguard. His attack was anticipated by Felix, who went to meet him with the Roman heavy infantry, the whole population joining him in the defence. The outcome of the ensuing engagement was that the Egyptian escaped with a few of his followers; most of his force were killed or taken prisoners; the remainder dispersed and stealthily escaped to their several homes.

The Egyptian impostor.

prophets and shall show great signs . . . they shall say unto you, Behold he is in the wilderness." Theudas was an earlier impostor of this type, and met with a similar fate, *A.* xx. 97.

[b] 4000 according to Acts xxi. 38; S. Paul was mistaken for this impostor.

264 (6) Κατεσταλμένων δὲ καὶ τούτων ὥσπερ ἐν
νοσοῦντι σώματι πάλιν ἕτερον μέρος ἐφλέγμαινεν.
οἱ γὰρ γόητες καὶ λῃστρικοὶ συναχθέντες πολλοὺς
εἰς ἀπόστασιν ἐνῆγον καὶ πρὸς ἐλευθερίαν παρ-
εκρότουν, θάνατον ἐπιτιμῶντες τοῖς πειθαρχοῦσιν
τῇ Ῥωμαίων ἡγεμονίᾳ καὶ πρὸς βίαν ἀφαιρή-
σεσθαι λέγοντες τοὺς ἑκουσίως δουλεύειν προαιρου-
265 μένους. μεριζόμενοι δ' εἰς τὴν χώραν κατὰ λόχους
διήρπαζόν τε τὰς τῶν δυνατῶν οἰκίας καὶ αὐτοὺς
ἀνῄρουν καὶ τὰς κώμας ἐνεπίμπρασαν, ὥστε τῆς
ἀπονοίας αὐτῶν πᾶσαν τὴν Ἰουδαίαν ἀναπίμ-
πλασθαι. καὶ οὗτος μὲν ὁ πόλεμος καθ' ἡμέραν
ἀνερριπίζετο.

266 (7) Ἑτέρα δὲ ταραχὴ συνίσταται περὶ Καισάρειαν τῶν ἀναμεμιγμένων Ἰουδαίων πρὸς τοὺς ἐν
αὐτῇ Σύρους στασιασάντων. οἱ μὲν γὰρ ἠξίουν
σφετέραν εἶναι τὴν πόλιν Ἰουδαῖον γεγονέναι τὸν
κτίστην αὐτῆς λέγοντες· ἦν δὲ Ἡρώδης ὁ βασιλεύς·
οἱ δὲ ἕτεροι τὸν οἰκιστὴν μὲν προσωμολόγουν
Ἰουδαῖον, αὐτὴν μέντοι γε τὴν πόλιν Ἑλλήνων
ἔφασαν· οὐ γὰρ ἂν ἀνδριάντας καὶ ναοὺς ἐγκαθ-
267 ιδρῦσαι Ἰουδαίοις αὐτὴν ἀνατιθέντα. διὰ ταῦτα
διημφισβήτουν[1] ἑκάτεροι, προῄει δ' αὐτοῖς τὸ φιλό-
νεικον εἰς ὅπλα καὶ καθ' ἡμέραν οἱ θρασύτεροι
παρ' ἀμφοῖν προεπήδων ἐπὶ μάχην· οὔτε[2] γὰρ
Ἰουδαίων οἱ γεραιοὶ τοὺς ἰδίους στασιαστὰς κατ-
έχειν οἷοί τε ἦσαν καὶ τοῖς Ἕλλησιν αἶσχος ἐδόκει
268 Ἰουδαίων ἐλαττοῦσθαι. προεῖχον δ' οἱ μὲν πλούτῳ
καὶ σωμάτων ἀλκῇ, τὸ δὲ Ἑλληνικὸν τῇ παρὰ

---

[1] Destinon: δὲ ἠμφισβήτουν mss.   [2] οὐδὲ PAML.

[a] Where S. Paul then probably lay a prisoner.

(6) No sooner were these disorders reduced than the inflammation, as in a sick man's body, broke out again in another quarter. The impostors and brigands, banding together, incited numbers to revolt, exhorting them to assert their independence, and threatening to kill any who submitted to Roman domination and forcibly to suppress those who voluntarily accepted servitude. Distributing themselves in companies throughout the country, they looted the houses of the wealthy, murdered their owners, and set the villages on fire. The effects of their frenzy were thus felt throughout all Judaea, and every day saw this war being fanned into fiercer flame.

(7) Another disturbance occurred at Caesarea,[a] where the Jewish portion of the population rose against the Syrian inhabitants. They claimed that the city was theirs on the ground that its founder, King Herod, was a Jew. Their opponents admitted the Jewish origin of its second founder, but maintained that the city itself belonged to the Greeks, since Herod would never have erected the statues and temples which he placed there had he destined it for Jews.[b] Such were the points at issue between the two parties, and the quarrel eventually led to an appeal to arms. Every day the more venturesome in either camp would rush into combat ; for the older members of the Jewish community were incapable of restraining their turbulent partisans, and the Greeks considered it humiliating to give way to the Jews. The latter had the advantage of superior wealth and physical strength, the Greeks that of the

[b] In *A.* xx. 173 their argument is that the older city, Strato's Tower, had not a single Jewish inhabitant.

τῶν στρατιωτῶν ἀμύνῃ· τὸ γὰρ πλέον Ῥωμαίοις
τῆς ἐκεῖ δυνάμεως ἐκ Συρίας ἦν κατειλεγμένον
καὶ καθάπερ συγγενεῖς ἦσαν πρὸς τὰς βοηθείας
269 ἕτοιμοι. τοῖς γε μὴν ἐπάρχοις φροντὶς ἦν ἀναστέλλειν τὴν ταραχὴν καὶ τοὺς μαχιμωτέρους ἀεὶ
συλλαμβάνοντες ἐκόλαζον μάστιξι καὶ δεσμοῖς. οὐ
μὴν τὰ πάθη τῶν συλλαμβανομένων ἐνεποίει τοῖς
καταλειπομένοις ἀνακοπὴν ἢ δέος, ἀλλ' ἔτι μᾶλλον
270 παρωξύνοντο πρὸς τὴν στάσιν. νικῶντας δέ ποτε
τοὺς Ἰουδαίους προελθὼν¹ εἰς τὴν ἀγορὰν ὁ Φῆλιξ
μετ' ἀπειλῆς ἐκέλευσεν ἀναχωρεῖν. τῶν δὲ μὴ
πειθομένων ἐπιπέμψας τοὺς στρατιώτας ἀναιρεῖ
συχνούς, ὧν διαρπαγῆναι συνέβη καὶ τὰς οὐσίας.
μενούσης δὲ τῆς στάσεως ἐπιλέξας ἑκατέρωθεν
τοὺς γνωρίμους ἔπεμψεν πρέσβεις ἐπὶ Νέρωνα
διαλεξομένους περὶ τῶν δικαίων.

271 (xiv. 1) Διαδεξάμενος δὲ παρὰ τούτου τὴν
ἐπιτροπὴν ὁ Φῆστος τὸ μάλιστα λυμαινόμενον τὴν
χώραν ἐπεξῄει· τῶν γοῦν λῃστῶν συνέλαβέν τε
272 πλείστους καὶ διέφθειρεν οὐκ ὀλίγους. ἀλλ' οὐχ
ὁ μετὰ Φῆστον Ἀλβῖνος τὸν αὐτὸν τρόπον ἐξ-
ηγήσατο τῶν πραγμάτων, οὐκ ἔστιν δὲ ἥντινα κα-
273 κουργίας ἰδέαν παρέλειπεν. οὐ μόνον γοῦν ἐν τοῖς
πολιτικοῖς πράγμασιν ἔκλεπτεν καὶ διήρπαζεν τὰς
ἑκάστων οὐσίας, οὐδὲ τὸ πᾶν ἔθνος ἐβάρει ταῖς
εἰσφοραῖς, ἀλλὰ καὶ τοὺς ἐπὶ λῃστείᾳ δεδεμένους
ὑπὸ τῆς παρ' ἑκάστοις βουλῆς ἢ τῶν προτέρων
ἐπιτρόπων ἀπελύτρου τοῖς συγγενέσιν, καὶ μόνος

¹ PM: παρελθών (-εῖν C) the rest.

ᵃ Porcius Festus died in office (A. xx. 200). A more
favourable estimate of his successor (Lucceius) Albinus is
given in A. xx. than in the War. There he begins by putting

support of the military ; for the troops stationed here
were mainly levied by the Romans from Syria, and
were consequently always ready to lend aid to their
compatriots. The magistrates, indeed, were at pains
to repress these disorders, and constantly arrested
the more pugnacious offenders and punished them
with the scourge and imprisonment ; but the sufferings of those arrested, so far from checking or in-
timidating the remainder, only served as a stimulus
to sedition. On one occasion when the Jews had
been victorious, Felix came forward into the market-
place and ordered them in menacing tones to retire ;
on their refusing to obey, he set his troops upon them,
when many were killed, their property being subsequently plundered. The quarrel, nevertheless, continuing, Felix selected the notables of the two parties
and sent them to Nero as deputies to discuss before
him their respective rights.

(xiv 1) Festus, who succeeded Felix as procurator, The last
proceeded to attack the principal plague of the three procurators:
country : he captured large numbers of the brigands Festus,
and put not a few to death. A.D. 60–62.

The administration of Albinus,[a] who followed Albinus,
Festus, was of another order ; there was no form of A.D. 62–64.
villainy which he omitted to practise. Not only did
he, in his official capacity, steal and plunder private
property and burden the whole nation with extraordinary taxes, but he accepted ransoms from their
relatives on behalf of those who had been imprisoned
for robbery by the local councils or by former
procurators ; and the only persons left in gaol as

down the *sicarii*, though he ends, on hearing of his supersession, by opening the prisons and thus filling the country
with brigands.

ὁ μὴ δοὺς τοῖς δεσμωτηρίοις ὡς πονηρὸς ἐγκατ-
274 ελείπετο. τηνικαῦτα καὶ τῶν νεωτερίζειν βουλο-
μένων ἐν Ἱεροσολύμοις ἐθάρσησαν αἱ τόλμαι, καὶ
χρήμασιν μὲν οἱ δυνατοὶ τὸν Ἀλβῖνον προσελάμ-
βανον ὥστε τοῦ στασιάζειν αὐτοῖς παρέχειν ἄδειαν,
τοῦ δημοτικοῦ δὲ τὸ μὴ χαῖρον ἡσυχίᾳ πρὸς τοὺς
275 Ἀλβίνου κοινωνοὺς ἀπέκλινεν. ἕκαστος δὲ τῶν
πονηρῶν ἴδιον στῖφος ὑπεζωσμένος αὐτὸς μὲν
ὥσπερ ἀρχιληστὴς ἢ τύραννος προανεῖχεν ἐκ τοῦ
λόχου, τοῖς δορυφοροῦσι δὲ πρὸς ἁρπαγὰς τῶν
276 μετρίων κατεχρῆτο. συνέβαινεν δὲ τοὺς μὲν ἀφ-
ῃρημένους ὑπὲρ ὧν ἀγανακτεῖν ἐχρῆν σιωπᾶν,
τοὺς ἀπλῆγας δέ, δέει τοῦ μὴ τὰ αὐτὰ παθεῖν,
καὶ κολακεύειν τὸν ἄξιον κολάσεως. καθόλου δὲ
ἡ μὲν παρρησία πάντων περικέκοπτο, τυραννὶς δ'
ἦν διὰ πλειόνων, καὶ τὰ σπέρματα τῆς μελλούσης
ἁλώσεως ἔκτοτε τῇ πόλει κατεβάλλετο.
277 (2) Τοιοῦτον δ' ὄντα τὸν Ἀλβῖνον ἀπέδειξεν
ὁ μετ' αὐτὸν ἐλθὼν Γέσσιος Φλῶρος ἀγαθώτατον
κατὰ σύγκρισιν. ὁ μέν γε λάθρα τὰ πολλὰ καὶ
μεθ' ὑποστολῆς ἐκακούργησεν, Γέσσιος δὲ τὰς
εἰς τὸ ἔθνος παρανομίας ἐπόμπευσεν, καὶ ὥσπερ
ἐπὶ τιμωρίᾳ κατακρίτων πεμφθεὶς δήμιος οὔτε
278 ἁρπαγῆς τινα τρόπον οὔτε αἰκίας παρέλιπεν. ἦν
δὲ ἐν μὲν τοῖς ἐλεεινοῖς ὠμότατος, ἐν δὲ τοῖς
αἰσχροῖς ἀναιδέστατος· οὔτε δὲ πλείω τις ἀπιστίαν
τῆς ἀληθείας κατέχεεν οὔτε ἐν τῷ πανουργεῖν
δολιωτέρας ὁδοὺς ἐπενόησεν. ᾧ τὸ μὲν κατ'
ἄνδρα κερδαίνειν μικρὸν ἐδόκει, πόλεις δ' ὅλας
ἐξεδίδυσκε καὶ δήμους ἀθρόους ἐλυμαίνετο, καὶ

ᵃ Literally " unbelief "; " was more successful in
smothering the truth " (Traill).

malefactors were those who failed to pay the price. Now, too, the audacity of the revolutionary party in Jerusalem was stimulated; the influential men among their number secured from Albinus, by means of bribes, immunity for their seditious practices; while of the populace all who were dissatisfied with peace joined hands with the governor's accomplices. Each ruffian, with his own band of followers grouped around him, towered above his company like a brigand chief or tyrant, employing his bodyguard to plunder peaceable citizens. The result was that the victims of robbery kept their grievances, of which they had every reason to complain, to themselves, while those who escaped injury cringed to wretches deserving of punishment, through fear of suffering the same fate. In short, none could now speak his mind, with tyrants on every side; and from this date were sown in the city the seeds of its impending fall.

(2) Such was the character of Albinus, but his successor, Gessius Florus, made him appear by comparison a paragon of virtue. The crimes of Albinus were, for the most part, perpetrated in secret and with dissimulation; Gessius, on the contrary, ostentatiously paraded his outrages upon the nation, and, as though he had been sent as hangman of condemned criminals, abstained from no form of robbery or violence. Was there a call for compassion, he was the most cruel of men; for shame, none more shameless than he. No man ever poured greater contempt[a] on truth; none invented more crafty methods of crime. To make gain out of individuals seemed beneath him: he stripped whole cities, ruined entire populations, and almost went the

431

μόνον οὐκ ἐκήρυξεν ἀνὰ τὴν χώραν πᾶσιν ἐξεῖναι
λῃστεύειν, ἐφ᾽ ᾧ μέρος αὐτὸς λήψεται τῶν λαφύ-
279 ρων. διὰ γοῦν τὴν ἐκείνου πλεονεξίαν πάσας
ἐρημωθῆναι συνέβη τὰς πόλεις[1] καὶ πολλοὺς τῶν
πατρίων ἠθῶν[2] ἐξαναστάντας φυγεῖν εἰς τὰς ἀλλοφύλους ἐπαρχίας.

280 (3) Μέχρι μὲν οὖν ἐν Συρίᾳ Κέστιος Γάλλος
ἦν διέπων τὴν ἐπαρχίαν, οὐδὲ πρεσβεύσασθαί τις
πρὸς αὐτὸν ἐτόλμησεν κατὰ τοῦ Φλώρου· παρα-
γενόμενον δὲ εἰς Ἱεροσόλυμα τῆς τῶν ἀζύμων
ἑορτῆς ἐνεστώσης περιστὰς ὁ δῆμος, οὐκ ἐλάττους
τριακοσίων μυριάδων, ἱκέτευον ἐλεῆσαι τὰς τοῦ
ἔθνους συμφορὰς καὶ τὸν λυμεῶνα τῆς χώρας
281 Φλῶρον ἐκεκράγεσαν· ὁ δὲ παρὼν καὶ τῷ Κεστίῳ
παρεστὼς διεχλεύαζεν τὰς φωνάς. ὅ γε μὴν
Κέστιος τὴν ὁρμὴν τοῦ πλήθους καταστείλας καὶ
δοὺς ἔμφασιν ὡς πρὸς τὸ μέλλον αὐτοῖς τὸν
Φλῶρον κατασκευάσειεν μετριώτερον, ὑπέστρεφεν
282 εἰς Ἀντιόχειαν. προέπεμπε δ᾽ αὐτὸν μέχρι Καισαρείας Φλῶρος ἐξαπατῶν καὶ πόλεμον ἤδη τῷ
ἔθνει σκοπούμενος, ᾧ μόνῳ συγκρύψειν τὰς ἑαυτοῦ
283 παρανομίας ὑπελάμβανεν· εἰρήνης μὲν γὰρ οὔσης
κατηγόρους ἕξειν ἐπὶ Καίσαρος Ἰουδαίους προσ-
εδόκα, πραγματευσάμενος δὲ ἀπόστασιν αὐτῶν τῷ
μείζονι κακῷ περισπάσειν τὸν ἔλεγχον ἀπὸ τῶν
μετριωτέρων. ὁ μὲν οὖν, ὡς ἂν ἀπορραγείη τὸ
ἔθνος, καθ᾽ ἡμέραν ἐπέτεινεν αὐτοῖς τὰς συμφοράς.
284 (4) Ἐν δὲ τούτῳ καὶ οἱ Καισαρέων Ἕλληνες,
νικήσαντες παρὰ Νέρωνι τῆς πόλεως ἄρχειν, τὰ

---

[1] τοπαρχίας LVRC Exc.
[2] Destinon from *A.* xx. 256 and Lat.: ἐθῶν mss.

length of proclaiming throughout the country that all were at liberty to practise brigandage, on condition that he received his share of the spoils. Certainly his avarice brought desolation upon all the cities, and caused many to desert their ancestral haunts and seek refuge in foreign provinces.[a]

(3) So long as Cestius Gallus remained in Syria discharging his provincial duties, none dared even to send a deputation to him to complain of Florus ; but when he visited Jerusalem on the occasion of the feast of unleavened bread, the people pressed round him, and a crowd of not less than three millions [b] implored him to have compassion on the calamities of the nation, and loudly denounced Florus as the ruin of the country. Florus, who was present at Cestius's side, scoffed at their outcry. Cestius, for his part, having quieted the excitement of the crowd, pledged himself to secure for them greater moderation on the part of Florus in future, and so returned to Antioch. Florus escorted him as far as Caesarea, playing upon his credulity, and already contemplating the prospect of war with the nation—his only hope of covering up his own enormities. For, if the peace were kept, he expected to have the Jews accusing him before Caesar ; whereas, could he bring about their revolt, he hoped that this larger crime would divert inquiry into less serious offences. In order, therefore, to produce an outbreak of the nation, he daily added to their sufferings.

(4) Meanwhile the Greeks of Caesarea had won their case at Caesar's tribunal,[c] and obtained from him the government of that city ; they brought back

The Jews complain to C. Gallus, governor of Syria. Passover, (?) A.D. 65.

A rising at Caesarea leads to war with Rome.

---

[a] Here the parallel narrative in the *Antiquities* ceases.
[b] An impossible figure.   [c] See § 270.

τῆς κρίσεως ἐκόμισαν γράμματα, καὶ προσ-
ελάμβανεν τὴν ἀρχὴν ὁ πόλεμος δωδεκάτῳ μὲν
ἔτει τῆς Νέρωνος ἡγεμονίας, ἑπτακαιδεκάτῳ δὲ
285 τῆς Ἀγρίππα βασιλείας, Ἀρτεμισίου μηνός. πρὸς
δὲ τὸ μέγεθος τῶν ἐξ αὐτοῦ συμφορῶν οὐκ ἀξίαν
ἔσχεν πρόφασιν. οἱ γὰρ ἐν Καισαρείᾳ Ἰουδαῖοι,
συναγωγὴν ἔχοντες παρὰ χωρίον, οὗ δεσπότης ἦν
τις Ἕλλην Καισαρεύς, πολλάκις μὲν κτήσασθαι
τὸν τόπον ἐσπούδασαν τιμὴν πολλαπλασίονα τῆς
286 ἀξίας διδόντες· ὡς δ᾽ ὑπερορῶν τὰς δεήσεις πρὸς
ἐπήρειαν ἔτι καὶ παρῳκοδόμει[1] τὸ χωρίον ἐκεῖνος
ἐργαστήρια κατασκευαζόμενος, στενήν τε καὶ
παντάπασιν βιαίαν πάροδον ἀπέλειπεν αὐτοῖς, τὸ
μὲν πρῶτον οἱ θερμότεροι τῶν νέων προπηδῶντες
287 οἰκοδομεῖν ἐκώλυον. ὡς δὲ τούτους εἶργεν τῆς
βίας Φλῶρος, ἀμηχανοῦντες οἱ δυνατοὶ τῶν
Ἰουδαίων, σὺν οἷς Ἰωάννης ὁ τελώνης, πείθουσι
τὸν Φλῶρον ἀργυρίου ταλάντοις ὀκτὼ διακωλῦσαι
288 τὸ ἔργον. ὁ δὲ πρὸς μόνον τὸ λαβεῖν ὑποσχόμενος
πάντα συμπράξειν, λαβὼν ἔξεισιν τῆς Καισαρείας
εἰς Σεβαστὴν καὶ καταλείπει τὴν στάσιν αὐτ-
εξούσιον, ὥσπερ ἄδειαν πεπρακὼς Ἰουδαίοις τοῦ
μάχεσθαι.
289 (5) Τῆς δ᾽ ἐπιούσης ἡμέρας ἑβδομάδος οὔσης,
τῶν Ἰουδαίων εἰς τὴν συναγωγὴν συναθροισθέν-
των, στασιαστής τις Καισαρεὺς γάστραν κατα-
στρέψας[2] καὶ παρὰ τὴν εἴσοδον αὐτῶν θέμενος

---

[1] προσῳκοδόμει VRC.
[2] Niese ingeniously conjectures καταστέψας "wreathed
like an altar"; cf. B. i. 378 where the words are confused,
but here no correction seems necessary.

---

[a] Nero's decision must have been given some years

434

with them the text of the decision, and it was now
that the war opened, in the twelfth year of the
principate of Nero, and the seventeenth of the reign c. May
of Agrippa, in the month of Artemisius.[a] The A.D. 66.
ostensible pretext for war was out of proportion to
the magnitude of the disasters to which it led. The
Jews in Caesarea had a synagogue adjoining a plot The affair
of ground owned by a Greek of that city ; this site of the
they had frequently endeavoured to purchase, offer- at Caesarea.
ing a price far exceeding its true value. The pro-
prietor, disdaining their solicitations, by way of insult
further proceeded to build upon the site and erect
workshops, leaving the Jews only a narrow and
extremely awkward passage. Thereupon, some of
the hot-headed youths proceeded to set upon the
builders and attempted to interrupt operations.
Florus having put a stop to their violence, the
Jewish notables, with John the tax-collector, having
no other expedient, offered Florus eight talents of
silver to procure the cessation of the work. Florus,
with his eye only on the money, promised them every
assistance, but, having secured his pay, at once
quitted Caesarea for Sebaste,[b] leaving a free field to
sedition, as though he had sold the Jews a licence to
fight the matter out.

(5) On the following day, which was a sabbath,
when the Jews assembled at the synagogue, they
found that one of the Caesarean mischief-makers had
placed beside the entrance a pot, turned bottom

earlier, since the decisive part in the matter was played by
Pallas (*A.* xx. 182), who died in 62 (Tac. *Ann.* xiv. 65). But
the decision led to increased trouble at Caesarea and *ultimately* to war (*A.* xx. 184). Artemisius is a month in spring
or early summer in the Macedonian calendar which is
followed throughout the *War*.   [b] Samaria.

ἐπέθυεν ὄρνεις. τοῦτο τοὺς Ἰουδαίους ἀνηκέστως
παρώξυνεν ὡς ὑβρισμένων [μὲν]¹ αὐτοῖς τῶν
290 νόμων, μεμιασμένου δὲ τοῦ χωρίου. τὸ μὲν οὖν
εὐσταθὲς καὶ πρᾶον ἐπὶ τοὺς ἡγεμόνας ἀναφεύγειν
ᾤετο χρῆναι, τὸ στασιῶδες δὲ καὶ ἐν² νεότητι
φλεγμαῖνον ἐξεκαίετο πρὸς μάχην. παρεσκευασμέ-
νοι δ' εἱστήκεσαν οἱ τῶν Καισαρέων στασιασταί,
τὸν γὰρ ἐπιθύσοντα προπεπόμφεσαν ἐκ συντάγ-
291 ματος, καὶ ταχέως ἐγένετο συμβολή. προσελθὼν
δὲ Ἰούκουνδος ὁ διακωλύειν τεταγμένος ἱππάρχης
τήν τε γάστραν αἴρει καὶ καταπαύειν ἐπειρᾶτο τὴν
στάσιν. ἡττωμένου δ' αὐτοῦ τῆς τῶν Καισαρέων
βίας Ἰουδαῖοι τοὺς νόμους ἁρπάσαντες ἀνεχώρησαν
εἰς Νάρβατα· χώρα τις αὐτῶν οὕτω καλεῖται
292 σταδίους ἑξήκοντα διέχουσα τῆς Καισαρείας· οἱ
δὲ περὶ τὸν Ἰωάννην δυνατοὶ δώδεκα πρὸς Φλῶρον
ἐλθόντες εἰς Σεβαστὴν ἀπωδύροντο περὶ τῶν πε-
πραγμένων καὶ βοηθεῖν ἱκέτευον, αἰδημόνως ὑπο-
μιμνήσκοντες τῶν ὀκτὼ ταλάντων. ὁ δὲ καὶ συλλαβὼν ἔδησεν τοὺς ἄνδρας, αἰτιώμενος ὑπὲρ τοῦ
τοὺς νόμους ἐξενεγκεῖν τῆς Καισαρείας.

293 (6) Πρὸς τοῦτο τῶν ἐν Ἱεροσολύμοις ἀγανάκτησις ἦν, ἔτι μέντοι τοὺς θυμοὺς κατεῖχον. ὁ δὲ
Φλῶρος ὥσπερ ἠργολαβηκὼς ἐκριπίζειν τὸν πόλεμον, πέμψας ἐπὶ τὸν ἱερὸν θησαυρὸν ἐξαιρεῖ
δεκαεπτὰ τάλαντα, σκηψάμενος εἰς τὰς Καίσαρος

¹ C: om. the rest.   ² om. ἐν Niese.

ᵃ An insinuation as acutely suggested by Reland, that the
Jews were lepers, for whom, under the Law, birds were to

upwards, upon which he was sacrificing birds.[a] This spectacle of what they considered an outrage upon their laws and a desecration of the spot enraged the Jews beyond endurance. The steady-going and peaceable members of the congregation were in favour of immediate recourse to the authorities ; but the factious folk and the passionate youth were burning for a fight. The Caesarean party, on their side, stood prepared for action, for they had, by a concerted plan, sent the man on to the mock sacrifice ; and so they soon came to blows. Jucundus, the cavalry commander commissioned to intervene, came up, removed the pot and endeavoured to quell the riot, but was unable to cope with the violence of the Caesareans. The Jews, thereupon, snatched up their copy of the Law and withdrew to Narbata, a Jewish district sixty furlongs distant from Caesarea.[b] Their leading men, twelve in number, with John at their head, waited upon Florus at Sebaste, bitterly complained of these proceedings and besought his assistance, delicately reminding him of the matter of the eight talents.[c] Florus actually had them arrested and put in irons on the charge of having carried off the copy of the Law from Caesarea. *The Jews quit Caesarea and vainly appeal to Florus.*

(6) This news roused indignation at Jerusalem, though the citizens still restrained their feelings. But Florus, as if he had contracted to fan the flames of war, sent to the temple treasury and extracted seventeen talents, making the requirements of the *Florus pillages the Temple : ferment at Jerusalem.*

be killed in an earthen vessel (Lev. xiv. 4 f.). The charge that Moses and the Israelites whom he led out of Egypt were lepers occurs constantly in the *Contra Apionem* (*e.g.* i. 279 ff.).

[b] The " toparchy " of Narbata is mentioned later, § 509.
[c] § 287.

294 χρείας. σύγχυσις δ' εὐθέως εἶχεν τὸν δῆμον, καὶ
συνδραμόντες εἰς τὸ ἱερὸν βοαῖς διαπρυσίοις τὸ
Καίσαρος ἀνεκάλουν ὄνομα καὶ τῆς Φλώρου τυραν-
295 νίδος ἐλευθεροῦν σφᾶς ἱκέτευον. ἔνιοι δὲ τῶν
στασιαστῶν λοιδορίας αἰσχίστους εἰς τὸν Φλῶρον
ἐκεκράγεσαν καὶ κανοῦν περιφέροντες ἐπῄτουν[1]
αὐτῷ κέρματα καθάπερ ἀκλήρῳ καὶ ταλαιπώρῳ.
τούτοις οὐκ ἀνετράπη τὴν φιλαργυρίαν, ἀλλ' ἐπὶ
296 τὸ μᾶλλον χρηματίσασθαι παρωργίσθη. δέον γοῦν
εἰς Καισάρειαν ἐλθόντα σβέσαι τὸ τοῦ πολέμου
πῦρ ἐκεῖθεν ἀρχόμενον καὶ τῆς ταραχῆς ἀνελεῖν
τὰς αἰτίας, ἐφ' ᾧ καὶ μισθὸν ἔλαβεν, ὁ δὲ μετὰ
στρατιᾶς ἱππικῆς τε καὶ πεζικῆς ἐπὶ Ἱεροσολύμων
ὥρμησεν, ἵνα τοῖς Ῥωμαίων ὅπλοις ἐργάσηται[2]
καὶ τῷ δέει καὶ ταῖς ἀπειλαῖς περιδύσῃ τὴν πόλιν.
297 (7) Ὁ δὲ δῆμος προδυσωπῆσαι τὴν ὁρμὴν
αὐτοῦ βουλόμενος ὑπαντᾷ τοῖς στρατιώταις μετ'
εὐφημίας καὶ τὸν Φλῶρον θεραπευτικῶς ἐκδέχε-
298 σθαι παρεσκευάσατο. κἀκεῖνος προπέμψας σὺν ἱππεῦσιν πεντήκοντα Καπίτωνα ἑκατοντάρχην ἀναχωρεῖν αὐτοὺς ἐκέλευσεν, καὶ μὴ πρὸς ὃν οὕτως
ἐλοιδόρησαν αἰσχρῶς εἰρωνεύεσθαι τὰς νῦν φιλο-
299 φρονήσεις· δεῖν γὰρ αὐτούς, εἴπερ γενναῖοί εἰσιν
καὶ παρρησιασταί, σκώπτειν μὲν αὐτὸν καὶ
παρόντα, φαίνεσθαι δὲ μὴ μόνον ἐν τοῖς λόγοις,
300 ἀλλὰ κἂν τοῖς ὅπλοις φιλελευθέρους. τούτοις
καταπλαγὲν τὸ πλῆθος, ἅμα καὶ τῶν περὶ Καπίτωνα ἱππέων εἰς μέσον φερομένων, διεσκεδάσθη
πρὶν ἀσπάσασθαι τὸν Φλῶρον ἢ τοῖς στρατιώταις

---

[1] ἀπήτουν PAM.
[2] +τὸ βουλόμενον C; cf. "ad quod uolebat uteretur" Lat.
and for τὸ β. A. xvi. 396.

imperial service his pretext.[a]   Instantly fired by this
outrage, the people rushed in a body to the temple
and with piercing cries invoked the name of Caesar,
imploring him to liberate them from the tyranny of
Florus.   Some of the malcontents railed on the procurator in the most opprobrious terms and carrying
round a basket begged coppers for him as for an
unfortunate destitute.   These proceedings, however,
far from checking his avarice, only provoked him to
further peculation.   Accordingly, instead of betaking
himself, as he should have done, to Caesarea, to extin-
guish the flames of war, there already breaking out,
and to root out the cause of these disorders—a task for
which he had been paid—he marched with an army[b] of
cavalry and infantry upon Jerusalem, in order to attain his object with the aid of the Roman arms, and by
means of intimidation and menaces to fleece the city.

(7) The citizens, anxious to forestall and make him
ashamed of his intention, went to meet the troops
with acclamations, and prepared to give Florus an
obsequious reception.   He, however, sent on ahead
a centurion, Capito, with fifty horsemen, and ordered
the Jews to retire and not to mock with this show of
cordiality one whom they had so grossly abused ; if
they were courageous and outspoken persons (so ran
his words) they ought to jeer at him in his very
presence and to show their love of liberty not only
in words but with arms in hand.   Dismayed by this
message and by Capito's cavalrymen charging into
their ranks, the crowd dispersed, before they had a
chance of saluting Florus or giving the soldiers proof

Florus at Jerusalem.

---

[a] Perhaps because their payment of tribute was in arrear,
§ 403 (Reinach).
[b] Apparently he had only a single cohort (§ 332).

φανερὸν ποιῆσαι τὸ πειθήνιον. ἀναχωρήσαντες
δὲ εἰς τὰς οἰκίας μετὰ δέους καὶ ταπεινότητος
ἐνυκτέρευσαν.[1]

301 (8) Φλῶρος δὲ τότε μὲν ἐν τοῖς βασιλείοις
αὐλίζεται, τῇ δ' ὑστεραίᾳ βῆμα πρὸ αὐτῶν
θέμενος καθέζεται, καὶ προσελθόντες οἵ τε ἀρχιερεῖς καὶ δυνατοὶ τό τε γνωριμώτατον τῆς πόλεως[2]
302 παρέστησαν τῷ βήματι. τούτοις ὁ Φλῶρος ἐκέλευσεν τοὺς λοιδορήσαντας αὐτὸν ἐκδοῦναι, φάμενος αὐτοὺς ἀπολαύσειν τῆς ἀμύνης, εἰ μὴ προ-
άγοιεν τοὺς αἰτίους. οἱ δὲ τὸν μὲν δῆμον ἀπέφηναν[3]
εἰρηνικὰ φρονοῦντα, τοῖς δὲ παραφθεγξαμένοις
303 ᾐτοῦντο συγγνώμην· ἐν γὰρ τοσούτῳ πλήθει θαυ-
μαστὸν μὲν οὐδὲν εἶναί τινας θρασυτέρους καὶ δι'
ἡλικίαν ἄφρονας, ἀμήχανον δὲ τῶν ἡμαρτηκότων
τὴν διάκρισιν ἑκάστου μετανοοῦντος καὶ δέει[4] ἃ
304 δέδρακεν ἀρνουμένου. δεῖν μέντοι γε ἐκεῖνον, εἰ
προνοεῖ τῆς κατὰ τὸ ἔθνος εἰρήνης καὶ βούλεται
Ῥωμαίοις περισώζειν τὴν πόλιν, μᾶλλον διὰ τοὺς
πολλοὺς ἀκαταιτιάτους συγγνῶναι καὶ τοῖς ὀλίγοις
πλημμελήσασιν ἢ δι' ὀλίγους πονηροὺς ταράξαι
δῆμον ἀγαθὸν τοσοῦτον.

305 (9) Πρὸς ταῦτα μᾶλλον παροξυνθεὶς ἐμβοᾷ τοῖς
στρατιώταις διαρπάζειν τὴν ἄνω καλουμένην
ἀγορὰν καὶ κτείνειν τοὺς ἐντυγχάνοντας. οἱ δ'
ἐπιθυμίᾳ κέρδους προσλαβόντες ἡγεμονικὴν παρα-
κέλευσιν οὐ μόνον ἐφ' ὃν ἐπέμφθησαν τόπον
ἥρπαζον, ἀλλ' εἰς πάσας ἐμπηδῶντες τὰς οἰκίας

---

[1] διενυκτέρευσαν VRC (the usual word in Josephus).
[2] + πᾶν VRC.   [3] ἀπέφαινον VRC.
[4] Destinon: δι' mss.

of their obedience. They retired to their homes
and passed the night in terror and dejection.

(8) Florus lodged at the palace, and on the following day had a tribunal placed in front of the building
and took his seat; the chief priests, the nobles, and
the most eminent citizens then presented themselves
before the tribunal. Florus ordered them to hand
over the men who had insulted him, declaring that
they themselves would feel his vengeance if they
failed to produce the culprits. The leaders, in reply,
declared that the people were peaceably disposed
and implored pardon for the individuals who had
spoken disrespectfully. It was not surprising, they
said, that in so great a crowd there should be some
reckless spirits and foolish youths; but to pick out
the delinquents was impossible, as everyone was now
penitent and would, from fear of the consequences,
deny what he had done. If, then, Florus cared for
the peace of the nation and wished to preserve the
city for the Romans, he ought to pardon the few
offenders for the sake of the many innocent, rather
than, because of a few rascals, to bring trouble upon
such a host of good citizens.

(9) This speech merely increased the exasperation *He delivers
of Florus, who now shouted to the soldiers to sack the city to
his soldiers
the agora known as the " upper market," [a] and to for plunder
kill any whom they encountered. The troops, whose massacre.
and*
lust for booty was thus backed by their general's
order, not only plundered the quarter which they
were sent to attack, but plunged into every house and

[a] The upper city or upper agora, viz. the south-west
quarter of the town. See *B.* v. 137 f. for the city hills:
(1) upper city [S.W.], (2) lower city or Akra [S.E.], (3) a
third which had disappeared in the time of Josephus
[probably N.E.]; with G. A. Smith, *Jerusalem*, ii. 448 note.

306 ἔσφαζον τοὺς οἰκήτορας. φυγὴ δ᾽ ἦν ἐκ τῶν
στενωπῶν καὶ φόνος τῶν καταλαμβανομένων,
τρόπος τε ἁρπαγῆς οὐδεὶς παρελείπετο, καὶ πολλοὺς τῶν μετρίων συλλαβόντες ἐπὶ τὸν Φλῶρον
ἀνῆγον· οὓς μάστιξιν προαικισάμενος ἀνεσταύ-
307 ρωσεν. ὁ δὲ[1] σύμπας τῶν ἐκείνης ἀπολομένων
τῆς ἡμέρας ἀριθμὸς σὺν γυναιξὶν καὶ τέκνοις, οὐδὲ
γὰρ νηπίων ἀπέσχοντο, περὶ τρισχιλίους[2] καὶ ἑξα-
308 κοσίους συνήχθη. βαρυτέραν τε ἐποίει τὴν συμφορὰν τὸ καινὸν τῆς Ῥωμαίων ὠμότητος· ὃ γὰρ
μηδεὶς πρότερον τότε Φλῶρος ἐτόλμησεν, ἄνδρας
ἱππικοῦ τάγματος μαστιγῶσαί τε πρὸ τοῦ βήματος
καὶ σταυρῷ προσηλῶσαι, ὧν εἰ καὶ τὸ γένος Ἰουδαῖον[3] ἀλλὰ γοῦν τὸ ἀξίωμα Ῥωμαϊκὸν ἦν.

309 (xv. 1) Κατὰ τοῦτον τὸν καιρὸν ὁ μὲν βασιλεὺς Ἀγρίππας ἔτυχεν εἰς τὴν Ἀλεξάνδρειαν
πεπορευμένος, ὅπως Ἀλεξάνδρῳ συνησθείη πεπι-
στευμένῳ τὴν Αἴγυπτον ὑπὸ Νέρωνος καὶ πεμ-
310 φθέντι διέπειν. τὴν ἀδελφὴν δὲ αὐτοῦ Βερνίκην
παροῦσαν ἐν Ἱεροσολύμοις καὶ τὴν παρανομίαν
τῶν στρατιωτῶν θεωμένην δεινὸν εἰσῄει πάθος,
καὶ πολλάκις τούς τε ἱππάρχους ἑαυτῆς καὶ
σωματοφύλακας πέμπουσα πρὸς Φλῶρον ἐδεῖτο
311 παύσασθαι τοῦ φόνου. καὶ ὁ μὲν οὔτε εἰς τὸ
πλῆθος τῶν ἀναιρουμένων οὔτε εἰς τὴν εὐγένειαν
τῆς παρακαλούσης, ἀλλ᾽ εἰς μόνον τὸ λυσιτελὲς
312 τὸ ἐκ τῶν ἁρπαγῶν ἀποβλέπων παρήκουσεν. ἡ
δ᾽ ὁρμὴ τῶν στρατιωτῶν ἐλύσσησεν καὶ κατὰ τῆς
βασιλίδος· οὐ μόνον γοῦν ἐν ὄμμασιν αὐτῆς ἠκί-
ζοντο τοὺς ἁλισκομένους καὶ διέφθειρον, ἀλλὰ

---

[1] ὁ γοῦν VRC.   [2] VRC: τριάκοντα PAM.
[3] ML: Ἰουδαίων or Ἰουδαῖοι the rest.

slaughtered the inmates. There ensued a stampede through the narrow alleys, massacre of all who were caught, every variety of pillage ; many of the peaceable citizens were arrested and brought before Florus, who had them first scourged and then crucified. The total number of that day's victims, including women and children, for even infancy received no quarter, amounted to about three thousand six hundred. The calamity was aggravated by the unprecedented character of the Romans' cruelty. For Florus ventured that day to do what none had ever done before, namely, to scourge before his tribunal and nail to the cross men of equestrian rank, men who, if Jews by birth, were at least invested with that Roman dignity.

(xv. 1) King Agrippa, at this moment, was absent, having gone to Alexandria to offer his congratulations to Alexander,[a] recently sent to take over the government of Egypt, with which he had been entrusted by Nero. Agrippa's sister Bernice, however, who was at Jerusalem, witnessed with the liveliest emotion the outrages of the soldiers, and constantly sent her cavalry-commanders and bodyguards to Florus to implore him to put a stop to the carnage. But he, regarding neither the number of the slain nor the exalted rank of his suppliant, but only the profit accruing from the plunder, turned a deaf ear to her prayers. The mad rage of the soldiers even vented itself upon the queen. Not only did they torture and put their captives to death under her eyes, but

Ineffectual appeal of Queen Bernice to Florus.

---

[a] Tiberius Alexander, previously procurator of Judaea (§ 220 note), and brother-in-law of Bernice (*A.* xix. 276 f.).

κἂν αὐτὴν ἀνεῖλον, εἰ μὴ καταφυγεῖν εἰς τὴν
βασιλικὴν αὐλὴν ἔφθη, κἀκεῖ διενυκτέρευσεν μετὰ
φυλακῆς δεδοικυῖα τὴν τῶν στρατιωτῶν ἔφοδον.
313 ἐπεδήμει δ' ἐν τοῖς Ἱεροσολύμοις εὐχὴν ἐκτελοῦσα
τῷ θεῷ· τοὺς γὰρ ἢ νόσῳ καταπονουμένους ἢ
τισιν ἄλλαις ἀνάγκαις ἔθος εὔχεσθαι πρὸ τριάκοντα ἡμερῶν ἧς ἀποδώσειν μέλλοιεν θυσίας οἴνου
314 τε ἀφέξεσθαι καὶ ξυρήσεσθαι[1] τὰς κόμας. ἃ δὴ
καὶ τότε τελοῦσα Βερνίκη γυμνόπους τε πρὸ τοῦ
βήματος ἱκέτευε τὸν Φλῶρον, καὶ πρὸς τῷ μὴ
τυχεῖν αἰδοῦς αὐτὴ[2] τὸν περὶ τοῦ ζῆν κίνδυνον
ἐπείρασεν.

315 (2) Ταῦτα μὲν οὖν ἑξκαιδεκάτῃ μηνὸς Ἀρτεμισίου συνηνέχθη, τῇ δ' ἐπιούσῃ τὸ μὲν πλῆθος
ὑπερπαθῆσαν εἰς τὴν ἄνω συνέρρευσεν ἀγορὰν καὶ
βοαῖς ἐξαισίοις περὶ τῶν ἀπολωλότων ἀνωδύρετο·
τὸ πλέον δὲ ἦσαν εἰς τὸν Φλῶρον ἐπίφθονοι φωναί.
316 πρὸς ὃ δείσαντες οἱ δυνατοὶ σὺν τοῖς ἀρχιερεῦσιν
τὰς ἐσθῆτας περιερρήξαντο, καὶ προσπίπτοντες
ἑκάστοις[3] ἐδέοντο παύσασθαι καὶ μὴ πρὸς οἷς
πεπόνθασιν εἰς ἀνήκεστόν τι τὸν Φλῶρον ἐρεθίζειν.
317 ἐπείσθη δὲ τὸ πλῆθος ταχέως αἰδοῖ τε τῶν παρακαλούντων καὶ κατ' ἐλπίδα τοῦ μηδὲν ἔτι τὸν
Φλῶρον εἰς αὐτοὺς παρανομήσειν.

318 (3) Ὁ δὲ σβεσθείσης τῆς ταραχῆς ἤχθετο καὶ
πάλιν αὐτὴν ἀνάψαι πραγματευόμενος τούς τε
ἀρχιερεῖς σὺν τοῖς γνωρίμοις μεταπέμπεται καὶ
μόνον ἔφη τεκμήριον ἔσεσθαι τοῦ μηδὲν ἔτι τὸν

---

[1] Dindorf: ξυρήσασθαι (-ίσασθαι) mss.
[2] Destinon: αὐτὴν mss.
[3] VRC (Lat. ?): ἕκαστος the rest.

---

[a] A Nazirite vow, cf. Acts xxi. 23-26. Thirty days was

they would have killed her also, had she not hastened
to seek refuge in the palace, where she passed the
night surrounded by guards, dreading an attack of
the troops. She was visiting Jerusalem to discharge
a vow to God ; for it is customary for those suffering
from illness or other affliction to make a vow to abstain from wine and to shave their heads during the
thirty days preceding that on which they must offer
sacrifices.[a] These rites Bernice was then undergoing,
and she would come barefoot before the tribunal and
make supplication to Florus, without any respect
being shown to her, and even at the peril of her life.

(2) These events took place on the sixteenth of
the month Artemisius. On the following day the
multitude, overcome with distress, flocked to the
upper *agora*, uttering terrific lamentations for the
dead, but the shouts of imprecation upon Florus pre-
ponderated. Alarmed at this outburst, the leading
men and the chief priests rent their clothes and,
falling at the feet of one after another of the mob,
implored them to desist, and not to provoke Florus,
after all they had endured, to some new and irreparable outrage. The multitude promptly complied,
alike out of respect for their petitioners, and in the
hope that Florus would spare them further enormities.

(3) The procurator was vexed at the extinction of
the tumult, and, with the object of relighting the
flames, sent for the chief priests and leading citizens
and told them that the people had but one way of
proving that they intended to refrain from any

Marginal notes: 3 June 66 A.D.[b] Mourning of the Jews. / Florus brings two cohorts from Caesarea,

the period of purification prescribed by the school of Shammai
for Nazirites completing a vow in Palestine ; the school of
Hillel was apparently more severe (Mishna, *Nasir*, iii. 6,
quoted by Schürer).

[b] According to Niese's calculation.

δῆμον νεωτερίσειν, εἰ προελθόντες ὑπαντήσουσιν
τοῖς ἀπὸ Καισαρείας ἀνιοῦσιν στρατιώταις· παρεγί-
319 νοντο δὲ δύο σπεῖραι. τῶν δ' ἔτι συγκαλούντων
τὸ πλῆθος προπέμψας διεδήλου τοῖς τῶν σπειρῶν
ἑκατοντάρχοις, ὅπως παραγγείλωσιν τοῖς ὑφ'
ἑαυτοὺς μήτε ἀντασπάσασθαι τοὺς Ἰουδαίους,
κἄν τι κατ' αὐτοῦ φθέγξωνται χρήσασθαι τοῖς
320 ὅπλοις. οἱ δ' ἀρχιερεῖς εἰς τὸ ἱερὸν τὴν πληθὺν
συναγαγόντες ὑπαντᾶν τοῖς Ῥωμαίοις παρεκάλουν
καὶ πρὸ ἀνηκέστου πάθους τὰς σπείρας δεξιοῦσθαι.
τούτοις τὸ στασιῶδες ἠπείθει, καὶ διὰ τοὺς
ἀπολωλότας τὸ πλῆθος ἔρρεπεν πρὸς τοὺς θρασυτέρους.
321   (4) Ἔνθα δὴ πᾶς μὲν ἱερεὺς πᾶς δ' ὑπηρέτης
τοῦ θεοῦ τὰ ἅγια σκεύη προκομίσαντες καὶ τὸν
κόσμον, ἐν ᾧ λειτουργεῖν ἔθος ἦν αὐτοῖς, ἀνα-
λαβόντες, κιθαρισταί τε καὶ ὑμνῳδοὶ μετὰ τῶν
ὀργάνων προσέπιπτον καὶ κατηντιβόλουν φυλάξαι
τὸν ἱερὸν κόσμον αὐτοῖς καὶ μὴ πρὸς ἁρπαγὴν
322 τῶν θείων κειμηλίων Ῥωμαίους ἐρεθίσαι. τοὺς
δ' ἀρχιερεῖς αὐτοὺς ἦν ἰδεῖν καταμωμένους μὲν
τῆς κεφαλῆς κόνιν,[1] γυμνοὺς δὲ τὰ στέρνα τῶν
ἐσθήτων διερρηγμένων.[2] ὀνομαστὶ δ' ἕκαστον τῶν
γνωρίμων καὶ κοινῇ τὸ πλῆθος ἱκέτευον μὴ δι'
ἐλαχίστης πλημμελείας προδοῦναι τὴν πατρίδα
323 τοῖς ἐπιθυμοῦσιν πορθῆσαι· τίνα γὰρ ἢ τοῖς
στρατιώταις φέρειν ὠφέλειαν τὸν ἀπὸ Ἰουδαίων
ἀσπασμὸν ἢ διόρθωσιν αὐτοῖς τῶν συμβεβηκότων
324 τὸ μὴ νῦν προελθεῖν; εἰ δὲ δὴ δεξιώσαιντο τοὺς

---

[1] LVRC (cf. § 601): τὴν κεφαλὴν κόνει PAM.
[2] περιερρηγμένων LVRC.

further revolutionary proceedings, namely to go out
and meet the troops coming up from Caesarea—two
cohorts being at the time on their way. Then, while _{and sends}
the leaders were still convening the people for the _{them private}
purpose, Florus sent word to the centurions of the _{instruc-}
cohorts to instruct their men not to return the salute _{tions.}
of the Jews, and if they uttered a word in disparage-
ment of himself, to make use of their arms. The
chief priests, meanwhile, having assembled the
multitude in the temple, exhorted them to meet the _{The priests}
advancing Romans and to prevent any irremediable _{urge the Jews to}
disaster by giving a courteous reception to the _{submit.}
cohorts. To this advice the factious party refused
to listen, and the crowd, influenced by their memory
of the fallen, inclined to the bolder policy.

(4) Then it was that every priest and every minister
of God, bearing in procession the holy vessels and
wearing the robes in which they were wont to per-
form their priestly offices, the harpers also and the
choristers with their instruments, fell on their knees
and earnestly implored the people to preserve for
them these sacred ornaments, and not to provoke the
Romans to pillage the treasures of the house of God.
Even the chief priests might then have been seen
heaping dust upon their heads, their breasts bared,
their vestments rent. They appealed by name to
each of the notables individually and to the people
as a whole not, by offending in so trifling a matter,
to deliver up their country to those who were eager
to sack it. " After all," they asked, " what would
the troops profit by receiving a salute from the
Jews ? What reparation for past events would they
themselves obtain by now refusing to go out ? If,
on the contrary, they welcomed these new-comers

προσιόντας ὡς ἔθος, Φλώρῳ μὲν ἀποκοπήσεσθαι
τὴν ἀφορμὴν τοῦ πολέμου, κερδήσειν δ' αὐτοὺς
τὴν πατρίδα καὶ τὸ μηδὲν παθεῖν πλέον. ἄλλως
τε καὶ τὸ πείθεσθαι στασιάζουσιν ὀλίγοις, δέον
αὐτοὺς δῆμον ὄντας τοσοῦτον συναναγκάζειν κἀκείνους συνευγνωμονεῖν,[1] δεινῆς ἀκρασίας εἶναι.
325 (5) Τούτοις μειλισσόμενοι τὸ πλῆθος ἅμα καὶ
τῶν στασιαστῶν οὓς μὲν ἀπειλαῖς, οὓς δὲ αἰδοῖ
κατέστειλαν. ἔπειτα ἐξηγούμενοι μεθ' ἡσυχίας
τε καὶ κόσμου τοῖς στρατιώταις ὑπήντων καὶ
πλησίον γενομένους ἠσπάσαντο· τῶν δὲ μηδὲν
ἀποκριναμένων οἱ στασιασταὶ Φλώρου κατεβόων.
326 τοῦτ' ἦν σύνθημα κατ' αὐτῶν δεδομένον· αὐτίκα
γοῦν οἱ στρατιῶται περισχόντες αὐτοὺς ἔπαιον
ξύλοις, καὶ φεύγοντας οἱ ἱππεῖς καταδιώκοντες
συνεπάτουν. ἔπιπτον δὲ πολλοὶ μὲν ὑπὸ Ῥωμαίων τυπτόμενοι, πλείους δ' ὑπ' ἀλλήλων βια-
327 ζόμενοι. δεινὸς δὲ περὶ τὰς πύλας ὠθισμὸς ἦν,
καὶ φθάνειν ἑκάστου σπεύδοντος βραδυτέρα μὲν ἡ
φυγὴ πᾶσιν ἐγίνετο, τῶν δὲ σφαλέντων ἀπώλεια
δεινή· πνιγόμενοι γὰρ καὶ κλώμενοι πλήθει τῶν
ἐπιβαινόντων ἠφανίζοντο, καὶ οὐδὲ πρὸς ταφήν
328 τις γνώριμος τοῖς ἰδίοις κατελείπετο. συνεισ-
έπιπτον[2] δὲ καὶ στρατιῶται παίοντες ἀνέδην τοὺς
καταλαμβανομένους καὶ διὰ τῆς Βεζεθὰ καλου-
μένης ἀνεώθουν τὸ πλῆθος, βιαζόμενοι παρελθεῖν
καὶ κρατῆσαι τοῦ τε ἱεροῦ καὶ τῆς Ἀντωνίας·

---

[1] συνευδαιμονεῖν PAL.
[2] Bekker: συνέπιπτον MSS.

---

[a] Or " New city," the northernmost suburb, included
within the unfinished wall of Agrippa I (*B.* v. 151 ff.).

with their customary courtesy, they would cut away
from Florus all ground for hostilities and gain for
themselves their country and freedom from further
molestation. And then, above all, what utter feeble-
ness it showed to be guided by a handful of rebels,
when they ought instead with their numerous body
to coerce even these malcontents to join in their
own rational policy ! ''

(5) By these remonstrances they succeeded in
soothing the multitude, while they quelled the rebels
partly by menaces, partly by appealing to their feelings of respect. Then, taking the lead, they advanced in quiet and orderly fashion to meet the
troops, and on the approach of the latter saluted
them. The cohorts making no response, the rebels
started clamouring against Florus. This was the
given signal for falling upon the Jews. In an instant
the troops were round them, striking out with their
clubs, and on their taking flight the cavalry pursued
and trampled them under their horses' feet. Many
fell beneath the blows of the Romans, a still larger
number under the pressure of their own companions.
Around the gates the crush was terrible ; as each
strove to pass in first, the flight of all was retarded,
and dreadful was the fate of any who stumbled ;
suffocated and mangled by the crowds that trod them
down, they were obliterated and their bodies so dis-
figured that their relatives could not recognize them
to give them burial. The troops pushed in with the
fugitives, mercilessly striking anyone who fell into
their hands, and so thrust the crowd back through
the quarter called Bezetha,[a] trying to force their way
through and occupy the temple and the castle of

Reception of the cohorts : a fresh collision.

449

ὧν καὶ Φλῶρος ἐφιέμενος ἐξῆγε τῆς βασιλικῆς
αὐλῆς τοὺς σὺν αὐτῷ καὶ πρὸς τὸ φρούριον ἐλθεῖν
329 ἠγωνίζετο. διήμαρτέν γε μὴν τῆς ἐπιβολῆς·[1]
ὁ γὰρ δῆμος ἄντικρυς ἐπιστραφεὶς εἶργεν τὴν
ὁρμήν,[2] καὶ διαστάντες ἐπὶ τῶν τεγῶν τοὺς Ῥωμαίους ἔβαλλον. καταπονούμενοι δὲ τοῖς ὕπερθεν
βέλεσιν καὶ διακόψαι τὸ τοὺς στενωποὺς ἐμφράξαν
πλῆθος ἀσθενήσαντες, ἀνεχώρουν εἰς τὸ πρὸς τοῖς
βασιλείοις στρατόπεδον.

330   (6) Οἱ δὲ στασιασταὶ δείσαντες μὴ πάλιν
ἐπελθὼν ὁ Φλῶρος κρατήσῃ τοῦ ἱεροῦ διὰ τῆς
Ἀντωνίας, ἀναβάντες εὐθέως τὰς συνεχεῖς στοὰς
331 τοῦ ἱεροῦ πρὸς τὴν Ἀντωνίαν διέκοψαν. τοῦτ᾽
ἔψυξεν τὴν Φλώρου πλεονεξίαν· τῶν γὰρ τοῦ
θεοῦ θησαυρῶν ἐφιέμενος καὶ διὰ τοῦτο παρελθεῖν
ἐπιθυμῶν εἰς τὴν Ἀντωνίαν, ὡς ἀπερράγησαν αἱ
στοαί, τὴν ὁρμὴν ἀνετράπη, καὶ μεταπεμψάμενος
τούς τε ἀρχιερεῖς καὶ τὴν βουλὴν αὐτὸς μὲν
ἐξιέναι τῆς πόλεως ἔφη, φρουρὰν δ᾽ ἐγκαταλείψειν
332 αὐτοῖς ὅσην ἂν ἀξιώσωσιν. τῶν δὲ πάντα περὶ
ἀσφαλείας καὶ τοῦ μηδὲν νεωτερίσειν ὑποσχομέ-
νων, εἰ μίαν αὐτοῖς καταλείποι σπεῖραν, μὴ μέντοι τὴν μαχεσαμένην, πρὸς γὰρ ταύτην ἀπεχθῶς
δι᾽ ἃ πέπονθεν ἔχειν τὸ πλῆθος, ἀλλάξας τὴν
σπεῖραν, ὡς ἠξίουν, μετὰ τῆς λοιπῆς δυνάμεως
ὑπέστρεψεν εἰς Καισάρειαν.

333   (xvi. 1) Ἑτέραν δὲ ἐπιβολὴν[3] τῷ πολέμῳ
πορίζομενος ἐπέστελλεν Κεστίῳ Ἰουδαίων ἀπό-

---

[1] L Lat.: ἐπιβουλῆς the rest.   [2] τῆς ὁρμῆς P: om. Lat.
[3] ἐπιβουλὴν PAM and second hand of L.

[a] *i.e.* the cohort which Florus himself had brought into
the city (§ 296) and which had sacked the Upper Market.

Antonia. Florus, with the same object in view, led
his men out from the court of the palace and struggled
to reach the fortress. But he was foiled in this
purpose ; for he found himself faced by the people,
who turned upon him and checked his advance, while
others, posting themselves along the roofs, kept the
Romans under continuous fire. Overwhelmed by
the missiles from above and incapable of cutting
their way through the crowds that blocked the
narrow alleys, the soldiers beat a retreat to their
camp adjoining the palace.

(6) Fearing, however, that Florus might return to
the attack and capture the temple by way of the
fortress Antonia, the Jewish revolutionaries instantly
mounted the porticoes which connect the two buildings and cut the communication. This manœuvre
cooled the cupidity of Florus ; for it was God's
treasures that he coveted and that had made him
so eager to reach Antonia, and now that the porticoes
were broken down, his ardour was checked ; he sent
for the chief priests and the council, and told them
that he intended to quit the city, but would leave
them whatever garrison they desired. In reply, they
undertook to maintain perfect order and to prevent
any revolution, provided that he left them a single
cohort, but not the one which had fought,[a] as the
people bore it a grudge on account of what they
had suffered from it. He, accordingly, changed the
cohort, as they requested, and with the remainder
of his forces returned to Caesarea.

(xvi. 1) With a view to providing further ground
for hostilities, Florus now sent a report to Cestius,

The Jews destroy the porticoes adjoining Antonia.

Florus evacuates Jerusalem.

Cestius sends an emissary to investigate the position.

451

στασιν καταψευδόμενος, τήν τε ἀρχὴν τῆς μάχης
περιθεὶς αὐτοῖς, καὶ δρᾶσαι λέγων ἐκείνους ἃ
πεπόνθεσαν. οὐ μὴν οὐδ' οἱ τῶν Ἱεροσολύμων
ἄρχοντες ἐσίγησαν, ἀλλ' αὐτοί τε καὶ Βερνίκη
τῷ Κεστίῳ περὶ ὧν Φλῶρος εἰς τὴν πόλιν παρηνό-
334 μησεν ἔγραφον. ὁ δὲ τὰ παρ' ἀμφοῖν ἀναγνοὺς
μετὰ τῶν ἡγεμόνων ἐβουλεύετο. τοῖς μὲν οὖν
αὐτὸν¹ ἐδόκει Κέστιον μετὰ στρατιᾶς ἀναβαίνειν
ἢ τιμωρησόμενον τὴν ἀπόστασιν, εἰ γέγονεν, ἢ
βεβαιοτέρους καταστήσοντα Ἰουδαίους καὶ συμ-
μένοντας, αὐτῷ δὲ προπέμψαι² τῶν ἑταίρων τὸν
κατασκεψόμενον τὰ πράγματα καὶ τὰ φρονήματα
335 τῶν Ἰουδαίων πιστῶς ἀναγγελοῦντα. πέμπει δή³
τινα τῶν χιλιάρχων Νεαπολιτανόν,⁴ ὃς ἀπὸ τῆς
Ἀλεξανδρείας ὑποστρέφοντι περιτυχὼν Ἀγρίππᾳ
τῷ βασιλεῖ κατὰ Ἰάμνειαν τόν τε πέμψαντα καὶ
τὰς αἰτίας ἐδήλωσεν.

336   (2) Ἔνθα καὶ Ἰουδαίων οἵ τε ἀρχιερεῖς ἅμα
τοῖς δυνατοῖς καὶ ἡ βουλὴ παρῆν δεξιουμένη τὸν
βασιλέα. μετὰ δὲ τὴν εἰς ἐκεῖνον θεραπείαν ἀπωδύροντο τὰς ἑαυτῶν συμφορὰς καὶ τὴν Φλώρου
337 διεξήεσαν ὠμότητα. πρὸς ἣν ἠγανάκτει μὲν
Ἀγρίππας, στρατηγικῶς δὲ τὴν ὀργὴν εἰς οὓς
ἠλέει Ἰουδαίους μετέφερεν, ταπεινοῦν αὐτῶν βουλόμενος τὰ φρονήματα καὶ τῷ μὴ δοκεῖν ἀδίκως
338 τι παθεῖν τῆς ἀμύνης ἀποτρέπων. οἱ μὲν οὖν, ὡς

---

¹ LC: αὐτῶν the rest: om. Lat.
² P: +τινὰ the rest.
³ Cardwell: δὲ or οὖν δὴ mss.
⁴ Νεοπολιτανόν here and below VRC (as in Vita 121).

falsely accusing the Jews of revolt, representing them as the aggressors in the recent fighting, and charging them with crimes of which in fact they were the sufferers. However, the magistrates of Jerusalem, on their side, did not remain silent : they, too, wrote to Cestius, as did also Bernice, on the subject of the iniquities perpetrated upon the city by Florus. Cestius, having read the dispatches from both parties, took counsel with his officers. They were of opinion that Cestius should go up in person to Jerusalem with an army, either to punish the authors of the revolt, if it was a fact, or to confirm the Jews in their allegiance, if they still remained loyal to Rome. The governor, however, decided first to send one of his colleagues to investigate the position of affairs and to present a faithful report to him of the temper of the Jews. He accordingly dispatched the tribune Neapolitanus, who fell in at Jamnia[a] with king Agrippa as he was returning from Alexandria, and informed him who it was that had sent him on this mission and what was its object.

Agrippa returns to Jerusalem.

(2) To Jamnia also came the chief priests of the Jews, the leading citizens and the council, to welcome the king. After paying homage to him, they proceeded to deplore the calamities which had befallen them and to recount the brutalities of Florus. Agrippa was indignant at their narrative, but diplomatically turned his resentment upon the Jews whom at heart he pitied, wishing to humiliate their pride and, by appearing to disbelieve that they had been at all ill-treated, to divert them from revenge.

Inquiry of Neapolitanus at Jerusalem.

---

[a] Jamnia (*Yebnah*) in Philistia not being on the direct route to Jerusalem from Caesarea (or Antioch), it is supposed that Neapolitanus went out of his way to meet Agrippa.

ἂν ὄντες ἔκκριτοι καὶ διὰ τὰς ἑαυτῶν κτήσεις
ἐπιθυμοῦντες εἰρήνης, συνίεσαν εὐνοϊκὴν τὴν ἐπί-
πληξιν τοῦ βασιλέως· ὁ δὲ δῆμος ἐκ τῶν Ἱεροσολύμων ἐπὶ ἑξήκοντα προελθὼν σταδίους ἐδεξιοῦτο
339 τὸν Ἀγρίππαν καὶ τὸν Νεαπολιτανόν. ἐκώκυον
δὲ καὶ τῶν ἀπεσφαγμένων αἱ γυναῖκες προεκ-
θέουσαι, καὶ πρὸς τὴν τούτων οἰμωγὴν ὁ δῆμος
εἰς ὀλοφυρμοὺς τραπόμενος ἐπικουρεῖν τὸν Ἀγρίππαν ἱκέτευεν, τοῦ τε Νεαπολιτανοῦ κατεβόων ὅσα
πάθοιεν ὑπὸ Φλώρου, καὶ παρελθοῦσιν εἰς τὴν
πόλιν τήν τε ἀγορὰν ἠρημωμένην ἐπεδείκνυσαν καὶ
340 πεπορθημένας τὰς οἰκίας. ἔπειτα δι’ Ἀγρίππα
πείθουσι τὸν Νεαπολιτανὸν σὺν ἑνὶ θεράποντι
περιελθεῖν μέχρι τοῦ Σιλωᾶ τὴν πόλιν, ἵνα γνῷ
Ἰουδαίους τοῖς μὲν ἄλλοις Ῥωμαίοις ἅπασιν
εἴκοντας, μόνῳ δ’ ἀπεχθανομένους Φλώρῳ δι’
ὑπερβολὴν τῆς εἰς αὐτοὺς ὠμότητος. ὁ δ’ ὡς
διοδεύσας πεῖραν ἱκανὴν ἔλαβεν τῆς πραότητος
341 αὐτῶν, εἰς τὸ ἱερὸν ἀναβαίνει. ἔνθα συγκαλέσας
τὸ πλῆθος, καὶ πολλὰ μὲν εἰς πίστιν αὐτοὺς τὴν
πρὸς Ῥωμαίους ἐπαινέσας, πολλὰ δὲ εἰς τὸ τηρεῖν
τὴν εἰρήνην προτρεψάμενος καὶ τοῦ θεοῦ προσ-
κυνήσας ὅθεν ἐξῆν τὰ ἅγια, πρὸς Κέστιον ἐπανῄει.
342 (3) Τὸ δὲ πλῆθος τῶν Ἰουδαίων ἐπί τε τὸν
βασιλέα καὶ τοὺς ἀρχιερεῖς τραπόμενον πέμπειν
κατὰ Φλώρου πρέσβεις ἠξίου πρὸς Νέρωνα καὶ
μὴ σιωπῶντας ἐπὶ τοσούτῳ φόνῳ καταλιπεῖν
ἑαυτοῖς ὑπόνοιαν ἀποστάσεως· δόξειν γὰρ αὐτοὶ

---

^a The pool of Siloam at the south-east extremity of the
city.
^b *i.e.* without passing the stone balustrade or parapet
(δρύφακτος, *soreg*), which separated the outer from the inner

They indeed, being men of position, and as owners of property desirous of peace, understood the benevolent intention of the king's reprimand. But the people of Jerusalem also came out to a distance of sixty furlongs from the city to welcome Agrippa and Neapolitanus ; the widows of the slain ran on in advance uttering piercing cries, and to their shrieks the people responded with lamentations, entreating Agrippa to succour them, and loudly declaiming to Neapolitanus all that they had suffered from Florus. When they entered the city the Jews showed them the *agora* a scene of desolation, and the houses plundered. Then, through the agency of Agrippa, they induced Neapolitanus to make the tour of the city as far as Siloam,[a] with a single attendant, in order to assure himself that the Jews were duly subordinate to all the Roman officials, Florus alone excepted, whom they hated for the excessive cruelty with which he had treated them. Having traversed the city and satisfied himself as to the amenable temper of the inhabitants, Neapolitanus went up to the Temple. Here he called the multitude together, highly commended them for their loyalty to the Romans and earnestly exhorted them to keep the peace ; then, after paying his devotions to the sanctuary of God from the permitted area,[b] he returned to Cestius.

(3) The Jewish populace now turning to the king and the chief priests pressed them to send an embassy to Nero to denounce Florus, and not to remain silent after so frightful a massacre, thereby leaving the Jews under the suspicion of revolt ; as they would be

The citizens press for an embassy to Nero.

court, entry to the latter being forbidden to Gentiles under pain of death (*B.* v. 193 f.).

κατάρξαι τῶν ὅπλων, εἰ μὴ φθάσαντες ἐνδείξαιντο
343 τὸν κατάρξαντα. φανεροὶ δ' ἦσαν οὐκ ἠρεμήσοντες,
εἰ τὴν πρεσβείαν τις ἀποκωλύοι.¹ Ἀγρίππᾳ δὲ
τὸ μὲν χειροτονεῖν Φλώρου κατηγόρους ἐπίφθονον,
τὸ περιιδεῖν δὲ Ἰουδαίους εἰς πόλεμον ἐκριπι-
344 σθέντας οὐδὲ² αὐτῷ λυσιτελὲς κατεφαίνετο. προσκαλεσάμενος δὲ εἰς τὸν ξυστὸν τὸ πλῆθος καὶ
παραστησάμενος ἐν περιόπτῳ τὴν ἀδελφὴν Βερνίκην ἐπὶ τῆς Ἀσαμωναίων οἰκίας, αὕτη γὰρ ἦν
ἐπάνω τοῦ ξυστοῦ πρὸς τὸ πέραν τῆς ἄνω πόλεως,
καὶ γέφυρα τῷ ξυστῷ τὸ ἱερὸν συνῆπτεν, Ἀγρίππας ἔλεξεν τοιάδε.

345 (4) " Εἰ μὲν ἑώρων πάντας ὑμᾶς πολεμεῖν
Ῥωμαίοις ὡρμημένους καὶ μὴ τοῦ δήμου τὸ
καθαρώτατον καὶ εἰλικρινέστατον εἰρήνην ἄγειν
προῃρημένους, οὔτ' ἂν παρῆλθον εἰς ὑμᾶς οὔτε
συμβουλεύειν ἐθάρρησα· περισσὸς γὰρ ὑπὲρ τοῦ τὰ
δέοντα ποιεῖν πᾶς λόγος, ὅταν ᾖ τῶν ἀκουόντων
346 πάντων πρὸς τὸ χεῖρον ὁμόνοια. ἐπεὶ δὲ τινὰς
μὲν ἡλικία τῶν ἐν πολέμῳ κακῶν ἀπείρατος, τινὰς
δὲ ἐλπὶς ἀλόγιστος ἐλευθερίας, ἐνίους δὲ πλεονεξία

¹ ἀποκωλύει PAM.   ² C: οὔτε the rest.

ᵃ The meaning of πρὸς τὸ πέραν τῆς ἄνω πόλεως is uncertain; Reinach renders "et sa façade regardait les
terrains qui font vis-à-vis à la ville haute."

ᵇ The Xystus, perhaps the gymnasium originally built by
Jason (2 Macc. iv. 9), was a place of exercise, apparently
mainly open to the air, with "polished" flag-stones from
which it took its name. Its exact position is uncertain;
it seems to have lain on the lower slopes of the western hill
(the upper city) above the Tyropoeon valley, which separated
the west and the east hills, or (G. A. Smith) in the valley
itself. The palace of the Hasmonaeans was to the west of it,
higher up the western hill; in this palace Agrippa I had

regarded as having commenced hostilities, unless
prompt measures were taken to denounce the real
aggressor. It was clear that they did not intend to
submit quietly to any opposition to the proposed
embassy. Agrippa saw how odious would be the
task of electing a body to accuse Florus, but realized
also the danger, even to himself, of letting the flames
now smouldering in Jewish breasts break out into
war. He, accordingly, summoned the people to the
Xystus and placed his sister Bernice in a commanding
position on the roof of the palace of the Hasmonaeans,
which stood above the Xystus on the opposite side
of the upper town *a* ; the Xystus was connected with
the Temple by a bridge.*b* Agrippa then delivered
the following speech *c* :—

(4) " Had I found you all bent on war with the
Romans, instead of seeing that the most honest and
single-minded members of the community are determined to preserve the peace, I should not have
presented myself before you, nor ventured to offer
advice ; for any speech in support of the right policy
is thrown away when the audience unanimously
favours the worse. But seeing that the stimulus to
war is for some of you mere youthfulness which lacks
experience of its horrors, for others an unreflecting
hope of regaining independence, for yet others

Speech of
Agrippa to
dissuade the
Jews from
war.

constructed an apartment which commanded a view of the
interior of the Temple (*A.* xx. 189 f.).

c On the accuracy of the information given in the following
speech, and apparently derived from some official source,
monographs have been written by Friedländer, *De fonte quo
Josephus*, B.J. ii. 16. 4, *usus sit* (Königsberg, 1873), and
Domaszewski, "Die Dislokation des römischen Heeres im
Jahre 66 n. Chr." (*Rheinisches Museum*, 1892, pp. 207-218).
I owe these references to Drs. Th. Reinach and E. Schürer.

τις παροξύνει καὶ τὸ παρὰ τῶν ἀσθενεστέρων, ἐὰν
τὰ πράγματα συγχυθῇ, κέρδος, ὅπως αὐτοί τε
σωφρονισθέντες μεταβάλωνται καὶ μὴ τῆς ἐνίων
κακοβουλίας οἱ ἀγαθοὶ παραπολαύσωσιν, ᾠήθην
δεῖν ἐπὶ τὸ αὐτὸ πάντας ὑμᾶς συναγαγὼν εἰπεῖν
347 ἃ νομίζω συμφέρειν. θορυβήσῃ δέ μοι μηδείς,
ἐὰν μὴ τὰ πρὸς ἡδονὴν ἀκούῃ· τοῖς μὲν γὰρ ἀνηκέστως ἐπὶ τὴν ἀπόστασιν ὡρμημένοις ἔνεστι καὶ
μετὰ τὴν ἐμὴν παραίνεσιν ταὐτὰ φρονεῖν, ἐμοὶ δὲ
διαπίπτει καὶ πρὸς τοὺς ἀκούειν ἐθέλοντας ὁ λόγος,
348 ἐὰν μὴ παρὰ πάντων ἡσυχία γένηται. οἶδα μὲν
οὖν ὅτι πολλοὶ τὰς ἐκ τῶν ἐπιτρόπων ὕβρεις καὶ
τὰ τῆς ἐλευθερίας ἐγκώμια τραγῳδοῦσιν, ἐγὼ
δὲ πρὶν ἐξετάζειν τίνες ὄντες τίσιν ἐπιχειρεῖτε
πολεμεῖν, πρῶτον διαζεύξω τὴν συμπλοκὴν τῶν
349 προφάσεων. εἰ μὲν γὰρ ἀμύνεσθε τοὺς ἀδικοῦντας,
τί σεμνύνετε τὴν ἐλευθερίαν; εἰ δὲ τὸ δουλεύειν
ἀφόρητον ἡγεῖσθε, περισσὴ πρὸς τοὺς ἡγεμόνας ἡ
μέμψις· καὶ γὰρ ἐκείνων μετριαζόντων αἰσχρὸν
350 ὁμοίως τὸ δουλεύειν. σκοπεῖτε δὲ καὶ καθ᾽ ἕκαστον τούτων ὡς ἔστιν μικρὰ τοῦ πολεμεῖν ἡ ὑπόθεσις, καὶ πρῶτά γε τὰ τῶν ἐπιτρόπων ἐγκλήματα.
θεραπεύειν γάρ, οὐκ ἐρεθίζειν χρὴ τὰς ἐξουσίας·
351 ὅταν δὲ τῶν μικρῶν ἁμαρτημάτων τοὺς ἐξονει-
δισμοὺς ποιῆσθε μεγάλους, καθ᾽ ἑαυτῶν τοὺς
458

perhaps avarice and the prospect of enriching themselves at the expense of the weak in the event of a
general convulsion, I, in order to bring these mis-
guided persons to reason and a better frame of mind,
and to prevent virtuous citizens from reaping the
consequences of the errors of a few, have thought it
my duty to call you all together and to tell you what
I conceive to be to your interest. If my remarks are
not to the liking of any of my audience, pray let him
not create a disturbance. For those who have irre-
vocably determined to rebel will still be at liberty,
after my exhortation, to retain their sentiments ;
but my words will be lost even upon those who are
anxious to hear them, unless you all give me a quiet
hearing.

"Now, I know that there are many who wax
eloquent on the insolence of the procurators and
pronounce pompous panegyrics on liberty ; but, for
my part, before examining who you are and who are
this people whom you are undertaking to fight, I
would first consider apart two distinct pretexts for
hostilities which have been confused. For, if your
object is to have your revenge for injustice, what
good is it to extol liberty ? If, on the other hand,
it is servitude which you find intolerable, to complain
of your rulers is superfluous ; were they the most
considerate of men, servitude would be equally
disgraceful.

"Consider then these arguments apart and how
weak, on either ground, are your reasons for going to
war ; and first the charges against the procurators.
The powers that be should be conciliated by flattery,
not irritated ; when you indulge in exaggerated
reproaches for minor errors, you only injure your-

*Your
motives for
war are
mixed.*

*(i) Your
accusations
against
individual
Roman pro-
curators do
not justify
war with
Rome.*

ὀνειδιζομένους ἀπελέγχετε, καὶ παρέντες τὸ λάθρα
καὶ μετ᾽ αἰδοῦς ὑμᾶς βλάπτειν πορθοῦσι φανερῶς.
οὐδὲν δὲ οὕτως τὰς πληγὰς ὡς τὸ φέρειν ἀνα-
στέλλει, καὶ τὸ τῶν ἀδικουμένων ἡσύχιον τοῖς
352 ἀδικοῦσι γίνεται διατροπή. φέρε δ᾽ εἶναι τοὺς
Ῥωμαίων ὑπηρέτας ἀνηκέστως χαλεπούς· οὔπω
Ῥωμαῖοι πάντες ἀδικοῦσιν ὑμᾶς οὐδὲ Καῖσαρ,
πρὸς οὓς αἴρεσθε¹ τὸν πόλεμον· οὐδὲ γὰρ ἐξ
ἐντολῆς ἥκει τις πονηρὸς ἀπ᾽ ἐκείνων, οὐδέ γε
τοὺς ὑπὸ τὴν ἀνατολὴν οἱ ἀφ᾽ ἑσπέρας ἐπιβλέ-
πουσιν· ἀλλ᾽ οὐδ᾽ ἀκούειν ταχέως τὰ ἐντεῦθεν ἐκεῖ
353 ῥάδιον. ἄτοπον δὲ καὶ δι᾽ ἕνα πολλοῖς καὶ διὰ
354 μικρὰς αἰτίας τηλικούτοις καὶ μηδὲ γινώσκουσιν
ἃ μεμφόμεθα πολεμεῖν. καὶ τῶν μὲν ἡμετέρων
ἐγκλημάτων ταχεῖα γένοιτ᾽ ἂν [ἡ]² διόρθωσις·
οὔτε γὰρ ὁ αὐτὸς ἐπίτροπος μενεῖ³ διὰ παντός, καὶ
τοὺς διαδεξομένους εἰκὸς ἐλεύσεσθαι μετριωτέρους·
κινηθέντα δ᾽ ἅπαξ τὸν πόλεμον οὔτ᾽ ἀποθέσθαι
355 ῥάδιον δίχα συμφορῶν οὔτε βαστάζειν. ἀλλὰ μὴν
τό γε νῦν ἐλευθερίας ἐπιθυμεῖν ἄωρον, δέον ὑπὲρ
τοῦ μηδὲ ἀποβαλεῖν αὐτὴν ἀγωνίζεσθαι πρότερον.
ἡ γὰρ πεῖρα τῆς δουλείας χαλεπή, καὶ περὶ τοῦ
356 μηδ᾽ ἄρξασθαι ταύτης ὁ ἀγὼν δίκαιος· ὁ δ᾽ ἅπαξ
χειρωθείς, ἔπειτα ἀφιστάμενος, αὐθάδης δοῦλός
ἐστιν, οὐ φιλελεύθερος. τότε τοιγαροῦν ἐχρῆν
πάνθ᾽ ὑπὲρ τοῦ μὴ δέξασθαι Ῥωμαίους ποιεῖν,
357 ὅτε⁴ ἐπέβαινεν τῆς χώρας Πομπήιος. ἀλλ᾽ οἱ μὲν
ἡμέτεροι⁵ πρόγονοι καὶ οἱ βασιλεῖς αὐτῶν, καὶ

---

¹ Cobet (cf. e.g. B. ii. 638): αἱρεῖσθε mss.
² om. PAL.   ³ μένει PAL.
⁴ +τὴν ἀρχὴν MVRC.   ⁵ ὑμέτεροι AL Lat.

ᵃ Or "turns the wrongdoer aside."

selves by your denunciation of those whom you
incriminate ; instead of maltreating you, as before,
in secret and with a sense of shame, they will now
despoil you openly. There is nothing to check
blows like submission, and the resignation of the
wronged victim puts the wrongdoer to confusion.[a]
Granted that the Roman ministers are intolerably
harsh, it does not follow that all the Romans are
unjust to you any more than Caesar ; yet it is against
them, against him, that you are going to war. It is
not by their orders that an oppressive governor
comes from them to us, and they cannot see in the
west their officers in the east ; it is not easy even
promptly to hear yonder the news from these parts.
How absurd it were, because of one man to make war
on a whole people, for trifling grievances to take arms
against so mighty a power, which does not even
know the nature of our complaints ! The wrongs
which we lay to their charge may be speedily rectified;
for the same procurator will not remain for ever, and
it is probable that the successors of this one will show
greater moderation on taking office. But war once
set on foot cannot be lightly either broken off or
carried through without risk of disaster.

" Passing to your present passion for liberty, I say
that it comes too late. The time is past when you
ought to have striven never to lose it. For servitude
is a painful experience and a struggle to avoid it once
for all is just ; but the man who having once accepted
the yoke then tries to cast it off is a contumacious
slave, not a lover of liberty. There was, to be sure,
a time when you should have strained every nerve to
keep out the Romans ; that was when Pompey
invaded this country. But our forefathers and their

(ii) Your
passion for
independ-
ence is
belated.

461

χρήμασιν καὶ σώμασιν καὶ ψυχαῖς ἄμεινον ὑμῶν
πολλῷ διακείμενοι, πρὸς μοῖραν ὀλίγην τῆς Ῥωμαίων δυνάμεως οὐκ ἀντέσχον· ὑμεῖς δὲ οἱ τὸ μὲν
ὑπακούειν ἐκ διαδοχῆς παρειληφότες, τοῖς πράγμασιν δὲ τῶν πρώτων ὑπακουσάντων τοσοῦτον
ἐλαττούμενοι, πρὸς ὅλην ἀνθίστασθε τὴν Ῥωμαίων
358 ἡγεμονίαν; καὶ Ἀθηναῖοι μὲν οἱ περὶ τῆς τῶν
Ἑλλήνων ἐλευθερίας παραδόντες ποτὲ καὶ πυρὶ
τὴν πόλιν, οἱ τὸν ὑπερήφανον Ξέρξην διὰ γῆς
πλεύσαντα καὶ διὰ θαλάσσης ὁδεύσαντα καὶ μὴ
χωρούμενον μὲν τοῖς πελάγεσι, πλατυτέραν δὲ
τῆς Εὐρώπης τὴν στρατιὰν ἄγοντα, οἷα δραπέτην
ἐπὶ μιᾶς νεὼς διώξαντες, περὶ δὲ τῇ σμικρᾷ
Σαλαμῖνι τὴν τοσαύτην Ἀσίαν κλάσαντες νῦν
δουλεύουσιν Ῥωμαίοις, καὶ τὴν ἡγεμονίδα τῆς
Ἑλλάδος πόλιν διοικεῖ τὰ ἀπὸ τῆς Ἰταλίας προσ-
359 τάγματα. Λακεδαιμόνιοι δὲ μετὰ Θερμοπύλας
καὶ Πλαταιὰς καὶ τὸν ἐρευνήσαντα τὴν Ἀσίαν
360 Ἀγησίλαον ἀγαπῶσιν τοὺς αὐτοὺς δεσπότας, καὶ
Μακεδόνες ἔτι φανταζόμενοι Φίλιππον καὶ τὴν
σὺν Ἀλεξάνδρῳ παρασπείρουσαν¹ αὐτοῖς τὴν τῆς
οἰκουμένης ἡγεμονίαν ὁρῶντες, φέρουσιν τὴν τοσαύτην μεταβολὴν καὶ πρὸς οὓς μεταβέβηκεν ἡ τύχη
361 προσκυνοῦσιν. ἄλλα τε ἔθνη μυρία πλείονος γέμοντα πρὸς ἐλευθερίαν παρρησίας εἴκει. μόνοι δ᾽
ὑμεῖς ἀδοξεῖτε δουλεύειν οἷς ὑποτέτακται τὰ πάντα;

¹ Dindorf's conjecture παρασπαίρουσαν is unnecessary;
the noun τύχην must be understood, but need not be
inserted, as it is by Destinon.

<hr />

ᵃ Alluding to the canal of Athos and the bridge across the
Hellespont.

ᵇ His campaigns in Asia against Tissaphernes and Phar-

kings, though in wealth and in vigour of body and soul far your superiors, yet failed to withstand a small fraction of the Roman army ; and will you, to whom thraldom is hereditary, you who in resources fall so far short of those who first tendered their submission, will you, I say, defy the whole Roman empire ?

" Look at the Athenians, the men who, to maintain the liberty of Greece, once consigned their city to the flames ; the men before whose pursuit the haughty Xerxes, who navigated the land and trod the sea,[a] Xerxes for whom the deep was too narrow and whose army overflowed Europe, fled like a fugitive slave on a single galley ; the men who, off the coast of little Salamis, broke the immense might of Asia. Those men today are the servants of the Romans and the city that was queen of Greece is governed by orders from Italy. Look at the Lacedaemonians : after Thermopylae and Plataea, after Agesilaus the explorer of Asia,[b] they are content to serve the same masters. Look at the Macedonians, who still cherish Philip in their imagination, still have before their eyes the vision of her [c] who with Alexander scattered broadcast for them the seeds of the empire of the world ; yet they submit to endure such a reversal of fate and bow before those to whom Fortune has transferred her favours. Myriads of other nations, swelling with greater pride in the assertion of their liberty, have yielded. And will you alone disdain to serve those to whom the universe is subject ?

Many great states have submitted to Rome:
(a) Athens,
(b) Sparta,
(c) Macedon.

nabazus in 396–394 B.C. were cut short by his recall to war at home.

[c] The goddess Fortune.

ποίᾳ στρατιᾷ, ποίοις πεποιθότες ὅπλοις; ποῦ
μὲν ὁ στόλος ὑμῖν διαληψόμενος τὰς Ῥωμαίων θα-
λάσσας; ποῦ δ᾽ οἱ ταῖς ἐπιβολαῖς ἐξαρκέσοντες
362 θησαυροί; πρὸς Αἰγυπτίους ἄρα καὶ πρὸς Ἄραβας
οἴεσθε κινεῖν τὸν πόλεμον; οὐ περισκέψεσθε τὴν
Ῥωμαίων ἡγεμονίαν; οὐ μετρήσετε τὴν ἑαυτῶν
ἀσθένειαν; οὐ τὰ μὲν ἡμέτερα[1] καὶ τῶν προσοίκων
ἐθνῶν ἡττήθη πολλάκις, ἡ δὲ ἐκείνων ἰσχὺς διὰ
363 τῆς οἰκουμένης ἀνίκητος; μᾶλλον δὲ καὶ ταύτης
ἐζήτησάν τι πλέον. οὐ γὰρ ἐξήρκεσεν αὐτοῖς ὅρος[2]
Εὐφράτης ὑπὸ τὴν ἀνατολήν, οὐδὲ τῶν προσ-
αρκτίων ὁ Ἴστρος, ἥ τε μεσημβρινὴ μέχρι τῶν
ἀοικήτων ἐρευνηθεῖσα Λιβύη καὶ Γάδειρα πρὸς
ἑσπέραν, ἀλλ᾽ ὑπὲρ ὠκεανὸν ἑτέραν ἐζήτησαν
οἰκουμένην καὶ μέχρι τῶν ἀνιστορήτων πρότερον
364 Βρεττανῶν διήνεγκαν τὰ ὅπλα. τί οὖν; ὑμεῖς
πλουσιώτεροι Γαλατῶν, ἰσχυρότεροι Γερμανῶν,
Ἑλλήνων συνετώτεροι, πλείους τῶν κατὰ τὴν
οἰκουμένην ἐστὲ πάντων; τί τὸ πεποιθὸς ὑμᾶς
365 κατὰ Ῥωμαίων ἐπαίρει; χαλεπὸν τὸ δουλεύειν,
ἐρεῖ τις. πόσῳ μᾶλλον Ἕλλησιν, οἳ τῶν ὑφ᾽ ἡλίῳ
πάντων προύχοντες εὐγενείᾳ[3] καὶ τοσαύτην νεμόμενοι χώραν ἐξ Ῥωμαίων ὑπείκουσιν ῥάβδοις,
τοσαύταις δὲ καὶ Μακεδόνες οἱ δικαιότερον ὑμῶν
366 ὀφείλοντες ἐλευθερίας ἀντιποιεῖσθαι. τί δ᾽ αἱ

---

[1] ὑμέτερα MLC Lat.   [2] Niese, Destinon : ὅλος mss.
[3] προύχοντες εὐγενείᾳ P : προύχειν εὐγενείᾳ δοκοῦντες καὶ ὄντες
A : προύχειν εὐγενείᾳ (or εὐγ. προυχ.) δοκοῦντες the rest.

---

[a] The Danube.   [b] Greek "Gadeira"; Cadiz.

" What are the troops, what is the armour, on ^{Contrast} which you rely ? Where is your fleet to sweep the Roman seas ? Where is your treasury to meet the cost of your campaigns ? Do you really suppose that you are going to war with Egyptians or Arabs ? Will you shut your eyes to the might of the Roman empire and refuse to take the measure of your own weakness ? Have not our forces been constantly defeated even by the neighbouring nations, while theirs have never met with a reverse throughout the whole known world ? Nay, even that world has not sufficed for their ambition. For, not content with having for their frontiers on the east the Euphrates, on the north the Ister,^a on the south Libya explored into desert regions, on the west Gades,^b they have sought a new world beyond the ocean and carried their arms as far as the Britons, previously unknown to history. I ask you, then, are you wealthier than the Gauls, stronger than the Germans, more intelligent than the Greeks, more numerous than all the peoples of the world ? What is it which inspires you with confidence to defy the Romans ?

" ' It is hard to serve,' you will tell me. How much harder for Greeks who, though noblest of all races under the sun and occupants of so vast a territory, are yet subservient to six rods of a Roman magistrate ^c ! A like number suffices to curb the Macedonians,^d who with better right than you might claim their liberty. And then the five hundred cities

Contrast your lack of resources with the might of the Roman Empire.

Other nations besides Greece and Macedon have bowed to Rome,

^c The lictor's *fasces*. Achaea, since 27 B.C. (except under Tiberius, when it was an imperial province, and for a short period under Nero, when Greece was proclaimed free) was a senatorial province governed by a proconsul of praetorian rank, who was attended by six lictors.

^d Another senatorial province.

465

πεντακόσιαι τῆς Ἀσίας πόλεις; οὐ δίχα φρουρᾶς
ἕνα προσκυνοῦσιν ἡγεμόνα καὶ τὰς ὑπατικὰς
ῥάβδους; τί χρὴ λέγειν Ἡνιόχους τε καὶ Κόλχους
καὶ τὸ τῶν Ταύρων φῦλον, Βοσπορανούς τε καὶ
τὰ περίοικα τοῦ Πόντου καὶ τῆς Μαιώτιδος ἔθνη;
367 παρ᾽ οἷς πρὶν μὲν οὐδ᾽ οἰκεῖος ἐγιγνώσκετο
δεσπότης, νῦν δὲ τρισχιλίοις ὁπλίταις ὑποτάσ-
σεται, καὶ τεσσαράκοντα νῆες μακραὶ τὴν πρὶν
368 ἄπλωτον καὶ ἀγρίαν εἰρηνεύουσι θάλασσαν. πόσα
Βιθυνία καὶ Καππαδοκία καὶ τὸ Παμφύλιον ἔθνος
Λύκιοί τε καὶ Κίλικες ὑπὲρ ἐλευθερίας ἔχοντες
εἰπεῖν χωρὶς ὅπλων φορολογοῦνται; τί δαί; Θρᾷκες
οἱ πέντε μὲν εὖρος, ἑπτὰ δὲ μῆκος ἡμερῶν χώραν
διειληφότες, τραχυτέραν τε καὶ πολλῷ τῆς ὑμετέρας
ὀχυρωτέραν καὶ βαθεῖ κρυμῷ τοὺς ἐπιστρατεύ-
σοντας[1] ἀνακόπτουσαν, οὐχὶ δισχιλίοις Ῥωμαίων
369 ὑπακούουσιν φρουροῖς; οἱ δ᾽ ἀπὸ τούτων Ἰλλυριοὶ
τὴν μέχρι Δαλματίας ἀποτεμνομένην Ἴστρῳ κατ-
οικοῦντες, οὐ δυσὶν μόνοις τάγμασιν ὑπείκουσιν,
μεθ᾽ ὧν αὐτοὶ τὰς Δακῶν ἀνακόπτουσιν ὁρμάς;
370 οἱ δὲ τοσαυτάκις πρὸς ἐλευθερίαν ἀναχαιτίσαντες
Δαλμάται καὶ πρὸς μόνον ἀεὶ χειρωθέντες τὸ

---

[1] PL: ἐπιστρατεύοντας or -εύσαντας the rest.

[a] The number agrees with that named by Philostratus
(*Lives of Sophists*, ii. 1. 4) ; the geographer Ptolemy reckons
only 140 (Reinach). Asia was senatorial with a governor of
consular rank.

[b] The Colchians, of whom the Heniochi were a tribe, were
settled on the east and south-east of the Black Sea.

[c] Inhabiting the Tauric Chersonese, the modern Crimea.

[d] The sea of Azov.

of Asia [a]: do they not, without a garrison, bow (d) Asia,
before a single governor and the consular *fasces*?
Need I speak of the Heniochi, the Colchians,[b]
the race of the Taurians,[c] the people of the Bos-
phorus, the nations bordering on the Euxine and
Lake Maeotis [d]? These peoples, who formerly
recognized no master, not even one from their own
ranks, are now in subjection to three thousand
soldiers, while forty battle-ships bring peace to that
once unnavigated and savage sea.[e] What strong
claims to liberty might be advanced by Bithynia,
Cappadocia, the Pamphylian nation, Lycians and
Cilicians? Yet they pay their tribute without resort
to arms.[f] Then, what of the Thracians, who are (e) Thrace,
spread over a country five days' march in breadth
and seven in length, a country more rugged and far
stronger than your own, the rigour of whose icy
climate repels an invader: do they not obey the
orders of two thousand Roman guards? [g] The
Illyrians, their neighbours, who inhabit the region (f) Illyria,
extending from Dalmatia to the frontier of the Ister,
are they not kept in check by no more than two
legions,[h] with whom they themselves unite to repel
the incursions of the Dacians? The Dalmatians, (g) Dalmatia,
too, who have so often reared their heads [i] for liberty,

[e] The numbers of troops and ships here mentioned cannot
be checked; the military occupation of these districts appears
to date from the annexation of the kingdom of Pontus on
the deposition of Polemon II c. A.D. 63.

[f] Or perhaps " without constraint of arms " (Reinach).

[g] Detached from the two legions stationed in Moesia;
Thrace, after several risings, was finally converted into a
Roman province in 46 A.D.

[h] The two legions of Moesia (not Illyria) are intended:
viz. VIII Augusta and VII Claudia (Tac. *Hist.* ii. 85).

[i] Greek " manes."

συλλεξάμενοι[1] τὴν ἰσχὺν πάλιν ἀποστῆναι, νῦν οὐχ
371 ὑφ' ἑνὶ τάγματι Ῥωμαίων ἡσυχίαν ἄγουσιν; ἀλλὰ
μὴν εἴ γέ τινας εἰς ἀπόστασιν ὤφειλον ἀφορμαὶ
μεγάλαι παροξύνειν, μάλιστα Γαλάτας ἐχρῆν, τοὺς
οὕτως ὑπὸ τῆς φύσεως τετειχισμένους, ἐξ ἀνατολῆς
μὲν ταῖς Ἄλπεσιν, πρὸς ἄρκτῳ δὲ Ῥήνῳ ποταμῷ,
μεσημβρινοῖς δὲ τοῖς Πυρηναίοις ὄρεσιν, ὠκεανῷ
372 δὲ πρὸς δυσμῶν.[2] ἀλλὰ καίτοι τηλικαῦτα μὲν
ἕρκη περιβεβλημένοι, πέντε δὲ καὶ τριακοσίοις
πληθύοντες ἔθνεσιν, τὰς δὲ πηγάς, ὡς ἄν τις εἴποι,
τῆς εὐδαιμονίας ἐπιχωρίους ἔχοντες καὶ τοῖς ἀγαθοῖς σχεδὸν ὅλην ἐπικλύζοντες τὴν οἰκουμένην,
ἀνέχονται Ῥωμαίων πρόσοδος ὄντες καὶ ταμιευό-
373 μενοι παρ' αὐτῶν τὴν οἰκείαν εὐδαιμονίαν. καὶ
τοῦθ' ὑπομένουσιν οὐ διὰ φρονημάτων μαλακίαν,
οὐδὲ δι' ἀγένειαν, οἵ γε διήνεγκαν ὀγδοήκοντα ἔτη
πόλεμον ὑπὲρ τῆς ἐλευθερίας, ἀλλὰ μετὰ τῆς
δυνάμεως Ῥωμαίων καὶ τὴν τύχην καταπλαγέντες,
ἥτις αὐτοῖς κατορθοῖ πλείονα τῶν ὅπλων. τοιγαροῦν ὑπὸ χιλίοις καὶ διακοσίοις στρατιώταις
δουλεύουσιν, ὧν ὀλίγου δεῖν πλείους ἔχουσι πόλεις.
374 οὐδὲ Ἴβηρσιν ὁ γεωργούμενος χρυσὸς εἰς τὸν ὑπὲρ
τῆς ἐλευθερίας ἐξήρκεσεν πόλεμον, οὐδὲ τὸ τοσοῦτον ἀπὸ Ῥωμαίων γῆς καὶ θαλάσσης διάστημα,

---

[1] Text emended by Niese: πρὸς τὸ μόνον ἀεὶ χειρ. τότε
συλλεξ. mss.
[2] δυσμαῖς MVRC.

---

[a] Apparently XI Claudia (cf. Tac. Hist. iii. 50).
[b] 400 according to Appian, Celt. i. 2, 300 according to
Plutarch, Caes. 15; the "nations" intended are the pagi or
"cantons," a subdivision of the civitates (Reinach).
[c] From the campaign of M. Fulvius Flaccus (125 B.C.),
which led to the foundation of the Provincia Narbonensis,

whose constant defeats have only led them to muster
their forces for a fresh revolt, do they not now live
in peace under a single Roman legion [a] ?

" But if there is one people above all others which (h) Gaul,
should be tempted by its grand opportunities to raise
the standard of revolt, it is surely the Gauls with their
magnificent natural ramparts, on the east the Alps,
on the north the river Rhine, on the south the chain
of the Pyrenees, on the west the ocean.   But, though
encompassed by such formidable barriers, though
swarming with a population of three hundred and
five nations,[b] possessing, so to say, in their native
soil the springs of prosperity and irrigating well-nigh
the whole world with the overflow of their products,
the Gauls are yet content to be treated as a source
of revenue to the Romans and to have their own
prosperous fortune meted out to them at their hands.
And this they tolerate, not from any lack of spirit or
because they are an ignoble race, they who for full
eighty years [c] fought for their independence, but
because they are overawed at once by the power of
Rome and by her fortune, which brings her more
triumphs even than her arms.   That is why they
submit to the orders of twelve hundred soldiers,[d]
they who have cities enough almost to outmatch that
number.[e]   Then the Iberians—neither the gold (i) Spain,|
which their soil produces, nor the vast extent of land
and sea which separates them from the Romans, nor

up to the end of Caesar's campaigns was a period of about
seventy-five years.
    [d] Two *cohortes urbanae* established at Lyons, one of which
(the eighteenth) is mentioned in Tac. *Hist.* i. 64, and the
other (the seventeenth) in an inscription, Mommsen, *Hermes*,
xvi. 645 (Reinach).
    [e] " More than 800 cities " (App. *Celt.* i. 2 ; Plut. *Caes.* 15),

φῦλά τε Λουσιτανῶν καὶ Καντάβρων ἀρειμάνια,
οὐδὲ γείτων ὠκεανὸς φοβερὰν καὶ τοῖς ἐπιχωρίοις
375 ἄμπωτιν ἐπάγων, ἀλλ᾽ ὑπὲρ τὰς Ἡρακλείους στή-
λας ἐκτείναντες τὰ ὅπλα καὶ διὰ νεφῶν ὁδεύ-
σαντες τὰ Πυρηναῖα¹ ὅρη, καὶ τούτους ἐδουλώσαντο Ῥωμαῖοι· φρουρὰ δ᾽ ἤρκεσεν τῶν οὕτως
δυσμάχων καὶ τοσοῦτον ἀπῳκισμένων ἓν τάγμα.
376 τίς ὑμῶν οὐκ ἀκοῇ παρείληφεν τὸ Γερμανῶν
πλῆθος; ἀλκὴν μὲν γὰρ καὶ μεγέθη σωμάτων
εἴδετε δήπου πολλάκις, ἐπεὶ πανταχοῦ Ῥωμαῖοι
377 τοὺς τούτων αἰχμαλώτους ἔχουσιν. ἀλλ᾽ οὗτοι
γῆν μὲν ἄπειρον νεμόμενοι, μείζω δὲ τῶν σωμάτων
ἔχοντες τὰ φρονήματα καὶ τὴν μὲν ψυχὴν θανάτου
καταφρονοῦσαν, τοὺς δὲ θυμοὺς τῶν ἀγριωτάτων
θηρίων σφοδροτέρους, Ῥῆνον τῆς ὁρμῆς ὅρον
ἔχουσιν καὶ Ῥωμαίων ὀκτὼ τάγμασιν δαμαζό-
μενοι δουλεύουσιν μὲν ἁλόντες, τὸ δ᾽ ὅλον αὐτῶν
378 ἔθνος φυγῇ διασώζεται. σκέψασθε δὲ καὶ τὸ
Βρεττανῶν τεῖχος οἱ τοῖς Ἱεροσολύμων τείχεσιν
πεποιθότες· καὶ γὰρ ἐκείνους περιβεβλημένους
ὠκεανὸν καὶ τῆς καθ᾽ ἡμᾶς οἰκουμένης οὐκ ἐλάσ-
σονα νῆσον οἰκοῦντας πλεύσαντες ἐδουλώσαντο
Ῥωμαῖοι, τέσσαρα δὲ τάγματα τὴν τοσαύτην
379 νῆσον φυλάσσει. καὶ τί δεῖ πολλὰ λέγειν, ὅπου

¹ Πυρηνίων PAM.

---

[a] VI Victrix, the legion which proclaimed Galba emperor
(Tac. *Hist.* v. 16; Suet. *Galba*, 10).

[b] Four in Upper, four in Lower Germany. In A.D. 69
(when the upper army numbered only three) the seven
legions were IV, XXI, XXII; I, V, XV, XVI. The eighth

the tribes of the Lusitanians and Cantabrians with
their fever for war, nor the neighbouring ocean, the
ebb and flow of whose tides terrifies the very inhabitants, none of these sufficed in their struggle for
independence ; no, the Romans carrying their arms
beyond the Pillars of Hercules, traversing through
clouds the mountains of the Pyrenees, have reduced
even them to servitude ; to guard this nation of
fighters, so stubborn, so remote, a single legion now
suffices.[a] Which of you has not heard tell of the
horde of Germans ? Nay, you have surely often seen (j) Germany
their stalwart and burly figures, for the Romans have
captives from that nation everywhere. This people
occupies an immense country, their hearts are even
greater than their stature, their souls disdainful of
death, their rage fiercer than that of the most savage
of beasts ; yet the Rhine sets a bound to their impetuosity and, tamed by eight Roman legions,[b] the
captured are reduced to slavery, while the rest of the
nation has found safety in flight. Again, consider
what a wall of defence had the Britons, you who put (k) Britain,
your trust in the walls of Jerusalem : the ocean
surrounds them, they inhabit an island no less in
extent than the part of the world in which we live ; [c]
yet the Romans crossed the sea and enslaved them,
and four legions [d] now secure that vast island. But

in A.D. 66 is thought to have been X Gemina. Mommsen,
Provinces, i. 118 f., 132, Domaszewski, *op. cit.* (§ 344 note).
  [c] *i.e.* Palestine. Or possibly ' the whole of our inhabited
continent ' ; for before Agricola's campaign of A.D. 84 the
Romans had a very imperfect conception of the size of
Britain (Merivale, *Romans under Empire*, vii. 90).
  [d] II Augusta, IX Hispana, XIV Gemina Martia Victrix
(recalled in 68), XX Valeria Victrix. Domaszewski, *op. cit.*,
cf. Mommsen, *Provinces*, i. 174, note 4.

καὶ Πάρθοι, τὸ πολεμικώτατον φῦλον, τοσούτων
ἄρχοντες ἐθνῶν καὶ τηλικαύτην περιβεβλημένοι
δύναμιν, ὁμήρους πέμπουσιν Ῥωμαίοις, καὶ ἔστιν
ἐπὶ τῆς Ἰταλίας ἰδεῖν ἐν εἰρήνης προφάσει δου-
380 λεύουσαν τὴν ἀπὸ τῆς ἀνατολῆς εὐγένειαν. πάντων δὴ σχεδὸν τῶν ὑφ᾽ ἡλίῳ τὰ Ῥωμαίων ὅπλα
προσκυνούντων ὑμεῖς μόνοι πολεμήσετε, μηδὲ τὸ
Καρχηδονίων τέλος σκοποῦντες, οἳ τὸν μέγαν
αὐχοῦντες Ἀννίβαν καὶ τὴν ἀπὸ Φοινίκων εὐ-
381 γένειαν ὑπὸ τὴν Σκιπίωνος δεξιὰν ἔπεσον; οὔτε δὲ
Κυρηναῖοι, τὸ Λακώνων γένος, οὔτε Μαρμαρίδαι,
τὸ μέχρι τῆς διψάδος ἐκτεταμένον φῦλον, οὔθ᾽ αἱ
φοβεραὶ καὶ τοῖς ἀκούουσιν Σύρτεις, Νασαμῶνές
τε καὶ Μαῦροι καὶ τὸ Νομάδων ἄπειρον πλῆθος
382 τὰς Ῥωμαίων ἀνέκοψαν ἀρετάς. τὴν δὲ τρίτην
τῆς οἰκουμένης μοῖραν, ἧς οὐδὲ ἐξαριθμήσασθαι
τὰ ἔθνη ῥᾴδιον, ὁριζομένην Ἀτλαντικῷ τε πελάγει
καὶ στήλαις Ἡρακλείοις καὶ μέχρι τῆς Ἐρυθρᾶς
θαλάσσης τοὺς ἀπείρους νέμουσαν Αἰθίοπας ἐχει-
383 ρώσαντο μὲν ὅλην, χωρὶς δὲ τῶν ἐτησίων καρπῶν,
οἳ μησὶν ὀκτὼ τὸ κατὰ τὴν Ῥώμην πλῆθος τρέ-
φουσιν, [καὶ][1] ἔξωθεν παντοίως φορολογοῦνται καὶ
ταῖς χρείαις τῆς ἡγεμονίας παρέχουσιν ἑτοίμους
τὰς εἰσφοράς, οὐδὲν τῶν ἐπιταγμάτων ὥσπερ
ὑμεῖς ὕβριν ἡγούμενοι, καίπερ ἑνὸς τάγματος
384 αὐτοῖς παραμένοντος. καὶ τί δεῖ πόρρωθεν ὑμῖν
τὴν Ῥωμαίων ὑποδεικνύναι δύναμιν, παρὸν ἐξ

¹ om. PAL.

---

[a] Reinach instances Tiridates I (king of Armenia and
brother of the king of Parthia), who in A.D. 63 did homage to
Nero and left his daughter in Rome as a hostage (Tac. *Ann.*
xv. 29 f.).

why enlarge, when the Parthians themselves, that (*l*) Parthia, race of finest warriors, lords of so many nations, provided with so vast an army, send hostages to the Romans, and the nobility of the east may be seen in Italy, under the pretext of peace, bending to the yoke ? [a]

" Thus, when almost every nation under the sun (*m*) does homage to the Roman arms, are you alone to Carthage, defy them, regardless of the fate of the Carthaginians, Cyrene, who, for all their pride in the great Hannibal and in tribes of the nobility of their Phoenician descent, fell beneath Africa, the hand of Scipio ? Neither Cyrenians, of Spartan breed, nor Marmaridae, that race that stretches to the regions of drought, nor Syrtes, whose very name strikes terror, Nasamons, Maurians, Numidians in their countless hosts, none have checked the valour of Rome. This third part of the inhabited world,[b] the mere enumeration of whose nations is no easy task, bounded by the Atlantic ocean and the pillars of Hercules, and supporting right up to the Red Sea Ethiopians innumerable, they have subdued it all ; and these peoples, besides their annual produce, which feeds for eight months of the year the populace of Rome, over and above this pay tribute of all kinds and ungrudgingly devote their contributions [c] to the service of the empire, far from seeing, as do you, an outrage in the orders which they receive, although but one legion [d] is quartered among them.

" But why seek so far afield for proofs of the power (*n*) Egypt of Rome, when I can find them at your very door, in and Alexandria.

---

[b] Africa.

[c] εἰσφορά in Attic Greek is a sort of super-tax.

[d] III Augusta, stationed in the senatorial or western portion of the province of Africa.

473

385 Αἰγύπτου τῆς γειτνιώσης, ἥτις ἐκτεινομένη μέχρις
Αἰθιόπων καὶ τῆς εὐδαίμονος Ἀραβίας, ὅρμος[1]
τε οὖσα τῆς Ἰνδικῆς, πεντήκοντα πρὸς ταῖς ἑπτα-
κοσίαις ἔχουσα μυριάδας ἀνθρώπων δίχα τῶν
Ἀλεξάνδρειαν κατοικούντων, ὡς ἔνεστιν ἐκ τῆς
καθ' ἑκάστην κεφαλὴν εἰσφορᾶς[2] τεκμήρασθαι, τὴν
Ῥωμαίων ἡγεμονίαν οὐκ ἀδοξεῖ, καίτοι πηλίκον
ἀποστάσεως κέντρον ἔχουσα τὴν Ἀλεξάνδρειαν
πλήθους τε ἀνδρῶν ἕνεκα καὶ πλούτου, πρὸς δὲ
386 μεγέθους· μῆκος μέν γε αὐτῆς τριάκοντα σταδίων,
εὖρος δ' οὐκ ἔλαττον δέκα, τοῦ δὲ ἐνιαυσιαίου
παρ' ὑμῶν φόρου καθ' ἕνα μῆνα πλέον Ῥωμαίοις
παρέχει καὶ τῶν χρημάτων ἔξωθεν τῇ Ῥώμῃ
σῖτον μηνῶν τεσσάρων· τετείχισται δὲ πάντοθεν
ἢ δυσβάτοις ἐρημίαις ἢ θαλάσσαις ἀλιμένοις ἢ
387 ποταμοῖς ἢ ἕλεσιν. ἀλλ' οὐδὲν τούτων ἰσχυρότερον εὑρέθη τῆς Ῥωμαίων τύχης, δύο δ' ἐγκαθ-
ήμενα τῇ πόλει τάγματα τὴν βαθεῖαν Αἴγυπτον
388 ἅμα τῇ Μακεδόνων εὐγενείᾳ χαλινοῖ. τίνας οὖν
ἐπὶ τὸν πόλεμον ἐκ τῆς ἀοικήτου παραλήψεσθε
συμμάχους; οἱ μὲν γὰρ ἐπὶ τῆς οἰκουμένης πάντες
εἰσὶν Ῥωμαῖοι, εἰ μή τις ὑπὲρ Εὐφράτην ἐκτείνει
τὰς ἐλπίδας καὶ τοὺς ἐκ τῆς Ἀδιαβηνῆς ὁμοφύλους
389 οἴεται προσαμυνεῖν.[3] οἱ δ' οὔτε δι' αἰτίαν ἄλογον

---

[1] ὅμορος VC Lat.   [2] συνεισφορᾶς P.
[3] Niese from Lat.: προσαμύνειν or ἐπαμύνειν mss.

---

[a] Diodorus Siculus, writing some seventy years earlier,
gives the population of Egypt as seven millions (i. 31,
Reinach), that of Alexandria as 300,000 (xvii. 52).

[b] Or, perhaps, " a centre for revolt."

[c] " Seven or eight," Strabo xvii. 1. 8 (Reinach) ; Strabo
agrees with Josephus as to the length.

Egypt? This country, which extends as far as
Ethiopia and Arabia Felix, which is the port for
India, which has a population of seven million five
hundred thousand souls,[a] exclusive of the inhabitants
of Alexandria, as may be estimated from the poll-
tax returns, this country, I say, does not disdain to
submit to Roman domination; and yet what an
incentive to revolt[b] she has in Alexandria, so popu-
lous, so wealthy, so vast! The length of that city
is thirty furlongs, its breadth not less than ten[c];
the tribute which she yields to Rome in one month
surpasses that which you pay in a year; besides
money she sends corn to feed Rome for four months;[d]
she is protected on all sides by trackless deserts, by
seas without ports, by rivers or lagoons. Yet none
of these assets proved a match for the fortune of
Rome, and two legions[e] stationed in the city curb
this far-reaching Egypt and the proud nobility of
Macedon.

"What allies then do you expect for this war?
Will you recruit them from the uninhabited wilds?
For in the habitable world all are Romans—unless,
maybe, the hopes of some of you soar beyond the
Euphrates and you count on obtaining aid from your
kinsmen in Adiabene.[f] But they will not, for any

You cannot expect aid from Jews beyond the Euphrates,

---

[d] The corn for the capital for the other eight months of the
year being furnished by Africa (§ 383).

[e] These in A.D. 69 were III and XXII (Tac. *Hist.* v. 1);
under Augustus there had been a third legion, Mommsen,
Provinces, ii. 273.

[f] Cf. *B.* i. 5 for these expectations. "Proselytes" would
have been a more correct term than "kinsmen"; the
dynasty of Adiabene, a region east of the Tigris on the
Parthian frontier, had under Claudius been converted to
Judaism (*A.* xx. 17 ff.). Some members of the royal family
fought on the side of the Jews (*B.* ii. 520, vi. 356).

τηλικούτῳ πολέμῳ συνεμπλέξουσιν ἑαυτούς, οὔτε
βουλευσαμένοις κακῶς ὁ Πάρθος ἐπιτρέψει· πρόνοια γὰρ αὐτῷ τῆς πρὸς Ῥωμαίους ἐκεχειρίας,
καὶ παραβαίνειν οἰήσεται τὰς σπονδάς, ἄν τις τῶν
390 ὑπ' αὐτὸν ἐπὶ Ῥωμαίους ἴῃ. λοιπὸν οὖν ἐπὶ τὴν
τοῦ θεοῦ συμμαχίαν καταφευκτέον. ἀλλὰ καὶ
τοῦτο παρὰ Ῥωμαίοις τέτακται· δίχα γὰρ θεοῦ
391 συστῆναι τηλικαύτην ἡγεμονίαν ἀδύνατον. σκέψασθε δ' ὡς ὑμῖν τὸ τῆς θρησκείας ἄκρατον, εἰ
καὶ πρὸς εὐχειρώτους πολεμοῖτε, δυσδιοίκητον,
καὶ δι' ἃ μᾶλλον τὸν θεὸν ἐλπίζετε σύμμαχον,
ταῦτ' ἀναγκαζόμενοι παραβαίνειν ἀποστρέψετε.
392 τηροῦντές γε μὴν τὰ τῶν ἑβδομάδων ἔθη καὶ
πρὸς μηδεμίαν πρᾶξιν κινούμενοι ῥᾳδίως ἁλώσεσθε,
καθάπερ οἱ πρόγονοι Πομπηΐῳ, ταύτας μάλιστα
τὰς ἡμέρας ἐνεργοὺς ποιησαμένῳ τῆς πολιορκίας,
393 ἐν αἷς ἤργουν οἱ πολιορκούμενοι· παραβαίνοντες δ'
ἐν τῷ πολέμῳ τὸν πάτριον νόμον οὐκ οἶδ' ὑπὲρ
ὅτου λοιπὸν ποιήσεσθε τὸν ἀγῶνα· σπουδὴ γὰρ
394 ὑμῖν μία τὸ μὴ τῶν πατρίων τι καταλῦσαι. πῶς
δ' ἐπικαλέσεσθε τὸ θεῖον πρὸς τὴν ἄμυναν οἱ
παραβάντες ἑκουσίως τὴν εἰς αὐτὸ θεραπείαν;
ἐπαναιροῦνται δὲ ἕκαστοι πόλεμον ἢ θείᾳ πεποιθότες ἢ ἀνθρωπίνῃ βοηθείᾳ· ὅταν δὲ τὴν παρ'
ἀμφοῖν τὸ εἰκὸς ἀποκόπτῃ, φανερὰν ἅλωσιν οἱ
395 πολεμοῦντες αἱροῦνται. τί δὴ κωλύει ταῖς ἑαυτῶν
χερσὶν διαχρήσασθαι τέκνα καὶ γυναῖκας καὶ τὴν
περικαλλεστάτην πατρίδα ταύτην καταφλέξαι; μα-

---

[a] *Cf. B.* i. 146; *A.* xiv. 63 ff.

frivolous pretext, let themselves be embroiled in so
serious a war, and, if they did contemplate such folly,
the Parthian would not permit it ; for he is careful
to maintain the truce with the Romans, and would
regard it as a violation of the treaty if any of his
tributaries were to march against them.

" The only refuge, then, left to you is divine assistance. But even this is ranged on the side of the
Romans, for, without God's aid, so vast an empire
could never have been built up. Consider, too, the
difficulty of preserving your religious rules from con-
tamination, even were you engaging a less formidable
foe ; and how, if compelled to transgress the very
principles on which you chiefly build your hopes of
God's assistance, you will alienate Him from you.
If you observe your sabbath customs and refuse to
take any action on that day, you will undoubtedly be
easily defeated, as were your forefathers by Pompey,
who pressed the siege most vigorously on the days
when the besieged remained inactive ; [a] if, on the
contrary, you transgress the law of your ancestors,
I fail to see what further object you will have for
hostilities, since your one aim is to preserve inviolate
all the institutions of your fathers. How could you
invoke the aid of the Deity, after deliberately
omitting to pay Him the service which you owe Him ?

" All who embark on war do so in reliance on the
support either of God or man ; but when, in all
probability, no assistance from either quarter is
forthcoming, then the aggressor goes with his eyes
open to certain ruin. What is there, then, to prevent
you from dispatching with your own hands your
children and wives and from consigning this sur-
passingly beautiful home of yours to the flames ?

nor from God, who is on the side of Rome.

Your religion will hamper you in war.

You have no allies ; be warned in time.

477

JOSEPHUS

νέντες γὰρ οὕτως τό γε τῆς ἥττης ὄνειδος κερ-
396 δήσετε. καλόν, ὦ φίλοι, καλόν, ἕως ἔτι ἐν ὅρμῳ
τὸ σκάφος, προσκέπτεσθαι[1] τὸν μέλλοντα χειμῶνα
μηδ' εἰς μέσας τὰς θυέλλας ἀπολουμένους[2] ἀναχθῆ-
ναι· τοῖς μὲν γὰρ ἐξ ἀδήλων ἐμπεσοῦσιν[3] δεινοῖς
τὸ γοῦν ἐλεεῖσθαι περίεστιν, ὁ δ' εἰς πρόδηλον
397 ἀπώλειαν ὁρμήσας καὶ προσονειδίζεται. πλὴν εἰ
μή τις ὑπολαμβάνει κατὰ συνθήκας πολεμήσειν
καὶ Ῥωμαίους κρατήσαντας ὑμῶν μετριάσειν, ἀλλ'
οὐκ εἰς ὑπόδειγμα τῶν ἄλλων ἐθνῶν καταφλέξειν
μὲν τὴν ἱερὰν πόλιν, ἀναιρήσειν δὲ πᾶν ὑμῶν τὸ
φῦλον· οὐδὲ γὰρ περιλειφθέντες φυγῆς εὑρήσετε
τόπον, ἁπάντων ἐχόντων Ῥωμαίους δεσπότας ἢ
398 δεδοικότων σχεῖν. ὁ δὲ κίνδυνος οὐ τῶν ἐνθάδε
μόνον, ἀλλὰ καὶ τῶν κατὰ τὰς ἄλλας κατοικούντων
πόλεις· οὐ γὰρ ἔστιν ἐπὶ τῆς οἰκουμένης δῆμος ὁ
399 μὴ μοῖραν ἡμετέραν ἔχων. οὓς ἅπαντας πολεμη-
σάντων ὑμῶν κατασφάξουσιν οἱ διάφοροι, καὶ δι'
ὀλίγων ἀνδρῶν κακοβουλίαν πᾶσα πλησθήσεται[4]
πόλις Ἰουδαϊκοῦ φόνου. καὶ συγγνώμη μὲν τοῖς
τοῦτο πράξασιν· ἂν δὲ μὴ πραχθῇ, λογίσασθε πῶς
πρὸς οὕτω φιλανθρώπους ὅπλα κινεῖν ἀνόσιον.
400 εἰσελθέτω δ' οἶκτος ὑμᾶς εἰ καὶ μὴ τέκνων καὶ
γυναικῶν, ἀλλὰ τῆς γε μητροπόλεως ταύτης καὶ
τῶν ἱερῶν περιβόλων. φείσασθε τοῦ ἱεροῦ καὶ
τὸν ναὸν ἑαυτοῖς μετὰ τῶν ἁγίων τηρήσατε· ἀφ-
έξονται γὰρ οὐκέτι Ῥωμαῖοι τούτων κρατήσαντες,

[1] περισκέπτεσθαι P.
[2] PA: ἀπολλυμένους L: ἀπὸ λιμένος MVRC (perhaps rightly).
[3] M: ἐπιπεσοῦσιν the rest.　　[4] P: πληρωθήσεται the rest.

By such an act of madness you would at least spare
yourselves the ignominy of defeat. It were well,
my friends, it were well, while the vessel is still in
port, to foresee the coming storm, and not to put
out into the midst of the hurricane to meet your
doom.[a] For to the victims of unforeseen disaster there
is left at least the meed of pity ; but he who rushes
to manifest destruction incurs opprobrium to boot.

" There may be some who imagine that the war will
be fought under special terms, and that the Romans,
when victorious, will treat you with consideration ;
on the contrary, to make you an example to the rest
of the nations, they will burn the holy city to the
ground and exterminate your race. Even the survivors will find no place of refuge, since all the peoples
of the earth either have, or dread the thought of
having, the Romans for their masters. The peril,
moreover, threatens not only us Jews here, but also
all who inhabit foreign cities ; for there is not a
people in the world which does not contain a portion
of our race.[b] All these, if you go to war, will be
butchered by your adversaries, and through the folly
of a handful of men every city will be drenched with
Jewish blood. Such massacre would be excusable ; but,
should it not take place, think what a crime it were
to take up arms against such humane opponents !
Take pity, then, if not on your children and your
wives, at least on your mother city and its sacred
precincts. Spare the temple and preserve for yourselves the sanctuary with its holy places [c] ; for the
Romans, once masters of these, will refrain their

[marginal note: Do not look for mercy; have pity on your race, your city and your Temple.*]*

---

[a] Or, with the other reading, " put out from harbour into
the midst of the hurricane."

[b] *Cf. Ap.* ii. 282.　　　　[c] Or " treasures."

JOSEPHUS

401 ὧν φεισάμενοι πρότερον ἠχαρίστηνται. μαρτύρο-
μαι δὲ ἐγὼ μὲν ὑμῶν τὰ ἅγια καὶ τοὺς ἱεροὺς
ἀγγέλους τοῦ θεοῦ καὶ πατρίδα τὴν κοινήν, ὡς
οὐδὲν τῶν σωτηρίων ὑμῖν καθυφηκάμην, ὑμεῖς δὲ
βουλευσάμενοι μὲν τὰ δέοντα κοινὴν σὺν ἐμοὶ τὴν
εἰρήνην ἕξετε, προαχθέντες δὲ τοῖς θυμοῖς χωρὶς
ἐμοῦ κινδυνεύσετε."

402 (5) Τοσαῦτα εἰπὼν ἐπεδάκρυσέν τε μετὰ τῆς
ἀδελφῆς καὶ πολὺ τῆς ὁρμῆς αὐτῶν ἔπαυσεν τοῖς
δακρύοις. ἀνεβόων δὲ οὐ Ῥωμαίοις, ἀλλὰ Φλώρῳ

403 δι᾽ ἃ πεπόνθασιν πολεμεῖν. πρὸς τοῦτο βασιλεὺς
Ἀγρίππας " ἀλλὰ τὰ ἔργα," ἔφη, " Ῥωμαίοις
ἤδη πολεμούντων ἐστίν· οὔτε γὰρ Καίσαρι δεδώ-
κατε τὸν φόρον καὶ τὰς στοὰς ἀπεκόψατε τῆς[1]

404 Ἀντωνίας. ἀποσκευάσαισθε[2] δ᾽ ἂν τὴν αἰτίαν
τῆς ἀποστάσεως, εἰ ταύτας τε συνάψετε πάλιν
καὶ τελέσετε τὴν εἰσφοράν· οὐ γὰρ δή γε Φλώρου
τὸ φρούριόν ἐστιν ἢ Φλώρῳ τὰ χρήματα δώσετε."

405 (xvii. 1) Τούτοις ὁ δῆμος ἐπείθετο, καὶ μετὰ
τοῦ βασιλέως τῆς τε Βερνίκης ἀναβάντες εἰς τὸ
ἱερὸν κατήρξαντο τῆς τῶν στοῶν δομήσεως, εἰς
δὲ τὰς κώμας οἵ τε ἄρχοντες καὶ βουλευταὶ με-
ρισθέντες τοὺς φόρους συνέλεγον· ταχέως δὲ τὰ
τεσσαράκοντα τάλαντα, τοσοῦτον γὰρ ἔλειπεν,

406 ἠθροίσθη. καὶ τοῦ μὲν πολέμου τότε οὕτω τὴν
ἀπειλὴν κατεῖχεν Ἀγρίππας, αὖθις δὲ ἐπειρᾶτο
πείθειν τὸ πλῆθος ὑπακούειν Φλώρῳ, μέχρις ἀντ᾽
αὐτοῦ πέμψει[3] Καῖσαρ διάδοχον· πρὸς ὃ παρ-
οξυνθέντες ἐβλασφήμουν εἰς τὸν βασιλέα καὶ τῆς

---

[1] τὰς PAL (cf. Lat. Antonianas).
[2] Dindorf: ἀπεσκευάσασθε or the like mss.
[3] M: πέμψῃ the rest.

hands no more, seeing that their forbearance in the past met only with ingratitude. As for me, I call your sanctuary and God's holy angels and our common country to witness, that I have kept back nothing which could conduce to your preservation ; as for you, if you decide aright, you will enjoy with me the blessings of peace, but, if you let yourselves be carried away by your passion, you will face, without me, this tremendous peril."

(5) Having spoken thus, he burst into tears, as did also his sister ; and his emotion much restrained the passion of his hearers. Still they began to cry out that they were not taking up arms against the Romans, but against Florus, because of all the wrong that he had done them. To this king Agrippa replied : " But your actions are already acts of war against Rome : you have not paid your tribute to Caesar, and you have cut down the porticoes communicating with Antonia. If you wish to clear yourselves of the charge of insurrection, re-establish the porticoes and pay the tax ; for assuredly the fortress does not belong to Florus, and it is not Florus to whom your money will go."

Agrippa's advice : " Pay your tribute and restore the porticoes."

(xvii. 1) Acting on this advice, the people went up to the temple, with the king and Bernice, and began the reconstruction of the porticoes, while the magistrates and the members of the council dispersed to the various villages and levied the tribute. The arrears, amounting to forty talents, were rapidly collected. Thus for the moment Agrippa dispelled the menace of war. Subsequently, he endeavoured to induce the people to submit to the orders of Florus until a successor was sent by Caesar to replace him. But this exasperated the Jews, who heaped abuse upon

πόλεως αὐτὸν ἐξεκήρυσσον, ἐτόλμων δέ τινες τῶν
407 στασιαστῶν καὶ λίθους ἐπ' αὐτὸν βάλλειν. ὁ δὲ
βασιλεὺς ἰδὼν τὴν ὁρμὴν ἤδη τῶν νεωτεριζόντων
ἀκατάσχετον καὶ χαλεπήνας ἐφ' οἷς προπεπηλά-
κιστο,¹ τοὺς μὲν ἄρχοντας αὐτῶν ἅμα τοῖς δυνατοῖς ἔπεμπε πρὸς Φλῶρον εἰς Καισάρειαν, ἵν'
ἐκεῖνος ἐξ αὐτῶν ἀποδείξῃ τοὺς τὴν χώραν
φορολογήσοντας, αὐτὸς δ' ἀνεχώρησεν εἰς τὴν
βασιλείαν.

408   (2) Κἂν τούτῳ τινὲς τῶν μάλιστα κινούντων
τὸν πόλεμον συνελθόντες ὥρμησαν ἐπὶ φρούριόν
τι καλούμενον Μασάδαν, καὶ καταλαβόντες αὐτὸ
λάθρα τοὺς μὲν Ῥωμαίων φρουροὺς ἀπέσφαξαν,
409 ἑτέρους δ' ἐγκατέστησαν ἰδίους. ἅμα δὲ καὶ κατὰ
τὸ ἱερὸν Ἐλεάζαρος υἱὸς Ἀνανία τοῦ ἀρχιερέως,
νεανίας θρασύτατος, στρατηγῶν τότε τοὺς κατὰ
τὴν λατρείαν λειτουργοῦντας ἀναπείθει μηδενὸς
ἀλλοτρίου δῶρον ἢ θυσίαν προσδέχεσθαι. τοῦτο
δ' ἦν τοῦ πρὸς Ῥωμαίους πολέμου καταβολή·
τὴν γὰρ ὑπὲρ τούτων θυσίαν καὶ² Καίσαρος ἀπ-
410 έρριψαν. καὶ πολλὰ τῶν τε ἀρχιερέων καὶ τῶν
γνωρίμων παρακαλούντων μὴ παραλιπεῖν τὸ ὑπὲρ
τῶν ἡγεμόνων ἔθος οὐκ ἐνέδοσαν, πολὺ μὲν καὶ
τῷ σφετέρῳ πλήθει πεποιθότες, καὶ γὰρ τὸ
ἀκμαιότατον τῶν νεωτεριζόντων συνήργει, μά-

¹ προπεπηλάκισται PA.   ² om. καὶ VRC.

ᵃ As opposed to the tribute already collected from Jerusalem and the environs (§ 405).
ᵇ Close to the Dead Sea, more than half-way down the
west coast, modern *Sebbeh*.
ᶜ *i.e.* "captain of the Temple" (Acts iv. 1, etc.), or *Sagan*,

the king and formally proclaimed his banishment Agrippa expelled from the city.
from the city ; some of the insurgents even ventured
to throw stones at him. The king, seeing that the
passions of the revolutionaries were now beyond
control, and indignant at the insults which he had
received, sent the magistrates and principal citizens
to Florus at Caesarea, in order that he might appoint
some of their number to collect the tribute in the
country [a] ; he then withdrew to his own dominions.

(2) And now some of the most ardent promoters Capture of Masada by Jewish insurgents, summer of A.D. 66.
of hostilities banded together and made an assault
on a fortress called Masada [b] ; and having gained
possession of it by stratagem, they slew the Roman
guards and put a garrison of their own in their place.
Another incident occurred at the same time in the Cessation of sacrifices for Rome.
Temple. Eleazar, son of Ananias the high-priest, a
very daring youth, then holding the position of
captain,[c] persuaded those who officiated in the Temple
services to accept no gift or sacrifice from a foreigner.
This action laid the foundation of the war with the
Romans ; for the sacrifices offered on behalf of that
nation and the emperor were in consequence rejected.[d] The chief priests and the notables earnestly
besought them not to abandon the customary offering
for their rulers, but the priests remained obdurate.
Their numbers gave them great confidence, supported
as they were by the stalwarts of the revolutionary

an official who in the hierarchy ranked next to the high
priest.

[d] These sacrifices, offered twice daily (*B.* ii. 197), were
instituted by Augustus and consisted of two lambs and a
bull (Philo, *Leg. ad Gaium,* 157, 317 Cohn). The expense,
according to Philo, was borne by the Emperor (ἐκ τῶν ἰδίων
προσόδων), according to Josephus (*Ap.* ii. 77) by the Jewish
nation.

λιστα δ' ἀφορῶντες εἰς τὸν Ἐλεάζαρον στρατηγοῦντα.

411 (3) Συνελθόντες γοῦν[1] οἱ δυνατοὶ τοῖς ἀρχιερεῦσιν εἰς ταὐτὸ καὶ τοῖς τῶν Φαρισαίων
γνωρίμοις ὡς ἐπ' ἀνηκέστοις ἤδη συμφοραῖς
ἐβουλεύοντο περὶ τῶν ὅλων· καὶ δόξαν ἀποπειραθῆναι τῶν στασιαστῶν λόγοις, πρὸ τῆς χαλκῆς
πύλης ἀθροίζουσι τὸν δῆμον, ἥτις ἦν τοῦ ἔνδον

412 ἱεροῦ τετραμμένη πρὸς ἀνατολὰς ἡλίου. καὶ
πρῶτον αὐτῶν πολλὰ πρὸς τὴν τόλμαν τῆς ἀποστάσεως χαλεπήναντες καὶ τὸ τηλικοῦτον ἐπι-
σείειν τῇ πατρίδι πόλεμον, ἔπειτα τὸ τῆς προφάσεως ἄλογον διήλεγχον, φάμενοι τοὺς μὲν
προγόνους αὐτῶν κεκοσμηκέναι τὸν ναὸν ἐκ τῶν
ἀλλοφύλων τὸ πλέον, ἀεὶ προσδεχομένους τὰς ἀπὸ

413 τῶν ἔξωθεν ἐθνῶν δωρεάς, καὶ οὐ μόνον οὐ δια-
κεκωλυκέναι θυσίας τινῶν, τοῦτο γὰρ ἀσεβέστατον,
ἀλλὰ καὶ τὰ βλεπόμενα καὶ[2] παραμένοντα [τὸν][3]
τοσοῦτον χρόνον ἀναθήματα περὶ τῷ ἱερῷ καθ-

414 ιδρυκέναι. αὐτοὺς δὲ νῦν ἐρεθίζοντας τὰ Ῥωμαίων ὅπλα καὶ μνηστευομένους τὸν ἀπ' ἐκείνων
πόλεμον καινοτομεῖν θρησκείαν ξένην, καὶ μετὰ
τοῦ κινδύνου καταψηφίσασθαι τῆς πόλεως ἀ-
σέβειαν, εἰ παρὰ μόνοις Ἰουδαίοις οὔτε θύσει τις

415 ἀλλότριος οὔτε προσκυνήσει. κἂν μὲν ἐπὶ ἰδιώτου
τις ἑνὸς τοῦτον εἰσφέρῃ τὸν νόμον, ἀγανακτεῖν
ὡς ὁριζομένης ἀπανθρωπίας, περιορᾶν δ' ὅτε

416 Ῥωμαῖοι καὶ ὁ Καῖσαρ ἔκσπονδος γίνεται. δεδοι-

---

[1] οὖν VRC.   [2] +τὰ mss.   [3] om. PAML.

---

[a] The gate of Corinthian bronze (*B.* v. 201), probably on

484

party ; but they relied above all on the authority of
the captain Eleazar.

(3) Thereupon the principal citizens assembled
with the chief priests and the most notable Pharisees
to deliberate on the position of affairs, now that they
were faced with what seemed irreparable disaster.
Deciding to try the effect of an appeal to the revolutionaries, they called the people together before the
bronze gate—that of the inner Temple facing east-
ward.[a] They began by expressing the keenest
indignation at the audacity of this revolt and at their
country being thus threatened with so serious a war.
They then proceeded to expose the absurdity of the
alleged pretext. Their forefathers, they said, had
adorned the sanctuary mainly at the expense of
aliens and had always accepted the gifts of foreign
nations ; not only had they never taken the sacrilegious step of forbidding anyone to offer sacrifice,
but they had set up around the Temple the dedicatory
offerings which were still to be seen and had remained
there for so long a time. But now here were these
men, who were provoking the arms of the Romans
and courting a war with them, introducing a strange
innovation into their religion, and, besides endanger-
ing the city, laying it open to the charge of impiety,
if Jews henceforth were to be the only people to allow
no alien the right of sacrifice or worship. Should
such a law be introduced in the case of any private
individual, they would be indignant at so inhumane
a decree ; yet they made light of putting the Romans
and Caesar outside the pale. It was to be feared,

*Expostula-
tion of the
Jewish
rulers.*

the east of the women's court and identical with " the
Beautiful gate " of Acts iii. 2 and " Nicanor's gate " of the
Mishna.

κέναι μέντοι μὴ τὰς ὑπὲρ ἐκείνων ἀπορρίψαντες
θυσίας κωλυθῶσι θύειν καὶ τὰς ὑπὲρ ἑαυτῶν,
γένηταί τε ἔκσπονδος τῆς ἡγεμονίας ἡ πόλις, εἰ
μὴ ταχέως σωφρονήσαντες ἀποδώσουσιν τὰς
θυσίας, καὶ πρὶν ἐξελθεῖν ἐφ᾽ οὓς ὑβρίκασιν τὴν
φήμην διορθώσονται τὴν ὕβριν.

417   (4) Ἅμα ταῦτα λέγοντες παρῆγον τοὺς ἐμ-
πείρους τῶν πατρίων ἱερεῖς, ἀφηγουμένους ὅτι
πάντες οἱ πρόγονοι τὰς παρὰ τῶν ἀλλογενῶν
θυσίας ἀπεδέχοντο. προσεῖχεν δὲ οὐδεὶς τῶν
νεωτεριζόντων, ἀλλ᾽ οὐδὲ προσῄεσαν[1] οἱ λει-
τουργοὶ[2] τὴν τοῦ πολέμου καταβολὴν ἐνσκευαζό-
418 μενοι. συνιδόντες οὖν οἱ δυνατοὶ τήν τε στάσιν
ἤδη δυσκαθαίρετον ὑπ᾽ αὐτῶν οὖσαν καὶ τὸν ἀπὸ
Ῥωμαίων κίνδυνον ἐπὶ πρώτους αὐτοὺς ἀφ-
ιξόμενον, ἀπεσκευάζοντο τὰς αἰτίας, καὶ πρέσβεις
οὓς μὲν πρὸς Φλῶρον ἔπεμπον, ὧν ἦρχεν υἱὸς
Ἀνανίου Σίμων, οὓς δὲ πρὸς Ἀγρίππαν, ἐν οἷς
ἦσαν ἐπίσημοι Σαῦλός τε καὶ Ἀντίπας καὶ
Κοστόβαρος προσήκοντες τῷ βασιλεῖ κατὰ γένος.
419 ἐδέοντο δὲ ἀμφοτέρων ἀναβῆναι μετὰ δυνάμεως
εἰς τὴν πόλιν καὶ πρὶν γενέσθαι δυσκαθαίρετον
420 ἐπικόψαι τὴν στάσιν. Φλώρῳ μὲν οὖν δεινὸν[3]
εὐαγγέλιον ἦν, καὶ προῃρημένος ἐξάπτειν τὸν
421 πόλεμον οὐδὲν ἀπεκρίνατο τοῖς πρεσβευταῖς· Ἀγρίππας δὲ κηδόμενος ἐπίσης τῶν τε ἀφισταμένων
καὶ πρὸς οὓς ὁ πόλεμος ἠγείρετο, βουλόμενός τε

---

[1] MLC: προσίεσαν the rest.
[2] λῃστρικοὶ PAM*: +καὶ PAL; the text is doubtful.
[3] τὸ δεινὸν C " the dire news was a godsend ": τοῦτο
δεινὸν MVR.

however, that, once they rejected the sacrifices for the Romans, they might not be allowed to offer sacrifice even for themselves, and that their city would be placed outside the pale of the empire, unless, with a speedy return to discretion, they restored the sacrifices and made amends for the insult before the report reached the ears of those whom they had insulted.

(4) In the course of these remonstrances they produced priestly experts on the traditions, who declared that all their ancestors had accepted the sacrifices of aliens. But not one of the revolutionary party would listen to them; even the Temple ministers failed to come to their support and were thus instrumental in bringing about the war. Thereupon, the leading citizens, perceiving that it was now beyond their power to suppress the insurrection and that they would be the first victims of the vengeance of Rome, took steps to exonerate themselves from blame, and dispatched two deputations, one to Florus, headed by Simon, son of Ananias, and another to Agrippa, including some eminent persons, Saul, Antipas and Costobar,[a] all members of the royal family. They besought them both to come up to the city with troops and to crush the revolt before it became insuperable. To Florus the news was a wonderful godsend; determined as he was to kindle the war, he gave the emissaries no reply. Agrippa, on the other hand, equally solicitous for the rebels and for the nation against which they were rising in arms, anxious that the Romans should

They obtain reinforcements from Agrippa.

---

[a] Saul and Costobar were brothers who, after the defeat of Cestius, made a timely exit from Jerusalem; Antipas, who remained, was slain by the insurgents (*B.* ii. 556 f., iv. 140).

Ῥωμαίοις μὲν Ἰουδαίους σώζεσθαι, Ἰουδαίοις δὲ
τὸ ἱερὸν καὶ τὴν μητρόπολιν, ἀλλ᾽ οὐδ᾽ ἑαυτῷ
λυσιτελήσειν τὴν ταραχὴν ἐπιστάμενος, ἔπεμπεν
τοὺς ἐπαμυνοῦντας[1] τῷ δήμῳ δισχιλίους ἱππεῖς,
Αὐρανίτας τε καὶ Βαταναίους καὶ Τραχωνίτας,
ὑπὸ Δαρείῳ μὲν ἱππάρχῃ, στρατηγῷ δὲ τῷ
Ἰακίμου Φιλίππῳ.

422 (5) Τούτοις θαρσήσαντες οἱ δυνατοὶ σὺν τοῖς
ἀρχιερεῦσιν καὶ πᾶν ὅσον τοῦ πλήθους εἰρήνην
ἠγάπα τὴν ἄνω καταλαμβάνονται πόλιν· τῆς
κάτω γὰρ τὸ στασιάζον ἐκράτει καὶ τοῦ ἱεροῦ.

423 χερμάσιν μὲν οὖν καὶ τοῖς ἐκηβόλοις ἀδιαλείπτως
ἐχρῶντο, καὶ συνεχεῖς ἦσαν βελῶν ἀφέσεις ἐξ
ἑκατέρων τῶν κλιμάτων· ἔστιν δ᾽ ὅτε καὶ κατὰ
λόχους ἐκτρέχοντες συστάδην ἐμάχοντο, τόλμαις
μὲν οἱ στασιασταὶ προέχοντες, ἐμπειρίᾳ δὲ οἱ

424 βασιλικοί. καὶ τούτοις μὲν ἦν ἀγὼν τοῦ ἱεροῦ
κρατῆσαι μάλιστα καὶ τοὺς μιαίνοντας τὸν ναὸν
ἐξελάσαι, τοῖς δὲ περὶ τὸν Ἐλεάζαρον στασιασταῖς πρὸς οἷς ἔσχον καὶ τὴν ἄνω πόλιν προσλαβεῖν.
ἑπτὰ μὲν οὖν ἡμέραις συχνὸς ἀμφοτέρων φόνος
ἐγίνετο, καὶ οὐδέτεροι τοῦ καταληφθέντος μέρους
εἶκον.

425 (6) Τῇ δ᾽ ἑξῆς τῆς τῶν ξυλοφορίων ἑορτῆς
οὔσης, ἐν ᾗ πᾶσιν ἔθος ἦν ὕλην τῷ βωμῷ προσ-
φέρειν, ὅπως μήποτε τροφὴ τῷ πυρὶ λείποι,

---

[1] L: ἐπαμύνοντας the rest.

not lose the Jews nor the Jews their Temple and
mother city, conscious, moreover, that he had nothing
to gain from this disorder, dispatched to the aid of
the citizens two thousand horse from Auranitis,
Batanaea, and Trachonitis, under Darius, as cavalry
commander, and Philip,[a] son of Jacimus, as general.

(5) Encouraged by these reinforcements, the leading men, the chief priests and all the people who
were in favour of peace occupied the upper city ; for
the lower city and the Temple were in the hands of
the insurgents. Stones and slings were incessantly
in action ; from one quarter and from the other there
was a continuous hail of missiles ; sometimes companies even sallied out and there was a hand-to-hand
engagement, the insurgents having the superiority
in daring, the king's soldiers in skill. The objective
of the royal troops was to capture the Temple and
to expel those who were polluting the sanctuary ;
Eleazar and the rebels strove to gain the upper
city in addition to the ground which they held
already. So for seven days there was great slaughter
on both sides, neither of the combatants surrender-
ing the portion of the town which he occupied. *Struggle between the pro-Romans and the insurgents.*

(6) The eighth day was the feast of wood-carrying,
when it was customary for all to bring wood for the
altar, in order that there might be an unfailing supply *The rebels, joined by the* sicarii,

(ἔπαρχος) of Agrippa II, are narrated at length in the *Life*
(46, etc.). His father Jacimus had held a high position
(according to one text as " tetrarch ") under Agrippa
(probably I) ; his grandfather Zamaris had been placed by
Herod the Great in charge of a colony of Babylonian Jews
in Batanaea (*A.* xvii. 23-29). Waddington's supposed
discovery of the name Darius on an inscription in
Trachonitis referring to Agrippa has been shown to be
erroneous (Dittenberger, *Orientis Graeci Inscr. Sel.* i. 422
Reinach).

διαμένει γὰρ ἄσβεστον ἀεί, τοὺς μὲν διαφόρους
τῆς θρησκείας ἐξέκλεισαν, τῷ δ' ἀσθενεῖ λαῷ
συνεισρυέντας πολλοὺς τῶν σικαρίων, οὕτως γὰρ
ἐκάλουν τοὺς λῃστὰς ἔχοντας ὑπὸ τοῖς κόλποις
ξίφη, προσλαβόντες θαρραλεώτερον ἥπτοντο τῆς
426 ἐπιχειρήσεως. ἡττῶντο δ' οἱ βασιλικοὶ πλήθει
τε καὶ τόλμῃ καὶ βιασαμένοις εἶκον ἐκ τῆς ἄνω
πόλεως. οἱ δὲ ἐπιπεσόντες τήν τε Ἀνανίου τοῦ
ἀρχιερέως οἰκίαν καὶ τὰ Ἀγρίππα καὶ Βερνίκης
427 ὑποπιμπρᾶσιν βασίλεια· μεθ' ἃ τὸ πῦρ ἐπὶ τὰ
ἀρχεῖα ἔφερον ἀφανίσαι σπεύδοντες τὰ συμβόλαια
τῶν δεδανεικότων καὶ τὰς εἰσπράξεις ἀποκόψαι
τῶν χρεῶν, ὅπως αὐτοί τε πλῆθος προσλάβωσιν
τῶν ὠφεληθέντων καὶ μετ' ἀδείας τοῖς εὐπόροις
ἐπαναστήσωσι τοὺς ἀπόρους. φυγόντων δὲ τῶν
428 πρὸς τῷ γραμματοφυλακείῳ τὸ πῦρ ἐνίεσαν. ἐπεὶ
δὲ τὰ νεῦρα τῆς πόλεως καταφλέξαντες ἐπὶ τοὺς
ἐχθροὺς ἐχώρουν, ἔνθα δὴ τῶν δυνατῶν καὶ τῶν
ἀρχιερέων οἱ μὲν εἰς τοὺς ὑπονόμους καταδύντες
429 διελάνθανον, οἱ δὲ σὺν τοῖς βασιλικοῖς εἰς τὴν
ἀνωτέρω καταφυγόντες αὐλὴν ταχέως ἀπέκλεισαν
τὰς θύρας, σὺν οἷς Ἀνανίας ὁ ἀρχιερεὺς Ἐζεκίας
τε ὁ ἀδελφὸς αὐτοῦ καὶ οἱ πρεσβεύσαντες πρὸς
Ἀγρίππαν ἦσαν. τότε μὲν οὖν τῇ νίκῃ καὶ τοῖς
ἐμπρησθεῖσιν ἀρκεσθέντες ἀνεπαύσαντο.

---

[a] *Cf.* Lev. vi. 12 f. According to the Mishna, *Taanith*,
iv. 5, the wood was carried by respective families on nine
separate days in the year, but the principal day was the
15th of Ab (July-August). Josephus, however (see § 430),
appears to place the feast on the preceding day, 14th Ab.
[b] Probably additions of Agrippa II to the old palace of
the Hasmonaeans (*cf. A.* xx. 189 f.).

of fuel for the flames, which are kept always burning.[a] The Jews in the Temple excluded their opponents from this ceremony, but along with some feebler folk numbers of the *sicarii*—so they called the brigands who carried a dagger in their bosom—forced their way in ; these they enlisted in their service and pressed their attacks more boldly than before. The royalists, now outmatched in numbers and audacity, were forced to evacuate the upper city. The victors burst in and set fire to the house of Ananias the high-priest and to the palaces of Agrippa and Bernice [b] ; they next carried their combustibles to the public archives,[c] eager to destroy the money-lenders' bonds and to prevent the recovery of debts, in order to win over a host of grateful debtors and to cause a rising of the poor against the rich, sure of impunity. The keepers of the Record Office having fled, they set light to the building. After consuming the sinews of the city in the flames, they advanced against their foes ; whereupon the notables and chief priests made their escape, some hiding in the underground passages,[d] while others fled with the royal troops to the palace situated higher up,[e] and instantly shut the gates ; among the latter were Ananias the high-priest, his brother Ezechias and the members of the deputation which had been sent to Agrippa. Satisfied with their victory and incendiary proceedings, the insurgents paused for that day.

[c] The Archives building was finally burnt down by the Romans (*B.* vi. 354) ; it is there spoken of as adjoining the Akra (or citadel, thought to be the old city of David) and the council-chamber (of the Sanhedrin).

[d] Or " sewers."

[e] The palace of Herod the Great on the highest terrace of the upper city, described in *B.* v. 176 ff.

430   (7) Τῇ δ' ἑξῆς, πεντεκαιδεκάτῃ δ' ἦν Λώου
μηνός, ὥρμησαν ἐπὶ τὴν Ἀντωνίαν καὶ τοὺς ἐν
αὐτῇ φρουροὺς δυσὶν ἡμέραις πολιορκήσαντες
αὐτούς τε εἷλον καὶ κατέσφαξαν καὶ τὸ φρούριον
431 ἐνέπρησαν. ἔπειτα μετέβαινον εἰς τὴν αὐλήν, εἰς
ἣν οἱ βασιλικοὶ κατέφυγον, καὶ διανείμαντες σφᾶς
αὐτοὺς εἰς τέσσαρα μέρη τῶν τειχῶν ἐπειρῶντο.
τῶν δ' ἔνδον πρὸς ἐκδρομὴν μὲν οὐδεὶς ἐθάρρει
διὰ τὸ πλῆθος τῶν ἐφεστώτων, διιστάμενοι δὲ
ἐπὶ τὰ θωράκια καὶ τοὺς πύργους ἔβαλλον τοὺς
προσιόντας, καὶ συχνοὶ τῶν λῃστῶν ὑπὸ τοῖς
432 τείχεσιν ἔπιπτον. οὔτε δὲ νυκτὸς οὔτε ἡμέρας
διέλειπεν ἡ συμβολή, τῶν μὲν στασιαστῶν ἀπ-
αγορεύσειν τοὺς ἔνδον οἰομένων ἐνδείᾳ τροφῆς, τῶν
δ' ἔνδοθεν καμάτῳ τοὺς πολιορκοῦντας.

433   (8) Κἀν τούτῳ Μανάημός τις, υἱὸς Ἰούδα τοῦ
καλουμένου Γαλιλαίου, σοφιστὴς[1] δεινότατος, ὁ
καὶ ἐπὶ Κυρηνίου ποτὲ Ἰουδαίους ὀνειδίσας ὅτι
Ῥωμαίοις ὑπετάσσοντο μετὰ τὸν θεόν, ἀναλαβὼν
434 τοὺς γνωρίμους ἀνεχώρησεν εἰς Μασάδαν, ἔνθα
τὴν Ἡρώδου τοῦ βασιλέως ὁπλοθήκην ἀναρρήξας
καὶ πρὸς τοῖς δημόταις ἑτέρους λῃστὰς καθ-
οπλίσας, τούτοις τε χρώμενος δορυφόροις, οἷα δὴ
βασιλεὺς ἐπάνεισιν εἰς Ἱεροσόλυμα καὶ γενόμενος
ἡγεμὼν τῆς στάσεως διέτασσεν τὴν πολιορκίαν.
435 ἀπορία δ' ἦν ὀργάνων, καὶ φανερῶς ὑπορύττειν
τὸ τεῖχος οὐχ οἷόν τε ἦν ἄνωθεν βαλλομένους·
ὑπόνομον δὴ πόρρωθεν ἐφ' ἕνα τῶν πύργων ὑπ-
ορύξαντες ἀνεκρήμνισαν αὐτόν, ἔπειτα τὴν ἀνέχουσαν

---

[1] ὃς ἦν σοφιστὴς VRC : Destinon suggests σοφιστὴς ⟨ἦν⟩ or
that the whole clause (to θεόν) is a gloss.

(7) On the next day, being the fifteenth of the month Lous,[a] they attacked Antonia, and, after a siege of two days, captured the garrison, put them to the sword and set fire to the fortress. They then repaired to the palace, in which the king's followers had taken refuge, and forming themselves into four sections made repeated assaults on the walls. None of the blockaded party ventured on a sally because of the large number of their assailants ; but, posted along the breastworks and towers, they showered missiles upon all who approached, and numbers of the brigands fell beneath the walls. The combat continued incessantly day and night, the insurgents hoping to exhaust the besieged through failure of supplies, the defenders to wear down the besiegers by fatigue.

They capture the fort Antonia and besiege the Romans and loyal citizens in Herod's palace.

(8) At this period a certain Menahem, son of Judas surnamed the Galilaean—that redoubtable doctor who in old days, under Quirinius, had upbraided the Jews for recognizing the Romans as masters when they already had God [b]—took his intimate friends off with him to Masada,[c] where he broke into king Herod's armoury and provided arms both for his fellow-townsmen and for other brigands ; then, with these men for his bodyguard, he returned like a veritable king to Jerusalem, became the leader of the revolution, and directed the siege of the palace. The besiegers, however, lacked engines, and, exposed as they were to missiles from the wall, found it impossible to undermine it under the enemy's eyes ; they accordingly started digging a mine at a distance, continued it as far as one of the towers, which they

Menahem assumes command of the rebels and directs the siege.

---

[a] Roughly the equivalent in the Macedonian calendar of the Hebrew Ab and of our August.

[b] See § 118.　　　　　[c] § 408.

436 ὕλην ἐμπρήσαντες ἐξῆλθον. ὑποκαέντων δὲ τῶν
στηριγμάτων ὁ μὲν πύργος ἐξαίφνης κατασείεται,
τεῖχος δ᾽ ἕτερον ἔνδοθεν ἀντῳκοδομημένον[1] δι-
εφάνη· τὴν γὰρ ἐπιβουλὴν[2] αὐτῶν προαισθόμενοι,
τάχα καὶ τοῦ πύργου κινηθέντος ὡς ὑπωρύττετο,
437 δεύτερον ἑαυτοῖς ἔρυμα κατεσκεύασαν. πρὸς ὃ τῶν
ἀδοκήτως ἰδόντων καὶ κρατεῖν ἤδη πεπεισμένων
κατάπληξις ἦν. οἱ δὲ ἔνδοθεν πρός τε τὸν Μανάημον καὶ τοὺς ἐξάρχοντας τῆς στάσεως ἔπεμπον
ἀξιοῦντες ἐξελθεῖν ὑπόσπονδοι, καὶ δοθὲν μόνοις
τοῖς βασιλικοῖς καὶ τοῖς ἐπιχωρίοις οἱ μὲν ἐξῄεσαν.
438 ἀθυμία δὲ τοὺς Ῥωμαίους καταλειφθέντας μόνους
ὑπέλαβεν· οὔτε γὰρ βιάσασθαι τοσοῦτον πλῆθος
ἐδύναντο καὶ τὸ δεξιὰς αἰτεῖν ὄνειδος ὑπελάμ-
439 βανον, πρὸς τῷ μηδὲ πιστεύειν, εἰ διδοῖτο. καταλιπόντες δὴ τὸ στρατόπεδον ὡς εὐάλωτον ἐπὶ
τοὺς βασιλικοὺς ἀνέφυγον πύργους, τόν τε Ἱππικὸν καλούμενον καὶ Φασάηλον καὶ Μαριάμμην.
440 οἱ δὲ περὶ τὸν Μανάημον εἰσπεσόντες ὅθεν οἱ
στρατιῶται διέφυγον ὅσους τε αὐτῶν κατελάμβανον μὴ φθάσαντας ἐκδραμεῖν διέφθειραν,
καὶ τὰς ἀποσκευὰς διαρπάσαντες ἐνέπρησαν τὸ
στρατόπεδον. ταῦτα μὲν οὖν ἕκτῃ Γορπιαίου
μηνὸς ἐπράχθη.

441 (9) Κατὰ δὲ τὴν ἐπιοῦσαν ὅ τε ἀρχιερεὺς
Ἀνανίας περὶ τὸν τῆς βασιλικῆς αὐλῆς εὔριπον
διαλανθάνων ἁλίσκεται καὶ πρὸς τῶν λῃστῶν
ἀναιρεῖται σὺν Ἐζεκίᾳ τῷ ἀδελφῷ, καὶ τοὺς
πύργους περισχόντες[3] οἱ στασιασταὶ παρεφύλαττον,

---

[1] ἀνοικοδομημένον PA.   [2] ἐπιβολὴν Niese.
[3] Naber after Lat. "circumsidentes": ἐπισχόντες mss.

shored up, and then, after setting light to the supports retired. When the props were consumed, the tower suddenly collapsed, but only to reveal another wall constructed in its rear ; for the besieged, foreseeing their stratagem, perhaps warned by the tower shaking during the mining operations, had provided themselves with a second rampart. This unexpected sight dismayed the assailants who believed that victory was already theirs. However, the garrison now sent to Menahem and the leaders of the insurrection a request for permission to quit the fortress under treaty. This was granted, but only to the king's troops and natives of the country, who came out accordingly. The Romans, left alone, were now despondent ; they despaired of forcing their way through such a multitude and were ashamed to sue for terms ; besides, even were they granted, they could put no faith in them. They, accordingly, abandoned their camp, as untenable, and retired to the royal towers, known as Hippicus, Phasael and Mariamme.[a] Menahem's followers, rushing into the quarters just deserted by the soldiers, killed all the stragglers whom they could lay hands on, rifled the baggage and set fire to the camp. These events took place on the sixth of the month Gorpiaeus.[b]

Evacuation of the palace.

(9) On the following day the high-priest Ananias was caught near the canal[c] in the palace grounds, where he was hiding, and, with his brother Ezechias, was killed by the brigands ; while the rebels invested and kept strict watch on the towers, to prevent any

Murder of Menahem

[a] These towers, built by Herod the Great and described in *B.* v. 161 ff., were on the old city wall (173) on the north side of the palace enclosure (176).

[b] =Hebrew Elul (August-September).

[c] For the canals in the palace gardens see *B.* v. 181.

442 μή τις τῶν στρατιωτῶν διαφύγοι.[1] τὸν δὲ Μανάημον ἥ τε τῶν ὀχυρῶν καταστροφὴ χωρίων
καὶ ὁ τοῦ ἀρχιερέως Ἀνανίου θάνατος ἐτύφωσεν
εἰς ὠμότητα, καὶ μηδένα νομίζων ἔχειν ἐπὶ τοῖς
443 πράγμασιν ἀντίπαλον ἀφόρητος ἦν τύραννος. ἐπ-
ανίστανται δὲ οἱ περὶ τὸν Ἐλεάζαρον αὐτῷ, καὶ
λόγον ἀλλήλοις δόντες, ὡς οὐ χρὴ Ῥωμαίων
ἀποστάντας δι' ἐλευθερίας πόθον καταπροέσθαι
ταύτην οἰκείῳ δημίῳ[2] καὶ δεσπότην φέρειν, εἰ
καὶ μηδὲν πράττοι βίαιον, ἀλλ' οὖν ἑαυτῶν
ταπεινότερον· εἰ γὰρ καὶ δέοι τινὰ τῶν ὅλων
ἀφηγεῖσθαι, παντὶ μᾶλλον ἢ ἐκείνῳ προσήκειν,
συντίθενται καὶ κατὰ τὸ ἱερὸν ἐπεχείρουν αὐτῷ·
444 σοβαρὸς γὰρ ἀναβεβήκει προσκυνήσων ἐσθῆτί τε
βασιλικῇ κεκοσμημένος καὶ τοὺς ζηλωτὰς ἐν-
445 όπλους ἐφελκόμενος. ὡς δ' οἱ περὶ τὸν Ἐλεάζαρον
ἐπ' αὐτὸν ὥρμησαν, ὅ τε λοιπὸς δῆμος [ἐπὶ τὰς
ὀργὰς][3] λίθους ἁρπάσαντες τὸν σοφιστὴν ἔβαλλον,
οἰόμενοι τούτου καταλυθέντος διατρέψειν ὅλην
446 τὴν στάσιν, πρὸς ὀλίγον[4] οἱ περὶ τὸν Μανάημον
ἀντισχόντες ὡς εἶδον πᾶν ἐπ' αὐτοὺς τὸ πλῆθος
ὁρμῆσαν, ἔφυγον ὅπῃ τις ἴσχυσεν, καὶ φόνος μὲν
ἦν τῶν καταληφθέντων, ἔρευνα δὲ τῶν ἀπο-
447 κρυπτομένων. καὶ διεσώθησαν ὀλίγοι λάθρα διαδράντες εἰς Μασάδαν, σὺν οἷς Ἐλεάζαρος υἱὸς
Ἰαείρου, προσήκων τῷ Μαναήμῳ κατὰ γένος,
448 ὃς ὕστερον ἐτυράννησεν τῆς Μασάδας. αὐτόν τε
τὸν Μανάημον εἰς τὸν καλούμενον Ὀφλᾶν συμ-
φυγόντα κἀκεῖ ταπεινῶς ὑπολανθάνοντα ζωγρή-

---

[1] Naber: διαφύγῃ mss.   [2] Destinon: δήμῳ mss.
[3] om. L Lat.   [4] C: +δὲ the rest.

---

[a] Greek "zealots."   [b] Text and meaning doubtful.

soldier from escaping. But the reduction of the
strongholds and the murder of the high-priest
Ananias inflated and brutalized Menahem to such an
extent that he believed himself without a rival in the
conduct of affairs and became an insufferable tyrant.
The partisans of Eleazar now rose against him ; they
remarked to each other that, after revolting from the
Romans for love of liberty, they ought not to sacrifice
this liberty to a Jewish hangman and to put up with
a master who, even were he to abstain from violence,
was anyhow far below themselves ; and that if they
must have a leader, anyone would be better than
Menahem. So they laid their plans to attack him
in the Temple, whither he had gone up in state to
pay his devotions, arrayed in royal robes and attended
by his suite of armed fanatics.[a] When Eleazar and
his companions rushed upon him, and the rest of
the people to gratify their rage[b] took up stones
and began pelting the arrogant doctor, imagining
that his downfall would crush the whole revolt,
Menahem and his followers offered a momentary
resistance ; then, seeing themselves assailed by the
whole multitude, they fled whithersoever they could ;
all who were caught were massacred, and a hunt
was made for any in hiding. A few succeeded in
escaping by stealth to Masada, among others Eleazar,
son of Jairus and a relative of Menahem, and subsequently despot of Masada.[c] Menahem himself,
who had taken refuge in the place called Ophlas[d]
and there ignominiously concealed himself, was

[c] *B.* vii. 275 ff. The siege of Masada ended the war in
Palestine.

[d] The 'Ophel (= " protuberance "), a region in the lower
city, " either the whole of the east hill south of the Temple
or some part of it " (G. A. Smith, *Jerusalem*, i. 154).

σαντες εἰς τὸ φανερὸν ἐξείλκυσαν καὶ πολλαῖς
αἰκισάμενοι βασάνοις ἀνεῖλον, ὁμοίως δὲ καὶ τοὺς
ὑπ' αὐτὸν ἡγεμόνας τόν τε ἐπισημότατον τῆς
τυραννίδος ὑπηρέτην Ἀψάλωμον.

449 (10) Ὁ μὲν οὖν δῆμος, ὡς ἔφην, εἰς ταῦτα
συνήργησεν ἐλπίζων τινὰ τῆς ὅλης στάσεως
διόρθωσιν· οἱ δ' οὐ καταλῦσαι τὸν πόλεμον
σπεύδοντες, ἀλλ' ἀδεέστερον πολεμεῖν, Μανάημον
450 ἀνῃρήκεσαν. ἀμέλει πολλὰ τοῦ δήμου τοῖς στρατιώταις ἀνεῖναι τὴν πολιορκίαν παρακαλοῦντος,
οἱ δὲ προσέκειντο χαλεπώτερον, μέχρι μηκέτι
ἀντέχοντες οἱ περὶ τὸν Μετίλιον, οὗτος γὰρ ἦν
τῶν Ῥωμαίων ἔπαρχος, διαπέμπονται πρὸς τοὺς
περὶ τὸν Ἐλεάζαρον ἐξαιτούμενοι μόνας τὰς
ψυχὰς ὑποσπόνδους, τὰ δ' ὅπλα καὶ τὴν λοιπὴν
451 κτῆσιν παραδώσειν λέγοντες. οἱ δὲ καὶ τὴν
ἱκεσίαν ἁρπάσαντες ἀνέπεμψαν πρὸς αὐτοὺς Γω-
ρίονά τε Νικομήδους[1] υἱὸν καὶ Ἀνανίαν Σαδούκι
καὶ Ἰούδαν Ἰωνάθου δεξιάν[2] τε καὶ ὅρκους δώσοντας. ὧν γενομένων κατῆγεν τοὺς στρατιώτας ὁ
452 Μετίλιος. οἱ δὲ μέχρι μὲν ἦσαν ἐν τοῖς ὅπλοις,
οὔτ' ἐπεχείρει τις τῶν στασιαστῶν αὐτοῖς οὔτ'
ἐνέφαινεν ἐπιβουλήν· ὡς δὲ κατὰ τὰς συνθήκας
ἅπαντες ἀπέθεντο τοὺς θυρεοὺς καὶ τὰ ξίφη καὶ
453 μηδὲν ἔτι ὑποπτεύοντες ἀνεχώρουν, ὥρμησαν ἐπ'
αὐτοὺς οἱ περὶ τὸν Ἐλεάζαρον καὶ περισχόντες
ἀνῄρουν οὔτε ἀμυνομένους οὔτε ἱκετεύοντας, μόνας
δὲ τὰς συνθήκας καὶ τοὺς ὅρκους ἀναβοῶντας.
454 οἱ μὲν οὖν οὕτως ὠμῶς ἀπεσφάγησαν ἅπαντες
πλὴν Μετιλίου, τοῦτον γὰρ ἱκετεύσαντα καὶ μέχρι
περιτομῆς ἰουδαΐσειν ὑποσχόμενον διέσωσαν μόνον,

---

[1] Nicodemi Lat.   [2] δεξιάς LVRC.

caught, dragged into the open, and after being subjected to all kinds of torture, put to death. His lieutenants, along with Absalom, his most eminent supporter in his tyranny, met with a similar fate.

(10) The people, as I said,[a] co-operated in this plot in the hope of its producing some radical cure for the revolt; but the conspirators, in killing Menahem, had no desire to end the war, but only to prosecute it at greater liberty. In fact, though the civilians urgently entreated the soldiers to abandon the siege, they, on the contrary, only pressed it more vigorously; until Metilius, the commander of the Roman garrison, unable to prolong his resistance, sent envoys to Eleazar, asking, under terms of capitulation, for no more than their lives, and offering to surrender their arms and all their belongings. The besiegers, grasping at this petition, sent up to them Gorion son of Nicomedes, Ananias son of Sadok, and Judas son of Jonathan, to give a pledge of security and to take the necessary oaths. That done, Metilius marched his men down. So long as the soldiers retained their arms, none of the rebels molested them or gave any indication of treachery; but when, in accordance with the covenant, they had all laid down their bucklers and swords and, with no suspicion remaining, were taking their departure, Eleazar's party fell upon them, surrounded and massacred them; the Romans neither resisting nor suing for mercy, but merely appealing with loud cries to " the covenant " and " the oaths." Thus, brutally butchered, perished all save Metilius; he alone saved his life by entreaties and promises to turn Jew, and even to be circumcised. To the

Capitulation and massacre of the Roman garrison.

---

[a] § 445.

τὸ δὲ πάθος Ῥωμαίοις μὲν ἦν κοῦφον, ἐκ γὰρ
ἀπλέτου δυνάμεως ἀπαναλώθησαν ὀλίγοι, Ἰουδαίοις[1]
455 δὲ προοίμιον ἁλώσεως ἔδοξεν. καὶ κατιδόντες
ἀνηκέστους μὲν ἤδη τὰς αἰτίας τοῦ πολέμου,
τὴν δὲ πόλιν τηλικούτῳ μιάσματι πεφυρμένην,
ἐξ οὗ δαιμόνιόν τι μήνιμα προσδοκᾶν εἰκὸς ἦν,
εἰ καὶ μὴ τὴν ἐκ Ῥωμαίων ἄμυναν, ἐπένθουν
δημοσίᾳ, καὶ πλήρης μὲν κατηφείας ἦν ἡ πόλις,
ἕκαστος δὲ τῶν μετρίων ὡς αὐτὸς ὑπὲρ τῶν
456 στασιαστῶν δίκας δώσων τετάρακτο. καὶ γὰρ
δὴ σαββάτῳ συνέβη πραχθῆναι τὸν φόνον, ἐν ᾧ
διὰ τὴν θρησκείαν καὶ τῶν ὁσίων ἔργων ἔχουσιν
ἐκεχειρίαν.

457 (xviii. 1) Τῆς δ' αὐτῆς ἡμέρας καὶ ὥρας,
ὥσπερ ἐκ δαιμονίου προνοίας, ἀνῄρουν Καισαρεῖς
τοὺς παρ' ἑαυτοῖς Ἰουδαίους, ὡς ὑπὸ μίαν ὥραν
ἀποσφαγῆναι μὲν ὑπὲρ δισμυρίους, κενωθῆναι δὲ
πᾶσαν Ἰουδαίων τὴν Καισάρειαν· καὶ γὰρ τοὺς
διαφεύγοντας ὁ Φλῶρος συλλαβὼν κατῆγεν[2] δεσμώ-
458 τας εἰς τὰ νεώρια. πρὸς δὲ τὴν ἐκ τῆς Καισαρείας πληγὴν ὅλον τὸ ἔθνος ἐξαγριοῦται, καὶ
διαμερισθέντες τάς τε κώμας τῶν Σύρων καὶ
τὰς προσεχούσας ἐπόρθουν πόλεις, Φιλαδέλφειάν
τε καὶ Ἐσεβωνῖτιν[3] καὶ Γέρασαν καὶ Πέλλαν καὶ

---

[1] Ἰουδαίων PAL Lat.   [2] κατήγαγε LVRC.
[3] Hudson: Σεβωνῖτιν L: Γεβ(ε)ωνίτιν the rest.

---

[a] The day of the month was perhaps 17th Elul (Gorpiaeus),
if we may identify the massacre as the event referred to in
the old Jewish calendar *Megillath Taanith*: " On the 17th of
Elul the Romans *evacuated* Judah and Jerusalem " (vi. (b)
in Zeitlin's edition, Philadelphia, 1922) ; Zeitlin's identifica-

Romans this injury—the loss of a handful of men out of a boundless army—was slight; but to the Jews it looked like the prelude to their ruin. Seeing the grounds for war to be now beyond remedy, and the city polluted by such a stain of guilt as could not but arouse a dread of some visitation from heaven, if not of the vengeance of Rome, they gave themselves up to public mourning; the whole city was a scene of dejection, and among the moderates there was not one who was not racked with the thought that he would personally have to suffer for the rebels' crime. For, to add to its heinousness, the massacre took place on the sabbath,[a] a day on which from religious scruples Jews abstain even from the most innocent acts.

(xviii. 1) The same day and at the same hour, as it were by the hand of Providence, the inhabitants of Caesarea massacred the Jews who resided in their city; within one hour more than twenty thousand were slaughtered, and Caesarea was completely emptied of Jews, for the fugitives were arrested by orders of Florus and conducted, in chains, to the dockyards. The news of the disaster at Caesarea infuriated the whole nation; and parties of Jews sacked the Syrian villages and the neighbouring cities,[b] Philadelphia, Heshbon and its district, Gerasa,

Massacre of the Jews at Caesarea by the Syrians.

Jewish reprisals.

tion of that event as the capitulation mentioned in § 437 is open to the double objection that no terms were then made with the Romans and that Josephus dates that incident on the 6th of the month. The Romans held out, it seems, for eleven days more.

[b] The enumeration following begins in the south of Decapolis, proceeds northwards, rounds Galilee, and then generally follows the coast line from north to south. Separate parties probably started from Peraea, Galilee, and Judaea.

JOSEPHUS

459 Σκυθόπολιν. ἔπειτα Γαδάροις καὶ Ἵππῳ καὶ τῇ
Γαυλανίτιδι προσπεσόντες τὰ¹ μὲν καταστρεψά-
μενοι, τὰ¹ δ' ὑποπρήσαντες ἐχώρουν ἐπὶ Κάδασα
τὴν Τυρίων καὶ Πτολεμαΐδα Γάβαν² τε καὶ
460 Καισάρειαν. ἀντέσχεν δ' οὔτε Σεβαστὴ ταῖς
ὁρμαῖς αὐτῶν οὔτε Ἀσκάλων, ἀλλ' ἐπὶ ταύταις
πυρποληθείσαις Ἀνθηδόνα καὶ Γάζαν κατέσκαπ-
τον. πολλαὶ δὲ περὶ³ ἑκάστην τούτων τῶν πόλεων
ἀνηρπάζοντο κῶμαι, καὶ τῶν ἁλισκομένων ἀνδρῶν
φόνος ἦν ἄπειρος.
461 (2) Οὐ μὴν οἱ Σύροι τῶν Ἰουδαίων ἔλαττον
πλῆθος ἀνῄρουν, ἀλλὰ καὶ αὐτοὶ τοὺς ἐν ταῖς
πόλεσιν λαμβανομένους ἀπέσφαττον οὐ μόνον κατὰ
μῖσος, ὡς πρότερον, ἀλλ' ἤδη καὶ τὸν ἐφ' ἑαυτοῖς
462 κίνδυνον φθάνοντες. δεινὴ δὲ ὅλην τὴν Συρίαν
ἐπεῖχεν ταραχή, καὶ πᾶσα πόλις εἰς δύο διῄρητο
στρατόπεδα, σωτηρία δὲ τοῖς ἑτέροις ἦν τὸ τοὺς
463 ἑτέρους φθάσαι. καὶ τὰς μὲν ἡμέρας ἐν αἵματι
διῆγον, τὰς δὲ νύκτας δέει χαλεπωτέρας· καὶ γὰρ
ἀπεσκευάσθαι τοὺς Ἰουδαίους δοκοῦντες ἕκαστοι
τοὺς ἰουδαΐζοντας εἶχον ἐν ὑποψίᾳ, καὶ τὸ παρ'
ἑκάστοις ἀμφίβολον οὔτε ἀνελεῖν τις προχείρως
ὑπέμενεν, καὶ μεμιγμένον ὡς βεβαίως ἀλλόφυλον
464 ἐφοβεῖτο. προυκαλεῖτο δὲ ἐπὶ τὰς σφαγὰς τῶν
διαφόρων καὶ τοὺς πάλαι πραοτάτους πάνυ
δοκοῦντας ἡ πλεονεξία· τὰς γὰρ οὐσίας τῶν
ἀναιρεθέντων ἀδεῶς διήρπαζον καὶ καθάπερ ἐκ
παρατάξεως τὰ σκῦλα τῶν ἀνῃρημένων εἰς τοὺς
σφετέρους οἴκους μετέφερον, ἔνδοξός τε ἦν ὁ

---

¹ Many mss. read τάς.   ² Γάβαλαν PAM.
³ καθ' A : om. P (reading ἑκάστη for -ην).

502

Pella, and Scythopolis. Next they fell upon Gadara, Hippos, and Gaulanitis, destroying or setting fire to all in their path, and advanced to Kedasa,[a] a Tyrian village, Ptolemais, Gaba,[b] and Caesarea. Neither Sebaste[c] nor Ascalon withstood their fury ; these[d] they burnt to the ground and then razed Anthedon and Gaza. In the vicinity of each of these cities many villages were pillaged and immense numbers of the inhabitants captured and slaughtered.

(2) The Syrians on their side killed no less a number of Jews ; they, too, slaughtered those whom they caught in the towns, not merely now, as before, from hatred, but to forestall the peril which menaced themselves. The whole of Syria was a scene of frightful disorder ; every city was divided into two camps, and the safety of one party lay in their anticipating the other. They passed their days in blood, their nights, yet more dreadful, in terror. For, though believing that they had rid themselves of the Jews, still each city had its Judaizers, who aroused suspicion ; and while they shrank from killing offhand this equivocal element in their midst, they feared these neutrals as much as pronounced aliens. Even those who had long been reputed the very mildest of men were instigated by avarice to murder their adversaries ; for they would then with im-punity plunder the property of their victims and transfer to their own homes, as from a battle-field, the spoils of the slain, and he who gained the most

Syria a scene of massacres.

---

[a] Kedesh-Naphtali, north-west of Lake Merom, " always at war with Galilee " (iv. 105).

[b] A pro-Roman town in Galilee, built by Herod the Great for his veteran cavalry (*B.* iii. 36, *Vita* 115).

[c] Samaria.

[d] Or rather the surrounding villages (Reinach).

465 πλεῖστα κερδάνας ὡς κατισχύσας πλειόνων. ἦν
δὲ ἰδεῖν τὰς πόλεις μεστὰς ἀτάφων σωμάτων καὶ
νεκροὺς ἅμα νηπίοις γέροντας ἐρριμμένους, γύναιά
τε μηδὲ τῆς ἐπ' αἰδοῖ¹ σκέπης μετειληφότα, καὶ
πᾶσαν μὲν τὴν ἐπαρχίαν μεστὴν ἀδιηγήτων
συμφορῶν, μείζονα δὲ τῶν ἑκάστοτε τολμωμένων
τὴν ἐπὶ τοῖς ἀπειλουμένοις ἀνάτασιν.²

466 (3) Μέχρι μὲν δὴ τούτων Ἰουδαίοις πρὸς τὸ
ἀλλόφυλον ἦσαν προσβολαί, κατατρέχοντες δὲ εἰς
Σκυθόπολιν τοὺς παρ' ἐκείνοις Ἰουδαίους ἐπείρα-
σαν πολεμίους· ταξάμενοι γὰρ μετὰ τῶν Σκυθο-
πολιτῶν καὶ τῆς ἑαυτῶν ἀσφαλείας ἐν δευτέρῳ
θέμενοι τὴν συγγένειαν, ὁμόσε τοῖς ὁμοφύλοις
467 ἐχώρουν. ὑπωπτεύθη δ' αὐτῶν καὶ τὸ λίαν πρό-
θυμον· οἱ γοῦν Σκυθοπολῖται δείσαντες μὴ νύκτωρ
ἐπιχειρήσωσι τῇ πόλει καὶ μετὰ μεγάλης αὐτῶν
συμφορᾶς τοῖς οἰκείοις ἀπολογήσωνται περὶ τῆς
ἀποστάσεως, ἐκέλευον αὐτούς, εἰ βούλονται τὴν
ὁμόνοιαν βεβαιῶσαι καὶ τὸ πρὸς τοὺς ἀλλοεθνεῖς
πιστὸν ἐπιδείξασθαι, μεταβαίνειν ἅμα ταῖς γενεαῖς
468 εἰς τὸ ἄλσος. τῶν δὲ ποιησάντων τὸ προσταχθὲν
χωρὶς ὑποψίας, δύο μὲν ἡμέρας ἠρέμησαν οἱ
Σκυθοπολῖται τὴν πίστιν αὐτῶν δελεάζοντες, τῇ
δὲ τρίτῃ νυκτὶ παρατηρήσαντες τοὺς μὲν ἀφυλά-
κτους, οὓς δὲ κοιμωμένους, ἅπαντας ἀπέσφαξαν
ὄντας τὸν ἀριθμὸν ὑπὲρ μυρίους καὶ τρισχιλίους,
τὰς δὲ κτήσεις διήρπασαν ἁπάντων.

469 (4) Ἄξιον δ' ἀφηγήσασθαι καὶ τὸ Σίμωνος

¹ L: αἰδῶ the rest.
² Eus.: ἀνάστασιν (μετάστασιν) mss.

ᵃ The Biblical Bethshan, modern *Beisan*, the one town of

covered himself with glory as the most successful murderer. One saw cities choked with unburied corpses, dead bodies of old men and infants exposed side by side, poor women stripped of the last covering of modesty, the whole province full of indescribable horrors; and even worse than the tale of atrocities committed was the suspense caused by the menace of evils in store.

(3) Thus far the Jews had been faced with aliens only, but when they invaded Scythopolis [a] they found their own nation in arms against them; for the Jews in this district ranged themselves on the side of the Scythopolitans, and, regarding their own security as more important than the ties of blood, met their own countrymen in battle. However, this excess of ardour brought them under suspicion: the people of Scythopolis feared that the Jews might attack the city by night and inflict upon them some grave disaster, in order to make amends to their brethren for their defection. They, therefore, ordered them if they wished to confirm their allegiance and demonstrate their fidelity to their foreign allies, to betake themselves and their families to the adjoining grove. The Jews obeyed these orders, suspecting nothing. For two days the Scythopolitans made no move, in order to lull them into security, but on the third night, watching their opportunity when some were off their guard, and others asleep, they slaughtered them all to the number of upward of thirteen thousand and pillaged all their possessions.[b]

(4) Mention may here be made of the tragic fate

Perfidy of the Scythopolitans to their Jewish allies.

the ten cities of Decapolis which lay west of the Jordan, between it and Mt. Gilboa.

[b] This incident is referred to again in the *Life*, § 26.

πάθος, ὃς υἱὸς μὲν ἦν Σαούλου τινὸς τῶν οὐκ
ἀσήμων, ῥώμῃ δὲ σώματος καὶ τόλμῃ διαφέρων
ἐπὶ κακῷ τῶν ὁμοφύλων ἀμφοτέροις κατεχρήσατο·
470 προϊὼν γοῦν ὁσημέραι πολλοὺς μὲν ἀνῄρει τῶν
πρὸς τῇ Σκυθοπόλει Ἰουδαίων, τρεπόμενος δὲ
πολλάκις αὐτοὺς ἅπαντας μόνος ἦν ῥοπὴ τῆς
471 παρατάξεως. περιέρχεται δ' αὐτὸν ἀξία ποινὴ
τοῦ συγγενικοῦ φόνου· ἐπεὶ γὰρ περισχόντες οἱ
Σκυθοπολῖται κατηκόντιζον αὐτοὺς ἀνὰ τὸ ἄλσος,
σπασάμενος τὸ ξίφος ἐπ' οὐδένα μὲν ὥρμησεν τῶν
πολεμίων, καὶ γὰρ ἑώρα τὸ πλῆθος ἀνήνυτον,
472 ἀναβοήσας δὲ μάλα ἐκπαθῶς '' ἄξιά γε ὧν ἔδρασα
πάσχω, Σκυθοπολῖται [καθ' ὑμῶν],[1] οἳ[2] τοσούτῳ
φόνῳ συγγενῶν τὴν πρὸς αὐτοὺς[3] εὔνοιαν ἐπιστωσά-
μεθα.[4] τοιγαροῦν οἷς ἄπιστον μὲν εὐλόγως εὕρηται
τὸ ἀλλόφυλον, ἠσέβηται δὲ εἰς ἔσχατα τὸ οἰκεῖον,
θνήσκωμεν ὡς ἐναγεῖς χερσὶν ἰδίαις· οὐ γὰρ
473 πρέπον ἐν[5] ταῖς τῶν πολεμίων. τὸ αὐτὸ δ' ἂν
εἴη μοι καὶ ποινὴ τοῦ μιάσματος ἀξία καὶ πρὸς
ἀνδρείαν ἔπαινος, ἵνα μηδεὶς τῶν ἐχθρῶν τὴν ἐμὴν
αὐχήσῃ σφαγὴν μηδ' ἐπαλαζονεύηται πεσόντι.''
474 ταῦτ' εἰπὼν ἐλεοῦσιν ἅμα καὶ τεθυμωμένοις ὄμμασιν περισκέπτεται τὴν ἑαυτοῦ γενεάν· ἦν δ'
αὐτῷ καὶ γυνὴ καὶ τέκνα καὶ γηραιοὶ γονεῖς.
475 ὁ δὲ πρῶτον [μὲν][6] τὸν πατέρα τῆς πολιᾶς ἐπι-
σπασάμενος διελαύνει τῷ ξίφει, μεθ' ὃν οὐκ
ἄκουσαν τὴν μητέρα, κἀπὶ τούτοις τήν τε γυναῖκα
καὶ τὰ τέκνα, μόνον οὐχ ὑπαπαντῶντος ἑκάστου
τῷ ξίφει καὶ σπεύδοντος φθάσαι τοὺς πολεμίους.

---

[1] om. Lat. Heg.: παρ' ὑμῶν Hudson. [2] ὅτι MLVRC.
[3] uos Lat.: uobis Heg. [4] PAL: ἐπιστωσάμην the rest.
[5] ἦν Bekker. [6] P Lat.: om. the rest.

of Simon, whose father, Saul, was a man of some Heroic
distinction. Endowed with exceptional physical death of
strength and audacity, he abused both gifts to the Simon the
detriment of his countrymen. Day by day he had Jewish
marched out and slain large numbers of the Jews who renegade.
were attacking Scythopolis ; often had he put their
whole force to flight, his single arm turning the scale
in the engagement. But now this slaughter of his kin
met with its due penalty. For when the Scythopolitans
had surrounded the grove and were shooting down
its occupants with their javelins, he drew his sword,
and then, instead of rushing upon one of the enemy,
whose numbers he saw were endless, he exclaimed in
a tone of deep emotion : " Justly am I punished for
my crimes, men of Scythopolis, I and all who by such
a slaughter of our kinsmen have sealed our loyalty
to you. Ah ! well, let us who have but naturally
experienced the perfidy of foreigners, us who have
been guilty of the last degree of impiety towards our
own people, let us, I say, die, as cursed wretches, by
our own hands ; for we are not meet to die at the
hands of the enemy. This, God grant, shall be at
once the fit retribution for my foul crime and the
testimony to my courage, that none of my foes shall
be able to boast of having slain me or glory over my
prostrate body." With these words he cast a glance
of mingled pity and rage over his family : he had
wife, children, and aged parents. First seizing his
father by his hoary hair, he ran his sword through
his body ; after him he killed his mother, who offered
no resistance, and then his wife and children, each
victim almost rushing upon the blade, in haste to
anticipate the enemy. After slaying every member

476 ὁ δὲ διελθὼν πᾶσαν τὴν γενεὰν καὶ περίοπτος
ἐπιστὰς τοῖς σώμασιν τήν τε δεξιὰν ἀνατείνας,
ὡς μηδένα λαθεῖν, ὅλον εἰς τὴν ἑαυτοῦ σφαγὴν
ἐβάπτισεν τὸ ξίφος, ἄξιος μὲν ἐλέους [ὁ][1] νεανίας
δι᾽ ἀλκὴν σώματος καὶ ψυχῆς παράστημα, τῆς
δὲ πρὸς ἀλλοφύλους πίστεως ἕνεκεν ἀκολούθοις
πάθεσι χρησάμενος.

477 (5) Πρὸς δὲ τὴν ἐν Σκυθοπόλει φθορὰν αἱ
λοιπαὶ πόλεις ἐπανίσταντο τοῖς καθ᾽ ἑαυτὴν Ἰουδαίοις ἑκάστη, καὶ πεντακοσίους μὲν ἐπὶ δισχιλίοις Ἀσκαλωνῖται, Πτολεμαεῖς δὲ δισχιλίους
478 ἀνεῖλον, ἔδησάν τ᾽ οὐκ ὀλίγους. καὶ Τύριοι
συχνοὺς μὲν διεχειρίσαντο, πλείους[2] δ᾽ αὐτῶν
δεσμώτας ἐφρούρουν, Ἱππηνοί τε καὶ Γαδαρεῖς
ὁμοίως τοὺς μὲν θρασυτέρους ἀπεσκευάσαντο,
τοὺς δὲ φοβεροὺς διὰ φυλακῆς εἶχον, αἵ τε λοιπαὶ
πόλεις τῆς Συρίας, ὅπως ἑκάστη πρὸς τὸ Ἰου-
479 δαϊκὸν ἢ μίσους ἢ δέους εἶχον. μόνοι δ᾽ Ἀν-
τιοχεῖς καὶ Σιδώνιοι καὶ Ἀπαμεῖς ἐφείσαντο τῶν
μετοικούντων καὶ οὔτε ἀνελεῖν τινας Ἰουδαίων
ὑπέμειναν οὔτε δῆσαι, τάχα μὲν καὶ διὰ τὸ
σφέτερον πλῆθος ὑπερορῶντες αὐτῶν πρὸς τὰ
κινήματα, τὸ πλέον δ᾽ ἔμοιγε δοκεῖν[3] οἴκτῳ πρὸς
480 οὓς οὐδὲν ἑώρων νεωτερίζοντας. Γερασηνοί τε
οὔτε εἰς τοὺς ἐμμείναντας ἐπλημμέλησαν καὶ τοὺς
ἐξελθεῖν ἐθελήσαντας προέπεμψαν μέχρι τῶν ὅρων.

481 (6) Συνέστη δὲ καὶ κατὰ τὴν Ἀγρίππα βασιλείαν ἐπιβουλὴ κατὰ Ἰουδαίων. αὐτὸς γὰρ ἐπεπό-
ρευτο πρὸς Κέστιον Γάλλον εἰς Ἀντιόχειαν, κατα-

---

[1] om. L.
[2] Lat. (plures): πλείστους PAML: τὸ πλεῖον or τὸ πλεῖστον
the rest.   [3] Niese: δοκεῖ MSS.

508

of his family, he stood conspicuous on the corpses,
and with right hand uplifted to attract all eyes,
plunged the sword up to the hilt into his own throat.
So perished a youth who, in virtue of his strength of
body and fortitude of soul, deserves commiseration,
but who by reason of his trust in aliens met the
consequent fate.

(5) As a sequel to the holocaust at Scythopolis, the
other cities rose against the Jews in their
respective territories. The inhabitants of Ascalon
slew 2500, those of Ptolemais 2000, besides putting
multitudes in irons. The Tyrians dispatched a considerable number, but imprisoned the majority in
chains ; similarly the people of Hippos and Gadara
made away with the more daring of their enemies
and kept the timid folk in custody ; and so with the
remaining cities of Syria, the action of each being
governed by their feelings of hatred or fear of
their Jewish neighbours. Only Antioch, Sidon and
Apamea[a] spared the residents and refused either to
kill or to imprison a single Jew ; perhaps, with their
own vast populations, these cities disdained the
possibility of Jewish risings, but what mainly influenced them, in my opinion, was their pity for men
who showed no revolutionary intentions. The people
of Gerasa[b] not only abstained from maltreating the
Jews who remained with them, but escorted to the
frontiers any who chose to emigrate.

(6) Even within Agrippa's dominion a plot was
formed against certain Jews. The king himself had
gone to visit Cestius Gallus at Antioch, leaving in

General rising against the Jews throughout Syria.

---

[a] On the Orontes, south of Antioch.
[b] In the south-east of Decapolis, north of the river Jabbok.

λέλειπτο δὲ διοικεῖν τὰ πράγματα τούτου τῶν
ἑταίρων τις τοὔνομα Νόαρος, Σοαίμῳ τῷ βασιλεῖ
482 προσήκων κατὰ γένος. ἧκόν δ' ἐκ τῆς Βατα-
ναίας ἑβδομήκοντα τὸν ἀριθμὸν ἄνδρες, οἱ κατὰ
γένος καὶ σύνεσιν τῶν πολιτῶν δοκιμώτατοι,
στρατιὰν αἰτοῦντες, ἵν', εἴ τι γένοιτο κίνημα καὶ
περὶ σφᾶς, ἔχοιεν ἀξιόχρεων φυλακὴν κωλύειν
483 τοὺς ἐπανισταμένους. τούτους ὁ Νόαρος ἐκπέμψας νύκτωρ τῶν βασιλικῶν τινας ὁπλιτῶν ἅπαντας
ἀναιρεῖ, τολμήσας μὲν τοὖργον δίχα τῆς Ἀγρίππα
γνώμης, διὰ δὲ φιλαργυρίαν ἄμετρον εἰς τοὺς
ὁμοφύλους ἑλόμενος ἀσεβεῖν τὴν βασιλείαν δι-
έφθειρεν· διετέλει τε ὠμῶς εἰς τὸ ἔθνος παρανομῶν,
μέχρι πυθόμενος Ἀγρίππας ἀνελεῖν μὲν αὐτὸν
ᾐδέσθη διὰ Σόαιμον, ἔπαυσεν δὲ τῆς ἐπιτροπῆς.
484 οἱ δὲ στασιασταὶ καταλαβόμενοί τι φρούριον, ὃ
καλεῖται μὲν Κύπρος, καθύπερθεν δ' ἦν Ἱεριχοῦντος, τοὺς μὲν φρουροὺς ἀπέσφαξαν, τὰ δ'
485 ἐρύματα κατέρριψαν εἰς γῆν. κατὰ δὲ τὰς αὐτὰς
ἡμέρας καὶ τῶν ἐν Μαχαιροῦντι Ἰουδαίων τὸ
πλῆθος ἔπειθεν τοὺς φρουροῦντας Ῥωμαίους ἐκ-
486 λείπειν τὸ φρούριον καὶ παραδιδόναι σφίσιν. οἱ
δὲ τὴν ἐκ βίας ἀφαίρεσιν εὐλαβηθέντες συντίθενται
πρὸς αὐτοὺς ἐκχωρήσειν ὑπόσπονδοι καὶ λαβόντες
τὰ πιστὰ παραδιδόασι τὸ φρούριον, ὅπερ φυλακῇ
κρατυνάμενοι κατεῖχον οἱ Μαχαιρῖται.

---

^a Called Varus in the parallel account in *Vita*, 48 ff. and
possibly in *B*. ii. 247.

^b King of Emesa (*Homs*, in N. Syria), mentioned in *B*. ii.
501 as furnishing a contingent to the Romans, and elsewhere. In *Vita* 52 Varus is called a descendant (? grandson) of another Soaemus, who had been "a tetrarch in the

charge of the government one of his friends named
Noarus,[a] a relative of King Soaemus.[b] At this juncture
there arrived from Batanaea a deputation of seventy
persons, pre-eminent among their fellow-citizens by
birth and ability, to ask for a body of troops in order,
in the event of trouble arising in their district, to be
in a position to repress the insurgents. Noarus sent
out by night some of the king's heavy infantry and
massacred the whole deputation. This outrageous
action he took without consulting Agrippa ; un-
bounded avarice led him thus deliberately and
impiously to murder his countrymen, to the great
injury of the kingdom. He continued this brutal
maltreatment of the nation until Agrippa, being
informed of his conduct, but withheld by respect for
Soaemus from putting him to death, deposed him from
his regency.[c] It was now that the insurgents took
the fortress called Cypros,[d] which dominated Jericho,
massacred the garrison and levelled the defences.
About the same time the Jewish population of
Machaerus[e] succeeded in inducing the Roman
garrison to evacuate that fortress and to hand it over
to them. The Romans, fearing that it would be
carried by assault, agreed to retire under treaty, and
having received the necessary pledges surrendered
the fort, which the people of Machaerus thereupon
occupied and garrisoned.

Massacre of Jews by Agrippa's viceroy.

Capture of the forts Cypros and Machaerus by the rebels.

Lebanon district," and is probably identical with the " king
of Ituraea " mentioned in Tac. *Ann.* xii. 23 (died A.D. 49).

[c] The story of Varus's aspirations to supplant Agrippa,
his further massacres of Jews, and his supersession is told in
detail in *Vita* 52-61.

[d] Built by Herod the Great and named after his mother
(*B.* i. 417).

[e] Above the east coast of the Dead Sea.

487 (7) Κατὰ δὲ τὴν Ἀλεξάνδρειαν ἀεὶ μὲν ἦν στάσις
πρὸς τὸ Ἰουδαϊκὸν τοῖς ἐπιχωρίοις ἀφ' οὗ χρησάμενος προθυμοτάτοις κατὰ τῶν Αἰγυπτίων Ἰουδαίοις Ἀλέξανδρος γέρας τῆς συμμαχίας ἔδωκεν
τὸ μετοικεῖν κατὰ τὴν πόλιν ἐξ ἰσομοιρίας[1] πρὸς
488 τοὺς Ἕλληνας. διέμεινεν δ' αὐτοῖς ἡ τιμὴ καὶ
παρὰ τῶν διαδόχων, οἳ καὶ τόπον ἴδιον αὐτοῖς
ἀφώρισαν, ὅπως καθαρωτέραν ἔχοιεν τὴν δίαιταν,
ἧττον ἐπιμισγομένων τῶν ἀλλοφύλων, καὶ χρη-
ματίζειν ἐπέτρεψαν Μακεδόνας· ἐπεὶ δὲ Ῥωμαῖοι
κατεκτήσαντο τὴν Αἴγυπτον, οὔτε Καῖσαρ ὁ
πρῶτος οὔτε τῶν μετ' αὐτόν τις ὑπέμεινεν τὰς
ἀπ' Ἀλεξάνδρου τιμὰς Ἰουδαίων ἐλαττῶσαι.
489 συμβολαὶ δ' ἦσαν αὐτῶν ἀδιάλειπτοι πρὸς τοὺς
Ἕλληνας, καὶ τῶν ἡγεμόνων πολλοὺς ὁσημέραι
παρ' ἀμφοῖν κολαζόντων ἡ στάσις μᾶλλον παρ-
490 ωξύνετο. τότε δ' ὡς καὶ ⟨τὰ⟩[2] παρὰ τοῖς ἄλλοις
ἐτετάρακτο, μᾶλλον ἐξήφθη τὰ παρ' ἐκείνοις.
καὶ δὴ τῶν Ἀλεξανδρέων ἐκκλησιαζόντων περὶ
ἧς ἔμελλον ἐκπέμπειν πρεσβείας ἐπὶ Νέρωνα,
συνερρύησαν μὲν εἰς τὸ ἀμφιθέατρον ἅμα τοῖς
491 Ἕλλησιν συχνοὶ Ἰουδαίων, κατιδόντες δὲ αὐτοὺς
οἱ διάφοροι παραχρῆμα [μὲν][3] ἀνεβόων πολεμίους
καὶ κατασκόπους λέγοντες· ἔπειτα ἀναπηδήσαντες
ἐπέβαλλον τὰς χεῖρας αὐτοῖς. οἱ μὲν οὖν λοιποὶ
φεύγοντες διεσπάρησαν,[4] τρεῖς δὲ ἄνδρας συλ-
492 λαβόντες ἔσυρον ὡς ζῶντας καταφλέξοντες. ἤρθη

---

[1] Destinon: ἐξ ἰσουμοίρας (sic) PA: ἐξ ἰσοτιμίας the rest.
[2] ins. Destinon.   [3] A: om. the rest.
[4] Naber with Lat.: διεφθάρησαν MSS.

---

[a] Josephus elsewhere states that this quarter was given
them by Alexander (*Ap.* ii. 35 with note). The privileges

512

(7) At Alexandria there had been incessant strife between the native inhabitants and the Jewish settlers since the time when Alexander, having received from the Jews very active support against the Egyptians, granted them, as a reward for their assistance, permission to reside in the city on terms of equality with the Greeks. This privilege was confirmed by his successors, who, moreover, assigned them a quarter of their own,[a] in order that, through mixing less with aliens, they might be free to observe their rules more strictly ; and they were also permitted to take the title of Macedonians. Again, when the Romans took possession of Egypt, neither the first Caesar nor any of his successors would consent to any diminution of the honours conferred on the Jews since the time of Alexander. They were, however, continually coming into collision with the Greeks, and the numerous punishments daily inflicted on the rioters of both parties by the authorities only served to embitter the quarrel. But now that disorder had become universal, the riots at Alexandria broke out more furiously than ever. On one occasion, when the Alexandrians were holding a public meeting on the subject of an embassy which they proposed to send to Nero, a large number of Jews flocked into the amphitheatre along with the Greeks ; their adversaries, the instant they caught sight of them, raised shouts of " enemies " and " spies," and then rushed forward to lay hands on them. The majority of the Jews took flight and scattered, but three of them were caught by the Alexandrians and dragged off to be burnt alive. Thereupon the whole Jewish

Riots at Alexandria : Greeks v. Jews.

bestowed on the Alexandrian Jews by the Ptolemies and the Romans are stated more fully in *Ap.* ii. 42-64.

δὲ πᾶν τὸ Ἰουδαϊκὸν ἐπὶ τὴν ἄμυναν, καὶ τὸ μὲν
πρῶτον λίθοις τοὺς Ἕλληνας ἔβαλλον, αὖθις δὲ
λαμπάδας ἁρπασάμενοι πρὸς τὸ ἀμφιθέατρον
ὥρμησαν, ἀπειλοῦντες ἐν αὐτῷ καταφλέξειν τὸν
δῆμον αὔτανδρον. κἂν ἔφθησαν τοῦτο δράσαντες,
εἰ μὴ τοὺς θυμοὺς αὐτῶν ἀνέκοψεν Τιβέριος
493 Ἀλέξανδρος ὁ τῆς πόλεως ἡγεμών. οὐ μὴν
οὗτός γε ἀπὸ τῶν ὅπλων ἤρξατο σωφρονίζειν,
ἀλλ᾽ ὑποπέμψας τοὺς γνωρίμους αὐτοῖς παύσασθαι
παρεκάλει καὶ μὴ καθ᾽ ἑαυτῶν ἐρεθίζειν τὸ Ῥωμαίων στράτευμα. καταχλευάζοντες δὲ τῆς παρα-
κλήσεως οἱ στασιώδεις ἐβλασφήμουν τὸν Τιβέριον.

494 (8) Κἀκεῖνος συνιδὼν ὡς χωρὶς μεγάλης συμφορᾶς οὐκ ἂν παύσαιντο νεωτερίζοντες, ἐπαφίησιν
αὐτοῖς τὰ κατὰ τὴν πόλιν Ῥωμαίων δύο τάγματα
καὶ σὺν αὐτοῖς δισχιλίους[1] στρατιώτας κατὰ τύχην
παρόντας εἰς τὸν Ἰουδαίων ὄλεθρον ἐκ Λιβύης·
ἐπέτρεψεν δ᾽ οὐ μόνον ἀναιρεῖν, ἀλλὰ καὶ τὰς
κτήσεις αὐτῶν διαρπάζειν καὶ τὰς οἰκίας κατα-
495 φλέγειν. οἱ δ᾽ ὁρμήσαντες εἰς τὸ καλούμενον
Δέλτα, συνῴκιστο γὰρ ἐκεῖ τὸ Ἰουδαϊκόν, ἐτέλουν
τὰς ἐντολάς, οὐ μὴν ἀναιμωτί· συστραφέντες γὰρ
οἱ Ἰουδαῖοι καὶ τοὺς ἄμεινον ὡπλισμένους ἑαυτῶν
προταξάμενοι μέχρι πλείστου μὲν ἀντέσχον, ἅπαξ
496 δ᾽ ἐγκλίναντες[2] ἀνέδην διεφθείροντο. καὶ παν-
τοῖος ἦν αὐτῶν ὄλεθρος, τῶν μὲν ἐν τῷ πεδίῳ
καταλαμβανομένων, τῶν δ᾽ εἰς τὰς οἰκίας συνωθουμένων. ὑπεπίμπρασαν δὲ καὶ ταύτας οἱ Ῥωμαῖοι

[1] πεντακισχιλίους LVRC Lat.
[2] Bekker: δὲ ἐκκλίναντες or δὲ κλίναντες MSS.

---

[a] And prefect (viceroy) of the whole province of Egypt;
see B. ii. 220 note and iv. 616.

colony rose to the rescue ; first they hurled stones at the Greeks, and then snatching up torches rushed to the amphitheatre, threatening to consume the assembled citizens in the flames to the last man. And this they would actually have done, had not Tiberius Alexander, the governor of the city,[a] curbed their fury. He first, however, attempted to recall them to reason without recourse to arms, quietly sending the principal citizens to them and entreating them to desist and not to provoke the Roman army to take action. But the rioters only ridiculed this exhortation and used abusive language of Tiberius.

(8) Understanding then that nothing but the infliction of a severe lesson would quell the rebels, he let loose upon them the two Roman legions stationed in the city,[b] together with two thousand soldiers, who by chance had just arrived from Libya to complete the ruin of the Jews ; permission was given them not merely to kill the rioters but to plunder their property and burn down their houses. The troops, thereupon, rushed to the quarter of the city called " Delta,"[c] where the Jews were concentrated, and executed their orders, but not without bloodshed on their own side ; for the Jews closing their ranks and putting the best armed among their number in the front offered a prolonged resistance, but when once they gave way, wholesale carnage ensued. Death in every form was theirs ; some were caught in the plain, others driven into their houses, to which the Romans set fire after stripping

The Roman soldiers let loose upon the Alexandrian Jews.

[b] *Cf.* § 387 note.
[c] The five quarters of Alexandria were called after the first five letters of the alphabet, two being occupied by Jews (Philo, *In Flaccum*, § 55 Cohn ; quoted by Reinach).

515

προδιαρπάζοντες τὰ ἔνδον, καὶ οὔτε νηπίων ἔλεος
αὐτοὺς οὔτε αἰδὼς εἰσήει γερόντων, ἀλλὰ διὰ
497 πάσης ἡλικίας ἐχώρουν κτείνοντες, ὡς ἐπικλυσθῆναι
μὲν αἵματι πάντα τὸν χῶρον, πέντε δὲ μυριάδες
ἐσωρεύθησαν νεκρῶν, περιελείφθη δ᾽ ἂν οὐδὲ τὸ
λοιπόν, εἰ μὴ πρὸς ἱκετηρίας ἐτράποντο. κατ-
οικτείρας δ᾽ αὐτοὺς Ἀλέξανδρος ἀναχωρεῖν τοὺς
498 Ῥωμαίους ἐκέλευσεν. οἱ μὲν οὖν ἐξ ἔθους τὸ
πειθήνιον ἔχοντες ἅμα νεύματι τοῦ φονεύειν ἐπαύσαντο, τὸ δημοτικὸν δὲ τῶν Ἀλεξανδρέων δι᾽
ὑπερβολὴν μίσους δυσανάκλητον ἦν καὶ μόλις
ἀπεσπᾶτο τῶν σωμάτων.

499   (9) Τοιοῦτον μὲν τὸ κατὰ τὴν Ἀλεξάνδρειαν
πάθος συνηνέχθη· Κεστίῳ δὲ οὐκέτι ἠρεμεῖν
ἐδόκει πανταχοῦ τῶν Ἰουδαίων ἐκπεπολεμωμένων.
500 ἀναλαβὼν δὲ ἀπὸ τῆς Ἀντιοχείας τὸ μὲν δωδέ-
κατον τάγμα πλῆρες, ἀπὸ δὲ τῶν λοιπῶν ἀνὰ
δισχιλίους ἐπιλέκτους, πεζῶν τε ἐξ σπείρας καὶ
τέσσαρας ἴλας ἱππέων, πρὸς αἷς τὰς παρὰ τῶν
βασιλέων συμμαχίας, Ἀντιόχου μὲν δισχιλίους
ἱππεῖς καὶ πεζοὺς τρισχιλίους, τοξότας πάντας,
Ἀγρίππα δὲ πεζοὺς μὲν τοὺς ἴσους ἱππεῖς δὲ
501 δισχιλίων ἐλάττους, εἵπετο δὲ καὶ Σόαιμος μετὰ
τετρακισχιλίων, ὧν ἦσαν ἱππεῖς ἡ τρίτη μοῖρα καὶ
τὸ πλέον τοξόται, προῆλθεν εἰς Πτολεμαΐδα.
502 πλεῖστοι δὲ κἀκ τῶν πόλεων ἐπίκουροι συνελέγη-

ᵃ Governor of Syria, ii. 280, etc.
ᵇ There were four legions in Syria, as there had been since
the time of Augustus (Tac. *Ann.* iv. 5, quoted by Reinach):
516

them of their contents ; there was no pity for infancy,
no respect for years : all ages fell before their
murderous career, until the whole district was
deluged with blood and the heaps of corpses numbered
fifty thousand ; even the remnant would not have
escaped, had they not sued for quarter. Alexander,
now moved to compassion, ordered the Romans to
retire. They, broken to obedience, ceased massacring at the first signal ; but the Alexandrian
populace in the intensity of their hate were not so
easily called off and were with difficulty torn from
the corpses.

(9) Such was the catastrophe which befell the
Jews of Alexandria. Cestius,[a] now that on all
sides war was being made upon the Jews, decided
to remain inactive no longer. He accordingly left
Antioch, taking with him the twelfth legion in full
strength, two thousand picked men from each of the
other legions,[b] and in addition six cohorts of infantry
and four squadrons of cavalry ; besides these he had
the auxiliary contingents furnished by the kings, of
which Antiochus [c] supplied two thousand horse and
three thousand foot, all archers, Agrippa an equal
number of foot and rather less than two thousand
horse, Soaemus [d] following with four thousand, of
which one-third were cavalry and the majority archers.
With these troops he advanced upon Ptolemais.
Further auxiliaries in very large numbers were

Cestius
Gallus takes
the field.

viz. III Gallica, VI Ferrata, X Fretensis, XII Fulminata ;
Mommsen, *Provinces*, ii. 63 note.

[c] Antiochus IV, king of Commagene (in N. Syria) from
A.D. 38 to 72, when he was deprived of his kingdom on the
charge of conspiracy (*B.* vii. 219 ff.).

[d] King of Emesa, § 481 note.

JOSEPHUS

σαν, ἐμπειρίᾳ μὲν ἡττώμενοι τῶν στρατιωτῶν,
ταῖς δὲ προθυμίαις καὶ τῷ κατὰ Ἰουδαίων μίσει
τὸ λεῖπον ἐν ταῖς ἐπιστήμαις ἀντιπληροῦντες.
παρῆν[1] δὲ καὶ αὐτὸς Ἀγρίππας Κεστίῳ τῆς τε
503 ὁδοῦ καὶ τῶν συμφερόντων ἐξηγούμενος. ἀναλαβὼν δὲ μέρος τῆς δυνάμεως Κέστιος ὥρμησεν
ἐπὶ πόλιν καρτερὰν τῆς Γαλιλαίας, Χαβουλὼν[2] καλεῖται[3], διορίζει δὲ ἀπὸ τοῦ ἔθνους τὴν Πτολεμαΐδα.
504 καὶ καταλαβὼν αὐτὴν ἔρημον μὲν ἀνδρῶν, ἀνα-
πεφεύγει γὰρ τὸ πλῆθος εἰς τὰ ὄρη, πλήρη δὲ
παντοίων κτημάτων, τὰ μὲν ἐφῆκεν τοῖς στρατιώταις διαρπάζειν, τὸ δὲ ἄστυ καίτοι θαυμάσας τοῦ
κάλλους, ἔχον τὰς οἰκίας ὁμοίως ταῖς ἐν Τύρῳ
καὶ Σιδῶνι καὶ Βηρυτῷ δεδομημένας, ἐνέπρησεν.
505 ἔπειτα τὴν χώραν καταδραμὼν καὶ διαρπάσας
μὲν πᾶν τὸ προσπῖπτον καταφλέξας δὲ τὰς πέριξ
506 κώμας ὑπέστρεψεν εἰς τὴν Πτολεμαΐδα. πρὸς δὲ
ταῖς ἁρπαγαῖς ἔτι τῶν Σύρων ὄντων καὶ τὸ πλέον
Βηρυτίων ἀναθαρσήσαντες οἱ Ἰουδαῖοι, καὶ γὰρ
ἀποκεχωρηκότα συνίεσαν Κέστιον, τοῖς ἀπο-
λειφθεῖσιν ἀδοκήτως ἐπέπεσον καὶ περὶ δισχιλίους
αὐτῶν διέφθειραν.
507 (10) Ὁ δὲ Κέστιος ἀναζεύξας ἀπὸ τῆς Πτολεμαΐδος αὐτὸς μὲν εἰς Καισάρειαν ἀφικνεῖται,
μοῖραν δὲ τῆς στρατιᾶς προέπεμψεν εἰς Ἰόππην,
προστάξας, εἰ μὲν καταλαβέσθαι δυνηθεῖεν τὴν
πόλιν, φρουρεῖν, εἰ δὲ προαίσθοιντο τὴν ἔφοδον,
508 περιμένειν αὐτόν τε καὶ τὴν ἄλλην δύναμιν. τῶν
δ' οἱ μὲν κατὰ θάλασσαν οἱ δὲ κατὰ γῆν ἐπει-

---

[1] συμπαρῆν MVRC.   [2] Niese (cf. iii. 38): Ζαβουλὼν mss.
[3] ἢ (or ᾗ) καλεῖται ἀνδρῶν mss.: ἀνδρῶν has probably come
in from the next sentence (Niese).

collected from the towns; these, though lacking the experience of the regulars, made good their deficiency in technical training by their ardour and their detestation of the Jews. Agrippa personally accompanied Cestius, to guide and to provide for the interests of the army. With a detachment of these troops, Cestius marched against a fortified city of Galilee, called Chabulon,[a] on the frontier of Ptolemais and Jewish territory. He found it deserted by its inhabitants, who had all fled up into the hills, but stocked with goods of all kinds, which he allowed his soldiers to pillage; the town itself, although he admired its beauty, with its houses built in the style of those at Tyre, Sidon, and Berytus, he set on fire. He next overran the district, sacking everything in his path and burning the surrounding villages, and then returned to Ptolemais. But while the Syrians and in particular those of Berytus were still occupied in pillage, the Jews, understanding that Cestius had departed, recovered courage, and, falling unexpectedly on the troops which he had left behind, killed about two thousand of them.

Capture of Chabulon

(10) Leaving Ptolemais and resuming his march, Cestius himself proceeded to Caesarea, but sent forward a detachment of his force to Joppa, with orders to garrison the town, if they succeeded in taking it by surprise, but if the inhabitants obtained previous intelligence of their approach, to await his arrival with the main body. These troops advancing rapidly in two parties, by sea and land, easily carried

and Joppa

---

[a] Called Chabolo in the *Life*, 213, etc., modern Kabul; it probably gave its name to the district presented by Solomon to Hiram (1 Kings ix. 13).

χθέντες ἀμφοτέρωθεν αἱροῦσιν τὴν πόλιν ῥᾳδίως·
καὶ μηδὲ φυγεῖν φθασάντων τῶν οἰκητόρων, οὐχ
ὅπως παρασκευάσασθαι πρὸς μάχην, ἐμπεσόντες
ἅπαντας ἀνεῖλον σὺν ταῖς γενεαῖς καὶ τὴν πόλιν
509 διαρπάσαντες ἐνέπρησαν· ὁ δὲ ἀριθμὸς τῶν φονευθέντων τετρακόσιοι πρὸς ὀκτακισχιλίοις. ὁμοίως
δὲ καὶ εἰς τὴν ὅμορον τῆς Καισαρείας Ναρβατηνὴν
τοπαρχίαν ἔπεμψεν συχνοὺς τῶν ἱππέων, οἳ τήν
τε γῆν ἔτεμον καὶ πολὺ πλῆθος διέφθειραν τῶν
ἐπιχωρίων, τάς τε κτήσεις διήρπασαν καὶ τὰς
κώμας κατέφλεξαν.

510   (11) Εἰς δὲ τὴν Γαλιλαίαν ἀπέστειλεν Και-
σέννιον Γάλλον ἡγεμόνα τοῦ δωδεκάτου τάγματος,
παραδοὺς δύναμιν ὅσην ἀρκέσειν πρὸς τὸ ἔθνος
511 ὑπελάμβανεν. τοῦτον ἡ καρτερωτάτη τῆς Γαλιλαίας πόλις Σέπφωρις μετ᾽ εὐφημίας δέχεται, καὶ
πρὸς τὴν ταύτης εὐβουλίαν αἱ λοιπαὶ πόλεις
ἠρέμουν. τὸ δὲ στασιῶδες καὶ ληστρικὸν πᾶν
ἔφυγεν εἰς τὸ μεσαίτατον τῆς Γαλιλαίας ὄρος, ὃ
κεῖται μὲν ἀντικρὺ τῆς Σεπφώρεως, καλεῖται δὲ
᾽Ασαμών. τούτοις ὁ Γάλλος ἐπῆγε τὴν δύναμιν.
512 οἱ δ᾽ ἕως μὲν ἦσαν ὑπερδέξιοι, ῥᾳδίως τοὺς ῾Ρω-
μαίους ἠμύναντο προσιόντας καὶ πρὸς διακοσίους
αὐτῶν ἀνεῖλον, περιελθόντων δὲ καὶ γενομένων ἐν
τοῖς ὑψηλοτέροις ἡττῶντο ταχέως, καὶ οὔτε γυμ-
νῆτες ὁπλίτας συστάδην ἔφερον οὔτε ἐν τῇ τροπῇ
τοὺς ἱππεῖς ἐξέφευγον, ὥστε ὀλίγους μὲν ἐν ταῖς
δυσχωρίαις διαλαθεῖν, ἀναιρεθῆναι δὲ ὑπὲρ δισχιλίους.

513   (xix. 1) Γάλλος μὲν οὖν ὡς οὐδὲν ἔτι ἑώρα
κατὰ τὴν Γαλιλαίαν νεωτεριζόμενον, ὑπέστρεφεν
μετὰ τῆς στρατιᾶς εἰς Καισάρειαν· Κέστιος δὲ

the town by an attack on both elements; the inhabitants had no time to fly, much less to prepare for defence, and the Romans, bursting in, slew them all with their families, and sacked and burnt the town; the victims numbered eight thousand four hundred. Cestius likewise dispatched a strong force of cavalry into the toparchy of Narbatene,[a] which borders on Caesarea; these ravaged the country, killed a large number of the inhabitants, pillaged their property and burnt their villages.

(11) To Galilee he sent Caesennius Gallus, commander of the twelfth legion, with such forces as he considered sufficient for the reduction of that province. Sepphoris, the strongest city in Galilee, received Gallus with open arms, and, following the sage advice of this city, the rest remained quiet. All the rebels and brigands in the district fled to the mountain in the heart of Galilee, which faces Sepphoris and is called Asamon[b]; against these Gallus led his troops. So long as the enemy held the superior position, they easily beat off the attacks of the Romans and killed some two hundred of them, but when the Romans turned their flank and gained the higher ground, they were quickly defeated; being lightly armed, they could not sustain the charge of the heavy-armed legionaries, nor when routed outdistance the cavalry; consequently a few only succeeded in concealing themselves in [c] broken ground, while more than two thousand perished. *and reduction of Galilee.*

(xix. 1) Gallus, seeing no further signs of revolt in Galilee, returned with his troops to Caesarea; where- *March of Cestius upon Jeruaslem.*

---

[a] *Cf.* ii. 291.   [b] Unidentified.
[c] Or perhaps " escaping over."

μετὰ πάσης τῆς δυνάμεως ἀναζεύξας ἐνέβαλεν εἰς
Ἀντιπατρίδα, καὶ πυθόμενος ἔν τινι πύργῳ
Ἀφεκοῦ καλουμένῳ συνηθροῖσθαι Ἰουδαίων δύναμιν οὐκ ὀλίγην, προύπεμψε τοὺς συμβαλοῦντας.
514 οἱ δὲ πρὶν εἰς χεῖρας ἐλθεῖν δέει τοὺς Ἰουδαίους
διεσκέδασαν, ἐπελθόντες δὲ ἔρημον τὸ στρατόπεδον
515 καὶ τὰς πέριξ κώμας ἐνέπρησαν. ἀπὸ δὲ τῆς
Ἀντιπατρίδος Κέστιος εἰς Λύδδα προελθὼν κενὴν
ἀνδρῶν τὴν πόλιν καταλαμβάνει· διὰ γὰρ τὴν τῆς
σκηνοπηγίας ἑορτὴν ἀναβεβήκει πᾶν τὸ πλῆθος εἰς
516 Ἱεροσόλυμα. πεντήκοντα δὲ τῶν παραφανέντων
διαφθείρας καὶ τὸ ἄστυ κατακαύσας ἐχώρει πρόσω,
καὶ διὰ Βαιθώρων ἀναβὰς στρατοπεδεύεται κατά
τινα χῶρον Γαβαὼ καλούμενον, ἀπέχοντα τῶν
Ἱεροσολύμων πεντήκοντα σταδίους.
517   (2) Οἱ δὲ Ἰουδαῖοι κατιδόντες ἤδη πλησιάζοντα
τῇ μητροπόλει τὸν πόλεμον, ἀφέμενοι τὴν ἑορτὴν
ἐχώρουν ἐπὶ τὰ ὅπλα, καὶ μέγα τῷ πλήθει θαρροῦντες ἄτακτοι [καὶ]¹ μετὰ κραυγῆς ἐξεπήδων
ἐπὶ τὴν μάχην, μηδὲ τῆς ἀργῆς ἑβδομάδος ἔννοιαν
λαβόντες· ἦν γὰρ δὴ τὸ μάλιστα παρ' αὐτοῖς
518 θρησκευόμενον σάββατον. ὁ δ' ἐκσείσας αὐτοὺς
τῆς εὐσεβείας θυμὸς ἐποίησεν πλεονεκτῆσαι καὶ
κατὰ τὴν μάχην· μετὰ τοσαύτης γοῦν ὁρμῆς τοῖς
Ῥωμαίοις προσέπεσον, ὡς διαρρῆξαι τὰς τάξεις
519 αὐτῶν καὶ διὰ μέσων χωρεῖν ἀναιροῦντας. εἰ δὲ
μὴ τῷ χαλασθέντι τῆς φάλαγγος οἵ τε ἱππεῖς

¹ om. PAL.

ᵃ In the plain of Sharon, north-east of Joppa.
ᵇ Or perhaps " called after Aphek." Several places of
the name are mentioned in the O.T. : this may be the Aphek
522

upon Cestius resumed his march with his entire army
and entered Antipatris.[a] Learning that a considerable
body of Jews had assembled in a tower called Apheku,[b]
he sent on a detachment to attack them. Fear, however, dispersed the Jews before any engagement took
place ; and the Romans, on invading their camp,
found it evacuated, and burnt it and the neighbouring villages. From Antipatris Cestius advanced to
Lydda[c] and found the city deserted, for the whole
population had gone up to Jerusalem for the Feast
of Tabernacles. Fifty persons who showed themselves he put to the sword, and after burning down
the town resumed his march ; and, ascending through
Beth-horon, pitched his camp at a place called
Gabao,[d] fifty furlongs distant from Jerusalem.

c. October
A.D. 66 (15-22
Tishri).

(2) The Jews, seeing the war now approaching the
capital, abandoned the feast and rushed to arms ;
and, with great confidence in their numbers, sprang
in disorder and with loud cries into the fray, with no
thought for the seventh day of rest, for it was the
very sabbath which they regarded with special
reverence.[e] But the same passion which shook
them out of their piety brought them victory in the
battle ; for with such fury did they fall upon the
Romans that they broke and penetrated their ranks,
slaughtering the enemy. Had not the cavalry, with
a body of infantry which was not so hard pressed as

A successful
Jewish
charge
outside
Jerusalem.

in Sharon (Jos. xii. 18, some LXX mss.), doubtfully identified
with *el Mejdel*, south-east of Caesarea.

[e] *Ludd*, south of Antipatris, at the point where the road
from the north joins the route from Joppa via Beth-horon to
Jerusalem.

[d] The O.T. Gibeon, modern *el Jib*, five or six miles north-
west of Jerusalem ; the distance given in *A.* vii. 283 is only
40 furlongs (stadia). For Beth-horon see § 547 note.

[e] Falling within the week of the Feast of Tabernacles.

ἐκπεριελθόντες ἐπήμυναν καὶ τοῦ πεζοῦ τὸ μὴ
σφόδρα κάμνον, κἂν ἐκινδύνευσεν ὅλῃ τῇ δυνάμει
Κέστιος. ἀπέθανον δὲ Ῥωμαίων πεντακόσιοι
δεκαπέντε· τούτων ἦσαν οἱ τετρακόσιοι πεζοί, τὸ
δὲ λοιπὸν ἱππεῖς· τῶν δὲ Ἰουδαίων δύο πρὸς τοῖς
520 εἴκοσι. γενναιότατοι δ' αὐτῶν ἔδοξαν οἱ Μονο-
βάζου τοῦ τῆς Ἀδιαβηνῆς βασιλέως συγγενεῖς,
Μονόβαζός τε καὶ Κενεδαῖος, μεθ' οὓς ὁ Περαΐτης
Νίγερ καὶ Σίλας ὁ Βαβυλώνιος αὐτομολήσας εἰς
τοὺς Ἰουδαίους ἀπ' Ἀγρίππα τοῦ βασιλέως·
521 ἐστρατεύετο γὰρ παρ' αὐτῷ. κατὰ πρόσωπον
μὲν οὖν ἀνακοπέντες Ἰουδαῖοι πρὸς τὴν πόλιν
ὑπέστρεφον, κατόπιν δὲ τοῖς Ῥωμαίοις ἐπὶ τὴν
Βεθώραν[1] ἀνιοῦσιν προσπεσὼν ὁ τοῦ Γιώρα Σίμων
πολὺ τῆς οὐραγίας ἐσπάραξεν καὶ συχνὰ τῶν
σκευοφόρων ἀποσπάσας ἤγαγεν εἰς τὴν πόλιν.
522 μένοντος δὲ τοῦ Κεστίου κατὰ χώραν τρισὶν
ἡμέραις οἱ Ἰουδαῖοι τὰ μετέωρα κατειληφότες
ἐπετήρουν τὰς παρόδους, δῆλοί τε ἦσαν οὐκ ἠρεμήσοντες ἀρξαμένων τῶν Ῥωμαίων ὁδεύειν.

523   (3) Ἔνθα δὴ κατιδὼν Ἀγρίππας οὐδὲ τὰ Ῥωμαίων ἀκίνδυνα, πλήθους ἀπείρου πολεμίων τὰ
ὄρη περισχόντος, ἔκρινεν ἀποπειραθῆναι τῶν Ἰουδαίων λόγοις· ἢ γὰρ πάντας πείσειν καταθέσθαι
τὸν πόλεμον ἢ τῶν ἐναντιωθέντων ἀποστήσειν τὸ
524 μὴ συμφρονοῦν. ἔπεμψεν οὖν τῶν παρ' ἑαυτῷ
τοὺς μάλιστα γνωρίμους ἐκείνοις, Βόρκιόν τε καὶ
Φοῖβον, δεξιάς τε παρὰ Κεστίου καὶ συγγνώμην
παρὰ Ῥωμαίοις ἀσφαλῆ περὶ τῶν ἡμαρτημένων

---

[1] PAL : Βαιθωρῶν the rest.

[a] King Monobazus, like his brother Izates, whom he had

the rest, wheeled round to the relief of the broken
line, Cestius and his whole army would have been in
jeopardy. The Roman killed were five hundred and
fifteen, of whom four hundred were infantry and the
rest cavalry ; the Jews lost but two and twenty. In
the Jewish ranks the most distinguished for valour
were Monobazus and Cenedaeus, kinsmen of Monobazus,[a] king of Adiabene ; next to them came Niger
of Peraea and Silas the Babylonian,[b] a deserter to
the Jews from the army of King Agrippa. The Jews,
when their frontal attack was checked, retired to the
city ; but from the back of their lines Simon, son of
Gioras, fell upon the Romans as they were mounting
towards Beth-horon, cut up a large part of their rearguard, and carried off many of the baggage mules,
which he brought with him into the city. While
Cestius for three days remained in his former quarters,
the Jews occupied the heights and kept guard on the
defiles, clearly not intending to remain inactive,
should the Romans begin to move.

(3) At this juncture, Agrippa, perceiving that,
with the enemy in such countless numbers in possession of the surrounding mountains, even a Roman
army was in a perilous position, decided to try the
effect of parley with the Jews ; he hoped either to
prevail on all to abandon hostilities, or at least to
detach from their opponents those who did not share
the views of the war party. He accordingly sent his
two friends, whom the Jews knew best, Borcius and
Phoebus, with an offer of a treaty on the part of
Cestius and of sure pardon for their misdoings on the

*Agrippa
vainly
attempts
a parley
with the
Jews.*

recently succeeded, and his mother Helena, was a convert
to Judaism ; *cf.* § 388 note.
  [b] Probably one of the colony of Babylonian Jews settled
in Batanaea (*Vita* 54 note).

ὑπισχνούμενος, εἰ τὰ ὅπλα ῥίψαντες πρὸς αὐτοὺς
525 μεταβάλοιντο. δείσαντες δ' οἱ στασιασταί, μὴ
πᾶν τὸ πλῆθος ἀδείας ἐλπίδι πρὸς τὸν Ἀγρίππαν
μεταβάληται, τοὺς ἀπ' αὐτοῦ πρεσβεύοντας ὥρ-
526 μησαν ἀνελεῖν. καὶ πρὶν ἢ φθέγξασθαι τὸν μὲν
Φοῖβον διέφθειραν, ὃ δὲ Βόρκιος τρωθεὶς ἔφθη
διαφυγεῖν· τοῦ δήμου δὲ τοὺς ἀγανακτήσαντας
λίθοις καὶ ξύλοις παίοντες εἰς τὸ ἄστυ συνήλασαν.
527 (4) Κέστιος δὲ τὴν πρὸς ἀλλήλους αὐτῶν ταραχὴν εὔκαιρον ἰδὼν εἰς ἐπίθεσιν, ἅπασαν ἐπῆγεν
τὴν δύναμιν καὶ τραπέντας μέχρι Ἱεροσολύμων
528 κατεδίωξεν. στρατοπεδευσάμενος δὲ ἐπὶ τοῦ καλουμένου Σκοποῦ, διέχει δ' οὗτος ἑπτὰ τῆς πόλεως
σταδίους, τρισὶ μὲν ἡμέραις οὐκ ἐπεχείρει τῇ
πόλει, τάχα τι παρὰ τῶν ἔνδον ἐνδοθήσεσθαι
προσδοκῶν, εἰς δὲ τὰς πέριξ κώμας ἐφ' ἁρπαγὴν
σίτου πολλοὺς διαφῆκεν τῶν στρατιωτῶν· τῇ
τετάρτῃ δέ, ἥτις ἦν τριακὰς Ὑπερβερεταίου
μηνός, διατάξας τὴν στρατιὰν εἰσῆγεν εἰς τὴν
529 πόλιν. ὁ μὲν οὖν δῆμος ὑπὸ τοῖς στασιασταῖς
ἔμφρουρος ἦν, οἱ δὲ στασιασταὶ τὴν εὐταξίαν τῶν
Ῥωμαίων καταπλαγέντες τῶν μὲν ἔξω τῆς πόλεως
μερῶν εἶκον, εἰς δὲ τὴν ἐνδοτέρω καὶ τὸ ἱερὸν
530 ἀνεχώρουν. Κέστιος δὲ παρελθὼν ὑποπίμπρησιν
τήν τε Βεζεθὰν προσαγορευομένην τὴν καὶ¹ Καινό-
πολιν καὶ τὸ καλούμενον Δοκῶν ἀγοράν, ἔπειτα
πρὸς τὴν ἄνω πόλιν ἐλθὼν ἀντικρὺ τῆς βασιλικῆς
531 αὐλῆς ἐστρατοπεδεύετο. κἂν εἴπερ ἠθέλησεν κατ'

¹ τὴν καὶ Reland: καὶ τὴν mss.

---

[a] A hill to the north-west and commanding a " view "

part of the Romans, if they would lay down their arms
and return to their allegiance. But the insurgents,
fearing that the prospect of an amnesty would induce
the whole multitude to go over to Agrippa, made a
murderous assault upon his emissaries. Phoebus
was slain before he had uttered a syllable ; Borcius
was wounded but succeeded in escaping. Any
citizens who raised indignant protests were assailed
with stones and clubs and driven into the town.

(4) Cestius, seeing that these internal dissensions
offered a favourable opportunity for attack, brought
up his whole force, routed the enemy, and pursued
them to Jerusalem. Having pitched his camp in the
region called Scopus,[a] distant seven furlongs from
the city, for three days he suspended all attack upon
it, expecting perhaps that the defenders would show
signs of surrender ; but he sent out to the surrounding villages numerous foraging parties to collect corn.
On the fourth day, the thirtieth of the month Hyper-
bereteaeus, he deployed his forces and led them into
the city. For the people were at the mercy of the
rebels, and the latter, overawed by the orderly discipline of the Romans, abandoned the suburbs and
retired upon the inner city and the Temple.[c] Cestius,
on entering, set fire to the district known as Bezetha
or " New City " and the so-called Timber Market ;
he then proceeded to the upper city and encamped
opposite the royal palace. Had he, at that particular

*Cestius
occupies the
suburb
Bezetha,*

*November [b]
A.D. 66*

(whence its name) of the city (*A.* xi. 329, where it is called
Saphein).
   [b] November 17, according to Niese's reckoning.
   [c] They abandoned the unfinished third wall (that of
Agrippa I, see § 218) as untenable ; Cestius advanced to the
second wall, enclosing the upper city ; for the northern
suburb Bezetha between the two walls *cf.* § 328.

αὐτὴν ἐκείνην τὴν ὥραν ἐντὸς τῶν τειχέων βιάσασθαι, παραυτίκα τὴν πόλιν ἔσχεν καὶ τὸν πόλεμον
συνέβη καταλελύσθαι[1]· ἀλλὰ γὰρ ὅ τε στρατοπεδάρχης Τυράννιος Πρῖσκος καὶ τῶν ἱππάρχων
οἱ πλεῖστοι χρήμασιν ὑπὸ Φλώρου δεκασθέντες[2]
532 ἀπέστρεψαν αὐτὸν τῆς ἐπιχειρήσεως. καὶ παρὰ
τὴν αἰτίαν ταύτην ὅ τε πόλεμος ἐπὶ τοσοῦτον
μῆκος προύβη καὶ ἀνηκέστων Ἰουδαίους συμφορῶν
ἀναπλησθῆναι συνέπεσεν.

533 (5) Ἐν δὲ τούτῳ πολλοὶ τῶν γνωρίμων δημο-
τῶν, Ἀνάνῳ τῷ Ἰωνάθου παιδὶ πεισθέντες, ἐκάλουν τὸν Κέστιον ὡς ἀνοίξοντες αὐτῷ τὰς πύλας.
534 ὁ δὲ καὶ πρὸς ὀργὴν ὑπεριδὼν καὶ μὴ πάνυ πι-
στεύσας διεμέλλησεν, ἕως οἱ στασιασταὶ τὴν προδοσίαν αἰσθόμενοι τοὺς μὲν περὶ τὸν Ἄνανον ἀπὸ
τοῦ τείχους κατέβαλον καὶ λίθοις παίοντες συνήλασαν εἰς τὰς οἰκίας, αὐτοὶ δὲ διαστάντες ἀπὸ[3]
τῶν πύργων τοὺς ἀποπειρωμένους τοῦ τείχους
535 ἔβαλλον. πέντε μὲν οὖν ἡμέραις πάντοθεν ἐπι-
χειροῦσιν τοῖς Ῥωμαίοις ἀμήχανος ἦν ἡ προσβολή,
τῇ δ' ἐπιούσῃ ἀναλαβὼν ὁ Κέστιος τῶν τε ἐπιλέκτων συχνοὺς καὶ τοὺς τοξότας κατὰ τὸ προσ-
536 άρκτιον ἐπεχείρει κλίμα τῷ ἱερῷ. Ἰουδαῖοι δὲ
ἀπὸ τῆς στοᾶς εἶργον, καὶ πολλάκις μὲν ἀπεκρούσαντο τοὺς τῷ τείχει προσελθόντας, τέλος
δὲ τῷ πλήθει τῶν βελῶν ἀνακοπέντες ἀνεχώρησαν.
537 τῶν δὲ Ῥωμαίων οἱ πρῶτοι τοὺς θυρεοὺς ἐξερεί-
σαντες εἰς τὸ τεῖχος καὶ κατὰ τούτων οἱ κατόπιν
ἄλλους οἵ τε ἑξῆς ὁμοίως τὴν καλουμένην παρ'
αὐτοῖς χελώνην ἐφράξαντο, καθ' ἧς τὰ βέλη

καταλύεσθαι PAML.   [2] L: δελεασθέντες the rest.
[3] ἐπὶ Bekker, Naber.

528

moment, decided to force his way through the walls,
he would have captured the city forthwith, and the
war would have been over; but his camp-prefect [a]
Tyrannius Priscus, with most of the cavalry commanders, bribed by Florus, diverted him from the
attempt. Hence it came about that the war was so
long protracted and the Jews drained the cup of
irretrievable disaster.

(5) Many of the leading citizens, at the instance and attacks the inner city and the Temple.
of Ananus, son of Jonathan,[b] now sent an invitation
to Cestius, promising to open the gates to him.
These overtures, however, partly from anger and
disdain, partly because he did not wholly credit them,
he hesitated to accept, until the insurgents, discovering the treason, pulled down Ananus and his
confederates from the wall and drove them, with
showers of stones, into their houses; then, posting
themselves on the towers, they kept up a fire on the
enemy who were attempting to scale the wall. For
five days the Romans pressed their attack on all
sides without success; on the sixth Cestius led a
large force of picked men with the archers to an
assault on the north side of the Temple. The Jews
from the roof of the portico resisted the attack and
time after time repulsed those who had reached the
wall, but at length, overpowered by the hail of
missiles, gave way. The front rank of the Romans
then planted their bucklers against the wall, those
behind them placed theirs upon the first row of
shields, and the rest did likewise, forming a screen
which they call " the tortoise," [c] from which the

[a] Quartermaster-general.
[b] Jonathan, probably the high-priest and first victim of the
sicarii (§ 256).
[c] *testudo.*

φερόμενα περιωλίσθανεν ἄπρακτα, μηδὲν δ' οἱ στρατιῶται κακούμενοι τὸ τεῖχος ὑπέσυρον καὶ τοῦ
ἱεροῦ τὴν πύλην ὑποπιμπράναι παρεσκευάζοντο.

538 (6) Δεινὴ δὲ τοὺς στασιαστὰς ἔκπληξις κατ-
έλαβεν, ἤδη τε[1] πολλοὶ διεδίδρασκον ἀπὸ τῆς
πόλεως ὡς ἁλωσομένης αὐτίκα. τὸν δὲ δῆμον
ἐπὶ τούτοις συνέβαινεν θαρρεῖν, καὶ καθὸ παρ-
είκοιεν οἱ πονηροί, προσῄεσαν αὐτοὶ τὰς πύλας
ἀνοίξοντες καὶ δεξόμενοι τὸν Κέστιον ὡς εὐεργέ-
539 την. ὃς εἰ βραχὺ τῇ πολιορκίᾳ προσελιπάρησεν,
κἂν εὐθέως τὴν πόλιν παρέλαβεν· ἀλλ' οἶμαι διὰ
τοὺς πονηροὺς ἀπεστραμμένος ὁ θεὸς ἤδη καὶ τὰ
ἅγια, τέλος λαβεῖν ἐπ' ἐκείνης τῆς ἡμέρας ἐκώλυσεν τὸν πόλεμον.

540 (7) Ὁ γοῦν Κέστιος, οὔτε τὴν τῶν πολιορκου-
μένων ἀπόγνωσιν οὔτε τοῦ δήμου τὸ φρόνημα
συνιδών, ἐξαίφνης ἀνεκάλεσεν τοὺς στρατιώτας
καὶ καταγνοὺς ἐπ' οὐδεμιᾷ πληγῇ τῶν ἐλπίδων
541 παραλογώτατα ἀπὸ τῆς πόλεως ἀνέζευξεν. πρὸς
δὲ τὴν ἀδόκητον αὐτοῦ τροπὴν ἀναθαρσήσαντες
οἱ λῃσταὶ κατὰ τῶν ὑστάτων ἐπεξέδραμον καὶ
542 συχνοὺς τῶν ἱππέων καὶ πεζῶν διέφθειραν. τότε
μὲν οὖν ἐν τῷ κατὰ τὸν Σκοπὸν αὐλίζεται στρατο-
πέδῳ Κέστιος, τῇ δ' ἐπιούσῃ προσωτέρω χωρι-
ζόμενος μᾶλλον ἐξεκαλέσατο τοὺς πολεμίους, καὶ
τοὺς ὑστάτους αὐτῶν προσκείμενοι διέφθειρον καὶ
καθ' ἑκάτερον τῆς ὁδοῦ περιόντες ἠκόντιζον εἰς
543 πλαγίους. οὔτε δὲ ἐπιστραφῆναι πρὸς τοὺς κατόπιν τιτρώσκοντας ἐθάρρουν οἱ τελευταῖοι, ἄπειρόν τι πλῆθος οἰόμενοι διώκειν, καὶ τοὺς κατὰ
πλευρὸν ἐγκειμένους ἀναστέλλειν οὐχ ὑπέμενον,

[1] Destinon : δὲ mss.

missiles, as they fell, glanced off harmlessly, while
the soldiers with immunity undermined the wall and
prepared to set fire to the gate of the Temple.

(6) A terrible panic now seized the insurgents,
many of whom were already slinking out of the city
in the belief that it was on the verge of capture. The
people [a] thereupon took heart again, and the more
the miscreants gave ground, the nearer did these
advance to the gates, to open them and welcome
Cestius as a benefactor. Had he but persisted for a
while with the siege, he would have forthwith taken
the city ; but God, I suppose, because of those
miscreants, had already turned away even from His
sanctuary and ordained that that day should not see
the end of the war.

(7) At any rate, Cestius, realizing neither the
despair of the besieged nor the true temper of the
people, suddenly recalled his troops, renounced his
hopes, without having suffered any reverse, and,
contrary to all calculation, retired from the city. On
this unexpected retreat, the brigands, plucking up
courage, sallied out upon his rear and killed a considerable number of cavalry and infantry. Cestius
passed that night in his camp at Scopus. The following day, by continuing his retreat, he invited further
opposition from the enemy ; hanging upon his heels
they cut up his rear, and enclosing the troops on
either side of the route poured their missiles on the
flanks of the column. The rear ranks did not dare
to round upon those who were wounding them from
behind, supposing that they were pursued by an
innumerable host ; nor did the rest venture to beat
off those who were pressing their flanks, being heavily

Unexpected and disastrous retreat of Cestius.

---

[a] *i.e.* the moderates.

αὐτοὶ μὲν ὄντες βαρεῖς καὶ δεδοικότες τὴν τάξιν
διασπᾶν, τοὺς δὲ Ἰουδαίους ὁρῶντες κούφους καὶ
πρὸς τὰς ἐπιδρομὰς εὐκόλους· ὥστε συνέβαινεν
αὐτοῖς πολλὰ κακοῦσθαι μηδὲν ἀντιβλάπτουσιν
544 τοὺς ἐχθρούς. παρ' ὅλην δὲ τὴν ὁδὸν παιόμενοι
καὶ τῆς φάλαγγος ἐκσειόμενοι κατέπιπτον, μέχρι
πολλῶν διαφθαρέντων, ἐν οἷς ἦν Πρῖσκος μὲν
στρατάρχης τάγματος ἕκτου, Λογγῖνος δὲ χιλίαρχος, ἔπαρχος δὲ ἴλης Αἰμίλιος Ἰούκουνδος ὄνομα,
μόλις εἰς Γαβαὼ¹ κατήντησαν ἐπὶ τὸ πρότερον
στρατόπεδον, τὰ πολλὰ καὶ τῶν σκευῶν ἀποβα-
545 λόντες. ἔνθα δύο μὲν ἡμέρας ἐπέμεινεν ὁ Κέστιος
ἀμηχανῶν, ὅ τι χρὴ ποιεῖν, τῇ τρίτῃ δὲ πολλῷ
πλείους τοὺς πολεμίους θεασάμενος καὶ πάντα τὰ
κύκλῳ μεστὰ Ἰουδαίων, ἔγνω καθ' ἑαυτοῦ τε βρα-
δύνας κἂν ἔτι μείνῃ πλείοσιν χρησόμενος ἐχθροῖς.

546 (8) Ἵνα δὴ² συντονωτέρα³ χρήσαιτο φυγῇ, τὰ
τὴν στρατιὰν ἀνθέλκοντα περικόπτειν προσέταξεν.
διαφθαρέντων δὲ τῶν τε ὀρέων καὶ τῶν ὄνων ἔτι
δὲ καὶ τῶν ὑποζυγίων, πλὴν ὅσα βέλη παρεκόμιζεν
καὶ μηχανάς, τούτων γὰρ διὰ τὴν χρείαν περι-
είχοντο καὶ μάλιστα δεδοικότες μὴ Ἰουδαίοις κατ'
αὐτῶν ἁλῷ, προῆγε τὴν δύναμιν κατὰ⁴ Βαιθώρων.
547 οἱ δὲ Ἰουδαῖοι κατὰ μὲν τὰς εὐρυχωρίας ἧττον
ἐπέκειντο, συνειληθέντων δ' εἰς τὰ στενὰ καὶ τὴν
κατάβασιν οἱ μὲν φθάσαντες εἶργον αὐτοὺς τῆς

---

¹ Γαβαὼν PA (cf. § 516). ² L Lat. (itaque): δὲ the rest.
³ Dindorf: συντομωτέρα mss. ⁴ ἐπὶ VRC.

ᵃ Perhaps identical with Jucundus, the cavalry commander
at Caesarea, § 291.

ᵇ From Upper Beth-horon (1730 feet) to Lower Beth-
horon (1240 feet); this famous pass has been the scene of
numerous defeats (G. A. Smith, *Historical Geography of the*

armed themselves and afraid of opening out their
ranks, while the Jews, as they saw, were light-armed
and prepared to dash in among them. The result
was that they suffered heavily, without any retaliation upon their foes. All along the route men were
continually being struck, torn from the ranks, and
dropping on the ground. At length, after numerous
casualties, including Priscus, the commander of the
sixth legion, Longinus, a tribune, and Aemilius
Jucundus,[a] commander of a troop of horse, with
difficulty the army reached their former camp at
Gabao, having further abandoned the greater part
of their baggage. Here Cestius halted for two days,
uncertain what course to pursue ; but, on the third,
seeing the enemy's strength greatly increased and
all the surrounding country swarming with Jews, he
decided that the delay had been detrimental to him
and, if further prolonged, would but increase the
number of his foes.

(8) To accelerate the retreat, he gave orders to
retrench all impedimenta. So the mules, asses, and all
the beasts of burthen were killed, excepting those
that carried missiles and engines of war ; these they
clung to for their own use, and, still more, from fear
of their falling into Jewish hands and being employed
against themselves. Cestius then led his army on
down the road to Beth-horon. On the open ground
their movements were less harassed by the Jews,
but, once the Romans became involved in the defiles
and had begun the descent,[b] one party of the enemy
went ahead of them and barred their egress, another

Scene in the
pass of
Beth-horon.

Holy Land, 210 f.). It was down this same road from Gibeon
on the plateau (2300 feet), through the two Beth-horons, to
the maritime plain that Joshua pursued the five Canaanite
kings (Jos. x. 10 f.).

ἐξόδου, ἄλλοι δὲ τοὺς ὑστάτους κατεώθουν εἰς τὴν
φάραγγα· τὸ δὲ πᾶν πλῆθος παρεκταθὲν ὑπὲρ τὸν
αὐχένα τῆς ὁδοῦ κατεκάλυπτε τὴν φάλαγγα τοῖς
548 βέλεσιν. ἔνθα καὶ τῶν πεζῶν ἀμηχανούντων
προσαμύνειν ἑαυτοῖς ἐπισφαλέστερος τοῖς ἱππεῦσιν
ὁ κίνδυνος ἦν· οὔτε γὰρ ἐν τάξει κατὰ τῆς ὁδοῦ
βαδίζειν ἐδύναντο βαλλόμενοι, καὶ τὸ πρόσαντες
549 ἐπὶ τοὺς πολεμίους ἱππάσιμον οὐκ ἦν· τὸ δὲ ἐπὶ
θάτερα κρημνοὶ καὶ φάραγγες, εἰς οὓς ἀποσφα-
λέντες κατεφθείροντο. καὶ οὔτε φυγῆς τις τόπον
οὔτε ἀμύνης εἶχεν ἐπίνοιαν, ἀλλ' ὑπ' ἀμηχανίας
ἐπ' οἰμωγὴν ἐτράποντο καὶ τοὺς ἐν ἀπογνώσεσιν
ὀδυρμούς· ἀντήχει δ' αὐτοῖς τὸ παρὰ Ἰουδαίων
ἐγκέλευσμα καὶ κραυγὴ χαιρόντων ἅμα καὶ τεθυ-
550 μωμένων. ὀλίγου δὲ δεῖν πᾶσαν ἂν ἥρπασαν τὴν
ἅμα Κεστίῳ δύναμιν, εἰ μὴ νὺξ ἐπέλαβεν, ἐν ᾗ
Ῥωμαῖοι μὲν εἰς τὴν Βεθώραν κατέφυγον, Ἰουδαῖοι δὲ πάντα τὰ κύκλῳ περισχόντες ἐφρούρουν
αὐτῶν τὴν ἔξοδον.

551 (9) Ἔνθα δὴ Κέστιος τὴν φανερὰν ὁδὸν ἀπογνοὺς δρασμὸν ἐβουλεύετο, καὶ διακρίνας τοὺς
εὐψυχοτάτους στρατιώτας ὡσεὶ τετρακοσίους ἐπ-
έστησεν τῶν δωμάτων, προστάξας ἀναβοᾶν τὰ
σημεῖα τῶν ἐν τοῖς στρατοπέδοις φυλάκων, ὅπως
[οἱ][1] Ἰουδαῖοι πᾶσαν οἴωνται τὴν δύναμιν κατὰ
χώραν μένειν· αὐτὸς δὲ τοὺς λοιποὺς ἀναλαβὼν
552 ἡσυχῇ τριάκοντα πρόεισιν σταδίους. ἕωθεν δὲ
Ἰουδαῖοι κατιδόντες ἔρημον τὴν ἔπαυλιν αὐτῶν
ἐπὶ τοὺς ἐξαπατήσαντας τετρακοσίους ἔδραμον,
κἀκείνους μὲν ταχέως κατηκόντισαν, ἐδίωκον δὲ
553 τὸν Κέστιον. ὁ δὲ τῆς τε νυκτὸς οὐκ ὀλίγον

[1] om. P.

drove the rearguard down into the ravine, while the main body lined the heights above the narrowest part of the route and covered the legions with showers of arrows. Here, while even the infantry were hard put to it to defend themselves, the cavalry were in still greater jeopardy ; to advance in order down the road under the hail of darts was impossible, to charge up the slopes was impracticable for horse ; on either side were precipices and ravines, down which they slipped and were hurled to destruction ; there was no room for flight, no conceivable means of defence ; in their utter helplessness the troops were reduced to groans and the wailings of despair, which were answered by the war-whoop of the Jews, with mingled shouts of exultation and fury. Cestius and his entire army were, indeed, within an ace of being captured ; only the intervention of night enabled the Romans to find refuge in Beth-horon.[a] The Jews occupied all the surrounding points and kept a look-out for their departure.

(9) Cestius, now despairing of openly pursuing his march, laid plans for secret flight. Selecting about four hundred of his bravest men, he posted them upon the roofs, with orders to shout out the watch-words of the camp-sentinels, that the Jews might think that the whole army was still on the spot ; he himself with the remainder then stealthily advanced another thirty furlongs. At daybreak the Jews, discovering that the enemy's quarters were deserted, rushed upon the four hundred who had deluded them, rapidly dispatched them with their javelins, and then hastened in pursuit of Cestius. He had gained much

Flight of Cestius.

---

[a] The lower Beth-horon at the foot of the pass.

προειλήφει καὶ συντονώτερον ἔφευγεν μεθ' ἡμέραν,
ὥστε τοὺς στρατιώτας ὑπ' ἐκπλήξεως καὶ δέους
τάς τε ἑλεπόλεις καὶ τοὺς ὀξυβελεῖς καὶ τὰ πολλὰ
τῶν ἄλλων ὀργάνων καταλιπεῖν, ἃ τότε Ἰουδαῖοι
λαβόντες αὖθις ἐχρήσαντο κατὰ τῶν ἀφέντων.
554 προῆλθον δὲ τοὺς Ῥωμαίους διώκοντες μέχρις
Ἀντιπατρίδος. ἔπειθ' ὡς οὐ κατελάμβανον, ὑποστρέφοντες τάς τε μηχανὰς ἦρον καὶ τοὺς νεκροὺς
ἐσύλων, τήν τε ἀπολειφθεῖσαν λείαν συνῆγον καὶ
μετὰ παιάνων εἰς τὴν μητρόπολιν ἐπαλινδρόμουν,
555 αὐτοὶ μὲν ὀλίγους ἀποβεβλημένοι παντάπασιν, τῶν
δὲ Ῥωμαίων καὶ τῶν συμμάχων πεζοὺς μὲν
πεντακισχιλίους καὶ τριακοσίους ἀνῃρηκότες,
ἱππεῖς δὲ ὀγδοήκοντα καὶ τετρακοσίους.[1] τάδε
μὲν οὖν ἐπράχθη Δίου μηνὸς ὀγδόῃ, δωδεκάτῳ τῆς
Νέρωνος ἡγεμονίας ἔτει.

556 (xx. 1) Μετὰ δὲ τὴν Κεστίου συμφορὰν πολλοὶ
τῶν ἐπιφανῶν Ἰουδαίων ὥσπερ βαπτιζομένης
νεὼς ἀπενήχοντο τῆς πόλεως. Κοστόβαρος γοῦν
καὶ Σάουλος ἀδελφοὶ σὺν Φιλίππῳ τῷ Ἰακίμου,
στρατοπεδάρχης δ' ἦν οὗτος Ἀγρίππα τοῦ βασιλέως, διαδράντες ἐκ τῆς πόλεως ᾤχοντο πρὸς
557 Κέστιον· ὁ δὲ σὺν τούτοις κατὰ τὴν βασιλικὴν
αὐλὴν πολιορκηθεὶς Ἀντίπας ὑπεριδὼν τὴν φυγὴν
αὖθις ὡς ὑπὸ τῶν στασιαστῶν διεφθάρη δηλώ-
558 σομεν. Κέστιος δὲ τοὺς περὶ Σάουλον ἀξιώσαντας
ἀνέπεμψεν εἰς Ἀχαΐαν πρὸς Νέρωνα τήν τε αὑτῶν

---

[1] PL: τριακοσίους the rest and Heg.: nongentis Lat.

---

[a] November 25 (Niese).

upon them during the night, and, when day came, quickened his flight to such a pace that the men in consternation and terror abandoned the battering-rams, catapults, and most of the other machines, which the Jews then captured and afterwards employed against those who had relinquished them. The Jews continued the pursuit as far as Antipatris, and then, failing to overtake the Romans, turned and carried off the machines, plundered the corpses, collected the booty which had been left on the route, and, with songs of triumph, retraced their steps to the capital. Their own losses had been quite inconsiderable ; of the Romans and their allies they had slain five thousand three hundred infantry and four hundred and eighty of the cavalry. This action took place on the eighth of the month Dius in the twelfth [b] year of Nero's principate.

November,[a]
A.D. 66.

(xx. 1) After this catastrophe of Cestius many distinguished Jews abandoned the city as swimmers desert a sinking ship. Thus the brothers Costobar and Saul [c] with Philip,[d] son of Jacimus, prefect of king Agrippa's army, fled from Jerusalem and joined Cestius. We shall tell later [e] how Antipas, who had been besieged with them in the royal palace and disdained to fly, was killed by the rebels. Cestius dispatched Saul and his companions, at their request, to Nero in Achaia, to inform him of the straits to

Eminent Jews quit Jerusalem.

Cestius reports to Nero.

[b] As the date of the accession of Nero was 13 October 54, it appears probable that Josephus is slightly in error, and that the battle of Beth-horon took place early in his thirteenth year.　　　　　　　　　　　　　　　　　[c] § 418.
[d] Philip had escaped from Jerusalem after the siege of the palace (*Vita* 46 ff.), and we are not told that he had returned.
[e] iv. 140.

δηλώσοντας ἀνάγκην καὶ τὰς αἰτίας τοῦ πολέμου
τρέψοντας εἰς Φλῶρον· τὴν γὰρ ἐπ' ἐκεῖνον ὀργὴν
κουφίσειν καὶ τοὺς ἑαυτοῦ κινδύνους ἤλπισεν.

559 (2) Κἂν τούτῳ Δαμασκηνοὶ τὴν τῶν Ῥωμαίων
φθορὰν πυθόμενοι τοὺς παρ' ἑαυτοῖς Ἰουδαίους
560 ἀνελεῖν ἐσπούδασαν. καὶ καθὸ μὲν εἶχον αὐτοὺς
ἐν τῷ γυμνασίῳ συνηθροισμένους πάλαι, διὰ τὰς
ὑποψίας τοῦτο πραγματευσάμενοι, ῥᾴστην τὴν
ἐπιχείρησιν ἐδόκουν, ἐδεδοίκεισαν δὲ τὰς ἑαυτῶν
γυναῖκας ἁπάσας πλὴν ὀλίγων ὑπηγμένας τῇ
561 Ἰουδαϊκῇ θρησκείᾳ· διὸ μέγιστος αὐτοῖς ἀγὼν
ἐγένετο λαθεῖν ἐκείνας, τοὺς δὲ Ἰουδαίους ὡς ἂν
ἐν στενῷ χωρίῳ, τὸν ἀριθμὸν μυρίους καὶ πεντακοσίους, πάντας ἀνόπλους ἐπελθόντες ὑπὸ μίαν
ὥραν ἀδεῶς ἀπέσφαξαν.

562 (3) Οἱ δὲ διώξαντες τὸν Κέστιον ὡς ὑπ-
έστρεψαν εἰς Ἱεροσόλυμα, τοὺς μὲν βίᾳ τῶν ἔτι
ῥωμαϊζόντων τοὺς δὲ πειθοῖ προσήγοντο, καὶ
συναθροισθέντες εἰς τὸ ἱερὸν στρατηγοὺς ἀπεδεί-
563 κνυσαν τοῦ πολέμου πλείονας. ᾑρέθη δὲ Ἰώσηπός
τε υἱὸς Γωρίονος καὶ ὁ ἀρχιερεὺς Ἄνανος τῶν τε
κατὰ τὴν πόλιν ἁπάντων αὐτοκράτορες καὶ μά-
564 λιστα τὰ τείχη τῆς πόλεως ἀνεγείρειν· τὸν γὰρ
τοῦ Σίμωνος υἱὸν Ἐλεάζαρον, καίπερ ὑφ' ἑαυτῷ
πεποιημένον τὴν Ῥωμαίων λείαν καὶ τὰ ἁρπαγέντα
Κεστίου χρήματα, πρὸς οἷς πολλὰ τῶν δημοσίων
θησαυρῶν, ὅμως οὐκ ἐπέστησαν ταῖς χρείαις,

---

[a] *i.e.* ex-high priest. Ananus, son of Ananus (the father
seems to be the Annas of the N.T.), a Sadducee, was appointed high priest by Agrippa II and deposed after three
months on account of his action in punishing James the
brother of " Jesus called Christ " (*A.* xx. 197 ff.). The harsh
character there given of him forms a strange contrast to the

which they were reduced, and to lay upon Florus the responsibility for the war ; for he hoped, by exciting Nero's resentment against Florus, to diminish the risk to himself.

(2) Meanwhile, the people of Damascus, learning of the disaster which had befallen the Romans, were fired with a determination to kill the Jews who resided among them. As they had for a long time past kept them shut up in the gymnasium—a precaution prompted by suspicion—they considered that the execution of their plan would present no difficulty whatever ; their only fear was of their own wives who, with few exceptions, had all become converts to the Jewish religion, and so their efforts were mainly directed to keeping the secret from them. In the end, they fell upon the Jews, cooped up as they were and unarmed, and within one hour slaughtered them all with impunity, to the number of ten thousand five hundred.

(3) The Jews who had pursued Cestius, on their return to Jerusalem, partly by force, partly by persuasion, brought over to their side such pro-Romans as still remained ; and, assembling in the Temple, appointed additional generals to conduct the war. Joseph, son of Gorion, and Ananus the high priest [a] were elected to the supreme control of affairs in the city, with a special charge to raise the height of the walls. As for Eleazar, son of Simon, notwithstanding that he had in his hands the Roman spoils, the money taken from Cestius, and a great part of the public treasure, they did not entrust him with office,

Massacre of the Jews in Damascus.

Selection of Jewish generals for the war.

picture drawn of him in the *War*. Here he is a leader of the moderate party, opposes the Zealots, and on being murdered by the mob receives an encomium worthy of a Pericles (*B.* iv. 319 ff.).

539

αὐτόν τε τυραννικὸν ὁρῶντες καὶ τοὺς ὑπ' αὐτῷ
565 ζηλωτὰς δορυφόρων ἔθεσι χρωμένους. κατ' ὀλίγον
γε μὴν ἥ τε χρεία τῶν χρημάτων καὶ γοητεύων
Ἐλεάζαρος ἐκπεριῆλθε τὸν δῆμον ὥστε αὐτῷ
πειθαρχεῖν περὶ τῶν ὅλων.

566 (4) Εἰς δὲ τὴν Ἰδουμαίαν ἑτέρους ἐπελέξαντο
στρατηγοὺς Ἰησοῦν υἱὸν Σαπφᾶ¹ τῶν ἀρχιερέων
ἕνα καὶ Ἐλεάζαρον ἀρχιερέως υἱὸν Νέου²· τῷ δ'
ἄρχοντι τότε τῆς Ἰδουμαίας Νίγερι, γένος δ' ἦν
ἐκ τῆς ὑπὲρ³ Ἰορδάνην Περαίας, διὸ καὶ Περαΐτης
ἐκαλεῖτο, προσέταξαν ὑποτάσσεσθαι τοῖς στρα-
567 τηγοῖς. ἠμέλουν δὲ οὐδὲ τῆς ἄλλης χώρας, ἀλλ'
εἰς μὲν Ἰεριχοῦν Ἰώσηπος ὁ Σίμωνος, εἰς δὲ τὴν
Περαίαν Μανασσῆς, Θαμνᾶ δὲ τοπαρχίας Ἰωάννης
ὁ Ἐσσαῖος στρατηγήσων ἐπέμφθη· προσκεκλήρωτο
568 δ' αὐτῷ Λύδδα καὶ Ἰόππη καὶ Ἀμμαοῦς. τῆς δὲ
Γοφνιτικῆς καὶ Ἀκραβεττηνῆς ὁ Ἀνανίου Ἰωάννης
ἡγεμὼν ἀποδείκνυται καὶ τῆς Γαλιλαίας ἑκατέρας
Ἰώσηπος Ματθίου· προσώρ   ιστο δὲ τῇ τούτου
στρατηγίᾳ καὶ Γάμαλα τῶν ταύτῃ πόλεων ὀχυ-
ρωτάτη.

569 (5) Τῶν μὲν οὖν ἄλλων στρατηγῶν ἕκαστος ὡς
εἶχεν προθυμίας ἢ συνέσεως διώκει τὰ πεπι-
στευμένα· Ἰώσηπος δὲ εἰς τὴν Γαλιλαίαν ἐλθὼν

---

¹ Niese: Σαπφὼ or Σαπφὰν mss.: Σαπφία Hudson (cf.
§ 599).
² Ἀνανίου Hudson.   ³ Niese: περὶ mss.

ᵃ No high priest of this name is known: if we read
Ananias with Hudson, Eleazar will be the son of Ananias
already mentioned as mainly responsible for the war (§ 409).
ᵇ § 520.
ᶜ i.e. his province was the north and west of Judaea;

because they observed his despotic nature, and that
his subservient admirers conducted themselves like
his bodyguard. Gradually, however, financial needs
and the intrigues of Eleazar had such influence with
the people that they ended by yielding the supreme
command to him.

(4) Other generals were selected for Idumaea,
namely, Jesus son of Sapphas, one of the chief priests,
and Eleazar, son of the high-priest Neus [a]; and the
existing governor of Idumaea, Niger, called the
Peraean [b] because he was a native of Peraea beyond
Jordan, received instructions to act under the orders
of these officers. Nor were the other districts
neglected ; Joseph, son of Simon, was sent to take
command at Jericho, Manasseh to Peraea, John the
Essene to the province of Thamna, with Lydda,
Joppa and Emmaus also under his charge.[c] John,
son of Ananias, was appointed commanding officer of
the provinces of Gophna and Acrabetta [d]; Josephus,
son of Matthias [e] was given the two Galilees, with
the addition of Gamala,[f] the strongest city in that
region.

(5) Each of these generals executed his commission   Josephus
to the best of his zeal or ability. As for Josephus,   organizes
on his arrival in Galilee, he made it his first care to   the defence
of Galilee.

Thamna is in the region of Mt. Ephraim ; for Emmaus see
§ 71 note.

    [d] *i.e.* of the N.E. of Judaea.

    [e] The historian. In his *Life* § 29, he tells us that his com-
mission was of a purely pacific nature—to disarm the dis-
affected. There is a noticeable change in the character and
style of the narrative where the historian turns to his personal
history and seems to take the pen into his own hand ; the
marks of the skilled assistant whose services he has hitherto
employed (*Ap.* i. 50) are less conspicuous.

    [f] In Gaulanitis, east of the sea of Galilee.

πρῶτον ἐφρόντισεν τῆς εἰς ἑαυτὸν εὐνοίας τῶν
ἐπιχωρίων, εἰδὼς ὅτι ταύτῃ πλεῖστα κατορθώσει,
570 κἂν τἆλλα διαμαρτάνῃ. συνιδὼν δ' ὅτι τοὺς μὲν
δυνατοὺς οἰκειώσεται μεταδιδοὺς τῆς ἐξουσίας
αὐτοῖς, τὸ δὲ πᾶν πλῆθος, εἰ δι' ἐπιχωρίων καὶ
συνήθων τὰ πολλὰ προστάσσοι, τῶν μὲν γηραιῶν
ἑβδομήκοντα τοὺς σωφρονεστάτους ἐπιλέξας ἐκ
τοῦ ἔθνους κατέστησεν ἄρχοντας ὅλης τῆς Γαλι-
571 λαίας, ἑπτὰ δ' ἐν ἑκάστῃ πόλει δικαστὰς τῶν
εὐτελεστέρων διαφόρων· τὰ γὰρ μείζω πράγματα
καὶ τὰς φονικὰς δίκας ἐφ' ἑαυτὸν ἀναπέμπειν
ἐκέλευσεν καὶ τοὺς ἑβδομήκοντα.
572 (6) Καταστησάμενος δὲ τὰ πρὸς ἀλλήλους
νόμιμα τῶν κατὰ πόλιν ἐπὶ τὴν ἔξωθεν αὐτῶν
573 ἀσφάλειαν ἐχώρει. καὶ γινώσκων Ῥωμαίους
προεμβαλοῦντας εἰς τὴν Γαλιλαίαν τἀπιτήδεια τῶν
χωρίων ἐτείχιζεν, Ἰωτάπατα μὲν καὶ Βηρσαβὲ
καὶ Σελάμην, ἔτι δὲ Καφαρεκχὼ καὶ Ἴαφα καὶ
Σιγὼφ τό τε Ἰταβύριον καλούμενον ὄρος καὶ
Ταριχαίας καὶ Τιβεριάδα, πρὸς δὲ τούτοις τὰ περὶ
Γεννησὰρ τὴν λίμνην σπήλαια κατὰ τὴν κάτω
καλουμένην Γαλιλαίαν ἐτειχίσατο, τῆς δὲ ἄνω
Γαλιλαίας τήν τε προσαγορευομένην Ἀκχαβάρων
574 πέτραν καὶ Σὲπφ καὶ Ἰαμνεὶθ καὶ Μηρώ. κατὰ
δὲ τὴν Γαυλανιτικὴν Σελεύκειάν τε καὶ Σωγαναίαν
καὶ Γάμαλαν ὠχύρωσεν· μόνοις δὲ Σεπφωρίταις
ἐφῆκε[1] καθ' ἑαυτοὺς τεῖχος ἀναδείμασθαι, χρημάτων τε εὐπόρους ὁρῶν ὄντας καὶ προθύμους

---

[1] Bekker: ἔφη PAL: ἀφῆκε the rest (Josephus uses ἐφιέναι,
not ἀφιέναι, in this sense).

win the affection of the inhabitants, knowing that
this would be of the greatest advantage to him,
however he might otherwise fail. He realized that
he would conciliate the leaders by associating them
with him in his authority, and the people at large, if
his orders were in the main given through the medium
of their local acquaintances. He, therefore, selected
from the nation seventy persons [a] of mature years
and the greatest discretion and appointed them
magistrates of the whole of Galilee, and seven
individuals in each city to adjudicate upon petty
disputes, with instructions to refer more important matters and capital cases to himself and the
seventy.

(6) Having established these principles for the He fortifies
internal regulation of the various towns, he proceeded the towns,
to take measures for their security from external
attack. Foreseeing that Galilee would bear the
brunt of the Romans' opening assault, he fortified the
most suitable places, namely, Jotapata, Bersabe,
Selame, Caphareccho, Japha, Sigoph, the mount
called Itabyrion,[b] Tarichaeae, and Tiberias; he
further provided with walls the caves in Lower
Galilee in the neighbourhood of the lake of Gen-
nesareth, and in Upper Galilee the rock known as
Acchabaron, Seph, Jamnith, and Mero. In Gaulanitis
he fortified Seleucia, Soganaea and Gamala.[c] The
inhabitants of Sepphoris alone were authorized by
him to erect walls on their own account, because he
saw that they were in affluent circumstances and,

---

[a] Cf. Vita 79. [b] Mt. Tabor.
[c] This enumeration of fortified places is repeated, with
some variations, in Vita 187 f.; the " caves " are there
identified as those of Arbela (see B. i. 304 f.).

575 ἐπὶ τὸν πόλεμον δίχα προστάγματος. ὁμοίως δὲ
καὶ Γίσχαλα Ἰωάννης ὁ Ληΐου καθ᾽ ἑαυτὸν ἐτείχιζεν Ἰωσήπου κελεύσαντος· τοῖς δ᾽ ἄλλοις ἐρύ-
μασιν ἅπασιν αὐτὸς συμπονῶν ἅμα καὶ προσ-
576 τάσσων παρῆν. κατέλεξεν δὲ καὶ δύναμιν ἐκ τῆς
Γαλιλαίας ὑπὲρ δέκα μυριάδας νέων ἀνδρῶν, οὓς
πάντας ἐκ¹ τῶν συλλεγομένων παλαιῶν ὅπλων
ἐγκατασκευαζόμενος ὥπλιζεν.

577 (7) Ἔπειτα συνιδὼν ἀήττητον τὴν Ῥωμαίων
ἰσχὺν γεγενημένην εὐπειθείᾳ μάλιστα καὶ μελέτῃ
τῶν ὅπλων, τὴν μὲν διδασκαλίαν ἀπέγνω τῇ
χρείᾳ διωκομένην, τὸ δ᾽ εὐπειθὲς ὁρῶν περιγινό-
μενον ἐκ τοῦ πλήθους τῶν ἡγεμόνων ῥωμαϊκώ-
τερον ἔτεμνεν τὴν στρατιὰν καὶ πλείους καθίστατο
578 ταξιάρχους. στρατιωτῶν τε γὰρ ἀπεδείκνυεν διαφοράς, καὶ τούτους μὲν ὑπέτασσεν δεκαδάρχαις
καὶ ἑκατοντάρχαις, ἔπειτα χιλιάρχοις, κἀπὶ τούτοις ἡγεμόνας ταγμάτων ἀδροτέρων ἀφηγου-
579 μένους. ἐδίδασκεν δὲ σημείων παραδόσεις καὶ
σάλπιγγος προκλήσεις τε καὶ ἀνακλήσεις, προσβολάς τε κεράτων καὶ περιαγωγάς, καὶ πῶς δεῖ
πρὸς μὲν τὸ κάμνον ἐπιστρέφειν ἐκ τοῦ περιόντος,
580 ἐν δὲ τῷ πονοῦντι συμπαθεῖν. ὅσα τε εἰς παρά-
στασιν ψυχῆς ἢ καρτερίαν συνετέλει σώματος
ἀφηγεῖτο· μάλιστα δ᾽ αὐτοὺς ἤσκει πρὸς τὸν
πόλεμον παρ᾽ ἕκαστα τὴν Ῥωμαίων εὐταξίαν
διηγούμενος, καὶ ὡς πολεμήσουσιν πρὸς ἄνδρας,
οἳ δι᾽ ἀλκὴν σώματος καὶ ψυχῆς παράστημα

¹ C : most mss. add τε.

ᵃ This conflicts with the account in the *Life* (§§ 30, etc.),
which represents Sepphoris as consistently pro-Roman ; *cf.*
B. ii. 511 (the welcome given to the Romans).

even without orders, eager for hostilities.[a] Similarly, John, son of Levi, fortified Gischala at his own expense, on the instruction of Josephus.[b] The other fortresses were all built under the personal superintendence of Josephus, who both assisted in and directed the operations. He, moreover, levied in Galilee an army of upwards of a hundred thousand young men, all of whom he equipped with old arms collected for the purpose.

(7) Another task remained. He understood that the Romans owed their invincible strength above all to discipline and military training; if he despaired of providing similar instruction, to be acquired only by long use, he observed that their discipline was due to the number of their officers, and he therefore divided his army on Roman lines and increased the number of his company commanders. He instituted various ranks of soldiers and set over them decurions and centurions, above whom were tribunes, and over these generals in command of more extensive divisions. He taught them the transmission of signals, the trumpet-calls for the charge and the retreat, attacks by the wings and enveloping manœuvres, how relief should be sent by the victorious portion to those who were hard pressed and aid extended to any in distress. He expounded all that conduces to fortitude of soul or bodily endurance; but above all he trained them for war by continually dwelling upon the good order maintained by the Romans and telling them that they would have to fight against men who by their vigour and intrepidity

and trains an army on Roman lines.

[b] On the contrary the *Life* states that John was the enemy of Josephus and fortified Gischala without consulting him (§§ 45, 189).

581 πάσης ὀλίγου δεῖν τῆς οἰκουμένης κρατοῦσιν. ἔφη
δὲ πεῖραν αὐτῶν λήψεσθαι τῆς κατὰ τὸν πόλεμον
πειθαρχίας καὶ πρὸ παρατάξεως, εἰ τῶν συνήθων
ἀδικημάτων ἀπόσχοιντο, κλοπῆς τε καὶ λῃστείας
καὶ ἁρπαγῆς, τοῦ τε ἐξαπατᾶν τὸ ὁμόφυλον, τοῦ
τε[1] κέρδος οἰκεῖον ἡγεῖσθαι τὴν βλάβην τῶν συν-
582 ηθεστάτων. διοικεῖσθαι γὰρ κάλλιστα τοὺς πολέμους παρ' οἷς ἂν ἀγαθὸν τὸ συνειδὸς ἔχωσιν
[πάντες][2] οἱ στρατευόμενοι, τοὺς δὲ οἴκοθεν φαύ-
λους οὐ μόνον τοῖς ἐπιοῦσιν ἐχθροῖς ἀλλὰ καὶ τῷ
θεῷ χρῆσθαι πολεμίῳ.
583 (8) Πολλὰ τοιαῦτα παραινῶν διετέλει. καὶ τὸ
μὲν ἕτοιμον εἰς παράταξιν αὐτῷ συνεκεκρότητο
πεζῶν μὲν ἓξ μυριάδες, ἱππεῖς δὲ πεντήκοντα καὶ
τριακόσιοι,[3] χωρὶς δὲ τούτων, οἷς ἐπεποίθει
μάλιστα, μισθοφόροι περὶ τετρακισχιλίους καὶ
πεντακοσίους· ἐπιλέκτους δὲ περὶ αὐτὸν εἶχεν
584 ἑξακοσίους φύλακας τοῦ σώματος. ἔτρεφον δὲ
πλὴν τῶν μισθοφόρων τὴν ἄλλην στρατιὰν αἱ
πόλεις ῥᾳδίως· τῶν γὰρ καταλεγέντων ἑκάστη
τοὺς ἡμίσεις ἐπὶ τὴν στρατείαν[4] ἐκπέμπουσα τοὺς
λοιποὺς ἐπὶ συμπορισμὸν αὐτοῖς τῶν ἐπιτηδείων
κατεῖχεν, ὡς τοὺς μὲν εἰς ὅπλα, τοὺς δὲ εἰς
ἐργασίαν διῃρῆσθαι, καὶ τοῖς τὰ σῖτα πέμπουσιν
ἀντιχορηγεῖσθαι παρὰ τῶν ὁπλιτῶν τὴν ἀσφάλειαν.
585 (xxi. 1) Διοικοῦντι δ' οὕτως τῷ Ἰωσήπῳ τὰ
κατὰ τὴν Γαλιλαίαν παρανίσταταί τις ἐπίβουλος
ἀνὴρ ἀπὸ Γισχάλων, υἱὸς Λητοῦ, Ἰωάννης ὄνομα,
πανουργότατος μὲν καὶ δολιώτατος τῶν ἐπισήμων

---

[1] τοῦ τε Dindorf : τὸ, τοῦ or τό τε the best mss.
[2] om. VRC Lat. and placed after στρατευόμενοι by AM :
perhaps a gloss.   [3] διακόσιοι καὶ πεντήκοντα VRC Lat.

had become masters of well-nigh the whole world.
He told them that he should test their military discipline, even before they went into action, by noting
whether they abstained from their habitual malpractices, theft, robbery and rapine, and ceased to
defraud their countrymen and to regard as personal
profit an injury sustained by their most intimate
friends. For, he added, the armies that are most
successful in war are those in which every combatant
has a clear conscience ; whereas those who were
depraved at heart would have to contend not only
with their adversaries but also with God.

(8) Such was the tenor of his unceasing exhortations. He had now mustered an army, ready for
action, of sixty thousand [a] infantry and three hundred
and fifty cavalry, besides some four thousand five
hundred mercenaries, in whom he placed most confidence ; he had also a bodyguard of six hundred
picked men about his person. These troops, the
mercenaries excepted, were maintained without
difficulty by the towns : each town sent out on service
only one half of its levy and kept back the remainder
to provide them with supplies ; thus one party was
told off for military, and the other for fatigue duty,
and in return for the corn which their comrades sent
them the men under arms assured them protection.

(xxi. 1) While Josephus was thus directing affairs
in Galilee, there appeared upon the scene an intriguer,
a native of Gischala, named John, son of Levi, the
most unscrupulous and crafty of all who have ever

Intrigues
and raids
of John of
Gischala.

---

[a] Contrast § 576, " over 100,000 " ; presumably the rest
were not yet " ready for action."

---

[4] Destinon : στρατιὰν MSS.

ἐν τοῖσδε τοῖς πονηρεύμασιν ἀπάντων, πένης δὲ
τὰ πρῶτα καὶ μέχρι πολλοῦ κώλυμα σχὼν τῆς
586 κακίας τὴν ἀπορίαν, ἕτοιμος μὲν ψεύσασθαι, δεινὸς
δ' ἐπιθεῖναι πίστιν τοῖς ἐψευσμένοις, ἀρετὴν ἡγούμενος τὴν ἀπάτην καὶ ταύτῃ κατὰ τῶν φιλτάτων
587 χρώμενος, ὑποκριτὴς φιλανθρωπίας καὶ δι' ἐλπίδα
κέρδους φονικώτατος, ἀεὶ μὲν ἐπιθυμήσας μεγάλων,
τρέφων δὲ τὰς ἐλπίδας ἐκ τῶν ταπεινῶν κακουρ-
γημάτων· λῃστὴς γὰρ ἦν μονότροπος, ἔπειτα καὶ
συνοδίαν εὗρεν τῆς τόλμης, τὸ μὲν πρῶτον ὀλίγην,
588 προκόπτων δ' ἀεὶ πλείονα. φροντὶς δ' ἦν αὐτῷ
μηδένα προσλαμβάνειν εὐάλωτον, ἀλλὰ τοὺς εὐεξίᾳ
σώματος καὶ ψυχῆς παραστήματι καὶ πολέμων
ἐμπειρίᾳ διαφέροντας ἐξελέγετο, μέχρι καὶ τετρακοσίων ἀνδρῶν στῖφος συνεκρότησεν, οἳ τὸ πλέον
ἐκ τῆς Τυρίων χώρας καὶ τῶν ἐν αὐτῇ κωμῶν
589 φυγάδες ἦσαν· δι' ὧν πᾶσαν ἐλῄζετο τὴν Γαλιλαίαν καὶ μετεώρους ὄντας ἐπὶ τῷ μέλλοντι πολέμῳ τοὺς πολλοὺς ἐσπάρασσεν.

590   (2) Ἤδη δ' αὐτὸν στρατηγιῶντα καὶ μειζόνων
ἐφιέμενον ἔνδεια χρημάτων κατεῖχεν. ἐπεὶ δὲ
τὸν Ἰώσηπον ὁρῴη[1] αὐτοῦ [σφόδρα][2] χαίροντα
τῷ δραστηρίῳ, πείθει πρῶτον μὲν αὐτῷ πι-
στεῦσαι τὸ τεῖχος ἀνοικοδομῆσαι τῆς πατρίδος,
ἐν ᾧ πολλὰ παρὰ τῶν πλουσίων ἐκέρδανεν·
591 ἔπειτα συνθεὶς σκηνὴν πανουργοτάτην, ὡς ἄρα

---

[1] M: ὁρῶν (without construction, reading H as N?) the rest.
[2] om. PM Lat.

---

[a] This portrait of John (blacker than any drawn of him in the *Life*) recalls Sallust's description of Catiline : " animus audax, subdolus, varius, *cuius rei lubet simulator ac dissimulator . . . nimis alta semper cupiebat . . .* agitabatur

548

gained notoriety by such infamous means. Poor at the opening of his career, his penury had for long thwarted his malicious designs ; a ready liar and clever in obtaining credit for his lies, he made a merit of deceit and practised it upon his most intimate friends ; while affecting humanity, the prospect of lucre made him the most sanguinary of men ; always full of high ambitions, his hopes were fed on the basest of knaveries.[a] For he was a brigand, who at the outset practised his trade alone, but afterwards found for his daring deeds accomplices, whose numbers, small at first, grew with his success. He was, moreover, careful never to take into partnership anyone likely to fall an easy prey to an assailant, but selected good, strapping fellows, with stout hearts and military experience. He ended by mustering a band of four hundred men, for the most part fugitives from the region of Tyre and the villages in that neighbourhood. With their help he plundered the whole of Galilee and harried the masses, whose minds were already distracted by the impending war.

(2) He was already aspiring to the command and had yet higher ambitions, but was checked by impecuniosity. Perceiving that Josephus was delighted at his energy, John first induced him to entrust him with the rebuilding of the walls of his native town, an undertaking in which he made a large profit at the expense of the wealthy citizens.[b] He next contrived to play a very crafty trick : with the avowed

His antagonism to Josephus.

---

magis magisque in dies animus ferox *inopia rei familiaris* " (*De Cat. coni.* 5).

[b] According to *Vita* 71 ff., John obtained permission from Josephus's colleagues to sell the imperial corn stored in Upper Galilee, and to devote the proceeds to the repair of the walls of Gischala.

φυλάττοιντο πάντες οἱ κατὰ τὴν Συρίαν Ἰουδαῖοι
ἐλαίῳ χρῆσθαι μὴ δι' ὁμοφύλων ἐγκεχειρισμένῳ,
592 πέμπειν αὐτοῖς ἐπὶ τὴν μεθορίαν ἐξητήσατο. συνωνούμενος δὲ τοῦ Τυρίου νομίσματος, ὃ τέσσαρας
Ἀττικὰς δύναται, τέσσαρας ἀμφορεῖς, τῆς αὐτῆς
ἐπίπρασκεν τιμῆς ἡμιαμφόριον. οὔσης δὲ τῆς
Γαλιλαίας ἐλαιοφόρου μάλιστα καὶ τότε εὐφορη-
κυίας, εἰς σπανίζοντας εἰσπέμπων πολὺ καὶ μόνος
ἄπειρόν τι πλῆθος συνῆγεν χρημάτων, οἷς εὐθέως
593 ἐχρῆτο κατὰ τοῦ τὴν ἐργασίαν[1] παρασχόντος. καὶ
ὑπολαβών, εἰ καταλύσειεν τὸν Ἰώσηπον, αὐτὸς
ἡγήσεσθαι τῆς Γαλιλαίας, τοῖς μὲν ὑφ' ἑαυτὸν
λῃσταῖς προσέταξεν εὐτονώτερον ἐγχειρεῖν ταῖς
ἁρπαγαῖς, ὅπως πολλῶν νεωτεριζομένων κατὰ τὴν
χώραν ἢ διαχρήσαιτό που τὸν στρατηγὸν ἐκ-
βοηθοῦντα λοχήσας ἢ περιορῶντα τοὺς λῃστὰς
594 διαβάλλοι πρὸς τοὺς ἐπιχωρίους. ἔπειτα διεφήμιζεν
πόρρωθεν ὡς ἄρα προδιδοίη[2] τὰ πράγματα Ῥωμαίοις Ἰώσηπος, καὶ πολλὰ τοιαῦτα πρὸς κατάλυσιν τἀνδρὸς ἐπραγματεύετο.
595 (3) Καθ' ὃν καιρὸν ἀπὸ Δαβαρίθθων κώμης
νεανίσκοι τινὲς τῶν ἐν τῷ μεγάλῳ πεδίῳ καθ-
εζομένων φυλάκων, ἐνεδρεύσαντες Πτολεμαῖον τὸν
Ἀγρίππα καὶ Βερνίκης ἐπίτροπον, ἀφείλοντο

[1] εὐεργεσίαν PAM Lat.: the text finds a parallel in
Acts xvi. 16.
[2] Dindorf: προδιδῴη mss.

[a] In the account in *Vita* (74 f.) there are again slight
differences. The persons to be protected from the forbidden
use of foreign oil are there not " all the Jews of Syria,"
but only those who had been confined by order in Caesarea
Philippi. In the *Life* John makes a profit of 10 : 1 (buying

object of protecting all the Jews of Syria from the use of oil not supplied by their own countrymen, he sought and obtained permission to deliver it to them at the frontier. He then bought up that commodity, paying Tyrian coin of the value of four Attic drachms for four *amphorae* and proceeded to sell half an *amphora* at the same price.[a] As Galilee is a special home of the olive and the crop had been plentiful, John, enjoying a monopoly, by sending large quantities to districts in want of it, amassed an immense sum of money, which he forthwith employed against the man who had brought him his gains. Supposing that, if he could get rid of Josephus, he would himself become governor of Galilee, he directed his band of brigands to push their raids more vigorously than ever; in the anarchy thus produced throughout the district, either the governor would go to the rescue, in which case he would find means of laying an ambush and making away with him, or if Josephus neglected to take measures against the brigands, he would calumniate him to his countrymen. Lastly, he had long since been spreading a report that Josephus intended to betray the country to the Romans, and in numerous similar ways he was scheming to ruin his chief.

(3) About this time some young men of the village of Dabarittha,[b] units of the guard posted in the great plain, laid an ambush for Ptolemy,[c] the overseer[d] of Agrippa and Bernice, and robbed him of all the

The affair of Dabarittha and Agrippa's stolen goods.

80 *sextarii* for 4 drachms and selling 2 *sextarii* for 1 drachm), here of 8 : 1.

[b] O.T. Daberath, modern *Deburieh*, under the western slopes of Mt. Tabor; the "great plain" is that of Esdraelon. *Cf.* the parallel account in *Vita* 126 ff.

[c] Ptolemy's wife, *Vita* 126.   [d] Or "finance officer."

πᾶσαν ὅσην ἦγεν ἀποσκευήν, ἐν ᾗ πολυτελεῖς τε
ἐσθῆτες οὐκ ὀλίγαι καὶ πλῆθος ἐκπωμάτων
596 ἀργυρῶν χρυσοῖ τε ἦσαν ἑξακόσιοι. μὴ δυνά-
μενοι δὲ διαθέσθαι[1] κρύφα τὴν ἁρπαγὴν πάντα
597 πρὸς Ἰώσηπον εἰς Ταριχαίας ἐκόμισαν. ὁ δὲ
μεμψάμενος αὐτῶν τὸ πρὸς τοὺς βασιλικοὺς
βίαιον τίθησιν τὰ κομισθέντα παρὰ τῷ δυνα-
τωτάτῳ τῶν Ταριχαιατῶν Ἀνναίῳ, πέμψαι κατὰ
καιρὸν τοῖς δεσπόταις προαιρούμενος· ὃ δὴ μέγιστον
598 αὐτῷ κίνδυνον ἐπήγαγεν. οἱ γὰρ ἁρπάσαντες ἅμα
μὲν ἐπὶ τῷ μηδεμιᾶς τυχεῖν μερίδος ἐκ τῶν
κεκομισμένων ἀγανακτοῦντες, ἅμα δὲ καὶ προ-
σκεψάμενοι τοῦ Ἰωσήπου τὴν διάνοιαν, ὅτι
μέλλοι τὸν πόνον αὐτῶν τοῖς βασιλεῦσιν χαρί-
ζεσθαι, νύκτωρ εἰς τὰς κώμας διέδραμον καὶ
πᾶσιν ἐνεδείκνυντο τὸν Ἰώσηπον ὡς προδότην·
ἐνέπλησαν δὲ καὶ τὰς πλησίον πόλεις ταραχῆς,
ὥστε ὑπὸ τὴν ἕω δέκα μυριάδας ὁπλιτῶν ἐπ᾽
599 αὐτὸν συνδραμεῖν. καὶ τὸ μὲν πλῆθος ἐν τῷ
κατὰ Ταριχαίας ἱπποδρόμῳ συνηθροισμένον πολλὰ
πρὸς ὀργὴν ἀνεβόα καὶ[2] καταλεύειν οἱ δὲ καίειν
τὸν προδότην ἐκεκράγεσαν· παρώξυνεν δὲ τοὺς
πολλοὺς ὁ Ἰωάννης καὶ σὺν αὐτῷ Ἰησοῦς τις
600 υἱὸς Σαπφία, τότε ἄρχων τῆς Τιβεριάδος. οἱ μὲν
οὖν φίλοι καὶ σωματοφύλακες τοῦ Ἰωσήπου, καταπλαγέντες τὴν ὁρμὴν τοῦ πλήθους, ἔφυγον πλὴν
τεσσάρων πάντες, αὐτὸς δὲ κοιμώμενος ἤδη προσ-
601 φερομένου τοῦ πυρὸς διανίσταται, καὶ παραινούν-
των φεύγειν τῶν τεσσάρων, οἳ παρέμειναν, οὔτε
πρὸς τὴν καθ᾽ ἑαυτὸν ἐρημίαν οὔτε πρὸς τὸ

---

[1] διελέσθαι PAML.   [2] + οἱ μὲν Hudson (after Lat.).

baggage which he was convoying, including a large number of rich vestments, a quantity of silver goblets and six hundred [a] pieces [b] of gold. Being unable to dispose secretly of such booty, they brought the whole to Josephus, then at Tarichaeae. He censured them for this act of violence to servants of the king, and committed the goods to the keeping of Annaeus, [c] the most important citizen of Tarichaeae, intending to return them to their legitimate owners when an opportunity presented itself. This action brought him into the greatest peril. For the plunderers, indignant at receiving no portion of the spoil, and divining the intention of Josephus to present the king and queen with the fruits of their labours, ran round the villages by night, denouncing Josephus to all as a traitor ; they also created a ferment in the neighbouring cities, with the result that at daybreak a hundred thousand men in arms had collected against him. The multitude, assembled in the hippodrome at Tarichaeae, made loud and angry demonstrations ; some clamoured for the stoning of the traitor, others to have him burnt alive ; the mob was instigated by John, [d] who was seconded by Jesus, son of Sapphias, then chief magistrate of Tiberias. The friends and bodyguard of Josephus, terrified at the assault of the crowd, all fled, with the exception of four [e] ; he himself was asleep and awoke only at the moment when his enemies were about to set fire to the house. His four faithful companions urged him to fly [f] ; but he, undaunted by the general

Josephus, denounced as a traitor at Tarichaeae,

---

[a] 500, *Vita* 127.   [b] Unspecified : " staters " (Reinach).

[c] Dassion and Jannaeus, friends of Agrippa, according to *Vita* 131.   [d] John is not mentioned in *Vita*.

[e] One (Simon), *Vita* 137.

[f] Simon advises Josephus to kill himself, *Vita ib.*

πλῆθος τῶν ἐφεστώτων καταπλαγεὶς προπηδᾷ,
περιρρηξάμενος μὲν τὴν ἐσθῆτα, καταπασάμενος[1]
δὲ τῆς κεφαλῆς κόνιν, ἀποστρέψας δὲ ὀπίσω τὰς
χεῖρας καὶ τὸ ἴδιον ξίφος ἐπιδήσας τῷ τένοντι.
602 πρὸς ταῦτα τῶν μὲν οἰκείως ἐχόντων καὶ μάλιστα
τῶν Ταριχαιατῶν οἶκτος ἦν, οἱ δ' ἀπὸ τῆς χώρας
καὶ τῶν πλησίον ὅσοις ἐδόκει φορτικὸς ἐβλασφήμουν, προφέρειν τε τὰ κοινὰ χρήματα θᾶττον
ἐκέλευον καὶ τὰς προδοτικὰς συνθήκας ἐξομολο-
603 γεῖσθαι· προειλήφεσαν[2] γὰρ ἐκ τοῦ σχήματος
οὐδὲν αὐτὸν ἀρνήσεσθαι τῶν ὑπονοηθέντων, ἀλλ'
ἐπὶ συγγνώμης πορισμῷ πάντα πεποιηκέναι τὰ
604 πρὸς τὸν ἔλεον. τῷ δ' ἦν ἡ ταπείνωσις προ-
παρασκευὴ στρατηγήματος, καὶ τεχνιτεύων τοὺς
ἀγανακτοῦντας καθ' αὑτοῦ κατ' ἀλλήλων στα-
σιάσαι, ἐφ' οἷς ὠργίζοντο πάνθ' ὁμολογήσων,[3]
605 ἔπειτα δοθὲν αὐτῷ λέγειν, "ἐγὼ ταῦτα," ἔφη,
"τὰ χρήματα οὔτε ἀναπέμπειν Ἀγρίππᾳ προ-
ῃρούμην οὔτε κερδαίνειν αὐτός· μὴ γὰρ ἡγησαίμην
ποτὲ ἢ φίλον τὸν ὑμῖν διάφορον ἢ κέρδος τὸ
606 φέρον τῷ κοινῷ βλάβην. ὁρῶν δέ, ὦ Ταρι-
χαιᾶται, μάλιστα τὴν ὑμετέραν πόλιν ἀσφαλείας
δεομένην καὶ πρὸς κατασκευὴν τείχους χρῄζουσαν
ἀργυρίου, δεδοικὼς δὲ τὸν Τιβεριέων δῆμον καὶ
τὰς ἄλλας πόλεις ἐφεδρευούσας τοῖς ἡρπαγμένοις,
κατασχεῖν ἡσυχῇ τὰ χρήματα προειλόμην, ἵν'
607 ὑμῖν περιβάλωμαι τεῖχος. εἰ μὴ δοκεῖ, προφέρω
τὰ κεκομισμένα καὶ παρέχω διαρπάζειν, εἰ δὲ

---

[1] καταμησάμενος L Suid.
[2] Bekker: προσειλήφεσαν MSS.
[3] ὁμολογήσειν ὑπισχνεῖτο C: Destinon and Niese suspect a
lacuna.

desertion or by the number of his assailants, rushed quells the rising by a ruse.
out with raiment rent and ashes sprinkled on his
head, his hands behind his back and his sword
suspended from his neck. At this spectacle his
familiar friends, the Tarichaeans in particular, were
moved to compassion, but the country-folk and those
of the neighbourhood who regarded him as a nuisance,
railed at him and bade him instantly produce the
public money and confess his treasonable compact ;
for they concluded from his demeanour that he would
deny none of the crimes of which they suspected him,
and had only made all this pitiable exhibition of
himself in order to procure their pardon. But, in
reality, this pose of humiliation was merely part of a
stratagem ; with the design of producing dissension
among his indignant opponents he promised to
make a full confession on the subject which had
roused their ire, and on obtaining permission to speak,
thus addressed them : " About this money—I had
no intention of either sending it to Agrippa or appropriating it myself ; far be it from me ever to reckon
as a friend one who is your foe, or as personal gain
anything involving loss to the community. But as I
saw, citizens of Tarichaeae, that your city above all
needed to be put in a state of defence and that it was
in lack of funds to construct ramparts ; as, moreover,
I feared that the people of Tiberias and of the other
cities had their eyes on these spoils, I decided quietly
to keep this money in order to encompass you with
a wall. If this does not meet your approval, I am
prepared to produce what was brought to me and
leave you to plunder it ; if, on the contrary, I have

καλῶς ὑμῖν ἐβουλευσάμην, ⟨μὴ⟩ κολάζετε[1] τὸν
εὐεργέτην."

608 (4) Ἐπὶ τούτοις οἱ Ταριχαῖαι μὲν αὐτὸν
ἀνευφήμουν, οἱ δ' ἀπὸ τῆς Τιβεριάδος σὺν τοῖς
ἄλλοις ἐκάκιζον καὶ διηπείλουν· καταλιπόντες δ'
ἑκάτεροι τὸν Ἰώσηπον ἀλλήλοις διεφέροντο. κἀκεῖνος θαρρῶν ἤδη τοῖς ᾠκειωμένοις, ἦσαν δὲ εἰς
τετρακισμυρίους Ταριχαῖαι, παντὶ τῷ πλήθει
609 παρρησιαστικώτερον ὡμίλει. καὶ πολλὰ τὴν προ-
πέτειαν αὐτῶν κατονειδίσας ἐκ μὲν τῶν παρόντων
Ταριχαίας ἔφη τειχίσειν, ἀσφαλιεῖσθαι δὲ ὁμοίως
καὶ τὰς ἄλλας πόλεις· οὐ γὰρ ἀπορήσειν χρημάτων, ἐὰν ὁμονοῶσιν ἐφ' οὓς δεῖ πορίζειν καὶ
μὴ παροξύνωνται κατὰ τοῦ πορίζοντος.

610 (5) Ἔνθα δὴ τὸ μὲν ἄλλο πλῆθος τῶν ἠπατημένων ἀνεχώρει καίτοι διωργισμένον, δισχίλιοι δ'
ἐπ' αὐτὸν ὥρμησαν ἔνοπλοι, καὶ φθάσαντος εἰς
τὸ δωμάτιον παρελθεῖν ἀπειλοῦντες ἐφεστήκεσαν.
611 ἐπὶ τούτοις Ἰώσηπος ἀπάτῃ δευτέρᾳ χρῆται·
ἀναβὰς γὰρ ἐπὶ τὸ τέγος καὶ τῇ δεξιᾷ καταστείλας τὸν θόρυβον αὐτῶν ἀγνοεῖν ἔφη, τίνων
ἀξιοῦσιν τυχεῖν· οὐ γὰρ κατακούειν διὰ τὴν τῆς
βοῆς σύγχυσιν· ὅσα δ' ἂν κελεύσωσιν πάντα
ποιήσειν, εἰ τοὺς διαλεξομένους ἡσυχῇ πέμψειαν
612 εἴσω πρὸς αὐτόν. ταῦτα ἀκούσαντες οἱ γνώριμοι
σὺν τοῖς ἄρχουσιν εἰσήεσαν. ὁ δὲ σύρας αὐτοὺς

---

[1] Text as emended by Hudson and Cobet, partly
supported by Lat.: εἰ (or εἰ δὲ) μὴ καλῶς ὑμῖν ἐβουλ. κολάζετε
mss.; the negative appears to have been misplaced.

[a] Or, perhaps, " unite with him in opposing the enemy
who ought to provide it " (from whom they should extract
it, viz. the Romans). [b] 600, *Vita* 145.

consulted your best interests, do not punish your benefactor."

(4) At these words the people of Tarichaeae applauded, but those from Tiberias and elsewhere vilified and threatened him ; and the two parties let Josephus alone and fell to quarrelling with each other. He, now relying on the supporters he had won—the Taricrhaeans numbered as many as forty thousand—proceeded to address the whole multitude more freely. He severely censured them for their precipitance, promised to fortify Taricchaeae with the funds at his disposal, and undertook to provide similar protection for the other cities as well ; money, he added, would be forthcoming, would they but agree who was the enemy against whom its provision was necessary,[a] instead of furiously attacking the man who provided it.

(5) Thereupon the majority of the deluded crowd withdrew, though still highly excited ; but two thousand [b] men in arms made a rush upon him. He was too quick for them and succeeded in regaining his lodging, which they beset with menacing cries. Josephus now had recourse to a second ruse. He mounted to the roof, quelled their clamour with a motion of his hand and said that he had no idea what they wanted, as their confused shouts prevented him from hearing them ; he would, however, comply with all their demands, if they would send in a deputation to confer quietly with him. On hearing that, the leaders of the party, with the magistrates, entered the house.[c] He then haled them to the most

Another attempt on Josephus's life frustrated by stratagem.

[c] In *Vita* 147 only one delegate is sent in ; he, besides being scourged, has one of his hands severed and suspended to his neck.

557

JOSEPHUS

εἰς τὸ μυχαίτατον τῆς οἰκίας καὶ τὴν αὔλειον
ἀποκλείσας ἐμαστίγωσεν, μέχρι πάντων τὰ
σπλάγχνα γυμνῶσαι· περιειστήκει δὲ τέως τὸ
πλῆθος δικαιολογεῖσθαι μακρότερα τοὺς εἰσελθόν-
613 τας οἰόμενον. ὁ δὲ τὰς θύρας ἐξαπίνης ἀνοίξας
ἡμαγμένους ἐξαφῆκεν τοὺς ἄνδρας καὶ τοσαύτην
τοῖς ἀπειλοῦσιν ἐνειργάσατο κατάπληξιν, ὥστε
ῥίψαντας τὰ ὅπλα φεύγειν.
614   (6) Πρὸς ταῦτα Ἰωάννης ἐπέτεινεν τὸν φθόνον
καὶ δευτέραν ἤρτυσεν ἐπιβουλὴν κατὰ τοῦ Ἰωσήπου. σκηψάμενος δὴ νόσον ἱκέτευσεν δι᾽ ἐπιστολῆς τὸν Ἰώσηπον ἐπιτρέψαι πρὸς θεραπείαν
αὐτῷ χρήσασθαι τοῖς ἐν Τιβεριάδι θερμοῖς ὕδασιν.
615 ὁ δέ, οὔπω γὰρ ὑπώπτευεν τὸν ἐπίβουλον, γράφει
τοῖς κατὰ τὴν πόλιν ὑπάρχοις ξενίαν τε καὶ τὰ-
πιτήδεια Ἰωάννῃ παρασχεῖν. ὧν ἀπολαύσας μετὰ
δύο ἡμέρας ἐφ᾽ ὃ παρῆν διεπράττετο, καὶ τοὺς
μὲν ἀπάταις τοὺς δὲ χρήμασι διαφθείρων ἀνέπειθεν
616 ἀποστῆναι Ἰωσήπου. καὶ γνοὺς ταῦτα Σίλας ὁ
φυλάσσειν τὴν πόλιν ὑπὸ Ἰωσήπου καθεσταμένος
γράφει τὰ περὶ¹ τὴν ἐπιβουλὴν αὐτῷ κατὰ τάχος.
ὁ δὲ Ἰώσηπος ὡς ἔλαβεν τὴν ἐπιστολήν, νυκτὸς
ὁδεύσας συντόνως ἑωθινὸς παρῆν πρὸς τὴν Τιβε-
617 ριάδα. καὶ τὸ μὲν ἄλλο πλῆθος αὐτῷ ὑπήντα,
Ἰωάννης δέ, καίτοι τὴν παρουσίαν ὑποπτεύσας
ἐπ᾽ αὐτόν, ὅμως πέμψας τινὰ τῶν γνωρίμων
ὑπεκρίνατο τὴν ἀσθένειαν καὶ κλινήρης ὢν ὑστε-

¹ κατὰ MVRC.

ᵃ Or "envy." The incidents at Tiberias in this and the
following chapter (§§ 614-623) are placed *before* the Tarichaeae affair (§§ 595-613) in the parallel narrative (*Vita* 84-
103). In the *Life* the "envy" (ἐφθόνησε 85) of John is
558

secluded portion of the building, closed the outer door, and had them scourged till he had flayed them all to the bone. The mob, meanwhile, remained standing round the house, supposing their delegates to be engaged in a prolonged parley. Suddenly Josephus had the doors thrown open and the men dismissed, all covered with blood, a spectacle which struck such terror into his menacing foes that they dropped their arms and fled.

(6) These proceedings intensified John's malice [a] and he devised a second plot against Josephus. Feigning sickness, he wrote to Josephus to request his permission to take the hot baths at Tiberias for the good of his health. Thereupon Josephus, whose suspicions of the conspirator were not yet aroused, wrote to his lieutenants in the town to give John hospitality and to provide for his needs. He, after enjoying these benefits for two days, proceeded to carry into effect the object of his visit : by deception or bribery he corrupted the citizens and endeavoured to induce them to revolt from Josephus. Hearing of this, Silas, whom Josephus had appointed to guard the town, hastened to inform his chief of the conspiracy. Josephus, on receipt of his letter,[b] set off and, after a rapid night march, reached Tiberias at daybreak. The whole population came out to meet him except John ; he, though suspecting that this visit boded ill for himself, sent one of his acquaintances with a message, pretending to be indisposed and bedridden, and so prevented from paying his

John of Gischala promotes opposition to Josephus at Tiberias.

explained by the popularity of Josephus ; here the context supplies no such link. This suggests that the *Life* has preserved the true connexion of events and lends support to Laqueur's theory that it is the older work.

[b] He was then at Cana (*Vita* 86).

618 ῥῆσαι τῆς θεραπείας ἔλεγεν. ὡς δὲ εἰς τὸ στά-
διον τοὺς Τιβεριεῖς ἀθροίσας ὁ Ἰώσηπος ἐπειρᾶτο
διαλέγεσθαι περὶ τῶν ἐπεσταλμένων, ὑποπέμψας
619 ὁπλίτας προσέταξεν αὐτὸν ἀνελεῖν. τούτους τὰ
ξίφη γυμνοῦντας ὁ δῆμος προϊδὼν ἀνεβόησεν· πρὸς
δὲ τὴν κραυγὴν ὁ Ἰώσηπος ἐπιστραφεὶς καὶ θεασάμενος ἐπὶ τῆς σφαγῆς ἤδη τὸν σίδηρον ἀπεπήδησεν
εἰς τὸν αἰγιαλόν· εἱστήκει δὲ δημηγορῶν ἐπὶ βου-
νοῦ τινος ἐξαπήχους τὸ ὕψος· καὶ παρορμοῦντος
ἐπιπηδήσας σκάφους σὺν δυσὶν σωματοφύλαξιν
εἰς μέσην τὴν λίμνην ἀνέφευγεν.[1]

620 (7) Οἱ στρατιῶται δ' αὐτοῦ ταχέως ἁρπάσαντες
τὰ ὅπλα κατὰ τῶν ἐπιβούλων ἐχώρουν. ἔνθα
δείσας ὁ Ἰώσηπος, μὴ πολέμου κινηθέντος ἐμ-
φυλίου δι' ὀλίγων φθόνον παραναλώσῃ τὴν πόλιν,
πέμπει τοῖς σφετέροις ἄγγελον μόνης προνοεῖν
τῆς ἑαυτῶν ἀσφαλείας, μήτε δὲ κτείνειν τινὰ
621 μήτ' ἀπελέγχειν τῶν αἰτίων. καὶ οἱ μὲν τῷ
παραγγέλματι πεισθέντες ἠρέμησαν, οἱ δ' ἀνὰ
τὴν πέριξ χώραν πυθόμενοι τήν τ' ἐπιβουλὴν καὶ
τὸν συσκευάσαντα συνηθροίζοντο κατὰ Ἰωάννου·
φθάνει δ' ἐκεῖνος εἰς Γίσχαλα φυγὼν τὴν πατρίδα.
622 συνέρρεον δὲ πρὸς τὸν Ἰώσηπον οἱ Γαλιλαῖοι κατὰ
πόλεις, καὶ πολλαὶ μυριάδες ὁπλιτῶν γενόμεναι
παρεῖναι σφᾶς ἐπὶ τὸν Ἰωάννην τὸν κοινὸν ἐπίβουλον ἐβόων· συγκαταφλέξειν γὰρ αὐτῷ καὶ τὴν
623 ὑποδεξαμένην πόλιν. ὁ δὲ ἀποδέχεσθαι μὲν αὐτῶν
ἔφασκεν τὴν εὔνοιαν, ἀνεῖργεν δὲ τὴν ὁρμήν,

---

[1] ἀνέφυγεν L.

respects.[a] But when Josephus had assembled the Tiberians in the stadium and was endeavouring to address them on the subject of the news which he had received, John secretly sent out some soldiers with orders to kill him. The people, seeing these men drawing their swords, raised a shout ; at their cries Josephus turned round, beheld the blade actually at his throat, leapt down to the beach—he had been standing, to harangue the people, on a hillock six cubits high—and jumping with two of his guards [b] into a boat that was moored hard by, escaped to the middle of the lake.

(7) His soldiers, however, hastily seized their arms and advanced against the conspirators. Thereupon Josephus, fearing that the outbreak of civil war might bring ruin upon the city, all for the misdeeds of a few envious individuals, sent instructions to his men to restrict themselves to providing for their own safety, to kill nobody and to call none of the culprits to account.[c] In accordance with these orders they took no further action ; but the inhabitants of the district, on learning of the plot and the contriver of it, mustered in force to attack John, who hastily made his escape to Gischala, his native place. The Galilaeans from one town after another flocked to Josephus ; myriads of men in arms came and protested that they were there to punish John, the public enemy, and that they would burn him alive with the city that harboured him. Josephus thanked them for their goodwill, but checked their im-

Josephus disperses John's followers,

[a] In *Vita* 91 John comes in person to meet Josephus, but hastily retires.

[b] James, his bodyguard, and Herod, a citizen of Tiberias, are his two companions in *Vita* 96.

[c] This sentence and the preceding have no parallel in *Vita*.

χειρώσασθαι συνέσει τοὺς ἐχθροὺς μᾶλλον ἢ
624 κτεῖναι προαιρούμενος. ἐκλαβὼν δὲ τοὺς ἀφ᾽
ἑκάστης πόλεως Ἰωάννῃ συναφεστῶτας κατ᾽
ὄνομα, προθύμως δὲ ἐνεδείκνυντο τοὺς σφετέρους
οἱ δημόται, καὶ διὰ κηρύκων ἀπειλήσας¹ ἐντὸς
ἡμέρας πέμπτης τῶν μὴ καταλιπόντων Ἰωάννην
τάς τε οὐσίας διαρπάσειν καὶ τὰς οἰκίας ἅμα ταῖς
625 γενεαῖς καταφλέξειν, τρισχιλίους μὲν ἀπέστησεν
εὐθέως, οἳ παραγενόμενοι τὰ ὅπλα παρὰ τοῖς
ποσὶν ἔρριψαν αὐτοῦ, σὺν δὲ τοῖς καταλειφθεῖσιν,
ἦσαν δ᾽ ὅσον εἰς δισχιλίους Σύρων φυγάδες,
ἀνέστελλεν² Ἰωάννην³ πάλιν ἐπὶ τὰς λαθραίους
626 ἐπιβουλὰς ἐκ τῶν φανερωτέρων. κρύφα γοῦν
ἔπεμπεν ἀγγέλους εἰς Ἱεροσόλυμα διαβάλλων τὸν
Ἰώσηπον ἐπὶ τῷ μεγέθει τῆς δυνάμεως, φάσκων
ὅσον οὐδέπω τύραννον ἐλεύσεσθαι τῆς μητρο-
627 πόλεως, εἰ μὴ προκαταληφθείη. ταῦθ᾽ ὁ μὲν δῆμος
προειδὼς οὐ προσεῖχεν, οἱ δυνατοὶ δὲ κατὰ φθόνον
καὶ τῶν ἀρχόντων τινὲς λάθρα τῷ Ἰωάννῃ χρήματα πρὸς συλλογὴν μισθοφόρων ἔπεμψαν, ὅπως
πολεμῇ⁴ πρὸς Ἰώσηπον· ἐψηφίσαντο δὲ καθ᾽ ἑαυτοὺς καὶ μετακαλεῖν αὐτὸν ἀπὸ τῆς στρατηγίας.
628 οὐ μὴν ἠξίουν ἀποχρήσειν τὸ δόγμα, δισχιλίους
δὲ καὶ πεντακοσίους ὁπλίτας καὶ τέσσαρας τῶν
ἐπιφανῶν ἄνδρας ἔστειλαν, τόν τε τοῦ Νομικοῦ

---

¹ A (margin): ἀπειλησάντων (·αντος L) the rest.
² ἀνέστειλεν L.   ³ Niese: Ἰωάννης mss.
⁴ πολεμήσωσιν PAM.

ᵃ "20 days," *Vita* 370.   ᵇ "4000," *Vita* 371.
ᶜ We should probably read "Tyrian" as in *Vita* 372 (*cf.*
§ 588 above).
ᵈ This episode (§§ 624 f.) is placed, probably correctly,

petuosity, preferring to overcome his enemies by diplomacy rather than by slaughter. Instead, he obtained from each city a list of names of those who had joined in John's revolt, this information being readily given by their fellow-citizens, and then issued a public proclamation that all who within five [a] days had not abandoned John would have their property seized and their houses burnt to the ground, along with their families. This threat immediately produced the desertion of three [b] thousand of his followers, who came to Josephus and threw down their arms at his feet ; with the remainder, some two thousand Syrian [c] fugitives, John, abandoning open hostilities, was again driven to resort to clandestine plots.[d]

He accordingly now sent secret emissaries to Jerusalem [e] to denounce Josephus as growing too great, declaring that he might at any moment appear at the capital as its tyrant, unless he were checked in time. The people, who foresaw these calumnies, attached no importance to them ; but their leaders, with some of the magistrates, from motives of envy, secretly supplied John with money to enable him to collect mercenaries and make war on Josephus. They further took it upon themselves to pass a decree recalling him from his command. As, however, they did not regard this decree as sufficient, they sent out a force of two thousand five hundred men [f] with four men of mark, namely, Joesdrus,[g] son of Nomicus,

and defeats his attempt to supplant him.

much later in the other narrative, after the conflict with the deputies from Jerusalem (*Vita* 368-372).

[e] The story of the attempt to supersede Josephus is narrated at much greater length in *Vita* 189-332.

[f] Only 600 soldiers and 300 citizens in *Vita* 200.

[g] Called Joazar or Jozar in *Vita*.

Ἰώεσδρον καὶ Ἀνανίαν Σαδούκι καὶ Σίμωνα καὶ
Ἰούδην Ἰωνάθου, πάντας εἰπεῖν δυνατωτάτους, ἵν᾿
οὗτοι τὴν πρὸς τὸν Ἰώσηπον εὔνοιαν ἀποστρέ-
ψωσιν, κἂν μὲν ἑκὼν παραγένηται, λόγον ὑποσχεῖν
ἐᾶν αὐτόν, εἰ δὲ βιάζοιτο μένειν, ὡς πολεμίῳ
629 χρῆσθαι. Ἰωσήπῳ δὲ παραγίνεσθαι μὲν στρατιὰν
ἐπεστάλκεσαν οἱ φίλοι, τὴν δ᾿ αἰτίαν οὐ προεδή-
λουν, ἅτε δὴ λάθρα τῶν ἐχθρῶν βεβουλευμένων.
διὸ καὶ μὴ προφυλαξαμένου τέσσαρες πόλεις
εὐθέως πρὸς τοὺς διαφόρους ἀπέστησαν ἐλθόντας,
Σέπφωρίς τε καὶ Γάβαρα¹ καὶ Γίσχαλα καὶ Τι-
630 βεριάς. ταχέως δὲ καὶ ταύτας προσηγάγετο δίχα
τῶν ὅπλων καὶ χειρωσάμενος στρατηγήμασιν τοὺς
τέσσαρας ἡγεμόνας τῶν τε ὁπλιτῶν τοὺς δυνατωτά-
631 τους ἀνέπεμψεν εἰς Ἱεροσόλυμα. πρὸς οὓς ὁ δῆμος
οὐ μετρίως ἠγανάκτησεν καὶ σὺν αὐτοῖς ὥρμησεν
τοὺς προπέμψαντας ἀνελεῖν, εἰ μὴ φθάσαντες ἀπέδρασαν.

632 (8) Ἰωάννην δὲ λοιπὸν ἐντὸς τοῦ Γισχάλων
τείχους ὁ παρὰ Ἰωσήπου φόβος ἐφρούρει. καὶ
μετ᾿ ὀλίγας ἡμέρας πάλιν ἀπέστη Τιβεριὰς ἐπι-
καλεσαμένων τῶν ἔνδον Ἀγρίππαν τὸν βασιλέα.
633 καὶ τοῦ μὲν μὴ καταντήσαντος ἐφ᾿ ἣν συντέτακτο
προθεσμίαν, Ῥωμαϊκῶν δ᾿ ὀλίγων ἱππέων κατ᾿
ἐκείνην τὴν ἡμέραν παραφανέντων, τὸν Ἰώσηπον
634 ἐξεκήρυσσον. τῷ² δ᾿ ἠγγέλη μὲν εἰς Ταριχαίας
ἡ ἀπόστασις εὐθέως, ἐκπεπομφὼς δὲ πάντας τοὺς

¹ Destinon with Lat. and *Vita* 203: Γάδαρα or Γάμαλα
MSS.
² R (corrector): τῶν the rest. VRC preserve the true text
in this clause.

Ananias, son of Sadok, Simon and Judas,[a] sons of Jonathan, all very able speakers, with the object of undermining the popularity of Josephus ; if he were prepared to leave without demur, they were to allow him an opportunity of rendering an account of himself, if he insisted on remaining, they were to treat him as a public enemy. Friends of Josephus had, meanwhile, sent him word that troops were on their way to Galilee, but gave no hint of the reason, as his adversaries had planned their scheme in secret conclave. Consequently he had taken no precautions and four cities went over to his opponents as soon as they appeared, namely, Sepphoris, Gabara, Gischala, and Tiberias. These,[b] however, he soon reclaimed without recourse to arms, and then by stratagem got the four leaders into his power with the best of their troops and sent them back to Jerusalem. The citizens were highly indignant at these individuals, and would have killed them, as well as their employers, had they not promptly taken flight.

(8) John from this time forth was confined by fear of Josephus within the walls of Gischala. A few days later Tiberias again revolted, the inhabitants having appealed to King Agrippa for aid. He did not arrive on the agreed date, but on that same day a small body of Roman cavalry happening to appear, the Tiberians issued a proclamation excluding Josephus from the city. Their defection was immediately reported to him at Tarichaeae. He had

Revolt of Tiberias

---

[a] For Judas, son of Jonathan, *Vita* 197 etc. has Jonathan.
[b] Gischala excepted.

στρατιώτας ἐπὶ σίτου συλλογὴν οὔτε μόνος ἐξ-
ορμᾶν ἐπὶ τοὺς ἀποστάντας οὔτε μένειν ὑπέμενεν,
δεδοικὼς μὴ βραδύναντος αὐτοῦ φθάσωσιν οἱ
βασιλικοὶ παρελθεῖν εἰς τὴν πόλιν· οὐδὲ γὰρ τὴν
ἐπιοῦσαν ἡμέραν ἐνεργὸν ἕξειν ἔμελλεν ἐπέχοντος
635 σαββάτου. δόλῳ δὴ¹ περιελθεῖν ἐπενόει τοὺς ἀποστάντας. καὶ τὰς μὲν πύλας τῶν Ταριχαίων ἀπο-
κλεῖσαι κελεύσας, ὡς μὴ προεξαγγείλειέ τις τὸ
σκέμμα τοῖς ἐπιχειρουμένοις, τὰ δ' ἐπὶ τῆς λίμνης
σκάφη πάντα συναθροίσας, τριάκοντα δ' εὑρέ-
θησαν καὶ διακόσια,² καὶ ναῦται τεσσάρων οὐ
πλείους ἦσαν ἐν ἑκάστῳ, διὰ τάχους ἐλαύνει πρὸς
636 τὴν Τιβεριάδα. καὶ τοσοῦτον ἀποσχὼν τῆς πόλεως
ἐξ ὅσου συνιδεῖν οὐ ῥᾴδιον ἦν, κενὰς τὰς ἁλιάδας
μετεώρους σαλεύειν ἐκέλευσεν, αὐτὸς δὲ μόνους
ἑπτὰ τῶν σωματοφυλάκων ἐνόπλους³ ἔχων ἔγγιον
637 ὀφθῆναι προσῄει. θεασάμενοι δ' αὐτὸν ἀπὸ τῶν
τειχῶν ἔτι βλασφημοῦντες οἱ διάφοροι καὶ διὰ
τὴν ἔκπληξιν πάντα τὰ σκάφη γέμειν ὁπλιτῶν
νομίσαντες ἔρριψαν τὰ ὅπλα καὶ κατασείοντες
ἱκετηρίας ἐδέοντο φείσασθαι τῆς πόλεως.

638   (9) Ὁ δὲ Ἰώσηπος πολλὰ διαπειλησάμενος αὐτοῖς καὶ κατονειδίσας, εἰ πρῶτον μὲν ἀράμενοι τὸν
πρὸς Ῥωμαίους πόλεμον εἰς στάσεις ἐμφυλίους
προαναλίσκουσιν τὴν ἰσχὺν καὶ τὰ εὐκταιότατα
δρῶσιν τοῖς ἐχθροῖς, ἔπειτα τὸν κηδεμόνα τῆς
ἀσφαλείας αὐτῶν ἀναρπάσαι σπεύδουσιν καὶ κλείειν

¹ L: δὲ the rest.   ² τριακόσια PA.
³ Destinon and others (a correction required by the
sequel, § 642): ἀνόπλους MSS.

ᵃ "I had dismissed my soldiers to their homes because,

566

just sent all his soldiers on a foraging excursion;[a] he
could neither go out alone to face the rebels nor
afford to remain idle, for fear that the king's troops,
profiting by his delay, might forestall him in occupying the town; on the following day, moreover, he
could take no action owing to the restrictions of the
sabbath. In this dilemma the idea occurred to him
of circumventing the rebels by a ruse. After order- checked by
ing the gates of Tarichaeae to be closed, in order that a ruse (a
no hint of his project might reach the city which
was the objective of his attack, he collected all the
boats which he could find on the lake—there were
two hundred and thirty, with no more than four
sailors on board each—and with this fleet sailed at
full speed for Tiberias. Keeping far enough from
the town to prevent the inhabitants from detecting
that his ships were unmanned, he let them ride in
the offing, while he, with no more than seven of his
armed guards, advanced within view of all. On
perceiving him from the walls, where they were still
heaping invectives upon him, his adversaries, imagining that all the boats were filled with troops, were
terrified, threw down their arms and, waving sup-
pliants' olive-branches, implored him to spare the
city.

(9) Josephus severely threatened and reproached
them, first for their folly, after taking up arms against
Rome, in wasting their strength beforehand upon
civil strife and so fulfilling their enemies' fondest
wishes; next for their eagerness to make away with
their guardian and protector, and their shamelessness

the next day being the sabbath, I desired to spare the
Tarichaeans annoyance from the presence of the military "
(*Vita* 159).

οὐκ αἰδοῦνται τὴν πόλιν αὐτῷ τῷ τειχίσαντι, προσδέχεσθαι τοὺς ἀπολογησομένους ἔφασκεν καὶ δι'
639 ὧν βεβαιώσεται¹ τὴν πόλιν. κατέβαινον δ' εὐθέως
δέκα τῶν Τιβεριέων οἱ δυνατώτατοι· καὶ τοὺς μὲν
ἀναλαβὼν μιᾷ τῶν ἁλιάδων ἀνήγαγεν πορρωτέρω,
πεντήκοντα δ' ἑτέρους τῆς βουλῆς τοὺς μάλιστα
γνωρίμους κελεύει προελθεῖν, ὡς καὶ παρ' ἐκείνων
640 πίστιν τινὰ βουλόμενος λαβεῖν. ἔπειτα καινοτέρας
σκήψεις ἐπινοῶν ἄλλους ἐπ' ἄλλοις ὡς ἐπὶ συν-
641 θήκαις προυκαλεῖτο. τοῖς δὲ κυβερνήταις ἐκέλευσεν
τῶν² πληρουμένων διὰ τάχους εἰς Ταριχαίας ἀνα-
πλεῖν καὶ συγκλείειν τοὺς ἄνδρας εἰς τὸ δεσμωτή-
ριον, μέχρι πᾶσαν μὲν τὴν βουλὴν οὖσαν ἑξακοσίων,
περὶ δὲ δισχιλίους τῶν ἀπὸ τοῦ δήμου συλλαβὼν
ἀνήγαγεν σκάφεσιν εἰς Ταριχαίας.

642 (10) Βοώντων δὲ τῶν λοιπῶν αἴτιον εἶναι μάλιστα τῆς ἀποστάσεως Κλεῖτόν τινα καὶ παρακαλούντων εἰς ἐκεῖνον ἀπερείδεσθαι τὴν ὀργήν,
ὁ Ἰώσηπος ἀνελεῖν μὲν οὐδένα προῄρητο, Λευὶν
δέ τινα τῶν ἑαυτοῦ φυλάκων ἐκέλευσεν ἐξελθεῖν,
643 ἵνα ἀποκόψῃ τὰς χεῖρας τοῦ Κλείτου. δείσας δὲ
ἐκεῖνος εἰς ἐχθρῶν στῖφος ἀποβήσεσθαι μόνος οὐκ
ἔφη. σχετλιάζοντα δὲ τὸν Ἰώσηπον ἐπὶ τοῦ
σκάφους ὁ Κλεῖτος ὁρῶν καὶ προθυμούμενον αὐτὸν
ἐπιπηδᾶν ἐπὶ τὴν τιμωρίαν ἱκέτευεν ἀπὸ τῆς ἀκτῆς
644 τὴν ἑτέραν τῶν χειρῶν καταλιπεῖν. κἀκείνου κατα-
νεύσαντος ἐφ' ᾧ τὴν ἑτέραν αὐτὸς ἀποκόψειεν
ἑαυτοῦ, σπασάμενος τῇ δεξιᾷ τὸ ξίφος ἀπέκοψεν
τὴν λαιάν· εἰς τοσοῦτον δέους ὑπὸ τοῦ Ἰωσήπου
645 προήχθη. τότε μὲν δὴ κενοῖς σκάφεσιν καὶ δορυφόροις ἑπτὰ τὸν δῆμον αἰχμαλωτισάμενος πάλιν

¹ Destinon : βεβαιώσηται or -ώσαιτο MSS.

in closing their city to him, who had built its walls ;
he declared himself ready, notwithstanding, to receive deputies who would offer an apology and assist
him to secure the town. At once ten citizens, the
principal men of Tiberias, came down ; these he
took on board one of the vessels and conveyed some
distance from the land. Next he required fifty more,
the most eminent members of the council, to come
forward, ostensibly to give him their word as well.
And so, always inventing some new pretext, he
called up one party after another, presumably to
ratify the agreement. As the boats were successively
filled, he gave orders to the skippers to sail with all
speed to Tarichaeae and to shut the men up in prison.
Thus, in the end, he arrested the whole council of six
hundred members and some two thousand other
citizens, and shipped them off to Tarichaeae.

(10) Those who were left indicated, with loud
cries, a certain Cleitus as the prime mover of the
revolt, and urged the governor to vent his wrath
upon him. Josephus, being determined to put no
one to death, ordered one of his guards, named Levi,
to go ashore and cut off Cleitus's hands. The soldier,
afraid to venture alone into the midst of a host of
enemies, refused to go. Cleitus, thereupon, seeing
Josephus on the boat fuming with anger and prepared
to leap out himself to chastise him, implored him
from the beach to leave him one of his hands. The
governor consenting to this, on condition that he cut
off the other himself, Cleitus drew his sword with his
right hand and severed the left from his body ; such
was his terror of Josephus. Thus, with empty ships
and seven guards, he captured, on that occasion, an

---

² + σκαφῶν Bekker (after Lat.).

Τιβεριάδα προσηγάγετο, μετὰ δ' ἡμέρας ὀλίγας
Σεπφωρίταις συναποστᾶσαν εὑρὼν¹ ἐπέτρεψε μὲν
646 διαρπάσαι τοῖς στρατιώταις, συναγαγὼν μέντοι
πάντα τοῖς δημόταις ἔδωκεν, τοῖς τε κατὰ Σέπφωριν ὁμοίως· καὶ γὰρ ἐκείνους χειρωσάμενος
νουθετῆσαι διὰ τῆς ἁρπαγῆς ἠθέλησεν, τῇ δ'
ἀποδόσει τῶν χρημάτων πάλιν εἰς εὔνοιαν προσηγάγετο.

647 (xxii. 1) Τὰ μὲν οὖν κατὰ Γαλιλαίαν ἐπέπαυτο
κινήματα, καὶ τῶν ἐμφυλίων παυσάμενοι θορύβων
ἐπὶ τὰς πρὸς Ῥωμαίους ἐτράποντο παρασκευάς,
648 ἐν δὲ τοῖς Ἱεροσολύμοις Ἄνανός τε ὁ ἀρχιερεὺς
καὶ τῶν δυνατῶν ὅσοι μὴ τὰ Ῥωμαίων ἐφρόνουν
τό τε τεῖχος ἐπεσκεύαζον καὶ πολλὰ τῶν πολε-
649 μιστηρίων ὀργάνων. καὶ διὰ πάσης μὲν τῆς
πόλεως ἐχαλκεύετο βέλη καὶ πανοπλία, πρὸς
ἀτάκτοις² δὲ γυμνασίαις τὸ τῶν νέων πλῆθος ἦν,
καὶ μεστὰ πάντα θορύβου, δεινὴ δὲ κατήφεια τῶν
μετρίων, καὶ πολλοὶ τὰς μελλούσας προορώμενοι
650 συμφορὰς ἀπωλοφύροντο. θειασμοί τε τοῖς εἰρήνην ἀγαπῶσιν δύσφημοι, τοῖς δὲ τὸν πόλεμον ἐξ-
άψασιν ἐσχεδιάζοντο πρὸς ἡδονήν, καὶ τὸ κατάστημα τῆς πόλεως πρὶν ἐπελθεῖν Ῥωμαίους ἦν
651 οἷον ἀπολουμένης. Ἀνάνῳ γε μὴν φροντὶς ἦν
κατὰ μικρὸν ἀφισταμένῳ τῶν εἰς τὸν πόλεμον
παρασκευῶν κάμψαι πρὸς τὸ συμφέρον τούς τε
στασιαστὰς καὶ τὴν τῶν κληθέντων ζηλωτῶν

¹ PA: ἑλὼν the rest.
² iussis Lat., *i.e.* τακταῖς " regular."

570

entire population, and once more reduced Tiberias to submission. But a few days later, discovering that the city had revolted again along with Sepphoris, he delivered it over to his soldiers to plunder it. However, he collected all the spoil and restored it to the townsfolk. He followed the same procedure at Sepphoris ; for that town also was subdued by him, and he wished to give the inhabitants a lesson by pillaging it, and then by restoring their property to regain their affection.

Reduction and pillage of Tiberias and Sepphoris.

(xxii. 1) The disturbances in Galilee were thus quelled ; and, their civil strife now ended, the Jews turned to preparations for the struggle with the Romans. In Jerusalem Ananus the high-priest and all the leading men who were not pro-Romans busied themselves with the repair of the walls and the accumulation of engines of war. In every quarter of the city missiles and suits of armour were being forged ; masses of young men were undergoing a desultory training ; and the whole was one scene of tumult. On the other side, the dejection of the moderates was profound ; and many, foreseeing the impending disasters, made open lamentation. Then, too, there were omens,[a] which to the friends of peace boded ill, although those who had kindled the war readily invented favourable interpretations for them. In short, the city before the coming of the Romans wore the appearance of a place doomed to destruction. Ananus, nevertheless, cherished the thought of gradually abandoning these warlike preparations and bending the malcontents and the infatuated so-called zealots to a more salutary policy ; but he

Preparations at Jerusalem for war. Winter of A.D. 66–67.

[a] A description of these is given later, vi. 288-315.

ἀφροσύνην, ἡττήθη δὲ τῆς βίας, κἂν τοῖς ἑξῆς
οἷου τέλους ἔτυχεν δηλώσομεν.

652 (2) Κατὰ δὲ τὴν Ἀκραβατηνὴν¹ τοπαρχίαν ὁ
Γιώρα Σίμων πολλοὺς τῶν νεωτεριζόντων συ-
στησάμενος ἐφ᾽ ἁρπαγὰς ἐτράπετο καὶ οὐ μόνον τὰς
οἰκίας ἐσπάρασσεν² τῶν πλουσίων, ἀλλὰ καὶ τὰ
σώματα κατηκίζετο, δῆλός τε ἦν ἤδη πόρρωθεν
653 ἀρχόμενος τυραννεῖν. πεμφθείσης δ᾽ ἐπ᾽ αὐτὸν
ὑπ᾽ Ἀνάνου καὶ τῶν ἀρχόντων στρατιᾶς, πρὸς
τοὺς ἐν Μασάδα λῃστὰς μεθ᾽ ὧν εἶχεν κατέφυγεν,
κἀκεῖ μέχρι τῆς Ἀνάνου καὶ τῆς τῶν ἄλλων
ἐχθρῶν ἀναιρέσεως μένων συνελῄζετο τὴν Ἰδου-
654 μαίαν, ὥστε τοὺς ἄρχοντας τοῦ ἔθνους διὰ τὸ
πλῆθος τῶν φονευομένων καὶ τὰς συνεχεῖς ἁρπαγὰς στρατιὰν ἀθροίσαντας ἐμφρούρους τὰς
κώμας ἔχειν. καὶ τὰ μὲν κατὰ τὴν Ἰδουμαίαν
ἐν τούτοις ἦν.

¹ Ἀκραβετινὴν PA.
² ἐτάρασσεν PAML Lat.

succumbed to their violence, and the sequel of our narrative will show the fate which befell him.[a]

(2) In the toparchy of Acrabatene Simon, son of Gioras, mustering a large band of revolutionaries, devoted himself to rapine ; not content with ransacking the houses of the wealthy, he further maltreated their persons, and plainly showed, even at that early date, that he was entering on a career of tyranny.[b] When Ananus and the magistrates sent an army against him, he fled with his band to the brigands at Masada,[c] and there he remained until Ananus and his other opponents were killed. Meanwhile, with his brigand friends, he worked such havoc in Idumaea, that the local magistrates, in consequence of the number of the slain and the continuous raids, raised an army and garrisoned the villages. Such was the condition of affairs in Idumaea.

Raids of Simon, son of Gioras, in Samaria and Idumaea.

[a] *B*. iv. 315 ff. ; for Ananus see the note on § 563 above.
[b] He becomes a prominent figure in the siege of Jerusalem.
[c] §§ 408, 433, 447.